COMMUNICATING
WITH STRANGERS

AN APPROACH
TO INTERCULTURAL
COMMUNICATION

THIRD EDITION

COMMUNICATING WITH STRANGERS

AN APPROACH TO INTERCULTURAL COMMUNICATION

WILLIAM B. GUDYKUNST
California State University, Fullerton

YOUNG YUN KIM
University of Oklahoma

Boston, Massachusetts   Burr Ridge, Illinois   Dubuque, Iowa
Madison, Wisconsin   New York, New York   San Francisco, California   St. Louis, Missouri

McGraw-Hill

A Division of The **McGraw·Hill** *Companies*

COMMUNICATING WITH STRANGERS:
An Approach to Intercultural Communication

This book is printed on acid-free paper.

5 6 7 8 9 0 DOC DOC 9 0

ISBN 0-07-034647-X

This book was set in Times Roman by Graphic World, Inc.
The editors were Marjorie Byers and David A. Damstra;
the production supervisor was Diane Ficarra.
The cover was designed by Karen K. Quigley.
R. R. Donnelley and Sons Company was printer and binder.

Library of Congress Cataloging-in-Publication Data
Gudykunst, William B.
    Communicating with strangers: an approach to intercultural communication / William B. Gudykunst, Young Yun Kim. — 3d ed.
        p.   cm.
    Includes bibliographical references.
    ISBN 0-07-034647-X
    1. Intercultural communication.   I. Kim, Young Yun.   II. Title.
HM258.G84   1997
320.2—dc20   96-4051
                                                        CIP

ABOUT
THE AUTHORS

William B. Gudykunst is a professor of speech communication at California State University, Fullerton. He received his B.S. and M.A. degrees in sociology from Arizona State University. After completing his M.A., Bill spent three years in the U.S. Navy stationed in Yokosuka, Japan. He became interested in intercultural communication while working as an Intercultural Relations Specialist in the Navy. Bill helped develop the intercultural relations seminar in Japan, which was designed to help naval personnel and their families adjust to living in Japan. After being released from active duty, Bill went to the University of Minnesota, where he completed his Ph.D. in 1977.

Bill's work focuses on developing a theory of interpersonal and intergroup effectiveness that can be applied to improving the quality of communication. Bill is the author of *Bridging Differences* (Sage, 1994), and coauthor of *Culture and Interpersonal Communication* (with S. Ting-Toomey, Sage, 1988), *Bridging Japanese/North American Differences* (with T. Nishida, Sage, 1994), and *Building Bridges* (with S. Ting-Toomey, S. Sudweeks, and L. Stewart, Houghton Mifflin, 1995). Among the books he has edited are *Intercultural Communication Theory* (Sage, 1983), *Intergroup Communication* (Edward Arnold, 1986), *Handbook of International and Intercultural Communication* (with M. Asante, Sage, 1989), *Communication in Japan and the United States* (State University of New York Press, 1994), and *Communication in Personal Relationships Across Cultures* (with S. Ting-Toomey and T. Nishida, Sage, 1996).

Young Yun Kim is a professor of communication at the University of Oklahoma, Norman, and formerly taught at Governors State University in Illinois. Young was born and raised in Seoul, Korea, where she received her B.A. degree from Seoul National University. In 1970, she moved to the United States and completed her M.A. degree at the University of Hawaii in conjunction with the East-West Center. She continued her graduate study at Northwestern University in Evanston, Illinois, where she received her Ph.D. degree in 1976. Young teaches courses and directs doctoral theses in the area of international, intercultural, and interethnic/interracial communication. Her research has been aimed primarily at explaining the role of communication in the cross-cultural adaptation process of immigrants, sojourners, and native-born ethnic minorities. Young has conducted original research in Asian, Hispanic, and American Indian communities and has published her work in journals such as *Communication Yearbook, Human Communication Research,* and *International Journal of Intercultural Relations.* She is the author or editor of a number of books, including *Interethnic Communication* (Sage, 1986), *Theories in Intercultural Communication* (Sage, 1988, with W. B. Gudykunst), *Communication and Cross-Cultural Adaptation* (Multilingual Matters, 1988), and *Becoming Intercultural* (Sage, in press). Young has served on the boards of directors of the International Communication Association and the Speech Communication Association. Presently, she is a member of the editorial boards of *Communication Research, Human Communication Research,* and *International Journal of Intercultural Relations.*

CONTENTS

PREFACE

This book is designed to be a text for a college course in intercultural communication, but anyone who communicates with people from other groups, either for pleasure or as part of his or her job, should find this book useful. Foreign Service Officers, Peace Corps volunteers, businesspersons in multinational or multiethnic corporations, social workers, teachers in integrated schools, staff members of hospitals in urban settings, and police officers dealing with ethnic communities, to name only a few groups, should find this book helpful in the performance of their work.

We focus on theoretical issues more than most authors of existing texts on intercultural communication. We believe that in order to understand the process of intercultural communication and to improve our intercultural effectiveness, we must have the conceptual tools to understand what is happening. Following Kurt Lewin, we believe that "there is nothing so practical as a good theory." Throughout the book, we apply the theories we have been developing over the last decade. Gudykunst's (1988b, 1993, 1995) theory of interpersonal and intergroup communication provides the conceptual foundation for most of the book. Kim's (1988, in press; Kim & Ruben, 1988) theories of adaptation and intercultural growth are used to organize Chapters 13 and 14. Although the book is grounded theoretically, we do not focus on presenting the theories. Rather, we "translate" the theories so that they can be applied to improving our communication with people from different cultures and/or ethnic groups.

To organize the various elements of the process of intercultural communication, we present a model of intercultural communication in Part One. Our model is based on the premise that communication between people from different cultures is essentially the same as communication between people from different subcultures. In fact, we go even further to assume that all interactions between people share essentially the same underlying communication process, which we outline in Part One.

We conceptualize the common underlying process of communication with people who are unknown and unfamiliar as communication with strangers. In this view, intercultural communication is a special case only in the sense that the unknown and unfamiliar qualities of strangers are primarily culturally based. This fact, in turn, permeates all other sources of interpersonal differences, including sociocultural, psychocultural, and environmental influences, on which we elaborate in Part Two.

Our communication with strangers presents the challenge of having to understand their cultural backgrounds and their communication patterns. As we acquire knowledge of how strangers express themselves and interpret the world, we also recognize the fundamental universalities of communication that are shared by people in all cultures. In Part Three, we look at some of the recognized variations in how we transmit and interpret messages and how these variations influence our communication with strangers.

The development of interpersonal relationships with strangers requires that we have some understanding of their culture and patterns of communication and that they have some understanding of ours. Being able to communicate effectively and to manage conflict plays a vital role in determining the nature and the quality of the relationships we establish with strangers. As our relationships with strangers become more meaningful, we begin to deal with the strangers, who in the meantime go through a process of cultural adaptation into our environment. Through cumulative experiences of communicating with strangers, we, as well as the strangers, may enter the process of becoming intercultural—a gradual change of psychic growth beyond our respective cultural parameters. Through intercultural communication, we are therefore able to broaden our perspective on life, people, and ourselves, and to expand our behavioral capacity to adapt in our changing world. In Part Four, we discuss these and other related topics.

We have thoroughly updated the third edition. This third edition is much more coherent than previous editions. The perspective introduced in Part One is carried throughout the book. We have removed overly complex language and added examples to illustrate our points. In updating the various chapters, we have omitted redundancies and dropped material not found useful in the previous editions. We have added research that has been conducted in the years that have passed since the second edition was published.

We expanded on our discussion of our assumptions about the nature of communication and culture in Chapter 1. In Chapter 2, we reorganized the overview of our approach, adding material on interpersonal versus intergroup behavior as well as new material on anxiety/uncertainty management and mindfulness. Chapter 3 now focuses exclusively on dimensions of cultural variability (the material on norms and rules previously in this chapter was moved to Chapter 6). We expanded the discussion of individualism-collectivism and low- and high-context communication, adding a discussion of individual level factors (i.e., personality, self construals, and values) that mediate the influence of cultural individualism-collectivism on communication behavior. We expanded the discussion of Hofstede's dimensions of cultural variability, presented a new theory of values, and added material on structural tightness. Chapter 4 now focuses on group memberships and social identities that influence our communication with strangers. We expanded our discussion of ethnic identity and added new material on identities based on gender, age, social class, and disabilities. Chapter 5 is still organized around the idea of expectations. We expanded our discussion of stereotypes and communication, and prejudice and communication, and added a section on responding to prejudice. In Chapter 6, we updated the material and added a new section on situational influences on communication. In addition, we incorporated the material on norms and rules previously included in Chapter 3.

The third part focuses on transmitting and interpreting messages. The perceptual and attributional processes are the focus of Chapter 7. The discussion of perception is new to this edition. The material on attributional processes was updated. Also included in this chapter is an updated discussion of how cognitive styles and patterns of thought influence our interpretation of messages. We reorganized and updated the discussion of differences in verbal messages across cultures in Chapter 8. The discussion of language in communicating with strangers was expanded (e.g., extensive new material on code-switching was added). We also added a new discussion of the causes of and solutions to problems of miscommunication with strangers. We revised the chapter on nonverbal communication. It focuses on the recognition/expression of emotions, on contact, on interpersonal synchrony, and on what happens when our nonverbal expectations are violated.

The final part was reorganized and expanded. This part now begins with the chapter on being effective. This chapter (Chapter 10) was expanded and updated. Chapter 11 is a new chapter on managing conflict with strangers. This chapter includes discussion of cultural and ethnic differences in conflict, intergroup conflict, constructive conflict management, and skills for managing conflict. Chapter 12 focuses on developing interpersonal relationships with strangers. Material on interpersonal relationships (e.g., from Chapter 4 in the second edition) was moved to this chapter. The chapter was updated and expanded. Chapters 13 ("Adapting to New Cultures"), 14 ("Becoming Intercultural"), and 15 ("Building Community") were updated and expanded.

In revising the book, we have added figures and tables to clarify and summarize material in the text. In addition, we have provided study questions and suggested readings at the end of each chapter.

In updating the various chapters, we have adapted material from other books we have written (e.g., Gudykunst, 1994; Gudykunst et al., 1995; Kim, in press). To illustrate, the material in Chapter 2 on identities based on age, gender, social class, and disabilities, as well as the material on perception in Chapter 7, was adapted from Gudykunst (1994), while the material on situational influences on communication in Chapter 6 was adapted from Gudykunst et al. (1995).

Several people have influenced our approach to the study of intercultural communication and we want to take this opportunity to recognize them. The work of Harry C. Triandis and of Edward T. Hall is cited in virtually every chapter of the book. These two pioneers have had a profound effect on our work and on that of most other scholars in the area. We also want to recognize the influence of Georg Simmel, whose concept of the stranger provides the foundation for our approach. Charles Berger's work on uncertainty and Walter Stephan and Cookie Stephan's work on anxiety also serve as intellectual roots of the approach we take in the book.

Before concluding, we also want to express our gratitude to friends and colleagues who contributed their time and expertise in reviewing various versions of the book. San Rao initially encouraged us to write the book, and Linda Fisher, our editor at Addison-Wesley for the first edition, was a constant source of support throughout the completion of the original version of the manuscript. Hilary Jackson, our editor at McGraw-Hill for the second edition, encouraged us to improve the book and make it more useful to students. Peggy Henderson facilitated getting the third edition into production.

We also want to thank the people who provided valuable suggestions for this third edition. Numerous colleagues and students have provided constructive suggestions for revising the book over the years since the first edition was published. We cannot name all the people individually, but we want them to know that we appreciate their feedback. We have attempted to incorporate as many of the suggestions we received over the years as possible.

Bill Gudykunst
Young Kim

COMMUNICATING WITH STRANGERS

AN APPROACH TO INTERCULTURAL COMMUNICATION

PART ONE

Conceptual Foundations

On April 8, 1960, the world entered a new era. On that date, the first attempt was made to "communicate" with extraterrestrial life as part of Project Ozma, organized by Frank Drake of the National Radio Astronomy Observatory in Green Bank, West Virginia. *Pioneer 10,* launched on March 3, 1972, included a six-by-nine-inch gold-plated aluminum plaque with a message for any extraterrestrial being coming across it. The plaque on *Pioneer 10* was designed by the astronomer Carl Sagan. The left side of the plaque contained a representation of the periods of pulsars to indicate the solar system of origin, while across the bottom the planets of the solar system were drawn with an indication that *Pioneer 10* originated on the third planet. The right side of the plaque contained drawings of unclothed male and female figures, the man having his right arm raised with the palm extending outward. Pictures of the plaque appeared in newspapers around the world when *Pioneer 10* was launched.

What does the plaque on *Pioneer 10* have to do with the study of intercultural communication? Think about it for a moment. Does the plaque have anything in common with our attempts to communicate with people from other cultures? The plaque illustrates what often happens when two people who do not share a common language try to communicate: They try to get their ideas across nonverbally. Reactions to the plaque when it appeared in newspapers around the world further illustrate what can happen when we use this method in our everyday encounters with people from other cultures. People in some cultures interpreted the man's gesture to be a universal gesture of friendliness, while people in other cultures interpreted it as one of hostility. We can only imagine how extraterrestrial beings would interpret the gesture; they might take it to mean that one arm of one of the sexes is permanently angled at the elbow while that of the other sex is not. The point is that gestures used by people in one culture often do not mean the same thing in another culture. Trying to communicate through nonverbal means may, therefore, lead to misunderstandings

In order to minimize misunderstandings when we communicate with people from other cultures, we need to understand the process of intercultural communication. The importance of understanding this process is called to our attention by two former presidents of the United States:

> So let us not be blind to our differences, but let us direct our attention to our common interests and to the means by which those differences can be resolved. And if we cannot end now our differences, at least we can make the world safe for diversity.

> John F. Kennedy

> It is . . . in our interest—and the interest of other nations—that Americans have the opportunity to understand the histories, cultures and problems of others, so that we can understand their hopes, perceptions and aspirations. [These efforts] will contribute to our capacity as a people and a government to manage our foreign affairs with sensitivity, in an effective and responsible way.

> Jimmy Carter

These two former presidents imply that understanding people of other cultures and their patterns of communication is important not only to decrease misunderstandings but also to make the world a safer place in which to live.

Throughout the book, we focus on the concepts necessary to understand people from other cultures, their patterns of communication, and our interactions with them. More specifically, our intent is to present a framework for understanding our encounters with people from other cultures and subcultures, for determining when misunderstandings occur, and for improving the effectiveness of our intercultural communication.

The purpose of Part One is to outline our perspective on communication in general and intercultural communication in particular. In Chapter 1, we specify the assumptions we make about the process of communication and define the two major terms, *communication* and *culture,* used in the book. Our approach to intercultural communication is presented in Chapter 2, where we examine the concept of the stranger and outline the model we use to organize the elements in the process of communication.

1

Introduction

Greetings. I am pleased to see that we are different.
May we together become greater than the sum of both of us.
Vulcan Greeting (*Star Trek*)

In the past, most human beings were born, lived, and died within a limited geographical area, never encountering people of other races and/or cultural backgrounds. Such an existence, however, no longer prevails in the world. Even members of once isolated groups of people like the Tasadays in the Philippines now frequently have contact with members of other cultural groups. McLuhan (1962) characterizes today's world as a "global village" because of the rapid expansion of worldwide transportation and communication networks (e.g., airplanes, communication satellites, and telephones). It is now possible for any person from an industrialized country to communicate with any person in another industrialized country within minutes by phone, fax, or videoconference, and within hours, face-to-face. In fact, we are at a point in history when important or interesting events, such as wars, presidential debates in the United States, major sporting events, and royal weddings in one country, often are transmitted simultaneously to more than 100 different countries.

The expansion of worldwide communication networks, combined with increases in travel for pleasure or business and in international migration of refugees, heightens our awareness of the need for understanding other cultures and their people. The work of the Presidential Commission on Foreign Language and International Studies (1979) illustrates this increased awareness. In its final report to the president of the United States, the commission points out that nothing less is at issue than the nation's security. At a time when the resurgent forces of nationalism and of ethnic and linguistic consciousness so directly affect global realities, the United States requires far more reliable capacities to communicate with its allies, analyze the behavior of potential adversaries, and earn the trust and sympathies of the uncommitted. Yet there is a widening gap between these needs and the [North] American competence to understand and deal successfully with other peoples in a world in a flux. (pp. 1–2)

The problems isolated by the presidential commission in 1979 are even more important today. The commission set forth a number of recommendations in order for the people of the United States to understand and deal successfully with other peoples of the world, including increased foreign language instruction, more international educational exchanges, citizen education in international affairs, and increases in international training for business and government personnel. Central to most of the commission's recommendations is the need for an increased awareness and understanding of communication between people from different cultures.

In a world of international interdependence, the ability to understand and communicate effectively with people from other cultures takes on extreme urgency. The need for intercultural understanding, however, does not begin or end with national boundaries. Within any nation, a multitude of racial and ethnic groups exist, and their members interact daily. Legislation and legal rulings in the United States on affirmative action, school busing, and desegregation underscore the importance of nondiscriminatory contact between members of different groups. The importance of good intergroup relations also is apparent when current demographic trends are examined. It is projected, for example, that in the near future, the workplace will change from a place dominated by European American (i.e., white) males to a place dominated by women, immigrants, and non-European American (i.e., nonwhite) ethnics (Hudson Institute, 1987). For work to be accomplished effectively in the multicultural organization, people of different groups need to understand one another's patterns of communication.

It is recognized widely that one of the characteristics separating humans from other animals is our development of culture. The development of human culture is made possible through communication, and it is through communication that culture is transmitted from one generation to another. Culture and communication are intertwined so closely that Hall (1959) maintains that "culture is communication" and "communication is culture." In other words, we communicate the way we do because we are raised in a particular culture and learn its language, rules, and norms. Because we learn the language, rules, and norms of our culture by a very early age (between five and ten years of age), however, we generally are unaware of how culture influences our behavior in general and our communication in particular.

When we communicate with people from other cultures, we often are confronted with languages, rules, and norms different from our own. Confronting these differences can be a source of insight into the rules and norms of our own culture, as well as a source of frustration or gratification. Although the presence of cultural differences may suggest the need for accommodation in our communication, it cannot be taken automatically as either a barrier to or a facilitator of effective communication (Ellingsworth, 1977). Communication between people from different cultures can be as effective as communication between people from the same culture (Taylor & Simard, 1975). In other words, communicating with a person from another culture may be either easier or more difficult than communicating with someone from the same culture.

One of the major factors influencing our effectiveness in communicating with people from other cultures is our ability to understand their cultures. It is impossible to understand the communication of people from other cultures if we are highly ethnocentric. Sumner (1940) characterizes ethnocentrism as the "view of things in which one's own group is the center of everything, and all others are scaled and rated with reference to it" (p. 27). Ethnocentrism leads us to see our own culture's ways of doing things as "right" and all others as "wrong." While the tendency to make judgments according to our own cultural standards is natural, it hinders our understanding of other cultures and the patterns of communication of their people. Becoming more culturally relativistic, on the other hand, can be conducive to understanding.

Cultural relativism suggests that the only way we can understand the behavior of others is in the context of their culture. Herskovits (1973) says behaviors must be understood "relative to the cultural background out of which they arise" (p. 14). No one cultural trait is "right" or "wrong"; it is merely "different" from alternative cultural traits. This is not to say we must never make value judgments of people in other cultures. Making them is often necessary. Postponing such value judgments, or recognizing their tentative nature, until adequate information is gathered and we understand the people from the other culture, however, greatly facilitates understanding and effective communication.

The purpose of this book is to provide the conceptual tools needed to understand culture, communication, the ways in which culture influences communication, and the process of communication between people from different cultures. Such knowledge is extremely important. In fact, it is necessary if we are to comprehend fully the daily events of today's multicultural world. The concepts discussed should help you better understand your communication with people from other cultures as well as international situations such as the holding of United States diplomats in Iran. Understanding the material presented also should help you not only analyze your intercultural encounters in order to determine where misunderstandings occur, but also determine how such misunderstandings can be minimized in future interactions.

Given this brief introduction, we define what we mean when we use the terms communication, culture, and intercultural communication. In the next section, we outline the assumptions we make about the nature of communication. Following that presentation, we examine the concept of culture and develop a working definition for intercultural communication. We conclude this chapter by presenting our plan for the book.

CONCEPTUALIZING COMMUNICATION

Everyone communicates and has a preconceived notion of what communication is and how it takes place. Our purpose here is to specify our preconceived notions about the nature of communication. It is not necessary for you to agree with our conceptualization; however, while reading the remainder of the book, remember that we take the ideas expressed here for granted. Because we take these ideas for granted, we present them as assumptions.

Assumption 1: Communication Is a Symbolic Activity

Communication involves the use of symbols. *Symbols* are things used to stand for, or represent, something else. Symbols are not limited to words; they also include nonverbal displays and objects (e.g., the flag). Virtually anything can be a symbol—written words, spoken words, gestures, facial expressions, flags, and so forth. Symbols have referents, or things they symbolize. A red light at an intersection, for example, symbolizes "stop." The important thing to remember is that symbols are symbols only because a group of people agree to consider them as such. There is not a natural connection between symbols and their referents; the relationships are arbitrary and vary from culture to culture. Bram (1955) points out that

> the relationship between symbols and the "things" which they symbolize is not a self-evident or natural one. . . . Symbols derive their specific function from group consensus or social convention and have no effect whatever (outside their rather trivial physical characteristics) on any person not acquainted with such consensus or convention. (p. 2)

Symbols are symbols because a group of people have agreed on their common usage.

One of the defining characteristics of a culture is the agreement among the people who share a culture on the general meaning of symbols. This general agreement does not imply, however, that all members of a culture share a common meaning for any given symbol. The meaning we attach to a symbol is a function of our culture, our ethnic group, our family, and our unique individual experiences. Two people *never* attach exactly the same meaning to a specific symbol. Within a culture, nevertheless, there is sufficient agreement so that people can communicate with relative clarity on most topics of communication.

It is the human ability to use symbols that makes possible the development of speech and language and the capacity to deal with relationships among people and objects in the absence of those people and objects. The meanings of symbols are learned through the process of socialization, the process of learning to be a member of our culture. Symbols may take on different meanings in different situations. In that respect, symbols differ from signs. Signs are concrete and fixed regardless of context (Dance, 1982). When a person shows a dog the palm of the hand, for example, that sign means "down" regardless of where the gesture is used.

Assumption 2: Communication Is a Process Involving the Transmitting and Interpreting of Messages

Since it is impossible to transmit electrical impulses directly from one person's brain to that of another person, it is necessary for us to put our ideas into codes that can be transmitted, either verbally or nonverbally. *Transmitting messages* refers to the process of putting our thoughts, feelings, emotions, or attitudes, for example, into a form recognizable by others. The symbols used may be written, verbal, nonverbal, mathematical, or musical, to cite only a few possibilities. We refer to the transmitted set of symbols as a message. *Interpreting messages* is the process of perceiving, or making sense of, incoming messages and stimuli from the environment.

The way that we transmit and interpret messages is influenced by our background—our culture, our ethnicity, our family upbringing—and our unique individual experiences (including our experiences with others and the emotions we have felt). Since no two people have exactly the same background or individual experiences, no two people transmit or interpret messages in the same way.

Messages can be transmitted from one person to another; *meanings cannot.* Since meanings are not determined solely by the message, the net result of any communication is a partial difference between the meanings held by the communicators. In other words, the meaning of the message one person transmits is never exactly the same as the meaning another person interprets. "To say that meaning in communication is never totally the same for all communicators is not to say that communication is impossible or even difficult—only that it is imperfect" (Fisher, 1978, p. 257).

The transmission and interpretation of messages are not static activities. We transmit and interpret messages at the same time. We interpret other people's messages at the same time we transmit messages to them. We may change what we are saying because of our interpretation of other people's messages while we are talking.

The fact that we transmit and interpret messages at the same time suggests that communication is a process. Berlo (1960) points out if we conceptualize communication as a *process,* "we view events and relationships as dynamic, on-going, ever-changing, continuous. . . . we also mean that it does not have a beginning, an end, a fixed sequence of events. It is not static, at rest. It is moving. The ingredients within a process interact: each affects all of the others" (p. 24). Viewing communication as a process, therefore, allows for recognition of its continuity, complexity, unrepeatability, and irreversibility.

Assumption 3: Communication Involves the Creation of Meaning

As indicated earlier, messages can be transmitted from one person to another, but meanings cannot. One of the reasons we cannot transmit meanings is the ambiguity inherent in the language we speak. Ortega y Gasset (1957) points out that man [or woman] when he [or she] sets himself [or herself] to speak, does so because he [or she] believes that he [or she] will be able to say what he [or she] thinks. Now, this is an illusion. Language is not up to that. It says more or less, a part of what we think, and raises an impenetrable obstacle to the transmission of the rest. It serves quite well for mathematical statements and proofs. . . . But in proportion as conversation treats of more important, more human, more "real" subjects than these, its vagueness, clumsiness, and confusion steadily increases. Obedient to the inveterate prejudice that "talking leads to understanding," we speak and listen in such good faith that we end by misunderstanding one another far more than if we remained mute and set ourselves to divine each other. Nay, more: since our thought is in large measure dependent on our language. (p. 245)

We also cannot transmit meanings because the meanings we attach to messages are a transaction among the message itself, such as what is said and how it is said; the channel used, such as whether the message was spoken or written; the situation in which the message is transmitted, for example, in an office or in a home; the people who transmit and interpret it; and the interaction that is taking place between the individuals.

The channel used to transmit a message influences how we interpret the message. A message transmitted face-to-face using the spoken word may be interpreted differently if it is said exactly the same way on a telephone answering machine. An order from the boss written in memo form will be interpreted differently from the same words given in person with a pleasant tone of voice. Similarly, messages transmitted over computer-mediated networks may be expressed differently from messages in handwritten letters or from those transmitted face-to-face. Computer-mediated messages, for example, make it easier to express anger. One manager reports that "before [computers], if I was really angry, it took time to find the person and vent my anger. A lot of the times I cooled down. . . . Now, I can just hit a button and in a matter of 30 seconds, send hate mail to dozens of people" (Scott, 1993, p. A33).

The situation in which a message is transmitted also influences its interpretation. The same message transmitted in two different locations might be interpreted very differently. If, for instance, we have a friend who is a physician and she or he says "How are you?" we will interpret the message one way at a party and another in the physician's office.

The situation also influences the degree to which we must elaborate our messages in order to be understood. Sometimes we must use concrete language and complete sentences to be understood. At other times, this type of elaboration is not necessary. In communicating with close friends in an informal situation, for example, we may use shorthand speech and slang. We would not, however, use the same speech patterns in our place of work when talking to our supervisor. At work we would use formal language.

The people involved in any particular encounter also influence the interpretation of the messages exchanged. If we know other people, we use our knowledge of them in interpreting their messages. If we do not know others, we use our stereotypes of their group memberships (our mental image of the groups) in interpreting their messages. The culture, ethnic group, social class, and age of the people involved influence how we interpret their messages.

Meanings also emerge out of the interaction that occurs. We always interpret other people's messages in terms of the messages they have transmitted to us during the same encounter and in terms of the messages we have transmitted to them during the same encounter. If it appears that we are attaching meanings to messages that differ from those of the person with whom we are communicating, we can negotiate a new meaning with that person. To illustrate, suppose you are having a conversation with a friend and you say, "My partner thinks that we should take a short trip over the weekend." You are using the word *partner* to refer to your romantic partner. If your friend says, "I didn't know you had a business," you would know there was a misunderstanding, and you could correct the problem by telling your friend that "partner" refers to the person you are dating.

To decrease our chances of misinterpreting other people's messages, we must be aware of how misinterpretations occur. Misinterpretations occur because:

(1) We can never know the state of mind—the attitudes, thoughts, and feelings—of other people.

(2) We depend on [messages], which are frequently ambiguous, to inform us about the attitudes and wishes of other people.

(3) We use our own coding system, which may be defective, to decipher these [messages].

(4) Depending on our state of mind at a particular time, we may be biased in our method of interpreting other people's behavior . . . .

(5) The degree to which we believe that we are correct in divining another person's motives and attitudes is not related to the actual accuracy of our belief. (Beck, 1988, p. 18)

Many of the ideas discussed throughout this book are designed to help us improve the accuracy of our interpretations and, in turn, improve the quality of our communication.

When we communicate, we present ourselves as we want others to see us and respond to how others present themselves to us. We modify how we see ourselves on the basis of the feedback we receive from others. If others consistently tell us we are incompetent, for example, we begin to see ourselves as incompetent. Through communication we can facilitate others' personal growth or destroy them. Gerbner (1978) refers to the latter possibility as "symbolic annihilation."

Assumption 4: Communication Takes Place at Varying Levels of Awareness

As we are socialized into our culture, we learn much of our behavior unconsciously. Learning to walk is a good illustration. No one told us how to walk. We just did it and, through trial and error, eventually mastered it. Much of our communication behavior was learned the same way. Because we learned much of it unconsciously, we are not usually aware of our behavior when we communicate.

A large amount of our social interaction occurs at very low levels of aware-ness (e.g., Abelson, 1976; Berger & Bradac, 1982; Langer, 1978, 1989). These writ-ers argue, and we concur, that we behave with low levels of awareness in situations we consider "normal," or routine.

When our communication is routine, it is based on our implicit theories of communication. Our *implicit personal theories of communication* are our uncon-scious, taken-for-granted assumptions about communication. As human beings, we "construct theories about social reality. [Our] theories have all of the features of the formal theories constructed by scientists. They employ concepts and relationships derived from observation; they provide a structure through which social reality is observed; they enable [us] to make predictions" about how other people will com-municate with us (Wegner & Vallacher, 1977, p. 21). We are not, however, highly aware of the theories we use to guide our behavior.

Since we are not aware that we are using implicit, unconscious theories to guide our behavior, we do not question our theories or think about how they can be modified. Not questioning our implicit theories leads us to assume that the predic-tions we make about other people's behavior (based on our implicit theories) are accurate. The predictions we make based on our implicit theories, however, are not always accurate. To be able to improve our accuracy in predicting other people's behavior, we must become aware of the implicit theories we use to guide our be-havior and think about how they can be improved.

Our implicit theories tell us with whom we should communicate, when we should communicate with others, what we should communicate, how we should communicate with others, how we should present ourselves when we communicate, what effective communication is, and how to interpret other people's communica-tion behavior. Because we learned our implicit personal theories of communication as we were growing up and as we live our lives, our theories are based on the cul-ture in which we were raised, our ethnic background, our gender, our social class, the region of the country in which we were raised, as well as on our unique indi-vidual experiences.

When we encounter new or novel situations, we become aware of our behav-ior (our behavior is enacted consciously). One difference to be expected between our communication with people from our own culture and people from other cultures, therefore, is the level of awareness we have of our behavior. We are more aware of our behavior with people who are from other cultures than we are of our behavior with people from our own culture. Our awareness is heightened because interaction with people from other cultures is less routine; it involves new and novel situations.

Assumption 5: Communicators Make Predictions About the Outcomes of Their Communication Behavior

Miller and Steinberg (1975) argue that "when people communicate, they make pre-dictions about the effects, or outcomes, of their communication behaviors; that is, they choose among various communicative strategies on the basis of how the per-son receiving the message will respond" (p. 7). They go on to recognize that our communication behaviors, including our predictions, are not always conscious. Miller and Steinberg suggest that our awareness of making predictions varies with the degree to which we are aware of alternative outcomes for the situation in which we find ourselves. The more aware we are of alternative outcomes, the more aware we are of making predictions. When our behavior is unconscious (outside of our awareness), generally we are not aware of making predictions. When our behavior is conscious, we are more aware of the predictions we make.

When we feel that others' behavior is predictable, we feel that there is rhythm to our interactions with them. We need to feel that there is a rhythm to our interactions with others to feel comfortable interacting with them (Turner, 1988). The rhythm we expect to take place varies depending on the context of our interaction. We expect one kind of predictability when we interact with a server in a restaurant, and another when we are talking with a close friend. When other people's behavior is not predictable, we feel anxiety.

If we do not feel a part of the interaction taking place, we will have a difficult time seeing other people's behavior as predictable. Our cultural, ethnic, and gender identities provide us with implicit predictions about other people's behavior. The categories in which we place others (e.g., based on their culture, ethnicity, age) also provide us with implicit predictions of their behaviors. When we categorize others, our stereotypes of the groups (e.g., the traits we associate with the groups) in which we categorize them are activated. Our stereotypes provide predictions of other people's behavior, and our interactions will appear to have rhythm if other people conform to our stereotypes. If other people do not follow our stereotypes, our interaction with them will seem as if it lacks rhythm.

Predictability tends to increase as relationships become more intimate (we have more predictability about friends than acquaintances), but within a specific relationship predictability fluctuates over time. There is a dialectic between predictability and novelty. We need both predictability *and* novelty to maintain our relationships. Predictability is necessary to know how to expect other people to behave, but novelty is needed to keep our relationships interesting and to facilitate effective communication. When we are not conscious of our communication behavior, however, we may focus exclusively on our need for predictability and ignore our need for novelty.

Assumption 6: Intention Is Not a Necessary Condition for Communication

Intentions are instructions we give ourselves about how to communicate (Triandis, 1977). When we think about what we want to do in a particular situation (i.e., engage in cognitive activity), we form intentions. Intention, therefore, is a cognitive construct—it is part of our thought processes. We may not be able to accomplish our intentions, however. Our intention, for example, may be to be nonjudgmental in our interactions with others, but in actuality we may be very judgmental.

Our assumption is derived from Watzlawick, Beavin, and Jackson's (1967) first axiom of communication: "one cannot not communicate" (p. 51, emphasis deleted). The basis for this axiom is that any behavior, or the absence of any be-havior, communicates something if there is someone in the environment to notice the behavior, or its absence. In making this assumption, we are not contending all behavior is communication; rather, communication occurs any time one person at-tributes meaning to his or her own or another person's behavior. Taking this view implies it is not necessary for a person to transmit a message intentionally in order to communicate. Many intercultural misunderstandings, in fact, are due to the un-intentional behavior of a person from one culture being perceived, interpreted, and reacted to by a person from another culture. In other words, behavior that is not meant to communicate is interpreted by another person and influences the messages that person sends.

It is important to recognize that intentions are only one source of our com-munication behavior. Our communication behavior also can be based on two other sources, habits or emotions (Triandis, 1977). We engage in much of our communi-cation behavior out of habit. We have learned scripts that we enact in particular sit-uations. *Scripts* are predetermined courses of action we have learned. The greeting ritual is one example. The ritual for greeting others reduces the vast amount of un-certainty and anxiety present in initial interactions to manageable portions, and al-lows us to interact with others as though there was relatively little uncertainty or anxiety. The norms and rules for the ritual provide us with predictions about how others will respond in the situation. When someone deviates from the script or we enter a new situation, we cannot fall back on the rituals' implicit predictions. Un-der those circumstances, we have to reduce our uncertainty and anxiety before we can make accurate predictions and communicate effectively.

Our communication behavior also can be based on our affect, feelings, or emo-tions. We often react to others on a strictly emotional basis. If we feel we were criticized, for example, we may become defensive and strike out at the other person without think-ing. We can, however, manage our emotional reactions cognitively. Our communication behavior can be based on any one of these three sources or on some combination.

Assumption 7: Every Communication Message Has a Content Dimension and a Relationship Dimension

Watzlawick, Beavin, and Jackson (1967) argue that every communication message can be interpreted on two levels: what is said (the content level), and how it is said (the relationship level). The content level specifies the substance of the message, while the relationship level indicates how the substance is to be interpreted. The re-lationship dimension is "only rarely defined deliberately or with full awareness" (p. 52); it is, therefore, usually transmitted and interpreted unconsciously. The con-tent level usually is transmitted verbally, while the relationship level tends to be transmitted nonverbally. A student, for example, can say "I want to discuss my grade" to a professor, but the tone of voice will tell the professor whether it is go-ing to be a friendly discussion or a hostile encounter.

The way we communicate offers a definition of the relationship between us. The children's saying "Sticks and stones may break my bones, but words will never hurt me" is not accurate. The words we choose and the way we say them to others can and do hurt others and our relationship with them. As we show later, cultures vary with respect to the emphasis they place on the content and the relationship levels of messages.

Assumption 8: Communicators Impose Structure on Their Interactions

Watzlawick, Beavin, and Jackson's (1967) third axiom states that "the nature of a relationship is contingent upon the punctuation of the communicational sequences between the communicants" (p. 59, emphasis deleted). *Punctuation of the sequence of events* means the grouping of elements into a recognizable pattern, or the imposition of structure on the communication process. Without this grouping of elements, or imposition of structure, interaction would be uninterpretable. People not only impose a beginning and an ending on a sequence of events but also interpret a particular event as being a "cause" or an "effect" of their behavior. A husband, for example, may say he drinks (an effect) because his wife always works late (a cause). The wife, in contrast, may say she works late (an effect) because her husband drinks (a cause).

Every time we communicate, we impose structure on the process. "Culturally, we share many conventions of punctuation which, while no more or less accurate than other views of the same events, serve to organize common and important interactional sequences" (Watzlawick, Beavin, & Jackson, 1967, p. 56). When communicating with people from our own culture, we usually are safe in assuming that the structure we impose is roughly the same as the one they impose. When communicating with people from another culture, however, we must determine how they impose structure on the process of communication if we are to interpret and predict their behavior accurately.

In summary, the assumptions outlined above present a relatively clear picture of how we view communication. We elaborate on our conceptualization in the next chapter, but the above specification of our assumptions is sufficient to demonstrate what we mean by communication. Those aspects of our assumptions necessary for delimiting communication are as follows: (1) it is a symbolic activity; (2) it is a process; (3) it involves the transmitting and interpreting of messages; (4) it involves creating meaning; (5) it takes place at varying levels of conscious awareness; and (6) intention is not necessary for it to take place.

Uncertainty and Anxiety

We communicate for many reasons. We communicate to inform someone about something, to entertain another person, to change another person's attitudes or behavior, and to reinforce our view of ourselves, to name only a few of the possibilities. No matter what our reason is for communicating, we always experience some degree of uncertainty (a cognitive response, or a response involving our thoughts) and anxiety (an affective, or emotional, response). High levels of uncertainty and anxiety inhibit effective communication.

Interacting with people from other cultures and/or ethnic groups is a novel situation for most people. Novel situations are characterized by high levels of uncertainty and anxiety. "The immediate psychological result of being in a new situation is lack of security. Ignorance of the potentialities inherent in the situation, of the means to reach a goal, and of the probable outcomes of an intended action causes insecurity" (Herman & Schield, 1960, p. 165). Attempts to deal with the ambiguity of new situations involves a pattern of information seeking (uncertainty reduction) and tension (anxiety) reduction (Ball-Rokeach, 1973).

Uncertainty refers to our inability to predict or explain others' behavior, feelings, attitudes, or values (Berger & Calabrese, 1975). When we reduce uncertainty about others and ourselves, understanding is possible. Understanding involves obtaining information, knowing, comprehending, and interpreting. Three levels of understanding can be differentiated: description, prediction, and explanation (Berger et al., 1976). Description involves specifying what is observed in terms of its physical attributes (i.e., drawing a picture in words). Prediction involves projecting what will happen in a particular situation, while explanation involves stating why something occurred.

We make predictions and create explanations all the time when we communicate. We rarely describe others' behavior, however. When we communicate with others, we typically interpret messages by attaching meaning directly to them. We do not stop to describe what we saw or heard before we interpret it. Rather, we interpret messages as we perceive them. The problem is that we base our interpretations on our life experiences, culture, or ethnic group memberships. Since our life experiences differ from the other person's, our interpretations of the other person's behavior may be incorrect. Incorrect interpretations often lead to misunderstandings.

Anxiety refers to the feeling of being uneasy, tense, worried, or apprehensive about what might happen. It is an affective (i.e., emotional) response, not a cognitive response as is uncertainty. While uncertainty results from our inability to predict others' behavior, "anxiety stems from the anticipation of negative consequences. People fear at least four types of negative consequences: psychological or behavioral consequences for the self, and negative evaluations by members of the outgroup and the ingroup" (Stephan & Stephan, 1985, p. 159).

Our ingroups are groups with which we identify that are important to us (Triandis, 1988). If we define our religious group as important and identify with being members of our religion, for example, our religious group is one of our ingroups. Other religious groups then become outgroups for us. We may, however, identify with many ingroups. When we interact with another person, we categorize that person by placing her or him into an ingroup or an outgroup. We experience more uncertainty and anxiety when we communicate with members of outgroups than when we communicate with members of ingroups.

Many other factors affect the amount of uncertainty and anxiety we experience in a particular situation. The degree to which we are familiar with the situation and know how to behave, the expectations we have for our own and others' behavior, and the degree to which we perceive ourselves to be similar to the other person, for example, influence our levels of uncertainty and anxiety. Our ability to reduce our uncertainty and anxiety, in turn, influences the degree to which we can communicate effectively.

We do not mean to imply that we want to reduce our uncertainty and anxiety totally when we communicate with strangers. Low levels of uncertainty and anxiety are not functional. If anxiety is too low, we do not care enough to perform well. If uncertainty is too low, there is little "mystery" and we get bored. Moderate levels of uncertainty and anxiety are desirable for effective communication and adaptation to new environments (Gudykunst, 1995). We examine uncertainty and anxiety in more detail in Chapter 2.

CONCEPTUALIZING CULTURE

Culture is a term that means many different things to different people. Some writers discuss culture in terms that suggest it is the same as society, while others define it in such a way that they can talk about male and female cultures. In order to clarify our conceptualization of culture, we will take a brief digression into the more general study of social organization. Through an understanding of social organization, we will generate a working definition for culture.

The Process of Social Organization

The study of social organization is concerned with the way in which human activity is coordinated or organized. Olsen (1978) contends that social life is "a process that is continually being created and recreated as individuals bring order and meaning to their collective social life" (p. 4). In other words, like communication, social life is a dynamic, ongoing process without a beginning or an end.

Social organization cannot come about unless some degree of "order" exists. Olsen (1978) differentiates three levels of ordering involved in social life: personal, social, and cultural. *Personal ordering* refers to the process that "gives coherence and stability to the various cognitive and affective psychological processes occurring within an individual" (p. 7). This level of ordering takes place within us as our minds bring together our feelings, attitudes, and needs into a coherent whole, which we call a personality.

For *social ordering* to exist, two or more individuals must interact with each other over time. Social interaction occurs whenever the behavior of one person influences another person's thoughts and/or behavior (Olsen, 1978). As individuals interact over time, ongoing social relationships are formed among them. When these patterns of behavior become stable, we can say social ordering takes place. Social ordering therefore "grows out of the interactions and relationships of individuals as these activities become patterned and recurrent through time" (Olsen, 1978, p. 7).

Obviously, different levels of social ordering occur. When two people interact for an extended period of time and their behavior becomes patterned, for example, one form of social ordering takes place (a friendship is formed). Similarly, when a man and a woman get married and have children and interact on a daily basis, their behavior becomes patterned and another type of social ordering occurs (a family). Furthermore, when people within some geographical area interact over time and their behavior becomes patterned, we again can say that social ordering develops (a society is "born"). If a group of people interact together over time and their behavior becomes patterned (i.e., social ordering has taken place), they develop shared agreements about how to interpret the world they inhabit. In other words, patterned and recurrent social interactions "give rise to shared sets of cultural ideas that symbolize, reflect and give meaning to the social order" (Olsen, 1978, p. 163).

Cultural ordering involves the development of a set of shared symbolic ideas associated with patterns of social ordering. Any group that develops social ordering also displays cultural ordering. Cultural ordering is associated not only with large collectivities (such as nations) but also with smaller collectivities (such as ethnic groups and families) that interact on an ongoing basis. To the extent collectivities are interrelated or overlap with each other, they share cultural ideas (Olsen, 1978).

A Working Definition for Culture

Olsen's (1978) analysis of the process of social organization specifies how cultural ordering emerges, but it does not adequately define culture. We use Keesing's (1974) definition of culture. His definition is long, but not overly technical:

> Culture, conceived as a system of competence shared in its broad design and deeper principles, and varying between individuals in its specificities, is then not all of what an individual knows and thinks and feels about his [or her] world. It is his [or her] theory of what his [or her] fellows know, believe, and mean, his [or her] theory of the code being followed, the game being played, in the society into which he [or she] was born. . . . It is this theory to which a native actor [or actress] refers in interpreting the unfamiliar or the ambiguous, in interacting with strangers (or supernaturals), and in other settings peripheral to the familiarity of mundane everyday life space; and with which he [or she] creates the stage on which the games of life are played. . . . But note that the actor's [or actress's] "theory" of his [or her] culture, like his [or her] theory of his [or her] language may be in large measure unconscious. Actors [or actresses] follow rules of which they are not consciously aware, and assume a world to be "out there" that they have in fact created with culturally shaped and shaded patterns of mind. We can recognize that not every individual shares precisely the same theory of the cultural code, that not every individual knows all the sectors of the culture . . . no one native actor [or actress] knows all the culture, and each has a variant version of the code. Culture in this view is ordered not simply as a collection of symbols fitted together by the analyst but as a system of knowledge, shaped and constrained by the way the human brain acquires, organizes, and processes information and creates "internal models of reality." (p. 89)

This definition suggests that culture is our theory of the "game being played" in our society. We use our theory of the game being played in interacting with the other people we encounter. It tells us how to communicate with others and how to interpret their behavior. We generally are not highly aware of the rules of the game being played, but we behave as though there is general agreement on the rules.

We learn to be members of our culture from our parents, from teachers in schools, from our religious institutions, from our peers, and from the mass media. Originally, we learn about our culture from our parents. Our parents begin to teach us the norms and communication rules that guide behavior in our culture. Norms are guidelines with a basis in morality for how we should behave or how we should not behave. Rules, in contrast, are guidelines for the ways we are expected to communicate. Rules are not based in morality (Olsen, 1978). Our parents do not explicitly tell us the norms and rules of our culture. They do not, for example, tell us that when we meet someone for the first time, we should stick out our right hands and shake three times. Rather, they teach us the norms and rules by modeling how to behave and correcting us when we violate a norm or rule.

Once we are old enough to interact with other children, they reinforce the norms and rules we learned from our parents. We also learn additional norms and rules of our culture from them. We learn from our peers, for example, how to be cooperative and how to compete with others. When we attend religious services or school, we learn other norms and rules of our culture. The other way we learn about our culture is through the mass media, especially television. Television teaches us many of the day-to-day norms of our culture and provides us with a view of reality. Television has become the medium through which most of us learn what others' expectations are for our behavior. It appears that the more television we watch, the more our views of reality overlap with others' (Gerbner et al., 1980).

Members of a culture do not all share exactly the same view of their culture (Keesing, 1974). No one member of a culture knows all aspects of the culture, and all members of a culture have a unique view of their culture. The theories that members of a culture share, however, overlap sufficiently so that the members can coordinate their behavior in everyday life. Olsen (1978) points out that

> as people communicate the meanings of their actions to each other and work out shared interpretations of activities and definitions of situations, they develop a common culture that is shared by all the participants. Shared culture in turn influences and guides—but does not fully determine—these people's collective activities by providing them with interpretations of social life, role expectations, common definitions of situations, and social norms. (p. 107)

Since we developed our individual implicit theories of communication while learning to be members of our culture, there is overlap in the implicit personal theories of communication members of the same culture use to guide their behavior.

Our culture influences our behavior directly through the norms and rules we use to guide our behavior when we interact with others. Our culture also indirectly affects our communication through the individual characteristics we learn when we are socialized into our culture. As we are socialized into our culture, we learn how we are expected to view ourselves (e.g., in the United States people learn to think of themselves as unique individuals). The way we view ourselves, in turn, influences the way we communicate. Figure 1.1 provides a visual summary of how culture influences our communication. We discuss this model in detail in Chapter 3 when we focus on culture.

Our culture provides us with a system of knowledge that generally allows us to know how to communicate with other people and how to interpret their behavior (Keesing, 1974). The term *culture* usually is reserved to refer to the systems of knowledge used by relatively large numbers of people (i.e., cultural ordering at the societal level). The boundaries between cultures usually, but not always, coincide with political, or national, boundaries between countries. We can speak, for example, of the culture of the United States, the Mexican culture, the Japanese culture, and so forth.

If the term *culture* is reserved for cultural ordering at the societal level, we need a term to use to refer to cultural ordering at lower levels of social ordering. The term traditionally used for this purpose is *subculture*. A *subculture,* therefore, involves a set of shared symbolic ideas held by a collectivity within a larger society. A subculture's set of cultural ideas generally is derived from the larger (societal) culture but differs in some respect. Although the term *subculture* often is used to refer to racial and/or ethnic groups, there obviously are other types of subcultures. We can, for example, talk about a student subculture, a medical subculture (people who work in medicine), a lower-class subculture, a middle-class subculture, or a business subculture, to name only a few. Each of these groups shares many common cultural ideas with a larger culture but has some that are unique.

Before proceeding, we must point out that we believe that our culture influences our communication and that our communication influences our culture. We focus throughout the remainder of the book, however, on the influence of culture on our communication. This influence is mostly out of our awareness. To communicate effectively with people from other cultures and/or ethnic groups, we must be aware of culture's influence on our communication.

Figure 1.1   Cultural influences on communication.

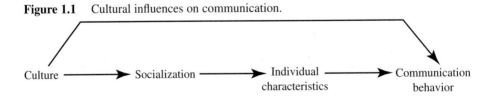

Culture ⟶ Socialization ⟶ Individual characteristics ⟶ Communication behavior

DIFFERENTIATING TERMINOLOGY

Given the preceding conceptualizations of communication and culture, we are now ready to present a working definition for intercultural communication. Putting the two conceptualizations together, we stipulate that *intercultural communication is a transactional, symbolic process involving the attribution of meaning between people from different cultures.* It should be noted that this definition does not suggest communication must be effective in order to be labeled intercultural. When we use the term *intercultural communication,* we are not implying that the communication is either effective or ineffective. Effectiveness is a separate dimension; thus to say that two people engaged in intercultural communication is not to say they understood each other. (In Chapter 10, we examine intercultural effectiveness, which is defined as minimizing misunderstandings when people from different cultures communicate.)

Many terms are used to refer to related aspects of communication. So that there is no confusion concerning how we use these terms and how they are used in the intercultural literature, we must introduce these terms. If intercultural communication refers to communication between people from different cultures, then *intracultural* communication refers to communication between people from the same culture. It should be remembered that we reserve the term *culture* for cultural ordering at the societal level. Thus, if we examine communication between two Japanese *or* between two Germans, we are looking at intracultural communication. On the other hand, if we observe communication *between* a Japanese *and* a German, we are looking at intercultural communication.

It should be noted here that we see the underlying communication processes in intercultural and intracultural communication as being essentially the same. The two forms of communication are not different in kind, only in degree. In other words, the variables influencing intercultural and intracultural communication are the same, but some variables have more of an influence on our communication in one situation than in another. Our ethnocentric attitudes, for example, influence our intercultural communication more than our intracultural communication, but our ethnocentric attitudes also influence our intracultural communication. We differentiate between intracultural and intercultural only for the sake of clarity in communicating with you, not to suggest they are different types of communication.

Another term that needs to be clarified is *cross-cultural.* While this term often is used as a synonym for intercultural, the term *cross-cultural* traditionally implies a comparison of some phenomenon across cultures. If, for example, we examine the use of self-disclosure in Japan *and* Germany, we are making a cross-cultural comparison. If we look at how Japanese use self-disclosure when communicating *with* Germans and how Germans use self-disclosure when communicating *with* Japanese, we are looking at intercultural communication.

If the term *culture* refers to societal cultures, then, as indicated earlier, a subculture is a subset of a culture having some different values, norms, and/or symbols that are not shared by all members of the larger culture. In other words, a subculture involves a set of ideas that arise from the larger culture but differ in some respects. With respect to our differentiation of terminology, the most important subcultures are races and ethnic groups. The labels *race* and *ethnic group* often are used interchangeably. Such usage is incorrect. A *race* is a group of people who are biologically similar. An *ethnic group,* on the other hand, is a group of people who share a common cultural heritage usually based on a common national origin or language. Jews are, therefore, an ethnic group, not a race. An ethnic group may be made up of many races, and, similarly, a race may consist of more than one ethnic group.

Even though the process of communication between people from different subcultures is essentially the same as the process of communication between people from different cultures, different terms often are used. The terms used to designate communication between people from different subcultures are not as clear as we would like, but at times it is useful to be able to differentiate the type of communication being discussed by using specific terms. We therefore stipulate that *interracial communication* refers to communication between people from different races and *interethnic communication* refers to communication between people from different ethnic groups. The differentration is not this simple, however. One culture may include several races and/or ethnic groups, and one race or ethnic group may exist in different cultures. This overlap leads to problems in labeling some forms of communication. If we look at communication between a white person from the United States and a black from Ghana, for example, are we observing interracial communication or intercultural communication? The answer, obviously, is both. As another example, what if a Jew from the United States is communicating with a Jew from Israel? Such communication is both intraethnic and intercultural. Such situations lead to conceptual confusion when we try to apply these terms.

Since the underlying processes in intracultural, intercultural, interracial, and interethnic communication are essentially the same and there is confusion as to when some of the terms are applicable, we need a way to refer to the common underlying process without differentiating between the different "types" of communication. The term intercultural communication is the most general; however, it is not adequate because it has specific connotations. The title of this book, *Communicating with Strangers,* hints at our solution to this problem. Anytime we communicate with people who are different and unknown and those people are in an environment unfamiliar to them, we are communicating with strangers. The people generally viewed as the most unknown and unfamiliar are those from different societal cultures, but people from different races or ethnic groups are also unknown and unfamiliar. In addition, people from our own culture can be unknown and unfamiliar in the same sense; for example, a new groom approaching his bride's family for the first time is a stranger, according to our use of the term. In Chapter 2, we elaborate on our conceptualization of strangers; for now it is sufficient to say that when we talk about communicating with strangers, we are referring to the underlying process shared in common by intracultural, intercultural, intraracial, interracial, intraethnic, and interethnic communication.

PLAN FOR THE BOOK

In the next chapter, we elaborate on our conceptualization of strangers and give an overview of the process of communicating with strangers. Also in Chapter 2, we present a model of communication used to organize the material covered in Parts Two and Three of the book.

In Part Two (Chapters 3 to 6), we examine the conceptual filters influencing our communication with strangers. The strategy employed in this part is to introduce the relevant concepts, examine how they vary across cultures, and apply them where feasible to our communication with strangers. Specifically, in Chapter 3, we examine the cultural influences on our communication with strangers. Chapter 4 focuses on the sociocultural influences on our communication with strangers, including our memberships in social groups. In Chapter 5, we look at social cognitive factors that create expectations when we communicate with strangers, our stereotypes and intergroup attitudes (ethnocentrism and prejudice)—the psychocultural influences. Chapter 6, the final chapter in Part Two, focuses on the environmental influences on our communication with strangers, including climate, geography, architecture, the situation, privacy regulation, territoriality, and temporality.

In Part Three (Chapters 7 to 9), we look at the transmitting and interpreting processes. Our strategy in this part is to introduce the concepts, to examine their variation across cultures, and to apply them to our communication with strangers. We begin, in Chapter 7, by examining cultural variations in interpreting, focusing on perception, attributional processes, cognitive styles, and patterns of thought. In Chapter 8, we look at cultural variations in verbal behavior, including language and patterns of thought. Cultural variations in nonverbal behaviors are examined in Chapter 9.

The final part of the book, Part Four (Chapters 10 to 15), considers selected aspects of intercultural interaction. The issues of intercultural communication effectiveness and perceived communication competence are discussed in Chapter 10. In Chapter 11, how we can effectively manage conflict with strangers is examined. Chapter 12 focuses on relationships between people from different subcultures or cultures, including friendships and marital relationships. In Chapter 13, we examine strangers' adaptation to new cultural environments. We examine both short-term adjustment and long-term acculturation of strangers in this chapter. Chapter 14 contains a discussion of the process of becoming intercultural, which is a desirable outcome to seek as a result of our communication with strangers. We conclude in Chapter 15 by discussing how cultural and ethnic differences can be used as resources in building community.

SUMMARY

The purpose of this chapter is to introduce the two major concepts, communication and culture, used throughout the remainder of this book. In light of the eight assumptions we make about the nature of communication, we stipulate that communication is a symbolic process involving the attribution of meaning. We reserve the term *culture* for the cultural ordering process associated with the societal level of social ordering. Intercultural communication, therefore, is stipulated to be communication between people from different societal cultures.

We take the position that the underlying process of communication between people from different cultures or subcultures is the same as the underlying process of communication between people from the same culture or subculture. Given the similarity of the underlying process and the confusion of existing terminology, we argue that what is needed is a way to refer to the underlying process that all types of communication (i.e., intracultural, interracial, interethnic, and intercultural) have in common. Since none of the present terms are adequate, we introduce our notion of communicating with strangers. By *communicating with strangers,* we mean communicating with people who are unknown and unfamiliar, including people from another culture and people from our own culture or subculture who are in an environment new to them.

STUDY QUESTIONS

1. Why do different people attach different meanings to symbols?
2. What factors influence the meanings we attach to messages?
3. Why can messages be transmitted from one person to another, while meanings cannot?
4. How do our implicit theories of communication influence the way we communicate?
5. How does predictability provide rhythm to our interactions?
6. Why are intentions not necessary for communication to take place?
7. What is the difference between the content and relationship dimensions of messages?
8. How do we impose structure on our communication?
9. Why are uncertainty and anxiety important aspects of communication?
10. What is meant by saying that "culture is our theory of the game being played"?
11. How do cross-cultural and intercultural communication differ?

SUGGESTED READING

Fisher, B. A. (1978). *Perspectives on human communication.* New York: Macmillan.
Olsen, M. (1978). *The process of social organization* (2nd ed.). New York: Holt, Rinehart, and Winston.
Triandis, H. C. (1994). *Culture and social behavior.* New York: McGraw-Hill.
Watzlawick, P., Beavin, J., & Jackson, D. (1967). *The pragmatics of human communication.* New York: Norton.

2

An Approach to the Study of Intercultural Communication

See at a distance an undesirable person;
See close at hand a desirable person;
Come closer to the undesirable person;
Move away from the desirable person.
Coming close and moving apart,
how interesting life is.
Gensho Ogura

Cultural variability in people's backgrounds influences their communication behavior. This cultural variability in communication leads many scholars studying intercultural communication to view it as a unique form of communication, differing in kind from other forms of communication (e.g., intracultural communication, communication between people from the same culture). This point of view, however, is not accepted widely. Sarbaugh (1979) points out that

> there appears to be a temptation among scholars and practitioners of communication to approach intercultural communication as though it were a different process than intracultural communication. As one begins to identify the variables that operate in the communication being studied, however, it becomes apparent that they are the same for both intracultural and intercultural settings. (p. 5)

We agree with Sarbaugh; not only are the variables the same, but the underlying communication process also is the same.

We believe that any approach to the study of intercultural communication must be consistent with the study of intracultural communication. In this chapter, and the remainder of this book, we present a perspective for the study of communication that is useful for understanding not only our communication with people from other cultures or subcultures, but also our communication with people from our own culture or subculture. We begin by looking at the linking concept in our view of communication, the concept of the stranger.

THE CONCEPT OF THE STRANGER

When we are confronted with cultural differences (and other forms of group differences, such as gender, ethnic, or class differences), we tend to view people from other cultures (or groups) as strangers. The term *stranger* is somewhat ambiguous in that it often is used to refer to aliens, intruders, foreigners, outsiders, newcomers, and immigrants, as well as any other person who is unknown and unfamiliar. Despite this ambiguity, "the concept of the stranger remains one of the most powerful sociological tools for analyzing social processes of individuals and groups confronting new social orders" (Shack, 1979, p. 2).

Simmel (1950/1908) views strangers as possessing the contradictory qualities of being both near and far at the same time:

> The unity of nearness and remoteness in every human relation is organized, in the phenomenon of the stranger, in a way which may be most briefly formulated by saying that in the relationship to him [or her], distance means that he [or she], who is also far, is actually near. . . . The stranger . . . is an element of the group itself. His [or her] position as a full-fledged member involves being both outside it and confronting it. (p. 402)

Strangers represent the idea of nearness because they are physically close and the idea of remoteness because they have different values and ways of doing things. Strangers are physically present and participating in a situation and, at the same time, are outside the situation because they are not members of the group.

Wood's (1934) view of the stranger is broader than Simmel's, and she adds a new dimension to describing strangers, meeting for the first time:

> We shall describe the stranger as one who has come into face-to-face contact with the group for the first time. . . . For us the stranger may be, as with Simmel, a potential wanderer who comes today and goes tomorrow, or he [or she] may come today and remain with us permanently. The condition of being a stranger is not . . . dependent upon the future duration of the contact, but it is determined by the fact that it was the first face-to-face meeting of individuals who have not known one another before. (pp. 43–44)

Wood, therefore, sees strangers as newly arrived outsiders.

Like Wood, Schuetz (1944) takes a broader view of the concept of the stranger than does Simmel. For Schuetz, the term *stranger* means "an adult individual . . . who tries to be permanently accepted or at least partially tolerated by the group which he [or she] approaches" (p. 499). This conceptualization includes not only the obvious cases of immigrants and sojourners to other cultures but also a person trying to join a closed club, a groom attempting to be accepted by the bride's family, a recruit entering the army, or any other person coming into a new and unfamiliar group. Schuetz argues that strangers do not understand the social world inhabited by the members of the group they approach. Parrillo (1980) succinctly summarizes Schuetz's perspective:

> Because this is a shared world, it is an intersubjective one. For the native, then, every social situation is a coming together not only of roles and identities, but also of shared realities—the intersubjective structure of consciousness. What is taken for granted by the native is problematic for the stranger. In a familiar world, people live through the day by responding to daily routine without questioning or reflection. To strangers, however, every situation is new and is therefore experienced as a crisis. (p. 3)

One of the defining characteristics of this view is that strangers may perceive their interactions in their new surroundings as a series of crises.

Herman and Schield (1960) take a similar position when they argue that the major problem strangers face in their new surroundings is "lack of security." Strangers do not have the knowledge necessary to understand fully their new environment or the communication of the people who live in it. Further, members of the host group do not possess information regarding individual strangers, even though they may have some information about the group or culture from which the strangers come. Since we do not have information regarding individual strangers, our initial impression of them must, therefore, be an abstract or categoric one (i.e., a stereotypic one). Strangers are classified on the basis of whatever information we can obtain. If the only information we have is their culture, we base our initial impression on this information. If we have additional information (their ethnicity, gender, class), we use that as well.

Strangers, as we conceive of them, are people who are members of different groups and unknown to us. It should be obvious that strangerhood is a figure-ground phenomenon—a stranger's status is always defined in relation to a host, a native, or some existing group. A person from the United States visiting another country and a person from another country visiting the United States are both strangers. A European American teacher in a predominantly African American school, a Native American working in a predominantly European American organization, a Vietnamese refugee in the United States, a new bride visiting the groom's family, and a Chicano moving into a predominantly European American neighborhood are all examples of strangers. In general, we include anyone entering a relatively unknown or unfamiliar environment under the rubric of stranger. This conceptualization, therefore, subsumes both Wood's and Schuetz's views on strangers.

Obviously, not everyone we meet for the first time is truly unknown and unfamiliar. Sometimes we are familiar with or know something about people we meet for the first time. Cohen (1972) argues that we can say our social interactions, not just our interactions with people we meet for the first time, vary with respect to the degree of strangeness and/or familiarity present in the interaction. Our interactions with close friends and relatives involve a high degree of familiarity, while our interactions with acquaintances and coworkers involve less familiarity and more strangeness. When we meet people for the first time, there may be any degree of strangeness and/or familiarity. When we meet a close friend of our best friend for the first time, for example, we may be somewhat familiar with that person already because of what our close friend has told us about her or him. When we meet a person from another subculture of our culture (e.g., a person from another ethnic group), in contrast, our interaction with that person usually involves more strangeness than familiarity. Because they do not share the same culture, our interactions with people from other cultures often involve the highest degree of strangeness and the least degree of familiarity.

Our use of the term *strangers* throughout this book refers to those people in relationships where there is a relatively high degree of strangeness and a relatively low degree of familiarity. Since our interactions with people from other cultures tend to involve the highest degree of strangeness and the lowest degree of familiarity, we focus on these interactions, but we also examine other interactions involving a relatively high degree of strangeness (e.g., those with members of different ethnic groups, social classes, ages).

As indicated earlier, strangerhood is a figure-ground phenomenon. When members of other groups approach our group in our environment, they are the strangers. When we approach other groups in their environment, we are the strangers. Harman (1987) points out that "in the dominant mode of social organization in western society—the metropolis—the stranger is not the exception but the rule. . . . strangeness is no longer a temporary condition to be overcome, but a way of life" (p. 44). She contends we are all strangers trying to become members of different groups or maintain our group memberships. Harman argues that "the defining characteristics of the modern stranger are cultural fluency and membership orientation. The expert navigator of the cultural world is one who may 'fit in' anywhere by being acutely aware of the cultural nuances" (p. 159). Kristeva (1991) also suggests that when we see others as strangers, we come to recognize the strangeness in ourselves. "By recognizing *our* uncanny strangeness we shall neither suffer from it or enjoy it from the outside. The [stranger] is within me, hence we are all [strangers]" (p. 192).

In looking at the general process of communication with strangers, we are able to overcome one of the major conceptual problems of many analyses of intercultural communication. The problem to which we refer involves the drawing of artificial distinctions between intracultural, intercultural, interracial, and interethnic communication. While some variables may take on more importance in one situation than in another (e.g., our ethnic prejudices may be more important in interethnic communication than in intraethnic communication), each of the situations is influenced by the same variables, albeit in varying degrees (e.g., in our intraethnic communication, our prejudices regarding sexism may be more of an influence than those regarding ethnicity). If the variables influencing each situation and the underlying process of communication are the same, it does not make sense to draw artificial distinctions between types of communication with those who are unfamiliar. By using the stranger as a linking concept, we can examine a general process, communicating with strangers, which subsumes intracultural, intercultural, interracial, and interethnic communication into one general framework. Before moving on, however, we find it worthwhile to reiterate some of the qualities of the stranger concept that help us understand our communication with people from different groups.

Levine (1979) points out that it is the dialectic between closeness and remoteness

> that makes the position of strangers socially problematic in all times and places. When those who would be close, in any sense of the term, are actually close, and those who should be distant are distant, everyone is "in his [or her] place." When those who should be distant are close, however, the inevitable result is a degree of tension and anxiety which necessitates some special kind of response. (p. 29)

Levine goes on to argue that

> group members derive security from relating in familiar ways to fellow group members and from maintaining their distance from nonmembers through established insulating mechanisms. In situations where an outsider comes into the social space normally occupied by group members only, one can presume an initial response of anxiety and at least latent antagonism. (p. 30)

As we indicated in Chapter 1, reducing anxiety is one of the major functions of communication when we interact with strangers. The anxiety we experience when interacting with strangers is a critical factor influencing our communication and one of the factors that differentiates communication with strangers from communication with people who are familiar. We discuss this concept in more detail later in this chapter.

Prior to presenting our organizing model of communication, we overview the process of communicating with strangers. Our focus in the next section is on differentiating how communication with strangers (i.e., intergroup communication) differs from our communication with people who are familiar (i.e., interpersonal communication).

INTERGROUP AND INTERPERSONAL BEHAVIOR

The communication processes underlying interpersonal and intergroup communication are the same. Different factors, nevertheless, are given different weights in the two types of communication. In this section, we present two different, but complementary, ways of differentiating between interpersonal and intergroup behavior.

Types of Data Used in Making Predictions

Miller and Steinberg (1975) argue that we use three types of data when we make predictions about other people's behavior. The first type of data we use is *cultural.* The people in any culture generally behave in a regular fashion because of their postulates, norms, and values. It is this regularity that allows us to make predictions on the basis of cultural data. Miller and Sunnafrank (1982) point out that

> knowledge about another person's culture—its language, dominant values, beliefs, and prevailing ideology—often permits predictions of the person's probable responses to certain messages. . . . Upon first encountering a stranger, cultural information provides the only grounds for communicative predictions. This fact explains the uneasiness and perceived lack of control most people experience when thrust into an alien culture: they not only lack information about the individuals with whom they must communicate, they are bereft of information concerning shared cultural norms and values. (pp. 226–227)

Cultural data are used to predict behavior of people from our own culture and people from other cultures.

Two major factors influence our predictive accuracy when we use cultural data. First, the more experiences at the cultural level we have, the better our predictive accuracy is. When we are confronting someone from our own culture, the experiences to which we refer are in our culture. When we are communicating with strangers, on the other hand, our accuracy depends on our experiences with their culture. If we know little or nothing about strangers' culture, our predictions will be more inaccurate than if we know a lot about their culture. Second, errors in predictions are made either because we are not aware of the strangers' cultural experiences or because we try to predict the behavior of strangers on the basis of cultural experiences different from the ones they have had, for example, when we make ethnocentric predictions on the basis of our own cultural experiences (Miller & Steinberg, 1975).

The second type of data used in making predictions is *sociological.* Sociological predictions are based on strangers' memberships in or aspirations to particular social groups. "Knowledge of an individual's membership groups, as well as the reference groups to which he or she aspires, permits numerous predictions about responses to various messages" (Miller & Sunnafrank, 1982, p. 227). Membership in social groups may be voluntary, or strangers may be classified as a member of a group because of certain characteristics they possess. Our predictions at the sociological level, for example, include those based on strangers' memberships in political or other social groups, the roles they fill, their gender, or their ethnicity. Miller and Sunnafrank (1982) argue that sociological-level data are the principal kind used to predict the behavior of people from the same culture. The major error in making predictions based on sociological-level data stems from the fact that strangers are members of many groups and when we communicate with strangers, we are not always sure which group's norms and values are influencing their behavior (Miller & Steinberg, 1975).

The final type of data used in making predictions about the outcomes of our communication behavior is *psychological.* Psychological predictions are based on the specific people with whom we are communicating. When using this type of data, we are concerned with how these people are different from and similar to other members of their culture and the groups to which they belong. When predictions are based on psychological data, "each participant relates to the other in terms of what sets the other apart from most people. They take into consideration each other's individual differences in terms of the subject and the occasion" (Dance & Larson, 1972, p. 56).

It is important to keep in mind that our predictions are rarely made on the basis of only one type of data. Once we have some psychological information about strangers with whom we are communicating, we use this information and combine it with our cultural and sociological data to make predictions about their behavior. Most of our predictions are some combination of the three levels of data, but one level often predominates.

For the purpose of the present analysis, we modify the labels for the three levels of data used in making predictions. Since all three levels are highly interrelated, we use labels reflecting the interrelations: *cultural, sociocultural,* and *psychocultural.* Our modification of the last two labels is intended only to emphasize that the three levels of data are interrelated, not to reflect a disagreement with Miller and Steinberg's (1975) conceptualization.

Our Identities Influence Our Behavior

We think about ourselves differently in different situations. The different ways we think about ourselves are our *identities.* In any particular situation, we may or may not be conscious of the identities influencing our behavior. Even though we may not be aware of the identities influencing our behavior, we act as though a clear identity is guiding our behavior (R. H. Turner, 1987).

Our identities can be grouped under three broad categories: human, social, and personal (J. C. Turner, 1987). Our human identities involve those views of ourselves that we believe we share with all other humans. It is important to recognize that "people and their cultures perish in isolation, but they are born or reborn in contact with other men and women, with men and women of another culture, another creed, another race. If we do not recognize our humanity in others, we shall not recognize it in ourselves" (Fuentes, 1992, Back cover). To understand our human identities, we have to look for those things we share in common with all other humans.

Our social identities involve those views of ourselves that we assume we share with other members of our ingroups. Ingroups are "groups of people about whose welfare [we are] concerned, with whom [we are] willing to cooperate without demanding equitable returns, and separation from whom leads to discomfort or even pain" (Triandis, 1988, p. 75). Our social identities may be based on the roles we play, such as student, professor, or parent; the demographic categories in which we are categorized, such as our nationality, ethnicity, gender, or age; and our membership in formal and informal organizations, such as a political party, voluntary organization, or social club.

Our personal identities involve those views of ourselves that differentiate us from other members of our ingroups—those characteristics that define us as unique individuals. Our personality characteristics, for example, are part of our personal identities. Our personal identities may involve views of ourselves as being intelligent, attractive, caring, and so forth.

Our different identities influence our behavior in different situations. Tajfel's (1978) distinction between intergroup and interpersonal behavior is based on which identity is guiding behavior:

> These differences can be conceived as lying on a continuum, one extreme of which can be described as being "purely" interpersonal and the other as being "purely" intergroup. What is meant by "purely" interpersonal is any social encounter between two or more people in which all interaction that takes place is determined by the personal relationship between the individuals and by their respective individual characteristics [e.g., personal identities generate behavior]. The "intergroup" extreme is that in which all of the behavior of two or more individuals towards each other is determined by their membership in different social groups or categories [e.g., social identities generate behavior]. (p. 41)

Tajfel's distinction is similar to Miller and Steinberg's (1975) discussion of making predictions based on cultural, sociological, or psychological data. Pure interpersonal behavior occurs when all predictions are made on the basis of psychological data. Pure intergroup behavior, on the other hand, takes place when all predictions are made on the basis of sociological and/or cultural data. Pure intergroup behavior takes place when no individual differences are recognized. The source of intergroup behavior is social identity, and the source of interpersonal behavior is personal identity.

Tajfel (1978) argues that it is impossible to conceive of pure interpersonal behavior, that no instance of it can be found. "It is impossible to imagine a social encounter between two people which will not be affected, at least to some minimal degree, by their mutual assignments of one another to a variety of social categories about which some general expectations concerning their characteristics and behavior exist in the mind of the interactants" (p. 41). Tajfel contends that social identities come into play even in relationships between husbands and wives and between close friends. It is possible, in contrast, to conceive of an example of pure intergroup behavior. Tajfel (1978) cites an example of a bomber crew on a mission against an enemy population. The bomber crew members are involved in pure intergroup behavior because they are not perceiving the enemy as individuals. If you have ever watched the television program *M*A*S*H*, you may recall the episode "Dear Sigmund," in which a U.S. bombardier limps into the 4077th for medical aid. While

Hawkeye is administering to his wounds, the flyer talks about how the war does not inconvenience him much. All he does is strap himself into his seat in the plane, fly over the enemy, push a button, and drop his bombs, returning to his wife in Tokyo every weekend. Hawkeye then asks the bombardier if he has ever seen the enemy, and the flyer says he has not. The bombardier is, therefore, engaged in a pure form of intergroup behavior. During his stay at the 4077th, however, the bombardier is put to work carrying the wounded into the operating room. During one trip into the operating room, he notices a young Korean child who is about to undergo surgery. He asks Hawkeye what happened to the child. Hawkeye tells him that a bomb exploded in the child's village. The bombardier then asks whether it was one of "ours" or one of "theirs." Colonel Potter responds by saying it doesn't make any difference whose bomb it was. The bombardier declares that it makes a difference to him. Hawkeye counters by saying it doesn't make any difference to the child. At this point, the bombardier begins to see the Koreans, on whom he has been dropping bombs, as individuals. Since he now recognizes individual differences, however slight, in the members of the other group, the bombardier's behavior will not be pure intergroup behavior.

Other conceptualizations suggest that the interpersonal-intergroup continuum oversimplifies the nature of communication involved (Giles & Hewstone, 1982; Gudykunst & Lim, 1986; Stephenson, 1981). Stephenson (1981), for example, argues that

> it is difficult to think of any social situation which may not have both intergroup and interpersonal significance. Making love, for example, may seem unambiguously interpersonal, yet a consideration of the objectives achieved by James Bond's sexual exploits should prevent our being overly sentimental about performance, even in that sphere. In any interaction with another, our apparent membership in different social groups—be it male, female, young, English, black, or European—is at least a potential allegiance which may be exploited by the other, such that we act in some sense as *representatives* of fellow members of those groups. When our nationality, sex, or occupation becomes salient in the interaction, this does not necessarily obliterate the interpersonal significance of the encounter; indeed, it may enhance it. (p. 195)

Stephenson's argument suggests that both interpersonal and intergroup factors operate in every situation.

Stephenson (1981) distinguishes between encounters that involve both high interpersonal and high intergroup salience and those that involve low interpersonal and high intergroup salience in terms of how negotiations take place. If they are conducted face-to-face, then they involve high interpersonal and high intergroup salience. When negotiations take place over the phone, by contrast, they involve high intergroup and low interpersonal salience. Stephenson believes the difference is that in the face-to-face situation, negotiators are aware of the interpersonal significance of their behavior, while they are much less aware of it when they negotiate over the phone. Situations that involve high interpersonal and low intergroup salience include most encounters between friends, lovers, mates, and so forth. Situations that involve low interpersonal and low intergroup salience encompass a large percentage of encounters between strangers, including interactions between strangers on public transportation, interactions between clerks and customers, and other encounters of this nature.

Interpersonal and intergroup salience can and does change within specific encounters (Coupland, 1980). In other words, both personal and social identities serve as generative mechanisms for behavior in the same encounter. This fact suggests that explanations of communication in social relationships must take both interpersonal and intergroup factors into consideration.

ANXIETY AND UNCERTAINTY MANAGEMENT

When we interact with strangers, our ability to communicate effectively is based, at least in part, on our ability to manage our anxiety and uncertainty (Gudykunst, 1995). In this section, we examine the nature of uncertainty, anxiety, and mindfulness (the cognitive process that allows us to manage our uncertainty and anxiety). We begin with uncertainty.

Uncertainty in Interactions with Strangers

The predictions we make when we are communicating are aimed at reducing the uncertainty present whenever we communicate with strangers. Berger and Calabrese (1975) point out that the primary concern anytime we meet someone new is uncertainty reduction. Berger (1979) modified that position, arguing that we try to reduce uncertainty when the person we meet will be encountered in the future, provides rewards to us, or behaves in a deviant fashion. Given that strangers, especially those from other cultures or ethnic groups, are likely to behave in a deviant fashion, it is reasonable to say we try to reduce uncertainty when we communicate with strangers more than we do when we communicate with people who are familiar.

The Nature of Uncertainty.   Berger and Calabrese (1975) point out that at least two distinct types of uncertainty are present in our interactions with strangers. First is the uncertainty we have about strangers' attitudes, feelings, beliefs, values, and behavior. We need to be able, for example, to predict which of several alternative behavior patterns strangers will choose to employ. An illustration is the situation when we meet a person we find attractive at a party. If we want to see this person again after the party, we try to think about different ways we can approach this person in order to persuade him or her to see us again. The different approaches we think about are the predictions of alternative behaviors that reduce our uncertainty. The second type of uncertainty Berger and Calabrese (1975) isolate involves explanations of strangers' behavior. Whenever we try to figure out why strangers behaved the way they did, we are engaging in explanatory uncertainty reduction. The problem we are addressing is one of reducing the number of possible explanations for the strangers' behavior. This type of uncertainty reduction is necessary if we are to understand their behavior and, thus, be able to increase our ability to predict their behavior in the future.

It appears that there is greater uncertainty in our initial interactions with strangers than with people who are familiar (Gudykunst, 1991). Higher uncertainty does not mean, however, that we will be motivated to reduce uncertainty more when we communicate with strangers than when we communicate with people who are familiar. While strangers may behave in a deviant fashion (e.g., not follow *our* norms or communication rules), they rarely are seen as sources of rewards and we may not anticipate seeing them again in the future. When we do not actively try to reduce our uncertainty regarding strangers' behavior, we rely on our categorizations of strangers to reduce our uncertainty and guide our predictions. As indicated earlier, that approach often leads to misunderstandings.

Minimum and Maximum Thresholds. Some degree of uncertainty exists in all relationships. We can never totally predict or explain other people's behavior. We all have maximum and minimum thresholds for uncertainty (Gudykunst, 1993). If our uncertainty is above the maximum threshold or below the minimum threshold, we feel uncomfortable and we will have difficulty communicating effectively. If our uncertainty is above our maximum threshold, we do not think we have enough information to predict or explain other people's behavior. Thus, we lack confidence in our predictions and explanations of other people's behavior. When there are norms or rules guiding behavior in a particular situation, the norms or rules allow us unconsciously to predict how others will behave, and our uncertainty therefore will be below our maximum threshold. Also, when we have some information about others so that we feel comfortable predicting how they will behave in the situation, our uncertainty will be below our maximum threshold. When our uncertainty is below our maximum threshold, we have sufficient confidence in the information we have to predict and explain other people's behavior.

If our uncertainty is below our minimum threshold, we think other people's behavior is highly predictable; we have a high level of confidence in our ability to predict other people's behavior. High levels of predictability, however, often are associated with boredom. When this situation occurs, there may not be sufficient novelty in our relationships for us to sustain interest in interacting with the other people, and we may not be motivated to communicate. It also is important to remember that confidence in our predictions does not mean that our predictions are accurate. When we see other people's behavior as highly predictable, we are likely to misinterpret their messages because we do not consider the possibility that our interpretations of their messages are wrong. In other words, overconfidence can breed misinterpretations.

Communicating effectively requires that our uncertainty be between our minimum and maximum thresholds (Gudykunst, 1995). If our uncertainty is above our maximum threshold or below our minimum threshold, we need to manage our uncertainty consciously to improve the effectiveness of our communication.

Uncertainty over Time.   Generally, as we get to know strangers, our uncertainty regarding their behavior tends to decrease (Hubbert, Guerrero, & Gudykunst, 1995). Uncertainty, however, does not always decrease as relationships change over time. It also can increase. When we first meet strangers, our uncertainty tends to be above our maximum threshold since we do not feel comfortable predicting their behavior. Once we meet strangers and see that they follow the rules of interacting, our uncertainty will drop below our maximum threshold. We will assume that we can use cultural norms to predict their behavior. As we get to know strangers in the United States, we use their attitudes, values, and beliefs to predict and explain their behavior (cultural differences in uncertainty reduction are discussed below).

While uncertainty tends to decrease as we get to know strangers, events may occur in our established relationships or strangers might do something we do not expect that increases our uncertainty. When, for example, we find out that others are engaged in competing relationships, when we lose closeness in a relationship, as well as when we find out that others have deceived or betrayed us, our uncertainty may increase (Planalp, Rutherford, & Honeycutt, 1988). The more surprised we are, the more our uncertainty is likely to increase. It is possible that our uncertainty may increase so much that it rises above our maximum threshold. If that situation occurs, we must reduce our uncertainty to feel comfortable interacting with the other person. We can reduce the uncertainty by seeking information, such as asking why the person behaved the way he or she did.

Depending on the nature of the event that increases our uncertainty and on how we manage the uncertainty, increases in uncertainty can have positive or negative consequences for our relationships with others. If we find out, for example, that our romantic partner is seeing someone else, that realization probably will increase our uncertainty above our maximum threshold. Depending on our partner's explanation, we may or may not be able to reduce our uncertainty about our partner's future behavior below our maximum threshold. If we cannot reduce our uncertainty, we might end the relationship. If we can reduce our uncertainty and we are confident that our romantic partner will not see others in the future, in contrast, our uncertainty probably will return to our comfort range.

In summary, our uncertainty regarding strangers' behavior fluctuates over time. If our uncertainty is above our maximum threshold or below our minimum threshold, we need to manage it consciously to increase the effectiveness of our communication. Figure 2.1 provides a visual summary of how uncertainty might change over time. The specific patterns that emerge depend on the two people involved in the relationship, what happens between them, and events external to the relationship (e.g., changes in the relationship between the two groups of which participants are members).

Uncertainty in Intergroup Encounters.   Many factors influence the amount of uncertainty we experience when we communicate with strangers (Gudykunst, 1988b, 1995). These factors include, but are not limited to, our expectations, our social identities, the perception of similarity between our group and the strangers'

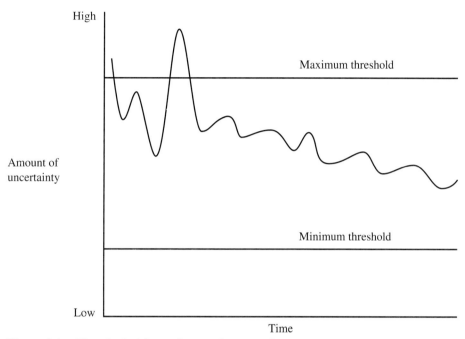

Figure 2.1   Hypothetical form of uncertainty over time.

groups, the degree to which we share communication networks with strangers, and the interpersonal salience of our contact with strangers.

Well-defined expectations (e.g., complex images of strangers and their groups) help us reduce uncertainty. The more well-defined our expectations are, the more confident we will be predicting strangers' behavior. We can have either well-defined positive or well-defined negative expectations. Well-defined expectations alone, however, do not necessarily help us explain strangers' behavior. To accurately explain strangers' behavior, we need to have accurate information regarding strangers' cultures and group memberships as well as about the individual strangers with whom we are communicating. We discuss several strategies for acquiring this information in Chapter 12.

Gudykunst (1988b) argues that the stronger our social identities are (i.e., the more important our group memberships are to how we define ourselves), the greater our predictive certainty regarding strangers' behavior. This claim, however, has to be qualified. Gudykunst and Hammer (1988b) report that strength of social identity reduces uncertainty only when we recognize that the strangers are from another group and when the strangers with whom we are communicating are perceived to be typical members of their group. When the strangers are perceived to be atypical members of their group, we do not treat them on the basis of their group membership; i.e., we see them as "an exception to the rule." In that case, our communication is influenced by our personal identities, not our social identities. When communication is based on our personal identities, we need information about the individual stranger with whom we are communicating to reduce uncertainty.

The degree to which our group is similar to the strangers' groups also influences our ability to reduce uncertainty (Gudykunst, 1988b). If we perceive that the strangers' groups are similar to our own ingroup, we have more confidence in our ability to predict strangers' behavior. Perceived similarity, however, may not increase our ability to explain strangers' behavior accurately because we may perceive similarities when we are actually different or perceive differences when we are actually similar. Knowledge of the actual similarities or dissimilarities between our group and the strangers' groups is necessary to reduce our explanatory uncertainty.

The degree to which we share communication networks with the strangers also influences the amount of uncertainty we experience when we communicate with strangers (Gudykunst, 1988b). The more we know the same people that the strangers with whom we are communicating know, the more we can reduce uncertainty. Further, the degree to which we want to establish an interpersonal relationship with the specific strangers contributes to the reduction of uncertainty. If we are physically or socially attracted to the strangers with whom we are communicating, our confidence in our ability to predict their behavior will increase. In addition, our cultural and linguistic knowledge of the strangers' culture helps us predict their behavior. The more we understand and can speak the strangers' language and the more knowledge we have of their culture, the more our uncertainty will be reduced. We will discuss the role of linguistic knowledge in more detail in Chapter 8.

Anxiety in Interactions with Strangers

When we communicate with strangers, we not only have a high level of uncertainty, we also have a high level of anxiety. The anxiety we experience when we communicate with strangers usually is based on negative expectations. Actual or anticipated interaction with members of different groups leads to anxiety.

Minimum and Maximum Thresholds.   We have maximum and minimum thresholds for anxiety (Gudykunst, 1993). If our anxiety is above our upper threshold, we are so uneasy that we do not want to communicate with others. If our anxiety is below our minimum threshold, not enough adrenaline is running through our system to motivate us to communicate with others. If we are to be motivated to communicate with others, our anxiety has to be below our maximum threshold and above our minimum threshold. The role of anxiety in interpersonal communication is similar to its role in our performance on tests. If we are too anxious, we do not perform well on tests. Similarly, if we are not at all anxious, we do not perform well. This argument is consistent with Janis' (1971) theory of anticipatory fear. He contends that moderate levels of fear lead to adaptive processes, while low and high levels do not. There is an optimal level of anxiety that facilitates our experiencing flow or having optimal experiences (Csikszentmihalyi, 1990).

If we are to communicate effectively with others, our anxiety needs to be below our maximum threshold and above our minimum threshold. When anxiety is above our maximum or below our minimum thresholds, we tend to process information in a very simplistic fashion. When our anxiety is too high, for example, we use only our stereotypes to predict other people's behavior. Since stereotypes are never accurate when applied to an individual, our predictions are inaccurate and our communication, therefore, is likely to be ineffective.

Individuals' minimum and maximum thresholds differ. One way that we can tell if our anxiety is above our maximum threshold is by paying attention to our "gut reaction." If we feel a few butterflies in our stomach, our anxiety probably is not above our maximum threshold. A few butterflies probably indicate a normal amount of anxiety, an amount between our minimum and maximum thresholds. When we do not feel any butterflies or nervousness, our anxiety is probably below our minimum threshold. If, however, we have a stomachache and the palms of our hands are sweating, our anxiety is probably above our maximum threshold. The physical indicators each of us can use will differ. By paying attention to our reactions, we can figure out when our anxiety is so high that we do not feel comfortable communicating, and when it is so low that we do not care what happens. Once we know where these points are, we can cognitively manage our anxiety.

Anxiety over Time.   Generally, as we get to know strangers, the anxiety we experience in interacting with them tends to decrease (Hubbert et al., 1995). We do not mean to imply, however, that anxiety continually decreases. While there is a general trend for our anxiety to decrease the more we get to know strangers, our anxiety can increase or decrease at any particular point in a relationship depending on what is going on in the relationship and how we interpret it.

When we first meet strangers, our anxiety might be above our maximum threshold, especially if we see strangers as attractive in some way or as a member of a different group. After we talk with strangers, our anxiety probably decreases somewhat, assuming that we see that strangers are not a threat to us. As our relationship with strangers becomes more intimate, our overall level of anxiety tends to decrease. As we get to know strangers, however, our anxiety fluctuates depending on the specific circumstances of our interaction. The first time we kiss a date, for example, our anxiety increases.

If we become extremely comfortable with strangers, our anxiety may drop below our minimum threshold. If this situation occurs, our motivation to communicate with strangers decreases and we may not make the effort to communicate. It is also possible, however, that something may occur in our relationship and our anxiety will increase dramatically, possibly rising above our maximum threshold. If we are involved in a romantic relationship, think that the relationship is going well, and want it to continue, our anxiety might increase dramatically if our partner told us that he or she wanted to break off the relationship.

In summary, our anxiety about communicating with strangers fluctuates over time. If our anxiety is above our maximum threshold or below our minimum threshold, we need to manage it consciously to communicate effectively. Figure 2.2 provides a visual summary of how anxiety might change over time. The specific pattern that emerges is a function of the two people involved, what happens in the relationship, and external events (e.g., the relationships between the groups of which individuals are members).

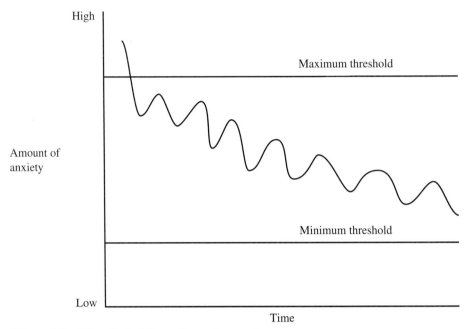

Figure 2.2   Hypothetical form of anxiety over time.

Anxiety in Intergroup Interactions.   Stephan and Stephan (1985) argue that we fear four types of negative consequences when interacting with strangers. First, we fear negative consequences for our self-concept. In interacting with strangers, we worry "about feeling incompetent, confused, and not in control. . . . [We] anticipate discomfort, frustration, and irritation due to the awkwardness of intergroup interactions" (Stephan & Stephan, 1985, p. 159). We also may fear the loss of self-esteem, that our social identities will be threatened, and that we will feel guilty if we behave in ways that offend strangers.

Second, we may fear that negative behavioral consequences will result from our communication with strangers. We may feel that strangers will exploit us, take advantage of us, or try to dominate us. We also may worry about performing poorly in the presence of strangers or worry that physical harm or verbal conflict will occur.

Third, we fear negative evaluations of strangers. We fear rejection, ridicule, disapproval, and being stereotyped negatively. These negative evaluations, in turn, can be seen as threats to our social identities. Recent research suggests that we perceive communication with people who are familiar as more agreeable and less abrasive than communication with strangers (Hoyle, Pinkley, & Insko, 1989).

Fourth, we may fear negative evaluations by members of our ingroups. If we interact with strangers, members of our ingroups may disapprove. We may fear that "ingroup members will reject" us, "apply other sanctions," or identify us "with the outgroup" (Stephan & Stephan, 1985, p. 160).

Several factors are associated with the amount of anxiety we experience when we communicate with strangers. Thinking about the behavior in which we need to engage when communicating with strangers, for example, can reduce our anxiety about interacting with them (Janis & Mann, 1977). Further, if we focus on finding out as much as we can about strangers and forming accurate impressions of them, the biases we have, based on our anxiety and negative expectations, will be reduced (Leary, Kowalski, & Bergen, 1988; Neuberg, 1989). Stephan and Stephan (1989) also found that the less intergroup contact we have experienced, the less ethnocentric we are; and the more positive our stereotypes are, the less intergroup anxiety we experience.

Stephan and Stephan (1985) isolate three broad categories of antecedents to intergroup anxiety: prior intergroup relations, intergroup cognitions (e.g., stereotypes and intergroup attitudes), and situational factors. The important aspects of prior intergroup relations that influence the amount of intergroup anxiety we experience when communicating with strangers are the amount of contact we have had with the strangers' groups and the conditions under which that contact occurred. Stephan and Stephan argue that the more contact we have had and the clearer the norms are for intergroup relations, the less intergroup anxiety we will experience. If, however, there has been prior conflict between our group and the strangers' groups or our economic and political interests do not coincide, we are likely to experience intergroup anxiety.

The way we think about strangers influences our affective reactions toward them. The important intergroup cognitions are our knowledge of strangers' cultures, our stereotypes, our prejudice, our ethnocentrism, and our perceptions of ingroup-outgroup differences (Stephan & Stephan, 1985). The less knowledge we have of strangers' groups, the more anxiety we will experience. Negative cognitive expectations (i.e., negative stereotypes and prejudice) lead to intergroup anxiety. The greater the differences (real or imagined) we perceive between our group and the strangers' groups, the more intergroup anxiety we will experience.

The situational factors that contribute to intergroup anxiety include the amount of structure in the situation in which contact occurs, the type of interdependence, the group composition, and the relative status of the participants. Stephan and Stephan point out that in structured situations, the norms provide guides for our behavior and reduce our anxiety. The more unstructured the situation is, therefore, the greater our intergroup anxiety. Situations in which we cooperate with strangers involve less anxiety than situations in which we compete with them. Further, we will experience less anxiety when we find ourselves in situations where our ingroup is in the majority than in situations where our ingroup is in the minority. Finally, we will experience less anxiety in situations where our ingroup has higher status than the strangers' groups than in situations where our ingroup has lower status.

Stephan and Stephan (1985) isolate cognitive, behavioral, and affective consequences of intergroup anxiety. While their focus is on the negative consequences, positive consequences also can occur. One of the behavioral consequences of anxiety is avoidance. We avoid strangers because it reduces our anxiety. When we are experiencing anxiety and cannot avoid strangers, we will terminate the interaction as soon as we can. Cognitively, intergroup anxiety leads to biases in information processing. The more anxious we are, the more likely we will attune to the behaviors we expected to see (e.g., those based on our stereotypes) and the more likely we are to confirm these expectations (i.e., we will not attune to behavior that is inconsistent with our expectations). The greater our anxiety, the more we will be self-aware and concerned with our self-esteem. When we are highly anxious, we therefore try to make our own group look good in comparison with other groups.

Mindfulness

To manage our uncertainty and anxiety, we must be conscious (i.e., mindful) of our communication. We do not, however, generally think much about our behavior. Much of our communication behavior, for example, is habitual. When we are communicating habitually, we are following scripts—"a coherent sequence of events expected by the individual involving him [or her] either as a participant or an observer" (Abelson, 1976, p. 33). Langer (1978) argues that when we first encounter a new situation, we consciously seek cues to guide our behavior. As we have repeated experiences with the same event, we have less need to think consciously about our behavior. "The more often we engage in the activity, the more likely it is that we rely on scripts for the completion of the activity and the less likely there will be any correspondence between our actions and those thoughts of ours that occur simultaneously" (Langer, 1978, p. 39).

As indicated earlier, when we are engaging in habitual or scripted behavior, we are not highly aware of what we are doing or saying. Borrowing an analogy from flying a plane, we might say that we are on automatic pilot. In Langer's (1978) terminology, we are mindless. Recent research, however, suggests that we do not communicate totally on automatic pilot. Rather, we pay sufficient attention so that we can recall key words in the conversations we have (Kitayama & Burnstein, 1988).

Langer (1989) isolates three characteristics of mindfulness: (1) creating new categories, (2) being open to new information, and (3) being aware of more than one perspective. One condition that contributes to being mindless is the *use of broad categories.* Categorization often is based on physical (e.g., gender, race) or cultural (e.g., ethnic background) characteristics, but we also can categorize others in terms of their attitudes (e.g., liberal or conservative) or approaches to life (e.g., Christian or Buddhist; Trungpa, 1973). Langer (1989) points out that "categorizing is a fundamental and natural human activity. It is the way we come to know the world. Any attempt to eliminate bias by attempting to eliminate the perception of differences is doomed to failure" (p. 154). Being mindful involves making more, not fewer, distinctions. When we are on automatic pilot, we tend to use broad categories to predict other people's behavior, for example, their culture, ethnicity, or sex, or the role they are playing. When we are mindful, we can create new categories that are more specific. Rather than using the broad category *professor,* for example, students can subcategorize professors into males/females, professors who are formal/professors who are informal, professors who call students by name/professors who do not call students by name, and so forth. The more subcategories we use, the more personalized the information we use to make predictions will be.

Mindfulness involves being *open to new information* (Langer, 1989). When we behave on automatic pilot in a particular situation, we tend to see the same thing occurring in the situation that we saw the previous time in the same situation. If we are consciously open to new information, however, we see the subtle differences in our own and other people's behavior that may take place. The more we think about how to behave in situations, the more appropriate and effective our behavior tends to be (Cegala & Waldron, 1992).

Being open to new information involves focusing on the process of communication that is taking place, not the outcome of our interactions with others:

> An outcome orientation in social situations can induce mindlessness. If we think we know how to handle a situation, we don't feel a need to pay attention. If we respond to the situation as very familiar (as a result, for example, of overlearning), we notice only minimal cues necessary to carry out the proper scenarios. If, on the other hand, the situation is strange, we might be so preoccupied with the thought of failure ("what if I make a fool of myself?") that we miss nuances of our own and others' behavior. In this sense, we are mindless with respect to the immediate situation, although we may be thinking quite actively about outcome related issues. (Langer, 1989, p. 34)

When we focus on the outcome, we miss subtle cues in our interactions with others which leads to misunderstandings. Focusing on the process of communication forces us to be mindful of our behavior and to pay attention to the situations in which we find ourselves (Langer, 1989).

To be mindful, we must also recognize that there is *more than one perspective* that can be used to understand or explain our interaction with others (Langer, 1989). Suppose a friend sprained her or his ankle and asked you to go to the local pharmacy for an Ace bandage. What would you do if the local pharmacy was out of Ace bandages (and there was only the one pharmacy available)? Most of us would probably return and tell our friend that the pharmacy was out of Ace bandages if we were acting on automatic pilot (Langer, 1989). If we were mindful, however, we might think to ask the pharmacist if there are alternatives to using an Ace bandage on a sprained ankle.

When we communicate on automatic pilot, we do not recognize alternative perspectives. The mindset we bring to communication situations limits our ability to see the choices we actually have about how to behave in most situations (Langer, 1989). When we communicate mindfully, however, we can look for the options that are available to us and not be limited by only those that come to mind in the situation. When we are communicating mindfully, we can use all the communication resources available to us rather than limit ourselves to those in our implicit personal theories of communication.

Recognizing alternative perspectives is critical to effective communication. Effective communication requires recognizing that other people use their own perspective to interpret our messages, and they may not interpret our messages the way we intended them. When we communicate on automatic pilot, we assume everyone uses the same perspective as we do. It is only when we are mindful of the process of our communication that we can determine how our interpretations of messages differ from other people's interpretations of those messages.

We often become conscious of our behavior when we enter new situations, such as communicating with strangers. Berger and Douglas (1982) list five conditions under which we are highly cognizant of our behavior:

> (1) in novel situations where, by definition, no appropriate script exists, (2) where external factors prevent completion of a script, (3) when scripted behavior becomes effortful because substantially more of the behavior is required than is usual, (4) when a discrepant outcome is experienced, or (5) where multiple scripts come into conflict so that involvement in any one script is suspended. In short, individuals will enact scripted sequences whenever those sequences are available and will continue to do so until events unusual to the script are encountered. (pp. 46–47)

It can be inferred that we are more aware of our behavior when communicating with strangers than we are when communicating with people who are familiar. The problem, however, is that we tend to be aware of outcomes, not the process of communication. Our mindfulness, therefore, does not increase our effectiveness.

Uncertainty, Anxiety, Mindfulness, and Effective Communication

In general, as our uncertainty and anxiety decrease, the better we get to know others. Uncertainty and anxiety, however, do not increase or decrease consistently over time. Uncertainty, for example, is not reduced every time we communicate with strangers. We may reduce our uncertainty the first time we communicate, but something may occur the second time we communicate (e.g., the stranger does something we did not expect) and our uncertainty might increase. Once we have established a relationship with strangers, we can expect our uncertainty and anxiety regarding strangers to fluctuate over time. As the relationship becomes more intimate, nevertheless, there should be a general pattern for uncertainty and anxiety to decease. There tends to be less uncertainty and anxiety in acquaintance relationships, for example, than in relationships with strangers, and there is less uncertainty and anxiety in friendships than in acquaintance relationships. At the same time, within any stage (e.g., acquaintance, friend) of a particular relationship, uncertainty and anxiety will fluctuate over time.

We do not want to try to reduce our anxiety and uncertainty totally. At the same time, we cannot communicate effectively if our uncertainty and anxiety are too high. If uncertainty and anxiety are too high, we cannot accurately interpret strangers' messages or make accurate predictions about strangers' behavior. If anxiety is above our maximum threshold, as it often is when we first meet strangers, we are too anxious to communicate effectively. When anxiety is above our maximum threshold, the way we process information becomes very simple, thereby decreasing our ability to predict strangers' behavior (Wilder & Shapiro, 1989). When uncertainty is above our maximum threshold, we do not think we can predict strangers' behavior. In most situations, however, there are sufficiently clear norms and rules for communication so that our uncertainty and anxiety are reduced below our maximum threshold. Even if our uncertainty and anxiety are below the maximum threshold, either or both may still be too high for us to communicate effectively. If we are to communicate effectively, our anxiety needs to be sufficiently low so that we can accurately interpret and predict strangers' behavior. When anxiety is too high, we communicate on automatic pilot and interpret strangers' behavior using our own cultural frame of reference.

If uncertainty and anxiety are low, we may not be motivated to communicate. If both uncertainty and anxiety are consistently below our minimum threshold in a particular relationship, for example, the relationship will become boring. Kruglanski (1989) points out that we all have a need to avoid closure on topics or people to allow for mystery to be maintained. When uncertainty is below our minimum threshold, we also become overconfident that we understand strangers' behavior and we do not question whether our predictions are accurate. If we are to communicate effectively, our uncertainty and anxiety both must be above our minimum threshold.

Uncertainty and anxiety do not necessarily increase and decrease at the same time. We may reduce our uncertainty and be highly anxious. Consider, for example, a situation in which we predict very confidently that something negative is going to happen. We also may reduce our anxiety and have high uncertainty. If we are to communicate effectively, our anxiety must be sufficiently low (well below maximum threshold, but above minimum) that we can reduce our explanatory uncertainty. If our anxiety is high, we must cognitively manage our anxiety (i.e., become mindful) if we are to communicate effectively (we discuss this process in detail in Chapter 10, on effectiveness).

When we have managed our anxiety, we need to try to develop accurate predictions and explanations for strangers' behavior. This attempt requires that we be mindful of our communication. When we communicate on automatic pilot, we predict and interpret strangers' behavior using our frame of reference. When we are mindful, in contrast, we are open to new information and aware of alternative perspectives (e.g., strangers' perspectives; Langer, 1989). If we focus on the process of our communication with strangers and try to understand how they are interpreting messages, we can increase the accuracy of our predictions and explanations for strangers' behavior. This approach inevitably will increase the effectiveness of our communication with strangers (effectiveness is discussed in more detail in Chapter 10).

AN ORGANIZING MODEL FOR STUDYING COMMUNICATION WITH STRANGERS

The model presented in this section is designed to serve two functions. First, it helps isolate and identify the elements influencing our communication with strangers. Second, the model serves as a guide to the organization of the material presented in Parts Two and Three of the book. Our purpose in developing the model is not to describe the process of communication with strangers, but rather, to organize the elements influencing the process so that they can be discussed systematically.

The model is diagrammed in Figure 2.3. In constructing the model, we attempted to find a workable compromise between complexity and simplicity. As it stands, the model contains all the major elements, yet is simple enough to be interpreted easily. The elements included in the model are transmitting and interpreting messages, as well as the cultural, sociocultural, psychocultural, and environmental influences on the communication process.

In examining the model, we must keep in mind that any model, out of necessity, excludes certain elements. The problem of premature closure, as the exclusion of elements is called, is unavoidable in constructing a model. In deciding which elements to include, we used two criteria: (1) Is the element useful in explaining our communication with strangers? and (2) Is there research available on the element's influence on communication?

Since each of the elements of the model is discussed in detail in Parts Two and Three of the book, the following is intended only as an introduction. Our purpose here, therefore, is to put the material presented in the next two parts of the book into context.

An Overview of the Model

Given our view of communication, we see transmitting and interpreting of communication messages to be an interactive process influenced by conceptual filters, which we categorize into cultural, sociocultural, psychocultural, and environmental factors. This interaction is illustrated in Figure 2.3 by the way the center circle, which contains the interaction between transmitting and interpreting of messages, is surrounded by three other circles representing cultural, sociocultural, and psychocultural influences. The circles are drawn with dashed lines to indicate that the elements affect, and are affected by, the other elements. The two persons represented in the model are surrounded by a dashed box representing the environmental influences. This box is drawn with a dashed rather than a solid line because the immediate environment in which the communication takes place is not an isolated environment, or "closed system." Most communication between people takes place in a social environment that includes other people who also are engaging in communication.

The message/feedback between the two communicators is represented by the lines from one person's transmitting to the other person's interpreting and from

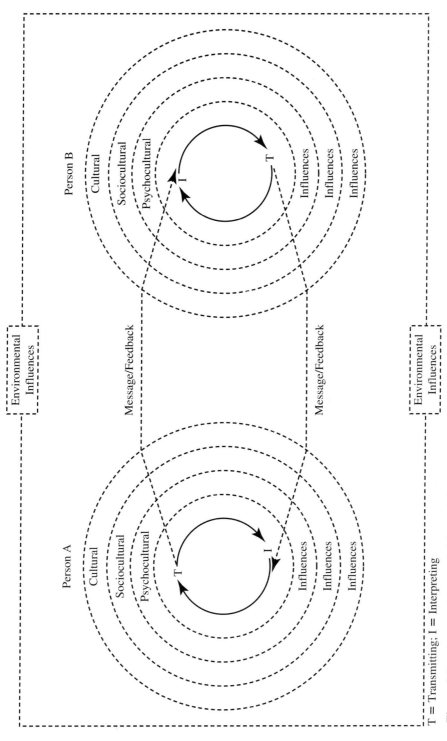

T = Transmitting; I = Interpreting

Figure 2.3   An organizing model for studying communication with strangers.

the second person's transmitting to the first person's interpreting. Two message/ feedback lines are shown to indicate that anytime we communicate, we are simultaneously engaged in transmitting and interpreting of messages. In other words, communication is not static; we do not transmit a message and do nothing until we receive feedback. Rather, we interpret incoming stimuli at the same time as we are transmitting messages.

The cultural, sociocultural, and psychocultural influences serve as conceptual filters for our transmit and interpret messages. By *filters,* we mean mechanisms that delimit the number of alternatives from which we choose when we transmit and interpret messages. More specifically, the filters limit the predictions we make about how strangers might respond to our communication behavior. The nature of the predictions we make, in turn, influences the way we choose to transmit our messages. Further, the filters delimit what stimuli we pay attention to and how we choose to interpret incoming messages.

Transmitting Messages

Since it is impossible to transmit electrical impulses directly from one person's brain to that of another person, it is necessary for us to put messages into codes that can be transmitted. Messages can be transmitted in many forms, but for the purpose of our analysis, two are most relevant: language (verbal codes) and nonverbal behaviors (we exclude codes such as mathematics, music, etc.). As indicated earlier, the process of transmitting messages is accomplished at varying levels of consciousness.

Language is one of the major vehicles through which we encode messages. Obviously, languages can differ from culture to culture. Culture and language are closely intertwined, with each influencing the other. Our language is a product of our culture, and our culture is a product of our language. The language we speak influences what we see and think, and what we see and think, in part, influences our culture.

Not only are messages transmitted verbally, but they also are encoded nonverbally. Nonverbal messages, like language, vary from culture to culture. Language is mostly a conscious activity, while nonverbal behavior is mostly an unconscious activity. That is, we generally are not aware of the messages we are encoding nonverbally through our gestures, facial expressions, or tones of voice, to name only a few behaviors. When we encounter nonverbal behaviors greatly different from our own (i.e., when communicating with strangers), however, we may become unusually conscious of those behaviors. We discuss the transmitting of messages in detail in Chapters 8 and 9.

Interpreting Messages

To a certain extent, interpreting messages is the opposite of transmitting messages. When we interpret a message, our perceptions depend on what the other person says verbally, what nonverbal behavior the other person exhibits, our own messages, our conceptual filters, and the context in which the message is received. In other words, how we interpret the messages encoded by strangers is a function of what they have transmitted, what we had previously transmitted to them, the context in which we are communicating, and our conceptual filters.

As indicated earlier, the way in which we process the incoming stimuli is partially a function of our conceptual filters. More specifically, the filters delimit the stimuli we observe and tell us how specific stimuli are to be interpreted. Consider strangers who are visiting Japan and are invited into a Japanese home, where it is expected that shoes be removed before entering the house. The strangers may see the Japanese family's shoes by the door but, because of their conceptual filters, not attribute any meaning to the stimuli and, therefore, walk into the house with shoes still on their feet. When the Japanese hosts become upset, the strangers will have no idea what they did wrong. The strangers' conceptual filters have delimited the stimuli to which they attribute meaning, thereby influencing the interpretations they make about the situation. We discuss interpreting messages in detail in Chapter 7.

Cultural Influences

The cultural influences include those factors involved in the cultural ordering process described in Chapter 1. For the purpose of our analysis, we focus on dimensions that explain similarities and differences across cultures. Is our culture dominated by concerns for the individual (i.e., individualism) or for the collectivity (i.e., collectivism)? These dimensions affect the values and the norms and rules that influence our communication behavior. *Values* are shared conceptions of the desired ends of social life and the means to reach those goals (Rokeach, 1972). They express a collective view of what is important and unimportant, good and bad. The norms and rules of a culture specify the acceptable and unacceptable behavior in our interactions with others. It is the norms and rules of a culture that allow its members to engage spontaneously in everyday social behavior without continually having to "guess" what other people are going to do. More formally, we can say that norms and rules are sets of expected behaviors for particular situations.

The dimensions of cultural variability (e.g., individualism-collectivism), values, and communication norms and rules that predominate in our culture influence how we transmit messages and interpret incoming stimuli when we communicate with strangers. Consider, for example, a visit to North America by strangers from a culture with a communication rule requiring that direct eye contact always be avoided. When interacting with these strangers, North Americans will try to establish direct eye contact. If the strangers do not look them in the eye when talking, the North Americans will assume that the strangers either have something to hide or are not telling the truth, since the communication rule in North America requires direct eye contact to establish one's sincerity. A rule of North American culture, therefore, has influenced the way in which North Americans interpret the strangers' behavior. It should be noted, however, that there are some subcultures in North America (e.g., the lower-class African American subculture) where this rule may not be applicable. We discuss cultural influences in detail in Chapter 3.

Sociocultural Influences

The sociocultural influences are those involved in the social ordering process. As indicated in Chapter 1, social ordering develops out of our interactions with others when the patterns of behavior become consistent over time (Olsen, 1978). We are members of groups either because we are born into them or because we join them. Groups we are born into include, but are not limited to, racial and ethnic groups, families, age groups, and gender groups. Groups we join include service groups (e.g., the Lions Club), occupational groups, religious groups, and ideological groups (e.g., Democratic and Republican parties, the Ku Klux Klan), to name only a few. The various groups of which we are members enforce sets of expected behaviors (norms and rules) and have shared values and, therefore, have an impact on how we communicate with strangers.

Our membership in social groups influences the way we see ourselves. Our self-concept is composed of at least two components: social identity and personal identity. Our social identities are derived from our membership in our social groups. Our personal identities are based on our unique individual experiences. The degree to which we identify with our groups and feel comfortable about ourselves as individuals influences our communication with strangers.

When we communicate with another person and make our predictions on the basis of a position that person holds in a group, we are engaging in a role relationship. The idea of position can best be illustrated by examples: clerk, judge, father, mother, boss, physician, professor, student, and so on. People filling one of these positions are expected to perform certain behaviors. The set of behaviors they are expected to perform is referred to as their role. Our role expectations influence how we interpret behavior and what predictions we make about people in a given role. Role expectations vary within any culture, but there is a tendency for them to vary more across cultures. If we do not know strangers' role expectations, we inevitably will make inaccurate interpretations and predictions about their behavior.

Psychocultural Influences

The variables included under the psychocultural influences are those involved in the personal ordering process. Personal ordering, you will recall, is the process giving stability to psychological processes. The variables influencing our communication with strangers include our stereotypes of and attitudes toward (e.g., ethnocentrism and prejudice) strangers' groups. Our stereotypes and attitudes create expectations of how strangers will behave. Our expectations, in turn, influence the way in which we interpret incoming stimuli and the predictions we make about strangers' behavior. Being highly ethnocentric, for example, leads us to interpret strangers' behavior from our own cultural frame of reference and to expect strangers to behave the same way we do. Using our frame of reference invariably leads to misinterpretations of the strangers' messages, as well as inaccurate predictions about their future behavior.

The influence of our expectations on our interpretation of strangers' behavior is mediated through the uncertainty and anxiety we are experiencing. If we are highly uncertain and/or anxious, we cannot interpret strangers' behavior accurately. If we are to communicate effectively, our anxiety needs to be sufficiently low so that we can make accurate predictions of strangers' behavior. We discuss psychocultural influences in detail in Chapter 5.

Environmental Influences

The environment in which we communicate influences our transmitting and interpreting of messages. The geographical location, climate, and architectural setting, as well as our perceptions of the environment, influence how we interpret incoming stimuli and the predictions we make about strangers' behavior. Since strangers may have different perceptions of and orientations toward the environment, they may interpret behavior differently in the same setting. As an illustration, a North American visiting a Colombian family would expect to engage in informal interaction in the living room. The Colombian host, on the other hand, probably would define the living room as a place for formal behavior. Each, therefore, would interpret the other's behavior in light of his or her own expectations and make predictions about the other's behavior on the basis of those same expectations. Such a situation, in all likelihood, would lead to misunderstanding. We discuss environmental influences in Chapter 6.

SUMMARY

Communication with people from our own culture, with people from other races or ethnic groups, and with people from other cultures shares the same underlying process. While communication in these different situations differs in degree, it does not differ in kind. Various names are available to label communication in these different situations, but ambiguity exists as to which label is appropriate for certain situations. Communication between a white person from South Africa and an African American person from the United States, for example, can be labeled as either intercultural or interracial communication.

Given the similarity of the underlying process of communication and the confusion in applying the various labels, we believe what is needed is a way to refer to the underlying process without referring to a particular situation. Talking about communication with strangers is a way to accomplish this end. Strangers can be conceived of as people who are unknown and unfamiliar and are confronting a group for the first time. An African American student in a mainly European American school, a Mexican student studying at a university in the United States, a groom meeting the bride's family for the first time, and a manager from the United States working in Thailand are all examples of strangers.

Intergroup communication is guided by our social identities and involves predicting strangers' behavior using cultural and sociocultural data. Interpersonal communication, in contrast, is guided by our personal identities and involves predicting others' behavior using psychological data. Both interpersonal and intergroup factors are present in virtually any encounter we have with another person. To communicate effectively in interpersonal or intergroup situations, we have to manage our anxiety and uncertainty. To accomplish this goal, we must be mindful. Being mindful involves creating new categories, being open to new information, and being aware of alternative perspectives.

Our communication with strangers is influenced by our conceptual filters, just as their communication with us is influenced by their filters. Our conceptual filters can be placed into four categories: cultural, sociocultural, psychocultural, and environmental. Each of these types of filters influences how we interpret messages encoded by strangers and what predictions we make about strangers' behavior. Without understanding strangers' filters, we cannot accurately interpret or predict their behavior.

STUDY QUESTIONS

1. How does the concept of the stranger help link interpersonal and intergroup communication?
2. Why is anxiety a typical reaction to encountering strangers?
3. Why is there greater uncertainty when we encounter strangers than when we encounter people who are familiar?
4. Why do misunderstandings occur when our uncertainty is below our minimum threshold?
5. How does uncertainty change over time as we communicate with others?
6. What factors influence the amount of uncertainty we have when we communicate with strangers?
7. Why do we have anxiety when we communicate with strangers?
8. Why do we make inaccurate predictions of strangers' behavior when our anxiety is above our maximum threshold?
9. How does anxiety change over time when we communicate with others?
10. What factors increase our anxiety when we communicate with strangers?
11. What are the consequences of high levels of anxiety?
12. What are the characteristics of mindfulness?
13. Why do we need to focus on being mindful of the process of communication (as opposed to the outcome) to communicate effectively with strangers?

SUGGESTED READING

Berger, C. R., & Bradac, J. (1982). *Language and social knowledge*. London: Edward Arnold.
Harman, L. (1987). *The modern stranger*. New York: Mouton de Gruyter.
Kristeva, J. (1991). *Strangers to ourselves*. New York: Columbia University Press.
Langer, E. (1989). *Mindfulness*. Reading, MA: Addison-Wesley.
Tajfel, H. (1982). *Human groups and social categories*. Cambridge, UK: Cambridge University Press.
Turner, J. (1987). *Rediscovering the social group*. London: Blackwell.

PART TWO

Influences on the Process of Communicating with Strangers

In Part One, we defined communication and culture, and overviewed the process of communicating with strangers. In this part, we examine, in depth, the major influences on our communication with strangers.

As indicated in Chapter 2, there are four major groups of influences on our communication with strangers: cultural, sociocultural, psychocultural, and environmental. Cultural influences include the dimensions on which cultures differ (e.g., individualism-collectivism). Sociocultural influences include those stemming from our membership in social groups, and our social identities. Psychocultural influences involve our expectations for strangers based on our stereotypes and the intergroup attitudes we hold, particularly ethnocentrism and prejudice. Environmental influences consist of the physical environment—geography, climate, and architecture; the situation in which communication occurs; the situational norms and rules guiding behavior; and our perceptions of the environment. Each of these groups of influences affects the way we interpret incoming stimuli and the predictions we make about strangers' behavior.

The focus of Part Two is on examining the variables making up each group of influences and looking at how they vary across cultures. In other words, this part is designed to be cross-cultural in nature. We believe knowledge of how these influences vary across cultures is a prerequisite to effective communication with strangers. Without an understanding of the cultural variation in the variables, it is impossible to make accurate predictions about strangers' behavior or to interpret incoming messages from them correctly. While the focus is on cross-cultural variations, we begin to apply these variations to our communication with strangers.

The four groups of influences examined in this part do not operate independently of one another; rather, each one is highly intertwined with each of the others. The culture in which we are raised, for example, has an influence on the groups to which we belong, the role relationships we learn, and the interpersonal relationships we form (the sociocultural influences), as well as on the way we categorize things and the attitudes we hold (the psychocultural influences). Further, our culture is influenced by the environment in which it exists and is affected by both sociocultural and psychocultural factors as well. Even though we separate the four groups of influences in the four chapters in this part, you should keep in mind as you read that they are highly interrelated.

3

Cultural Influences
on the Process

Human beings draw close to one another
by their common nature, but habits
and customs keep them apart.
Confucian Saying

We examine the cultural influences on our communication with strangers in this chapter. There are two general approaches to examining cultural processes. One approach is to look at how a particular culture works from the inside. When using this approach, we are concerned with trying to understand the behavior of people in a culture from their point of view. Another approach to understanding culture is to compare one culture with another. When using this approach, we use predetermined categories to examine selected aspects of the cultures being studied. In other words, the objective is to understand how the cultures compare with respect to some particular quality. These approaches are referred to as emic and etic, respectively (Pike, 1966). Our approach throughout this chapter is etic in nature because we want to present perspectives that will help you understand how cultures are similar and different.

In order to understand similarities and differences in communication across cultures, we must have a way of talking about how cultures differ and how they are similar. Cultural differences cannot be explained by saying that "Yuko communicates indirectly because she is Japanese" or that "Kim communicates directly because she is from the United States." Such statements tell us only *how* people in Japan and the United States communicate; they do not tell us *why* there are differences between the way people communicate in the United States and Japan. There has to be some aspect of the cultures in Japan and the United States that is different and that difference, in turn, explains why Japanese communicate indirectly and people from the United States communicate directly. In other words, variables on which cultures can be different or similar can be used to explain communication across cultures. We refer to these variables as dimensions of cultural variability.

It is important to recognize that communication is unique within each culture and, at the same time, that systematic similarities and differences exist. These similarities and differences can be explained and predicted theoretically through the use of dimensions of cultural variability (e.g., individualism-collectivism). In individualistic cultures, for example, individuals take precedence over groups, while in collectivistic cultures, groups take precedence over individuals (Triandis, 1988). Systematic variations in communication can be explained by cultural differences in individualism and collectivism. Members of individualistic cultures, for example, emphasize person-based information to predict each other's behavior, and members of collectivistic cultures emphasize group-based information to predict each other's behavior (Gudykunst & Nishida, 1986a).

There are general patterns of behavior that are consistent in individualistic cultures, and there are general patterns of behavior that are consistent in collectivistic cultures. Individualism and collectivism, however, are manifested in unique ways in each culture. In the Japanese culture, for example, collectivism involves a focus on the concepts of *wa* (roughly translated as "harmony"), *amae* (roughly translated as "dependency"), and *enryo* (roughly translated as "reserve" or "restraint") (Gudykunst & Nishida, 1994). Other collectivistic cultures emphasize different cultural constructs as part of their collectivistic tendencies. Understanding communication in any culture, therefore, requires culture general information (i.e., where the culture falls on the various dimensions of cultural variability) and culture specific information (i.e., the specific cultural constructs associated with the dimension of cultural variability). Our purpose in this chapter is to focus on the general patterns and illustrate how the dimensions of cultural variability can be used to explain communication across cultures.

Cultures differ on many dimensions. We begin by focusing on individualism-collectivism, the dimension that is used most frequently throughout the remainder of the book. We then discuss Hofstede's (1980) dimensions of cultural variability, Kluckhohn and Strodtbeck's (1961) value orientations, Parsons' (1951) pattern variables, and structural tightness. These dimensions of cultural variability provide ways to understand how communication differs across cultures, even if we do not have information about specific cultures. If we meet people from another culture, for example, and we do not know their cultural background (or we know the culture, but do not have any information about it), we can make reasonable interpretations of their behavior if we understand the dimensions of cultural variability discussed in this chapter.

Before proceeding, we need to draw a distinction between the two different levels of analysis: cultural and individual. General tendencies exist in every culture on each of the dimensions of cultural variability. These general tendencies within a culture are at the cultural level of analysis. As indicated in Chapter 1, however, not all members of a culture share the general tendencies of their culture. Figure 3.1 diagrams how individualistic and collectivistic tendencies might differ in Japan and the United States. Although most people in the United States have individualistic tendencies, some people do have collectivistic tendencies. Similarly, although most people in Japan have collectivistic tendencies, some people do have individualistic tendencies. Cultural-level tendencies, therefore, do not predict the behavior of all

Figure 3.1   Hypothetical distribution of individualistic (a) and collectivistic (b) tendencies in two cultures.

(*a*) *Individualistic Tendencies*

(*b*) *Collectivistic Tendencies*

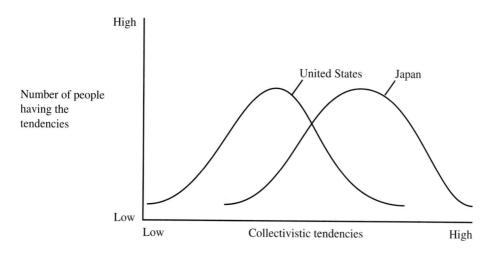

individual members of a culture. To understand individuals' behavior, we must understand the individual characteristics that mediate the influence of cultural-level tendencies on individual communication. To date, most research has been on isolating individual characteristics that mediate the influence of cultural individualism-collectivism on communication. These factors are discussed in the next section.

INDIVIDUALISM-COLLECTIVISM

Individualism-collectivism is the major dimension of cultural variability used to explain cross-cultural differences and similarities in communication across cultures. It also is the dimension with the clearest individual-level equivalents of the cultural-level tendencies. We begin our discussion of individualism-collectivism by looking at cultural-level tendencies.

Cultural-Level Individualism-Collectivism

Individuals' goals are emphasized more than group goals in individualistic cultures. Group goals, in contrast, take precedence over individuals' goals in collectivistic cultures. In individualistic cultures, "people are supposed to look after themselves and their immediate family only," while in collectivistic cultures, "people belong to ingroups or collectivities which are supposed to look after them in exchange for loyalty" (Hofstede & Bond, 1984, p. 419).

The emphasis in individualistic societies is on individuals' initiative and achievement, while emphasis is placed on belonging to groups in collectivistic societies. Individualistic cultures, for example, promote self-realization:

> Chief among the virtues claimed by individualist philosophers is self-realization. Each person is viewed as having a unique set of talents and potentials. The translation of these potentials into actuality is considered the highest purpose to which one can devote one's life. The striving for self-realization is accompanied by a subjective sense of rightness and personal well-being. (Waterman, 1984, pp. 4-5)

Collectivistic cultures, in contrast, require that individuals fit into the group. This tendency is illustrated by the Kenyan culture:

> In Kenyan tribes nobody is an isolated individual. Rather, his [or her] uniqueness is a secondary fact. . . . First, and foremost, he [or she] is several people's contemporary. His [or her] life is founded on these facts economically, socially and physically. In this system group activities are dominant, responsibility is shared and accountability is collective. . . . Because of the emphasis on collectivity, harmony and cooperation among the group tend to be emphasized more than individual function and responsibility. (Saleh & Gufwoli, 1982, p. 327)

These descriptions clearly illustrate the focus on the individual in individualistic cultures, and the focus on groups in collectivistic cultures.

Importance of Ingroups.   Triandis (1988) argues that the relative importance of ingroups is one of the major factors that differentiate individualistic and collectivistic cultures. Ingroups are groups that are important to their members. Individualistic cultures have many specific ingroups (family, religion, social clubs, profession, to name only a few) that might influence behavior in any particular social situation. Since they are many ingroups, individual ingroups, therefore, exert relatively little influence on behavior. In collectivistic cultures, there are few general ingroups (work group, university, family, to name the major ingroups that influence behavior in collectivistic cultures) that have a strong influence on behavior across situations. People in individualistic cultures tend to be universalistic and apply the same value standards to all. People in collectivistic cultures, in contrast, tend to be particularistic and, therefore, apply different value standards for members of their ingroups and outgroups.

While the ingroup may be the same in individualistic and collectivistic cultures, the sphere of its influence is different. The sphere of influence in an individualistic culture is very specific (i.e., the ingroup affects behavior in very specific circumstances), while the sphere of influence in a collectivistic culture is very general (i.e., the ingroup affects behavior in many different aspects of a person's life). In the individualistic culture of the United States, for example, the university people attend generally influences their behavior only when they are at the university or at an alumni event. In collectivistic cultures like Japan and Korea, in contrast, the university people attend influences their behavior throughout their adult lives.

Collectivistic cultures emphasize goals, needs, and views of the ingroup over those of the individual; the social norms of the ingroup, rather than individual pleasure; shared ingroup beliefs, rather than unique individual beliefs; and cooperation with ingroup members, rather than the maximizing of individual outcomes. Ingroups have different rank-orders of importance in collectivistic cultures; some cultures, for example, put family ahead of all other ingroups, while others put company ahead of other ingroups (Triandis, 1988). The company often is considered the primary ingroup in Japan (Nakane, 1970), for instance, while the family is the primary ingroup in many other collectivistic cultures (e.g., Latin America).

Individualism-collectivism is expected to affect communication mainly through its influence on group identities and the differentiation between ingroup and outgroup communication. While cultures tend to be predominantly either individualistic or collectivistic, both individualism and collectivism exist in all cultures. Parsons (1951), for example, suggests that a self orientation involves the "pursuit of private interests" (p. 60), while a collectivity orientation involves the "pursuit of the common interests of the collectivity" (p. 60). He points out that the same behavior can be simultaneously self and collectivity oriented. To illustrate this position, Parsons points to a department head in an organization whose actions may be aimed toward her or his own welfare, the department's welfare, the firm's welfare, and even society's welfare at the same time.

Individualistic and Collectivistic Cultural Values.   Rokeach (1972) contends that values "have to do with modes of conduct and end-states of existence.

To say that a person 'has a value' is to say that he [or she] has an enduring belief that a specific mode of conduct or end-state of existence is personally and socially preferable to alternative modes of conduct or end-states of existence" (pp. 159–160).

To illustrate individualistic and collectivistic values, we compare the values that predominate in the individualistic culture of the United States with those that predominate in the collectivistic Arabic cultures. We begin by looking at seven principal values that Vander Zanden (1965) argues guide behavior in the United States:

> 1. Materialism. [North] Americans are prone to evaluate things in material and monetary terms. . . . [North Americans] tend to get quite excited about things as opposed to ideas, people, and aesthetic creations.
> 2. Success. . . . Part of the [North] American faith is that "There is always another chance" and that "If at first you do not succeed, try, try again." If we ourselves cannot succeed, then we have the prospect for vicarious achievement through our children.
> 3. Work and Activity. . . . Work and activity are exalted in their own right; they are not merely means by which success may be realized; in and of themselves they are valued as worthwhile.
> 4. Progress. A belief in the perfectibility of society, [humankind], and the world has been a kind of driving force in [North] American history. . . . [North] Americans tend to equate "the new" with "the best."
> 5. Rationality. [North] Americans almost universally place faith in the rational approach to life. We continuously search out "reasonable," "time-saving," and "effort-saving" ways of doing things.
> 6. Democracy. "Democracy" has become almost synonymous with "the [North] American way of life." . . . We extol the Declaration of Independence with its insistence that "all [people] are created equal" and "governments (derive) their just power from the consent of the governed."
> 7. Humanitarianism. . . . Philanthropy and voluntary charity have been a characteristic note of [North] America. More recently, more attention has been given to numerous programs for social welfare, with government playing an active role. (pp. 67–69)

Obviously, not all these values are held by every person living in the United States. They are, however, values that tend to be held by a majority of the people, especially in the middle-class subculture, and, therefore, can be considered characteristic of the United States. The first five values in the list are individualistic values.

As a contrast to the North American values outlined, consider Arab values derived from the Bedouin culture (desert dwellers). While only a small percentage (about 10 percent) of present-day Arabs are Bedouins, contemporary Arab culture holds the "Bedouin ethos as an ideal to which, in theory at least, it would like to measure up" (Patai, 1976, p. 73). Patai isolates five values predominating in the Bedouin culture:

1. *Hospitality.* The value of hospitality is aimed at meeting a more general goal of strengthening the group. This value requires a family to receive and give asylum to anyone who comes and requests it. While the actual practice of hospitality varies in villages and urbanized areas, it is still a value held by the vast majority of Arabs (Patai, 1976).
2. *Generosity.* Generosity is tied very closely with the rules of Islam and the Muslim duty of *zakat* (paying a part of one's wealth to the poor). "Lavish generosity in traditional Arab society counterbalances the accumulation of wealth and the development of extreme riches and poverty" (Patai, 1976, p. 87).
3. *Courage.* Courage "means essentially the ability to stand physical pain or emotional strain with such self-control that no sound or facial expression betrays the trial one is undergoing" (Patai, 1976, p. 89). It is sometimes difficult to distinguish this value from the concept of bravery, which requires that Arabs be willing to give their life for the group, according to Patai.
4. *Honor.* In the Arab world, honorable behavior is that "which is conducive to group cohesion and group survival, that which strengthens the group and serves its interest; while shameful behavior is that which tends to disrupt, endanger, impair, or weaken the social aggregate" (Patai, 1976, p. 90).
5. *Self-respect.* "Arab ethics revolve around a single focal point, that of self-esteem or self-respect. The most important factor on which the preservation of this self-esteem depends is the sexual behavior of the women for whom the Arab is responsible: his daughters and sisters" (p. 96). This value is group-based because self-respect depends on other group members' behavior.

These five values clearly are collectivistic, and they are very different from the individualistic values in the United States. (Note: Schwartz, 1994b, argues that individualistic and collectivistic values are not the only cultural values that systematically vary.)

Horizontal Versus Vertical Cultures. Triandis (1995) argues that individualistic and collectivistic cultures can differ according to whether relations among people in the culture are horizontal or vertical. People are not expected to stand out from others in horizontal cultures. In horizontal cultures, people tend to see themselves as the same as others, and there is an emphasis on valuing equality. People are expected to try to stand out from others in vertical cultures. In vertical cultures, people tend to see themselves as different from others, and equality is *not* valued highly.

In horizontal, collectivistic cultures, high value is placed on equality, but little value is placed on freedom (Triandis, 1995). In Japan, for instance, there is a saying, "The nail that sticks out, gets hammered down," which illustrates that members of the culture are not expected to stand out. In vertical, collectivistic cultures (e.g., India), individuals are expected to fit into the group and, at the same time, they are allowed or expected to try to stand out in the group. People in vertical, collectivistic cultures do not value equality or freedom. In vertical, individualistic cultures (e.g., the United States, Britain, France, Germany), people are expected to act as individuals and try to stand out from others. People in these cultures place low value on equality and high value on freedom. In horizontal, individualistic cultures (e.g., Sweden, Norway), people are expected to act as individuals but, at the same time, not stand out from others. People in these cultures place high value on equality and freedom.

In summary, individualism-collectivism has been used widely to explain cultural differences in different types of behavior (see Triandis, 1990, for a summary). Kashima (1989), however, points out that there are problems with using dimensions of cultural variability to explain individual-level behavior. One problem area is that of developing causal explanations; it is impossible to test causal explanations of behavior on the basis of cultural-level explanations (e.g., culture cannot be controlled in an experiment). The second problem area is in mapping individualistic and collectivistic cultures. Hofstede (1980) and the Chinese Culture Connection (1987) present cultural-level scores regarding various dimensions of cultural variability, including individualism-collectivism. When specific samples are collected, however, they do not necessarily correspond with the cultural-level scores. When college students are sampled in Japan and the United States, for example, the Japanese college students often are more individualistic than the college students in the United States (Gudykunst, Gao, Schmidt et al., 1992; Triandis et al., 1988). If we are to overcome these problems, ways to study individualism-collectivism at the individual level are needed.

Individual Factors That Mediate the Influence of Cultural Individualism-Collectivism on Individual Behavior

At least three different individual characteristics mediate the influence of individualism-collectivism on individuals' communication: personalities, values, and self construals. Figure 3.2 schematically illustrates how the influence of cultural indi-

Figure 3.2   The influence of individualism-collectivism on communication.

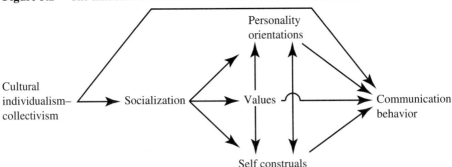

vidualism-collectivism on communication is mediated by these factors. This relationship should be kept in mind as you read the remainder of this section. We begin with personality orientations.

Personality Orientations.   The effect of cultural individualism-collectivism on communication is mediated by our personalities. Triandis et al. (1985), for example, propose idiocentrism and allocentrism as the personality orientations we learn as a function of individualism and collectivism, respectively. They report that allocentrism is correlated positively with social support, and negatively with alienation and anomie in the United States. Idiocentrism, in contrast, is correlated positively with an emphasis on achievement and perceived loneliness in the United States.

Gudykunst, Gao, Nishida, et al. (1992) report that the more idiocentric people are in the United States, the less sensitive they are to others' behavior. The more idiocentric Japanese are, the less sensitive they are to others' behavior, the less they pay attention to others' status characteristics, and the less concern they have for behaving in a socially appropriate fashion. Gudykunst, Gao, and Frankly-Stokes (in press) note that the more idiocentric Chinese and English are, the less they pay attention to others' status characteristics and the less concerned they are with behaving in a socially appropriate fashion.

Idiocentric individuals in individualistic cultures see it as natural to "do their own thing" and disregard needs of their ingroups, while allocentric individuals in individualistic cultures are concerned about their ingroups (Triandis et al., 1988). Allocentric individuals in collectivistic cultures "feel positive about accepting ingroup norms and do not even raise the question of whether or not to accept them," while idiocentric individuals in collectivistic cultures "feel ambivalent and even bitter about acceptance of ingroup norms" (Triandis et al., 1988, p. 325).

Yamaguchi (1994) argues that collectivism at the individual level involves the tendency to give priority to the collective self over the private self, especially when the two are in conflict. He found that the more collectivistic Japanese are, the more sensitive they are to others and the less they have a tendency to want to be unique. Yamaguchi, Kuhlman, and Sugimori (1992) found that these tendencies extend to people in Korea and the United States.

Individual Values.   The second way that the influence of cultural individualism-collectivism on communication is mediated is through the values we hold (see Schwartz, 1994a, and Schwartz & Sagiv, 1995, for discussions of individual values). Ball-Rokeach, Rokeach, and Grube (1984) argue that our values are the core of our personalities. They contend that our values serve as the major component of our personalities that helps us maintain and enhance our self-esteem. Feather (1995) reports that the type of values we hold influences the valences (positiveness/negativeness) we attach to different behaviors. Feather (1990) points out that our values influence the way we define situations, but they are not tied to specific situations.

Schwartz (1992) isolates 11 motivational domains of values. Value domains specify the structure of values and consist of specific values. Specific values fall in each of the domains [example values are given in brackets below]:

1. *Self-direction.* "Independent thought and action—choosing, creating, and exploring" (p. 5). [independence, freedom, curiosity]
2. *Stimulation.* "Excitement, novelty, and challenge in life" (p. 8). [exciting life, daring]
3. *Hedonism.* "Pleasure or sensuous gratification for oneself" (p. 8). [pleasure, enjoyment of life]
4. *Achievement.* "Personal success through demonstrated competence" (p. 8). [social recognition, capability, ambition]
5. Power. "Attainment of social status and prestige, and control or dominance over people" (p. 9). [authority, wealth, social recognition]
6. *Security.* "Safety, harmony, and stability of society, of relationships, and of self" (p. 9). [family security, social order, health]
7. *Conformity.* "Restraint of actions, inclinations, and impulses likely to upset or harm others and to violate social expectations or norms" (p. 9). [obedience, politeness, self-discipline]
8. *Tradition.* "Respect, commitment and acceptance of the customs and ideas that one's culture or religion imposes on the individual" (p. 10). [respect for tradition, humility, moderation]
9. *Spirituality.* "Endow life with meaning and coherence in the face of seeming meaninglessness of everyday existence" (p. 10). [meaning in life, inner harmony, devoutness]
10. *Benevolence.* "Preservation and enhancement of the welfare of people with whom one is in frequent social contact" (p. 11). [helpfulness, loyalty, responsibility]
11. *Universalism.* "Understanding, appreciation, tolerance, and protection for the welfare of *all* people and for nature" (p. 12). [equality, world at peace, social justice]

Schwartz argues that the interests served by the 11 value domains can be individualistic, collectivistic, or mixed. The value domains of stimulation, hedonism, power, achievement, and self-direction serve individual interests; the value domains of tradition, conformity, and benevolence serve collective interests; and the value domains of security, universalism, and spirituality serves mixed interests.

Schwartz (1990) contends that individualistic and collectivistic values do not necessarily conflict. With respect to individualistic values, he points out that

> hedonism (enjoyment), achievement, self-direction, social power, and stimulation values all serve self interests of the individual, but not necessarily at the expense of any collectivity. . . . These same values might be promoted by leaders or members of collectivities as goals for their ingroup. (p. 143)

With respect to collectivistic tendencies, Schwartz indicates that

> prosocial, restrictive conformity, security, and tradition values all focus on promoting the interests of others. It is other people, constituting a collective, who benefit from

the actor's [or actress's] concern for them, self-restraint, care for their security, and re-spect for shared traditions. But this does not necessarily occur at the expense of the actor [or actress]. (p. 143)

Individuals, therefore, can have both individualistic and collectivistic tendencies. While people can hold both individualistic and collectivistic values, one type tends to predominate. In the United States, for example, there are collective tendencies and some subcultures tend to be collectivistic, but most people hold individualistic values.

Self Construals. The third way the influence of cultural individualism-collectivism on communication is mediated is through the way we conceive of our-selves (e.g., Kashima, 1989; Markus & Kitayama, 1991, 1994a, 1994b; Triandis, 1989). Triandis, for example, argues that cultural variations in individualism-collectivism can be linked directly to the ways members of cultures conceive of themselves. The focus on self construal is important because how individuals con-ceive of the self is one of the major determinants of their behavior. The most widely used conceptualization of self construal is that of Markus and Kitayama (1991).

Markus and Kitayama (1991) contend that people use different construals of the self: the independent and the interdependent construals of the self. While Markus and Kitayama draw on work in which the authors discuss individualism-collectivism (e.g., Hofstede, 1980; Schwartz & Bilsky, 1990), they do not link independent and interdependent construals of the self directly to individualism-collectivism. We believe, however, that there is a direct relationship: The inde-pendent construal of self *predominates* in individualistic cultures, and the inter-dependent construal of self *predominates* in collectivistic cultures.

People in individualistic cultures emphasize an independent construal of the self. The independent construal of self involves the view that an individual's self is a unique, independent entity (see Figure 3.3). Geertz (1975), for example, describes the self "as a bounded, unique, more or less integrated motivational and cognitive universe, a dynamic center of awareness, emotion, judgment, and action organized into a distinctive whole and set contrastively both against other such wholes and against a social and natural background" (p. 48). Individualists' cultural "goal of in-dependence requires construing oneself as an individual whose behavior is orga-nized and made meaningful primarily by reference to one's own internal repertoire of thoughts, feelings, and action, rather than by reference to the thoughts, feelings, and actions of others" (Markus & Kitayama, 1991, p. 226).

The important tasks for people emphasizing an independent self construal are to be unique, strive for their own goals, express themselves, and be direct (e.g., "say what you mean"; Markus & Kitayama, 1991). Individuals' self-esteem is based on their ability to express themselves, and their ability to validate their internal attrib-utes (Markus & Kitayama, 1991).

People in collectivistic cultures (e.g., Asian, African, Latin American, and southern European cultures) emphasize an interdependent construal of the self. Markus and Kitayama (1991) point out that "experiencing interdependence entails seeing oneself as part of an encompassing social relationship and recognizing that

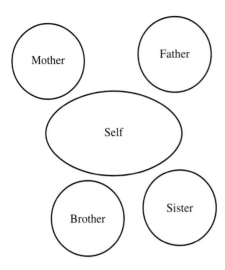

Figure 3.3   Independent self construals in family.

one's behavior is determined, contingent on, and, to a large extent, organized by what the actor [actress] perceives to be the thoughts, feelings, and actions of *others* in the relationship" (p. 227; see Figure 3.4). The construal of the self in relation to specific others guides behavior in specific social situations. Depending on the situation, different aspects of the interdependent self will guide people's behavior. If the behavior is taking place at home, the family interdependent self guides behavior; if the behavior is taking place on the job, the coworker interdependent self guides behavior.

The important tasks for people emphasizing an interdependent self construal are to fit in with the ingroup, act in an appropriate fashion, promote the ingroup's goals, occupy their proper place, be indirect, and read other people's minds (Markus & Kitayama, 1991). Markus and Kitayama also point out that "giving in is not a sign of weakness; rather it reflects tolerance, self-control, flexibility, and maturity" (p. 229). Self-esteem is based on people's ability to adjust to others, and their ability to maintain harmony in the social context when an interdependent self construal predominates (Markus & Kitayama, 1991).

As indicated earlier, independent construals of the self *predominate* in individualistic cultures and interdependent construals of the self *predominate* in collectivistic cultures. It is important to recognize, however, that everyone has both an independent and an interdependent construal of the self. Further, people with predominately interdependent construals of the self exist in individualistic cultures like that of the United States or Australia, and people with predominately independent construals of the self exist in collectivistic cultures like that of Japan or Korea. The critical issue is which self construal predominates to influence individuals' behavior and which self construal individuals use in guiding their behavior in a particular situation.

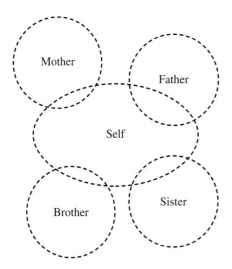

Figure 3.4   Interdependent self construals in family.

Low-Context and High-Context Communication

Individualism-collectivism provides a powerful explanatory framework for understanding cultural similarities and differences in interpersonal communication. There are cultural differences in the communication processes that predominate in individualistic and collectivistic cultures. These differences are best explained in terms of low- and high-context communication.

Characteristics of Low-Context and High-Context Communication.   Hall (1976) differentiates between low- and high-context communication. A high-context communication or message is one in which "most of the information is either in the physical context or internalized in the person, while very little is in the coded, explicit, transmitted part of the message (Hall, 1976, p. 79). A low-context communication or message, in contrast, is one in which "the mass of information is vested in the explicit code" (p. 70). Hall points out that

> people raised in high-context systems expect more of others than do the participants in low-context systems. When talking about something that they have on their minds, a high-context individual will expect his [or her] interlocutor to know what's bothering him [or her], so that he [or she] doesn't have to be specific. The result is that he [or she] will talk around and around the point, in effect putting all the pieces in place except the crucial one. Placing it properly—this keystone—is the role of his [or her] interlocutor. (p. 98)

These expectations clearly are different from those used in low-context communication where information is embedded mainly in the messages transmitted.

Members of individualistic cultures predominately use low-context communication and tend to communicate in a direct fashion, while members of collectivistic cultures predominately use high-context messages and tend to communicate in an indirect fashion. Levine (1985) describes communication in the collectivistic Amhara culture in Ethiopia:

> The Amhara's basic manner of communicating is indirect, often secretive. Amharic conversation abounds with general, evasive remarks, like *Min yeshallal?* ("What is better?") when the speaker has failed to indicate what issue he [or she] is referring to, or *Setagn!* ("Give me!") when the speaker fails to specify what it is he [or she] wants. When the speaker then is quizzed about the issue at hand or the object he [or she] desires, his [or her] reply still may not reveal what is really on his [or her] mind; and if it does, his [or her] interlocutor will likely as not interpret that response as a disguise. (p. 25)

Levine goes on to describe communication in the individualistic culture of the United States:

> The [North] American way of life, by contrast, affords little room for the cultivation of ambiguity. The dominant [North] American temper calls for clear and direct communication. It expresses itself in such common injunctions as "Say what you mean," "Don't beat around the bush," and "Get to the point." (p. 28)

These descriptions suggest that high-context communication is ambiguous and indirect, while low-context communication is direct and unambiguous.

Conversational Maxims.   Grice (1975) isolates four assumptions regarding coordinated social interaction that are characteristic of low-context communication. First, individuals should not give others more or less information than necessary (quantity maxim). Second, people should state only that which they believe to be true with sufficient evidence (quality maxim). Third, individuals' contributions should be pertinent to the context of conversations (relevancy maxim). Fourth, people should avoid obscure expressions, ambiguity, excessive verbosity, and disorganization (manner maxim). These conversational maxims are not characteristic of high-context communication.

Direct communication (Grice's, 1975, manner maxim) involves transmitting verbal messages that "embody and invoke speakers' true intentions," while indirect communication involves transmitting verbal messages that "camouflage and conceal speakers' true intentions" (Gudykunst & Ting-Toomey, 1988, p. 100). Indirect communication emphasizes listeners' abilities to infer speakers' intentions, while direct communication emphasizes speakers' ability to express their intentions (K. Okabe, 1987; R. Okabe, 1983; Yum, 1988b). K. Okabe (1987) points out, as examples, that someone being direct might say "The door is open" when asking someone to close the door, while someone being indirect might say "It is somewhat cold today."

R. Okabe (1983) suggests that low-context communication involves the use of categorical words such as certainly, absolutely, and positively. High-context communication, in contrast, is expressed through the use of qualifiers such as maybe, perhaps, and probably (R. Okabe, 1983, p. 34) in their conversation. Qualifier words are used to avoid leaving an assertive impression with the listener.

High-context communication involves the use of indirect, implicit, ambiguous words. When individuals' responses to others' messages are indirect and ambiguous, the responses may not appear to be relevant to what others said (e.g., they appear to violate Grice's, 1975, relevancy maxim). In order to communicate successfully using high-context communication, listeners must infer how what speakers say is relevant to what they said. Listeners also must infer speakers' intentions accurately to understand utterances correctly. Yum (1988b) contends that to be competent high-context communicators, people must "hear one and understand ten" (p. 384). This saying emphasizes the importance of receivers' sensitivity and abilities to capture the nonverbal aspect of indirect communication.

Consistent with Grice's (1975) quality maxim, speaking one's mind and telling the truth are "characteristic of a sincere and honest person" using low-context communication (Hofstede, 1991). People using low-context communication are expected to communicate in ways that are consistent with their feelings (Hall, 1976). People using high-context communication, in contrast, are expected to communicate in ways that maintain harmony in their ingroups. Doing so may involve people's transmitting messages that are inconsistent with their true feelings (Hall, 1976).

Speaking one's mind and telling the truth in low-context communication require that individuals be open with others. Openness involves revealing "personal information about the self in communicative interactions" (Norton, 1978, p. 101). Personal information is necessary to predict behavior when low-context communication is being used (Gudykunst & Ting-Toomey, 1988). When individuals are open, they are not reserved and they are approachable. Open communicators also are not secretive, and they are relatively frank with others (Norton, 1978).

Openness is not characteristic of high-context communication. In high-context communication, individuals do not reveal large amounts of personal information about themselves. Personal information is not used to predict behavior in high-context communication. Rather, group-based information (e.g., background, group memberships, status, age) is needed (Gudykunst & Nishida, 1986a). Communicators perceived as competent high-context communicators are not open, but tend to be reserved (R. Okabe, 1983). Being reserved is considered active, not passive, behavior in collectivistic cultures.

Low-context communication also involves being precise (Grice's, 1975, quantity maxim), while high-context communication involves the use of understatements. As indicated earlier, Grice's (1975) quantity maxim states that individuals' contributions to conversations should provide neither more nor less information than is required. High-context communication, in contrast, is not precise. Rather, high-context communication involves using understatements, or providing the least amount of information possible to allow listeners to infer speakers' intentions, and using pauses and silences in everyday conversation. R. Okabe (1983) argues that high-context communication requires transmitting messages through understatement and hesitation rather than through superlative expression (the opposite of Grice's, 1975, quantity maxim). In high-context communication, there is a negative association between the number of spoken words people use and the images other people have of them, especially in terms of their trustworthiness. People who use few words are viewed as more trustworthy than people who use many words (Lebra, 1987).

Closely related to the lack of emphasis on spoken words is the use of silence. In low-context communication, silence is space to be filled (Mare, 1990). People using low-context communication tend to experience a general discomfort with silence because it interrupts the flow of conversations. Silence often is interpreted by people using low-context communication as violating the quantity maxim. Silence also can be viewed as violating the relevancy maxim when individuals are using low-context communication. In high-context communication, in contrast, "silence is a communicative act rather than mere void in communicational space" (Lebra, 1987, p. 343). Lebra argues that silence can be used to indicate truthfulness, disapproval, embarrassment, and disagreement.

Individualism-Collectivism and Low-Context and High-Context Communication

High-context communication can be characterized as being indirect, ambiguous, and understated, with speakers being reserved and sensitive to listeners. Low-context communication, in contrast, can be characterized as being direct, explicit, open, precise, and consistent with one's feelings. As indicated earlier, these patterns of communication are compatible with collectivism and individualism, respectively.

Individuals use low- and high-context messages depending upon their relationship with the person with whom they are communicating. People in the individualistic culture of the United States, for example, use low-context communication in the vast majority of their relationships (Hall, 1976). They may, however, use high-context messages when communicating with a twin or their spouse of 20 years. In those relationships, it is unnecessary to be direct and precise to be clearly understood. People in Asian, African, and Latin collectivistic cultures, in contrast, tend to use high-context messages when they communicate most of the time. They, nevertheless, also use low-context messages in some relationships (e.g., close friendships).

Research on cultural differences in communication supports Gudykunst and Ting-Toomey's (1988) argument that low- and high-context communication styles are a function of individualism-collectivism. Members of individualistic cultures, for example, are more affect oriented (i.e., they base their behavior on their feelings; Frymier, Klopf, & Ishii, 1990) and more inclined to talk (Gaetz, Klopf, & Ishii, 1990) than are members of collectivistic cultures. Members of individualistic cultures are motivated to communicate interpersonally to achieve affection, pleasure, and inclusion more than are members of collectivistic cultures (Fernandez-Collado, Rubin, & Hernandez-Sampieri, 1991). Members of collectivistic cultures pay more attention to others' behavior and more attention to others' status characteristics than do members of individualistic cultures (Gudykunst, Gao, Nishida, et al., 1992). Members of collectivistic cultures are more concerned with avoiding hurting others and imposing on them than are members of individualistic cultures (Kim, 1994). Members of individualistic cultures are more concerned with clarity in conversations (Kim, 1994) and view clarity as necessary for effective communication (Kim & Wilson, 1994) more than do members of collectivistic cultures. Members of individualistic cultures perceive direct requests as the most effective strategy for accomplishing their goals, while members of collectivistic cultures perceive direct requests as the least effective strategy (Kim & Wilson, 1994).

As indicated earlier, not all members of individualistic cultures are individualists, and not all members of collectivistic cultures are collectivists (Triandis et al., 1985). Individuals' communication styles are dependent upon the degree to which the individuals have internalized the values of the culture in which they are socialized, and the way their culture socializes people to see themselves (e.g., as independent, unique individuals or individuals embedded in social groups). It, therefore, is necessary to examine the way the influence of cultural individualism-collectivism is mediated by individual factors.

With regard to the individual level, Markus and Kitayama (1991) argue that an independent self construal (one individual-level aspect of individualism) is associated with being unique, expressing the self, realizing internal attributes, and being direct. They suggest that an interdependent self construal (one individual-level component of collectivism), in contrast, is associated with belonging (fitting in), occupying one's proper place, engaging in appropriate action, and being indirect. Individuals use independent and interdependent self construals in different situations, and depending on their culture or ethnicity, they tend to use one more than the other.

Gudykunst and Nishida (1994) point out that "when a person's goal is to assert him- or herself as a unique person (individualism), he or she must be direct so that others will know where he or she stands" (p. 40). Kim, Sharkey, and Singelis (1994) observe that using interdependent self construals is associated with concern for others' feelings and using independent self construals is associated with a concern for clarity in conversations. Singelis and Brown (1995) report that interdependent self construals are related to using high-context communication styles, while independent self construals are not related to using high-context communication styles. Singelis and Sharkey (in press) note that independent self construals are correlated negatively with embarrassability, while Sharkey and Singelis (1993) observe that independent self construals are correlated negatively with social anxiety.

Gudykunst et al. (1996) report that independent self construals and individualistic values positively influence the use of dramatic communication, the use of feelings to guide behavior, openness of communication, and preciseness of communication. Interdependent self construals and collectivistic values positively influence the tendency to use indirect communication and to be interpersonally sensitive.

In summary, people in individualistic cultures predominantly use low-context communication, but they also use high-context communication at times. People in collectivistic cultures, in contrast, predominately use high-context communication, but they also use low-context communication at times. Table 3.1 summarizes the characteristics of individualistic and collectivistic cultures, and provides example cultures for the two orientations.

Given the overview of individualism-collectivism, we turn our attention to other dimensions of cultural variability. Our emphasis in the following discussion is on the cultural level of analysis because individual-level equivalents of these dimensions have not been isolated. We begin with Hofstede's (1980) dimensions of cultural variability.

Table 3-1 INDIVIDUALISTIC AND COLLECTIVISTIC CULTURES

Individualistic	Collectivistic
Major Characteristics	
Emphasis on individual's goals	Emphasis on ingroup's goals
Self-realization	Fitting into the ingroup
Little difference between ingroup and outgroup communication	Large difference between ingroup and outgroup communication
Independent self construal	Interdependent self construal
"I" identity	"We" identity
Saying what you are thinking	Avoiding confrontations in ingroup
Low-context communication that is direct, precise, and absolute	High-context communication that is indirect, imprecise, and probabilistic
Example Cultures	
Australia	Brazil
Belgium	China
Canada	Colombia
Denmark	Egypt
Finland	Greece
France	India
Germany	Japan
Great Britain	Kenya
Ireland	Korea
Israel	Mexico
Italy	Nigeria
Netherlands	Panama
New Zealand	Pakistan
Norway	Peru
South Africa	Saudi Arabia
Sweden	Thailand
Switzerland	Venezuela
United States	Vietnam

*The cultures listed are based on the *predominant* tendencies in the cultures.

HOFSTEDE'S DIMENSIONS OF CULTURAL VARIABILITY

Hofstede (1980, 1983) empirically derived four dimensions of cultural variability in his large-scale study of a multinational corporation. The first dimension isolated in his study, individualism, already has been discussed. The other three dimensions are uncertainty avoidance, power distance, and masculinity-femininity.

Uncertainty Avoidance

Uncertainty avoidance deals with the degree to which members of a culture try to avoid uncertainty. In comparison with members of cultures low in uncertainty avoidance, members of cultures high in uncertainty avoidance have a lower tolerance "for uncertainty and ambiguity, which expresses itself in higher levels of anxiety and energy release, greater need for formal rules and absolute truth, and less tolerance for people or groups with deviant ideas or behavior" (Hofstede, 1979, p. 395). In high uncertainty avoidance cultures, aggressive behavior of self and others is acceptable; however, individuals prefer to contain aggression by avoiding conflict and competition. There is a strong desire for consensus in cultures high in uncertainty avoidance; therefore, deviant behavior is not acceptable. Members of high uncertainty avoidance cultures also tend to display emotions more than members of low uncertainty avoidance cultures. Members of low uncertainty avoidance cultures have lower stress levels and weaker superegos, and accept dissent and taking risks more than members of high uncertainty avoidance cultures.

Hofstede (1991) points out that uncertainty avoidance should not be equated with risk avoidance. People in

> uncertainty avoiding cultures shun ambiguous situations. People in such cultures look for a structure in their organizations, institutions, and relationships which makes events clearly interpretable and predictable. Paradoxically, they are often prepared to engage in risky behavior to reduce ambiguities, like starting a fight with a potential opponent rather than sitting back and waiting. (p. 116)

Hofstede summarizes the view of people in high uncertainty avoidance cultures as "what is different, is dangerous" (p. 119), and the credo of people in low uncertainty avoidance cultures as "what is different, is curious" (p. 119).

Hofstede (1980) reports that in comparison with members of low uncertainty avoidance cultures, members of high uncertainty avoidance cultures resist change more, have higher levels of anxiety, have higher levels of intolerance for ambiguity, worry about the future more, see loyalty to their employer as more of a virtue, have a lower motivation for achievement, and take fewer risks. In organizations, workers in high uncertainty avoidance cultures prefer a specialist career, prefer clear instructions, avoid conflict, and disapprove of competition between employees more than do workers in low uncertainty avoidance cultures.

Uncertainty avoidance is useful in understanding differences in how strangers are treated. People in high uncertainty avoidance cultures try to avoid ambiguity and, therefore, develop rules and rituals for virtually every possible situation in which they might find themselves, including interacting with strangers. Interaction with strangers in cultures high in uncertainty avoidance may be highly ritualistic and/or very polite. If people from high uncertainty avoidance cultures interact with strangers in a situation where there are not clear rules, they may ignore the strangers—treat them as though they do not exist.

Different degrees of uncertainty avoidance exist in every culture, but one general tendency is predominant. Cultures that tend to be high in uncertainty avoidance include, but are not limited to, Egypt, Argentina, Belgium, Chile, France, Greece, Guatemala, Japan, Korea, Mexico, Peru, Portugal, and Spain. Cultures that tend to be low in uncertainty avoidance include, but are not limited to, Canada, Denmark, England, Hong Kong, India, Jamaica, Sweden, and the United States.

Power Distance

Power distance is "the extent to which the less powerful members of institutions and organizations accept that power is distributed unequally" (Hofstede & Bond, 1984, p. 419). Individuals from high power distance cultures accept power as part of society. As a result, superiors consider their subordinates to be different from themselves and vice versa. Members of high power distance cultures see power as a basic fact in society and stress coercive or referent power, while members of low power distance cultures believe power should be used only when it is legitimate and prefer expert or legitimate power.

In summarizing the differences between cultures low in power distance and cultures high in power distance, Hofstede (1991) points out that

> in small power distance countries there is limited dependence of subordinates on bosses, and a preference for consultation, that is, *interdependence* between boss and subordinate. The emotional distance between them is relatively small: subordinates will quite readily approach and contradict their bosses. In large power distance countries there is considerable dependence of subordinates on bosses. Subordinates respond by either *preferring* such dependence (in the form of autocratic or paternalistic boss), or rejecting it entirely, which in psychology is known as *counterdependence:* that is dependence, but with a negative sign. (p. 27)

The power distance dimension focuses on the relationships between people of different statuses (e.g., superiors and subordinates in organization).

Hofstede (1980) reports that parents in high power distance cultures value obedience in their children, and students value conformity and display authoritarian attitudes more than those in low power distance cultures. In organizations, close supervision, fear of disagreement with a supervisor, lack of trust among coworkers, and directed supervision are all manifested more in high power distance cultures than in low power distance cultures. Further, Hofstede notes that members of low power distance cultures see respect for the individual and equality as antecedents to "freedom," while members of high power distance cultures view tact, servitude, and money as antecedents to "freedom." Antecedents to "wealth" in low power distance cultures include happiness, knowledge, and love. Inheritance, ancestral property, stinginess, deceit, and theft, in contrast, are viewed as antecedents to "wealth" in high power distance cultures.

Power distance is useful in understanding strangers' behavior in role relationships, particularly those involving different degrees of power or authority. People from high power distance cultures, for example, do not question their superiors' orders. They expect to be told what to do. People in low power distance cultures, in contrast, do not necessarily accept superiors' orders at face value; they want to know why they should follow them. When people from the two different systems interact, misunderstanding is likely unless one, or both, understand the other person's system.

Low and high power distance tendencies exist in all cultures, but one tends to predominate. Cultures in which high power distance tends to predominate include, but are not limited to, Egypt, Ethiopia, Ghana, Guatemala, India, Malaysia, Nigeria, Panama, Saudi Arabia, and Venezuela. Cultures in which low power distance tends to predominate include, but are not limited to, Austria, Canada, Denmark, Germany, Ireland, Israel, New Zealand, Sweden, and the United States.

Masculinity-Femininity

High masculinity involves a high value placed on things, power, and assertiveness, while systems in which people, quality of life, and nurturance prevail are low on masculinity or high on femininity (Hofstede, 1980). Cultural systems high on the masculinity index emphasize differentiated sex roles, performance, ambition, and independence. Conversely, systems low on masculinity value fluid sex roles, quality of life, service, and interdependence.

Hofstede (1980) reports that in comparison with people in feminine cultures, people in masculine cultures have stronger motivation for achievement, view work as more central to their lives, accept their company's "interference" in their private lives, have higher job stress, have greater value differences between men and women in the same position, and view recognition, advancement, or challenge as more important to their satisfaction with their work.

Masculinity-femininity is useful in understanding cultural differences and similarities in opposite-sex and same-sex relationships. People from highly masculine cultures, for example, tend to have little contact with members of the opposite sex when they are growing up. They tend to see same-sex relationships as more intimate than opposite-sex relationships. For people from a feminine culture to communicate effectively with strangers from a masculine culture, especially if they are male and female, they must understand the others' orientation toward sex roles.

As with the other dimensions of cultural variability, both masculinity and femininity tendencies exist in all cultures; one, however, tends to predominate. Cultures in which masculinity tends to predominate include, but are not limited to, Austria, Italy, Jamaica, Japan, Mexico, Switzerland, and Venezuela. Cultures in which femininity tends to predominate include, but are not limited to, Chile, Costa Rica, Denmark, Finland, Netherlands, Norway, and Sweden. The United States falls in the middle on this dimension.

Confucian Work Dynamism

Hofstede (1980, 1983) observed the four dimensions discussed in this section (individualism-collectivism, power distance, uncertainty avoidance, masculinity-femininity) in his study of a large multinational company. The dimensions may have a western bias because of the methodology used in collecting the data. The Chinese Culture Connection (1987; the Chinese Culture Connection is a group of researchers organized by Michael Bond at the Chinese University of Hong Kong) tested Hofstede's conclusions using a methodology with a Chinese bias. They found four dimensions of cultural variability: Confucian work dynamism, integration, human-heartedness, and moral discipline. Three of these dimensions correlate with dimensions observed in Hofstede's study: Integration correlates with individualism, moral discipline correlates with power distance, and human-heartedness correlates with masculinity-femininity. The only dimension that does not correlate with one of Hofstede's dimensions is Confucian work dynamism.

Confucian work dynamism dimension involves eight values. Four values are associated positively with the dimension: ordering relationships, thrift, persistence, and having a sense of shame. Four are negatively associated with the dimension: protecting one's face, personal steadiness, respect for tradition, and reciprocation. The Chinese Culture Connection (1987) argues that the four positively loaded items reflect a hierarchical dynamism present in Chinese society, while the four negatively loaded items reflect "checks and distractions" to this dynamism.

The Confucian work dynamism dimension is consistent with Confucianism. Hofstede (1991) summarizes the tenets of Confucianism by isolating four key principles:

> 1. The stability of society is based on unequal relationships between people. . . .
> 2. The family is the prototype for all social organizations. . . .
> 3. Virtuous behavior towards others consists of not treating others as one would not like to be treated oneself. . . .
> 4. Virtue with regard to one's task in life consists of trying to acquire skills and education, working hard, not spending more than necessary, being patient, and persevering. (p. 165, italics omitted)

The Confucian work dynamism dimension was isolated by asking Chinese respondents in different countries to indicate the extent to which the Chinese values applied in the country in which they resided.

KLUCKHOHN AND STRODTBECK'S VALUE ORIENTATIONS

Value orientations are "complex but definitely patterned . . . principles . . . which give order and direction to the ever-flowing stream of human acts and thoughts as these relate to the solution of 'common human' problems" (Kluckhohn & Strodtbeck, 1961, p. 4). The theory of value orientations is based on three assumptions: (1) people in all cultures must find solutions to a limited number of common human problems; (2) the available solutions to these problems are not unlimited, but vary within a range of potential solutions; and (3) while one solution tends to be preferred by members of any given culture, all potential solutions are present in every culture.

Kluckhohn and Strodtbeck (1961) posit five problems for which all cultures must find solutions. Posed as questions, these problems are as follows: (1) What is the innate character of human nature (human nature orientation)? (2) What is the relationship of people to nature (person-nature orientation)? (3) What is the focus of human life with respect to time (time orientation)? (4) What is the focus of human activity (activity orientation)? and (5) What is the relationship of one person to another (relational orientation)? As indicated above, every culture must find a solution to each of these problems. The solutions available, however, are limited for each of the problems.

Human Nature Orientation

The human nature orientation deals with the innate character of human nature (Kluckhohn & Strodtbeck, 1961). The potential solutions to this problem appear relatively obvious: Humans can be seen as innately good, innately evil, or a mixture of good and evil. It is not quite that simple, however. Humans can be viewed not only as either good or evil but also as either able to change (mutable) or not able to change (immutable). In addition, we must recognize that viewing human nature as a mixture of good and evil is not the same as viewing human nature as neutral. If we combine these various aspects, we find that there are six potential solutions to this problem: (1) humans are evil but mutable; (2) humans are evil and immutable; (3) humans are neutral with respect to good and evil; (4) humans are a mixture of good and evil; (5) humans are good but mutable; and (6) humans are good and immutable.

When this orientation is applied to the United States, it is not always easy to decide which solution predominates. People in the United States inherited a view of human nature as evil but mutable from their Puritan predecessors. In this view, discipline and self-control are seen as necessary if humans are to change. Some subcultures within the United States definitely adopt this solution (e.g., the Hutterites), but the predominant view in the middle-class subculture of the United States is probably the view of human nature as a mixture of good and evil.

Person-Nature Orientation

Three potential types of relations exist between humans and nature: mastery over nature, harmony with nature, and subjugation to nature (Kluckhohn & Strodtbeck, 1961). These solutions are relatively straightforward and are illustrated best by examples.

In industrialized societies like the United States, the mastery-over-nature view tends to predominate. This orientation involves the view that all natural forces can and should be overcome and/or put to use by humans; examples are damming rivers, moving mountains, and controlling illness through medicine.

The harmony-with-nature orientation draws no distinctions between human life, nature, and the supernatural—any one is just an extension of another. The Cheyenne Indians of North America, for example, see themselves as living in harmony with nature. In their view, "human aspirations are realizable not so much through the appeasement of whimsical spirit beings and gods as through action that fits the conditions of environmental organization and functioning" (Hoebel, 1960, p. 85). This orientation also predominates in other Native American groups, such as the Navajo, as well as in many Asian cultures, including those of China and Japan.

The final solution to this problem, subjugation to nature, predominates in cultures like those of the Spanish Americans of the southwestern United States, according to Kluckhohn and Strodtbeck (1961). They cite as an example sheepherders who believe there is nothing that can be done to control nature if it threatens—neither land nor flock can be protected from storms.

Time Orientation

The temporal focus of human life can be directed on the past, the present, or the future (Kluckhohn & Strodtbeck, 1961). The concern here is not with hours, days, weeks, months, or even years, but rather with a broader concept of time. People in any culture must, of course, come to terms with all three solutions, but, as pointed out above, one solution tends to predominate in a particular culture.

The past orientation predominates in cultures placing a high value on tradition. This orientation predominates in cultures worshipping ancestors (e.g., the Shinto religion in Japan) or emphasizing strong family ties. Also included here are cultures where there is some degree of traditionalism and aristocracy (e.g., England).

The present orientation predominates where people pay relatively little attention to what has gone on in the past and what might happen in the future. In this orientation, the past is seen as unimportant, and the future is seen as vague and unpredictable. The Navajo Indians of northern Arizona, for example, have this orientation. To them, only the here and now is real; the future and the past have little reality (Hall, 1959).

The future orientation predominates where change is valued highly. In this orientation, the future generally is viewed as "bigger and better," while being "old-fashioned" (the past) is scorned. Both Kluckhohn and Strodtbeck (1961) and Hall (1959) see this orientation as predominating in the United States.

Activity Orientation

Human activity can be handled in three ways: doing, being, and being-in-becoming (Kluckhohn & Strodtbeck, 1961). The predominant orientation in the United States is doing. A doing orientation involves a focus upon those types of activities that have outcomes external to the individual, that can be measured by someone else. Activities must be tangible. In appraising a person, people in the United States tend to ask questions like "What did he or she do?" or "What has she or he accomplished?" According to this orientation, if you are sitting at your desk thinking, you are not doing anything because your thoughts cannot be externally measured.

The being orientation is almost the extreme opposite of the doing orientation. This orientation involves "a spontaneous expression of what is conceived to be 'given' in the human personality" (Kluckhohn & Strodtbeck, 1961, p. 16). An example of this orientation is the Mexican fiesta, which reveals pure impulse gratification.

The final activity orientation, being-in-becoming, is concerned with who we are, not what we have accomplished. The focus of human activity is on striving for an integrated whole in the development of the self. The best example of this orientation may be Zen Buddhist monks, who spend their lives in contemplation and meditation to fully develop the self. This view also was manifested in the self-improvement movement of the 1960s and 1970s in the United States. Maslow's (1970/1954) self-actualized person, for example, is in a constant state of being-in-becoming.

Relational Orientation

This value orientation is consistent with the broad dimension of cultural variability, individualism-collectivism, discussed above, but there are sufficient differences that it needs to be discussed here. Kluckhohn and Strodtbeck (1961) isolate three potential ways in which humans can define their relationships to other humans: individualism, lineality, and collaterality. As we might expect, individualism is the predominant orientation in the United States. This orientation is characterized by the autonomy of the individual; in other words, individuals are seen as unique, separate entities. In this orientation, individual goals and objectives take priority over group goals and objectives.

The lineality orientation, on the other hand, focuses on the group, with group goals taking precedence over individual goals. The crucial issue in the lineality orientation, according to Kluckhohn and Strodtbeck (1961), is the continuity of the group through time. Specific individuals are important only for their group memberships. One example of this orientation is the aristocracy of many European countries.

Collaterality, the third relational orientation, also focuses on the group, but not the group extended through time. Rather, the focus is on the laterally extended group (an individual's most immediate group memberships in time and space). The goals of the group take precedence over those of the individual. In fact, in this orientation, people are not considered except vis-à-vis their group memberships. One example of this orientation is the identification of the Japanese with the company for which they work or the university from which they graduated.

Applying the Orientations

Like the other dimensions of cultural variability, value orientations can be used to understand our communication with strangers. Consider two cultures that appear relatively similar on the surface, England and the United States. While there are surface similarities, there are also basic differences in value orientations, which can cause misunderstandings between people from the two cultures. For the purpose of illustration, consider the time dimension. In the United States, the future orientation tends to predominate, while in England, the past orientation does. "Indeed, some of the chief differences between the peoples of the United States and England derive from their somewhat varying attitudes toward time. Americans have difficulty understanding the respect the English have for tradition, and the English do not appreciate the typical American's disregard for it" (Kluckhohn & Strodtbeck, 1961, p. 15).

As another example, we can look at the relational orientation. People in the United States see themselves as individuals first and members of groups second, while people in many collectivistic cultures like Japan see themselves as members of groups first and foremost (either lineal or collateral orientation). When people with these two orientations come into contact, especially in the business world, there are often misunderstandings. Consider a manager from the United States in Japan whose subordinates (all Japanese) negotiate a very large business deal. The tendency in the United States would be to decide which individual is responsible for the deal and to reward him or her in some way. The manager from the United States would, therefore, naturally seek out an individual to reward. Assuming he or she locates an individual in the department and proceeds to reward that individual, what might the consequences be for the person selected? Many writers on Japanese business argue that this person might be ostracized from his or her work group because of being singled out. By being singled out, the person has assumed a self-definition outside his or her membership in the group. In Japan, the group, not the individual, would be rewarded.

PARSONS' PATTERN VARIABLES

Another view of cultural variability is Parsons' (1951) concept of pattern variables. A *pattern variable* is "a dichotomy, one side of which must be chosen by an actor [or actress] before the meaning of a situation is determinate for him [or her], and thus before he [or she] can act with respect to that situation" (Parsons & Shils, 1951, p. 77). In other words, pattern variables are mutually exclusive choices individuals make prior to engaging in action. These choices are made both consciously and unconsciously; however, they are generally made unconsciously since they are learned during the socialization process at an early age. Parsons' first pattern variable, self orientation–collective orientation, is identical to individualism-collectivism and, therefore, is omitted here.

Affectivity–Affective Neutrality

The affectivity–affective-neutrality orientation is concerned with the nature of the gratification that we seek (Parsons, 1951). Do we look for immediate gratification from the situation at hand (affectivity), or do we delay gratification by expressing self-restraint (affective neutrality)? Affectivity is associated with emotional responses throughout Parsons' writings. Affective neutrality, on the other hand, is associated with people's responding from a more cognitive (nonemotional) level. The United States typically is characterized as having an affective-neutrality orientation, while Latin American cultures usually are characterized as showing an affectivity orientation. People from the United States, therefore, are more likely to base decisions on cognitive information, while people from cultures with an affectivity orientation are more likely to base their decisions on emotional responses.

Universalism-Particularism

This orientation is concerned with modes of categorizing people or objects (Parsons, 1951). The categorization of people or objects in terms of some universal or general frame of reference is a universalistic orientation. The categorization of people or objects in specific categories is a particularistic orientation. Universalistic interaction generally follows a standardized pattern, while particularistic interaction is unique to the situation. Given this distinction, we expect individualistic cultures like the United States to be characterized by universalistic orientation, while a particularistic orientation tends to predominate in collectivistic cultures like those in Asia. People from cultures in which a universalistic orientation predominates communicate with strangers in the same way in a variety of situations, while people from cultures in which a particularistic orientation predominates communicate with strangers differently in different situations.

Diffuseness-Specificity

The universalism-particularism orientation as a pattern variable is concerned with how we categorize people or objects (Parsons, 1951). The diffuseness-specificity orientation is concerned with how we respond to people or objects. If a person or an object is responded to in a holistic manner, a diffuseness orientation is displayed. If a particular aspect of a person or an object is responded to, on the other hand, a specificity orientation is used. In collectivistic cultures, there is a tendency for a diffuseness orientation to predominate, while the specificity orientation tends to prevail in individualistic cultures like that of the United States. When people from a culture in which a diffuseness orientation predominates interact with a waiter or waitress, for example, they respond to the waiter or waitress as a whole person, not just to his or her role. People from cultures in which the specificity orientation predominates, in contrast, respond to the waiter or waitress only in a more role-specific way.

Ascription-Achievement

Are objects or people treated in terms of qualities ascribed to them or in terms of qualities they have achieved (Parsons, 1951)? With an ascription orientation, people are judged on qualities inherent in them (e.g., gender or family heritage). The prevalent orientation in the United States is achievement, while that in many other cultures (e.g., India) is ascription. People from cultures in which an ascription orientation predominates base their sociocultural predictions about others' behavior on the groups into which the others were born (gender, age, race, ethnic group, caste, etc.). People from cultures in which an achievement orientation predominates, on the other hand, base their sociocultural predictions on group memberships others have achieved through their own efforts (occupational group, social class, etc.).

Instrumental-Expressive Orientation

What is the nature of the goals we seek in our interactions with others (Parsons, 1951)? Are our interactions a means to another goal (instrumental), or are our interactions an end in and of themselves (expressive)? In the expressive orientation, interactions are valued because they are important, not because they will lead to anything else. Instrumental interactions, in contrast, are valued only because they help the person reach another goal. The instrumental orientation is the predominant pattern in the United States, while the expressive orientation predominates in many other cultures (e.g., Arab or Latin American cultures). People from cultures in which an expressive orientation predominates tend to value friendships for their own sake more than do people from cultures in which an instrumental orientation predominates.

Applying the Pattern Variables

The six pattern variables presented above can be used to analyze cultural differences. One specific illustration of such use is Lipset's (1963) comparison of Great Britain, Canada, Australia, and the United States. The results of his study indicate "the United States emphasizes achievement, egalitarianism, universalism, and specificity. Canada is lower than the United States on all of these dimensions. Great Britain in turn ranks lower than Canada. Australia was found more egalitarian but less achievement-oriented, universalistic, and specific" (Zavalloni, 1980, p. 89). Thus, although these cultures appear very similar on the surface, their underlying orientations toward action are significantly different. A person from one culture who does not recognize the differences in how underlying orientations influence strangers inevitably makes errors in predicting the strangers' behavior. To make accurate predictions about strangers' behavior, we must understand their postulates, the things they take for granted.

STRUCTURAL TIGHTNESS

Structural tightness focuses on the norms, rules, and constraints cultures place on members' behavior. Norms and rules are discussed in depth in Chapter 6, but for our present purpose, we can define *norms* as guidelines for behavior based on the moral code and rules as guidelines for behavior that are not based on the moral code (Olsen, 1978). Tight cultures impose many rules and constraints on behavior, while loose cultures place few *rules* and constraints on behavior (Triandis, 1994).

In tight cultures, the norms and rules of the culture tend to be clear and people are expected to follow them (Pelto, 1968). If members violate the norms or rules of the culture, sanctions are imposed on them (i.e., they are punished in some way, which may vary from a disapproving glance to being ostracized from the group). In loose cultures, the norms and rules may not be very clear, and people are allowed to deviate from them to some degree (Pelto, 1968). The norms and rules in loose cultures tend to be elastic, rather than rigid as in tight cultures. When norms and rules are violated in loose cultures, the sanctions are not as severe as they are in tight cultures.

Triandis (1994) argues that cultural homogeneity (people are similar) tends to lead to structural tightness. One reason for this tendency is that similarity among members of a culture tends to lead to agreement about behavior that is correct in specific situations. Cultural heterogeneity (people are different) tends to lead to cultural looseness. One reason for this tendency is that it is difficult to get people who are different to agree on what behavior is correct in a particular situation. The degree to which there is a need for coordinated action also influences the degree of structural tightness. The greater the need for coordinated action, the more tight the culture.

Mosel (1973) points out a relationship between the looseness or tightness of the social structure and the predictability of behavior. He believes behavior is much more predictable in a tight social structure than in a loose social structure. The degree of certainty we have about how another person will behave, therefore, decreases as we go from a culture with a tight social structure to one with a loose social structure.

The United States tends to be a loose culture, but it is not as loose as Thailand. Phillips (1965) reports that behavior in Thailand is not highly disciplined or regimented, and it lacks regularity. In companies, he observes that there may not be clear hours employees are expected to work. Phillips also notes that employees may decide to quit a job and just stop coming to work, rather than formally resigning. The reasons for leaving may vary from being bored, wanting to take a trip, or wanting to go home (e.g., to the home village for a person working in a city). In general, Thais see behavior as unpredictable and life is viewed as a series of accidents.

To illustrate the problems of intercultural communication in a highly loose social structure, we can look at a North American businessman working in Thailand (this example is drawn from *The Bridge,* Summer, 1979, p. 19). After spending some time in Thailand, the North American businessman discovers that the deadlines he imposed for his Thai subordinates are not being met. The employees verbally agree to complete the work on time; in other words, they agree to meet the supervisor's role expectation. When it is time to turn in their work, however, they fail to do so and the North American becomes increasingly upset with their behavior. In order to understand the problem, the businessman talks about it with several Thai supervisors. Each of the Thai supervisors tells the North American the same thing, *Mai pen rai*, a Thai saying meaning roughly, "Don't worry about it; it doesn't really matter." This example suggests that a tremendous amount of variation from the ideal role is tolerated in Thai culture.

Japan is an example of a tight culture (Embree, 1950). Hearn (1956), an early observer of Japanese society, notes that "the only safe rule of conduct in a Japanese settlement is to act in all things according to local custom; for the slightest divergence from the rule will be observed with disfavor" (p. 100). Benedict (1946) also observes that Japan is a "rigidly chartered world" where the value of a person is measured by his or her ability to carry out "all the rules of good behavior" (p. 225). While the rules are rigid, there are groups of people who are not expected to follow the rules (Edgerton, 1985). Drunks, mentally ill people, and foreigners, for example, can violate rules without harsh penalty because they are not responsible for their behavior (drunks and mentally ill) or are not expected to know the rules (foreigners).

The tightness of the Japanese culture is seen in the concepts of *on* and its reciprocal, *ongaeshi*. *On* and *ongaeshi* involve a reciprocal set of obligations between a superior and a subordinate. "*On* is a beneficence handed down from one's superior. It institutes an obligation (*ongaeshi*) to the superior on the part of the person who receives its benefit. By its very nature, *on* always connotes a hierarchical relation between two specific [people]" (Beardsley, 1965, p. 94). Although the superior-inferior aspect of the *on-ongaeshi* relationship is not explicitly stated, it is accepted by all parties. Beardsley (1965) points out that the person filling the superior role may be one of four types: (1) "a class superior," for example, an employer; (2) "a kin superior," for example, a person's grandparent or parent; (3) "an age-status superior," for example, a teacher; and (4) "a superior in a limited situation," for example, the person who arranges one's marriage. Once an *on-ongaeshi* relationship is begun, the inferior has an obligation for loyalty to the superior for as long as the relationship lasts, with little or no deviation being permitted.

SUMMARY

In this chapter, we examine dimensions of cultural variability that allow us to understand why patterns of communication are similar or different across cultures. Individualism-collectivism is the dimension of cultural variability most widely used to explain communication across cultures. Low-context communication is the predominant mode of communication in individualistic cultures, and high-context communication is the predominant mode of communication in collectivistic cultures. The influence of cultural individualism-collectivism on communication is mediated by our personalities, our values, and our self construals.

Hofstede's dimensions of cultural variability, Kluckhohn and Strodtbeck's value orientations, Parsons' pattern variables, and structural tightness also can be used to explain variations in communication behavior across cultures. By understanding where strangers' cultures fall on the various dimensions of cultural variability guiding their behavior, we can increase our ability to interpret and predict their behavior accurately, thereby decreasing the likelihood of misunderstandings.

STUDY QUESTIONS

1. What are the differences between the emic and etic approaches to the study of culture?
2. Why do we use dimensions of cultural variability to explain similarities and differences in behavior across cultures?
3. Why do ingroups have more influence on behavior in collectivistic cultures than in individualistic cultures?
4. Why is there an emphasis on independent self construals in individualistic cultures and interdependent self construals in collectivistic cultures?
5. Why does low-context communication predominate in individualistic cultures and high-context communication predominate in collectivistic cultures?
6. Why is ambiguity a major problem in high uncertainty avoidance cultures, but not in low uncertainty avoidance cultures?
7. How can we use power distance to understand cultural variation in communication behavior?
8. What differences would you expect in same-sex and opposite-sex communication in masculine and feminine cultures?
9. How does the activity orientation explain cultural variability in communication?
10. How does universalism-particularism influence the way people communicate?
11. How does the structural tightness of a culture influence the predictability of members' behavior?

SUGGESTED READING

Edgerton, R. (1985). *Rules, exceptions, and social order.* Berkeley: University of California Press.

Hall, E. T. (1976). *Beyond culture.* New York: Doubleday.

Hofstede, G. (1980). *Culture's consequences.* Beverly Hills, CA: Sage.

Hofstede, G. (1991). *Culture and organizations.* New York: McGraw-Hill.

Kim, U., Triandis, H. C., Kagitcibasi, C., Choi, S. C., & Yoon, G. (Eds.). (1994). *Individualism-collectivism: Theory, method, and application.* Thousand Oaks, CA: Sage.

Kluckhohn, F., & Strodtbeck, F. (1961). *Variations in value orientations.* New York: Row, Petersen.

Triandis, H. C. (1995). *Individualism-collectivism.* Boulder, CO: Westview.

4

Sociocultural Influences on the Process

*In every situation the person seems to know what group he [or she] be-
longs to and to what group he [or she] does not belong. He [or she]
knows more or less clearly where he [or she] stands, and this position
largely determines his [or her] behavior.*

Kurt Lewin

Our communication with strangers is influenced by our culture and by the group
memberships we form within our culture. Our purpose in this chapter is to examine the sociocultural influences on the intercultural communication process. We
examine the influence of our memberships in social groups, our social identities,
and our role relationships on our communication with strangers. Each of these
factors is influenced by our culture and each in turn influences the others. Our
membership in social groups, for example, influences our social identities and
how we look at our role relationships. We begin by looking at our membership in
social groups.

MEMBERSHIPS IN SOCIAL GROUPS

A *social group* is "two or more individuals who share a common social identification of themselves or . . . perceive themselves to be members of the same social category" (Turner, 1982, p. 15). Many different aspects of our group memberships influence our communication with strangers. We begin by looking at membership and
reference groups.

84

Membership and Reference Groups

We are members of many different social groups, such as our family, social class, racial group, ethnic group, sex, occupational group, and nationality. If we are conscious of belonging to a group or social category, we refer to that group as a *membership group*. Janis and Smith (1965) isolate several factors that lead us to maintain our associations with our membership groups. First, we obtain positive rewards from memberships in groups, including affection and friendship. Second, we desire to avoid the social isolation that can take place without close group ties, while at the same time, we desire to obtain the status and prestige associated with membership in certain groups. Finally, restraints act upon us to keep us in certain groups, even if we prefer to leave. We cannot, for example, choose our race or ethnic group.

There is a difference between those groups to which we actually belong and those groups to which we would like to belong. When we look to another group for guidance in determining our behavior, that group is a *reference group*. Sarbin and Allen (1968) define a reference group as

> a group which a person values. It is often used to explain behavior oriented toward audiences not physically present. A reference group may be a membership or nonmembership group, a single other person . . . a category of people, or even nonexistent groups or categories of people, for example, the future generation, God, ancestors. (p. 532)

In other words, a reference group is a group to which we look for guidance in how to behave. The closer our values coincide with those held by a particular group, the greater is the likelihood we will view the group as a reference group (Sarbin & Allen, 1968).

One of the largest membership groups to which we belong is our nation. A nation usually is defined in terms of historical, political, social, and economic events shared by a group of people. Such a conceptualization ignores the degree of consensus of the people about their membership in the group, or nation. Emerson (1960) proposes that "the simplest statement that can be made about a nation is that it is a body of people who feel they are a nation; and it may be that when all the fine-spun analysis is concluded this will be the ultimate statement as well" (p. 102).

All of us are members of majority groups and minority groups. Schaefer (1979) isolates five characteristics of minority group membership. First, members of minority groups are treated differently from members of a majority group by members of the majority group. This inequality usually takes the form of segregation, prejudice, and discrimination. Second, members of minority groups have either physical or cultural characteristics that make them stand out from the majority group. Third, because minority groups stand out, membership in them is not voluntary. Fourth, members of a minority group tend to associate with and marry other members of their group. Finally, "members of a minority group are aware of their subordinate status, which leads to strong group solidarity" (Schaefer, 1979, p. 8). The term *minority group* is not viewed positively by many non-European Americans in the United States today. We avoid the use of this classification whenever possible, but there are a few points where it is necessary to use it.

Wirth (1945) distinguishes between two types of minority groups. *Racial groups* possess "racial marks, . . . the most visible and permanent marks with which we are afflicted" (p. 347). *Ethnic groups,* in contrast, possess distinctive linguistic, religious, cultural, or national characteristics. The distinction between racial and ethnic groups, however often is a difficult distinction to make. Several writers argue that the concept of race should be dropped from both popular and scientific use. Montagu (1952), for example, suggests a broad definition of ethnic group, which encompasses the concept of race:

> An ethnic group represents one of a number of populations, which together comprise the species *Homo sapiens,* but individually maintain their differences, physical or cultural, by means of isolating mechanisms such as geographic and social barriers. These differences will vary as the power of the geographic and social boundaries vary. Where these boundaries are of low power, neighboring ethnic groups will integrate or hybridize one another. Where the barriers are of high power, such ethnic groups will tend to remain distinct from each other or replace each other geographically or ecologically. (pp. 87–88)

Montagu (1972) contends that substituting the term *ethnic group* for *race* would help avoid the negative connotations associated with racial terms and lead to increased investigation and discussion.

There also is another reason to focus on ethnicity rather than race. Our biological race does not influence our communication. Our ethnicity, in contrast, does influence our communication. Ethnicity influences our communication because it is based on a shared cultural heritage. We use the term *ethnicity* rather than *race* whenever possible.

In addition to nation, minority-majority, race, and ethnicity, other group memberships influence our communication with strangers. These include, but are not limited to, female-male, social class, able-bodied–disabled, and young-old. Like nation, social class, minority-majority, race, and ethnicity, these social groups are the basis for classifying people as members of an ingroup or an outgroup. We discuss social identities based on these group memberships later in this chapter.

Ingroups and Outgroups

As part of our socialization into our membership groups, we are taught to interact with members of certain groups of people because of their ethnic heritage, religion, or social class, to name only a few of the groups. The groups with which we are taught to associate are referred to as ingroups. More formally, *ingroups* are "groups of people about whose welfare [we are] concerned, with whom [we are] willing to cooperate without demanding equitable returns, and separation from whom leads to discomfort or even pain" (Triandis, 1988, p. 75). The groups of people with whom we are taught *not* to associate, in contrast, are referred to as outgroups. *Outgroups* are groups of people about whose welfare we are not concerned, and groups with whom we require an equitable return in order to cooperate. The tendency to draw a distinction between ingroups and outgroups is universal among humans (Brewer & Campbell, 1976).

There are several consequences of the formation of ingroups and outgroups. First, there is a tendency for us to expect other members of our ingroups to behave and think similarly to the way we do (Tajfel, 1969a). Second, as members of ingroups, we have a tendency to put our own groups in a favorable light when they are compared with outgroups (Brewer, 1979). Both of these consequences influence the way we categorize and use information about strangers, who are, by definition, members of outgroups. Third, we have less anxiety about interacting with members of our ingroups than about interacting with members of outgroups (Stephan & Stephan, 1985). Fourth, we tend to be more accurate in predicting the behavior of members of our ingroups than we are in predicting the behavior of members of outgroups (Gudykunst, 1995).

Our ingroups are not necessarily limited to our families or ethnic groups. When dealing with people from other cultures, we may define people from our own culture as the ingroup and the outgroups as people from other cultures. In such an instance, the tendency is for us to judge the behavior of people in the other culture (the outgroup) in terms of our cultural standards.

The images ingroup members have of outgroups are passed on to children from adults. Levine (1965) argues that

> the images of an out-group that adults pass on to children are affected by the amount of direct experience the adults have had with members of the out-group and by the amount of conspicuous difference (in physical features, dress, language, and occupational specialization) between the in-groups and the out-groups. (p. 49)

Not only are images of outgroups passed on to children from adults; they also are reinforced by peer group interactions within a culture.

As would be expected given our discussion of individualism-collectivism in Chapter 3, there are cultural differences in communication with members of ingroups and outgroups. Wetherall (1982), for example, notes that both Europeans (individualistic) and Polynesians (collectivistic) in New Zealand display bias when interacting with people from other groups, but Polynesians moderate their discrimination and show greater generosity to outgroup members compared with Europeans. Wetherall's findings are compatible with Feldman's (1968) field study in Paris, Boston, and Athens. Feldman observes that outgroup members were "treated better" in Athens (the most collectivistic) than in Boston and Paris (both individualistic). Feldman's results, however, may be unique to Greece, where foreigners and guests are perceived as potential members of the ingroup. Strangers in other collectivistic cultures generally are not viewed as potential members of the ingroup (Triandis, 1988).

THE NATURE OF SOCIAL IDENTITIES

The most important component of our self-concept influencing our communication with strangers is our social identities. Tajfel (1972) contends that we constantly strive to define ourselves regarding the world in which we live. One of the major cognitive "tools" we use in this process is social categorization. *Social categorization* is "the ordering of social environment in terms of groupings of persons in a manner which makes sense to the individual" (Tajfel, 1978, p. 61), for example, men and women, students and professors, Vietnamese Americans and African Americans.

The strategies we use in social categorization are learned through socialization into the various social groups to which we belong. Once we become aware of belonging to one or more social groups, our social identities begin to form. *Social identities* are those parts of an "individual's self-concept which derives from his [or her] knowledge of his [or her] membership in a social group (or groups) together with the value and emotional significance attached to that membership" (Tajfel, 1978, p. 63). Our social identities can be based on membership in demographic categories (e.g., nationality, ethnicity, gender, age, social class), the roles we play (e.g., student, professor, parent), membership in formal or informal organizations (e.g., political parties, social clubs), association or vocation (e.g., scientist, artist, gardener), or membership in stigmatized groups (e.g., homeless person, person with AIDS; see Deaux et al., 1995, for a study of the parameters of social identities).

Characteristics of Social Identities

We identify and evaluate ourselves in terms of the groups to which we belong and the characteristics of those groups (e.g., their status, skin color, gender, ability to reach goals). Our group memberships can contribute either positive or negative aspects to our social identities. For the group membership to contribute positive aspects to our social identities, our group (ingroup) must compare favorably with other relevant groups (outgroups). A positive social identity therefore is ensured by our interpreting strangers' behavior and behaving in such a manner that the ingroup is evaluated positively when compared with outgroups.

Brewer (1991) argues that our social identities emerge from the tension between our need to be seen as similar to and to fit in with others, and our need to be seen as unique. The need to be seen as similar allows us to identify with different groups and involves the general process of *inclusion.* The need to be seen as unique is based on the general process of *differentiation,* or making ourselves stand out from others. In individualistic cultures, like that of the United States, balancing these two tensions usually involves emphasizing differentiation more than inclusion. In collectivistic cultures, in contrast, balancing the tensions usually involves emphasizing inclusion more than differentiation.

Smith and Bond (1983) point out that some social identities, such as ethnicity and gender, are important in most situations. Other social identities, in contrast, are important only when they are distinctive, when there are only a few people holding the social identity present in the situation. If a lower-class person is alone in a group of upper-middle-class people, for example, his or her social class identity will be activated. If there is an equal number of lower-class and upper-middle-class people present, on the other hand, social class identities may not be activated.

The degree to which we perceive strangers to be typical members of their groups also influences whether we activate our social identities (Smith & Bond, 1993). If we are interacting with a member of another ethnic group and perceive this person to be a typical member of her or his group, for example, we will activate our ethnic identity. If we do not perceive the other person to be a typical member of his or her group, on the other hand, we may not activate our ethnic identity. Rather, we will use another social identity to guide our behavior.

The social relations between groups also affects whether social identities are activated (Smith & Bond, 1993). If good relations exist between ethnic groups, for instance, ethnic identities may not be activated when members of different ethnic groups interact. If relations between ethnic groups are hostile, in contrast, ethnic identities will be activated when members of different groups interact.

Dimensions of Social Identities

Deaux (1991) argues that social identities differ on two dimensions: voluntary-involuntary and desirable-undesirable. A *voluntary identity* is one that we can choose, while an *involuntary identity* is one where we do not necessarily have free choice (others may categorize us in an involuntary identity). *Desirable identities* are those we think are positive and *undesirable identities* are those we think are negative. The voluntary nature of identity influences the amount of effort we need to maintain the identity; voluntary identities require more effort and work than involuntary identities. The desirability dimension influences the degree to which we express our identities or hide them (Deaux, 1991). This dimension, therefore, influences the degree to which we feel pride or shame from expressing our identities. We feel pride expressing desirable identities and shame from expressing identities that we perceive to be undesirable.

Table 4.1 displays one group of people's perceptions of various social identities on these dimensions. Your perceptions of the identities in Table 4-1 may be different from those listed. There is not widespread agreement on the desirability of some social identities. Gay/lesbian, for example, is one of the social identities listed as undesirable in Table 4-1. Obviously, not everyone would agree that gay/lesbian is an undesirable social identity. One consequence of viewing gay/lesbian as an undesirable social identity, however, is that gay-bashing has become widespread in the United States in recent years. People who can hear also often view deafness as an undesirable identity. Deaf people do not necessarily agree with this assessment. Lane (1993), for example, points out:

> If the birth of a Deaf child is a priceless gift, then there is only cause for rejoicing, as at the birth of a black child, or an Indian one. Medical intervention is inappropriate, even if a perfect "cure" were available. Invasive surgery on healthy children is morally

wrong. We know that, as members of a stigmatized minority, these children's lives will be full of challenge but, by the same token, they have a general contribution to make to their own community and the larger society. (pp. 490–491)

Viewing strangers' social identities as undesirable is communicated to them in the way we transmit our messages to them. To communicate effectively or to develop intimate relationships with strangers, we must be aware of our biases and mindfully manage them when we transmit messages and interpret strangers' messages.

A difference often exists between our subjective social identities (those we use to define ourselves) and our objective characteristics (the groups into which others might categorize us; Deaux, 1991). We, therefore, need to keep in mind that strangers may not see the groups into which we categorize them as important aspects of their identities, and strangers may categorize us in ways we do not consider important.

Our social identities are relatively consistent over time (Deaux, 1991). In any given interaction and at any given time, one social identity tends to predominate to influence our behavior. The importance of our identities, our background, and the situational characteristics influence which identity guides our behavior. To illustrate, "the individual entering a classroom brings out the professor or student identity; the individual moving into an operating room takes on the identity of surgeon, nurse, or patient" (Deaux, 1991, p. 85).

As indicated earlier, the characteristics of the situation influence the importance we place on our social identities. If we find ourselves in a situation where

Table 4-1   ONE GROUP'S PERCEPTIONS OF SOCIAL IDENTITIES*

Voluntary, Desirable Identities	Voluntary, Undesirable Identities
Catholic	Alcoholic
Club member	[Drug Addict]
Democrat/Republican	Gay/Lesbian
Feminist	Smoker
Friend	
Husband/Wife	
Mother/Father	
Student	

Involuntary, Desirable Identities	Involuntary, Undesirable Identities
African American	[Blind person]
Daughter/Son	Deaf person
Hispanic	[Disabled person]
Jew	Old person
Man	
Woman	

*Adapted from Deaux and Ethier (1990) as reported in Deaux (1991). The perceptions presented here are those of one group of people. Your perceptions of the identities may be different. The identities in brackets have been added to further illustrate how other identities tend to be perceived.

people sharing our identity are in a numerical minority, that identity becomes important to us. Most European Americans, for example, do not think much about their ethnicity, but when they find themselves in an area predominated by another ethnic group, this identity becomes important. Finally, strangers' actions can influence the identity we choose to guide our behavior. If strangers communicate with us on the basis of their ethnic identity, for example, we will probably use our ethnic identity to guide our behavior.

Collective Self-Esteem

Social identity theory (e.g., Tajfel, 1978) suggests that we try to achieve positive social identities in our interactions with strangers. Luhtanen and Crocker (1992) contend that there are individual differences in the degree to which we have positive social identities. *Collective self-esteem* is the degree to which we generally evaluate our social groups positively. Crocker and Luhtanen (1990) argue that our level of collective self-esteem moderates the degree to which we try to protect or enhance our social identities when they are threatened. When our social identities are threatened and we derogate the outgroup threatening our social identities, our collective self-esteem increases (Branscombe & Wann, 1994).

There are four components to our collective self-esteem (Luhtanen & Crocker, 1992). First, private collective self-esteem involves the degree to which we evaluate our social groups positively. Second, membership esteem involves the degree to which we evaluate ourselves as good members of the social groups to which we belong. Third, public collective self-esteem involve our perceptions about how others evaluate our social groups. Fourth, the importance of our group memberships involves the degree to which our group memberships are central to how we define ourselves.

We can have different levels of collective self-esteem for the different social identities we have. We may, for example, have high collective self-esteem for our ethnic identity and low collective self-esteem for our gender identity.

Cross-Cultural Variability in Social Identities

In the United States and most other western cultures, the self is viewed in individualistic terms. Geertz (1975), for example, illustrates this view when he describes the "western" self "as a bounded, unique, more or less integrated motivational and cognitive universe, a dynamic center of awareness, emotion, judgment, and action organized into a distinctive whole and set contrastively both against other such wholes and against a social and natural background" (p. 48). Self-actualization and/or self-realization are viewed as important goals in individualistic cultures. Self-esteem in individualistic cultures is based on how well a person can stand on his or her own feet.

Members of collectivistic cultures view the self differently. In collectivistic cultures, the self is defined in relation to others. People, for example, might define themselves on the basis of the company for which they work, the university they attended, and so forth. In some collectivistic cultures, individuals may deny their own self-importance. Denying self importance occurs in Japan, especially when individuals are communicating with someone of higher social status (Doi, 1986). In some collectivistic cultures, there is not an ethical category for the person. Read (1955), for example, describes the self-concept in the Gahuku-Gana culture of New Guinea. He points out that in this culture, people do not "separate the individual from the social context and, ethically speaking, grant him [or her] an intrinsic moral value apart from that which attaches to him [or her] as the occupant of a particular status" (p. 257). Read goes on to argue that the value of people "does not reside in themselves as individuals or persons; it is dependent on the position they occupy within a system of inter-personal and inter-group relationships" (p. 250).

Overall, it appears that members of collectivistic cultures emphasize social identities more than do members of individualistic cultures. Gabrenya and Wang (1983), for example, observe that Chinese use more group-oriented self-conceptions than do people in the United States. Cousins (1989) obtains similar results when comparing the United States and Japan. Bond and Chueng's (1983) research, however, suggests that individualism-collectivism may not explain all the variability in social identities. They note that Hong Kong Chinese and North Americans emphasize family roles more than Japanese, while Japanese mention sex and age more than do the other two groups. These differences may be due to masculinity-femininity; highly masculine cultures like Japan emphasize gender and age more and family less than feminine cultures. Further, social roles based on hierarchical group memberships (e.g., caste, social class) are influenced by cultural variations in power distance.

Given this overview of social identity, we turn our attention to specific social identities that influence our communication with strangers.

SOCIAL IDENTITIES INFLUENCING OUR COMMUNICATION WITH STRANGERS

There are many social identities that could influence our communication with strangers. In this section, we discuss seven major identities: cultures, ethnic groups, gender, disability, age, social class, and roles. We begin with cultural identities.

Cultural Identities

Our cultural identity involves the degree to which we identify with our culture. If a person is born and raised in the United States, for example, his or her cultural identity involves the degree to which she or he identifies with being an "American." Billig (1995) argues that our national culture identities are "flagged" in the media through the use of symbols and habits of language. Symbols and language usage remind us of our culture, but they operate mindlessly, beyond our conscious awareness. Two dimensions of our cultural identities affect our communication with strangers from other cultures: the strength of our identification, and the content of our identity.

Members of a culture vary in the strength of their identification with their culture. Some people strongly identify with being members of their culture, while others weakly identify with their culture. The strength of our identification with our culture varies from situation to situation. "Americans," for example, may not identify strongly with their culture when they are in the United States, but when they visit another country and there are very few other "Americans" around, the strength of their identification will increase.

The content of our cultural identity involves the things we associate with being a member of our culture. One way to define the content of our cultural identity is by looking at the values we hold. Our identities, for example, can be either individualistic or collectivistic. The content of the cultural identity for "Americans" who strongly identify with their culture will involve holding individualistic values. The content of the cultural identities of "Americans" who do not strongly identify with their culture, in contrast, may involve holding collectivistic values. Gudykunst, Nishida et al.'s (1992) study reveals that North Americans who strongly identify with their culture value freedom, pleasure, social recognition, and independence more than North Americans who weakly identify with their culture and more than Japanese who strongly identify with their culture. Japanese who strongly identify with their culture value self-sacrifice, harmony, and tradition more than Japanese who weakly identify with their culture and more than North Americans who strongly identify with their culture.

Ethnic Identities

Another important social identity that influences our communication with strangers is our ethnic identity. The way we react toward strangers often is based on our assumptions about their ethnicity; for example, we impose ethnic labels on strangers. When we impose labels on strangers, however, we may not impose the labels the strangers would use to describe themselves (Barth, 1969). DeVos (1975) suggests that ethnicity involves the use of some aspect of a group's cultural background to separate themselves from others. Giles and Johnson (1981), in contrast, see an ethnic group as "those individuals who identify themselves as belonging to the same ethnic category" (p. 202).

In actuality, we impose an ethnic label on strangers *and* strangers claim an ethnic group when they interact with us. A European American interacting with a Chinese American, for instance, may view the other person as an "Asian American," while the Chinese American may see him- or herself as "Chinese." The use of different categories will affect the communication that occurs between the two people.

Anytime we categorize ourselves as members of a group, we also categorize strangers as not members of our group and, therefore, members of another group (Turner, 1987). Categorization of ethnicity may be based on cultural, social, psychological, or biological characteristics (Gorden, 1964; see Stanfield, 1995, for various theories of ethnicity).

Yinger (1994) isolates three primary ingredients used in defining ethnic groups:

(1) The group is perceived by others in the society to be different in some combination of the following traits: language, religion, race, or ancestral homeland with its related culture; (2) the members also perceive themselves to be different; and (3) they participate in shared activities built around their (real or mythical) common origin and culture. (pp. 3–4)

Yinger argues that if any one of these three ingredients is present in an interaction, ethnicity is influencing what is happening.

Assimilation Versus Pluralism. There have been changes in recent years in the way people in the United States view ethnicity. In the past, an assimilationist view of ethnicity predominated and was not questioned. *Assimilation* refers to the process of giving up one culture and taking on the characteristics of another. Park (1950), for example, argues that the "cycle of contact, competition, accommodation, and eventual assimilation [among ethnic groups] is apparently progressive and unreversibile" (p. 13). The assimilation view often leads to the use of race as a metaphor, where "Americanness" is defined as "white" (Morrison, 1992, p. 42). Explaining the culture of the United States by using this metaphor will not work, however, when European Americans become a numerical minority sometime in the next century. The changes in the ethnic composition of the United States are redefining what it means to be an "American." "The deeper significance of America's becoming a majority nonwhite society is what it means to the national psyche, to individuals' sense of themselves and their nation—their idea of what it is to be an American" (Henry, 1990, p. 30).

More recently, a pluralistic view of ethnicity has predominated. In the *pluralistic* view, ethnicity "is an internal attitude which predisposes, but does not make compulsory, the display of ethnic identification in interaction. When it facilitates self-interest, ethnic identity will be made self-evident; it is left latent when it would hinder" (Hraba & Hoiberg, 1983, p. 385). When members of a group decide to exert their ethnicity depends upon the particular circumstances in which they find themselves (Glazer & Moynihan, 1975).

Ethnic Identity and Behavior. While the degree to which we assert our social identities varies from situation to situation, the general degree to which we identify with particular groups, especially our ethnic group, appears to remain relatively stable over time. Alba (1990) defines *ethnic identity* as "a person's subjective orientation toward his or her ethnic origins" (p. 25). Roosens (1989) points out that asserting an ethnic identity helps us define who we are; it offers

commonality in language, a series of customs and symbols, a style, rituals, and appearance, and so forth, which can penetrate life in many ways. These trappings of ethnicity are particularly attractive when one is continually confronted by others who live differently. . . . If I see and experience myself as a member of an ethnic category or group, and others—fellow members and outsiders—recognize me as such, "ways of being" become possible for me that set me apart from the outsiders. These ways of being contribute to the *content* of my self-perceptions. In this sense, I *become* my ethnic allegiance; I experience any attack on the symbols, emblems, or values (cultural elements) that define my ethnicity as an attack on myself. (pp. 17–18)

Our ethnicity, therefore, influences all aspects of our lives.

Alba (1990) argues that there has been a transformation regarding how ethnic identity is manifested for whites in the United States. He concludes that ethnic distinctions based on ancestry from specific European countries are fading and that these identities are being replaced by a "new" ethnic group, "one based on ancestry from *anywhere* on the European continent" (p. 3). As evidence for this change, Alba points to the tremendous intermarriage between whites from different European countries—three of every four marriages between whites involves crossing country-of-origin boundaries. Alba notes that partners in marriages where the two trace their origins to different European countries do not perceive their partners to be from different ethnic groups. We refer to this group as European Americans.

European Americans often do not recognize their ethnicity or do not strongly identify with the group (Kleg, 1993). The reason is that European Americans are members of the dominant ethnic group in the United States. Kleg also points out that

> the popular notion that ethnics are somewhat different or exotic, along with the fact that members of the national ethos do not perceive anything special about their own culture, probably contribute to the lack of identification. The cliché of not being able to see the forest for the trees is quite appropriate in this case. (p. 52)

European Americans also may feel disassociated from their ethnic group because non-European Americans' ethnicity is stressed and romanticized (Kleg, 1993).

Symbolic Ethnicity.   In describing the way ethnic identity is manifested among European Americans in the United States, Alba (1990) points out that European Americans choose whether to express ethnic identity and that they vary in the degree of importance they attach to it. He concludes that Gans' (1979) notion of symbolic ethnicity accurately describes the manifestation of ethnicity among European Americans today. *Symbolic ethnicity* refers to "the desire to retain a sense of being ethnic, but without any deep commitment to the ethnic social ties and behavior" (Alba, 1990, p. 306). Similarly, Waters (1990) points out that

> the reality is that [European American] ethnics have a lot more choice and room for maneuver than they themselves think they do. The situation is very different for members of racial minorities, whose lives are strongly influenced by their race or national origin regardless of how much they choose not to identify themselves in ethnic or racial terms. (p. 157)

European Americans, however, do not recognize the differences between their experience of ethnicity and the way non-European Americans experience it (Waters, 1990). The voluntary aspect of European Americans' asserting their ethnicity and the enjoyment they receive from expressing it (e.g., it is asserted at ethnic celebrations) make it difficult for them to understand the way ethnicity affects non-European Americans.

The influence of ethnic identity for non-European Americans is illustrated by the way Gotanda (1991), a Japanese American playwright, describes his experiences. Gotanda was raised in the United States, but lived in Japan. His time in Japan helped him understand his ethnicity:

> After I'd been living in Japan for about a year, I had an extraordinary experience. . . . I was walking down the streets and I looked over to my left and I saw a bank of televisions all lined up, and they were filled with a Japanese newscaster. I looked up at the billboard and there was a Japanese face, I looked at the magazines on display and they were filled with Asian faces; I looked ahead and I saw a sea of people coming toward me, all about my same height, with black hair, with skin that looked exactly like mine. . . . What I experienced for the first time was this extraordinary thing called anonymity—the sense of being able to be part of a group, of everything around me reinforcing what I was. I didn't have to second guess my obviousness, to be constantly aware that I was different. . . . in that instant in Tokyo something lifted from me, and I was able to move freely. . . . Of course, the longer I was in Japan the more I became aware of the fact that I wasn't strictly Japanese either, that I would never be Japanese Japanese—that I was Japanese-American. (pp. 9–10)

Gotanda's experience clearly illustrates that ethnicity is not "symbolic" for non-European Americans in the United States.

Language and Ethnic Identity.   Skin color and national origin are only two of the markers used to define ethnicity. The language we speak also marks boundaries between our ethnic group and others in informal conversations with acquaintances and friends, as well as in formal communication situations (e.g., when we talk to our supervisors at work). Rodriguez (1982) illustrates the importance of language in describing the effect of hearing his father speak English to a European American gas station attendant when he was growing up:

> I cannot forget the sounds my father made as he spoke. At one point his words slid together to form one word—sounds as confused as the threads of blue and green oil in the puddle next to my shoes. His voice rushed through what he had left to say. And, toward the end, reached falsetto notes, appealing to his listeners' understanding. I looked away to the lights of passing automobiles. I tried not to hear anymore. (p. 15)

In contrast to the alienation he felt when he heard his father speaking English, he felt comfort when members of his family spoke to him in Spanish:

> A family member would say something to me and I would feel specially recognized. My parents would say something to me and I would feel embraced by the sounds of their words. Those words said: I am speaking with ease in Spanish. I am addressing you in words I never use with los gringos. I recognize you as someone special, close, like no one outside. You belong with us. In the family. (p. 15, italics omitted)

Speaking their native language creates solidarity among members of different ethnic groups.

Ethnic Labels.   Another way language affects our ethnic identity is through the labels we use to define ourselves. The labels strangers use regarding their ethnic group membership can tell us a lot about their orientations. A person who labels himself a *Chicano* or herself a *Chicana,* for example, defines himself or herself differently than a person who uses the label *Mexican American* (see Gimenez, Lopez, & Munoz, 1992). The person who defines himself as a Chicano or herself as a Chicana probably has political goals (e.g., promoting "La Raza") that the person who defines himself or herself as a Mexican American does not. Communicating effectively with either individual requires knowing why she or he prefers one label or another.

In the 1990s, it appears that the vast majority of blacks prefer to use the label *African American* when they refer to themselves. Two individuals provide the reasons for the use of this term:

> I grew up in a time when "black" was the accepted term. It was used on application forms and among family and friends. I changed to African American because it seemed more accurate and more enduring to our culture.
>
> [In the past] I didn't prefer "black," it was just used. However, when I began to realize that the term "black" was just making us be seen in terms of skin color (and not including our ethnic heritage), I embraced the term African American. After all, a "white, American, Irish person" is Irish American. We've done just as much for the country, and we have a heritage from *our* mother land, so why not express it! (Larkey, Hecht, & Martin, 1993, p. 19)

There is *not* a hyphen in the label African American. In fact, most non-European Americans no longer use a hyphen for their ethnicity (e.g., Japanese American, Mexican American). While it may seem like a minor point, omitting or including a hyphen may be interpreted as providing self-concept support (omitting it) or denying a self-concept (including it). We, therefore, need to pay attention to the labels strangers use to refer to themselves.

Concern over the use of ethnic labels is not limited to African Americans. Many people born in Mexico, Puerto Rico, and Cuba find the panethnic term (i.e., a term used for all of these cultures combined) *Hispanic* archaic and offensive (e.g., see Gonzalez, 1992). A majority of participants in a recent Latino Political Survey report that they prefer the term Latino over Hispanic (summarized in Gonzalez, 1992). Even the pronunciation of the term can be a statement of identity (the preferred pronunciation is lah-TEEN-oh). Sandra Cisneros (the author of *Woman Hollering Creek*) points out that "to say Latino is to say you came to my culture in a manner of respect" (quoted by Gonzalez). Cisneros believes that people who prefer the term *Hispanic* want to fit into the mainstream culture (that is, give up their original culture), while people who use *Latino* want to maintain their ethnicity.

All panethnic terms (e.g., Latino, Asian Americans) are misleading since they imply homogeneity across the groups included under the term. People who come from Mexico, Cuba, and Puerto Rico, for example, share some similarities based on a common language, but there are many cultural differences between the three groups that cannot be ignored. Respondents in the Latino Political Survey clearly indicate that they prefer labels based on their country of origin (e.g., Mexican American, Cuban American), rather than panethnic terms like Latino (Gonzalez, 1992). Similarly, first-generation Asian Americans may share a collectivistic upbringing, but there are many differences between Chinese Americans, Japanese Americans, Korean Americans, and Vietnamese Americans, to name only a few of the Asian groups often lumped together.

The labels strangers use regarding their ethnic group membership can tell us a lot about them. To communicate effectively with strangers, we must know which label they prefer. Such knowledge is important because effective communication requires that we support others' self-concepts, including their preferred ethnic identity.

Strength and Content of Ethnic Identity.   The labels we use for our ethnicity influence our communication. To fully understand how our ethnicity influences our communication, however, we must also take into consideration the strength and content of our ethnic identity. As is the case with our cultural identity, we vary in the degree to which we identify with our ethnic group (see Root, 1995, for how people with multiple identities act). Some of us strongly identify with our ethnic group, and some of us weakly identify with our ethnic group. Recognizing this difference is critical to effective communication with strangers.

Often someone in the mass media will say that we should ignore ethnic differences and strive for a "color-blind" society. If everyone weakly identified with his or her ethnic group, this goal might make sense. We may be able to ignore ethnic group differences when interacting with strangers who weakly identify with their ethnic group. If strangers strongly identify with their ethnic group, in contrast, we cannot ignore group differences. When strangers strongly identify with their ethnic group and we ignore their ethnicity when we interact with them, we are *not* supporting their self-concept. Not supporting their self-concepts is a problem because self-concept support is necessary for strangers to be satisfied with their communication with us (Hecht, Ribeau, & Alberts, 1989).

The content of our ethnic identity can be described similarly to the content of our cultural identity. In other words, the content of our ethnic identity may be highly individualistic or highly collectivistic. The content of our ethnic identity depends on our national heritage and the strength of our identity. If someone's national heritage can be traced to a collectivistic culture and she or he strongly identifies with his or her ethnic group, then the content of the identity will tend to be collectivistic values. If the person does not strongly identify with his or her ethnic group, in contrast, the content of her or his identity would not tend to involve strongly holding collectivistic values. Whether this person will hold individualistic values depends on his or her cultural identity. If the person is an "American" who

Table 4-2   INTERACTION BETWEEN CULTURAL AND ETHNIC IDENTITIES

		Cultural Identity	
		Weak	**Strong**
Ethnic Identity	**Weak**	Neither cultural nor ethnic identity has a strong influence on behavior.	Behavior generally is based on cultural identity.
	Strong	Behavior generally is based on ethnic identity.	Behavior is based on either cultural or ethnic identity, depending on the situation.

strongly identifies with her or his cultural identity, then his or her values will prob- ably be individualistic.

The preceding suggests that in order to understand strangers' communication, we must understand their cultural and ethnic identities (see Table 4-2). Strangers who weakly identify with their culture and strongly identify with their ethnic group will tend to base their communication on their ethnic identity. Strangers who strongly identify with their culture and weakly identify with their ethnic group, in contrast, will tend to base their communication on their cultural identity. Strangers who strongly identify with both their cultural identity and their ethnic identity will choose which identity to use to guide their behavior in specific situations. They may choose, for example, to base their communication at work on their cultural identity, and to base their communication at home on their ethnic identity. Strangers who weakly identify with both their cultural identity and their ethnic identity will tend to base their communication on other social identities or their personal identities. These people, however, may base their communication on their cultural or ethnic identities if others categorize them on the basis of those identities and act on the basis of that categorization.

In summary, the way we define ourselves and the way others define us with respect to our ethnicity influences our communication. To communicate effectively with strangers, we need to understand how they define their ethnic identity. Our sup- porting the ethnic identity strangers prefer and strangers' supporting the way we want to be viewed will help us communicate effectively.

Gender Identities

One of the major social identities affecting our communication is our gender and the way we define gender roles. Differences in the way men and women relate to the world affect their social identities. Tajfel (1978) argues that social identity involves a cognitive process of differentiation and comparison. Some contend that males engage in differentiation more than women. Women's social identity, in contrast, of- ten is viewed as being based more on communal processes than differentiation processes (e.g., Williams, 1984). Further, "women are more inclined [than men] to value relationships with other people from groups other than their own" (Skevington, 1989, p. 56).

It is not our biological sex that influences our communication, but rather our gender roles. *Gender roles* are "the psychological traits and the social responsibilities that individuals have and feel are appropriate for them because they are male or female" (Pleck, 1977, p. 182). Bem (1974) isolates four gender roles: feminine, masculine, undifferentiated, and androgynous. Feminine gender roles involve exhibiting a high degree of stereotypical feminine traits and behaviors (e.g., compassion, gentleness, sensitivity to others' needs, understanding, warmth). Masculine gender roles involve exhibiting a high degree of stereotypical masculine traits and behaviors (e.g., aggressiveness, competitiveness, forcefulness, self-reliance). Undifferentiated gender roles exist when individuals do not exhibit high degrees of either masculine or feminine traits or behaviors. Androgynous gender roles involve exhibiting high degrees of *both* masculine and feminine traits and behaviors. Bem (1993) argues that gender roles provide a lens that influences the way we look at the world. She goes on to point out that traditionally gender oriented individuals (i.e., highly masculine men and highly feminine women) tend to organize and recall information on the basis of gender.

Cultural differences exist in gender roles. Hofstede (1980) argues that in highly masculine cultures, there are clearly differentiated gender roles. In these cultures, there is a tendency for masculine and feminine gender roles to predominate. Hofstede points out that in highly feminine cultures, there are not clearly differentiated gender roles. In these cultures, undifferentiated and androgynous gender roles tend to predominate. Research on gender role ideology (e.g., Best & Williams, 1984) and family gender role development (e.g., Salamon, 1977) supports Hofstede's claims.

Important differences exist in the ways men and women communicate in the United States. Beck (1988), for example, points out that women tend to see questions as a way of keeping a conversation going. Men, in contrast, see questions as requests for information. Women tend to make connections between what their partners said and what they have to say. Men, on the other hand, do not use conversational bridges as much and may appear to ignore what their partners just said in a conversation. Men tend to view aggressiveness as a way of communicating, while women tend to interpret aggressiveness as an attack. Women may discuss problems and only be looking for reassurances. Men, on the other hand, interpret the discussion of a problem as a request for a solution. These differences can be viewed in terms of subcultural differences. In this view, men and women are seen as being socialized into different subcultures with different beliefs about the nature of communication and learning different rules for communication (Maltz & Borker, 1982; Tannen, 1990). Men and women come from different "subcultures which have different conceptions of what constitutes friendly conversation, different rules for engaging in such conversations and different rules for interpreting interaction behavior" (Henley & Kramarae, 1991, p. 24).

Women are viewed as being socialized to develop close relationships with others (Maltz & Borker, 1982) and to be involved with others (Tannen, 1990).

Women are socialized to view talk as important to developing and maintaining relationships (Tannen, 1990). Men, in contrast, learn to assert their dominance (Maltz & Borker, 1982) and to be independent (Tannen, 1990). Men learn to see talk as a way of establishing their dominance and, therefore, not central to intimate relationships where dominance is not important. Men tend to see talk as weakening intimate relationships (Tannen, 1990). Misunderstandings that occur between women and men are due to interpreting cues from the other group by using their own group's rules (Maltz & Borker, 1982).

Identities Based on Disabilities

Another social identity that affects our communication is whether or not one of the people is disabled. Individuals categorize others on the basis of their physical appearance and evaluate novel appearances negatively (McArthur, 1982). When nondisabled people communicate with people who are visibly disabled in some way, they tend to experience uncertainty and anxiety, and avoid interaction when possible (e.g., there is a bias toward the ingroup). Nondisabled people communicating with a person in a wheelchair, for example, predict more negative outcomes and are less aware of the person in the wheelchair than when they are communicating with other nondisabled individuals (Grove & Werkman, 1991). Similar observations can be made about interactions with other people whom we view as stigmatized (e.g., those who are blind or deaf, AIDS victims, the mentally ill; see Goffman, 1963). The bias toward the ingroup is a two-way street. There is a sign, for example, in the American Sign Language with the right index finger circling forward in front of the forehead, which indicates a deaf person who thinks like a hearing person. The sign is *not* meant as a compliment and its use demonstrates a bias toward the deaf ingroup (Barringer, 1993).

Members of a group with a disability can be seen as sharing a common culture. Reagan (1995) contends that there is a deaf cultural community in the United States. Members of this group share a common language (the American Sign Language) and an awareness of their deaf identity. Hearing-impaired people who are acculturated into the hearing world, however, do not share this common identity. Members of the deaf culture also share communication rules (e.g., eye contact, use of facial expressions) and cultural artifacts (e.g., the technological devices that help them live in a hearing society).

Coleman and DePaulo (1991) point out that the visibility of others' conditions influences whether nondisabled people see them as disabled:

> External markers of a disability, such as the use of sign language by the deaf, canes and guide dogs by the blind, and wheelchairs by amputees and paraplegics, render those special conditions even more salient. However, even conditions almost completely invisible can be perceived as disabling and can engender miscommunications if they are known to others. . . . For example, women who have recently had mastectomies may find themselves to be the object of unusual regard in their initial interactions with others immediately following the surgery. (p. 64)

Coleman and DePaulo also suggest that conditions that are not physically disabling (e.g., facial scars) may be psychologically disabling.

Coleman and DePaulo (1991) argue that both nondisabled and disabled individuals contribute to miscommunications when they interact. The nondisabled, for example, have negative stereotypes of the disabled. Disabled people are seen as "dependent, socially introverted, emotionally unstable, or depressed, hypersensitive, and easily offended, especially with regard to their disability" (p. 69). Nondisabled people may expect that disabled people will view them as prejudiced against the disabled. When nondisabled people interact with the disabled, the nondisabled may experience anxiety, fear, and surprise. These reactions often are displayed nonverbally (e.g., in the voice or on the face), even though the nondisabled may try to control their reactions.

Disabled people also contribute negative expectations to their interactions with nondisabled individuals. Coleman and DePaulo (1991) point out that the disabled may be "bitter and resentful about their disability" (p. 75). Disabled people also may expect to be perceived negatively by nondisabled individuals; "for example, blind people think that sighted persons perceive them as slightly retarded and hard of hearing" (p. 75). It is important to recognize that disabled persons' disabilities may affect their communication with nondisabled people. Blind people, for example, cannot make eye contact, and hearing-impaired people who read lips cannot pick up nuances of communication in tone of voice.

There are idioms in English such as "the blind leading the blind" and "that's a lame excuse" to which disabled individuals react negatively (Pogrebin, 1987). Also, the labels that the nondisabled use to refer to the disabled can cause problems in communication. "A man who wears leg braces says the issue is accuracy. I'm not handicapped; people's attitudes about me handicap me" (Pogrebin, 1987, p. 218). Differently abled and physically challenged also do not appear to be accepted widely by disabled individuals. Pogrebin quotes Harilyn Rousso, a psychotherapist with cerebral palsy, as saying:

> Friends who care most sometimes think they're doing you a favor by using euphemisms or saying "I never think of you as disabled." The reason they don't want to acknowledge my disability is that they think it is so negative. Meanwhile, I'm trying to recognize it as a valued part of me. I'm more complex than my disability and I don't want my friends to be obsessed by it. But it's clearly there, like my eye color, and I want my friends to appreciate and accept me with it. (p. 219)

Some disabled prefer the label cripple or gimp because they are not euphemisms and recognize the realities facing the disabled. As with members of different ethnic groups, it is important that we know what the individuals with whom we are communicating want to be called.

Age Identities

Members of other groups do not have to be disabled for us to experience uncertainty and anxiety and want to avoid communicating with them; for example, young people often avoid communicating with old people. Individuals categorize others on the basis of age when they guess ages on the basis of others' physical appearance, when others disclose their age, when others make references to age categories (e.g., indicating they are retired), and when others talk about experiences in the past. Age-based identities can take place at the beginning of interactions with others or emerge out of communication with others (Coupland, Nussbaum, & Coupland, 1991).

Rose (1965) argues that several factors have contributed to the development of age-based identities in the United States: (1) the growing number of old people; (2) the development of retirement communities, which segregates old people; (3) the increase in retirement, which decreases interaction between young and old on the job; (4) the amount of money available to older people; and (5) the emergence of groups and organizations exclusively for old people. Older people demonstrate

> all of the signs of group identification. There is a desire to associate with fellow-agers, especially in formal associations, and to exclude younger adults from these associations. There are expressions of group pride. . . . There are manifestations of a feeling of resentment at "the way older people are being mistreated," and indications of their taking social action to remove the sources of their resentment. (p. 14)

Intergeneration interaction, therefore, is clearly a form of intergroup communication.

Young people view elderly people as less desirable interaction partners than are other young people or middle-aged people (Tamir, 1984). When young people are communicating with the elderly, they use several different strategies to adapt their behavior (Coupland et al., 1988). First, young people adapt their behavior by overaccommodating to the elderly because they assume the elderly are handicapped (e.g., hard of hearing). Second, young people communicate with the elderly in ways that reflect the attitude that the elderly are dependent on the young. This strategy allows young people to control the elderly. Third, young people may speak differently than do the elderly to establish their identity as young people (e.g., using slang the elderly do not understand). Fourth, young people may overaccommodate to the elderly to nurture them (e.g., young people might use baby talk when talking to the elderly). Fifth, young people may not adapt their behavior to the elderly. The elderly, in turn, may perceive young people not adapting their behavior as lack of interest in them.

The elderly also use strategies in adapting their behavior to the young (Coupland et al., 1988). First, the elderly may not accommodate their behavior to the young. One reason for this behavior is that they may have little contact with young people and may not know how to adapt their behavior. Second, the elderly may use self-protecting strategies because they anticipate negative interactions with young people. Third, the elderly may anticipate that they will not perform well when they communicate with young people. Fourth, the elderly may engage in self-stereotyping (e.g., they may have negative stereotypes of being old). Fifth, the elderly may speak differently from the way young people do because they want to establish their social identity.

Self-concept support is necessary for effective intergenerational communication. One of the major concerns of older people is maintaining healthy self-concepts. Older people's self-concepts are threatened by the process of aging and by attitudes toward old people (Tamir, 1984). Tamir argues that "lack of self-affirmation by others can lead to a vicious circle of decreasing self-worth and continued negative and self-effacing encounters" (p. 36). Older people will find interactions with younger people who support the older people's self-concept more satisfying than they will interactions with younger people who do not support their self-concepts.

There are cross-cultural differences in intergenerational communication. In collectivistic cultures, for example, old people have high status and, therefore, young people tend to show respect to them. Age, however, does not tend to provide status in individualistic cultures.

Social Class Identities

We identify with a social class whether we are aware of it or not. Social class

> is much more than a convenient pigeonhole or merely arbitrary divisional unit—like minutes, ounces, I.Q. points or inches—along a linear continuum. It is a distinct reality which embraces the fact that people live, eat, play, mate, dress, work, and think at contrasting and dissimilar levels. These levels—social classes—are the blended product of shared and analogous occupational orientations, educational backgrounds, economic wherewithal, and life experiences. Persons occupying a given level need not be conscious of their class identity. But because of their approximately uniform backgrounds and experiences and because they grew up perceiving or "looking at things" in similar ways, they will share comparable values, attitudes, and lifestyles. (Hodges, 1964, p. 13)

The social class to which we belong may be the class with which we identify if we are satisfied with our position in society. Alternatively, if we are seeking upward mobility, our class identity may be based on the social class to which we aspire.

Sociologists tend to divide the social classes in the United States into upper class, upper middle class, middle class, lower middle class, and lower class. No matter how the class structure is divided, we sort ourselves and others into social classes when we interact with them. The criteria we use for sorting ourselves and others is usually based on income, occupation, education, beliefs/attitudes, style of life, or kind of family (Jackman & Jackman, 1983). Fussell (1983) points out that we also can tell people's social class by their hometown, their houses, their yards, the decorations in their houses, as well as the clothes they wear and the cars they drive.

Our class identities influence the way we communicate. We can tell strangers' class background from the way they speak. Using the standard dialect (e.g., the dialect used by newscasters on national broadcasts) is attributed higher social status than using a nonstandard dialect. Fussell, for example, points out that the use of double negatives (e.g., "I can't get no satisfaction") and ungrammatical numbers (e.g., "He don't," "I wants it") clearly distinguishes lower-class speakers from middle-class speakers. The way people pronounce words and the vocabulary they use distinguish between middle-class and upper-middle or upper-class speakers.

Role Identities

As indicated earlier, we have social identities based on the roles we play. Sarbin and Allen (1968) point out that role, "a term borrowed directly from the theater, is a metaphor intended to denote that conduct adheres to certain 'parts' (or positions) rather than the players who read or recite them" (p. 489). In other words, a *role* is a set of behavioral expectations associated with a particular position in a group. Examples of positions include, but are not limited to, professor, student, father, mother, physician, lawyer, judge, police officer, clerk, and customer. The behaviors you expect professors, for example, to perform are considered their role.

Role Expectations. Once we learn the role expectations associated with the positions we hold, we try to conform to those expectations when we communicate on automatic pilot. Our tendency to conform to a role is a function of how clearly the role is defined and how much consensus there is on how people are expected to behave in that role. The greater the clarity of the role definition and the greater the consensus on the role expectations, the more we tend to conform to role expectations (Stryker & Stratham, 1985). Our tendency to conform is due to the fact that role expectations are taken for granted (Bem, 1970). Since we take the behavioral expectations for granted, we often assume that our roles cannot be redefined. We can, however, choose to redefine our roles when we are mindful of our communication.

Other people do not always share our role expectations, and they may have different expectations for our roles than we do. We may fulfill our own role expectations and not those expectations other people have for us, or we may fulfill other people's expectations and not our own. Failure to live up to role expectations is traumatic to some degree. The trauma we experience when we do not meet role expectations is due partly to other people's responses to our performance (Stryker & Stratham, 1985). We want to perform our roles adequately so that other people will view us as competent. It is important, however, to recognize that cooperation from other people is necessary for us to perform our roles adequately. For instructors to perform their roles adequately, for example, the students in the class must cooperate and meet student role expectations, too. If instructors try to hold a discussion in class and the students do not participate, the instructors will not be able to meet role expectations.

Cross-Cultural Variability in Role Identities. One area where there are often different behavioral expectations across cultures is in the *degree of personalness* expected in a role relationship. In the United States, when interpersonal relationships do not exist between people filling positions, role relationships tend to be impersonal. In many other cultures, people are expected to treat others in role relationships in a personal way. Consider a Kenyan student's reaction to waiters in the United States: "Waiters extend courtesy to get a bigger tip or because the manager is around. They are very impersonal; it's just a job to them" (Feig & Blair, 1975, p. 31). In Kenya, waiters and waitresses are expected to see customers as people.

As a further illustration of expectations of personalness in role relationships, consider North Americans in Athens and their Greek coworkers. Triandis (1967) found that Greeks perceive North American behavior in organizations as "'inhumanly' legalistic, rigid, cold, and over concerned with efficiency" (p. 21). Even though Greek organizations are highly complex bureaucracies, "decisions are often taken on the basis of friendship and following strictly personal norms. . . . Greeks cannot understand the distinction between 'work behavior' and 'friendship behavior'" (p. 21). Thus, Greeks tend to place a high degree of importance on personalness in role relationships. A similar tendency occurs among Mexican bank employees (Zurcher, 1968).

The dimension of the degree of personalness expected in role relationships is related directly to Parsons's (1951) pattern variable of diffuseness or specificity (discussed in Chapter 3). Specifically, an expectation of impersonalness stems from a specificity orientation, the tendency to respond to specific aspects (i.e., the role) of another person. In contrast, an expectation of personalness stems from a diffuse orientation, the tendency to respond to others as total persons.

Role relationships also differ across cultures with respect to the *degree of formality* expected in the relationship. In the United States, interaction between people in a role relationship may be informal (e.g., students might call professors by their first names). Role relationships in many other cultures, however, tend to be highly formal. A Turkish woman talking about the student-teacher relationship illustrates this pattern; she says, "You're supposed to fear the teacher like you fear Allah. When he [or she] comes into the class, all stand up. When you meet him [or her] on the street, you bow" (Feig & Blair, 1975, p. 39). Iranians display a similar attitude: "a professor who allows himself [or herself] to be treated without the utmost respect or one who confesses ignorance on a subject is not generally taken seriously by Iranian students. 'The average student,' said one man, 'loses respect for a teacher when he [or she] is too friendly and common with his [or her] pupils'" (Feig & Blair, 1975, p. 83).

Another area where there are cultural differences in the nature of role relationships is the *degree of hierarchy* present in the relationship. In the United States, role relationships may be hierarchical, but this aspect generally is not stressed. In other cultures, the hierarchical nature of the relationship is critical. Role relationships in Vietnam, for example, involve high degrees of hierarchy. Social relations, including role relationships, between Vietnamese are influenced by Confucianism. Liem (1980) points out that Confucianism is a doctrine of social hierarchies that "defines, by rigid rules, the attitudes which each member of the society should have" (p. 15). With respect to the employer-employee relationship, Liem points out that

> the Vietnamese employee considers his [or her] employer as his [or her] mentor. As such, the latter is expected to give guidance, advice, and encouragement, and the former is supposed to execute orders, to perform his [or her] task quietly, and not to ask questions or have doubt about the orders. Because of his [or her] concept of the relationship, the Vietnamese employee does not voice his [or her] opinion to the boss; he [or she] just listens to his [or her] orders. (p. 16)

Obviously, such an expectation differs from the employer-employee relationship in western cultures.

Asian cultures are not the only cultures having hierarchical role relationships; many African cultures have similar role expectations. The clientship relationship of the Kanuri culture in the Bornu province of Nigeria, for example, involves a wide-ranging hierarchical relation between a patron and a client. Tessler, O'Ban, and Spain (1973) describe the relationship, indicating that

> the term clientship refers to the diffuse relationship between two individuals (adult males), one of whom is considered the superior or patron and the other the subordinate or client. It is a diffuse relationship because the patron may demand a wide range of services from the client, while the client may expect a wide range of considerations from his patron. . . . In general two types of client relationships may be distinguished: the apprentice-master relationship and the "simple" dependence relationship. For both, the relationship is entered into on a voluntary basis after initiation by the subordinate and with the agreement of the superior. . . . they both "agree with" or are satisfied with the behavior of the other. The stress on behavior in such agreements reflects their mutual trust in the willingness and ability of each to meet the role expectations of the other. (pp. 144–146)

The clientship relationship clearly involves a high degree of hierarchy.

The hierarchical nature of social relations in general, and role relationships in particular, often is reflected in the language of the culture. In Japanese, for example, different verb endings are used depending on whether you are talking to people of equal status, higher status, or lower status. Thus, any time people speak in Japan, they are placing themselves into the social hierarchy.

SUMMARY

Our communication with strangers is influenced by the groups to which we belong, the roles we fill, and the ways we define interpersonal relationships. Our membership groups and our reference groups influence the values, as well as the norms and rules, we learn. As part of our socialization into these groups, we are taught to avoid people from certain other groups (our outgroups). The orientation we learn toward outgroups causes us unconsciously to try to put our ingroup in a more favorable light when it is compared with the outgroups. This tendency in turn often leads us to make inaccurate attributions and predictions about the behavior of strangers from the outgroup.

Our social identities influence our communication more than our personal identities when we communicate with strangers. Depending on how we categorize strangers, the social identity guiding our behavior may be our cultural identities, ethnic identities, gender identities, social class identities, age group identities, and so forth. Supporting strangers' identities is critical if we want to form an on-going relationship with them. If we interact with strangers from another ethic group who do not strongly identify with their ethnic group and we focus on their ethnicity, we are not supporting their self-concept. Also, if we interact with strangers who strongly identify with their ethnic group and we act as though their ethnicity does not matter, we will not be supporting their self-concept.

Our role identities also influence our communication with strangers. We learn what behavior is expected in different roles as we are socialized into our culture and membership groups. Since roles tend to vary across cultures, it is necessary to know strangers' role expectations if we are to understand and accurately predict their behavior.

STUDY QUESTIONS

1. How does distinguishing between membership and reference groups help us understand our own and strangers' communication?
2. Why is it more useful to focus on ethnicity rather than race in understanding communication behavior?
3. How does drawing a distinction between ingroups and outgroups affect our communication with strangers?
4. What is the relationship between social categorization and social identities?
5. How does collective self-esteem influence our social identities?
6. What is the difference between cultural and ethnic identities? Why is it important to consider the strength and content of cultural and ethnic identities to understand strangers' communication?
7. How do European Americans and non-European Americans experience ethnicity differently?
8. How does language influence ethnic identity?
9. Why is it important to recognize the labels strangers use to define their ethnicity?
10. How can gender differences in communication be explained?
11. How do disabled and nondisabled people contribute to misunderstandings in communication?
12. How is intergenerational communication a form of intergroup communication?
13. Why is our communication with members of other social classes a form of intergroup communication?

SUGGESTED READING

Abrams, D., & Hogg, M. (Eds.). (1990). *Social identity theory: Constructive and critical advances.* New York: Springer-Verlag.

Alba, R. (1990). *Ethnic identity.* New Haven, CT: Yale University Press.

Billig, M. (1995). *Beyond nationalism.* London: Sage.

Hogg, M., & Abrams, D. (1988). *Social identifications.* London: Routledge.

Root, M. (Ed.). (1995). *The multiracial experience.* Thousand Oaks, CA: Sage.

Tajfel, H. (Ed.). (1982). *Social identity and intergroup relations.* Cambridge, UK: Cambridge University Press.

Waters, M. (1990). *Ethnic options.* Berkeley: University of California Press.

5

Psychocultural Influences on the Process

The great common door through which most forms of
negativity enter is premature expectation. . . .
All expectations are a judgment.

Hugh Prather

In the preceding two chapters, we examined how our socialization within our culture and how the social relationships we form within our culture influence our communication with strangers. Our analysis would be incomplete if we did not go one step further and examine processes occurring within individuals. The focus of this chapter, therefore, is on those influences we have labeled *psychocultural*. More specifically, we look at psychological factors that influence expectations when we communicate with strangers. Our expectations of strangers are, at least in part, a function of the stereotypes we hold and the attitudes we have toward strangers' groups. We begin by looking at the nature of expectations and how they are created.

THE NATURE OF EXPECTATIONS

Berger, Wagner, and Zelditch (1985) define *expectation states* as "self-other relational structures that organize behavior among interactants" (p. 32). *Expectations,* therefore, involve our anticipations and predictions about how others will communicate with us. Our expectations are derived in large part from the social norms and communication rules that we learned as children. They also emerge from our experiences with others, observations of our own behavior, the mass media, and our ingroups. Other factors, however, also create expectations. When we communicate with strangers, expectations emerge from our intergroup attitudes and the stereotypes we hold. In addition to these social cognitive factors, expectations are created by our affect or emotional responses to others. The expectations we have for strangers' behavior influences the uncertainty and anxiety we experience when we communicate with them. Generally, the more positive our expectations, the more our predictive uncertainty and anxiety are reduced (Gudykunst, 1988b).

"People who interact develop expectations about each others' behavior, not only in the sense that they are able to predict the regularities, but also in the sense that they develop preferences about how others *should* behave under certain circumstances" (Jackson, 1964, p. 225). Our culture and ethnicity provide guidelines for appropriate behavior and the expectations we use in judging competent communication. Burgoon and Hale (1988) point out, for example, that in the European American middle-class subculture in the United States

> one expects normal speakers to be reasonably fluent and coherent in their discourse, to refrain from erratic movements or emotional outbursts, and to adhere to politeness norms. Generally, normative behaviors are positively valued. If one keeps a polite distance and shows an appropriate level of interest in one's conversational partner, for instance, such behavior should be favorably received. (p. 61)

The problem is that norms for what is a polite distance and what constitutes an emotional outburst vary across cultures and across subcultures within a culture.

If strangers violate our expectations to a sufficient degree that we recognize the violation, we become aroused and have to assess the situation (Burgoon & Hale, 1988). In other words, the violation of our expectations leads to some degree of mindfulness. We may, however, become mindful of the outcome of the interaction and not the process of the interaction. Becoming mindful of the outcome, *will not* facilitate effective communication. Mindfulness of the process, in contrast, *will* facilitate effective communication.

Burgoon and Hale (1988) argue that the degree to which the other person provides us with rewards affects how we evaluate the violation and the person committing the act. As used here, the term rewards does not refer to money (although it might be a consideration if the other person is our boss or a client). Rather, *rewards* are the benefits we obtain from our interactions with the other person. If the other person provides us with rewards, we choose the most positive of the possible interpretations of violations that have multiple possible interpretations; "for example, increased proximity during conversation may be taken as a sign of affiliation if committed by a high reward person but as a sign of aggressiveness if committed by a low reward person" (Burgoon & Hale, 1988, p. 63).

Burgoon and Hale (1988) suggest that positively evaluated violations of our expectations should have positive consequences for our communication with violators (e.g., not lead to misinterpretations, increase intimacy). Negatively evaluated violations, in contrast, generally lead to negative outcomes (e.g., misinterpretations, decreases in intimacy). There are, however, exceptions for negative violations.

Burgoon and Hale point out that if the other person provides rewards and commits an extreme violation of our expectations, positive outcomes (e.g., higher credibility and/or interpersonal attraction) are possible.

Stephan (1985) contends that we often believe our expectations have been fulfilled when we communicate with strangers, regardless of how the stranger behaves. Stephan suggests that we tend not to change our behavior when others disconfirm our expectations. He goes on to point out that the

> affective consequences of confirmation or disconfirmation depend to a great degree on whether the expectancy is positive or negative. Confirmation of positive expectancies and disconfirmation of negative expectancies would be expected to elicit favorable affective responses to the behavior, such as pride and happiness. Disconfirmation of positive expectancies and confirmation of negative expectancies may lead to negative affect, such as sadness or low self-esteem or resentment and hostility directed toward the self or the holder of the expectancy. (p. 637)

Burgoon and Hale (1988), however, point out that whether the other person can provide rewards influences how we interpret the confirmation or disconfirmation of our expectations.

Our intergroup expectations for strangers' behavior are the result of many factors. In the next two sections of this chapter, we focus on two social cognitive factors, intergroup attitudes (e.g., ethnocentrism and prejudice) and the stereotypes we have of strangers, that create expectations when we communicate with strangers. We begin by looking at stereotypes.

STEREOTYPES

Lippman (1922) refers to stereotypes as "pictures in our heads." He points out that stereotypes have both a cognitive and affective component:

> [Stereotyping] is not merely a way of substituting order for the great blooming, buzzing confusion of reality. It is not merely a shortcut. It is all these things and more. It is a guarantee of our self-respect; it is the projection upon the world of our own sense of value, our own position and our own rights. The stereotypes are, therefore, highly charged with feelings that are attached to them. (pp. 63–64)

Stereotypes, therefore, are cognitive representations of another group that influence our feelings toward members of that group.

Hewstone and Brown (1986) isolate three aspects of *stereotypes* as mental representations:

> 1 Often individuals are categorized, usually on the basis of easily identifiable characteristics such as sex or ethnicity.

2 A set of attributes is ascribed to all (or most) members of that category. Individuals belonging to the stereotyped group are assumed to be similar to each other, and different from other groups, on this set of attributes.
3 The set of attributes is ascribed to any individual member of that category. (p. 29)

Hewstone and Brown's view of stereotypes is consistent with that of most other writers who see stereotypes as mental representations of other groups.

One problem with conceiving stereotypes as mental representations is the assumption that we ascribe traits to all or most members of a group. We often ascribe traits to a small percentage of a group. Stagnor and Lange (1994), for example, find that on average, we associate positive traits with about 60 percent of a group and negative traits with about 50 percent of a group. They, therefore, suggest that we conceive of stereotypes as the extent to which a characteristic is associated strongly with the relevant category in our memory.

Tajfel (1981) draws a distinction between stereotypes and *social stereotypes:*

> "stereotypes" are certain generalizations reached by individuals. They derive in large measure from, or are an instance of, the general cognitive process of categorizing. The main function of the process is to simplify or systematize, for purposes of cognitive and behavioral adaptation, the abundance and complexity of the information received from its environment by the human organism. . . . But such stereotypes can become *social* only when they are shared by large numbers of people within social groups. (pp. 146–147)

Some of our stereotypes are unique and based on our individual experiences, but some are shared with other members of our ingroups. The stereotypes we share with others are our social stereotypes. We may know what the social stereotype of a group is, but still hold a different view of the group (Devine, 1989).

Social stereotypes often are used in the media, and we learn many of our stereotypes from the media. Anyone who watches Saturday morning cartoons, for example, knows that villains are non-Europeans. The frequent use of "dirty old man" in the media contributes to sterotypes of aging. Additionally, aging is depicted as involving evil, failures, and unhappiness in television dramas (Arnoff, 1974). Similarly, disabled people often are presented as bitter, self-pitying, and maladjusted, while nondisabled people are portrayed as not having trouble accepting the disableds' identities (Longmore, 1987). Virtually all stereotypes of non-Europeans, the old, and the disabled presented in the media are negative and inaccurate.

Stereotypes also are used in advertising. A recent advertisement for a cleaning service, for example, indicated that the company is "German thoroughness, Swedish spotlessness, Polish flexibility, Discrete as a Swiss bank, Cheap as Russian promises." While some of these descriptions are positive stereotypes, others are negative and will be offensive to members of those groups.

Our stereotypes are multidimensional images. Vassiliou et al. (1972) contend that stereotypes vary along six dimensions:

1. *Complexity.* The number of traits assigned to the other group.
2. *Clarity.* (a) *Polarization* of the judgments on each trait dimension, that is, the extent to which people from one group assign non-neutral values of the trait to people from another group. (b) *Consensus,* that is, agreement among people in assigning the trait to another group.
3. *Specificity-Vagueness.* The extent to which the traits are specific or vague (abstract).
4. *Validity.* The extent to which the stereotypes correspond to substantially realistic assignment of traits.
5. *Value.* The favorability of the assigned traits.
6. *Comparability.* The extent to which the framework of the perceiver is involved in the stereotyping so that a comparison is made between autostereotype (group looking at self) and heterostereotype (one group looking at another). (pp. 90–91)

All stereotypes vary along each of these dimensions. When stereotypes involve substantially realistic assignments of traits to a group of people (i.e., are valid), Bogardus (1959) refers to them as "sociotypes."

Vassiliou et al. (1972) differentiate between normative and nonnormative stereotypes formed by members of an ingroup prior to contact with an outgroup. A normative stereotype is a "cognitive norm for thinking about a group of people" (p. 112) based on information gained from education, the mass media, and/or historical events. A nonnormative stereotype, on the other hand, is not formed on the basis of information from such sources. When one group does not have a normative stereotype about another group with whom friendly relations exist, the members of the group begin thinking about the other group as being "like us." Nonnormative stereotypes, in other words, are purely projective in nature. North Americans, for example, tend to have little information about Greeks; therefore, if they have had no previous contact with Greeks, they are likely to project their image of themselves and see Greeks as very similar to themselves. If friendly relations do not exist, the stereotype of the outgroup formed by the ingroup will then be a normative one.

Vassiliou et al. (1972) argue that "contact has the effect of changing the stereotypes to match the sociotypes; that is, it increases the validity of the stereotypes" (p. 114). It should be noted, however, that although contact has a tremendous influence on nonnormative stereotypes, it has a lesser influence on normative stereotypes. More specifically, contact increases the clarity of nonnormative stereotypes but has little or no effect on the clarity of normative stereotypes. Further, contact with members of the outgroup increases the complexity and specificity of the ingroup's stereotype of them.

Stereotypes and Communication

Stereotypes provide the content of our social categories. We have social categories in which we place people, and it is our stereotype that tells us what people in that category are like. Stereotypes, therefore, reduce our uncertainty and increase our confidence in predicting strangers' behavior. Stereotypes, however, do not increase the accuracy of our predictions (see below for more details). Stereotyping is the result of our tendency to overestimate the degree of association between group membership and psychological attributes. While there may be some association between group membership and psychological characteristics of members, it is much smaller than we assume when we communicate on automatic pilot. Only 28 to 37 percent of the people in a culture, for example, have the traits attributed to them (Wallace, 1952). In some cases, there is more similarity between people in the same occupation across cultures than there is between people in different occupations within a culture (Inkeles, 1974).

Our stereotypes tend to be activated automatically when we categorize strangers and when we are not communicating mindfully (see von Hippel, Sekaquaptewa, & Vargas, 1995). We, therefore, cannot not stereotype when we communicate on automatic pilot. Our tendency to stereotype automatically is enhanced when we are highly anxious. Wilder (1994) points out that "when anxiety distracts persons from careful attention to the environment, they rely more on cognitive structures such as social stereotypes in making judgments of others" (pp. 87–88). Islam and Hewstone (1993) report that the greater our anxiety, the less variability we see in outgroups (i.e., the more we assume members of outgroups are alike).

Our stereotypes influence the way we process information. We remember more favorable information about our ingroups and more unfavorable information about outgroups (Hewstone & Giles, 1986). The information we remember, in turn, affects the way we interpret incoming messages from members of ingroups and outgroups. Our processing of information is "biased in the direction of maintaining the preexisting belief systems. . . . These processes, then, can produce the *cognitive confirmation* of one's stereotypic beliefs" (Hamilton, Sherman, & Ruvolo, 1992, p. 138).

Our stereotypes also create expectations regarding how members of other groups will behave. Unconsciously, we assume that our expectations are correct and behave as though they are. Hamilton and his associates (1992) point out that

> stereotypes operate as a source of expectancies about what a group as a whole is like (e.g., Hispanics) as well as about what attributes individual group members are likely to possess (e.g., Juan Garcia). Their influence can be pervasive, affecting the perceiver's attention to, encoding of, inferences about, and judgments based on that information. And the resulting interpretations, inferences, and judgments typically are made so as to be consistent with preexisting beliefs that guided them. (p. 142)

We, therefore, unconsciously try to confirm our expectations when we communicate with strangers.

Our stereotypes constrain strangers' patterns of communication and engender stereotype-confirming communication. In other words, stereotypes create self-fulfilling prophecies. We tend to see behavior that confirms our expectations even when it is absent. We ignore disconfirming evidence when communicating on automatic pilot. Hamilton and his associates (1992) point out that perceivers can influence a person with whom they interact by constraining the person's behavior. However, perceivers typically do not recognize this influence or take it into consideration when interpreting the target's behavior. Although a target person's behavior may be affected by perceiver-induced constraints, it is often interpreted by the perceiver as a manifestation of the target's personality. (p. 149)

Snyder and Haugen (1995) suggest that our tendency to engage in confirming behaviors depends on our goal in the interaction. If our goal is to adjust to the other person and have smooth interactions, we tend to engage in confirming behaviors. If our goal is to gather information about the other person, in contrast, we do not necessarily engage in confirming behaviors.

Steele (cited in Watters, 1995) proposes an alternative explanation for stereotype-confirming behaviors. He argues that confirming others' stereotypes may be due to stereotype vulnerability. Stereotype vulnerability does not involve consciously or unconsciously accepting a stereotype, but rather, it emerges from having to contend with the stereotype when mental abilities are already taxed. Steele argues that stereotype vulnerability has broad implications:

I think much of what is mistaken for racial animosity in America today is really stereotype vulnerability. Imagine an [African American] man and a [European American] man meeting for the first time. Because the [African American] knows the stereotype of his group, he attempts to deflect those negative traits, finding ways of trying to communicate, in effect, "Don't think of me as incompetent." The [European American], for his part, is busy deflecting the stereotype of his group: "Don't think of me as a racist." Every action becomes loaded with the potential of confirming the stereotype, and you end up with two people struggling with the phantoms they're only half aware of. The discomfort and tension is often mistaken as racial animosity. (p. 47)

The problem is that the two people are being mindful of the outcome (i.e., "Don't think of me as incompetent" and "Don't think of me as a racist"), rather than being mindful of the communication process that is taking place between them (Langer, 1989).

When we communicate on automatic pilot, we do not cognitively process all the information about others that is available to us (Johnston & Macrae, 1994). As indicated earlier, we tend to process information that is consistent with our stereotypes and our stereotypes do not change. We can process all the information available to us if we are mindful of our communication. When we process all the information available to us, our stereotypes of strangers change (see the final section of the chapter for more details). Also, when we are highly involved in an interaction and receive information inconsistent with our stereotypes from a highly credible source, we tend to change our stereotypes (Johnston & Coolen, 1995).

Stereotypes, in and of themselves, do not lead to miscommunication and/or communication breakdown. If, however, inaccurate or negative stereotypes are held rigidly, they lead to inaccurate predictions of strangers' behavior and misunderstandings. Simple stereotypes of other groups also can lead to misunderstandings. In order to increase our effectiveness in communicating with strangers, we need to increase the complexity of our stereotypes (e.g., include a large number of traits in the stereotype and differentiate subgroups within the group being stereotyped) and question our unconscious assumption that most, if not all, members of a group fit a single stereotype (Stephan & Rosenfield, 1982).

Devine (1989) argues that conscious control of our reactions when our stereotypes are activated is necessary to control our prejudice:

> Nonprejudiced responses are . . . a function of intentional controlled processes and require a conscious decision to behave in a nonprejudiced fashion. In addition, new responses must be learned and well practiced before they can serve as competitive responses to the automatically activated stereotype-congruent response. (p. 15)

Von Hippel, Sekaquaptewa, and Vargas (1995) argue that people who are not highly prejudiced "suppress or replace their automatically activated stereotypes" (p. 224). This position is consistent with Langer's notion that mindfulness is necessary to reduce prejudice.

Accuracy of Predictions Based on Stereotypes

Individual members of a group may or may not fit a stereotype we have of that group. Ting-Toomey (1989) isolates four possible options for the relationship between how individuals identify with a group and the way they behave: (1) individuals may see themselves as typical group members and behave typically, (2) individuals may see themselves as typical group members and behave atypically, (3) individuals may see themselves as atypical group members and behave atypically, and (4) individuals may see themselves as atypical group members and behave typically. The situation is actually more complicated, however, because our perceptions of the other person as a typical or an atypical member of her or his group may not be the same as hers or his.

The accuracy of our predictions depends on whether the traits that we include in our stereotype of another group are similar to the ones in that group's stereotype of its own group (i.e., are our stereotypes valid?). If the traits we apply to another group agree with the traits members of that group apply to themselves, our stereotype should lead to accurate interpretations of the behavior of members of the group who are typical. Valid stereotypes, however, will lead to misinterpretations of the behavior of atypical members of the group.

When we place someone in a category, our stereotype of people in that category helps us predict his or her behavior if we perceive that person is typical of her or his group. We are able to reduce our uncertainty because we assume that our stereotypes tell us how typical group members communicate (Krauss & Fussell, 1991). If the other person has informed us of his or her category membership, our predictions may be accurate. If, for example, we are communicating with a woman from Mexico and she tells us she is a Chicana, not a Mexican American, we can make some accurate predictions of her behavior if our stereotypes of people from Mexico differentiates Chicanos/Chicanas from Mexican Americans.

If our stereotype does not include this differentiation, then our predictions will probably not be accurate. It is rare, however, for others to tell us their group memberships directly (Kellermann, 1993).

Rather than using strangers' self-categorizations (the group memberships they announce), we tend to base our categorizations on skin color, dress, accents, the car a person drives, and so forth (Clark & Marshall, 1981). The cues we use, however, are not always accurate ways to categorize others (i.e., an inaccurate categorization occurs when we put someone in a category in which he or she would not place her- or himself). Recall from Chapter 4 that we vary in the degree to which we identify with our ethnic groups and cultures. If we categorize strangers who do not identify strongly with their ethnic group and who do identify strongly with their culture on the basis of their ethnicity, our prediction will, in all likelihood, be inaccurate. Predictions based on ethnicity will probably be accurate only for strangers who identify strongly with their ethnic group and do not identify strongly with their culture.

Another source of inaccuracy in our predictions based on our stereotypes is that the boundaries between many social groups are fuzzy (Clark & Marshall, 1981). What, for example, is the boundary between educated and uneducated people? or between young and old? Even skin color may not be a good predictor of category membership. There are, for example, light-colored African Americans who look like European Americans. These individuals may be categorized as European American soley on the basis of skin color. They may, however, identify strongly with being African American. Similarly, dark-skinned African Americans may not identify strongly with their ethnic group. Obviously, predictions about their behavior based on skin color will be inaccurate.

Even if others are typical members of the group in which we categorize them, the inferences we make about them on the basis of their group membership may not be accurate. One reason is that our stereotypes may not be valid (i.e., our stereotypes of their group are different from their stereotypes of the group). Another reason our predictions may not be accurate is that the group membership we are using to categorize them may not be affecting their behavior in the current situation. We are all members of many social groups that influence our behavior and provide us with different social identities. When communicating with strangers, we might categorize them on the basis of one group membership (e.g., ethnicity) and assume that their social identities based on this category are influencing their behavior. The strangers, however, may be basing their behavior on a different social identity (e.g., social class, gender, role). To increase our accuracy in making prediction, we must try to understand which social identity is guiding strangers' behavior in a particular situation.

In summary, stereotypes are the content of the categories when we are categorizing people. The stereotypes we hold have a direct influence on our communication with strangers. Our initial predictions about strangers' behavior must, out of necessity, be based on the stereotypes we have about the strangers' culture, race, or ethnic group. To the degree that our stereotypes are accurate, we can make accurate cultural-level predictions about strangers' behavior. If our stereotypes are inaccurate, we cannot make correct attributions about strangers' behavior. Further, if we rigidly hold our stereotypes and are not willing to question them, we can never reach the point where we know strangers as individuals (i.e., we can never make psychocultural predictions about their behavior), and our attributions about an individual strangers' behavior will continue to be incorrect.

INTERGROUP ATTITUDES

An *attitude* "is a learned predisposition to respond in an evaluative (from extremely favorable to extremely unfavorable) manner toward some attitude object" (Davidson & Thompson, 1980, p. 27). Attitudes predispose us to behave in a positive or negative manner toward various objects or people.

Attitudes generally are conceptualized as having three components: cognitive, affective, and conative (McGuire, 1969). The cognitive component involves our beliefs about the attitude object. Rokeach (1972) defines a *belief* as " any simple proposition, conscious or unconscious, inferred from what a person says or does, capable of being preceded by the phrase 'I believe that'" (p. 113). Examples of beliefs include "blacks are musical," "the Irish are heavy drinkers," and "the Japanese are ambitious." The affective component of an attitude involves our emotional or evaluative reaction to the attitude object. Thus, the affective component refers to our subjective evaluation of the positive or negative aspects of the attitude object. The conative component of an attitude involves our behavioral intentions toward the attitude object (e.g., an intention to avoid members of the outgroup).

Intergroup attitudes serve several functions for the people who hold them. By functions, we mean what the attitudes do for people who hold them, or in other words, the uses of attitudes. Katz (1960) proposes four general functions any attitude can serve:

1. *The utilitarian or adjustment function.* We hold some attitudes because they are useful in our culture; they lead to the attainment of rewards.
2. *The ego-defensive function.* We hold some attitudes because they allow us to protect our self image (ego). These attitudes allow us to avoid admitting uncomfortable things about ourselves.
3. *The value-expressive function.* We hold some attitudes because we want to express those parts of our lives that are important to us.
4. *The knowledge function.* We hold some attitudes because they allow us to structure or organize incoming stimuli in a way that makes sense to us.

These functions can have positive and negative consequences. Negative intergroup attitudes, for example, increase our confidence in predicting strangers' behavior, but they also decrease the accuracy of our predictions (Gudykunst, 1988b). Negative intergroup attitudes also lead to anxiety in interacting with strangers (Stephan & Stephan, 1985). We begin our discussion of intergroup attitudes with the most general attitude, ethnocentrism.

Ethnocentrism

The word *ethnocentrism* is derived from two Greek words: *ethnos,* or "nation," and *kentron,* or "center." This derivation suggests that ethnocentrism occurs when our nation is seen as the center of the world. In common usage, however, the concept is applied more broadly. Sumner (1940) defines *ethnocentrism* as

> the technical name for the view of things in which one's own group is the center of everything, and all others are scaled and rated with reference to it. . . . the most important fact is that ethnocentrism leads people to exaggerate and intensify everything in their own folkways which is peculiar and which differentiates them from others. It therefore strengthens the folkways. (p. 13)

In other words, ethnocentrism refers to our tendency to identify with our ingroup (e.g., ethnic or racial group, culture) and to evaluate outgroups and their members according to its standards. *Everyone is ethnocentric to some degree.* Because we are ethnocentric, we tend to view our own cultural values and ways of doing things as more real, or as the "right" and natural values and ways of doing things. One major consequence of such a view is that our ingroup's values and ways of doing things are seen as superior to the outgroups' values and ways of doing things. Another consequence of ethnocentrism is that it leads us to be anxious about interacting with strangers (Stephan & Stephan, 1992).

Ethnocentrism is not the same as xenophobia. *Xenophobia* is a "fear of strangers" (Kleg, 1993, p. 153). Kleg points out that this fear is natural and we all have "some degree of fear of others who seem strange and different" (p. 153). One reason for xenophobia is that people who are strange are perceived as threats to the predictability and stability of our social worlds.

Ethnocentrism is not usually deliberate. Often the expression of ethnocentrism is a function of how we are socialized. People born and raised in the United States, for example, are taught many subtle cues suggesting the United States is the center of the world. Consider the major league baseball championship series played between the winners of the two leagues. Is it called the United States Series? No, obviously not; it is called the World Series, implying that no other nation has baseball teams (granted there are now Canadian teams in the World Series, but no Japanese, Korean, or Mexican teams). Another example of the tendency for people in the United States to view their country as the center of the world is in the use of the term *American.* Citizens of the other members of the Organization of American States (OAS) from North, Central, and South America are also "Americans."

The existence of ethnocentrism is not limited to recent historic times or to the United States. The early Greeks used the term *barbarikos* ("barbarians") to refer to those people living around them who did not speak Greek. Because they did not speak Greek, the ancient Persians and Egyptians were considered to be inferior by the Greeks. In current times, many languages have a word with a very similar meaning. The Japanese word *gaijin,* for example, means "foreigner," a person who is not Japanese, and often is used with a condescending overtone.

Ethnocentrism exists in all cultures. Klass and Hellman (1971) point out that ethnocentrism often is expressed in the way people draw their maps:

> There is nothing unusual about this type of thinking: the Chinese, who called their country the Middle Kingdom, were convinced that China was the center of the world, and similar beliefs were held by other nations—-and still are held. The British drew the Prime Meridian of longitude to run through Greenwich, near London. Europeans drew maps of the world with Europe at the center, [North] Americans with the New World at the center. (p. 61)

The way we draw maps clearly reflects ethnocentrism involving seeing our group as the center of the world.

The opposite of ethnocentrism is cultural relativism. *Cultural relativism* involves trying to understand others' behavior in the context of the culture or group of the person engaging in the behavior (Herskovits, 1973). We cannot understand others' behavior if we use our own cultural or ethnic frame of reference to interpret their behavior. Kurt Vonnegut, Jr., says:

> I didn't learn until I was in college about all other cultures, and I should have learned that in first grade. A first grader should understand that his or her culture isn't a rational invention; that there are thousands of other cultures and they all work pretty well; that all cultures function on faith rather than truth; that there are lots of alternatives to our own society. Cultural relativity is defensible and attractive. It also is a source of hope. It means we don't have to continue this way if we do not like it.

Some degree of cultural relativism is necessary to understand strangers' behavior. Cultural relativism, however, should not be extended to moral relativism (this issue is discussed in more detail in Chapter 15).

Functions and Dysfunctions of Ethnocentrism. Ethnocentrism is related closely to the attitude of nationalism. Rosenblatt (1964) believes both attitudes arise from a comparison of ingroups with outgroups. The attitudes differ, however, in that ethnocentrism focuses on cultural patterns of behavior, while nationalism focuses on a nation's political ideology. Rosenblatt argues that high levels of both nationalism and ethnocentrism serve several functions that maintain the integrity of the ingroup:

1. GROUP SURVIVAL—Groups with high ethnocentrism and high nationalism are more likely to survive the threats of external forces.
2. TANGIBLE PAYOFFS—Administrative efficacy is promoted (e.g., power in policy making decisions, division of labor, promotion of group welfare).
3. INCREASED HOMOGENEITY—Groups will have more homogeneous attitudes, greater cohesiveness, and increased conformity.
4. GREATER VIGOR AND PERSISTENCE—Problems affecting the group are addressed with persistence and energy.
5. GREATER EASE OF STRIVING AGAINST OUTSIDERS—Relations against outgroups are executed with greater ease because of strong commitments to group maintenance.

6. DECREASED SOCIAL DISORGANIZATION—Intragroup organization increases.

7. INCREASED TENURE OF LEADERS—Leaders are more likely to remain in the leadership position.

8. NEW DISSENSION—Intragroup conflicts arise frequently amid the strain toward homogeneity.

9. MISPERCEPTION OF OUTGROUPS—Attributions to out-group members are not accurate because of misperceptions.

10. FACILITITION OF LEARNING—Learning correct in-group behavior is easier when the pressures to conform are pervasive. (Rosenblatt, 1964, summarized in Burk, 1976, pp. 21–22)

Ethnocentrism, therefore, has positive and negative functions for the ingroup.

High levels of ethnocentrism and nationalism are functional when they satisfy needs in the lives of group members and when the ingroup is strengthened or becomes more cohesive (Burk, 1976). Ethnocentric attitudes serve all four of the functions Katz (1960) isolates. The utilitarian function involves the notion that if we are highly ethnocentric, we tend to conform to our culture and, thus, be in a better position to obtain its rewards. Ethnocentrism also helps us protect ourselves from uncomfortable things about ourselves (e.g., we can put down parts of another culture, thereby elevating the qualities of our own). An ethnocentric attitude also serves a value-expressive function. Specifically, this attitude allows us to express our values as the true and correct ones to hold. Finally, ethnocentrism serves the knowledge function; it allows us to structure a set of beliefs about people in other cultures on the basis of our own culture.

High levels of ethnocentrism and nationalism are also dysfunctional. Burk (1976) argues that the extremes of these attitudes are dysfunctional when they lead to hostility and conflict with outgroup members. "When the in-group feeling develops to the extent that the members of a particular society feel their way of life is so superior to all others that it is their duty to change other people to their way of thinking and doing (if necessary by force), then this attitude becomes a menace" (Holmes, 1965, p. 347). High levels of ethnocentrism and nationalism, therefore, are one cause of wars. Catton (1961) hypothesizes that "ethnocentrism is a factor which enables homo sapiens to engage in war despite rational considerations to the contrary" (p. 205).

High levels of ethnocentrism are also dysfunctional with respect to effective communication with strangers. Specifically, high levels of ethnocentrism lead to misperception of members of outgroups; this misperception causes us to make inaccurate attributions about strangers' behavior. In other words, a high level of ethnocentrism leads us to interpret strangers' behavior using our own cultural frame of reference, thereby possibly distorting the meaning of the strangers' behavior. If we do not understand strangers' behavior, effective communication is probably impossible.

A Consequence of Ethnocentrism: Communicative Distance.   The attitudes we hold influence the way we speak to other people. The speed with which we talk or the accent we use may be varied in order to generate different feelings of distance between us and strangers with whom we communicate (i.e., to make the distance seem smaller or greater). Peng (1974) uses the concept of *communicative distance* to explain this linguistic diversity:

> A communicative distance cannot be measured directly. It is not even visible. But we can be sure of its presence when we hear certain words or expressions. In other words, our awareness of a communicative distance in the midst of a conversation depends to a large extent on certain linguistic devices which serve, from the speaker's point of view, to set up the communicative distance, or from the hearer's point of view, to let the hearer know that it has already been set up by the speaker. (p. 33)

We, therefore, establish communicative distances between ourselves and others when we speak with them.

Lukens (1978) expands Peng's conceptualization of communicative distance to cover *ethnocentric speech,* which is reflected in three communicative distances: (1) the distance of indifference, (2) the distance of avoidance, and (3) the distance of disparagement. Lukens goes on:

> In essence, speech in accordance with the three communicative distances may be used: (1) to demonstrate lack of concern for persons of other cultures and reflect an insensitivity to cultural differences (the distance of indifference), (2) to avoid or limit the amount of interaction with out-groups (the distance of avoidance), and (3) to demonstrate feelings of hostility towards out-groups and to deride or belittle them (the distance of disparagement). (p. 41)

Lukens associates each of the three distances with a different level of ethnocentrism (low, moderate, and high, respectively).

The *distance of disparagement* reflects animosity of the ingroup toward the outgroup (Lukens, 1978). It arises when the two groups are in competition for the same resources and involves attacking strangers' self-concepts. Lukens indicates that at this distance, imitation and mockery of speech styles are characteristic. The use of "baby talk" with the elderly is one example of language perceived as mockery by the group toward whom it is directed.

The distance of disparagement is characterized by the use of pejorative expressions and ethnophaulisms. Ehrlich (1973) specifies three types of ethnophaulisms: (1) ethnic names used as a disparagement (e.g., "Irish confetti," "Jewbird"); (2) explicit group devaluations (e.g., "luck of the Irish," "Jew them down"); and (3) disparaging nicknames (e.g., "Polack," "jungle bunny," "honky"). If you are familiar with the television program *All in the Family,* you will recognize that Archie Bunker used all three types of ethnophaulisms. Palmore (1962) notes that all racial and ethnic groups use ethnophaulisms and they usually express unfavorable stereotypes. His study also reveals that when ethnophaulisms are directed toward other races, physical characteristics generally are highlighted. When ethnophaulisms are directed toward people from the same racial group, on the other hand, highly visible cultural differences usually are highlighted. Further, the number of ethnophaulisms we use is related to the degree of our ethnocentrism, and the use of ethnophaulisms can intensify our ethnocentrism. Palmore concludes that "we may discover that ethnophaulisms are essential for the existence of such forms of ethnocentrism as chauvinism, pejorative stereotypes, scapegoats, segregation, and discrimination" (p. 445).

The *distance of avoidance* is established in order to avoid or minimize contact with members of an outgroup (Lukens, 1978). One technique commonly used to accomplish this goal is the use of an ingroup dialect. "The emphasizing of an ethnic dialect and other linguistic differences between the in-group and outsiders may be purposefully used by in-group members to make themselves appear esoteric to the out-group thus lessening the likelihood for interaction" (p. 45). At this distance, members of the ingroup also may use terms of solidarity. Feelings of cultural pride and solidarity are increased through the use of such expressions as "black power," "black is beautiful," and "red power." In establishing this distance, ingroup members extensively use jargon common to their group.

The *distance of indifference* is the speech form used to "reflect the view that one's own culture is the center of everything" (Lukens, 1978, p. 42). This distance, therefore, reflects an insensitivity to strangers' perspectives. One example of the speech used at this distance is "foreigner talk," the form of speech used when talking to people who are not native speakers of a language. It usually takes the form of loud and slow speech patterns, exaggerated pronunciation, and simplification (e.g., deletion of articles). Downs (1971) points out that "we tend to believe that, if we speak slowly enough or loudly enough, anyone can understand us. I have done this myself quite without realizing it, and others have tried to reach me in the same way in Japanese, Chinese, Thai, Punjabi, Navajo, Spanish, Tibetan, and Singhalese" (p. 19). The distance of indifference is also characterized by the use of idiomatic expressions, such as "black sheep," "black list," "black magic," "low person on the totem pole," "Indian giver," "Jew them down," "Mexican standoff," and "the blind leading the blind," that suggest indifference to other groups' points of view.

While we agree that the three levels of communicative distance are manifested in speech patterns and are based on differing levels of ethnocentrism, we believe the trichotomy is incomplete as it now stands. As indicated earlier, ethnocentrism is only one side of the coin, the other side being the attitude of cultural relativism. Cultural relativism, as indicated earlier, involves the view that all cultures are of equal value and the values and behavior of a culture can be judged only by using that culture as a frame of reference. Often ethnocentrism and cultural relativism are discussed separately; that is, they are seen as two distinct attitudes. We believe, however, that ethnocentrism and cultural relativism are opposite sides of the same coin. If we adopt this view, a high level of ethnocentrism and a high level of cultural relativism can be seen as opposite end points of an attitudinal continuum. We can label at least five different points on the continuum: high ethnocentrism, moderate ethnocentrism, low ethnocentrism/low cultural relativism, moderate cultural relativism, and high cultural relativism. Each of these five points should be reflected in a different level of communicative distance. Lukens' (1978) analysis addresses the first three, but not the last two.

The level of moderate cultural relativism reflects none of the characteristics of Lukens' three distances. Rather, this level reveals a sensitivity to cultural differences. The speech at this level reflects our desire to decrease the communicative distance between ourselves and strangers. This distance is labeled the *distance of sensitivity.* Speech at this distance reflects a sensitivity to group differences, but the groups are not necessarily viewed as equal. When speaking at this distance, for example, we would use the term for strangers' ethnic groups that they prefer rather than the term we usually use.

The level of high cultural relativism reflects our desire to minimize the distance between ourselves and strangers. This distance involves an attitude of equality, one where we demonstrate we are interpreting the language and behavior of strangers in terms of their culture. This distance is labeled the *distance of equality.* Speech at this distance avoids evaluating other groups. The use of "he or she" instead of the generic "he," for example, illustrates equality between males and females.

Ethnic Prejudice

The term *prejudice* stems from the Latin word *praejudicium* which means "precedent," or "a judgment based on previous decisions and experiences" (Allport, 1954, p. 7). While prejudice can be positive or negative, there is a tendency for most of us to think of it as negative. Consistent with this view, Allport defines *negative ethnic prejudice* as "an antipathy based on a faulty and unflexible generalization. It may be felt or expressed. It may be directed toward a group as a whole, or toward an individual because he [or she] is a member of that group" (p. 10).

Prejudice typically is conceived as an attitude. Smith (1994, p. 299) points out that this view usually takes the following form:

Negative stereotype: *Members of Group A are dirty, hostile, lazy, . . .*

leads to

Prejudiced attitude: *I don't like A's*

leads to

Discrimination: *I prefer to avoid A's, exclude them from good jobs, . . .*

Smith, however, argues that prejudice can be viewed as an emotion. He defines prejudice as a "social emotion experienced with respect to one's social identity as a group member, with an outgroup member as a target" (p. 304). When prejudice is seen as an emotion, the logic takes the following form:

Appraisals: *A member of Group A is receiving benefits that are undeserved and paid for by my tax dollars*

leads to

> **Prejudiced emotion:** *I feel anger and resentment at A's*
>
> leads to
>
> **Discrimination:** *I want to harm A's by reducing food stamps and welfare benefits* . . . (p. 305)

Prejudice can be manifested in emotions such as fear, disgust, contempt (dislike), anger, and jealousy. Most research on prejudice views it as an attitude; we, therefore, focus on this view here.

We tend to think of prejudice in terms of a dichotomy; either we are prejudiced or we are not. It is more useful, however, to think of the strength of our prejudice as varying along a continuum from low to high. This approach suggests that *we all are prejudiced to some degree.* We also all are racist, sexist, agist, and so on to some degree. As is the case with ethnocentrism, prejudice is natural and unavoidable. It is the result of our being socialized as members of our ingroups. Even people with low levels of prejudice prefer to interact with people who are similar to themselves because such interactions are more comfortable and less stressful than interactions with strangers.

We also can think of prejudice as varying along a second continuum ranging from very positive to very negative. We tend to be positively prejudiced toward our ingroup and negatively prejudiced toward outgroups. It is possible, however, to be positively prejudiced toward outgroups and negatively prejudiced toward an ingroup. The valence (positive or negative) of our prejudice must be taken into consideration in trying to understand our reactions to violations of our expectations. The tendency over the years has been for younger European Americans to be have a more positive view of African Americans than do older European Americans. Recent research, however, suggests this trend may have come to an end. An Anti-Defamation League survey indicates that 35 percent of European Americans over age 50 are highly prejudiced against African Americans, while 23 percent of those between 30 and 49 years of age and 31 percent of those between 18 and 29 are highly prejudiced (*Los Angeles Times,* June 12, 1993, p. A25).

People who are highly prejudiced tend to ignore information not consistent with their faulty and inflexible generalization. Allport (1954) presents an excellent example of the process used by a highly prejudiced person when confronted with contradictory information:

> *Mr. X:* The trouble with Jews is that they only take care of their own group.
> *Mr. Y:* But the record of the Community Chest campaign shows that they give more generously, in proportion to their numbers, to the charities of the community, than do non-Jews.
> *Mr. X:* That shows they are always trying to buy favor and intrude into Christian affairs. They think of nothing but money; that is why there are so many Jewish bankers.
> *Mr. Y:* But a recent study shows that the percentage of Jews in the banking business is negligible, far smaller than the percentage of non-Jews.
> *Mr. X:* That's just it; they don't go in for respectable business; they are only in the movie business or run night clubs. (pp. 13–14)

Thus, highly prejudiced people tend to alter their beliefs to justify their attitude when confronted with contradictory information. Allport refers to this process as rationalization.

What if people changed their minds after being confronted with accurate information? Allport (1954) argues "errors of prejudgment" are different from prejudice. If people do not change a prejudgment when given new information, they are prejudiced; however, if they rectify an erroneous prejudgment on the basis of the new information, they are not highly prejudiced.

Functions of Prejudice. Prejudice, like ethnocentrism, is functional for people who hold the attitude. Brislin (1979) examines the functions of prejudice using Katz's (1960) scheme. The first function prejudice performs is to help us either avoid punishment or obtain rewards in our culture (utilitarian function). Brislin (1979) points out "people want to be well liked by others in their culture. If such esteem is dependent upon rejecting members of a certain group, then it is likely that people will indeed reject members of the outgroup" (p. 29).

The second function prejudice performs is to protect us from information that might damage our self-image (ego-defensive function). Brislin (1979) argues that people who are not successful in their chosen occupation can blame their lack of success on members of the outgroup (who may be seen as a bunch of cheaters) rather than admit to any personal inadequacies if they are highly prejudiced.

Another function that prejudice performs is to allow us to express important aspects of our lives (value-expressive function). Brislin (1979) points out that people of one religion may react negatively toward members of another religion "because they see themselves as standing up for the one true God (as defined by their religion)" (p. 30).

The final function that prejudice serves is to assist us in organizing the world around us (knowledge function). Prejudice allows us to behave in accordance with the categories we have constructed, rather than on the basis of the actual incoming stimuli. Aronson (1972) provides an example of how highly prejudiced people interpret incoming stimuli so that they are consistent with their attitude:

> Prejudiced people see the world in ways that are consistent with their prejudice. If Mr. Bigot sees a well-dressed, [European American] Protestant sitting on a park bench sunning himself [or herself] at three o'clock on a Wednesday afternoon, he thinks nothing of it. If he sees a well-dressed [African American] doing the same thing, he is liable to leap to the conclusion that the person is unemployed—and he becomes infuriated, because he assumes that his hard-earned taxes are paying that shiftless good-for-nothing enough in welfare subsidies to keep him in good clothes. If Mr. Bigot passes Mr. [European American's] house and notices that a trash can is overturned and some garbage is strewn about, he is apt to conclude that a stray dog has been searching for food. If he passes Mr. Garcia's house and notices the same thing, he is inclined to become annoyed, and to assert that "those people live like pigs." Not only does prejudice influence his conclusions, his erroneous conclusions justify and intensify his negative feelings. (p. 174)

The attributions we make about strangers are influenced by the attitudes we hold about the groups to which they belong.

Prejudice and Communication.   Prejudice should not be confused with its behavioral counterpart, discrimination. Williams (1947) defines *discrimination* as "the degree that individuals of a given group who are otherwise formally qualified are not treated in conformity with these nominally universal institutionalized codes" (p. 39). In other words, discrimination involves behaving in such a way that members of an outgroup are treated disadvantageously.

What is the relationship between prejudice and discrimination? Do highly prejudiced people always discriminate? Do people with a relatively low level of prejudice always engage in nondiscriminatory behavior? If attitudes always guided behavior, then the answer to these two questions would be a simple yes; however, attitudes are not the only factor influencing behavior. A simple yes, therefore, is not sufficient.

Merton (1957) presents a model of the possible relationships between prejudice and discrimination. His model suggests it is conceivable for people who have low levels of prejudice to discriminate under certain circumstances:

1. *Prejudiced discriminators, or "active bigots."* For this group of people, there is consistency between attitudes and behavior. Prejudiced discriminators openly express their beliefs about outgroups and openly practice discriminatory behavior.

2. *Prejudiced nondiscriminators, or "timid bigots."* This group's behavior is not consistent with their attitudes. Timid bigots believe many of the stereotypes about outgroups and also feel hostility toward them, but do not express their beliefs. Timid bigots do not express their beliefs because of their desire to conform and not to violate social norms or laws. If there were no laws or social pressure, timid bigots would discriminate.

3. *Nonprejudiced discriminators, or "fair-weather liberals."* Like timid bigots, fair-weather liberals do not behave in accordance with their attitudes. Probably the key word for this group of people is *expediency.* When people around them discriminate or talk in a prejudicial manner, fair-weather liberals will take the expedient course of action and keep quiet. The major reason for the inconsistency between attitudes and behavior is the social norms of the situation.

4. *Nonprejudiced nondiscriminators, or "all-weather liberals."* There is no inconsistency between the attitudes and behavior of all-weather liberals. Merton argues that this group of people is likely to discuss the issues of prejudice and discrimination with others and will not keep quiet when faced with people who discriminate or talk in a prejudicial manner.

Obviously, these four types of people will communicate with strangers differently.

Taylor, Wright, and Porter (1994) point out that when people experience discrimination, they tend to perceive that the discrimination is directed toward their group, rather than toward them as individuals. They conclude that this is related to the identity guiding the behavior. Since social identities guide intergroup behavior where discrimination occurs, the focus is on group memberships, not personal characteristics. With a focus on group memberships in these situations, it would be expected that people would perceive others' behavior as directed toward the group.

As Merton's typology suggests, there are individual differences in discrimination. Well-intentioned European Americans, for example, do not discriminate against African Americans, but European Americans who are not well intentioned do (Dovido et al., 1989). The degree to which we discriminate also is a function of the norms guiding behavior in the situation. When there are clear situational norms for appropriate intergroup behavior, we tend not to engage in discrimination (Gaertner & Dovidio, 1986). We do engage in discrimination, however, when the situational norms suggest that it is justifiable or is not inappropriate (Frey & Gaertner, 1986).

Crosby, Bromley, and Saxe (1980) contend that European Americans in the United States generally try to express nonbigoted ideologies and behave in a nondiscriminatory fashion, but at the same time, they have not internalized the feelings that correspond to the attitudes expressed. Sears (1988) argues that not internalizing the feelings is due to symbolic racism existing in the United States today. Sears suggests that *symbolic racism* is "not racism composed of derogations of and antagonism toward [African Americans] *per se,* or of support for formal inequality." Rather, it blends "some [anti-African American] feeling with the first and proudest of traditional [North] American values, particularly individualism" (p. 54). While there is support for his conceptualization, Sears reports research which suggests that current social attitudes may be due to egalitarianism, not individualism.

Billig and his associates (1988) suggest that there is an ambivalence inherent in our racial discourse (talk). Billig et al. point out that even individuals who are highly authoritarian (and, therefore, expected to hold negative views of other groups) tend to qualify verbally the views of other groups so that they appear reasonable. Billig et al. also note that people who appear very liberal "introduce innuendos and . . . cast aspersions in the most polite and outwardly 'reasonable' ways" (p. 107). If people are going to make a negative comment about strangers, for example, they preface their comment with a claim of not being prejudiced. One interviewee in van Dijk's (1984) study, for example, responds in this way:

> [Interviewer]: Did you ever have any unpleasant experiences [with foreigners]?
> [Interviewee]: I have nothing against foreigners. But their attitude, their aggression is scaring. We are no longer free here. You have to be careful. (p. 65)

Nayo (1995), an African American law professor, reports that a European American woman approached her after a meeting, saying that "the media have made such monsters of black men that I find myself afraid when I meet two black men on the street" (p. B7). Here the blame is placed on the media.

Another strategy we use in expressing prejudiced views is to explain our personal experiences. Verkuyten, de Jung, and Masson (1994) point out that personal "examples and stories make events factual, give firm ground to one's statements, making them independent of the speaker's own (prejudicial) concerns. In this way, the credibility, the rationality, and the expertise of the speaker is established" (p. 296). This strategy allows moderately prejudiced communicators to "excuse themselves for not being more racist" (p. 296).

Myrdal (1944) argues that people in the United States have a dilemma regarding interethnic relations. The "American Dilemma"

> is the ever-raging conflict between, on the one hand, the valuations preserved on the general plane which we shall call the American Creed, where the American thinks, talks, and acts under the influence of high national and Christian percepts, and on the other hand, the valuations on specific planes of individual and group living where . . . . group prejudices against particular persons or types of people, and all sorts of miscellaneous wants, impulses, and habits dominate his [or her] outlook. (p. xxi)

People in the United States, therefore, experience inner conflict regarding members of other ethnic groups. We have both favorable and unfavorable attitudes that are not necessarily related to each other. With respect to African Americans, European Americans are disposed "(a) to be in sympathy with [African Americans] as a group that is unfairly disadvantaged by past and present discrimination but also (b) to be critical of them for not doing enough to help themselves" (Hass et al., 1992, p. 787). When we are aware of these incompatible beliefs, we experience psychological discomfort and anxiety.

Billig and his associates (1988) claim that the ambivalence inherent in qualified prejudiced discourse does not reflect simply an inconsistency between attitudes and impression management. Rather, they suggest that it indicates that we have "dilemmatic" or dialectical thoughts—we may be prejudiced and tolerant at the same time. The prejudiced pole of the dialectic is manifested when we communicate on automatic pilot, and the tolerance pole of the dialectic is manifested when we communicate "mindfully."

Van Dijk (1984) observes that prejudiced talk clusters in four categories: (1) "they are different (culture, mentality)"; (2) "they do not adapt themselves"; (3) "they are involved in negative acts (nuisance, crime)"; and (4) "they threaten our (social, economic) interests" (p. 70). While van Dijk did his study in the Netherlands, these same types of prejudiced talk consistently are overheard in the United States.

The way we talk about people who are different is, in large part, a function of how we want to be seen by our ingroup. Wilder and Shapiro (1991) report that the presence of ingroup members leads us to identify strongly with the ingroup and see outgroup members as typical of their group. van Dijk (1984) points out that people "adapt" their discourse to the rules and constraints of interaction and communication social settings. Especially when delicate topics, such as "foreigners," are concerned, social members will strategically try to realize both the aims of positive self-presentation and those of effective persuasion. Both aims, however, derive from the position of social members within their group. Positive self-presentation is not just a defense mechanism of individuals as persons, but also as respected, accepted, and integrated social members of ingroups. And the same holds for the persuasive nature of prejudiced talk; people do not merely lodge personal complaints or uneasiness about people of other groups, but intend to have their experiences, their evaluations, their opinions, their attitudes, and their actions shared by other members of the ingroup. (p. 154)

Everyone engages in prejudiced talk to some degree. It is inevitable. We can, however, reduce the degree to which we engage in prejudiced talk if we are mindful of our communication.

Other Forms of Prejudice: Sexism and Ageism

Negative ethnic prejudice is not the only type of prejudice affecting our communication with strangers. Prejudice against any group influences communication with members of that group. Space does not permit us to discuss all other forms of prejudice. We briefly examine two: sexism and ageism.

Sexism. *Sexism* occurs when we assign characteristics to others based on their sex (Nilsen et al., 1977). While we can be sexist toward either males or females, sexism usually is viewed as prejudice against women. Sexism is manifested by viewing women as genetically inferior, supporting discriminatory practices against women, engaging in hostility toward women who do not fulfill traditional sex roles, not supporting the women's movement, using derogatory names to refer to women or negatively stereotyping women, and treating women as sexual objects (Benson & Vincent, 1980). While both men and women are sexist, men tend to be more sexist than women. If we look at individual sex roles, however, it appears that masculine men and feminine women are more sexist than men and women who are androgenous or have an undifferentiated sex role (Faulkender, 1985).

Sexism is manifested mainly through our language. There are three major forms of sexism in language: (1) the ignoring of women, (2) the way women are defined, and (3) the deprecation of women (Henley, Hamilton, & Thorne, 1985). The first way that language usage is sexist is in how *women are ignored*. Probably the main way that our language usage ignores women is through the use of masculine words to include both males and females (Schmidt, 1991). There are many words in the English language, for example, that include the word *man* that traditionally have been meant to include women. Examples of these words include, but are not limited to, chairman, mailman, spokesman, and mankind. Another way that women are ignored in language usage is through the use of *he* as a generic pronoun. Many of us learned that when we write or talk, pronouns for males can be used to refer to both males and females. Including both males and females, however, is not how we actually process the information. The use of male pronouns elicits a vision of a male for the reader or listener (Schneider & Hacker, 1973).

The second way that our language usage can be sexist is in *how women are defined*. One way women are defined is in our tendency to address a woman by her first name in situations where we would not address a man by his first name (McConnell-Ginet, 1978). Also "women, much more than men, are addressed through terms of endearment such as honey, cutie, and sweetie, which function to devalue women by depriving them of their name while renaming them with trivial terms" (Schmidt, 1991, p. 30).

The third way that our language is sexist is in *deprecating women*. In English, for example, there are over 200 terms to call a woman sexually promiscuous, but fewer than 25 to call a man sexually promiscuous (Stanley, 1977). While there are more masculine terms (more than 350) in the English language than feminine terms (fewer than 150), there are more negative feminine terms than masculine (Nilsen, 1977).

Ageism.   "Many, if not most, of the 'problems of aging' stem from or are exacerbated by prejudice and discrimination against the aged" (Palmore, 1982, p. 333). *Ageism* involves negative attitudes toward people who are older than we are (usually people we consider "old"). Teenagers, for example, may be prejudiced against people over 30, while a person who is middle-aged may be prejudiced against people who are retired. Ageism is based on "a deep-seated uneasiness on the part of the young and middle-aged—a personal revulsion to and distaste for growing older" (Butler, 1969, p. 243). It also can emerge from competition between the groups (young and old) over scarce resources and jobs (Levin & Levin, 1980). Overall, attitudes toward aging tend to be negative (Palmore, 1982).

Ageism is manifested in our language usage. While the term "old" has connotations of experience, skill, and wisdom, it also is used in derogatory terms used for others (e.g., "old hag," "old fogey"; Covey, 1988). There is a wide variety of terms in the English language referring to old people with negative overtones (e.g., "battleaxe," "geezer"), and the attributes used to talk about the elderly (e.g., "cantankerous," "grumpy") often have negative connotations (Nuessel, 1984). More than one-half of the jokes in English about aging reflect a negative view of old people, with a greater portion of jokes about women than about men being negative. Terms such as aged and elderly are perceived to be negative, while terms such as senior citizen and retired person are evaluated more positively by people of all age groups (Barbato & Freezel, 1987).

Responding to Ethnocentrism and Prejudice

We can influence the amount of ethnocentric speech or prejudiced talk in which others engage. When we express culturally relative or antiprejudiced sentiments, others are less likely to make ethnocentric prejudiced comments in our presence (Blanchard, Lilly, & Vaughn, 1991). When we are bystanders, we "can define the meaning of events and move others toward empathy and indifference. [We] can promote values and norms of caring, or by passivity or participation in the system

[we] can affirm the perpetrators" (Staub, 1989, p. 87). If we find that other people are making prejudiced remarks in our presence, we can point out that this type of speech is not acceptable to us. If we do not, we are being morally exclusive. We could say something like "I'd prefer you did not put down other groups in my presence." By simply stating our opinion in this way, we decrease the likelihood that others will continue to make prejudiced remarks in our presence. If we do not speak out when other people make prejudiced comments or behave in a discriminatory manner, we are partly responsible for the consequences of the remarks or behavior.

Dignity and Integrity.   Dignity and integrity play a large role in ethical behavior, and help explain why it is necessary to say something when others engage in prejudicial behavior or make prejudiced comments. Dignity involves a minimal level of self-respect (Pritchard, 1991). It refers to feeling worthy, honored, or respected as a person. Being moral involves maintaining not only our own sense of dignity but others' sense of dignity as well.

Pritchard (1991) contends that personal integrity reflects our view of what is important. Personal integrity is linked closely to moral integrity. Moral integrity requires "a somewhat unified moral stance. . . . Those with moral integrity can be expected to refuse to compromise moral standards for the sake of personal expediency" (Pritchard, 1991, p. 90). The Aspen Declaration on Character Education isolates six core values that make up a unified moral stance: (1) respect, (2) responsibility, (3) trustworthiness, (4) caring, (5) justice and fairness, and (6) civic virtue and citizenship. With respect to moral integrity, Pritchard (1991) argues it is important to recognize that

> when morality conflicts with other considerations, morality should prevail. Contemporary philosophers refer to this as the *overridingness* of morality. . . . The overridingness of morality need require only that one's conduct be limited to what is morally acceptable. That is, one should not choose immoral or morally objectionable courses of action over those that are morally acceptable. (pp. 225–226)

The overridingness of morality must be a major concern any time we communicate with strangers, see others communicate with strangers, or overhear others talk about strangers.

Behaving in a moral fashion requires that we respect others and their moral views (Guttmann, 1992). We do not have to agree with others' views of morality to respect them; we only have to see their views as based on a moral system. Guttmann (1992) contends that if people disregard the views of others, they are not worthy of respect. This view has clear implications for what often is referred to as hate speech (i.e., speech that puts down others because of their membership in a group). Gutmann argues that there is "no virtue in misogyny, racial or ethnic hatred" (p. 22). She goes on to point out that racist and anti-Semitic remarks (hate speech) are not defensible on moral grounds. "Hate speech violates the most elementary moral injunction, to respect the dignity of all human beings" (p. 23). Galston (1991) takes a similar position when he says that the language of rights is morally incomplete. To say that "I have a right to do X" [e.g., engage in hate speech] is not to conclude that "X is the right thing for me to do." . . . Rights give reasons to others not to interfere with me in the performance of the protected acts; however, they do not in and of themselves give me sufficient reason to perform the acts. There is a gap between rights and right ness that cannot be closed without a richer moral vocabulary—one that involves principles of decency, duty, responsibility, and the common good, among others. (p. 8)

Etzioni (1993) suggests that our rights are limited by the rights of others; we can do what we want only if it does not harm others.

Guttmann (1992) contends that we have a moral obligation to respond when we hear others engage in hate speech. Etzioni (1993) concurs, arguing that *"if we care about attaining a higher level of moral conduct than we now experience, we must be ready to express our moral sense"* (p. 36). Etzioni's position does not mean that we should not disagree with members of other groups. We can and should articulate our disagreements with others, but we must do so in a respectable fashion.

Moral Inclusion-Exclusion.   "Moral exclusion occurs when individuals or groups are perceived as *outside the boundary in which moral values, rules, and considerations of fairness apply.* Those who are morally excluded are perceived as nonentities, expendable, or undeserving; consequently, harming them appears acceptable, appropriate, or just" (Optow, 1990, p. 1). Optow (1990) argues that there are three attitudes associated with being morally inclusive. First, people who are morally inclusive assume that considerations of fairness apply to all people. Second, people who are morally inclusive are willing to provide a share of community resources to others who need them. Third, people who are morally inclusive are willing to make sacrifices to help others.

Optow (1990) isolates two major factors that lead us to behave in a morally exclusive fashion. When we are engaged in group conflict, for example, ingroup cohesiveness is high, but at the same time, concern for fairness for members of outgroups is low. Another factor that contributes to moral exclusiveness is feeling unconnected to the other person or group. When we feel connected to others in any way, in contrast, we feel attraction and empathy, and we engage in helpful behavior toward others. Such behavior is morally inclusive. When we see someone within our moral community (i.e., those we believe should be treated morally) harmed, we perceive an injustice to have taken place. If we harm others in our moral community, we will feel shame, guilt, remorse, or self-blame. When we see someone outside our moral community harmed, we may not perceive that his or her rights are being violated and we may not be concerned. When this situation occurs, we are being morally exclusive.

The Reverend Martin Niemoeller, a Protestant minister who was imprisoned in Dachau, a concentration camp in Germany in 1938, illustrates one of the problems with being morally exclusive when he said:

In Germany, the Nazis first came for the communists, and I didn't speak up because I wasn't a communist. Then they came for the Jews, and I didn't speak up because I wasn't a Jew. Then they came for the trade unionists, and I didn't speak up because I wasn't a trade unionist. Then they came for the Catholics, but I didn't speak up because I was a Protestant. Then they came for me, and by that time there was no one left to speak for me. (from a wall at the Holocaust Museum in Washington, DC)

Clearly, if we are morally exclusive toward others, others will be morally exclusive toward us.

Moral exclusion can take many forms. It can range from slavery, genocide, political repression, and violations of human rights to failing to recognize undeserved suffering in others. The Holocaust during World War II and the My Lai massacre during the Vietnam War are examples of severe moral exclusion. Moral exclusion, however, occurs in everyday interactions, too. If we distance ourselves from others psychologically, ignore our responsibility to others, glorify violence, behave in a prejudicial fashion, or allow others to behave in a prejudicial fashion, we are being morally exclusive.

CHANGING OUR EXPECTATIONS OF STRANGERS

In the preceding sections, we discussed two of the major attitudes influencing our communication with strangers. The next issue that needs to be addressed involves the question of whether the attitudes of ethnocentrism and prejudice and our stereotypes, once developed, are set for life or if contact with strangers changes attitudes.

Brewer and Miller (1988) argue that when we communicate with strangers, there are three ways that our experiences with individual strangers can generalize to change our attitudes toward and stereotypes of their groups:

1. *Change in attitudes toward the group as a whole.* This is the most direct form of generalization, where positive experiences with individual members of a broad social category lead to alterations in the affect and stereotypes associated with the group as a whole.

2. *Increased complexity of intergroup perceptions.* This form of generalization involves a change in the perceived heterogeneity of category structure. Instead of perceiving the out-group category as a relatively homogeneous social group, the individual comes to recognize variability among category members. Attitudes toward the category as a whole may not be altered, but affect and stereotypes are differentiated among various "sub-types" of the general category.

3. *Decategorization.* In this form of generalization, the meaningfulness of the category itself is undermined. Based on the frequency or intensity of exposure to individual members of a social group, the utility of category membership as a basis for identifying or classifying new individuals is reduced. (p. 316)

Each of these forms of generalization deserves brief discussion.

CHANGE IN ATTITUDES TOWARD THE GROUP AS A WHOLE

Many people assume that if we have contact with members of other groups, our attitudes toward those groups will become more positive. This result, however, is not necessarily the case. Research on intergroup contact suggests that contact can promote better relations between groups or increase hostility between groups. The question that needs to be answered is, When does contact lead to better relations between groups?

In his review of research on intergroup contact, Stephan (1985) isolates 13 characteristics of the contact situation that are necessary for positive attitude change toward a social group to occur as a result of our individual contact with specific strangers:

1. Cooperation within groups should be maximized and competition between groups should be minimized.
2. Members of the in-group and the out-group should be of equal status both within and outside the contact situation.
3. Similarity of group members on nonstatus dimensions (beliefs, values, etc.) appears to be desirable.
4. Differences in competence should be avoided.
5. The outcomes should be positive.
6. Strong normative and institutional support for the contact should be provided.
7. The intergroup contact should have the potential to extend beyond the immediate situation.
8. Individuation of group members should be promoted.
9. Nonsuperficial contact (e.g., mutual disclosure of information) should be encouraged.
10. The contact should be voluntary.
11. Positive effects are likely to correlate with the duration of the contact.
12. The contact should occur in a variety of contexts with a variety of in-group and out-group members.
13. Equal numbers of in-group and out-group members should be used. (p. 643)

Although this list is long, Stephan points out that it is incomplete. If we want to design a program to reduce prejudice or ethnocentrism, we, therefore, must make sure that the contact we arrange meets as many of these conditions as possible.

Increased Complexity of Intergroup Perceptions

This form of generalization involves seeing the social category as heterogeneous (i.e., different), rather than homogeneous (i.e., alike). In other words, we can increase the complexity of our intergroup perceptions by recognizing how members of a social category are different. Think of the social groups males and females. Are all males and all females the same? Obviously, the answer is no. We see differences among males and among females and place them in subcategories. Females, for example, may categorize males into "male chauvinists" and "feminists."

Increasing the complexity of our intergroup perceptions is consistent with Langer's notion of mindfulness. As you may recall from Chapter 2, one aspect of becoming mindful of our communication is the creation of new categories. Creating new categories for Langer means differentiating among the individuals within the broad social categories we use. It means increasing the number of "discriminations" we make—using specific rather than global labels (e.g., a person with a lame leg, rather than "a cripple"). When we are mindful of differences among the members of the various outgroups with whom we communicate, our expectations are based on the subcategories, not the broader social category.

Decategorization

Decategorization occurs when we communicate with strangers on the basis of their individual characteristics, rather than the categories in which we place them (i.e., communication is interpersonal, not intergroup). In order to accomplish this goal, we must differentiate individual strangers from their groups. Differentiation alone, however, is not sufficient for decategorization or personalization to occur.

When we personalize or decategorize our interactions with strangers, personal identity takes on more importance than social identity.

> To illustrate this distinction, consider the statement "Janet is a nurse." This description can be psychologically represented in one of two ways. It could mean that Janet is subordinate to (i.e., a specific instance of) the general category of nurses. Or it could mean that being a nurse is subordinate to (i.e., a particular characteristic of) the concept of Janet. The former interpretation is an example of category-based individuation, and the latter is an example of personalization. (Brewer & Miller, 1988, p. 318)

The difference lies in how we process the information. If we focus on the strangers' personal identities, we can decrease the degree to which their social identities affect our expectations.

Changing our attitudes toward outgroups, increasing the complexity of our intergroup perceptions, and decategorization can all change our expectations of strangers. To create positive expectations and improve our relations with members of other groups, we need to use all three processes simultaneously.

In conclusion, the answer to the question posed at the beginning of this section, therefore, is that our stereotypes and attitudes of ethnocentrism and prejudice are not set for life; they can and do change on the basis of our communication with strangers. We can develop accurate or favorable stereotypes and become less ethnocentric and prejudiced if we have contact with strangers under favorable conditions. If we have contact with strangers under unfavorable conditions (e.g., nonrewarding, superficial contact with strangers of lower status), we must consciously analyze the interaction so it does not increase our prejudice and ethnocentrism. We do not mean to suggest that being ethnocentric and prejudiced is "bad."

Holding such attitudes is natural and unavoidable. Rather, we are suggesting that in order to communicate effectively with strangers, we must understand their behavior, and in order to understand their behavior, we must be able at least to suspend, or to manage, our stereotypes, ethnocentrism, and prejudice.

SUMMARY

The stereotypes we develop and the intergroup attitudes we hold are learned as part of our socialization into our culture and the various groups of which we are members. In turn, the intergroup attitudes and the stereotypes we develop create expectations for how strangers will behave.

The stereotypes we hold provide the initial predictions we make about strangers' behavior at both the cultural and sociocultural levels. To the degree that our stereotypes are valid, we will be able to make accurate predictions about strangers' behavior. Also, if we are not willing to question our stereotypes, we will never be able to make accurate psychocultural predictions about strangers. In other words, if our stereotypes are rigidly held, we will never get to know strangers as individuals.

The two major attitudes influencing our communication with strangers are prejudice and ethnocentrism. High levels of either of these attitudes lead us to misinterpret strangers' behavior. Being very ethnocentric, for example, impels us to interpret strangers' behavior by using our own cultural standards. This tendency inevitably causes us to misinterpret strangers' behavior and to make inaccurate predictions about their behavior, thereby increasing the likelihood of misunderstandings. Since it is natural for everyone to be prejudiced and ethnocentric to some degree, we must consciously control our attitudinal responses if we are to communicate effectively with strangers.

STUDY QUESTIONS

1. How do expectations influence our communication with strangers?
2. Why are stereotypes a natural product of the communication process?
3. How do stereotypes influence our communication?
4. How does the use of stereotypes lead to inaccurate predictions?
5. How does ethnocentrism have positive consequences? negative consequences?
6. How does ethnocentrism influence the distances we create from strangers?
7. How is prejudice different from ethnocentrism? How are the two similar?
8. How does prejudice influence the way we communicate with strangers?
9. How do we adapt the way we talk about strangers?
10. How is sexism manifested in our language usage?
11. How is ageism manifested in our language usage?
12. Why is it important that we respond to others when they engage in prejudiced behavior or speak in a prejudiced manner?
13. How can we change our expectations for strangers' behavior?

SUGGESTED READING

Essed, P. (1991). *Understanding everyday racism.* Thousand Oaks, CA: Sage.

Kleg, M. (1993). *Hate, prejudice and racism.* Albany: State University of New York Press.

Leyens, J., Yzerbyt, V., & Schadron, G. (1994). *Stereotypes and social cognition.* Thousand Oaks, CA: Sage.

Mackie, D., & Hamilton, D. (Eds.). (1994). *Affect, cognition, and stereotyping.* New York: Academic Press.

Potter, J., & Wetherell, M. (1987). *Discourse and social psychology.* London: Sage.

van Dijk, T. (1984). *Prejudice in discourse.* Amsterdam: Benjamins.

Whilock, R., & Slayden, D. (Eds.). (1995). *Hate speech.* Thousand Oaks, CA: Sage.

Zanna, M., & Olsen, J. (Eds.). (1994). *The psychology of prejudice.* Hillsdale, NJ: Erlbaum.

6

Environmental Influences
on the Process

*Physical concepts are free creations of the
human mind, and are not, however it may seem,
uniquely determined by the external world.*
Albert Einstein

The purpose of this chapter is to complete our examination of the major influences on our communication behavior. In the preceding three chapters, we looked at the cultural, sociocultural, and psychocultural influences on our communication with strangers. In this chapter, we examine the environmental influences on our communication behavior.

The environment in which interaction occurs influences the communication taking place. These environmental influences, however, are generally outside our awareness. The environmental influence on behavior is so strong that Lewin (1936) includes it as one of the two factors in his definition of behavior: $B = f(P,E)$, where B = behavior, P = person, and E = environment. Lewin believes the behavior in which we engage is a function of us and the person with whom we are communicating, as well as of the environment within which the interaction takes place. In Lewin's analysis, the environment is divided into the physical environment and the psychological environment, or what people think about the physical environment. Both aspects of the environment influence communication. To illustrate the influence of the psychological environment, we need only look at the research on the influence of different types of rooms on behavior. When we enter a room, we rarely feel indifferent about it (Saarinen, 1948). Mintz (1956) found that prolonged exposure to an "ugly" room brings about such reactions "as monotony, fatigue, headache, sleep, discontent, irritability, hostility, and avoidance of the room" (p. 466). Exposure to a "beautiful" room, on the other hand, brings about "feelings of comfort, pleasure, enjoyment, importance, energy, and a desire to continue [the] activity" (p. 466).

The physical setting and the situation in which communication occurs define what is proper. Obviously, such settings as an office behind closed doors, an elevator, a living room, a bedroom, and a formal dining room suggest different forms of communication within any particular culture. People within a culture are taught during the socialization process what is appropriate to talk about in each of these different settings. Deutsch (1954) observes that "it is evident that behavior settings are 'coercive' primarily because there exist shared frames of reference of collective action as to what is appropriate behavior in a given behavior setting or with a given behavior-object" (p. 194). (The preceding should not be taken to suggest the same communication cannot occur in different settings, because it can and does.) The setting in which the communication occurs also performs the additional function of defining boundaries about how to interpret messages. The same message transmitted in different settings can have two entirely different meanings. A physician asking a member of the opposite sex to remove his or her clothes means one thing in the physician's office, for example, but an entirely different thing in a bedroom; only the context tells the receiver how to interpret the message. A "social act is always interpreted in relation to some normative context" (Deutsch, 1961, p. 398).

The physical setting takes on increased importance for at least two reasons when we communicate with strangers. First, what is appropriate behavior in a particular setting can differ across cultures. In some cultures (e.g., the United States), being in the living room of a home calls for informal behavior, while in other cultures, being in the living room calls for formal behavior. Second, when we communicate with strangers, the strangers are often in a physical setting unfamiliar to them. The strangers, therefore, may not know what behavior is expected in that setting. The strangers also may not have the "sense of place" necessary to understand in an ordered fashion what is going on in their lives (Downs & Stea, 1977).

We divide our discussion of the environmental influences on our communication with strangers into four sections: the physical environment, the situation, situational norms and rules, and the psychological environment. The *physical environment,* as we are using the term, involves geography, climate, landscape, and architecture. The situation is the setting in which communication occurs. The norms and rules guiding our behavior are a function of the situation in which our communication takes place. The psychological environment encompasses our perceptions of the physical environment and the situation, our perceptual and cognitive beliefs about the environment, and how we use the environment when we interact with one another.

THE PHYSICAL ENVIRONMENT

The physical environment in which our communication occurs influences how we communicate. If you are sitting on the deck of your house in shorts looking at the

Pacific Ocean in January, you will be in a different frame of mind than if you are driving in the middle of a blizzard in the midwest. In addition to the climate, the geographical location and the built environment in our culture influence the way we communicate. We begin our discussion of the physical environment by looking at geography and climate.

Geography and Climate

Few anthropologists would disagree "with the general statement that environment is an important conditioner of culture" (Meggers, 1954, p. 801). Meggers argues that "the primary point of interaction between a culture and its environment is in terms of subsistence, and the most vital aspect of environment from the point of view of culture is its suitability for food production" (p. 802). The geographical location of a culture also has other influences. "It would seem almost obvious that mountains or flat terrain, barren or fertile land, and the availability of resources, particularly of water, would affect human institutions and thereby alter the forms of social behavior" (Barnlund, 1968, p. 512).

Another factor in the physical environment closely associated with geography is climate, including temperature and humidity. Climatic factors have subtle influences on behavior. Hippocrates observed that

> Asia (Minor) differs widely from Europe in the nature of all its inhabitants and its vegetation. . . . the one region is less wild than the other, the character of its inhabitants is milder and more gentle.The cause of this is the temperate climate, because it lies toward the east midway between risings of the sun, further away than is Europe from the cold. (cited by Biswas, 1984, p. 6)

Huntington (1945) argues that living in the midlatitudes produces the greatest productivity and efficiency. McClelland (1961) concurs, arguing that climate affects the achievement of people in different societies. Further, it often is pointed out that murder rates in the United States increase during the summer months when the temperature and humidity rise.

Climate also influences the frequency and the form of the interactions taking place in a culture. Some cultures exist in climates so hot and muggy that it is impossible to do business during certain parts of the day. When strangers from a more moderate climate visit these cultures, they must make adjustments if they are to cope with the differences.

Climatic variations also exist within cultures. Andersen, Lustig, and Andersen (1990) examined the influence of climate in the United States on interpersonal communication. They found that "the southern culture is more verbally dominant, opinionated, intolerant, and authoritarian than are relatively more northern US cultures" (p. 305). Their data also suggest that northerners are more touch avoidant, open, and confirming than southerners. Andersen et al. suggest that in the United States, individuals might proactively choose their place of residence to match their communication needs. They suggest that sun lovers and outdoor recreationists might be more attracted to the sunbelt and the corresponding arousal, esteem, social independence, and isolation that it provides. Other individuals, who prefer closer social networks, more interpersonal dependence, and less arousal might be happier in the social climates that the more northern latitudes create. (p. 306)

While this explanation might work for highly mobile cultures like the United States, it does not explain the effect of climatic differences on behavior around the world. People in the vast majority of the cultures in the world are not as geographically mobile as people in the United States and cannot choose the climate in which they want to live.

Architecture and Landscape

Those aspects of the environment constructed by the human population of a culture also influence our communication behavior. Borrowing an analogy from the theater, we might say that the architecture and landscape, combined with the geography and climate, provide the stage for the human players. "The streets of Calcutta, the avenues of Brazilia, the Left Bank of Paris, the gardens of Kyoto, the slums of Chicago, and the canyons of lower Manhattan provide dramatically different backgrounds for human interaction" (Barnlund, 1968, p. 512). The physical structure of buildings, as well as the way they are decorated, is influenced by culture and also influences the interaction occurring within them. Winston Churchill often is quoted as saying, "We shape our buildings, and afterwards our buildings shape us." Conversations on the same topic held in an adobe house in New Mexico and a Japanese house in Kyoto will, in all likelihood, not be the same. Many aspects of architecture and landscape vary across cultures; however, we focus here on the aspect most central to people's lives—housing.

Rapoport (1969) argues that while the physical environment influences the way houses are designed and constructed, the design of houses also is influenced by the culture in which they are built. Human shelter varies from buildings with one room to structures with several hundred. Not only do the physical aspects of houses (e.g., construction material, size, shape, layout of rooms) differ across cultures, but how the house and its parts are defined and perceived also varies. Is the house, for example, a place where visitors are entertained, or is it reserved for only close friends and family? Do certain rooms in the house have a single function (e.g., sleeping), or is the same room used for several different functions (e.g., sleeping, eating, and entertaining guests)? Obviously, tremendous variation exists in the construction and perception of houses within any one culture; nevertheless, many similarities remain relatively constant. These similarities may not be obvious until houses based on other cultural assumptions are confronted. In order to illustrate cross-cultural variations in housing, we look at Japanese, Arab, German, and Latin American homes.

In most houses in the United States, particular rooms are designated to fill specific functions (e.g., eating in the dining room, sleeping in the bedroom). These distinctions, however, are not made in traditional Japanese homes (the distinctions, however, are made in many contemporary Japanese homes). The same room often is used for dining, entertaining, and sleeping. This combining of functions is accomplished through the use of very little furniture in traditional Japanese homes (and traditional rooms in contemporary houses). Rooms are separated by sliding walls (those made with rice paper are called *shoji*), rather than by fixed walls as in the United States. In a traditional Japanese home, therefore, people cannot go into their own room and lock the door to be alone. Floors in a traditional Japanese home are covered with straw mats *(tatami)*; therefore, people remove their shoes upon entering a house.

What furniture there is in a Japanese home usually is found in the center of the room rather than around the edges as in the United States. The multipurpose room usually has one single low table, which is used for many activities (e.g., studying, eating). Rather than sitting in chairs by the table, Japanese sit on cushions that can be moved easily when it is time for the room to change its function. When it is time to sleep, the table and cushions are removed, thick sleeping mats *(futons)* are laid out, and the room becomes a bedroom.

While the Japanese do not tend to make the distinctions made in the United States between dining room, living room, and bedroom, they do make a distinction between the bath and toilet. In the United States, the bath and toilet are found in the same room, while in Japan, the two rooms are separate. The bath *(ofuro)* is only for bathing (becoming clean), not for the "dirty" function of using the toilet *(otearai)*.

In contrast to Japanese homes, Arab homes tend to have a lot of space, very high ceilings, and unobstructed views (Hall, 1966). The desire for an unobstructed view is so strong that one way to get even with neighbors is to obstruct the view from their home. Hall (1966) points to a structure built by a person in Beirut that is several stories high but only four feet wide. The house is referred to as the "spite house" by local residents because it was built for the purpose of punishing neighbors by blocking their view of the Mediterranean.

Like people in the United States, but unlike the Japanese, Arabs tend to entertain guests in their homes. The amount and type of contact guests have in a house, however, is determined by their relationship with the family. In a typical Arab home, all rooms look alike, with the function of each room decided by the family, but one room usually is set aside for entertaining guests. In this room, the family displays heirlooms, souvenirs, and the best furnishings (Condon & Yousef, 1975). Guests who are not longtime friends usually are entertained in this room and may never see any other part of the house. By entertaining guests in the most formal part of the home and introducing them only to selected family members, "the guest is honored and the family status is reflected" (Condon & Yousef, 1975, p. 160). As guests become accepted by the family, they may see other parts of the house. Indicators of this change in status are increases in the length of visits and opportunities to meet family members of the opposite sex (Arabs may be friends for years without meeting their friends' family members of the opposite sex).

German homes tend to be surrounded by hedges and fences in order to ensure privacy, a pervasive value in German life (Condon & Yousef, 1975). "The ideal German home has a foyer or entryway that leads visitors into the house without exposing them to specific rooms and a resultant loss of privacy for the family members" (Condon & Yousef, 1975, p. 165). The most formal room in the house is the living room *(wohnsimmer),* which is used for entertaining guests. Unlike children in the United States, German children who are old enough to greet guests are expected to come into the living room when a guest arrives and remain for the length of the visit, speaking only when someone speaks to them.

A typical German home, like a typical German office, is characterized by large furniture and heavy doors (Hall, 1966). The large furniture, according to Hall, is used so guests will not be tempted to move the furniture and change the order of the room. A heavy door performs two functions. First, because of its weight, the door serves a soundproofing function when closed, thus fulfilling the German desire for privacy. Second, since the door typically is closed, in both homes and offices, it preserves the "integrity of the room and provides a protective boundary between people" (Hall, 1966, p. 136).

The typical middle-class Colombian home is built much closer to the street than is the typical North American home (Gorden, 1974). Generally, the front yard is very small, while the backyard is large and enclosed with a high fence. Each house abuts the houses on either side. There is no yard space between houses; only double walls separate houses. This pattern of constructing houses is different from the common one in North America, but the two patterns appear to be aimed at the same goal—privacy. Gorden observes that "privacy in the United States is obtained by increasing the open space between a person and his [or her] neighbor, while in Bogota it is achieved by abutting walls with no doors or windows" (p. 16).

Colombians tend to invite kinfolk into their homes, but not coworkers or neighbors. People may work side by side for years, and live near each other, but never see the inside of each other's homes. Gorden (1974) points out that the house "is more strictly a family thing in the sense of a tendency to exclude nonrelatives and to include relatives beyond the nuclear family" (pp. 22–23).

The various rooms in a Colombian home have functions different from those of the same rooms in a North American home. The living room, for example, in a Colombian home is a formal room not used for family gatherings. A bedroom, in contrast, may be used for family gatherings and entertaining friends. In discussing problems North Americans had when living with Colombian host families, Gorden (1974) points out that

> some misunderstandings between the [North] American guest and the Colombian host hinge upon the basic difference in their assumptions regarding the function of a bedroom. Both cultures accept the bedroom as a place to sleep, to make conjugal love, and to read, but beyond that there is little agreement. The [North] American thinks of it (particularly when he [or she] is in a foreign country) as a place to retreat, to find privacy, to study, to listen to records. The Colombian host families did not agree on all these things. The señora thinks of her bedroom as being a place to socialize with her friends, to watch television with members of the family and with friends. (p. 51)

North Americans taking refuge in the bedroom, therefore, often are perceived as "aloof" by the Colombian host family.

In trying to make sense of cultural differences in housing, Altman and Gauvain (1981) proposed a dialectical relationship encompassing culture, behavior, and the home environment. They contend that the home environment that predominates in a culture reflects the degree to which members of the culture try to cope with two sets of dialectical opposites: identity-communality and accessibility-inaccessibility. The *identity-communality dialectic* involves the degree to which houses reflect the uniqueness and individuality of the occupants (i.e., the personal or family identity of the occupants) or the ties of the occupants (i.e., their communality) with the larger culture. The *accessibility-inaccessibility dialectic* reflects the degree to which the home environment emphasizes the openness or closedness of the occupants to outsiders. The differences Altman and Gauvain observed can be related to individualism-collectivism. It appears that middle-class homes in individualistic cultures are separated from the community at large through the use of front yards, backyards, gates, and lawns. The furniture and decor of homes in individualistic cultures illustrate the desire of the occupants to differentiate themselves from others. In middle-class homes in collectivistic cultures, in contrast, the architectural design of the home is integrated with central plazas, a community center, or other neighborhood dwellings. The furniture and decor in these homes expresses the group identity and the communal desire of getting together.

THE SITUATION

One approach we could use to understand how situations influence our communication is to examine the objective characteristics of the situation, such as the physical location (whether it is a classroom or living room in a home) and its characteristics. The objective characteristics of situations, however, are not good predictors of our behavior (Cody & McLaughlin, 1985). A better predictor of how people behave in a particular situation is how they perceive the situation. Understanding what is required of us in a particular situation helps us manage our uncertainty and anxiety.

Situations can be divided into two broad components: the scene and the participants (Brown & Fraser, 1979). The *scene* tells us the setting and the purpose of the interaction. The *setting* includes the locale of the interaction, the time of the interaction, and the bystanders observing the interaction. The *purpose* of the interaction focuses on the type of activity in which the individuals are engaged and the subject matter of the conversation. The type of activity involves the individuals' goals for the interaction and the roles they are filling, such as professor or student, clerk or customer, and friend. The subject matter includes the task being completed and the specific topic of conversation.

The *participants* are divided into two components: the individual participants and the relationships between the participants (Brown & Fraser, 1979). Two aspects of the *individual participants* are relevant. People act not only as individuals, on the basis of their personality, physical appearance, moods, or attitudes, but also as members of social groups, such as members of their culture, ethnic group, class, sex, or age group. Two aspects of the *relationship between participants* influence their behavior: the interpersonal relations between the people communicating (such as whether they like each other or whether they know each other) and the roles/categories they are filling (such as the relative difference in power and status between the people).

The participants' perceptions of the situation are critical to understanding their behavior in any situation (Brown & Fraser, 1979). Understanding how perceptions of situations influence our communication behavior is important in improving the quality of our communication. Let's begin by looking at the setting.

Setting

The setting for communication involves the locale of the interaction with others, the time of our interaction, and the bystanders who observe our interaction. The physical space in which interaction occurs and the "props" that are present influence the way we communicate. Large spaces provide opportunities for communication different from those provided by small spaces. Space divided into many regions, such as offices or hallways, leads to types of communication different from those of open spaces. The physical appearance of the locale also affects our communication. Where interactions take place "offers a host of cues that tell people how to orient themselves" (Turner, 1988, p. 156). The cues provided by the locale of our interaction make coordination of our behavior easier and allow for smoother interaction. Without the cues that are provided by the locale, we would have to seek information to know how to expect others to act in specific situations.

Who is present (bystanders) in the situation also influences our communication. The status of the people who are observing our behavior influences how we present ourselves (Goffman, 1959). We tend to be more concerned with how we present ourselves if there are high-status bystanders than if the bystanders are low in status. We try to gain other people's favor and use self-enhancing statements more when there are high-status bystanders than when low-status bystanders are present (Ralston, 1985).

The degree to which we are familiar with bystanders also influences how we present ourselves in particular situations. Since people with whom we are familiar already have an impression of us, we tend to be more concerned about the impression we make on unfamiliar bystanders than on familiar bystanders. The familiarity of the bystanders also influences the way we explain our behavior in situations. The more familiar the people are, the more likely we are to provide justifications for our behavior (try to explain our internal states and how they affect our behavior; Cody & McLaughlin, 1985). Justifications of our behavior, however, do not appear to work well with people we do not know.

Purpose

The purpose of our interaction with others is based on the type of activity in which we are engaged and the subject matter we are discussing. Let's begin with type of activity.

The type of activity in which we are engaged influences the scripts we use to guide our behavior. The more we engage in particular activities, the more likely we are to learn scripts for the activity. A *script* is "a coherent sequence of events expected by the individual, involving him [or her] either as a participant or an observer" (Abelson, 1976, p. 33). Scripts are cognitive structures that help us understand the situations in which we find ourselves. Scripts, therefore, help us reduce the uncertainty we have about various situations (Berger & Bradac, 1982). We learn scripts by participating in the situation or by observing others participate (Abelson, 1976). We have learned both task oriented and nontask oriented scripts. In a situation, we have to figure out whether we have a script for the situation and what our role in the script is. This process, however, takes place at relatively low levels of awareness. Once we recognize the script, we know basically how we are expected to behave in the situation and we can communicate on automatic pilot. Scripts provide guides for the conversations we have in different scenes. It is important to keep in mind that people in different cultures learn different scripts for behavior.

The *task* on which we are working and the topic being discussed affect our communication in any situation. Whether we define situations as cooperative or competitive influences our perceptions of the task, and whether we define situations as intimate or superficial influences how we approach the topic. *Cooperation* involves "acting together, in a coordinated way at work, leisure, or in social relationships, in the pursuit of shared goals, the enjoyment of the joint activity, or simply furthering the relationship" (Argyle, 1991, p. 4). Defining a task as cooperative involves recognizing that the efforts of at least two people are needed and that there is a need for complementary skills and knowledge to accomplish the task. Defining tasks as cooperative has at least two major effects on our communication with others (Argyle, 1991). First, cooperation leads to positive feelings for the others participating in the task. Second, cooperation leads to interpersonal attraction toward the people with whom we are cooperating.

Our individualistic and collectivistic cultural identities influence the degree to which we perceive situations as cooperative or competitive. Collectivists in Hong Kong, for example, perceive situations as more cooperative than do individualists in Australia. Individualists in Australia, in contrast, perceive the same situations as more competitive than collectivists in Hong Kong (Forgas & Bond, 1985).

We perceive the *topic of conversations* to vary on the intimate-superficial dimension of situations. Some topics are perceived to be more intimate than others. In the United States, for example, telling someone where we were born, what we do for a living,what our political party affiliation is, and so forth is considered relatively superficial. Telling someone about our love life, in contrast, is considered intimate. There appears to be consistency in the topics considered to be intimate and superficial across cultures. Tastes and opinions are viewed as most appropriate topics for conversation, while physical attributes and personality traits are the least preferred topics for conversation, for example, in both Japan and the United States (Barnlund, 1975).

Individual Participants

We perceive the people with whom we interact as members of social groups and as individuals. Stable characteristics of individuals, such as their personalities, physical appearance, and interests, influence how they respond to us and how we respond to them in specific situations (Brown & Fraser, 1979). In addition to stable characteristics such as our personalities, our moods, attitudes, and emotions influence how we respond in situations and how others respond to them (Brown & Fraser, 1979). These characteristics differ from our personality in that our moods, emotions, and attitudes are temporary.

Our moods, emotions, and attitudes are not the only temporary aspects of our behavior that influence how others respond to us in different situations. Our speech patterns also influence the impressions others form of us and the ways they respond to us. "Standard [dialect] speakers are more positively perceived and judged than nonstandard [dialect] speakers" (Haslett, 1990, p. 332; this issue is discussed in more detail in Chapter 8).

Our group memberships and strangers' group memberships influence how we define various situations. The ways that we are socialized into the various groups of which we are members tell us how to define situations and how to expect others to behave in these situations. Strangers' group memberships influence whether we define situations as interpersonal or intergroup in nature. When we define situations as interpersonal in nature, our personal identities influence our behavior more than our social identities, and our predictions of others' behavior are based mainly on their unique characteristics (psychological data). When we define situations as mainly intergroup in nature, our social identities influence our behavior more than our personal identities, and our predictions of other people's behavior are based on their group memberships or the roles they fill (cultural or sociological data).

Some of the groups into which we categorize strangers involve some degree of stigmatization. Stigmatization involves discounting others because they are different (Goffman, 1963). Our expectations for how strangers we perceive to be stigmatized will behave in a situation are different from our expectations for those we do not perceive to be stigmatized. Strangers who are disabled, for example, often are perceived to be stigmatized by nondisabled people. Whether or not we perceive a person to be disabled influences how we communicate with her or him. A blind person describes how a taxi driver's communication changed when the taxi driver found out that he was blind:

> I could tell at first that the taxi driver didn't know that I was blind because for a while there he was quite a conversationalist. Then he asked me what these sticks were for (a collapsible cane). I told him it was a cane, and then he got so different. . . . He didn't talk about the same things as he did at first. (Davis, 1977, p. 85)

It appears that the taxi driver initially defined the situation as interpersonal in nature, but when he discovered that the passenger was blind, he redefined the situation as intergroup in nature.

Relationships Between Participants

The relationships between the participants in situations influence their communication. Both the interpersonal relations and the role/categories the individuals are filling affect the way people behave in situations. One of the major factors influencing the interpersonal relations between participants as individuals is the degree to which they are attracted to each other. Probably the most important factors influencing the attraction between participants as individuals is the degree to which they perceive themselves to be similar. When we are free to choose the people with whom we communicate, we tend to select people like us (Rogers & Bhowmik, 1971). It often is assumed that communication between people who are similar is more effective than communication between dissimilar people. Although this assumption is accepted widely, *moderate dissimilarities* between communicators who are generally similar may bring about more effective communication (Simons, Berkowitz, & Moyer, 1970).

The roles we are filling influence our communication in terms of the degree to which we define situations as formal or informal. In the United States, for example, if we are interacting with our boss in a work situation, we probably define the situation as formal. If we are interacting with our boss at a party, on the other hand, we might define the situation as informal. At the party, people in the United States may assume that the boss is filling the role of friend and, therefore, define the situation as informal rather than formal.

The extent to which we define a situation as formal or informal influences many aspects of our behavior. When we define situations as formal, we tend to use standard speech patterns (Furnham, 1986). When we view the situation as informal, in contrast, we may use a nonstandard dialect, such as a speech dialect based on our ethnicity or the region of the country in which we live. When talking in formal situations, we also speak slowly and attempt to use correct grammar. In informal situations, we may speak rapidly and not worry as much about our grammar.

How we categorize other people influences our communication in terms of the degree to which we define situations as between people who are equal or between people who are unequal. When the participants in a social situation are not equal in status, the higher-status people can define the situation by the speech patterns they use (Giles & Hewstone, 1982). Respect and authority often are established by using standard, formal speech patterns rather than using nonstandard dialects (such as a regional or ethnic dialect) and informal speech patterns. Once status is established through the use of formal language, for example, people can switch to using informal language to develop a relaxed atmosphere. If the higher-status people begin using a speech pattern designed to define the situation as informal and their authority is questioned, they are likely to switch to more formal speech patterns. If the lower-status people perceive that they are being treated unfairly in a particular situation, they can choose to redefine the situation with the speech patterns they use. The lower-status people, for example, might use their in-group speech patterns to change the definition of the situation from being based on status factors to defining the situation in terms of demonstrating solidarity with members of the ingroup.

SITUATIONAL NORMS AND RULES

Norms and rules specify the acceptable means to achieving the ends of social life in a culture. The means consist of the proscriptions and prescriptions for acceptable behavior. When the standards of acceptable behavior have moral or ethical connotations, we refer to them as norms; when there are no moral or ethical connotations in the standards, we refer to them as rules (Olsen, 1978).

Differentiating Between Norms and Rules

Norms can be defined as "rules of conduct," "blueprints for behavior," and "cultural expectations." Gibbs (1965) isolates three attributes of a *norm:* "(1) a collective evaluation of behavior in terms of what ought to be; (2) a collective expectation as to what behavior will be; [and] (3) particular reactions to behavior including attempts to apply sanctions or otherwise induce a particular kind of behavior" (p. 590). *Norms,* therefore, can be defined as socially shared guidelines for expected and accepted behaviors, violation of which leads to some form of sanction. Sanctions can vary from a disapproving look to ostracism from the group to death.

Social life is possible to the extent we take into account the existence of other people and their expected responses to our behavior. When the expectations are shared by a group of people, we can say a norm exists. Once norms are formed and we have internalized them, we tend to follow them whether or not we want to. Birenbaum and Sagarin (1976) point out that

> most people are aware that rules exist in all areas of life and take them into account when engaged in or anticipating interaction with other people. This awareness is part of the organized character of social life. . . . even when people dislike or reject a rule, it may be extremely difficult for them not to obey it, for much everyday life involves opportunities to demonstrate social competency, a factor that may override the will to disobey. Often obedience to the rule is simply reflexive, whereas transgression is effortful. (p. 4)

Two aspects of Birenbaum and Sagarin's position deserve brief elaboration. First, they are using the terms *rules* and *norms* interchangeably. Although this usage is common among people writing on norms, there are some people who use the terms differently. Olsen (1978), for example, believes norms have an ethical or moral connotation that is lacking in rules. Rules, in contrast, are developed for reasons of expediency, because they allow people to coordinate their activities more easily.

To illustrate, Olsen cites rules such as driving on the same side of the road to keep traffic running smoothly and requiring citizenship and registration in order to vote. (As noted earlier, we distinguish between norms and rules.)

The second aspect of the above quotation requiring comment is Birenbaum and Sagarin's argument that obedience to norms and rules is reflexive. Obedience to a norm or rule can be reflexive, however, only if you grow up in the culture where the rule exists and internalize it from a very early age. If a person socialized into one culture is living in or visiting another culture, obedience to the norms and rules of the host culture probably is effortful, and transgression may be reflexive. Following norms and rules in cultures other than those in which we were raised requires that we be mindful of our behavior.

Sumner (1940) divides norms into three categories: folkways, mores, and laws. Sumner views *folkways* as those pervasive everyday activities widely accepted by the people of a culture. Folkways include, but are not limited to, such actions as the way we greet others, the way we dress, the way we eat, the way we smell, the way we say good-bye, and other such actions that are widely accepted. Since folkways do not have moral or ethical connotations, they are more accurately considered rules (which are defined below) rather than norms by our terminology. *Mores,* according to Sumner, are those norms expressing strong moral demands on an individual's behavior; they are the norms believed necessary for collective action. Examples of mores include commandments derived from religious doctrine, incest taboos, and rules about what is acceptable to eat (e.g., in the United States, it is unacceptable to eat the meat of dogs, cats, and people). The final category of norms discussed by Sumner is laws. *Laws* are norms codified by a political entity such as a nation, state, or city. A law may be derived from either the folkways or the mores of a culture.

As indicated earlier, *rules* differ from norms in that rules do not have moral or ethical connotations. Noesjirwan (1978) points out that

> rules provide a statement of expected or intended behaviour and its outcome. As such, rules provide a number of related functions that serve to order social life and render it meaningful. Rules provide a set of mutual expectations, thus rendering the behaviour of each person predictable and understandable to the other. . . . The rules partly serve to define the meaning a situation has, and to define the meaning that any given action has within a situation. (pp. 305–306)

Rules, therefore, perform many of the same functions that norms do in establishing coordinated activities among individuals.

The violation of any norm or rule brings some form of sanction on the person committing the violation. The sanctions vary from a disapproving glance to the loss of life. The sanctions imposed for violation of a folkway are through interpersonal channels. If, for example, you were to "slurp" your soup in public in the United States, you probably would receive only disapproving glances from the people who heard you (of course, they may also make comments to their friends about your impolite behavior). If, on the other hand, you do *not* slurp your soup in some cultures, you may receive disapproving glances. Similarly, if you were to wear informal clothes (e.g., your best jeans) to a black-tie dinner, people would look at you disapprovingly and make comments about your lack of appropriate attire, but they would not use more severe sanctions. The violation of mores, in contrast to that of folkways, brings about more severe sanctions. An extreme example of a mos (singular of mores) in the United States is that we do not eat dogs or cats (there is a prohibition on eating dogs and cats). If people find out that you ate dog or cat meat, they will, in all likelihood, avoid you (you will be ostracized). Violations of laws obviously bring about legal sanctions. These sanctions, of course, can vary from a verbal reprimand from a judge to the death penalty.

The people of a culture are aware of some of the norms and rules guiding their behavior and unaware of many others. Even if people are aware that the norm exists, however, they probably cannot articulate all the specific behavioral expectations associated with the norm. This lack of awareness is illustrated by something as simple as a handshake. Shaking hands is a communication rule when greeting people for the first time in the United States; but what are the rules for shaking hands? Can you tell a person who has never shaken hands before, for example, someone from Mars, all the rules necessary for him or her to shake hands "correctly"? Many people would say that you grip the other person's extended hand and pump up and down. But is it that simple? What would you do if you met a person for the first time and she or he extended the left hand? That obviously isn't appropriate because we shake hands with the right hand. What if the other person extends the right hand but does not hold on to your hand (i.e., uses a "limp" grip)? Is this acceptable? No, probably not. What if the person uses the "correct" grip with the right hand and when you shake hands doesn't stop, but continues to pump up and down, up and down. How would you feel? Comfortable? Uncomfortable? Probably uncomfortable because the rule is that we pump our hands a few (one or two) times and stop. We could go on, but by now you get the point that shaking hands is not as simple as it initially seems. It is a complex process with many subtle expectations. We may not be able to explain all the expectations, but we know when they are violated.

One way to become aware of norms and communication rules guiding our behavior is to have them violated. When we interact with people from the same culture, our expectations generally are not violated often because people of the same culture share similar expectations. When we communicate with strangers, however, our behavioral expectations may be violated with much greater frequency because strangers probably learned a different set of norms in their culture. When our expectations are violated, we may react to the other person negatively; this is a "normal" reaction. There is also the possibility of positive outcomes, however. When our expectations are violated, for example, we can gain tremendous insight into the norms of our culture and how they influence our behavior. In addition, we come to see alternative behavioral patterns, which we might prefer. In other words, confronting cultural differences offers the possibility of personal growth and/or cultural change.

Cultural Differences in Norms and Rules

There are patterned cultural differences in norms and rules. We begin by looking at how the dimensions of norms and rules vary across cultures. Next, we examine cultural variations in the justice and reciprocity norms. We conclude by examining representative cross-cultural studies of rules.

Dimensions of Norms and Rules.   Rules (and norms) vary along four dimensions: (1) level of understanding, (2) specificity of actions, (3) range, and (4) homogeneity, or consensus (Cushman & Whiting, 1972). Both rules and norms can vary with respect to level of understanding. Cushman and Whiting argue that the greater the need for coordination in human activity, the greater is the degree of accuracy in understanding of the rules (and norms). Given our discussion of individualism-collectivism, we can argue there is a greater need for coordination of activity in collectivistic cultures than in individualistic cultures. There also is a correspondingly greater degree of accuracy in the understanding of rules (and norms) in collectivistic cultures than in individualistic cultures.

In addition to varying with respect to level of understanding, rules (and norms) vary with respect to the specificity of the actions required or permitted in a situation in which a rule applies and in terms of the span of situations in which particular actions are permitted or required (the range of rules). When rules have a large range and a low degree of specificity, Cushman and Whiting (1972) contend, habitual communication behavior emerges. Given the conceptualizations of individualism-collectivism, we can infer that rules (and norms) are more specific and have more range in collectivistic cultures than in individualistic cultures. In other words, rules (and norms) are more specific with respect to the behaviors permitted or required in a situation in collectivistic cultures than in individualistic cultures. Further, rules (and norms) tend to be less situation-specific (have a large range) in collectivistic cultures than in individualistic cultures, where the same rule may apply to more limited situations.

As indicated earlier, rules (and norms) also vary with respect to the degree of consensus there is about them. "The homogeneity of a rule system refers to the degree to which accurate understandings of standard usage are evenly distributed among participants in a communication system" (Cushman & Whiting, 1972, p. 233). Given the nature of collectivistic cultures, they tend to be more homogeneous than are individualistic cultures like that of the United States. Because of the homogeneity of their culture, members of collectivistic cultures are more likely to exhibit coordinated activity than are members of individualistic cultures.

Justice Norms.   There are two main orientations toward justice: the equity norm and the equality norm. The *equity norm* involves rewarding or punishing people on the basis of their effort. It is tied closely to the notion of "deservingness." The *equality norm,* in contrast, is based on rewarding or punishing people equally regardless of their input.

People in individualistic cultures tend to subscribe to the equity norm, while people in collectivistic cultures tend to subscribe to the equality norm with ingroup members. Mahler, Greenberg, and Hayashi (1981), for example, found that Japanese students prefer the equality norm for distributing rewards, while students in the United States preferred the equity norm. Leung and Bond (1982, 1984) examined justice norms in Hong Kong and the United States. They found that students in the United States prefer the equity norm and Chinese students prefer the equality norm. When students were asked to allocate rewards to ingroup and outgroup members, the Chinese used the equality norm with ingroup members more than with outgroup members.

Reciprocity Norm.   The *reciprocity norm* involves two conditions: "(1) people should help those who have helped them, and (2) people should not injure those who have helped them" (Gouldner, 1960, p. 171). The reciprocity norm is an implicit contract that binds people together.

Ting-Toomey (1986b) argues that members of individualistic cultures follow a voluntary reciprocity norm, while members of collectivistic cultures use an obligatory reciprocity norm. A voluntary reciprocity norm is based on individuals' free will and free choices. An obligatory reciprocity norm is based on requirements necessary to maintain membership in a group. Ting-Toomey also contends that members of individualistic cultures engage in short-term reciprocity (i.e., reciprocate shortly after others engage in behavior). Members of collectivistic cultures, in contrast, engage in long-term reciprocity (i.e., engage in reciprocity over the course of the relationship, not necessarily immediately following others' behavior).

Cultural Variability in Communication Rules.   Noesjirwan (1978) demonstrates how rules can be seen to vary systematically across cultures. In her study of Indonesia (collectivistic) and Australia (individualistic), she finds little systematic variation in 69 different rules, or value statements, while there are many between-culture variations in the same statements. Her study reveals, for example, different rules for dealing with other people in waiting rooms and at bus stops. The rule in both situations in Indonesia requires one to talk to any other person present. The rule for Australians in both situations, in contrast, requires one to ignore any other person present.

Argyle and Henderson (1984) argue that there are six "universal" rules in personal relationships: (1) one should respect others' privacy, (2) one should look the other person in the eye during conversations, (3) one should or should not discuss that which is said in confidence with the other person, (4) one should or should not indulge in sexual activity with the other person, (5) one should not criticize the other person in public, and (6) one should repay debts, favors, or compliments no matter how small. In testing these six rules in Hong Kong, Japan, Italy, and Britain, Argyle and his associates (1986) found that the respect-privacy rule received the strongest endorsement across cultures. The keeping-confidence rule received strong support in all cultures except Japan. The public-criticism rule was endorsed more strongly in Japan and Hong Kong than in Italy and Britain.

This finding is to be expected given that Japan and Hong Kong are collectivistic cultures and Italy and Britain are individualistic cultures. Harmony is maintained in collectivistic cultures by avoiding criticism.

This brief overview of rules should suffice to demonstrate that to communicate effectively with strangers, we must attempt to understand their rules. Noesjirwan (1978) illustrates the importance of understanding strangers' rules when she points out that "given a knowledge of the rule/value structure of the two cultures it becomes possible to predict, among other things, the likely sources of misunderstanding and conflict between those cultures, and the likely difficulties in adjustment faced by a person of one culture moving to the other" (p. 314). Should you find yourself moving from one culture to another (i.e., you are a stranger in a new culture), probably the first rule you should try to ascertain is the one regarding how members of the new culture are to communicate with strangers.

THE PSYCHOLOGICAL ENVIRONMENT

As we indicated earlier, the psychological environment refers to our perceptual and cognitive beliefs about the physical environment and how we use the physical environment when we interact with one another. Ittelson (1973) argues there are at least five levels at which we relate to the surrounding environment: (1) we have feelings about the environment, (2) we are oriented spatially within the environment, (3) we categorize phenomena in the environment, (4) we organize the environment in terms of relationships among its features, and (5) we manipulate the environment. Each of these levels can influence our behavior. Some writers, in fact, believe the psychological environment is more important than the physical environment in influencing behavior. Dubos (1981) observes that

> in addition to the influences that reach us from the outside—the world external to us—there are other influences that exist in the individual mind of each of us and that constitute our private conceptual environment. Whether primitive or poorly informed, or sophisticated and learned, each one of us lives as it were in a private world of his [or her] own. In fact, the conceptual environment may be more important than the external environment because it affects all aspects of our lives. (p. 31)

Dubos' observation suggests that we must understand strangers' perceptions of the psychological environment to communicate effectively with them.

Although very little cross-cultural research exists on differences in psychological environments, there is some relevant work that can be examined. In this section, we look at three aspects of the psychological environment: perceptions of privacy, the use of time, and the "interaction potential" of the environment.

Privacy

The concept of privacy is intertwined closely with our perceptions of the environment. Altman (1975) defines *privacy* as the "selective control of access to the self or to one's group" (p. 18). Privacy, therefore, is a mechanism that allows us to control our interaction with others. Altman differentiates between *desired privacy,* "how much or how little contact is desired at some moment in time," and *achieved privacy,* "the actual degree of contact that results from interaction with others" (p. 10). To the extent desired and achieved privacy match, we have controlled the interaction.

Altman (1975) views privacy as a dialectical process. He argues that the oppositional qualities of being closed and being open to social interaction vary over time. Our desire for privacy shifts depending on our mood and the circumstances in which we find ourselves. At the core of Altman's conceptualization is that when we regulate our privacy, we are regulating our interpersonal boundaries—the dividing lines between ourselves and others.

Altman (1975) and Altman and Chemers (1980a) argue that while the specific mechanisms for privacy vary across cultures, every culture has some method for regulating it. Privacy regulation, therefore, can be considered a cultural universal.

There is more than one type of privacy. Westin (1970) outlines four types of privacy: solitude, intimacy, anonymity, and reserve. Solitude, according to Westin, is when we are alone and cannot be observed by others, while intimacy occurs when a dyad or small group of people separate themselves from others to be alone. When we are "lost in a crowd," not expecting to be recognized by others, Westin says we are anonymous. The final type of privacy, reserve, involves "the creation of a psychological barrier against unwanted intrusion" (Westin, 1970, p. 32).

In the United States, privacy often is regulated through the use of closed doors. A closed door—whether it leads to a bedroom, den, office, or bathroom—sends the message "leave me alone!" (Altman, 1975). People in the United States tend to use other physical barriers (e.g., fences, hedges) in addition to doors as ways to achieve privacy. Such use of physical barriers is not necessarily the case in some other cultures. Hall (1966) observes that people in England do not tend to have private offices; instead, they conduct their business in open spaces. Privacy in England is achieved by speaking softly and by directing one's voice carefully, not by closing doors.

Privacy in many cultures is regulated psychologically, rather than through the use of environmental barriers. Geertz points out, for example, that in Java, it is impossible to regulate privacy through manipulation of the environment because the people do not put up physical barriers between themselves and outsiders. To North Americans, therefore, it often appears that there is no privacy at all in a Javanese household. This is not the case, however. Geertz points out that

> people speak softly, hide their feelings and even in the bosom of a Javanese family you have the feeling that you are in a public square and must behave with appropriate decorum. Javanese people shut people out with a wall of decorum, . . . with emotional restraint, and with a general lack of candor in both speech and behavior. It is not, in short, that the Javanese do not wish or value privacy, but merely that because they put up no physical or social barriers against the physical ingress of outsiders into their household life they must put up psychological ones and surround themselves with barriers of a different sort. (cited in Westin, 1970, p. 16)

Thus, Javanese privacy regulation can be described as "reserve," according to Westin's four categories.

Privacy also is regulated through the use of territory (territory is discussed in detail in Chapter 9). The concept of territory in the social sciences is very similar to its everyday usage (e.g., "my turf"). "Territorial behavior is a self/other boundary-regulation mechanism that involves personalization of or marking of a place or object and communication that it is 'owned' by a person or group" (Altman, 1975, p. 107). In other words, territorial behavior is the personalizing of an area in order to regulate communication. Perception of what constitutes "owned" territory obviously can vary across cultures. Hall (1966) compares the use of territorial boundaries in Germany and the United States. If you are standing on the porch of a house with the screen door closed, for example, you are considered to be "outside" the house in the United States. Similarly, if you "poke" your head into the door of an office, you still are considered to be outside the office. In Germany, the person in both of these situations is considered to be "inside," or within the other person's territory. Germans consider people to be inside their territory if they can see inside; if you can see, you are intruding.

Gudykunst and Ting-Toomey (1988) argue that privacy regulation is influenced by individualism-collectivism and that the way privacy is regulated affects the degree to which people self-disclose. They suggest that in individualistic cultures, people use physical space to assert their privacy and to provide a boundary between themselves and others. Because privacy is controlled through the use of physical space, individualists can allow themselves to be assessable through verbal self-disclosure. In collectivistic cultures, in contrast, people do not use physical space to control privacy or to set up a boundary between themselves and others. Rather, they use psychological mechanisms to control their privacy. Since psychological mechanisms are used, collectivists must be careful about how they allow themselves to be assessable through the use of verbal self-disclosure.

Baker and Gudykunst (1990) isolate differences in how individualists from the United States and collectivists from Japan indicate to others that they want privacy on a particular topic of conversation. The predominate way the individualists indicate a desire for privacy is to not be attentive to the person with whom they are communicating when the particular topic was discussed. The collectivists, in contrast, use indirect verbal communication (e.g., being evasive, starting to talk about something else).

Before we proceed, one final aspect of privacy must be mentioned briefly—the issue of crowding. Crowding is different from density. Density of population involves the concentration of people within a certain geographical area (e.g., the number of people per square mode). It is a physical indicator with no psychological meaning. *Crowding,* on the other hand, is a psychological phenomenon; it is the subjective feeling associated with too little space. According to Altman's definition of privacy, "crowding occurs when a privacy regulation system malfunctions, such that more social contact occurs than was originally desired" (Altman & Chemers, 1980a, p. 374). Altman and Chemers argue that when crowding is perceived, psychological stress is generated. This stress, in turn, motivates us to make increased attempts to return to the desired level of social interaction.

Although there is yet no research across cultures comparing responses to crowding, a few general observations can be made. People in some cultures have developed coping mechanisms for dealing with high levels of population density. The Japanese, for example, have a very high population density (a population approximately one-half of that of the United States in a geographical area about the size of Montana), which requires the development of sophisticated coping mechanisms. One of these mechanisms is to treat people who are encountered in public, but who are unknown as "nonpersons," that is, as if they were not there. Treating people as if they are not there is accomplished through the use of psychological methods of privacy regulation rather than physical methods.

One major problem in communicating with strangers occurs when a person from a culture using physical methods of privacy regulation visits, lives, or works in a culture using psychological methods of privacy regulation. A North American visiting Japan, for example, invariably feels crowded and evaluates the people as being "pushy" or having no concern for others, when in fact they just have a different privacy regulation system.

Temporality

Cultures develop temporal patterns of life that are part of the psychological environment. These patterns define when it is appropriate to do certain things (e.g., sleep, eat, arrive for meetings), as well as how many things it is appropriate to do at the same time. Hall (1959) distinguishes between monochronic and polychronic time patterns. *Monochronic time* involves compartmentalization; people compartmentalize their time and schedule one event at a time. *Polychronic time,* in contrast, does not involve compartmentalization; people tend to engage in several activities at the same time. People in monochronic time cultures tend to perceive time as a linear progression marching from the past into the future. They tend to treat time as a tangible, discrete entity, which can be "saved," "borrowed," "divided," "lost," and even "killed." People in polychronic time cultures, on the other hand, tend to treat time in a holistic way and to place a primary value on the activities occurring in time, rather than on the clock time itself. Polychronic time cultures stress completion of transactions rather than adherence to schedules. Thus in many polychronic time systems, punctuality is not as sacred as it is in monochronic time systems. If something important needs to be completed, the polychronic time person can sacrifice the next scheduled activity more readily than can the monochronic time person. It is not uncommon in a monochronic time system to see some of the most exciting activities being stopped abruptly simply because "time is up."

Hall (1959) equates the use of monochronic time with cultures characterized by low levels of involvement among people and the use of polychronic time with cultures characterized by high levels of involvement among people. Cultures like those of the United States and most of Europe, which are characterized by low levels of involvement among their people, tend to have compartmentalized time schedules. Cultures like those of Latin America and the Arab states, in contrast, which are characterized by high levels of involvement among their people, tend to use polychronic time patterns in which several activities are scheduled for the same time.

African cultures generally are viewed as polychronic time systems that are not very clock-bound. Africans do have their objective time systems, but these are based more on seasonal cycles, natural events, and biological rhythms and are therefore generally more flexible, less rigid, and less segmented (Harris & Moran, 1979). Because of this relative flexibility, Africans tend to consider people in a hurry with suspicion and distrust. Since trust is very important among them, they want to sit and talk—get to know the other person—even in business transactions. If a North American businessperson appears to them to be too task oriented, for example, the Africans may interpret it as planned foul play, arrogance, or insincerity.

Another example illustrates the difference between the two systems. Members of the United States Foreign Service assigned to an Arab country for the first time are bound to feel "insulted" when they arrive for a meeting with their Arab counterpart and find several other people in the counterpart's office doing business at the same time. There is, however, no reason to feel insulted; they have just encountered a different time pattern.

The Sioux Indians provide another example of a differing orientation toward time. Hall (1959) gives an account of a Sioux Indian school superintendent concerning the time behavior of his culture:

> During a long and fascinating account of the many problems which his tribe was having in adjusting to our way of life, he suddenly remarked: "What would you think of a people who had no word for time? My people have no word for 'late' or for 'waiting,' for that matter. They don't know what it is to wait or to be late." (p. 25)

These differences may be due to the language spoken. This issue is discussed in more detail in Chapter 8.

We can observe similar variations in temporal orientation between urban and rural areas. Such large urban areas as New York City present an extremely time-bound and monochronic temporal environment. Most remote rural areas and small towns, on the other hand, still maintain a less rigid, less segmented, and less hurried temporal environment.

Another aspect of time that varies across cultures involves the time of arrival for appointments. Hall (1959) differentiates five time intervals for arriving late for appointments: (1) "mumble something" period, (2) slight apology period, (3) mildly insulting period, (4) rude period, and (5) downright insulting period. In the United States, for example, if you are 5 minutes late for an appointment, you mumble something about why you were late and that is sufficient. If you are 10 to 15 minutes late, you would probably make a slight apology to the person with whom you have the appointment. If you are 45 to 60 minutes late for an appointment, you are being downright insulting (and probably should get down on your knees and beg for forgiveness). Other cultures are not as time conscious as the United States. In Latin American and Arab cultures, time is treated differently. It is not unusual for a person to be 45 minutes late for an appointment; however, this period is not considered an insult, but is seen as falling into the "mumble something" category. A North American who has an appointment to do business in Latin America often finds this "cavalier" attitude toward time frustrating; similarly, a Latin American doing business in North America finds the more "rigid" time schedule frustrating.

Interaction Potential of the Environment

The final aspect of the psychological environment to be discussed is the "interaction potential" of the environment. The *interaction potential* is the potential the environment provides for interacting with strangers. The type of contact individuals have the opportunity to have with members of other groups depends on the structural conditions of the environment (Jaspars & Warnaen, 1982). Kanter (1977) argues that feeling "different" depends on the relative numbers of people present. In organizations, for example, Kanter contends that when there are "tokens," or only a few people who are not part of the majority group (i.e., strangers), these people feel more pressure to conform. Because of this pressure, strangers may try to become invisible.

Blau and Schwartz (1984) argue that group memberships provide structural constraints in the establishment of intergroup relationships. They contend that the size of the ingroup influences the amount of contact people have with members of outgroups; as the size of the ingroup increases, the likelihood of contact with members of the outgroup decreases and the more likely people are to interact with members of their own group. Blau and Schwartz also suggest that the more heterogeneous the environment (i.e., increases in the number of different groups represented in the environment), the more intergroup contact occurs.

Blau and Schwartz's (1984) theory suggests that the more strangers from the same group there are in an environment, the less likely the strangers will interact with members of the ingroup. This argument is supported by extensive research. Hoffman (1985), for example, found that as the relative numbers of strangers increases in organizations (i.e., there are more strangers), the strangers' communication with members of their own group increases. In related research, Hallinan and Smith (1985) found that opportunities for contact influenced the development of interracial friendships in children. Children from the numerical minority group developed more interracial friendships than children from the numerical majority.

Another way of understanding the influence of the cultural composition of the environment is to look at the institutional completeness of the community. Breton (1964), for example, argues that the degree to which immigrants are assimilated into local communities depends on the availability of ethnic institutions (e.g., churches, markets, publications) to meet their needs. In comparing immigrants from 30 different ethnic backgrounds in Montreal, Breton found that the more complete the ethnic institutional support for the immigrants, the more likely they were to develop personal ties within their ethnic group and not with majority members of the local community. Inglis and Gudykunst's (1982) study comparing Korean immigrants in Hartford, Connecticut, (which has a low level of institutional completeness) with Koreans from Kim's (1978b) study in Chicago (which has a relatively complete institutional system) supported Breton's conclusion.

In summary, in order to understand strangers' behavior, we must take into consideration their relative numbers in the environment. The fewer strangers from a particular group there are in the environment, the more likely the strangers are to seek out contact with members of the ingroup. As the number of strangers from a particular group increases, there is a tendency for them to associate with other strangers from their group. One of the major reasons is that people tend to be attracted to people who are similar to themselves, assuming there are other people in the environment who are like them. We discuss the effects of similarity in more detail in Chapter 10.

SUMMARY

The environment and our perceptions of the environment influence our communication with strangers, as well as our communication as strangers. The physical environment—geography, climate, landscape, and architecture—influences our feelings, emotions, and attitudes, which in turn influence our communication behavior. In addition, certain aspects of the physical environment have a direct impact on the predictions we make about others' behavior and the way we interpret incoming stimuli. A North American exchange student (a stranger) visiting a Colombian family in the living room of their home, for example, probably would predict that informal behavior is called for in that setting and would act accordingly. Such a prediction, however, would not be accurate since the living room in a Colombian home is set aside for formal behavior. In order to make accurate predictions and correctly interpret incoming stimuli, we must know how the person with whom we are communicating defines the setting in which our communication is taking place. This knowledge is necessary when we are communicating with strangers on our "home turf," as well as when we are strangers on others' "home turf."

Situations are an important aspect of the environment that influences our behavior. The physical setting provides important cues that we use in determining how we should communicate. Our purpose in the situation also plays a large role in determining how we communicate in that particular situation. The people who are present and our relationship with them tell us whether we should speak formally, use a standard dialect, avoid certain topics of discussion, and so forth.

The norms and rules of our culture tell us the prescribed and proscribed methods for behaving in specific situations. Since norms and rules tend to vary systematically across cultures, our behavioral expectations tend to be violated with greater frequency when we communicate with strangers than when we communicate with people who are known. Knowing the norms and rules guiding strangers' behavior, as well as those guiding our own behavior, can help us communicate more effectively with strangers.

Our perceptions of the environment also have a direct influence on how we interpret incoming stimuli and make predictions about others' behavior. People in some cultures perceive physical barriers (e.g., closed doors, fences) as regulators of their privacy, while people in other cultures do not perceive physical barriers as a mechanism of privacy regulation. Rather, they perceive privacy as being regulated by psychological barriers (e.g., pretending the other person is not there). Misunderstandings can occur whenever people from one type of culture find themselves to be strangers in another type of culture. As strangers, they will be unable to find the privacy they want or desire because people of the host culture do not recognize the same barriers. Similarly, the hosts, in all likelihood, will misinterpret the strangers' behavior.

STUDY QUESTIONS

1. How do geography and climate influence the way we communicate?
2. How do architecture and landscape influence our communication?
3. Why does having cues provided by the locale in which we communicate make our interactions smoother than if we did not have those cues?
4. How do bystanders influence the way we communicate?
5. How does cooperation differ across cultures?
6. How does stigmatization influence communication?
7. Why do moderate dissimilarities when people are generally similar facilitate effective communication?
8. How does status—both our own and the other person's—influence communication?
9. How are norms and rules similar and different?
10. How do the dimensions of norms and rules vary across cultures?
11. How do the justice norms vary across cultures?
12. How does the reciprocity norm vary across cultures?
13. Why is achieving privacy a dialectical process?
14. How does privacy differ across cultures?
15. How does the use of territory differ across cultures?
16. How do monochronic and polychronic use of time differ?
17. What factors influence the interaction potential of the environment?

SUGGESTED READING

Altman, I. (1975). *The environment and social behavior.* Monterey, CA: Brooks/Cole.
Altman, I., & Chemers, M. (1980). *Culture and environment.* Monterey, CA: Brooks/Cole.
Argyle, M., Furnham, A., & Graham, J. (1981). *Social situations.* Cambridge, UK: Cambridge University Press.
Forgas, J. (Ed.). (1985). *Language and social situations.* New York: Springer-Verlag.
Hall, E. T. (1983). *The dance of life.* New York: Doubleday.

PART THREE

Interpreting and
Transmitting Messages

Culture affects our communication in various ways. It provides us with patterned ways of dealing with information in our environment. It influences what we perceive, how we interpret messages, and how we respond to messages both verbally and nonverbally. Culture shapes and colors our image of reality and conditions the way we think.

Our communication patterns are often subtle, elusive, and unconscious. It is difficult for even well-informed members of a culture to explain why, in their own culture, the custom is thus-and-so rather than so-and-thus. It would be hard, for example, to explain the "rule" governing the precise time in a relationship when the other person becomes a friend. It simply "feels right." Fortunately, members of the same culture share a great number of such taken-for-granted assumptions about interpersonal relationships and the corresponding "appropriate" behavior.

For strangers, however, many of the hidden assumptions and modes of behavior are not shared. As many people who visit a foreign country soon discover, communicationg with the natives can often be a challenging and novel experience. In the following chapters, we present material designed to help us better understand our message interpreting and transmitting when we communicate with strangers. In Chapter 7, we examine interpreting messages, the most fundamental process of receiving and processing information from the environment. Specifically, we discuss the perceptual process, how we make sense of strangers' behavior (i.e., attribution processes), how our cognitive styles influence our interpreting of strangers' messages, and how our patterns of thought influence our perceptions of strangers. In Chapter 8, we take up language and verbal behavior. The focus there is on

165

the Sapir-Whorf hypothesis, elaborated and restricted codes, and the factors that influence our language choices when we communicate with strangers (i.e., language vitality, language attitudes, second language competence, communication accommodation, and code-switching). Finally, in Chapter 9, we consider the recognition and expression of emotions, the differences between contact and noncontact cultures, and what happens when our nonverbal behavioral expectations are violated when we communicate with strangers.

7

Interpreting Messages

*What has been thought of as mind is actually
internalized culture. The mind culture process
which has evolved over the past four or more million
years is primarily concerned with "organization" and,
furthermore, the organization of "information" as it
is channeled (and altered by the senses) to the brain.*

Edward T. Hall

The way that we interpret strangers' messages affects the way we respond to them. Interpreting messages involves perceiving the cues strangers transmit and attributing meaning to those cues. The way we perceive the cues strangers transmit and attribute meaning to those cues is influenced by our social cognitive styles (e.g., the way we think about people) and our patterns of thought, logic, and reasoning. We can increase the accuracy of our perceptions and the attributions about strangers' behavior if we are mindful of our communication behavior.

Initially, we discuss how we perceive strangers' behavior. Second, we look at how we make sense of strangers' behavior—the process of making attributions. Next, we look at the cognitive styles that influence how we receive and organize information from the environment (i.e., field-independence/field-dependence, category width, uncertainty orientation, and cognitive complexity). Finally, we explore cultural variations in patterns of thought by examining cultural variability in world views, systems of logic, and patterns of reasoning.

PERCEPTUAL PROCESSES

Perception involves our awareness of what is taking place in the environment. Three critical aspects of perceptions influence our communication with strangers. First, our perceptions are selective. That is, we do not perceive all of the information available to us in the specific environment in which our communication takes place. Second, our perceptions involve categorization. When we perceive people and objects while communicating on automatic pilot, we unconsciously put them in categories. Third, rigid categories inhibit effective communication. To the extent that our categories are rigid, we are unable to see individual characteristics of the people with whom we are communicating and our communication, therefore, will not be as effective as it could be. We begin by looking at the selective nature of our perception.

Our Perceptions Are Selective

If we had to pay attention to all the stimuli in our environment, we would experience information overload. In the interest of not overloading ourselves with too much information, we limit our attention to those aspects of the other person or the situation that are essential to what we are doing (Bruner, 1958). We might perceive, for example, the color of a person's skin, but not notice its texture. Watts (1966) points out that

> to notice is to select, to regard some bits of perception, or some features of the world, as more noteworthy, more significant than others. To these, we attend, and the rest we ignore—for which reason . . . attention is at the same time ignore-ance (i.e., ignorance) despite the fact that it gives us a vividly clear picture of what we choose to notice. Physically, we see, hear, smell, taste, and touch innumerable features that we never notice. (p. 29)

Our perceptions of others, therefore, are highly selective.

Bateson (1979) points out that the process of selecting information from the environment and forming images takes place unconsciously. We do not consciously decide on the things to which we pay attention. We are conscious of what we see, but what we see is manufactured in our brains. What we see does not really exist because "all experience is subjective" (Bateson, 1979, p. 31). Presuppositions and expectations influence the cues that we select from the environment and what we see (expectations were discussed in Chapter 5).

Ittelson and Cantril (1954) contend that perceptions are always a function of our interaction with specific people in specific situations. We react to people on the basis of the way we perceive the people in the interaction, *not* as entities independent of our interaction with them. Each person's perceptions are unique; they are based on culture, ethnicity, sex, background experiences, and needs. Our perceptions overlap with others' perceptions to the extent that we share common experiences (e.g., culture, ethnicity, past interaction). To the extent that our perceptions overlap with others', our uncertainty is reduced. Although perceptions are based on our interactions with others, we tend mistakenly to assume that our perceptions are "real" and external to ourselves.

We assume that we perceive and observe others in an unbiased fashion. This assumption, however, is mistaken. Our perceptions are highly selective and biased. Assuming that our perceptions are unbiased leads us to make inaccurate predictions about strangers' behavior. Our group memberships and social identities (e.g., our culture, ethnic group, gender, age) are major sources of bias in our perceptions. We unconsciously activate our social identities when we interact with strangers. When we communicate on automatic pilot, we perceive strangers' behavior on the basis of the social identities we have activated. If we meet strangers from another ethnic group, for example, our ethnic identities will guide our behavior. We will unconsciously expect strangers' behavior to be based on their ethnic identities as well. This expection will lead to our perceptions' being highly selective, and we may not notice behavior inconsistent with our stereotype of the strangers' ethnic group.

Our past experiences are another source of bias in our perceptions. If, for example, a person's mother was quiet before she exploded and got angry with him or her, that person may perceive that others are getting angry when they are quiet. Our previous experiences with a particular person also can bias our perceptions of that person's current behavior. Our emotional states also bias our perceptions. Moods provide a lens through which we interpret our own and others' behavior. Other biases in perceptions are a function of the categorization process and our expectations.

Perceptions Involve Categorizations

When we select information from the environment, we need to organize it in some way by finding meaningful patterns. This task is accomplished by putting things or people into categories. As indicated in Chapter 2, categorization is a fundamental aspect of thought. It allows "us to structure and give coherence to our general knowledge about people and the social world, providing typical patterns of behavior and the range of likely variation between types of people and their characteristic actions and attributes" (Cantor, Mischel, & Schwartz, 1982, p. 34).

When we categorize, we group objects (people or things) according to aspects they have in common and ignore aspects they do not have in common. Our categorizations, therefore, are based on only selected aspects of the thing or person. In categorizing, we have to ignore some aspects in order to classify a person or thing. Once we have created a category, we assume that objects within that category are similar and that objects in other categories are different. Strangers can be classified, for example, as members of our culture or not members of our culture, but in creating this classification, we ignore other important qualities of the strangers (e.g., their ethnicity is similar to ours, their occupation is similar to ours). Once formed, however, the category influences how we respond to strangers.

When we categorize things or people, we draw distinctions among them and create boundaries between categories. Zerubavel (1991) points out that "things assume a distinctive identity only through being differentiated from other things, and their meaning is always a function of the particular mental compartment in which we place them" (p. 3). Once the categories are formed, we tend to take them for granted and assume there are gaps between them. These gaps enhance our view of categories as being separate and distinct. DeBono (1991) contends that the process of drawing distinctions often leads to drawing distinctions between things that actually are quite similar. When we create categories, we run the risk of treating them as solid and permanent (deBono refers to this process as using "rock logic"). It is important to keep in mind, however, that we created the categories in the first place and that the gaps between the categories are a function of the way we created the categories. If, for example, we use color of skin to create the categories African American and European American, we must keep in mind that not all African Americans are dark-skinned and not all European Americans are light-skinned.

Rigid Categories Inhibit Accurate Perceptions

Creating gaps between the categories formed is a natural part of the perceptual process. What creates problems in communication is the rigidity with which the boundaries between categories are maintained. Zerubavel (1991) points out that

> the most distinctive characteristic of the rigid mind is its unyielding, obsessive commitment to the mutual exclusivity of mental entities. The foremost logical prerequisite of a rigid classification is that a mental item belong to no more than one category. . . . the rigid mind cherishes sharp, clear-cut distinctions among mental entities. (p. 34)

People with rigid categories try to classify each thing or each person into only a single category. Encountering something that does not fit clearly into only one category threatens the cognitive structure of a person with a rigid category system. People with rigid category systems experience anxiety or fear when confronted with something or someone that cannot be categorized (Zerubavel, 1991). Additionally, forcing things or people into mutually exclusive categories biases perceptions.

If we hold categories rigidly, we will not recognize individual variations within our categories or consider recategorizing strangers on the basis of new information. Such rigidity leads to inaccurate predictions of strangers' behavior. If categories are rigid, we may categorize strangers as disabled, for example, and then see *all* disabled people as alike. All disabled people, however, are not alike. To communicate effectively with strangers who are disabled, we must be able to recognize how they are like other disabled people and how they are different from other disabled people.

We draw boundaries and categorize strangers to make sense of the world. We draw a boundary between ourselves and strangers, for example, so that we will feel distinct. We have a need not only to be distinct but also to feel connected. If we draw a rigid boundary between ourselves and strangers, we will fail to see how we are connected to strangers. When we base our communication with strangers on our social identities, for example, we fail to see the human identities we share with strangers and we may become morally exclusive. Balancing our needs for distinction (autonomy) and connection requires flexible categories. Zerubavel (1991) argues that "flexibility entails the ability to be both rigid and fuzzy. Flexible people notice structures yet feel comfortable destroying them from time to time" (p. 120). If our mental structures are flexible and elastic, we can "break away from the mental cages in which we so often lock ourselves" (p. 122). DeBono (1991) refers to this process as using "water logic." Having flexible categories is necessary for us to be mindful and to communicate effectively. If we know we have rigid categories, we can consciously choose to be more flexible when we are mindful of our communication.

When we are mindful, one thing we can do to overcome the biases in our perceptions is to look for exceptions. Weiner-Davis (1992) points out that recognizing a single exception helps us stop our cognitive distortions that are due to either/or thinking. If, for example, we categorize a stranger as not talkative, we would try to think of times that he or she *is* talkative. When we recognize that there are times that she or he is talkative, we will not view him or her in exactly the same way as before (i.e., she or he is not always quiet). This change in our perceptions will lead to more accurate perceptions of the stranger.

Perception Checking

If two people are communicating, it is likely that they are perceiving what is going on differently. Much of the time when we communicate with members of our own cultures, small differences in perceptions are not problematic. At times, however, even small differences in perceptions can lead to ineffective communication. This result is especially likely when we communicate with strangers. If strangers do not tell us directly what they are thinking or feeling, our perceptions can be inaccurate. When such a situation occurs, perception checking is a valuable skill to use to increase the accuracy of our predictions and interpretations of strangers' behavior.

Perception checking provides us with an opportunity to make sure our interpretations of strangers' behavior are accurate before we act. Perception checking helps reduce our uncertainty about strangers' behavior. Checking perceptions also can reduce anxiety for both people involved because it helps each person recognize that his or her need for a common, shared view of the world is being met. Perception checking, therefore, increases the likelihood that we will communicate effectively.

Perception checking involves three processes. First, we have to describe strangers' behavior. Second, we tell strangers our interpretations of their behavior. In doing so, we *must* refrain from evaluating strangers' thoughts or feelings. Third, we need to ask strangers if our perceptions are accurate. An example of a perception check would be, "You are smiling. I guess you're happy. Are you?" This statement describes the other person's behavior, tells our perception without any evaluation, and asks the other person if our perception is correct. If we are not sure what the person feels, we can still check our perceptions: "I'm not sure from your facial expression whether you are hurt or angry. Which is it?" is a form of perception check.

Sometimes we may think we are checking our perceptions when we actually aren't. If we do not describe our perceptions without evaluation and ask if they are correct, we are not checking our perceptions. Simply asking a question is not perception checking. "Are you angry with me?" and "Why are you mad at me?" are not perception checks. Speaking for the other person also is not checking our perceptions. If we said, "You're always depressed," we are not checking our perception. If we said, "You have not smiled in the last two weeks. I assume you are depressed. Are you?" we would be checking our perceptions. Also, if we express a judgment, we are not checking our perceptions. If someone expressed a feeling and we said, "Why on earth would you feel that way?" we would not be checking our perception. We would be judging the other person's feeling.

There are a few important things to keep in mind about perception checking. If the person doing the perception checking does not change his or her perceptions when the other person says, "No. I'm not feeling . . .," then the perception check will not improve the quality of communication. Rather, it will inhibit the possibility of effective communication, because the other person will interpret the relational message being transmitted to mean that the person doing the perception checking does not want to understand her or his feelings.

The person responding to the perception check also has a responsibility for the quality of the communication taking place. For communication to be effective, the person responding to the perception check needs to tell the truth. If someone says to us, "You appear angry. Are you?" we need to tell the truth. If we are angry and say "no," then our anger will still influence the way we communicate. If we say "no," then for communication to be effective, we have a responsibility to act as though we are not angry.

Checking our perceptions is *not* something most of us do in our everyday communication. Using this skill in everyday communication with others may feel awkward at first because we do not have a script for perception checking. The more we use it, however, the more natural it will become. Also, the more we engage in perception checking, the more likely we will develop a script for doing it, and the more likely that it will become one of our resources for communication when we are on automatic pilot.

It is important to keep in mind that perception checking involves direct communication and, therefore, has an individualistic bias. If you are an individualist communicating with a collectivist, it is important to keep in mind that collectivists may not feel comfortable answering direct questions. In that case, you may have to ask your perception checking questions indirectly.

Perception checking is one of the simplest and most powerful techniques we can use to improve the quality of our communication with strangers. We, nevertheless, are not suggesting that you use perception checking all the time. Use it when you think that there is a chance that your perceptions may not be accurate or when it is important that you base your behavior on accurate perceptions.

When we perceive strangers' behavior, we organize the information by using various categories. Once we have organized the information, we try to make sense of strangers' behavior. This process involves making attributions about strangers' behavior.

MAKING ATTRIBUTIONS

Jones and Nisbett (1972) argue that people who are engaging in behavior interpret their behavior differently than do people who are observing it. They suggest that people usually attribute their own behavior to situational factors, while observers attribute the behavior to qualities of the people being observed. Nisbett et al. (1973) offer two explanations for these divergent perspectives. The first is simply a perceptual one. The attention of the people engaging in the behavior is focused on situational cues with which their behavior is coordinated. It therefore appears to people engaging in behavior that their behavior is a response to these situational cues. For observers, however, it is not the situational cues that are salient, but rather the behavior. Observers are more likely to perceive the cause of others' behavior to be a trait or quality inherent in the person exhibiting it. This view suggests that when we communicate with strangers, our retroactive explanations of their behavior arc likely to focus on characteristics of the strangers (e.g., their cultural background or group membership). The second explanation suggested by Nisbett et al. stems from a difference in the nature and extent of information possessed. In general, the people engaging in the behavior know more about their own past behavior and present experiences than do observers. This difference in information may prevent people engaging in the behavior from interpreting their behavior in terms of personal characteristics, while allowing observers to make such an interpretation. To illustrate,

> if an actor [or actress] insults another person, an observer may be free to infer that the actor [or actress] did so because the actor [or actress] is hostile. The actor [or actress], however, may know that he [or she] rarely insults others and may believe that his [or her] insult was a response to the most recent in a series of provocations from the person he [or she] finally attacked. The difference in information available to the actor [or actress] and observer is, of course, reduced when the actor [or actress] and observer know one another well but is always present to a degree. (Nisbett et al., 1973, p. 155)

It is important, therefore, to keep in mind when we are trying to make sense of strangers' behavior that the information we have about them is incomplete.

When we communicate with strangers, there is an increased likelihood we will attribute the cause of their behavior to one particular characteristic—namely, their cultural background or group membership. In other words, we are not likely to attribute the cause of others' behavior to their culture if they come from the same culture we do, but since strangers often come from another culture or ethnic group, their origin or background is a plausible explanation for their behavior.

We begin our discussion of making sense of strangers' behavior by looking at the individual attribution process. Following this discussion, we look at the social nature of attributions and the attribution errors we make in communicating with strangers.

Individual Attributions

Heider (1958) believes that we act as naive or intuitive scientists when we are trying to make sense of the world. He suggests that we are motivated by practical concerns such as our needs to simplify and comprehend our environment, and to predict others' behavior. In order to meet these needs, we try to get beneath external appearances to isolate stable underlying processes, which he calls dispositional properties. Heider contends that others' motives are the dispositions we use most frequently in giving meaning to our experiences. He also points out that it is not our experiences, per se, but our interpretations of our experiences, that constitute our reality.

Kelley (1967) argues that when observing others' behavior, we attempt to make attributions about the effect of the environment on their behavior by ruling out individual explanations for the behavior. We organize our observations into a cube with these three dimensions: person × object × situation. In the person dimension, we compare the person engaging in the behavior with others; in the object dimension, we compare the different objects of the person's behavior; in the situation dimension, we vary the context in which the behavior occurs. We then use a covariation principle to assess the degree to which the behavior occurs in the presence and absence of the various causes.

The analysis of covariation is based on several principles. The *principle of consistency* deals with the extent to which the behavior occurs across time and location, given the same stimulus. The *distinctiveness principle* involves the extent to which other objects bring about the same behavior. The *consensus principle* deals with the degree to which people other than the person involved engage in the same behavior.

It may appear that the attributional process takes a long time. In actuality, we go through this analysis very quickly when we have complete information. While Kelley's attributional cube explains our attributions when we have complete information, it may not describe our everyday interactions when we do not have complete information. Kelley (1972) argues that in the presence of incomplete data, we infer meaning based on implicit theories, or preconceptions, we have about how specific causes are associated with specific effects. Our causal schemata permit "economical and fast attributional analysis, by providing a framework within which bits and pieces of information can be fitted in order to draw reasonably good inferences" (p. 152).

Social Attributions

Heider's (1958) and Kelley's (1967) explanations of the individual attribution process do not take into account that we are members of social groups. It, therefore, is necessary to look at the influence of group memberships on the attribution process. When group membership is taken into consideration, the process is called social attribution. *Social attributions* are concerned with how members of one social group explain the behavior of their own members and members of other social groups.

Hewstone and Jaspars (1984) isolate three propositions regarding the social nature of attributions:

> (1) Attribution is social in origin (e.g., it may be created by, or strengthened through, social interaction, or it may be influenced by social information).
>
> (2) Attribution is social in its reference or object (e.g., an attribution may be demanded for the individual characterized as a member of a social group, rather than in purely individual terms; or for a social outcome, rather than any behavior as such).
>
> (3) Attribution is social in that it is common to the members of a society or group (e.g., the members of different groups may hold different attributions for the same event). (pp. 379–380; italics omitted)

Hewstone and Jaspars argue that we enhance our social identities when we make social attributions. They also point out that our social attributions usually are based on the social stereotypes we share with other members of our ingroups. Our social attributions, however, can also be based on ethnocentrism.

Most writing on individual and social attributions is based on the assumption that observers know what the behavior they are observing means. This assumption, however, is questionable when we communicate with strangers. Detweiler (1975) points out that

> the process of cross-cultural attributions should not be the same as within-culture attribution. There are unique factors which may yield different attributions interculturally than intra-culturally. First, it is important to recognize that attributions are based upon our knowledge of cultural expectations. Hence, it is hypothesized that whether or not the actor [or actress] is from one's own culture or a different culture should have a major impact on the inference process. Second, to the degree that this cultural difference is recognized by the observer, inferences will be limited. (pp. 593–594)

The models proposed by individual attribution theorists, therefore, need modification for intercultural encounters. In examining the nature of intercultural attributions, Jaspars and Hewstone (1982) conclude:

> (1) Behavior of members of other groups perceived as out-of-role and unexpected from the perspective of one's own group is more likely to lead to person attribution.
>
> (2) Since social categorization in terms of cultural differences is probably very salient in such situations, the person attribution will be associated with the perceived differences in culture.
>
> (3) The same behavior which gives rise to person attribution cross-culturally may lead to a situational attribution within a particular group or culture because social categorization does not covary with the behavior, but is constant. (p. 139)

Making attributions about strangers' behavior, therefore, introduces additional ways that we can make inaccurate attributions.

Hewstone and Brown (1986) argue that when we perceive ourselves and others in individual terms (e.g., our personal identities generate our behavior) or when we see an outgroup member as atypical, we tend to make person-based attributions. Person-based attributions, in turn, lead us to look for personal similarities and differences between us and the other person. When we perceive ourselves and others as members of groups (e.g., our social identities generate our behavior), we tend to make category-based attributions. Category-based attributions then lead us to look for differences between our ingroup and the relevant outgroup.

The nature of the attributions we make is important and can determine whether or not our relations with members of other groups will improve. When members of different groups are working together and fail on their task, members of the ingroup usually blame the outgroup for the failure. Such attributions do not help improve intergroup relations and can, in fact, have a negative influence. If ingroup members are somehow prevented from blaming the outgroup for the failure, cooperation that results in failure does not result in increased bias toward the outgroup (Worchel & Norwell, 1980).

Errors in Attributions

The attributions we make about strangers' behavior are often inaccurate. Our errors in explaining strangers' behavior occur because there are several biases that affect our attributional processes. We tend to see our own behavior as normal and appropriate (*egocentric bias;* Kelley, 1967). We, therefore, explain strangers' behavior that is different from ours as a function of their personal characteristics. The specific personal characteristics we use to explain strangers' behavior depends on how we are thinking about ourselves and the strangers.

Sometimes we think about ourselves and others as unique individuals, and sometimes we think of ourselves and others as members of social groups. How we think about ourselves and others influences the characteristics we use to explain strangers' behavior. When we think about ourselves and strangers in individual terms and when our behavior is guided by our personal identities, we tend to make person-based attributions (Hewstone & Brown, 1986). When we see a member of an outgroup as not typical of her or his group, we also make person-based attributions. When making person-based attributions, we focus on characteristics of strangers as unique individuals in explaining their behavior. We might, for example, use strangers' intelligence or personalities as explanations for their behavior. When we perceive ourselves and strangers as members of groups and our behavior is guided by our social identities, we tend to make group-based attributions. When we make group-based attributions, we focus on strangers' membership in social groups as explanations for their behavior.

We have a tendency to overestimate the influence of personal characteristics and underestimate the influence of situational factors when we explain strangers' behavior (*fundamental attribution error;* Ross, 1977). We are most likely to make the fundamental attribution error when we are explaining strangers' behavior that we perceive to be negative. Often when strangers engage in behavior that we perceive to be positive, we will explain their behavior as a function of the situation. We tend to think that strangers behave positively because they have to—because of situational demands.

The opposite pattern occurs when we are trying to explain our own behavior. We tend to explain our positive behavior or successes by using our personal characteristics and our negative behavior or failures by using situational factors (*ego-protective bias;* Kelley, 1967). When we act in a positive fashion, we explain the behavior by thinking that we are "good people," but when we do something negative, such as yelling at another person, we do not think we are "bad people." Rather, we think that the behavior was necessary given the situation.

We have a tendency to stop looking for explanations for our own or strangers' behavior once we have found a relevant and reasonable explanation for the behavior (*premature closure;* Taylor & Fiske, 1978). When we communicate on automatic pilot, we do not think about a large number of alternative explanations for our own or strangers' behavior. Rather, we tend to stop searching for explanations when we have found a reasonable one.

We also have a tendency to overemphasize negative information about strangers' behavior (*principle of negativity;* Kanouse & Hanson, 1972). When we try to explain strangers' behavior while communicating on automatic pilot, we tend to focus on those aspects of their behavior we perceive to be negative. We, therefore, often interpret strangers' behavior more negatively than it actually is.

The Ultimate Attribution Error

Pettigrew (1979) proposes that the *ultimate attribution error* is "a systematic patterning of intergroup misattributions shaped in part by prejudice" (p. 464). He points out that our tendency to attribute behavior to dispositional or personal characteristics is enhanced when strangers are perceived to engage in negative behavior. When strangers engage in what is perceived to be positive behavior, in contrast, our tendency is to treat them as "exceptions to the rule" and to discount dispositional explanations for the behavior. We, therefore, attribute the behavior to situational factors.

When our expectations are confirmed by strangers' behavior, we rely on strangers' dispositions associated with our stereotype of their group and do not bother to consider other explanations for the behavior (Pyszczynski & Greenberg, 1981). When strangers do not confirm our expectations, we tend to attribute their behavior to external factors (Stephan & Rosenfield, 1982).

The ultimate attribution error is illustrated in a study of perceptions of "shoving" (Duncan, 1976). In this study, students were shown a videotape of one person (either an African American or a European American) shoving another person (either an African American or a European American). European American respondents attributed the shoving to dispositional causes (i.e., race) when the person doing the shoving was African American, but not when the person was European

American. The respondents also thought the shove was more violent when it was administered by an African American than when administered by a European American.

With respect to the ultimate attribution error, Pettigrew (1978) concludes that

> across-group perceptions are more likely than within-group perceptions to include the following:
>
> 1. For acts perceived as antisocial or undesirable, behavior will be attributed to personal, dispositional causes. Often these internal causes will be seen as innate characteristics, and role requirements will be overlooked. ("He shoved the white guy, because blacks are born violent like that.")
>
> 2. For acts perceived as prosocial or desirable, behavior will be attributed either: (a) to the situation—with role requirements receiving more attention ("Under the circumstances, what could the cheap Scot do, but pay the check?"); (b) to the motivational, as opposed to innate, dispositional qualities ("Jewish students make better grades, because they try so much harder"); or (c) to the exceptional, even exaggerated "special case" individual who is contrasted with his/her group—what Allport (1954) called "fence-mending" ("She is certainly bright and hardworking—not at all like other Chicanos"). (p. 39; italics omitted)

It is very likely that we will make the ultimate attribution error when communicating with strangers on automatic pilot. To reduce the possibility of making this error when making attributions about the behavior of strangers, we must be mindful of our interpretations of their behavior.

Cultural Variability in Attribution Processes

Ehrenhaus (1983) argues that the types of attributions people make in individualistic and collectivistic cultures differ. Members of collectivistic cultures are sensitive to situational features and explanations, and tend to attribute others' behavior to the context, situation, or other factors external to the individual. Members of individualistic cultures, in contrast, are sensitive to dispositional characteristics and tend to attribute others' behavior to characteristics internal to the individual (e.g., personality).

Miller (1984) observes that people in India (collectivistic) make greater reference to contextual factors and less reference to dispositional factors than do people in the United States (individualistic) when explaining others' behavior. Similar results emerge in research on attributions about reasons for promotions and demotions in organizations in India and the United States (Smith & Whitehead, 1984), and the use of self-serving biases in dealing with success and failure experiences in Japan and the United States (Kashima & Triandis, 1986).

Forgas and Bond (1985) report that Chinese in Hong Kong differentiate between episodes based on equal/unequal (power distance) and communal/individual (individualism) dimensions. Australians also use equal/unequal dimensions to differentiate between episodes, but interpretations placed on the dimension are different from those of the Chinese and consistent with the difference between the two cultures' scores on power distance.

Misattributions in Communicating with Strangers

To get an idea of the misattributions that can occur when we communicate with strangers, consider the following example presented by Triandis (1975, pp. 42–43). The example is drawn from the files of his colleague George Vassiliou, a Greek psychiatrist, and it involves a segment of interaction between a supervisor from the United States and a subordinate from Greece. In the segment, the supervisor wants the employee to participate in decisions (a norm in the United States), while the subordinate expects to be told what to do (a norm in Greece):

Behavior	Attribution
American: How long will it take you to finish this report?	American: I asked him to participate. Greek: His behavior makes no sense. He is the boss. Why doesn't he tell me?
Greek: I do not know. How long should it take?	American: He refuses to take responsibility. Greek: I asked him for an order.
American: You are in the best position to analyze time requirements.	American: I press him to take responsibility for his own actions. Greek: What nonsense! I better give him an answer.
Greek: 10 days.	American: He lacks the ability to estimate time; this estimate is totally inadequate.
American: Take 15. It is agreed you will do it in 15 days?	American: I offer a contract. Greek: These are my orders. 15 days.

In fact the report needed 30 days of regular work. So the Greek worked day and night, but at the end of the 15th day, he still needed one more day's work.

American: Where is my report?	American: I am making sure he fulfills his contract. Greek: He is asking for the report.
Greek: It will be ready tomorrow.	(Both attribute that it is not ready.)
American: But we agreed that it would be ready today.	American: I must teach him to fulfill a contract. Greek: The stupid, incompetent boss! Not only did he give me wrong orders, but he does not appreciate that I did a 30-day job in 16 days.
The Greek hands in his resignation.	The American is surprised. Greek: I can't work for such a man.

Clearly, the attributions the Greek and the American make for each other's behavior are incorrect. Such incorrect attributions lead to misunderstandings.

The misattributions we make regarding strangers' behavior are influenced by the dimensions of cultural variability discussed in Chapter 3. Not understanding how individualism-collectivism influences communication can easily lead to misinterpretations of the behavior of strangers from other cultures. A member of a collectivistic culture, who identifies with the group, for example, may offer personal opinions by using the pronoun *we* when stating a personal opinion. A member of an individualistic culture would perceive such a statement as being something that the group may do or believe, but not necessarily interpret the statement as the speaker's opinion. This misinterpretation will result in misunderstanding if the cultural differences in the use of personal pronouns is ignored.

Triandis (1975) points out that if North Americans do not understand Greeks' distinction between ingroup and outgroup, they cannot understand their politeness behavior:

> Some [North] Americans find Greeks extremely rude. They come to this conclusion from observations of Greeks in public settings—subways, busses, streets. They fail to recognize that Greeks have two sets of social behaviors; one set is used with their ingroup, and another with their outgroup. In an ingroup, which a Greek defines as "family and friends and other people who are concerned with my welfare," Greeks are extremely polite. In outgroups they are rude. If the sample of behavior to which a foreigner has access is limited to outgroup social behavior, he [or she] will mistakingly assume that all Greek social behavior is rude. This will, of course, have consequences for his [or her] own social behavior. Once he [or she] assumes that the other person is rude, he [or she] is likely to behave in a rude way toward him [or her], which will elicit rude behavior, thus confirming his [or her] perceptions. (p. 67)

Not understanding the ingroup-outgroup distinction in Greece leads North Americans to make mistattributions about Greeks' behavior.

Another example of how differences in individualism-collectivism can lead to misunderstanding involves how face is negotiated. *Face* is defined as the public self-image (Ting-Toomey, 1988). Face can be based on our need for inclusion or our need for autonomy. Further, we can have a concern for our own face or a concern for another's face. Problems in communication may occur when there is a difference in interpretation of the face-concern being used. In collectivistic cultures, the concern for face is predominately other-oriented. In individualistic cultures, the concern is self-oriented. Misunderstandings may occur when individualists fail to give face to collectivists when they interact.

The issue of giving face, especially to people with higher status, is important in collectivistic cultures. When people from individualistic cultures violate this expectation, the violation can have major consequences for their relationship. Brislin and his associates (1986) present an example of this issue in the context of business negotiations between individuals in Japan and the United States:

> Phil Downing . . . was involved in the setting up of a branch of his company that was merging with an existing Japanese counterpart. He seemed to get along very well with the executive colleagues assigned to work with him, one of whom had recently been

> elected chairman of the board when his grandfather retired. Over several weeks'
> discussion, they had generally laid out some working policies and agreed on strate-
> gies that would bring new directions needed for development. Several days later . . .
> the young chairman's grandfather happened to drop in. He began to comment on how
> the company had been formed and had been built up by the traditional practices,
> talking about some of the policies the young executives had recently discarded.
> Phil expected the new chairman to explain some of the new innovative and develop-
> mental policies they had both agreed upon. However, the young man said nothing;
> instead, he just nodded and agreed with his grandfather. Phil was bewildered and
> frustrated . . . and he started to protest. The atmosphere in the room became im-
> mediately tense . . . A week later the Japanese company withdrew from the nego-
> tiations. (pp. 155–156)

The young chairman of the Japanese company was giving his grandfather face by
agreeing with him. This behavior however, did not negate any of the negotiations
he had with Phil. Phil obviously did not understand. By protesting and disagreeing
with the grandfather, Phil not only failed to give face to the grandfather, he also
threatened the grandfather's face.

Face issues also can lead to misunderstanding in interethnic encounters in the
United States. In the European American middle-class subculture, for example, re-
fusing to comply with a directive given by a superior is attributed as a face-
threatening act. In the African American subculture, however, "stylin" includes re-
fusing to comply as part of a verbal game people play. This difference can be a
problem when European American teachers interact with African American students and neither understand the others' communication style:

> The [European American] teachers, not realizing the play argument was a salient
> speech event in the children's speech community, took literally the child's refusal to
> comply, often with disastrous results for the child's reputation. Such children can
> be seen as recalcitrant and possibly emotionally disturbed [by European American
> teachers]. (Erickson, 1981, pp. 6–7)

Not understanding the communication rules strangers use often leads to misattributions for their behavior.

As indicated in Chapter 3, Hall (1976) sees interpersonal bonds in an individualistic culture as fragile and notes that people in such a culture move away or
withdraw with relative ease if a relationship is not developing satisfactorily. The
bonds between people in a collectivistic culture, in contrast, are stronger, and thus
there is a tendency to allow for considerable bending of individual interests for the
sake of the relationship.

Not understanding the role of context in individualistic and collectivistic cultures also can lead to inaccurate interpretations of communication. One area where
misunderstandings may occur in communication between members of individualistic and collectivistic cultures is in the directness of speech used. As indicated in
Chapter 3, members of individualistic cultures tend to use a direct style of speech.
Members of collectivistic cultures, in contrast, tend to use an indirect style of

speech. The problems when people from individualistic and collectivistic cultures interact is illustrated in Tannen's (1979) study of Greek–North American communication. Tannen (1979) notes that Greeks tend to employ an indirect style of speech and interpret others' behavior on the basis of the assumption that others also are using the same style. North Americans, in contrast, use a direct style of speech and assume others are using the same style. Tannen observes that when Greeks and North Americans communicate, there often are misunderstandings due to these differences in style of speech. She goes on to point out that overcoming misunderstandings due to direct-indirect style differences is difficult because "in seeking to clarify, each speaker continues to use the very strategy which confused the other in the first place" (p. 5). To resolve the misunderstandings, obviously one of the people involved must recognize that the differences in styles are creating the problem, try to accurately interpret the other person's messages, and then shift her or his style of speech.

Tannen (1975) reports a conversation between a husband (nonnative speaker [NNS] of English who learned indirect rules) and a wife (native speaker [NS] using direct communication styles) that illustrates these differences:

> NS (wife): Bob's having a party. Wanna go?
> NNS (husband): OK.
> NS: (later) Are you sure you wanna go?
> NNS: OK, let's not go. I'm tired anyway.

In this conversation, the husband interpreted the wife's questions as an indirect indication that she did not want to go.

Misattributions also result from the way people in individualistic and collectivistic cultures try to reduce uncertainty, particularly in initial interactions with strangers. Consider how uncertainty is reduced in the United States and Japan. In the European American middle-class subculture in the United States, people try to obtain information about others' attitudes, feelings, and beliefs to reduce their uncertainty. In Japan, on the other hand, people must know others' status and background in order to reduce uncertainty and know which version of the language to use (there are different ways to speak to people who are superiors, equals, and inferiors). Japanese, therefore, introduce themselves by saying things like, "'I belong to Mitsubishi Bank.' and immediately asking . . . 'What is your job?' 'How old are you?' and 'What is the name of your company?'" (Loveday, 1982, pp. 4–5). These questions are designed to gather the information necessary for a Japanese to communicate with a stranger. They are perceived, however, as "rude" and "nosey" by North Americans.

COGNITIVE STYLES

Cognitive style refers to the ways in which we structure our beliefs and attitudes about the world and the way we respond to incoming messages (Miller & Steinberg,

1975). In this section, we focus on four cognitive styles that have a major influence on the way we perceive incoming messages from strangers and make attributions about strangers' behavior: field independence/field dependence, category width, uncertainty orientation, and cognitive complexity.

Field Independence and Field Dependence

Field dependence and *field independence* refer to how people rely on visual or other information in space in making judgments about the orientations of themselves and of objects in space (Witkin et al., 1962), global versus analytical style, and the degree to which a person differentiates between self and nonself. Jahoda (1980) describes the salient features of field-independent individuals:

> Field-independent people have a higher ability to extract a constituent part than field-dependent people who find it difficult to break up such an organized whole analytically. Similarly, in the intellectual sphere, relative field-independent people display greater skill in solving the particular type of problem which requires isolating certain elements from their context and making use of it in a different context. It was also originally suggested that field-dependent individuals were more sensitive to the prevailing social field and therefore more likely to respond to social cues or conform to social pressures. (p. 100)

Clear linkage exists between these characteristics of the field-dependent and field-independent cognitive styles and high-context and low-context communication patterns. The field-dependent cognitive style corresponds closely to the perceptual mode of the high-context communication style, while the field-independent cognitive style is related closely to the perceptual pattern of the low-context communication style. Both perspectives provide useful conceptual tools for understanding cross-cultural variations in information decoding patterns.

There appear to be cultural variations in field independence and field dependence. Witkin and Berry (1975) conclude that the evidence

> suggests that a relatively field-dependent cognitive style, and other characteristics of limited differentiation, are likely to be prevalent in social settings characterized by insistence on adherence to authority both in society and in the family, by the use of strict or even harsh socialization practices to enforce this conformance, and by tight social organizations. In contrast, a relatively field-independent cognitive style and greater differentiation are likely to be prevalent in social settings that are more encouraging of autonomous functioning, which are more lenient in their childrearing practices, and which are loose in social organization. (p. 46)

This analysis suggests that field dependence should predominate in high power distance cultures and field independence in low power distance cultures (Gudykunst & Ting-Toomey, 1988).

Category Width

Category width "refers to the range of instances included in a cognitive category" (Pettigrew, 1982, p. 200). Consider the question, Is a pane of glass in the wall that is 1 inch wide and 12 feet high a window? A narrow categorizer would probably say no, while a wide categorizer would probably say yes. Wide categorizers have more latitude than narrow categorizers in what they include in a category.

Detweiler (1978) summarizes the differences in narrow and wide categorizing by pointing out that *category width*

> is a term used to describe the amount of discrepancy tolerable among category members—how similar do things have to be to be called by the same name? A narrow categorizer might put only highly similar things in the same category, whereas a broad categorizer might put more discrepant things in the same category. (p. 263)

Pettigrew (1982) suggests that individual differences in category width are related to more general information-processing strategies people use. Broad categorizers, for example, tend to perform better than narrow categorizers on tasks that require holistic, integrated information processing. Narrow categorizers, in comparison, tend to perform better than broad categorizers on tasks that require detailed, analytic information processing.

There are several other differences between narrow and broad categorizers that are worth noting. Rokeach (1951), for example, observes that broad categorizers include concepts like Buddhism, capitalism, Christianity, democracy, Judaism, and socialism in the same category (e.g., beliefs or doctrines), while narrow categorizers do not. Rokeach also reports that narrow categorizers are more ethnocentric than broad categorizers. Research further indicates that narrow categorizers "react more to change, seek less prior information, and are more confident of their performances" than broad categorizers (Pettigrew, 1982, p. 207).

Detweiler (1975) demonstrates that category width influences the attributions European Americans make about people who are culturally similar (another European American) or culturally dissimilar (a person from Haiti) who engage in either positive or negative behavior. He indicates that narrow categorizers

> assume that the effects of behavior of a person from another culture tell all about the person, even though he [or she] in fact knows nothing about the actor's [or actress's] cultural background. He [or she] seems to make strong judgments based on the positivity or negativity of the effects of the behavior as evaluated from his [or her] own cultural viewpoint. Contrarily, when making attributions to a person who is culturally similar, the narrow [categorizer] seems to view the similarity as overshadowing the behavior. Thus, positive effects are seen as intended, and negative effects are confidently seen as unintended. (p. 600)

These findings suggest that narrow categorizers may have trouble making accurate attributions about messages from both people who are culturally similar and people who are culturally dissimilar.

Wide categorizers have a very different orientation. When making attributions about a culturally dissimilar person, a wide categorizer

> seems to assume that he [or she] in fact doesn't know enough to make "usual" attributions. Thus, behaviors with negative effect result in less confident and generally more neutral attributions when judgments are made about a person from a different culture. Conversely, the culturally similar person who causes a negative outcome is rated relatively more negatively with greater confidence by the wide [categorizer], since the behavior from one's own cultural background is meaningful. (Detweiler, 1975, p. 600)

Wide categorizers, therefore, are more likely than narrow categorizers to search for the appropriate interpretation of a culturally dissimilar person's behavior.

Uncertainty Orientation

Another cognitive style that influences our perceptions of strangers and our decoding of their messages is our orientation toward uncertainty. Sorrentino and Short (1986) point out

> that there are many people who simply are not interested in finding out information about themselves or the world, who do not conduct causal searches, who could not care less about comparing themselves with others, and who "don't give a hoot" for resolving discrepancies or inconsistencies about the self. Indeed, such people (we call them certainty oriented) will go out of their way not to perform activities such as these (we call people who *do* go out of their way to do such things uncertainty oriented). (pp. 379–380)

These differences influence how we think about ourselves and how we try to make sense of strangers' behavior.

Uncertainty oriented people integrate new and old ideas and change their belief systems accordingly. They evaluate ideas and thoughts on their own merit and do not necessarily compare them with others. Uncertainty oriented people want to understand themselves and their environment. *Certainty oriented* people, in contrast, like to hold on to traditional beliefs and have a tendency to reject ideas that are different. Certainty oriented people maintain a sense of self by not examining themselves or their behavior.

When we communicate on automatic pilot, we tend to be either certainty oriented or uncertainty oriented. Those of us who tend to be certainty oriented should keep in mind that we can choose to be more uncertainty oriented when we are mindful of our communication.

Cognitive Complexity

The complexity of our cognitive systems also affects the way we perceive strangers and interpret their messages (Applegate & Sypher, 1983). We use constructs to differentiate others when we communicate (Kelly, 1955). *Constructs* are perceptual categories used to organize our thoughts. A panhandler, for example, might use the construct "looks generous-does not look generous" in deciding whom to approach to ask for money. When communicating with strangers, we might use constructs such as similar-dissimilar, empathic–not empathic, extroverted-introverted, honest-dishonest, trustworthy–not trustworthy, and so forth in trying to understand their behavior. Cognitively complex people use more constructs to understand other people than do cognitively simple people.

It is not just the complexity of our cognitive system, however, that is important to how we communicate. The quality of the constructs we use in understanding others also is important (Clark & Delia, 1977). Determining quality is based on the relevance of the constructs to the situation in which we use them. If, for example, we are trying to improve the effectiveness of our communication with other people, assessing whether they are generous–not generous will not be very useful and, therefore, the quality of our constructs will be low. Assessing the degree to which other people are trustworthy–not trustworthy, in contrast, will be useful in improving the quality of our communication because this construct is directly related to communication.

Werner (1957) argues that "whenever development occurs it proceeds from a state of relative globality and lack of differentiation to a state of increasing differentiation, articulation, and hierarchic integration" (p. 126). The more differentiations we make in an area, the more complex our cognitive systems. If we make a large number of differentiations, we are said to be cognitively complex; if we make only a few, cognitively simple.

Cognitively complex people form impressions of others that are more extensive and differentiated, and better represent the behavioral variability of others than do cognitively simple people (O'Keefe & Sypher, 1981). Honess (1976) also points out that cognitively complex people seek out unique features of their environments more than do cognitively simple people. Cognitively simple people tend to seek information that is consistent with their prior beliefs. These differences support the argument that the more complex our cognitive systems, the more effective our communication (Wiseman & Abe, 1986).

In applying the concept of cognitive complexity to intercultural interactions, Davidson (1975) argues that

> the relation between complexity and cross-cultural effectiveness is assumed to exist because a cognitively simple person has a single framework within which to evaluate the observed behavior of others in the target culture. Thus, when a behavior which he [or she] does not understand takes place, he [or she] is likely to evaluate it ethnocentrically. A complex person, on the other hand, has several frameworks for the perception of the same behavior. He [or she] might, for example, suspend judgment and obtain more information before evaluating the behavior. (p. 80)

Detweiler's (1980) research supports this speculation.

Gudykunst (1995) argues that cognitive complexity is related directly to the management of uncertainty and anxiety when communicating with strangers. He argues that the more complex our cognitions are, the greater is our ability to manage our uncertainty and anxiety. It is important to keep in mind that if we tend to be cognitively simple when communicating on automatic pilot, we can choose to process information in a complex fashion when we are mindful of our communication.

PATTERNS OF THOUGHT

The way people in a culture think influences the way they interpret messages they receive from others. In this section, we examine three aspects of our patterns of thought: world view, systems of logic, and patterns of reasoning. These three aspects of patterns of thought are interrelated highly and they are separated here only to organize our discussion.

World View

"Every social group has a world view—a set of more or less systematized beliefs and values in terms of which the group evaluates and attaches meaning to the reality that surrounds it" (Kraft, 1978, p. 407). Kraft points out that the existence of a world view (*Weltanschauung* in the original German) is observed in every known group, but members of different groups vary in the degree to which they can articulate their world views. People have a difficult time articulating their world views mainly because such views are learned throughout the socialization process and tend to be unconscious. World views are accepted without questioning as "the way things are."

Kraft (1978) argues that a world view serves five important functions for the people of a culture. First, a world view performs an explanatory function for the members of a culture; it provides "explanations of how and why things got to be as they are and why they continue that way" (p. 408). Second, a world view performs an evaluational and validating function; that is, it provides the criteria for evaluating and validating the ends and means of the group. The third function a world view performs is psychological reinforcement. A world view provides ways for people to gain reinforcement for their beliefs in times of anxiety and crisis. This reinforcement may take the form of rituals in which the people participate or of individual activities which reinforce basic beliefs. Fourth, a world view performs an integrating function. "It systematizes and orders for them their perceptions of reality into an overall design" (p. 410). Finally, a world view provides an adaptational function for members of a culture. In times of social change, a world view gives people the means to allow them to adapt to the change that is taking place.

One way to illustrate differences in world views is to compare collectivistic and individualistic world views. Wei (1980) compares world views by looking at two specific dimensions: (1) cosmic patterns or ways of perceiving the world (Kraft's integrating function), and (2) philosophy of history (Kraft's explanatory function).

In individualistic cultures, people see the cosmos as created and controlled by a divine power. Since the cosmos is controlled by a supernatural power, there are laws of nature that must be followed. The view in collectivistic cultures, in contrast, is one of a "harmoniously functioning organism consisting of an orderly hierarchy of interrelated parts and forces which, though unequal in their status, are equally essential for the total process" (Wei, 1980, p. 4). The collectivistic view sees the cosmos as a self-operating system not controlled by an external source. Stemming from these general views of the cosmos are two epistemological questions: (1) What is the nature and source of knowledge? and (2) How do we come to know? In the west, "the fundamental question is how I can transcend myself to reach the other, either the external inanimated world or people surrounding me. In this question there is a basic dichotomy between the knower and things to be known" (Wei, 1980, p. 5). An example of the eastern view is seen in the Chinese orientation: "The Chinese distinguish two kinds of knowledge. The first is to investigate things, to know about the second is to know the illustrious way of the universe—the tao. The first kind of knowledge is one way of achieving the second, which is the true knowledge" (Wei, 1980, p. 8).

There also are differences between individualistic and collectivistic cultures with respect to the second aspect of world view, philosophy of history. The issue here is the meaning of history and the influence of specific events on history as a whole. In individualistic cultures, history is seen mainly as a "linear historical pattern toward progress" (Wei, 1980, p. 12). There are two different views, a sacred view stemming from the Judeo-Christian tradition and a secular view stemming from the philosophy of progress originating with Voltaire. In collectivistic cultures, in contrast, people see history as cyclical in nature. The themes of destruction and renovation, for example, are common throughout Buddhist and Hindu writings.

Differences in world views influence our communication with strangers. Consider, for example, a business delegation from North America meeting with strangers from a collectivistic culture to decide whether or not their two companies should work together on a joint venture. Based only on their differing world views, it might be expected that misunderstandings will occur. The North Americans would analyze all the facts and would develop a direct argument as to whether or not the two companies should do business together. The strangers, in contrast, would base their decision on a synthesis of all the data and on their intuition as to whether or not the idea is a good one and, in addition, would discuss the issues in an indirect rather than a direct method. Obviously, if one of the groups does not understand the other's world view and adapt its communication accordingly, misunderstanding is going to occur.

Systems of Logic

Observers of individualistic cultures characterize the predominant mode of thinking as logical, analytic, action oriented, and linear. The most characteristic form is known as scientific induction, which emphasizes concentrating attention on the "raw materials" provided by the senses and applying rational principles to those raw materials to bring them into a more or less orderly and self-consistent whole. Gulick (1962) describes individualistic thinking in the main as "the effort to make a coherent and verifiable 'world construct,' and to impose [human's] will on nature and society" (p. 127). Such mental characteristics of the individualists have given great impetus to the development of natural science and technology.

An associated characteristic of individualistic cultures, particularly that of the United States, is the tendency to see the world in terms of dichotomies (Stewart, 1972). This characteristic is illustrated by the individualistic tendency to think in terms of good-evil, right-wrong, true-false, and beautiful-ugly. Stewart describes this tendency to polarize as "simplifying the view of the world, predisposing to action and providing individuals with a typical method of evaluating and judging by means of a comparison" (p. 29).

While sharing a great deal of commonality with thinking in individualistic cultures in general, thinking by the people in the United States is distinguishable from that of Europeans by its heavier emphasis on empirical facts, induction, and operationalism. Stewart (1972) comments:

> For [North] Americans, the world is composed of facts—not ideas. Their process of thinking is generally inductive, beginning with facts and then proceeding to ideas. But the movement from the concrete to the more abstract is seldom a complete success, for [North] Americans have a recurrent need to reaffirm their theories and . . . their ideas require validation by application and by becoming institutionalized. (pp. 22–23)

The operational style of thinking tends to produce a stress on consequences and to result in a disregard for the empirical world as such. What is important is the ability of the individual to affect the empirical world. Such operationally oriented thinking in the United States has led to the prevailing cultural values of pragmatism and functionalism.

Europeans are characterized as attaching primacy to ideas and theories. Their deductive and abstract style of thinking gives priority to the conceptual world. Although the empirical world is not necessarily ignored, it often is treated with a symbolic and demonstrational attitude. Deductive thinkers are likely to have much more confidence in their ideas and theories, so it suffices for them to show one or two connections between their concepts and the empirical world. They do not feel compelled to amass facts and statistics, as is the way in the United States, and they tend to generalize from one concept to another concept, or to facts, by means of logic. Europeans have a greater faith and trust in the powers of thought, while people in the United States place a greater significance on their methods of empirical observation and measurement (Stewart, 1972). Although the cultures of the United States and Western Europe are in some respects dissimilar, they share certain basic characteristics of individualistic cultures. Even though the relative significance placed on empirical observation and verification and on the deductive and the inductive processes of deriving knowledge differs between the two cultural groups, they both emphasize a fundamental cognitive pattern that is logical, categorical, linear, and analytic.

Compared with those of individualistic cultures, the thinking patterns used in collectivistic cultures are characterized as relational, integrative, holistic, and intuitive. Asians, for example, are observed to have a central mode of thinking that is not concerned as much with logic and analysis as it is with intuitive "knowing" and meditative introspection and contemplation. Asians tend to emphasize the unity between the subjective and the objective realms of the inner and the outer conditions, and thus engage less in analyzing a topic divisively by breaking it down into smaller units as North Americans often do. What seems to be of central importance in Asian thinking is a certain repose of the personality in which it "feels" it is "grasping" the inner significance of the object of contemplation. The direct sense of rapport with the outer object—whether a person, idea, or thing—is the primary end result of Asian thinking (Gulick, 1962, p. 127).

The intuitive thinking of collectivists tends to de-emphasize the power of analysis, classification, precision, and abstraction, and the result is perhaps not as effective in attaining accurate "facts" about the object. Intuitive thinking, on the other hand, allows holistic and intimate identification with all the contextual cues in a communication transaction, thus making the perceptual patterns of collectivists highly contextual. The intuitive style of thinking provides a powerful cognitive mechanism for developing a harmonious rapport with the other person and the environment. This mechanism enables collectivists to be sensitive to the most subtle undercurrents of emotion and mood in a particular communication event and interpersonal relationship without having to engage in a deliberate attempt to analyze the situation logically.

Okabe (1983) illustrates the differences between collectivistic and individualistic logic by comparing Japan and the United States:

> [North] American logic and rhetoric value "step-by-step," "chain-like" organization, as frequently observed in the "problem-solution" pattern or in the "cause-to-effect" or "effect-to-cause" pattern of organization. . . . By contrast, Japanese logic and rhetoric emphasize the importance of a "dotted," "point-like" method of structuring a discourse. No sense of rigidity . . . is required in the Japanese-speaking society, where there is instead a sense of leisurely throwing a ball back and forth and carefully observing each other's response. (pp. 29–30)

He goes on to point out that North Americans rely on facts, figures, and quotations to support their arguments, while Japanese use more subjective and ambiguous forms of support.

Heimann (1964) compares logic in the United States and India. She argues that the differences are illustrated by comparing two Greek and Sanskrit terms:

> the Greek term *heteros* means literally "the other." As such it gains with Aristotle the meaning of "the worse," "the lesser." Western logic clings to the established order and is reluctant to accept the vague otherness. The Sanskrit equivalent is *para*. It, too, means the "other" but as such the "higher and better." It is here where the fundamental difference between western and Indian logic and its ethical implications lies. The thing in hand, while being clearly observable and distinct, is of definite value for the

Westerner. The "other" for him [or her] is thus something disquietingly vague, while the "other" is of positive value for the Indian because of its very vagueness. (p. 149)

These observations are consistent with the differences in low- and high-context communication discussed in Chapter 3.

Ornstein (1972) suggests a possible physiological explanation for the observed perceptual and cognitive variations across cultures. He believes the two cerebral hemispheres of the human brain process different kinds of information and the operating characteristics of the two likewise differ. The left hemisphere is involved predominantly with analytic, logical thinking; speech; and mathematical functions. Its mode of operation is primarily linear; it seems to process information sequentially. The right hemisphere is more holistic, direct, and relational in its mode of operation. It is responsible for orientation in space, intuition, and imagination, and is able to integrate information in a nonlinear, diffused fashion. In normal people, of course, the two hemispheres operate interdependently, integrating both sides of the brain. The differential emphasis in the specialized hemispheric functions, however, appears to correspond very closely to the variations in the patterns of information processing in collectivistic and individualistic cultures.

The cultural variations in thinking isolated here do not mean individualists think using only logic and reason and collectivists think using only intuition. The differences discussed involve the *relative* emphasis that members of different cultures place on particular methods of thinking, rather than absolute differences in kind. While collectivists do think and reason, as well as use their intuitive mode of seeing things without logical analysis, the significance of knowledge through intuition is accepted and valued more extensively in collectivistic cultures than in individualistic cultures. Similarly, individualistic thinking involves intuitive processes, but individualists tend to de-emphasize the importance of such awareness through intuition and to value instead the outcome of logical, analytic thinking processes.

Patterns of Reasoning

Glenn (1981) isolates two dimensions that can be used to describe patterns of reasoning across cultures: abstractive-associative and universalism-particularism. When knowledge is acquired through direct experience with the environment, it is associative. When thought is codified into precise meanings, abstraction takes place. Associative patterns are diffuse, indefinite, and rigid, while abstract patterns tend to be articulated, definite, and flexible. Glenn points out that

associative reasoning is marked by "arbitrary" ties between informational units. Abstractive reasoning is marked by (1) the definition of information that is relevant to a given situation, and (2) the definition of the relationship between informational units. . . . The primary process for the acquisition of knowledge appears to be associative. Abstraction appears as the primary process of the organization of knowledge. (p. 57)

The use of associative thought does not readily allow new or novel information to be integrated. Triandis (1984) argues that associative patterns of information processing depend upon oral, face-to-face communication and those who depend on these patterns find it difficult to follow written instructions (which require abstraction).

While associative and abstract thought exist in all cultures, one tends to predominate. An emphasis on associative thought is related to determining identity from ascription, and an emphasis on abstraction is related to deriving identity from achievement because achievement requires the use of abstraction (Gudykunst & Ting-Toomey, 1988).

The second dimension of patterns of reasoning is universalism-particularism (Glenn, 1981). Universalism involves seeing the world through conceptualizations that are reflected in definitions of words. Universalistic processing does not take into consideration experiences that make individuals different; it is abstract. Particularization, in contrast, recognizes specifics; it tends to be associative (Glenn, 1981). Particularistic information processing starts with specific observations and extracts generalizations, while universalistic begins with broad categories and determines how observations fit the categories. These tendencies correspond to inductive and deductive processes, respectively. Triandis (1984) points out that particularistic thought tends to be probabilistic and universalistic thought tends to be absolutistic. It appears that universalistic patterns of thought dominate in cultures high in uncertainty avoidance, while particularistic patterns of thought dominate in cultures low in uncertainty avoidance (Gudykunst & Ting-Toomey, 1988).

SUMMARY

In this chapter, we examine some of the factors that influence our interpretation of messages when we communicate with strangers. Perception involves our awareness of what is taking place in the environment. Three critical aspects of perceptions influence our communication with strangers. First, our perceptions are a function of the specific people and the specific environment in which our communication takes place. Second, our perceptions involve categorization. When we perceive people and objects while communicating on automatic pilot, we unconsciously put them in categories. Third, rigid categories inhibit effective communication. To the extent that our categories are rigid, we are unable to see individual characteristics of the people with whom we are communicating and our communication, therefore, will not be as effective as it could be.

The attributions we make about strangers' behavior are social in nature. When we communicate with strangers, we tend to overemphasize the importance of group memberships in explaining their behavior.

The way we interpret incoming messages from strangers is, in part, a function of our cognitive styles. The degree to which we are field-dependent or field-independent, the degree to which we are a wide or narrow categorizer, the degree to which we are certainty or uncertainty oriented, and the degree to which we are cognitively simple or complex all influence the way we decode messages from strangers.

The way we interpret messages from strangers also is affected by the predominate patterns of thought in our culture. Whether we use chainlike or dotlike logic influences the way we draw inferences about the meaning of strangers' behavior.

STUDY QUESTIONS

1. Why are our perceptions biased?
2. What is the role of categorization in the perception process?
3. How do rigid categories inhibit effective communication?
4. How are individual and social attributions different?
5. What are the major errors that occur when we try to make sense of strangers' behavior?
6. What is the ultimate attribution error?
7. How do attributions differ in individualistic and collectivistic cultures?
8. How do differences in individualism and collectivism lead to misattributions?
9. How does category width influence our communication with strangers?
10. Why are cognitively complex people more effective than cognitively simple people?
11. How does uncertainty orientation influence our communication with strangers?
12. How are systems of logic different in individualistic and collectivistic cultures?
13. How does our pattern of reasoning influence our communication with strangers?

SUGGESTED READING

Bruner, J. (1986). *Actual minds, possible worlds.* Cambridge, MA: Harvard University Press.

deBono, E. (1991). *I am right—you are wrong: From rock logic to water logic.* New York: Viking.

Glenn, E. (1981). *Man and mankind.* Norwood, NJ: Ablex.

Kearney, M. (1984). *World view.* Novato, CA: Chandler & Sharp.

Zerubavel, E. (1991). *The fine line: Making distinctions in everyday life.* New York: Free Press.

8

Verbal Messages

Those who know do not talk.
Those who talk do not know.
Lao Tszu

Every culture has a system of language with which people are able to communicate with one another. The specific language we speak is learned in a cultural context and it reflects the culture. Over time, changes in the language spoken by a group of people also change the culture. Babies learn language as they are socialized into their culture. As babies grow, they begin to perceive that people in the environment behave in rather stable ways toward objects and toward each other. Babies also begin to understand specific linguistic patterns used in their environment. Through their gradual development of knowledge about and the use of language, children eventually learn to behave in the manner set forth by their elders and hence come to understand and participate in that culture. The particular language children learn, in turn, exerts a powerful influence on their interaction with the environment. By specifying or highlighting what in the environment is relevant or irrelevant, the language spoken influences the nature of children's experiences.

Language and culture are so intertwined that Agar (1994) suggests we use the term languaculture rather than language and culture separately (see Pinker, 1994, for an alternative perspective). In this chapter, however, we separate the two and look at the role of language in our communication with strangers. We begin by looking at the nature of language. Next, we examine the factors that influence cross-cultural variations in language usage. Following that discussion, we look at cultural variations in verbal messages. We conclude by discussing the use of language in our communication with strangers.

194

THE NATURE OF LANGUAGE

All human languages contain elements that are universal and elements that are unique. Languages are all rule-governed. *Phonological rules* tell speakers how the sounds of their language are combined to form words. *Grammatical rules* tell speakers how to order words (e.g., nouns, objects, verbs) to form sentences. *Semantic rules* tell speakers the relationship between words and the things to which they refer. *Pragmatic rules* tell speakers how to interpret the meaning of utterances. The rules of a language are a function of the speech community using the language. *Speech communities* are groups of people who use similar rules to guide how they use language and interpret others' use of language (Hymes, 1974).

Within speech communities, there are *speech situations,* occasions when individuals speak to each other (Hymes, 1974). Different speech situations (e.g., parties, classes, job interviews) are chacterized by different types of speech. Speech situations are composed of *speech events,* activities that have rules governing the use of speech (e.g., getting-to-know-you conversations, formal speeches). The same speech event can take place in different speech situations (e.g., getting-to-know-you conversations take place at parties, sporting events, in the office). Speech events are composed of speech acts. *Speech acts* involve uttering identifiable words that are perceived as coherent to members of the speech community.

The language spoken in a speech community serves at least three functions. First, the *informative* function of language is to provide others with information or knowledge. Second, the *expressive* function of language is to tell others our attitudes, feelings, and emotions. Third, the *directive* function of language is used to direct others (e.g., causing or preventing some action).

Several characteristics of language are important to understanding its role in communication (Hockett, 1958). First, the elements of a language can be combined in new meaningful utterances *(productivity).* Second, language exhibits *discreteness* because we are able to perceive different sounds as discrete from one another. Third, language is *self-reflexive;* it can be used to refer to itself. Fourth, language can be used to refer to things that are not present *(displacement).* Fifth, language is *arbitrary.* Words are symbols and, therefore, there is not a direct connection between the words and the things they represent.

CULTURAL VARIATIONS IN LANGUAGE USAGE

In communication between members of differing linguistic or cultural groups, the degree of shared meaning in experiencing the reality is likely to be minimal, particularly when the differences between the two linguistic systems are considerable. An English-speaking person, for example, will have fewer commonalities with a Chinese-speaking stranger than with a German-speaking stranger. The similarity of the language systems influences the degree to which people perceive the world in similar ways. One reason is that our language influences the way we think. This is the basis for the Sapir-Whorf hypothesis.

The Sapir-Whorf Hypothesis

Drawing on the work of Sapir (1925/1970), Whorf (1956) theorizes that language is not merely a reproducing instrument for expressing ideas; rather, it is itself the shaper of ideas. Whorf argues that there is a relationship between culture and language and the associated differences in the ways speakers of different languages view the world. He believes every language plays a prominent role in actually molding the perceptual world of the people who use it.

> We dissect nature along lines laid down by our native languages. The categories and types that we isolate from the world of phenomena we do not find there. On the contrary, the world is presented in a kaleidoscopic flux of impressions which has to be organized by our minds and this means largely by the linguistic systems in our mind. (Whorf, 1952, p. 5)

This view of the relationship between language and culture is commonly known as the Sapir-Whorf hypothesis.

Whorf (1956) concentrates on the structural differences between the Hopi language and European languages. In his analysis of plurality, for instance, Whorf notes that English uses a plural form for both cyclic nouns (nouns that refer to days, years, or other units of time) and aggregate nouns (nouns that have a physical referent, such as apples). The Hopi, on the other hand, do not use cyclic nouns in the same way they use aggregate nouns. In the Hopi language, cycles do not have plurals; they have duration. Thus the Hopi equivalent for the English "he stayed ten days" is "he stayed until the eleventh day. " Further, the Hopi language does not possess tenses, which in most European languages place time in a sequence of distinct units of past, present, and future. A speaker of English expresses an event happening in the present in one of two constructions, for example, "he runs" or "he is running." The speaker of the Hopi language can select from a much wider variety of present tenses, which depend on the speaker's knowledge or lack of knowledge concerning the validity of the statement being made, for example, "I know that he is running at this very moment," "I know that he is running at this moment even though I cannot see him," "I am told that he is running," and so on (Farb, 1979, p. 445). Worf contends that the grammatical differences in how people speak Hopi and English refer to time affects how the people view time. Hopi's, for example, do not tend to have a sense of "being on time" (Hall, 1959).

Another illustration of the role of language in the way people think about the world is how bilinguals answer questions differently depending on the language used to ask the questions. Ervin-Tripp (1964), for example, reports the responses of Japanese women who are bilingual to the same questions presented on different days in Japanese and in English. One woman's responses are as follows:

1. WHEN MY WISHES CONFLICT WITH THOSE OF MY FAMILY . . .
   (Japanese) it is a time of great unhappiness.
   (English) I do what I want.
2. I WILL PROBABLY BECOME . . .

(Japanese) a housewife.
(English) a teacher.
3. REAL FRIENDS SHOULD . . .
(Japanese) help each other.
(English) be very frank. (p. 96)

These responses clearly indicate that different approaches to the world emerge according to whether Japanese bilinguals are thinking in Japanese or in English. It should be noted, however, that Japanese world views do not completely disappear when Japanese are speaking in English. Beebe and Takahashi (1989), for example, argue that many Japanese perform face-threatening acts in a Japanese fashion even when they are speaking in English.

The Sapir-Whorf hypothesis is accepted enthusiastically by some scholars and attacked by others. The weakness of the Sapir-Whorf hypothesis lies in the impossibility of generalizing about entire cultures and then attributing these generalizations to the languages spoken in them. Farb (1979), for example, argues that because of the absence of clocks, calendars, and written histories, the Hopis obviously have a different view of time than do speakers of European languages, but such an observation is not the same as proving that these cultural differences are caused by the differences between the Hopi language and European languages.

Whorf (1956) does not attempt to draw inferences as to the thought world of a people from the simple fact of the presence or absence of specific grammatical categories in a given language. Sapir and Whorf view the cultural significance of linguistic form as lying on a much more submerged, profound level than the overt one of a definite cultural pattern. The concepts of time and matter Whorf (1956) reports for the Hopi "do not depend so much upon any one system (e.g., tense or nouns) within the grammar as upon the ways of analyzing and reporting experiences which have become fixed in the language as integrated 'fashions of speaking' and which cut across the typical grammatical classifications" (p. 44). Thus the true value of the Sapir-Whorf hypothesis is not in providing a definitive and deterministic relationship between specific linguistic categories and the thought patterns of the people in a cultural system, but in articulating the profound alliance of language, mind, and the total culture of the speech community. Clearly, the language we speak influences, but does not determine, the way we look at the world. Few students of language doubt this interpretation of the hypothesis.

Restricted and Elaborated Codes

Bernstein (1966) provides a theoretical perspective that helps us understand the speech patterns (or verbal behaviors) of individuals in different groups. Bernstein hypothesizes that our speech patterns are necessarily conditioned by our social context. The social context is not only the specific interpersonal relational context in which a dyadic speech interaction occurs but also the broader social structure, such as society and the cultural environment. Bernstein argues that speech emerges in one of two types of codes, restricted or elaborated.

Restricted codes involve message transmission through verbal (word transmission) and nonverbal (intonation, facial features, gestures) channels. Restricted codes rely heavily on the hidden, implicit cues of the social context (such as interpersonal relationships, physical and psychological environment, and other contextual cues). Bernstein (1966) explains that

> speech is played out against a backdrop of assumptions common to the speakers, against a set of closely shared interests and identifications, against a system of shared expectations; in short, it presupposes a local cultural identity which reduces the need for the speakers to elaborate their intent verbally and to make it explicit. (pp. 433–434)

Restricted codes resemble jargon or "shorthand" speech, in which the speaker is almost telegraphic. When we are with a close friend, for example, we often find ourselves making only a brief reference to something; yet we are reminded by such a reference of a wealth of experiences or concepts. The question "Bill, how was it?" can be responded to spontaneously by Bill without his having to ask what was meant by "it." An outsider would have difficulty understanding the question because of the lack of shared experiences. Jargon used by a given group also represents a type of restricted code. Code words used by doctors, engineers, prisoners, or street gangs, or between family members and close friends are highly implicit in meaning and are known primarily to the members of such groups.

Speakers using elaborated codes employ verbal amplification to communicate, placing relatively little reliance on nonverbal and other contextual cues. Whereas new information emerges primarily through nonverbal channels with restricted codes, the verbal channel is the dominant source of information with elaborated codes. Bernstein (1966) further explains elaborated codes by contrasting them to restricted codes:

> Speakers using a restricted code are dependent upon these shared assumptions. The mutually held range of identifications defines the area of common intent and also the range of the code. The dependency underpinning the social relation generating an elaborated code is not of this order. With an elaborated code the listener is dependent upon the verbal elaboration of meaning. (p. 437)

Context, therefore, is not critical in understanding elaborated codes.

Bernstein's conceptualization of restricted and elaborated codes closely corresponds to Hall's (1976) high- and low-context messages, discussed in Chapter 3. As mentioned earlier, implicit messages (contextual cues) are emphasized in high-context messages, and explicit verbal messages are of central importance in low-context messages. The heavy reliance of users of restricted codes on nonverbal and other contextual cues describes the common communication patterns of collectivistic cultures; the primary reliance on elaborated, explicit verbal messages describes the communication patterns of individualistic cultures.

Hall (1976) characterizes the written Chinese language as a highly restricted language. To be literate in Chinese, one must understand the implicit meaning and significance of the characters and Chinese history. One must also know the spoken pronunciation system in which there are four tones and a change of tone means a change of meaning. Understanding a restricted, high-context linguistic system such as Chinese requires not only a functional knowledge of the culture and history but also a sensitivity to the specific social context in which a particular communication transaction occurs. Many Asian languages, for example, Chinese, Japanese, and Korean, are sensitive to the social status of the addressee. These languages implicitly or explicitly indicate the other person's social position relative to the speaker. This is usually done by using either "honorific" prefixes or suffixes or certain words having respectful or derogatory implications. Certain nouns, pronouns, and verbs can be used only when speaking to or of a superior; a second group of words having the same basal meanings can be used only when speaking to or of an equal; a third group can be used only when speaking to or of an inferior. This verbal pattern reflecting a sensitivity to hierarchical context is absent from most contemporary European languages, with the exception of the formal and informal forms of *you,* such as *Du* (casual) and *Sie* (formal) in German and *tu* (casual) and *usted* (formal) in Spanish.

CULTURAL VARIATIONS IN VERBAL MESSAGES

Given the general conceptualizations by Sapir and Whorf, Bernstein, and Hall of the relationship between culture and verbal messages, we will examine specific cross-cultural variations in the use of verbal messages. How might individuals in collectivistic cultures perceive the meaning and function of verbal messages in the total context of communication differently from the way people in individualistic cultures perceive them? How might cultures differ in stressing the importance of verbal precision and explicitness? How might cultures vary in their perception and use of silence? What communicative functions can silence play in cultures? Understanding these and other related issues is vital to increasing our understanding of the communication patterns of strangers, as well as our own patterns of communication.

Cultural Attitudes Toward Verbal Messages

Since all cultures have a system of language, the importance of verbal messages in interpersonal communication appears to be universally acknowledged. Cultures differ, however, in the importance placed on words and talk. The long tradition of the study of rhetoric in North America and Europe demonstrates the importance given to verbal messages. This rhetorical tradition reflects in a profound way the cultural pattern of logical, rational, and analytic thinking. In the United States, speech is considered an object of inquiry, more or less independent of its communicative context, and it can be taken out of its social context. The speaker and the listener are viewed as separate entities who are in a relationship defined primarily through the verbal messages. A primary function of speech in this tradition is to express one's ideas and thoughts as clearly, logically, and persuasively as possible, so speakers can be fully recognized for their individuality in influencing others.

In collectivistic cultures, a systematic study of speech as persuasion has not been developed as fully into a distinct academic discipline as it has in individualistic cultures. The Asian attitude toward speech and rhetoric, for example, is characteristically a holistic one—the words are only part of, and are inseparable from, the total communication context, which includes the personal characters of the parties involved and the nature of the interpersonal relationships between them. This attitude does not mean words are considered less important in Asian cultures than they are in the United States. Rather, verbal messages are considered an important and integral part of the total communication process in Asian cultures, inseparably interconnected with such concepts as ethics, psychology, politics, and social relations. In this holistic approach to speech and communication, verbal messages primarily serve the function of enhancing social integration and harmony rather than promoting the speaker's individuality or self-motivated purposes. Dialogue aimed at social harmony, rather than at the well-being of a specific speaker, naturally tends to lack arguments and persuasive fervor. Oliver (1971) observes that "perhaps most basic of all is the cardinal devotion of the Asian mind to the related concepts of unity and harmony" (p. 10).

Rather than encouraging the expression of individuality through the articulation of words, the tradition of collectivistic cultures stresses the value of strict adherence to culturally defined social expectations and rules. The primary emphasis is placed not on the technique of constructing and delivering verbal messages for maximum persuasiveness but on conformity to the already established social relationships defined by the position of the individual speaker in the society. In such a rhetorical context, one is expected to possess a moral and intellectual integrity and a keen sensitivity to subtle and implicit contextual cues surrounding the total communication process. Without the contextual base, the speaker's verbal articulation and delivery are perceived as less meaningful, if not superficial or even deceitful.

A related attitude in collectivistic cultures is a strong recognition or acceptance of the limitations and biases inherent in the language used to express ideas, thoughts, and feelings. Unlike the United States and other individualistic cultures, the orientation of collectivistic cultures can be characterized as bordering on a "mistrust" of words. Words are considered useful tools of human expression only to the extent that the user recognizes their limitations and biases. In Buddhism, for example, language is considered deceptive and misleading with regard to the matter of understanding the truth. Similarly, Confucianism cautions that one should not speak carelessly and speech should be guided by the time and place. Even today, these religious teachings are deeply rooted in the minds of Asians. Commenting on Japanese communication patterns, Yoshikawa (1978) observes that

> what is often verbally expressed and what is actually intended are two different things. What is verbally expressed is probably important enough to maintain friendship, and it is generally called "Tatame" which means simply "in principle," but what is not

verbalized counts most "Honne" which means "true mind." Although it is not expressed verbally, you are supposed to know it by "kan" [which means] "intuition." (p. 228)

When the true mind is not expressed, words cannot be trusted.

Direct and Indirect Forms of Verbal Behavior

The attitude toward forms of verbal communication is related to the relative importance of context in the culture (Hall, 1976). The cautious attitude toward words in collectivistic cultures, for example, is manifested in moderate or suppressed expression of negative and confrontational verbal messages, whenever possible. In general, members of collectivistic cultures tend to be concerned more with the overall emotional quality of the interaction than with the meaning of particular words or sentences. Courtesy often takes precedence over truthfulness, in accord with the cultural emphasis on the maintenance of social harmony as the primary function of speech. This concern for social harmony leads members of collectivistic cultures to give an agreeable and pleasant answer to a question when a literal, factual answer might be unpleasant or embarrassing (Hall & Whyte, 1979).

In certain high-context, Asian languages (such as Chinese, Japanese, and Korean), the language structures themselves promote ambiguity. In the Japanese language, for example, verbs come at the end of sentences, and, therefore, one is not able to understand what is being said until the whole sentence has been uttered. In addition, the Japanese language is quite loose in logical connection. As Morsbach (1976) describes it, one can talk for hours without clearly expressing one's opinion to another. Even in ordinary conversation, a Japanese person may say *hai* ("yes") without necessarily implying agreement. Frequently, *hai* is intended by the speaker, and is expected by the listener, to mean "I understand what you are saying."

Okabe (1983) illustrates cultural differences in direct and indirect forms of communication by comparing the United States and Japan:

> Reflecting the cultural value of precision, [North] Americans' tendency to use explicit words is most noteworthy in their communicative style. They prefer to employ such categorical words as "absolutely," "certainty," and "positively." . . . The English syntax dictates that the absolute "I" be placed at the beginning of the sentence in most cases, and that the subject-predicate relation be constructed in an ordinary sentence. . . . By contrast, the cultural assumptions of interdependence and harmony require that Japanese speakers limit themselves to implicit and even ambiguous use of words. In order to avoid leaving an assertive impression, they like to depend more frequently on qualifiers such as "maybe," "perhaps," "probably," and "somewhat." Since Japanese syntax does not require the use of a subject in a sentence, the qualifier-predicate is the predominant form of sentence construction. (p. 36)

The tendency among Asians to use subdued and ambiguous verbal expressions is not limited to communication situations in which one would express disagreement, embarrassment, doubt, or anger. Even when expressing strong personal affection, they commonly prefer a style of hesitancy and indirectness. Asians can even be suspicious of the genuineness of direct verbal expressions of love and respect. Excessive verbal praise or compliments sometimes are received with feelings of embarrassment.

Mizutani (1981) uses the example of a "higher-up" coming into a room that is cold and noticing that the window is open to illustrate how indirectness allows members of a Japanese group to maintain harmony. While the higher-up might say something like, *"'Samui-ja nai-ka, sono mado-o shimete-kure'* (Aren't you cold? Please close the window)" (p. 31), this language does not take into consideration the human relations among the group. The higher-up can avoid giving a direct order by saying something like *"samui-nee"* (It's cold in here) and hope that one of the people in the room understands the unspoken meaning and responds with *"'A, soo-ka, mado-ga akete-atta'* (Oh that's right. The window's open)" (p. 31). Mizutani argues that not all Japanese would respond indirectly in this situation, but that the majority of Japanese probably would unless there was a special relationship between themselves and the people in the room that would allow them to be direct.

Sometimes what appears to be ambiguous to outsiders is not ambiguous to insiders. Japanese, for example, often appears ambiguous to nonnative speakers because the meaning of Japanese sentences must be determined within the situational context in which the sentences are uttered (or written). Mizutani (1981) provides several examples. If a guest enters a room (e.g., an office), the host might offer the guest a seat by just saying *doozo* ("please"). Clearly implied to another Japanese would be "have a seat." If the guest does not recognize that the word "please" comes in a particular situational context, then he or she will be confused. To further understand this tendency, consider two people who are out drinking and there is only beer on the table. If one person says to the other, *"'Nomimasen-ka'* (Won't you have [some]?)" (p. 48), it would be understood that the referent is beer. If the person said *"'Biiru-o nomimasen-ka'* (Won't you have some beer?)" (p. 48), then the other person would understand that other drinks are available, but the person making the offer has selected beer.

Language use in Puerto Rico (a collectivistic culture) shares many commonalities with language use in the Asian cultures. Morris (1981) makes five generalizations about the use of discourse in Puerto Rico:

> (1) In Puerto Rican society, one's place and one's sense of oneself depends on an even, disciplined, and unthreatening style of behavior. . . .
> (2) In language one must take great care not to put oneself or others at risk, and one must reduce the risk of confrontation to the lowest degree possible. This implies a systematic blurring of meaning—that is, imprecision and indirectness. . . .
> (3) This implies a constant problem of interpretation, testing, probing, second-guessing, and investigation, but conducted indirectly. . . .
> (4) The personal value of the individual—and so the validity of his [or her] words—will be determined by what he [or she] actually *does,* not what he [or she] *says.* . . .
> (5) Information does not come in discrete "bits," but as complex indicators of fluid human relationships, the "bits" being inextricable from the constant, implicit negotiation of meaning. (pp. 135–136)

As with other forms of indirect communication, what is not said may be as important as what is said in Puerto Rico.

In comparison with Asian and Puerto Rican forms of verbal expression, the forms used by people in the United States are more direct, explicit, and exact; silence is consciously avoided in interpersonal communication. Good and competent communicators are expected to say what they mean and to mean what they say. If North Americans discover that someone spoke dubiously or evasively with respect to important matters, they are inclined to regard the person thereafter as unreliable, if not dishonest. Most of the European individualistic cultures, such as the French, the German, and the English, show a similar cultural tradition. These cultures give a high degree of social approval to individuals whose verbal behaviors in expressing ideas and feelings are precise, explicit, straightforward, and direct.

Cultural differences in the importance placed on context also influence the attention individuals pay to social roles when they use language. Okabe (1983), for example, points out that English is a person-oriented language and Japanese is a status-oriented language. When context is not emphasized (e.g., as in English), messages must be adapted to the specific person with whom we are communicating. When context is important (e.g., as in Japanese), messages must take the context into consideration. Status is a large part of the context in high power distance cultures. Albert's (1972) study of language use in Burundi (a collectivistic culture) illustrates the importance of roles. She observes that

> distinctions are made according to the social roles of those present: the degree of formality, publicity or privacy, and the objectives of the speech situation. Together, social role and situational prescriptions determine the order of precedence of speakers, relevant conventions of politeness, appropriate formulas and styles of speech, including extralinguistic signs, and topics of discussion. (p. 86)

In Burundi, language reflects the hierarchical social order that exists in the culture.

Direct and indirect forms of communication also are related to the use of a third party in social intercourse. Stewart (1972) cites an example in Thai culture where business between two people may be conducted indirectly by means of an emissary rather than directly by a face-to-face confrontation of the principals involved. This indirectness extends to other aspects of social interaction, even those that strangers may consider rather personal, intimate, and sensitive, such as choosing a mate or attempting to resolve conflicts between spouses. The use of an intermediary allows both sides to accommodate one another or to withdraw without losing face. Stewart (1972) illustrates one implication of these different orientations (Asian indirectness and North American preference for direct confrontation) in discussing the use of interpreters. He points out that North Americans see the interpreter "as a window pane that transmits the message from one language to the other; but in cultures where a third-person role is customary, the interpreter's role may become a much more active one, to the consternation of the [North] American who is likely to interpret it as inefficiency or perhaps disloyalty" (p. 53).

Elaborated Versus Understated Interaction Style

The elaborated versus understated dimension focuses on the degree to which talk is used (Gudykunst & Ting-Toomey, 1988). An *elaborated style* refers to the use of expressive language in everyday conversation. Expressive language can involve the use of exaggeration or animation. An *understated style,* in contrast, involves extensive use of silence, pauses, and understatements in conversation. The French, Arabs, Latin Americans, and Africans tend to use an exaggerated interaction style, while the Chinese, Japanese, Korean, and Thai tend to use an understated interaction style. Individualists in the United States tend to fall somewhere in the middle of the continuum. To understand this dimension with respect to the communication style used by individualists in the United States, we need to make two types of comparisons: comparing the elaborated style with that used by individualists in the United States, and comparing the understated style with that used by individualists in the United States.

As indicated earlier, the elaborated style can be based on either exaggeration or animation. The verbal communication style used in the Arabic language is an example of the exaggerated style:

> An Arab feels compelled to overassert in almost all types of communication because others expect him [or her] to. If an Arab says exactly what he [or she] means without the expected assertion, other Arabs may still think that he [or she] means the opposite. For example, a simple "No" by a [male] guest to the host's request to eat more or drink more will not suffice. To convey the meaning that he is actually full, the [male] guest must keep repeating "No" several times, coupling it with an oath such as "By God" or "I swear to God." . . . an Arab often fails to realize that others, particularly foreigners, may mean exactly what they say even though their language is simple. (Almaney & Alwan, 1982, p. 84)

The Arab proclivity to use verbal exaggerations is probably responsible for more diplomatic misunderstandings between the United States and Arab countries than any other single factor (Cohen, 1987).

The French also use an elaborated style in conversations with people close to them. The French style, however, is expressive in terms of animation, not exaggeration. For the French, a conversation must be "engaged, sustained, fueled, and revived if it is 'dragging.' Once we [the French] permit a conversation to begin, we owe it to ourselves to keep it from dying, to care for it, to guide it, to nourish it, and to watch over its development as if it were a living creature" (Carroll, 1988, p. 24). French conversations are like a spider's web: "we can see the exchanging words as playing the role of the spider, generating the threads which bind the participants. The ideal French conversation would resemble a perfect spider's web: delicate, fragile, elegant, brilliant, of harmonious proportions, a work of art" (Carroll, 1988, p. 25). This animated interaction style, however, is reserved for close relationships and it is used in informal situations. In "serious conversations," long, uninterrupted responses and attentive listening are used.

Ethnic differences also exist within the United States in the use of animated interactional styles. There are, for example, differences between the European

American and African American verbal interaction styles (Kochman, 1990). African Americans' verbal interaction style tends to be emotionally animated and expressive, while European Americans' verbal interaction style tends to be restrained and subdued. These style differences often lead to misunderstandings in intergroup encounters. Interethnic miscommunication arises when African Americans perceive European Americans as verbally detached and distant, and conversely, the European Americans interpret the verbal style and tone of African Americans as emotionally threatening and intimidating. Even routine conversations can escalate to conflict because of the basic stylistic, conversational differences when people communicate on automatic pilot. Recognizing and dealing with differences in verbal styles requires mindfulness.

The understated style involves the use of understatements, pauses, and silences in conversations (Gudykunst & Ting-Toomey, 1988). More generally, this style involves *not* emphasizing talk in interactions. European Americans see talk as more important and enjoyable than do native-born Chinese or Chinese Americans (Wiemann, Chen, & Giles, 1986). European Americans are more likely than the other two groups to initiate conversations with others and to engage in conversations when opportunities present themselves. Chinese Americans are more likely to engage in these activities than are native-born Chinese. European Americans also see talk as a means of social control, while native-born Chinese see silence as a control strategy. The differences in beliefs about talk between Chinese and European Americans are due to individualism-collectivism:

> Individualists have a choice among many groups . . . to which they do belong, and usually belong to these groups because they volunteer. Collectivists . . . are born into a few groups and are more or less stuck with them. So, the collectivists do not have to go out of their way and exert themselves to be accepted, while individualists have to work hard to be accepted. Hence, the individualists often speak more, try to control the situation verbally, and do not value silence. (Triandis quoted in Giles et al., 1992, p. 11)

Valuing silence should not be taken to suggest that collectivists do not engage in small talk or gossip, because they do. They also engage in a lot of talk with members of the ingroup. Collectivists, however, do not see talk as important as individualists do in developing relationships with others.

Cultures that do not value talk tend to value silence. Silence tends to be valued more in collectivistic cultures than in individualistic cultures. Lebra (1987), for example, isolates four meanings of silence in Japan: truthfulness, social discretion, embarrassment, and defiance. Japanese view truth as occurring only inside the person. Activities regarding the outer self do not involve an individual's true feelings and, therefore, frequently involve distortion, deception, or "moral falsity." A person who speaks little is trusted more than a person who speaks a great deal. In Japan, truthfulness emerges from silences, not words. Silence also allows Japanese to be socially discreet and "to gain social acceptance or to avoid social penalty" (Lebra, 1987, p. 347). At times, talking may be dangerous and require that the person tell the truth. In such instances, silence allows the person to avoid social disapproval. Silence also saves Japanese from embarrassment. Verbally expressing emotions to each other, for example, may cause a traditional married couple in Japan to become embarrassed. Japanese also may indicate disagreement or anger with someone else by being silent.

Silence is valued by some groups within the United States. Asian Americans who hold collectivistic values, for example, will value silence in conversations. Silence also is valued by many Native Americans. Apache Indians, for example, see silence as appropriate in contexts where social relations between individuals are unpredictable and involve high levels of uncertainty. They also prefer silence over talk in situations where role expectations are unclear (Basso, 1970).

Stylistic differences with respect to succinctness and silence can create problems in interethnic communication in North America. Native Americans in Canada and Alaska, for example, prefer more silence in conversations than do European Americans (Scollon & Wong-Scollon, 1990). For the Native Americans, conversations are seen as threatening because other people may try to change them. Conversations, therefore, are avoided unless everyone's opinions are known in advance. European Americans, in contrast, "feel that the main way to get to know the point of view of people is through conversation with them" (Scollon & Wong-Scollon, 1990, p. 263).The conversational paradox in this case also lies in the fact that one of the primary functions of talk is to bridge relational distance for European Americans. European Americans tend to reserve silence for intimate relationships. For the Native Americans, silence is used to protect the sense of vulnerable self from strangers, while talk is used when the relationship becomes more intimate.

Topic Management and Turn-Taking in Conversations

In our conversations with others, we have to coordinate our turn-taking, "that is, who speaks when and for how long. . . . Coordination is accomplished by a system that allows or obligates certain parties to talk at certain times" (Clark, 1985, p. 181). In addition to focusing on the need for coordination, how we take turns reflects who controls the conversation (Wiemann, 1985). Turns must be managed sequentially in conversations on a moment-by-moment basis (Sacks, Schegloff, & Jefferson, 1974).

Several properties of conversations are important in understanding turn-taking (Sacks, Schegloff, & Jefferson, 1974). Generally, one person talks at a time, and when one speaker is finished, another talks. While two (or more) people speaking at the same time is common in conversations, the overlaps do not last long. Generally, there is no gap, or only a small gap, between when one person finishes speaking and another person begins. The order and length of turns in conversations are not fixed. The relative distributions of turns in conversations also are not fixed.

Conversations are mutually constructed by the participants. The person speaking and the people listening have an equal responsibility for managing who talks when and what is discussed. Our conversations are "constructed on an utterance-by-utterance basis, with each subsequent utterance to some extent dependent on preceding ones for its sensibility and appropriateness" (Wiemann, 1985, p. 93). We define our relationships with others by the way we communicate with them. How we hold conversations with people lays the foundation for our future relationship with them. If we want to develop a relationship with another person, we want to "get off on the right foot." Getting off on the right foot is accomplished, at least in part, by how we negotiate turn-taking in our initial conversations. The way we take turns in conversations influences how cooperation will develop in the relationship; it also has implications for how control will be managed in the relationship. By making choices about when to change speakers, we define who is in control of our conversations and what the relationship is at that time (Wiemann, 1985). In handling turn-taking in conversations, we often deal with control issues in the relationship before we are consciously aware of them.

The ways that we take turns and manage topics in conversations differ across cultures. Individualism-collectivism influences topic management and turn distribution in conversations. Japanese (collectivists), for example, "take short turns, distribute their turns relatively evenly, and continue to distribute their turns evenly regardless of who initiates a topic" (Yamada, 1990, p. 291). North Americans (individualists), in contrast, "take long monologic turns, distribute their turns unevenly, and the participant who initiates a topic characteristically takes the highest proportion of turns in that topic" (p. 291). Collectivists organize topics interdependently, while individualists organize topics independently.

The way we manage conversations also is affected by individualism-collectivism. Collectivists use verbal and nonverbal complementary expressions and repetition to support others when they speak and maintain negotiations. Individualists, in contrast, use less synchronizing behaviors and repetition. Individualists tend to use feedback devices (e.g., questions, comments) to indicate they are attentive, while collectivists tend to use back channeling (e.g., brief utterances which make conversation flow smoothly) to accomplish this purpose. When North American "speakers orient attention, they focus on the specific topical content. Japanese speakers only value the emphatic interactional behavior and tend to consider the message exchange secondary" (Hayashi, 1990, p. 188).

Collectivists send back channel signals to the person with whom they are communicating more than do individualists (e.g., White, 1989). Back channel signals are the verbalizations we use to tell the other person that we are listening. To the extent that people are competent in using the back channeling techniques of members of other cultures when speaking their language, effective communication is facilitated (LoCastro, 1987).

One area where problems occur when non-Japanese are speaking Japanese is in the use of *aizuchi*. *Aizuchi* is used frequently in Japanese conversations as a way for the listener to let the speaker know that he or she is listening. A lack of awareness by the nonnative speaker of the rules for using *aizuchi* can create problems. Mizutani (1981, pp. 83–84) provides the following example to illustrate this point:

Japanese: *Moshi moshi.* (Hello.)

Foreigner: *Moshi moshi.* (Hello.)

Japanese: *Ee, kochira, anoo, Yamamoto-desu-ga.* (Uuh, this is err, Yamamoto.)

Foreigner: . . .

Japanese: *Moshi moshi.* (Are you there?)

Foreigner: *Moshi moshi.* (Hello.)

Japanese: *Kochira, Yamamoto-desu-ga. Johnsonsan-wa* . . . (This is Yamamoto. Is Mr./Ms. Johnson . . .)

Foreigner: . . .

Japanese: *Moshi moshi.* (Are you there?)

The caller identified himself in the third line and expected that the listener would provide *aizuchi* to indicate that he or she was paying attention. When no *aizuchi* was provided, the caller assumed that the listener was not following the conversation. The caller, therefore, used *moshi moshi* to determine if the listener was still there. This pattern is repeated later in the conversation when no *aizuchi* is provided. When non-Japanese are able to use *aizuchi*, misunderstandings decrease.

Persuasive Strategies

One important aspect of verbal communication that needs to be addressed before we look at language use in communicating with strangers is how the verbal strategies people use to persuade others vary across cultures. In the previous chapter, we examined patterns of reasoning. These patterns of reasoning can be linked directly to the strategies people use to persuade others. Universalism and abstraction (Glenn, 1981), for example, lead to an axiomatic-deductive style of persuasion (i.e., begin with generalities and proceed to specifics or start from fundamental principles and then discuss their implications). Particularism and associative thought, in contrast, are related to a factual-inductive style of persuasion (i.e., begin with relevant facts and draw conclusions from them). Both of these styles involve an affective-neutrality orientation (Parsons, 1951) toward persuasion. An affective-neutrality orientation toward persuasion is related to the affective-intuitive style of persuasion (i.e., using affective or emotional messages to persuade).

Members of collectivistic cultures take the context into consideration and select strategies that are appropriate to the context. Members of individualistic cultures, in contrast, focus on the person they are trying to persuade and use strategies that may be perceived as socially inappropriate (Gudykunst & Ting-Toomey, 1988).

Hirokawa and Miyahara (1986) report on the strategies managers in corporations in the United States and Japan use to persuade their subordinates. The first situation involves how the manager tries to persuade consistently tardy employees to change their behavior. Japanese managers indicate that they appeal to the employees' "duty" (e.g., "It is your duty as a responsible employee of this company to begin work on time"). North American managers prefer to "threaten" the employees (e.g., "If you don't start reporting to work on time, I will have no choice but to dock your pay") or to give an "ultimatum" (e.g., "If you can't come to work on time, go find yourself another job"). The second situation in this study involves how the managers persuade employees to give their ideas and suggestions to managers. Japanese managers tend to prefer to use "altruistic" strategies (e.g., "For the sake of the company, please share your ideas and suggestions with us") or appeal to "duty" (e.g., "Remember that it is your duty as a good company employee to suggest how we can improve the overall performance of the company"). North American managers prefer to make "direct requests" (e.g., "I want you to feel free to come to me with any ideas you have for improving the company"), to make "promises" (e.g., "Don't hesitate to offer ideas and suggestions because we always reward good suggestions"), or to "ingratiate" themselves to the employees (e.g., "You are one of our best people and I really value your judgment, so please feel free to come to me with ideas you have").

Burgoon et al. (1982) report that in comparison with European Americans, Asian Americans prefer to use the strategies of "promise" (e.g., "If you comply, I will reward you"), "positive expertise" (e.g., "If you comply, you will be rewarded by the nature of things"), "pregiving" (e.g., rewarding the person before making the request), "liking" (e.g., acting friendly to get the other person in a good frame of mind), "positive altercasting" (e.g., "A person with 'good' qualities would comply"), "negative altercasting" (e.g., "Only a person with 'bad' qualities would not comply"), "positive self-feeling" (e.g., "You will feel better about yourself if you comply"), and "positive self-esteem" (e.g., "People you value will think better of you if you comply"). All these strategies tend to involve high degrees of social acceptability.

Cross-cultural research on advertising supports the argument made here. Han and Shavitt (1994), for example, report that magazine advertisements in the United States emphasize benefits to individuals, personal success, and independence more than Korean advertisements. Korean advertisements, in contrast, emphasize ingroup benefits, harmony, and family integrity more than advertisements in the United States. Han and Shavitt also note that advertisements in the United States aimed at individual benefits are more persuasive than advertisement aimed at ingroup benefits, and the reverse is true in Korea.

LANGUAGE USAGE IN COMMUNICATING WITH STRANGERS

Cross-cultural variations in languages and verbal communication styles influence how people from different cultures communicate. Language variations within cultures also influence the way people communicate (see Ting-Toomey & Korzenny,

1989, for recent research). Each of us, for example, speaks a dialect. "Dialect refers to all the differences between varieties of a language, those in pronunciation, word usage, and syntax" (Chaika, 1982, p. 132). Sometimes the difference between language and dialect is not clear-cut. Chaika (1982) points out that

> political boundaries, in themselves, often determine whether two speech varieties will be considered different languages or not. For instance, some varieties of Swedish and Norwegian are mutually comprehensible, but they are considered different languages because they are separated by national borders. Conversely, the so-called dialects of Chinese are as different as French from Italian, but being spoken in one country they are not considered different languages. (p. 133)

Chaika (1982) argues that how we speak is tied very closely to how we define ourselves. She points out that in highly mobile cultures like the United States, "speech is likely to be the most reliable determiner of social class or ethnic group" (p. 139).

Several aspects of language and dialect usage are important in understanding our communication with strangers. Our attitudes toward other languages and dialects influence how we respond to others, whether we learn other languages, when we use other languages or dialects, and whether we accommodate to people with whom we are communicating. We begin our discussion of language in our communication with strangers by looking at the vitality of languages and linguistic groups.

Ethnolinguistic Vitality

Giles, Bourhis, and Taylor (1977) argue that the degree to which group members will act as a group when interacting with members of outgroups is influenced by the group's *ethnolinguistic vitality,* the range and importance of the functions served by language usage. They isolated three factors that contribute to a group's vitality: the group's social status, the demographic characteristics of the group, and the institutional support for the group's language or dialect. The social status variables include those which exert an influence on the prestige of a language group, such as the economic, social, and language status of that particular social group. Giles, Bourhis, and Taylor contend that the higher a group's social status, the greater its vitality. The demographic variables are those related to the size of the group and its distribution within specific areas and the country as a whole. Group size includes the group's absolute numbers, birth rate, number of mixed marriages, immigration and emigration, while distribution refers to the concentration as well as proportion of the group compared with an outgroup. As would be expected, the larger the group, the greater its vitality (Giles et al., 1977). Finally, institutional support refers to the representation of the language use in institutions such as churches, businesses, and government agencies. The greater the institutional support for a language group, the greater its validity (Giles et al., 1977).

Giles et al. (1977) isolate two types of group vitality: subjective and objective. Subjective group vitality is a group's societal position as perceived by its members, while objective group vitality is associated with the group's relative position based on the available "objective" data. They propose that the more vitality an ethnolinguistic group has, the more likely the group will survive as a distinctive linguistic group in a multilingual setting. Conversely, an ethnolinguistic group that has little or no group vitality will eventually cease to exist as a distinctive group.

Gao, Schmidt, and Gudykunst (1994) describe objective characteristics of Mexican Americans' ethnolinguistic vitality in Phoenix. In terms of demographic factors, they point out that Mexican Americans constitute "13.2 percent of the total population. Between 1970 and 1980, the Mexican American population grew by 43 percent. Projections suggest that by 1990, 15 percent of the Phoenix population will be Mexican American" (p. 335). With respect to social status, they point out that "the yearly mean family income for Mexican Americans in 1980 was $17,426, while Anglo families earned $24,559. The majority of Mexican Americans are employed by the construction industry and the service sector. Because of low educational attainment (43 percent are high school graduates), many Mexican Americans have not been integrated into the growing economy" (p. 335). For institutional support, Gao and her associates point out that "there are three Spanish speaking radio stations and one television station in Phoenix. Mexican Americans in Arizona proportionately hold more established, recognized and visible positions of leadership than in any other state. . . . Most Mexican Americans in the Phoenix area (63 percent) speak Spanish at home and the overwhelming majority are bilingual" (p. 335). Gao and her associates' study reveals that Mexican Americans' subjective perceptions of their group's vitality in the Phoenix area correspond closely with the objective situation.

A number of researchers have compared different ethnic group's perceptions of ethnolinguistic vitality within cultures. Giles, Rosenthall, and Young's (1985) study of ethnolinguistic vitality perceptions of Greek and Anglo Australians, for example, reveals that the two groups agree that Anglos' vitality is higher on certain status and institutional support items, but disagree about each other's sociostructural positions. Bourhis and Sachdev's (1984) research indicates that a relationship exists between perceived vitality and language attitudes (discussed below). Young, Giles, and Pierson's (1986) research suggests that proficiency in the ingroup and outgroup language also influences perceived vitality.

Gao, Schmidt, and Gudykunst (1994) contend that ethnic identity has a significant influence on perceived group vitality. The general trend is for respondents who identify strongly with their ethnic group to perceive that their group has higher vitality than those who do not identify strongly with their group. This pattern is compatible with social identity theory (e.g., Tajfel, 1978) and recent studies of the effect of social identity on language attitudes (e.g., Hogg, Joyce, & Abrams, 1984).

If members of a group perceive their language to have high vitality, that perception will strengthen their ethnic identity (Giles & Johnson, 1987). Because of its influence on strengthening identity, perceiving language vitality also decreases uncertainty and anxiety. Perceived vitality of a language also affects attitudes toward specific languages or dialects, the motivation of individuals in "minority" groups to learn the language of the dominant group, and the language or dialect people choose to use when they communicate. We discuss language attitudes first.

Language Attitudes

The language or dialect we speak influences how others judge us and whether they are willing to help us. A study by Gaertner and Bickman (1971) illustrates the influence of dialect on whether others will help us. African American and European American callers, making phone calls from a phone booth, pretended to have gotten a wrong number using the last of their change. After discovering they had a wrong number, the callers asked the person on the other end to help them by calling the correct number. The results indicate that African Americans who received phone calls were equally likely to help a European American or an African American caller. European Americans, in contrast, helped European Americans more frequently than they helped African Americans. Given that the only information the person receiving the call had about the person making the call was his or her dialect, the results demonstrate that dialect influences the degree to which others will help.

Generally, speakers using a standard dialect are rated high on competence, intelligence, industriousness, and confidence, as well as other traits associated with socioeconomic status. Speakers using nonstandard dialects, in contrast, are rated lower than standard speakers on these dimensions, even by nonstandard dialect speakers (see Bradac, 1990, for a review). Our language attitudes are influenced by our stereotypes and the situation in which the language is used. Social class also influences language attitudes. Chaika (1982) points out that speaking "properly"

> is a matter of great concern to the educated middle class, which above all wishes to be identified as educated. Its members' being recognized as those to be listened to hinges strongly on language. When people say they want to know the right way to speak, they do not mean the right way to communicate their ideas but, rather, the right way to announce that those ideas are to be respected, to be listened to. (p. 239)

We, therefore, cannot understand others' language usage unless we take their social class into consideration.

Ryan, Giles, and Sebastian (1982) suggest that language attitudes can be characterized in terms of two interrelated dimensions, standardization and vitality. Ryan, Hewstone, and Giles (1984) summarize these dimensions as follows:

> Standardization is the more static dimension, referring to the extent to which norms for correct usage . . . have been codified, adopted, and promoted for a particular variety. This might be accomplished through the compilation of dictionaries and grammars while the acceptance of a variety may be advanced by elites and government. . . . Vitality is the more dynamic dimension, reflecting the range and importance of functions served by language varieties . . . and the social pressures toward shift in language use. (pp. 143–144)

Changes in language attitudes are due mostly to changes in perceived vitality (changes in standardization also occur with changes in vitality). As people perceive the vitality of a language or dialect increasing, its use is viewed more positively.

Edwards (1985) draws several conclusions regarding the research on language attitudes. He points out that

> all language varieties can reflect [social] identity. There is a regularity in research findings here: non-standard forms attract high ratings in terms of group solidarity, while standard ones are seen to reflect higher competence. Thus, even dialects lacking in social prestige retain a claim upon their speakers. In this sense, a bidialectal person is like one for whom bilingualism is a stable quantity—identity can be carried in an original variety while another is added for instrumental reasons. . . . Dialectical adjustment according to the perceived demands of context reflects a motivation for success *and* original marker retention. (p. 167)

Our language attitudes clearly influnce how we respond to strangers.

Language attitudes are important, in and of themselves. They also are important because they influence our desire to learn other languages.

Second Language Competence

There are numerous explanations of second language learning (see Gardner, 1985, for reviews of major theories), but only the intergroup model takes into consideration the intergroup factors relevant to second language learning. Wc, therefore, focus on that model here.

Giles and Byrne (1982) argue that second language learning cannot be explained unless the relations between the groups are taken into consideration. Garrett, Giles, and Coupland (1989) isolate five factors that contribute to members of a "minority" group learning the language of the "dominant" group.

The first factor in Garrett, Giles, and Coupland's (1989) model involves how the minority language is viewed. If members of an ethnic group identify weakly with their group or do not view language as an important part of their identity, they are likely to try to learn the dominant language. If members of minority groups view their language as an important part of their identity, they will try to learn the dominant language to the extent that it does not threaten their identity or they have other ways to preserve their ethnic identity.

Second, if members of the ethnic group perceive few alternatives to their "subordinate" status and view the chance of its changing as small, they will try to learn the dominant language. They will also try to learn the dominant language if they perceive cognitive alternatives to their status and realize that these can be met by learning the dominant language.

Third, members of minority groups will try to learn the dominant language to the extent that they perceive the boundaries between their group and the dominant group to be soft and open. In other words, if they believe that learning the dominant language will help them be accepted in the dominant group, they will try to learn the language.

Fourth, members of minority groups will try to learn the dominant language to the extent that they derive satisfactory social identities from other group memberships. That is, they are members of other social categories that provide them with satisfactory identities.

Finally, if members of minority groups perceive the vitality of their group to be low, they will attempt to learn the dominant group language. They also will try to learn the dominant language if they believe learning it will contribute to the vitality of their ingroup.

In addition to these five intergroup factors, Garrett, Giles, and Coupland, (1989) isolated three sociolinguistic factors that contribute to second language learning. First, the more similar the dominant language and the majority language, the more likely members of minorities are to learn the dominant language. Second, there must be exposure to the dominant language for it to be learned (i.e., members of the minority group must have contact with speakers of the dominant language). Third, there must be use of the dominant language for it to be learned (i.e, members of the minority group need to have the opportunity to use the dominant language in a variety of contexts).

Garrett, Giles, and Coupland's research generally supports the model they propose. Other support for the model is provided by Giles and Johnson (1987), Hall and Gudykunst (1986), and Kelley et al. (1993).

The theory outlined here is not limited to members of minority groups learning the dominant language; it applies equally to a person from one culture learning the language of another culture. Once the dominant or second language is learned, there is the remaining issue of what effects its use has on the communication that takes place. If we are competent in strangers' languages, that competence reduces our uncertainty and anxiety when we communicate with them (Gudykunst, 1995). Linguistic competence also influences our ability to accommodate our communication and code-switch when we communicate with strangers. We discuss these issues in the next two sections.

Communication Accommodation

In attempting to provide a systematic explanation for the persistence of linguistic diversity, Tajfel (1974, 1978) suggests that when members of one group interact with strangers of another, they compare themselves on a number of value dimensions with the strangers. He claims these intergroup social comparisons lead group members to search for characteristics of their own group that will enable them to differentiate themselves favorably from the outgroup (as discussed in detail in Chapter 4). Such positive ingroup distinctiveness not only allows individuals personal satisfaction in their own group membership but also affords them a positive social identity. Applying this psychological process to speech behavior, Giles (1973) describes the tendency to accentuate (i.e., emphasize) linguistic difference as *speech divergence.* Some individuals in interaction with others shift their speech in their desire for their listeners' social approval. One tactic, consciously or unconsciously conceived, is for them to modify their speech in the direction of the listeners' speech patterns, a process Giles terms *speech convergence.*

Giles, Bourhis, and Taylor (1977) suggest that when members of a subordinate group accept their inferior status, they attempt to converge into the dominant group socially and psychologically by means of speech convergence. If, on the other hand, they consider their inferior status to be illegitimate and the intergroup situation to be unstable, they seek "psychological distinctiveness" by redefining their group attributes in a socially and psychologically more favorable direction. They also might seek distintinctivenss linguistically and, hence, in interaction with a member of the outgroup, accentuate their own ingroup characteristics by means of speech divergence, using their own dialect, accent, jargon, or other form of speech variation.

There is a tendency for members of ingroups to react favorably to outgroup members who converge linguistically toward them (Giles & Smith, 1979). Giles and Byrne (1982) point out that as an outgroup's members begin to learn the speech style of the ingroup, ingroup members may diverge in some way to maintain linguistic distinctiveness. Reaction to outgroup members' speech convergence depends on the intent ingroup members attribute to the outgroup members (Simard, Taylor, & Giles, 1976).

Genesse and Bourhis (1982) observe that ingroup members' evaluation of outgroup members' language usage in conversations is based on situational norms in the initial stages of conversations and on interpersonal accommodation later in the conversation. Bourhis (1985) claims that following situational norms is the strategy used most frequently in early stages of hostile intergroup encounters. In later stages of conversations, however, individuals adopt strategies based on their goals, their desire to assert their group identity, and their affective response to the other person.

Giles et al. (1986) argue that communication convergence is a function of a speaker's desire for (1) social approval, (2) high communication efficiency, (3) shared self- or group-presentation, and (4) an appropriate identity definition. For communication convergence to occur, a match must exist between the speaker's view of the recipient's speech style and the actual style used, and the specific speech style used must be appropriate for both speaker and recipient. Divergence, in contrast, is a function of the speaker's desire (1) for a "contrastive" self-image, (2) to dissociate from the recipient, (3) to change the recipient's speech behavior, and (4) to define an encounter in intergroup terms. Divergence also occurs when recipients use a speech style that deviates from a norm that is valued and consistent with the speaker's expectations regarding the recipient's performance. If strangers accommodate to our communication style and we perceive their intent to be positive, our uncertainty and anxiety in communicating with them will be reduced.

Gallois et al. (1995) argue that our cultural background affects how we respond to linguistic convergence by strangers. They suggest that

> individualists may react to convergence from outgroup interlocutors in a relatively positive manner, and converge toward the outgroup speaker reciprocally. With oftentimes softer group boundaries, their thresholds for allowing linguistic penetration by outgroup members may be lower [than collectivists' thresholds]. Conversely, people

from collectivistic cultures, who perceive harder boundaries [than do individualists], may react to attempts at communication convergence more negatively, and may diverge from them more if they perceive the convergence as overstepping a valued cultural or national boundary [than individualists]. (p. 131)

Members of collectivistic cultures, therefore, are more likely to diverge from outgroup members than are members of individualistic cultures.

Code-Switching

There is extensive research on attempts to isolate the factors that influence which code (i.e., language or dialect) people use (see Gudykunst et al. 1989; Sachdev & Bourhis, 1990, for sources). The code that is used is in part a function of the vitality of the languages or dialects of the speakers involved and the desire for the communicators to accommodate to the person with whom they are communicating. There are also "normative" factors that contribute to code choice. Studies of immigrants in the United States who speak English as a second language, for example, suggest that English is used in public formal settings, while the native language is used in informal, nonpublic settings. This conclusion is supported by research in other countries (e.g., Philippines, Paraguay, Israel, Nigeria) as well. The topic of conversation also affects the code used. People who speak more than one language tend to use their native language when discussing stressful or exciting topics.

In addition to choosing a particular code according to the topic of conversation and the setting, people may switch languages to show warmth and group identification (Gumperz & Hernandez-Chavez, 1972). Recall Rodriquez's explanation (in the ethnic identity section of Chapter 4) of the effect speaking in Spanish had on his feelings of being bonded to his family. Similarly, immigrants tend to use their first language when discussing life in the native country. Using the first language to discuss life in the native country reinforces cultural heritage and fills a need to "identify with compatriots" (Chaika, 1982, p. 239).

Chaika (1982) points out that people sometimes switch codes for emphasis or to see if a stranger belongs to the ingroup. She argues that

the switch from one language to another, in itself, has meaning. No matter what else a switch means, it reinforces bonds between speakers. Such switching can obviously only occur between those who speak the same language. It may be done in the presence of nonspeakers as a way of excluding them, just as jargon may. (p. 238)

The language or dialect people select, therefore, reinforces their social identity.

Scotton (1983) argues that individuals choose the code in which they speak in order to negotiate relationships with others. She believes that the choice is based on a negotiation principle which directs a person to "choose the form of your conversational contribution [i.e., the code] such that it symbolizes the set of rights and obligations which you wish to be in force between speaker and addressee for the current exchange" (p. 116). In any situation, one code is unmarked (i.e., considered to be the standard code in that situation) and other codes are considered to be marked to some degree. Which codes are considered marked or unmarked depends on the speakers and the situation. An upper-level management person in Nairobi speaking in an office transaction, for example, would choose English as the un-marked choice (Scotton, 1990). A lower-level employee, in contrast, would choose Swahili as the unmarked code.

Scotton (1990) contends that "making the unmarked choice in a convention-alized exchange is a negotiation of normative and predicted behavior" (p. 92). In conventionalized exchanges, the unmarked choice usually is relatively clear. One upper-level management person in Nairobi, for example, would choose to speak in English to another upper-level employee if he or she wanted to negotiate predictable behavior. A person can choose, however, to use an unmarked code in a convention-alized exchange. When this choice is made, the person is trying to negotiate an out-come different from the expected one. This strategy is used to change the social dis-tance between people. A lower-level employee in Nairobi choosing to speak to an upper-level employee in English instead of Swahili, for example, might be at-tempting to decrease the social distance between them.

Switching from an unmarked choice in a conventionalized exchange involves trying to negotiate new rights and obligations in the situation. "Marked switches are always disruptive, because they are disputing the status quo" (Scotton, 1990, p. 98). They can have positive or negative consequences depending on whether they in-crease or decrease the social distance between the participants. Scotton (1983) iso-lates two maxims which guide these changes. The *deference* maxim says to "show deference in your code choice to those from whom you desire something, espe-cially to negotiate face-threatening acts" (Scotton, 1990, p. 98). The *virtuosity* maxim involves making a linguistic choice on the basis of the linguistic ability of the speaker or person being addressed.

In nonconventionalized exchanges, the unmarked code is not necessarily clear (Scotton, 1990). In such a situation, the speaker proposes an unmarked code and if the person being addressed accepts this choice (i.e., responds in this code), she or he accepts the rights and obligations that go with speaking in that code. If the per-son being addressed chooses another code, he or she is trying to negotiate a differ-ent identity with the person speaking.

The degree to which different codes are mixed depends on how multilingual the society is. In the United States, European Americans do not engage in extensive code-switching. In other societies that are multilingual, there is extensive code-switching. Where there is extensive code-switching, code-switching tends to be motivated by a desire to maximize the positive benefits of the code being used and minimize the negative aspects of code usage. Southworth (1980), for example, points out that in South India

in many situations it is not only possible, but socially necessary, to use more than one language in the course of an interaction. Thus, rules of formality may indicate English, whereas ethnic solidarity demands Tamil or Malayalam. In other cases, informality (in a domestic context, for example) may require Tamil or Malayalam, but individuals of different ethnic backgrounds may require some speakers to add a certain proportion of another language to the mix. (p. 140)

Obviously, the degree to which code switches are made depends on the linguistic abilities of the people involved.

Code-switching is linked to ethnic identity in organizations. Banks (1987), for example, argues that the boundary (e.g., the line separating) between marked (e.g., use of ethnic dialect) and unmarked (e.g., "standard" dialect) ethnic discourse is soft and permeable, while the boundary between low- and high-power positions in the organization is harder and less permeable. Banks draws four conclusions regarding ethnic discourse in organizations. First, members of minority groups must cross the soft boundary from ethnically marked to unmarked discourse before crossing the boundary from low- to high-power positions. Second, crossing the boundary from ethnically marked to unmarked discourse is a function of the individuals' strategies to maximize rewards, as well as the norms, values for discourse in the organization (e.g., does the organization value speaking English). Third, there is an implicit promise from the organization he studied that if members of minorities cross the boundary from ethnically marked to unmarked discourse, they will have the opportunity to cross the boundary from low- to high-power position. Finally, individuals who cross the boundary from ethnically marked to unmarked discourse "subtract from" their ethnic identities (i.e., using unmarked discourse takes away from the strength of their ethnic identity).

San Antonio (1987) contends that language-in-use also is a marker of ethnic identity in a United States company in Japan. In the company she observed, the official policy is that only English is to be spoken. While that is the official policy of the company, the actual English ability of the Japanese ranges from no ability to speak English to almost native proficiency. San Antonio's data suggest that the use of English by Japanese employees is a way the employees take on the identity of being a Japanese with whom the North Americans can work. North American managers interpret the use of English and following North American communication rules (e.g., use of first names, joking) positively and not using English, negatively. The Japanese who are fluent in English in this company "protect" employees who do not speak English by speaking up in meetings and answering North Americans' questions. Speaking English, therefore, "adds" to their chosen identity in this situation.

Miscommunication in Intercultural Discourse

Miscommunication implies that things have gone wrong in the interaction between two people. While miscommunication can occur when any two people communicate, it is more likely to occur when native speakers (NSs) of one language communicate with nonnative speakers (NNSs) of that language (e.g., when NSs of English communicate with NNSs whose native language is not English). Gass and Varonis (1991) divide problems of communication in NS-NNS interaction into two categories: nonengagement and miscommunication.

Gass and Varonis (1991) isolate two types of nonengagement: noncommunication and communication breakoff. *Noncommunication* occurs when an NS or NNS avoids communicating with the other person. This situation could involve going out of the way to avoid interacting with the other person or consciously choosing to speak only to other members of one's ingroup. One reason noncommunication might occur is that NSs perceive that the energy necessary to communicate with NNSs is greater than what they will gain from the interaction. *Communication breakoff* occurs when NSs or NNSs end a conversation that is taking place. The main reason such a breakoff usually occurs is that the people breaking off the conversation perceive that continuing the conversation is not in their best interest.

Gass and Varonis (1991) also isolate two types of miscommunication: misunderstanding and incomplete understanding. *Misunderstanding* is a "simple disparity between the speaker's and hearer's semantic analysis of a given utterance" (Milroy, 1984, p. 15). When misunderstandings occur, the participants do not recognize that there is a problem. *Incomplete understanding,* in contrast, occurs when "one or more participants perceive that something has gone wrong" (Milroy, 1984, p. 15). When incomplete understanding occurs, at least one of the participants clearly recognizes that there is a problem.

When misunderstandings occur, neither participant recognizes that a problem occurs during the interaction. After the interaction is over, however, one or both of the participants might recognize that there was a problem. The person who recognizes the problem can choose to ignore the problem or to try to figure out what the problem was (for one method of determining what is causing such problems, see the discussion of description, interpretation, and evaluation in Chapter 10). Once the participant figures out what the problem was, he or she can choose to ignore the problem or to correct it. The decision that the person makes probably depends on the nature of the relationship between the people and the importance of the conversation. If, for example, the relationship between the two people is not close, the participant may choose to ignore the problem. If the relationship is close, in contrast, the participant may choose to correct the problem. Similarly, participants may choose to ignore the problem in conversations they do not think are important and to correct problems in conversations they think are important.

When incomplete understandings occur, at least one of the participants recognizes that there is a problem during the conversation. This situation is more likely to occur when participants are mindful of their communication rather than when they communicate on automatic pilot. The person who recognizes the problem can choose to ignore the problem or to try to correct it. The factors that influence this choice probably are similar to those that influence the choices regarding miscommunication after the interaction. If a decision to correct the problem is made, the participants must negotiate to correct the incomplete understanding. After attempting to negotiate the incomplete understanding, participants need to decide whether they have corrected the problem or not. If they have not corrected the problem, they must decide whether to try again or to ignore the problem.

When NNSs have low levels of competence in NSs' languages, both parties tend to assume that problems in communication will occur. When NNSs have high levels of competence, in contrast, there is an increased tendency for them not to recognize problems. Since the participants "assume they understand each other, they are less likely to question interpretations" of each other's messages (Gumperz & Tannen, 1979, p. 315). Varonis and Gass (1985) argue that this is the most "dangerous" type of situation because participants are confident of their interpretations of others' messages, but their interpretations actually are inaccurate.

Gass and Varonis (1984) argue that familiarity is one of the major factors that influence NSs' ability to comprehend NNSs. The more familiar NSs are with the topic of the conversation, the easier it is for them to comprehend NNSs' speech. Familiarity with the NNSs' speech and their accent also facilitates comprehension. The more familiar English speakers are in general with Japanese who are speaking English and with their accents, the more easily they can comprehend a specific Japanese person who is speaking English. Finally, familiarity with specific NNSs facilitates NSs' comprehension of their speech.

Misunderstandings and incomplete understanding can emerge from pragmatic errors. As indicated earlier, pragmatic rules tell us how to interpret the meaning of utterances. Riley (1989) argues that *pragmatic errors* are "the result of an interactant imposing the social rules on his [or her] communicative behavior in a situation where the social rules of another culture would be more appropriate" (p. 234). He isolates four types of pragmatic errors we make in intercultural interactions: pragmalinguistic, sociopragmatic, inchoactive, and nonlinguistic (the first two originally were isolated by J. Thomas, 1983).

Pragmalinguistic errors are language-specific errors that involve the pragmatic force of an utterance having different meanings in two languages or that occur when speech strategies are inappropriately transferred from one language to another (J. Thomas, 1983). English speakers who speak aggressively when speaking in Japanese, for example, are making pragmalinguistic errors because Japanese speakers humble themselves. French hotel receptionists who hand back a passport to a foreign visitor saying "please," also are making these errors (by translating word for word what would be said in French into English).

Sociopragmatic errors "stem from cross-culturally different perceptions of what constitutes appropriate linguistic behavior" (J. Thomas, 1983, p. 99). These errors are a function of *not* perceiving the situation or categorizing the other people involved in accordance with the cultural norms they are using. If a professor from Japan, for example, is visiting a professor in the United States and immediately after introductions asks "How old are you?" the Japanese professor is making a sociopragmatic error because he or she is using Japanese cultural communication rules (e.g., categorizing people on the basis of age).

Inchoactive errors are a function of "a failure to appreciate the 'true' value of discourse" (Riley, 1989, p. 237). This type of error is a function of the cultural value placed on talk and silence, discussed earlier in this chapter. Scollon and Scollon (1981), for example, argue that problems of communication between European Americans and Athbaskan Indians are due to different orientations toward talk and silence. European Americans "talk to strangers to get to know them" and Athbaskan Indians "get to know someone in order to be able to speak. "If we do not understand the values people place on talk and silence, we will inevitably make errors in interpreting their speech.

Nonlinguistic errors are errors that occur as a result of misinterpreting non-verbal cues strangers use (Riley, 1989). Riley argues that there are situations where responses to behaviors may require a verbal response and situations where no verbal response is required, but a nonverbal response is required. Nonverbal messages are discussed in the next chapter.

Riley (1989) argues that there are many strategies that can be used to correct pragmatic errors when they occur. Correcting errors, however, requires some awareness that an error has occurred. He isolates seven strategies for correcting pragmatic errors: (1) evasion (including message abandonment and change of focus); (2) paraphrase (including approximation, circumlocution, description, and word coinage); (3) transfer (including literal translation and language switch); (4) appeals (for assistance, clarification, or feedback); (5) nonverbal strategies (gesture, drawing, writing); (6) checks (giving further information, examples); and (7) simplification (of grammar or vocabulary). Any of these strategies can be used to correct pragmatic errors and negotiate meanings when we communicate with strangers.

Language Usage and Uncertainty Reduction

The language strangers use influences how we reduce uncertainty. Berger and Bradac (1982) suggest four alternative models with respect to the relationship between language and uncertainty reduction:

> *Model 1* specifies that we use others' language to develop hypotheses about their group affiliations. On the basis of these hypotheses, judgments of similarity are made. The greater the similarity we perceive, the more our uncertainty is reduced.

> *Model 2* specifies that we use others' language to make a judgment of their psychological traits. We then use these psychological traits to judge how similar others are to us. The more similarity we perceive, the more our uncertainty is reduced.

> *Model 3* combines Models 1 and 2. It posits that we use language to make a judgment of others' group memberships. On the basis of others' group memberships, we make assumptions about their psychological traits. On the basis of traits, we make assumptions about how similar they are to us.

> *Model 4* suggests that we make judgments of similarity directly from the language others use.

These four models are valid in different situations (Berger & Bradac, 1982).

Gudykunst and Ting-Toomey (1990) suggest that the validity of the models varies depending on the interpersonal and intergroup characteristics of the interaction. When intergroup factors are very important and interpersonal factors are not very important, we tend to use language to make judgments of group affiliations which lead to judgments of similarity (Model 1). When intergroup factors are very important and interpersonal factors also are very important, a judgment of group membership is used to make judgments of psychological traits, which form the basis for judgments of similarity (Model 3). When intergroup factors are not very important and interpersonal factors are very important, language leads directly to judgments of psychological traits, which lead to judgments of similarity (Model 2). Finally, when neither interpersonal or intergroup factors are very important, language usage leads directly to judgments of similarity (Model 4).

SUMMARY

In this chapter, we considered some of the cultural, sociological, and psychological dimensions of language and verbal behavior. The theoretical perspective provided by Sapir and Whorf warns us not to consider language to be merely a medium through which we express our thoughts and feelings. Language is much more than that. As we acquire language, we acquire culture, which, in turn, conditions our perception, thinking, and behavior.

Following Bernstein's conceptualization of language and social context, various languages can be placed on a continuum of restricted and elaborated codes. This continuum of linguistic variations closely coincides with Hall's continuum of high-context to low-context communication messages. While restricted codes are a predominant mode of linguistic and verbal behavior in collectivistic cultures, elaborated codes are relied on heavily for thinking processes and social interaction in individualistic cultures.

In addition, we note how language ties us emotionally to the speech community to which we belong. Through group identification with our language, we develop both a sense of identification with our own speech community and a feeling of distinctiveness from other speech communities. A foreign diplomat visiting the United States (a stranger) may choose to speak at a press conference in his or her own language rather than in English. This deliberate choice of speech mode commonly is respected as a symbolic assertion of the national sovereignty represented by the diplomat. On the other hand, the heartwarming speech given by Pope John Paul II while visiting the United States constituted a friendly and respectful gesture to the public in that he addressed his audience in English.

Understanding cultural and subcultural variations in the social meaning of verbal behavior as outlined in this chapter is a crucial step toward a greater understanding of ourselves and the strangers we meet. On the basis of such understanding, we may try to develop empathy and patience for strangers whose primary language and modes of verbal behavior are different from our own, thereby decreasing our anxiety and increasing our ability to understand and predict their behavior.

STUDY QUESTIONS

1. What is the Sapir-Whorf hypothesis?
2. How are restricted and elaborated codes similar to low- and high-context messages?
3. Why is there little rhetorical tradition in Asian cultures?
4. How do direct and indirect styles of verbal communication differ? Which styles predominate in individualistic and collectivistic cultures?
5. How do elaborated and understated styles of communication differ?
6. What does the way we take turns in conversations tell us about our relationships with others?
7. How do turn taking and topic management differ in individualistic and collectivistic cultures?
8. How does ethnolinguistic vitality influence the way members of different groups communicate with each other?
9. How are standard and nonstandard dialects evaluated?
10. What factors contribute to members of a minority group learning the majority group's language?
11. What factors contribute to our converging toward or diverging from others in conversations?
12. When do people who speak English as a second language tend to speak English and when do they tend to speak their native language?
13. What are the differences between misunderstanding and incomplete understanding?

SUGGESTED READING

Agar, M. (1994). *Language shock: Understanding the culture of conversation.* New York: Morrow.

Coupland, N., Giles, H., & Wiemann, J. (Eds.). (1991). *"Miscommunication" and problematic talk.* Thousand Oaks, CA: Sage.

Edwards, J. (1985). *Language, society, and identity.* Oxford, UK: Blackwell.

Giles, H., & Coupland, N. (1991). *Language: Contexts and consequences.* Pacific Grove, CA: Brooks/Cole.

Ting-Toomey, S., & Korzenny, F. (Eds.). (1989). *Language, communication, and culture.* Thousand Oaks, CA: Sage.

Whorf, B. L. (1956). *Language, thought, and reality.* New York: Wiley.

9

Nonverbal Messages

How stupid [are they] who would
patch the hatred in [their] eyes
with the smile of [their] lips.
Kahlil Gibran

Just as our verbal behaviors are influenced by our culture, our nonverbal behaviors reflect many of the cultural patterns we acquire throughout the socialization process. The way in which we move about in space when communicating with others is based primarily on our physical and emotional responses to environmental stimuli. While our verbal behaviors are mostly explicit and are processed cognitively, our nonverbal behaviors are spontaneous, ambiguous, often fleeting, and often beyond our conscious awareness and control. When we communicate with strangers, our understanding of the interaction is limited by the strangers' unfamiliar nonverbal behaviors. From greetings to expressions of feelings, we may find ourselves feeling uncomfortable because of strangers' nonverbal behavior. Since our perceptions of nonverbal behaviors are rarely conscious, we may not know exactly why we are feeling uncomfortable.

Hall (1966) refers to the largely unconscious phenomenon of nonverbal communication as the hidden dimension of culture. It is considered hidden because, unlike verbal messages, nonverbal messages are embedded in the contextual field of communication. In addition to the situational and relational cues of a particular communication transaction, nonverbal messages provide us with important contextual cues. Together with verbal and other contextual cues, nonverbal messages help us interpret the total meaning of our communication with strangers.

Our purpose in this chapter is to examine cultural variability in nonverbal behaviors and to identify how nonverbal behaviors influence our communication with strangers. We begin, however, with a brief overview of nonverbal communication.

THE NATURE OF NONVERBAL COMMUNICATION

Language and nonverbal cues are similar in some ways and different in others. First, nonverbal cues are discrete, as is language. Nonverbal cues can be separated from one another. Second, some nonverbal cues are created on the basis of agreement among the members of a group using them and, therefore, they are arbitrary, as are symbols. "The finger," for example, is an obscene gesture in the United States, but other cultures use different gestures with the same meaning as "the finger." Other nonverbal cues are not arbitrary. A smile, for instance, is recognized around the world to represent happiness (this is not to say that smiles cannot be used in other circumstances as well). Third, language involves displacement (i.e., the ability to use language to refer to things that are not present), but nonverbal cues do not. Nonverbal cues are limited to referring to things that are present. Finally, language and nonverbal cues differ in terms of their relative weight in determining meaning. In general, "adults place more reliance on nonverbal cues than verbal ones in determining meaning" (Burgoon, Buller, & Woodall, 1989, p. 155). This tendency to rely more on nonverbal cues is especially true when the verbal and nonverbal messages are inconsistent.

Nonverbal cues serve several functions in interaction (Ekman & Friesen, 1969). First, nonverbal cues may *repeat* the verbal message. Second, nonverbal cues may *contradict* the verbal cues. In English, when people tell us with a flat tone of voice that they love us, we are likely to interpret the flat tone of voice as contradicting the verbal message. Third, nonverbal cues can *substitute* for the verbal cues. Fourth, nonverbal messages may *complement* the verbal message. Fifth, nonverbal cues can *accent* part of the verbal message. Sixth, nonverbal cues can *regulate* the flow of conversations.

We use various types of nonverbal behavior when we communicate with others. First, our *physical appearance* provides nonverbal cues that others use to make judgments about us. Second, the way we use space (called *proxemics*) helps us regulate intimacy and control our sensory exposure to others. Third, the way we move our bodies (called *kinesic behavior*) provides information about us to others. Fourth, the way we use our voice (called *paralanguage*) tells others how we define the relationship between ourselves and them. Fifth, the degree to which we *touch* others and the degree to which we allow others to touch us provides cues to how we see our relationships.

Often nonverbal behaviors are discussed as either universal or culture-bound. The distinction, however, is not that simple. LaFrance and Mayo (1978) point out that there are at least three layers of nonverbal behavior:

The innermost core represents nonverbal behaviors considered to be universal and innate; facial expressions of some emotional states belong to this core. Next come the nonverbal behaviors that show both uniformity and diversity; members of all cultures display affect, express intimacy, and deal with status but the particular signs of so doing are variable. Finally, there are culture-bound nonverbal behaviors which manifest great dissimilarity across cultures—language-related acts such as emblems [nonverbal cues with a direct verbal translation; e.g., "V" for victory], illustrators [nonverbal cues which directly accompany speech; e.g., cues which illustrate what is being said nodding our head to accompany verbal agreement in the United States], and regulators [cues which regulate the back and forth flow of speaking and listen ing; e.g., looking at speaker when listening and looking away when talking in European American culture] show diversity most clearly. (p. 73)

Nonverbal behaviors, therefore, vary from universality to dissimilarity across cultures.

CROSS-CULTURAL VARIABILITY IN NONVERBAL MESSAGES

In this section, we examine cultural variability in nonverbal messages. We begin by looking at the recognition and expression of emotions. Next, we examine how the desire for contact influences cultural differences in nonverbal behaviors. Finally, we discuss the process of interpersonal synchronization.

Emotion Expression and Recognition

People everywhere experience feelings such as happiness, sadness, and anger and exhibit a great deal of similarity in their expressions of these human emotions. Darwin (1872) observed certain similarities in the expressive behavior of humans with different cultural backgrounds and interpreted these as being due to characteristics inborn in all humans. Darwin contends that emotional facial expressions are inherited because they were biologically adaptive in earlier times. The main purpose of emotional expression today is to signal internal emotional states to others. Biologists, biologically oriented anthropologists, and psychologists repeatedly emphasize the innate similarities in human expressive behavior.

The innate view of emotional expression has been challenged repeatedly. LaBarre (1947), for example, suggests that emotional expression is culturally based. Similarly, Birdwhistell (1963) advances the hypothesis that no expressive movement has a universal meaning and that all movements are a product of culture, not biologically inherited or inborn.

Ekman (1972) integrates these two views on human emotional expression into a neurocultural theory of facial expressions of emotion. Ekman agrees that facial expressions of emotion are inherited. He also believes that cultural constraints play a very important role in shaping how emotions are expressed. Ekman suggests that cultural *display rules* are learned within our culture, and these rules tell us when to express emotions and when not to expose them. Cultural display rules lead us to intensify, deintensify, neutralize, or mask the facial display to comply with the normative demands of specific situations in our culture (see Bond, 1993, for cultural display rules in Chinese culture). There also are cultural *decoding rules,* which tell us how to interpret emotions when they are displayed. Matsumoto and Kudoh (1993) argue that North Americans, for example, associate more positive characteristics with people who smile than do Japanese.

Universals in Emotion Recognition.   There has been extensive research on the universal aspects of emotion recognition. Izard (1968, summarized in Izard, 1980), for example, had individuals classify photographs of facial expressions into one of eight categories (interest-excitement, enjoyment-joy, surprise-startle, distress-anguish, disgust-contempt, anger-rage, shame-humiliation, and fear-terror) of emotions. His research reveals that there is high agreement in the United States, Germany, Sweden, France, Switzerland, Greece, and Japan on the category of emotion represented in the photographs. Data from Ekman and Friesen's (1971) study in Brazil, Chile, and Argentina yield similar results for six of the eight emotions (interest-excitement and shame-humiliation were omitted).

Ekman and his associates' (1987) study supports the argument that there are universal facial expressions of emotions. Research in 10 cultures (Estonia, Germany, Greece, Hong Kong, Italy, Japan, Scotland, Sumatra, Turkey, and the United States) indicates that agreement is not limited to conditions in which observers are limited to seeing one emotion for each facial expression. In this study there was agreement on which emotion was strongest and which was second strongest. Ekman et al. (1987) also observe agreement on the relative strength of the emotions expressed.

In addition to recognition of facial expression of emotions, it appears that there is agreement also on recognition of vocal emotional expressions. Beier and Zautra (1972), for example, note that non-English-speaking Japanese and Polish students are as accurate at decoding vocal emotional expressions in English as are students in the United States. Another study by Bezooijen, Otto, and Heenan (1983) indicates that Dutch, Taiwanese, and Japanese adults are similarly able to identify Dutch vocal expressions of emotion.

Matsumoto, Wallbott, and Scherer (1989) summarize many of the recent findings that have emerged from the cross-cultural study of emotions. They contend that there is universality in the recognition of six emotions in facial expressions—anger, disgust, fear, happiness, sadness, and surprise. In addition, they also believe that recognition of contempt probably is universal. Scherer and Wallbott (1994) argue that research in 37 cultures supports the universality of the expression of these seven emotions. Matsumoto, Wallbott, and Scherer (1989) point out that people across cultures recognize not only the primary facial expression, but also the secondary emotion being expressed. In addition to recognizing the emotion being expressed, people appear to agree on the relative intensity of the emotion being expressed.

Matsumoto and his colleagues also isolate universal aspects of emotional experiences. There appears, for example, to be consistency in antecedents for some emotions. To illustrate, birth of new family members elicits joy; and strangers, novel situations, and risky situations tend to elicit fear. Further, anger and disgust appear to occur most frequently and fear least frequently across cultures. Situations leading to sadness appear to be experienced most intensely, while situations eliciting shame and guilt are experienced least intensely.

Before discussing cultural differences in emotions, we must point out two caveats regarding accuracy in the recognition of emotions. Rosenthal and his associates' (1979) study indicates that the accuracy of interpreting role-plays of emotions varies, but respondents in all cultures are more accurate than would be expected by chance. The differences in accuracy that emerge appear to be a function of cultural similarity. The most accurate interpretations are made by respondents from cultures similar to that of the United States (e.g., Australia), where the role-plays were constructed, and the least accurate interpretation were from respondents in cultures very different from the United States (e.g., New Guinea). Ducci et al.'s (1982) study of the recognition of western emotions in Ethiopia suggests that familiarity with western culture is related to accuracy of recognizing emotions.

In summary, after reviewing research on the recognition and expression of emotions, Izard (1980) concludes that

> robust cross-cultural data . . . lend strong support to Darwin's thesis that the expressions of the emotions are innate and universal. Some studies suggest that universality is limited to certain primary or fundamental emotions. However, even some blends (expressions representing components of two or more fundamental emotions) are correctly identified across certain cultures, though blends do not yield as high agreement as unitary expressions when naive judges are used. Although the expressions and inner experiences that characterize the fundamental emotions are innate and universal, there are numerous cultural differences in attitudes toward emotions and their expression. (p. 216)

Understanding the expression of emotions, therefore, requires that we also examine how culture influences the display rules used.

Cultural Differences in Expression of Emotions.   Matsumoto, Wallbott, and Scherer (1989) isolate several differences in the expression of emotions. Rather than discussing differences between specific cultures, we focus here on systematic variations in emotions across cultures. There is some evidence that cultural differences in the expression of emotions, for example, may be related to the dimensions of cultural variability discussed in Chapter 3.

Gudykunst and Ting-Toomey (1988) note that attitudes toward some emotions are consistent with Hofstede's (1980) dimensions of cultural variability. They observe, for example, that people in masculine cultures tend to experience distress more than people in feminine cultures. They argue that since masculine cultures emphasize achievement and excellence, people in the culture experience distress if they do not achieve or excel. Feminine cultures, in contrast, emphasize serving and not trying to do better than others. Failure to accomplish those goals should not lead to distress.

Gudykunst and Ting-Toomey (1988) point out that people in high uncertainty avoidance cultures experience less joy from relationships than do people in low uncertainty avoidance cultures. This finding is reasonable given that relationships are guided by strict rules in high uncertainty avoidance cultures and that the rules are much more flexible in low uncertainty avoidance cultures.

Gudykunst and Ting-Toomey's (1988) report that nonvocal (e.g., reactions that include the use of the body) and verbal reactions to emotions are associated with individualism. People in individualistic cultures display more nonvocal and vocal reactions to emotions than do people in collectivistic cultures. This finding is consistent with the descriptions of individualistic and collectivistic cultures presented in Chapter 3.

Matsumoto (1989) extends Gudykunst and Ting-Toomey's research. He examines the perception of emotions in 15 cultures. Matsumoto concludes that

> cultures high in power distance and low in individualism stress hierarchy and group cohesion ("collectivity"), while individuality is minimized. In these cultures, the communication of negative emotions threatens group solidarity and interpersonal social structure. On the other hand, cultures low in power distance and high in individualism may sanction the communication of these emotions more, as they relate to individual freedom to express and perceive negative emotions. As such, they do not threaten social structures and groups to the same extent found in high power distance, low individualism cultures. (p. 101)

Understanding cultural differences in emotion expression requires using at least two dimensions of cultural variability.

Matsumoto (1991) theoretically links individualism-collectivism and power distance to the expression of emotions. He argues that since subjugating individuals' goals to group goals is more important in collectivistic cultures than in individualistic cultures, members of collectivistic cultures will emphasize emotional displays that facilitate group cooperation, harmony, and cohesion more than will members of individualistic cultures. He also points out that "members of individualistic cultures display a wider variety of emotional behaviors than members of collectivistic cultures. Collective cultures are not as tolerant of wide ranges of individual variations, and thus frown upon such variation" (p. 132).

The specific emotions displayed depend on the context and target of the emotion. To illustrate this conclusion, Matsumoto (1991) provides examples regarding expressing negative emotions when with a member of the ingroup in collectivistic cultures. In a public context, it would be inappropriate to display the emotion because it would reflect negatively on the ingroup. In addition, if the emotion is a reaction to an ingroup member and is experienced in private with the ingroup member, it would be inappropriate to express the emotion because it would disturb the harmony of the group. If the emotion is a reaction to an outgroup member, however, it would be acceptable to express it because the expression would foster cohesion in the ingroup.

Matsumoto (1991) goes on to argue that people in individualistic cultures are more likely to express positive and not to express negative emotions with members of the outgroup than are members of collectivistic cultures. We disagree with his argument. Members of collectivistic cultures avoid establishing intimacy with members of outgroups and, therefore, they would not display positive emotions in their presence. Virtually all analyses of individualism-collectivism suggest that members of collectivistic cultures avoid negative behaviors with the ingroup or with people of higher status, but not with the outgroup. Friesen's (1972) study illustrates how negative emotions are avoided with members of the ingroup. He notes that students in Japan (collectivistic) and the United States (individualistic) experienced similar affect when viewing a stressful film alone. When viewing the film with a member of the ingroup, however, the students in the United States displayed more negative affect than the students from Japan. Triandis and his associates (1988) provide an explanation for the display of negative affect toward members of the outgroup in collectivistic cultures. They point out that in collectivistic cultures, a "do whatever you can get away with" orientation applies toward members of outgroups. Members of outgroups in collectivistic cultures often are treated as nonpersons (e.g., Nakane, 1974). Cole (1990) reports that members of collectivistic cultures are more dominating with members of outgroups when trying to resolve conflict than are members of individualistic cultures. Given this line of reasoning, we believe that members of collectivistic cultures are more likely to express negative emotions with members of outgroups than are members of individualistic cultures.

Matsumoto (1991) also links power distance to the expression of emotions. He argues that people in high power distance cultures will display emotions that preserve status differences, while people in low power distance cultures will display emotions that minimize status differences. People in high power distance cultures, for example, would express positive emotions to people higher in status and negative emotions to people lower in status. Matsumoto illustrates his argument by comparing Japan and the United States. He suggests that

> status differs among retail clerks, department managers, store managers, and regional directors in the retail business. Japanese department managers would not hesitate to display negative emotions to their retail clerks (lower status). The retail clerks, meanwhile, would not dare display negative emotions back to the department manager. The combination of rules clearly differentiates status differences between the department manager and the clerks. [North] American department managers, however, would be more likely to treat their clerks as equals, minimizing status differences by displaying less negative emotions and more positive emotions to reduce friction. (p. 133)

These speculations, however, must be considered tentative because there is little difference between Japan and the United States in terms of power distance (Hofstede, 1980).

The line of theorizing and research outlined in this section is in its infancy. The findings to date, however, suggest that individualism-collectivism and power distance provide coherent theoretical explanations for some of the similarities and differences in the display of emotions across cultures.

Before proceeding, we need to present an alternative explanation for cultural differences in the display of emotions. It is possible that individualism-collectivism and power distance do not directly influence the display of emotions, but rather, influence the way people perceive situations in which they experience emotions. The perceptions of the situation, in turn, influence the display of emotions. Preliminary evidence from research in the United States and India supports this explanation. Roseman et al. (1995) report that members of the two cultures respond with similar emotions when they perceive the situation the same way, but their perceptions of situations often differ. More research is needed, however, to test this explanation.

Contact

In the preceding section, we used dimensions of cultural variability (e.g., individualism-collectivism) to explain similarities and differences in the display of emotions. One way to organize some of the research on nonverbal behavior is to use Hall's (1966) work on contact and noncontact cultures. Hall (1966) argues that people regulate intimacy by controlling sensory exposure through the use of interpersonal distance and space. He argues that cultures can be differentiated in terms of the degree of contact preferred by their members. Cultures in which the people tend to stand close and touch a lot are referred to as high contact cultures, while cultures in which people stand apart and tend not to touch are referred to as low contact cultures.

Hecht, Andersen, and Ribeau (1989) suggest that Hall's (1966) distinction is related to Mehrabian's (1971) immediacy dimension of meaning. *Immediacy* is the evaluative dimension of meaning, and it involves judgments of close-far, positive-negative, and good-bad that are used to indicate psychological closeness to others. Mehrabian contends that people approach persons and things high in immediacy and avoid persons or things low in immediacy. Immediacy behaviors reflect sensory stimulation, indicate attentiveness, and communicate liking (Mehrabian, 1971). The behaviors associated with immediacy are "(a) close conversational distance, (b) direct body and facial orientation, (c) forward lean, (d) increased and direct gaze, (e) positive reinforcers such as smiling, head nods, and pleasant facial expressions, (f) postural openness, (g) frequent gesturing, and (h) touch" (Burgoon, Buller, & Woodall, 1989, p. 315). In combination, these behaviors suggest immediacy. Taken individually, however, these behaviors may only indicate the intensity of interaction. When we are angry with other people, for example, we may engage in the same amount of eye contact as we do when we are attracted to them. When we are attracted to someone, we also will lean forward and have a pleasant look on our face.

The immediacy nonverbal behaviors are highly interrelated. Increases in one of the behaviors may be associated with decreases in another in order to keep the message balanced (Burgoon, Buller, & Woodall, 1989). If we move closer to someone, for example, we may decrease our eye contact to maintain the same degree of psychological closeness to the other person. When the various immediacy behaviors are combined, the psychological closeness is increased. It is important to recognize that the immediacy behaviors described here apply in the United States, especially the European American subculture. Immediacy behaviors differ across cultures and across ethnic groups in the United States.

When Hall's (1966) and Mehrabian's (1971) schemes are combined, we can talk about cultures varying along a continuum from high contact to low contact. People in high contact cultures evaluate "close" as positive and good, and evaluate "far" as negative and bad. People in low contact cultures evaluate "close" as negative and bad, and "far" as positive and good. This conceptualization of the importance of contact helps us organize a lot of the past research on nonverbal behavior. We look next at research on territoriality and sensory involvement.

Territoriality.   Altman and Chemers (1980a) see *territorial behavior* as involving the "control or ownership of a place or object on a temporary or permanent basis" (p. 121). The place or object may be large or small, and the possession of either a group or person. Territorial behavior serves several functions, including providing status and identity for the people who own or control the territory. Altman and Chemers divide the types of territory we use into three categories: primary, secondary, and public.

Primary territories are controlled or owned by individuals or groups and are central to the lives of the people. Examples of primary territory are homes, offices, farms, community property, and so forth. Others must be invited into primary territories. Uninvited intrusions into primary territory will lead to defensive behavior. The "inability to control a primary territory successfully may be a serious affront to the psychological well-being of a person or group" (Altman & Chemers, 1980a, p. 130).

Secondary territories are not as psychologically central to people. These territories may be places like the neighborhood street or bar, social clubs, and other places where there is a combination of public and private usage of the territory. Altman and Chemers (1980a) point out that secondary territories involve the potential for misunderstandings. Since they involve both public and private usage, strangers may not realize that there is a private aspect to secondary territories.

Public territories are available for people who have permission to use them on a temporary basis. Public territories include, but are not limited to, forms of public transportation (e.g., trains, planes, taxis), parks, tables in restaurants, beaches, and so forth. Public territories are not as central to people's lives as primary and secondary territories. Altman and Chemers (1980a) point out that in many "parts of the world certain groups within cultures are denied access to public facilities on the basis of their ethnicity, nationality, religion, or social class" (p. 135).

It is important to keep in mind that the way people mark their primary, secondary, and public territories varies across cultures. There also is variability across cultures in how the different forms of territories contribute to individuals' definitions of themselves. Native Americans in the northwestern part of North America, for example, use totem poles to mark their territory and to reflect their clan and lineage—their social identities. Offices in the United States usually are decorated with photos, mementos, and the like to reflect the occupant's personal identity.

In addition to the way they use territory in general, people vary in the way they use physical space—how they perceive, organize, and behave in their spatial environment. Hall (1966) suggests, for example, that human proxemic behavior can be classified into three general categories:

1. The *fixed feature,* such as spatial behavior in relation to an immovable and unchangeable environmental structure (e.g., organization of a town, architecture of a building);
2. The *semifixed feature,* which is conditioned by an environmental structure that is not permanently fixed (e.g., seating arrangement, furniture arrangement); and
3. The *dynamic feature,* which is codetermined by an individual's movement in space and by the movements of others with whom the person interacts.

These three categories, of course, are not mutually exclusive, but are interrelated in any actual spatial behavior. The way two college roommates live in a dormitory, for example, is influenced by the space as structured by their room and the building, as well as by the physical conditions of the university campus and the town in which the campus is located.

Of particular interest here are the dynamic aspects of interpersonal space. The dynamic interpersonal space is controlled, in part, by the nature of the relationship between interactants. In general, the more intimate a relationship, the more people permit each other to come close. Ashcraft and Scheflen (1976) observe that

> in the early stages of courtship, distance may be an issue of negotiation. But as courtship escalates, whatever the earlier distancing arrangements, the space between partners is reduced drastically. It disappears altogether in the physical union of copulation. (p. 7)

It appears that the closer the distance between people, the closer the relationship is across cultures. The distance people expect to have between themselves and others in a particular relationship (e.g., friend), however, varies across cultures.

Hall (1966) proposes four spatial zones used in social relations in the United States:

1. *Intimate distance* (0–1.5 feet) usually is maintained only between intimates or close associates, and not often in public. At this distance, a rich array of cues can be exchanged, including heat, smell, fine visual details, and touch.
2. *Personal distance* (1.5–4 feet) is a transitional distance where rich communication possibilities still exist.

3. *Social distance* (4–12 feet) is the distance of business and general public contact. Office desks, furniture arrangements in public settings, and chair locations in homes generally put people somewhere in this zone. One can still receive a fair number of communication cues, but they are not fine-grained.
4. *Public distance* (12-25 feet) usually is reserved for formal occasions, public speakers, or high-status figures. At this distance, only gross cues are available and such cues as smell, heat, and fine visual and vocal details are lost.

These spatial zones, however, are not the same in all cultures.

Sussman and Rosenfeld's (1982) study of how interpersonal distance is used by Japanese (low contact), North Americans (moderate contact), and Venezuelans (high contact) indicates that when they speak their native languages, Japanese sit the farthest apart, Venezuelans the closest, and the North Americans in the middle. They also note that when speaking English, the Japanese and Venezuelans used interpersonal distances approximating those used by the North Americans. Other research supports the conclusion from Sussman and Rosenfeld's study. Engebretson and Fullmer (1970), for example, observe that Japanese use greater interpersonal distances than Japanese Americans and European Americans in Hawaii. Watson and Graves' (1966) research suggests that Arabs prefer a closer sitting distance than North Americans. Little (1968) notes that members of Mediterranean cultures (e.g., Greece, Southern Italians; high contact) prefer closer interpersonal distances than Northern Europeans (moderate contact). Northern Europeans tend to use interactional distances similar to those of North Americans (Sommer, 1968).

How people in different cultures react to violations of their personal space appears to be related to individualism-collectivism. Gudykunst and Ting-Toomey (1988), for example, suggest that "members of individualistic cultures tend to take an active, aggressive stance when their space is violated, while members of collectivistic cultures tend to assume a passive, withdrawal stance when their personal space is violated" (p. 125).

Sensory Involvement. In general, people in high contact cultures prefer greater sensory involvement with the person with whom they are communicating than do people in low contact cultures. Sussman and Rosenfeld (1982) conclude that sensory involvement is "high among South Americans, Southern and Eastern Europeans, and Arabs, and low among Asians, Northern Europeans, and North Americans" (p. 66).

Almaney and Alwan (1982) compare the use of sensory information in Arab cultures (high contact) with such use in other cultures. They contend that

> to the Arab, to be able to smell a friend is reassuring. Smelling is a way of being involved with another, and to deny a friend his [or her] breath would be to act ashamed. In some rural Middle Eastern areas, when Arab intermediaries call to inspect a prospective bride for a relative, they sometimes ask to smell her. Their purpose is not

to make sure she is freshly scrubbed; apparently what they look for is any lingering odor of anger or discontent. The Burmese [high contact] show their affection during greeting by pressing mouths and noses upon the cheek and inhaling the breath strongly. The Samoans [high contact] show affection by juxtaposing noses and smelling heartily. In contrast, [North] Americans [moderate contact] seem to maintain their distance and suppress their sense of smell. (p. 17)

Differences in use of smell can create misunderstandings when people from different cultures communicate. Hall (1983) points out that when Arabs interact with North Americans, the Arabs often feel sensory deprivation and become alienated because of the lack of close social contact. The North Americans, in contrast, are anxious because of too much social contact.

Touch also is an aspect of sensory involvement. People in Latin American and Middle Eastern cultures engage in many more tactile behaviors than do people in the United States and Northern Europeans (e.g., Engebretson & Fullmer, 1970; Shuter, 1976; Watson, 1970). People in Asian cultures, in contrast, tend to engage in less touching behavior than North Americans and North Europeans (Barnlund, 1975; Sechrest, 1969). Watson (1970) argues that Far Eastern cultures are low touch, North American cultures are moderate touch, and Mediterranean cultures are high touch.

In general, there is more touching behavior in high contact cultures than in low contact cultures. Other dimensions of cultural variability, however, will influence the type of touching that occurs. Masculinity, for example, should affect the amount of touching that occurs between males and females. It would be expected that people in highly masculine cultures would avoid opposite-sex touching more than people in low masculine (feminine) cultures. Existing research appears to support this speculation. Jones and Remland's (1982) research indicates that people in the Far Eastern cultures (low contact, high masculinity) avoided touching members of the opposite sex the most, and members of the Mediterranean cultures (high contact, moderate masculinity) avoid opposite-sex touching less than people in the Far Eastern cultures, but more than people in the United States (moderate contact, low masculinity).

Smell and touch are not the only senses that differ across cultures. There also are differences in eye contact. The differences have to do with the extent to which people engage in eye contact and the situations in which they engage in eye contact. Members of low contact cultures (e.g., Asian cultures) tend to avoid eye contact when speaking and listening. Members of moderate contact cultures (e.g., Australia, Northern Europe, United States), in contrast, engage in more eye contact than do members of low contact cultures (e.g., Hall, 1966; Noesjirwan, 1978). Members of high contact cultures (e.g., Mediterranean cultures) engage in more eye contact than do members of moderate contact cultures (e.g., Watson & Graves, 1966).

People in individualistic cultures tend to learn to engage in eye contact when listening to others rather than when speaking. The listeners' eye contact is interpreted as an indication that they are indeed listening to the speaker. Members of other cultures (e.g., African cultures) learn to avoid eye contact when listening to others, especially when the person speaking is of higher status than the person listening (Byers & Byers, 1972). This pattern carries over to African Americans in the United States; that is, African Americans tend to look down (rather than engage in eye contact) to show respect when interacting with someone of higher status. European Americans often interpret this lack of eye contact as indicating that African Americans are inattentive or uninterested, or that they are lying (European Americans' learn to look people in the eye to indicate they are telling the truth). European Americans' eye contact behavior, on the other hand, may be interpreted as aggressive by African Americans.

One final aspect of sensory involvement is how people use their voice. Members of high contact cultures tend to speak loudly (Hall, 1959; Watson & Graves, 1966). In Arab cultures, for example, loudness is viewed as indicating strength and sincerity, while softness is viewed as reflecting deviousness and weakness. Members of moderate contact cultures tend to speak more softly than members of high contact cultures, and members of low contact cultures tend to speak the softest.

Interpersonal Synchronization

Once people begin to interact, they unconsciously move in synchrony (in whole or in part); failing to do so is disruptive to others around them. Nonverbal cues are critical to providing such rhythm in our interactions with others. Without rhythm in our interactions, we could not synchronize our behavior with others. *Interpersonal synchronization* refers to convergent rhythmic movements between two people on both the verbal and the nonverbal levels (Hall, 1983). Every facet of human behavior is involved in this rhythmic process. When synchronization occurs, our behavior is rhythmic. A sense of synchronization in our interactions with others plays "a crucial role in our ability to talk to each other, to work with each other, and to fall and stay in love" (Douglis, 1987, p. 37).

Interpersonal synchrony or convergence is achieved when the nonverbal behavior between two individuals is unique to the dyad (two people), flexible, smooth, and spontaneous (Knapp, 1983). Interpersonal misalignment, or divergence, occurs when the nonverbal behavior between two individuals is stylized, rigid, awkward, and hesitant (Knapp, 1983). Interpersonal synchrony is related to liking, rapport, and attention, while interpersonal misalignment is related to disliking and indifference.

Interpersonal synchronization is most evident when we watch two lovers talk:

> Without realizing it, after a while they actually begin to mirror each other's movements. She, facing him, leans on her right elbow as he leans on his left. They shift postures at the same time. They reach for their wine glasses, raise them and drink simultaneously, an unthinking toast to their closeness.
>
> Rhythms may even betray love at first sight to a careful observer before the lovers themselves realize what is happening. Over the course of an evening, a newly acquainted but smitten couple will begin to synchronize first head and arm movements. Then more body parts will join the mating dance, until the two are dancing as one. (Douglis, 1987, p. 42)

Observing that other people's behavior is synchronized is a good predictor of their mutual involvement (Douglis, 1987).

It is important to recognize that the rhythms we expect in our interactions are learned in our culture, our ethnic group, and the region of the country in which we live. Many problems that occur when people from different groups communicate can be traced to different rhythms of interaction. Nonnative speakers of English, for example, may stress the wrong words in a sentence or fail to stress words when they should. This misalignment in the vocal nonverbal behavior throws off the rhythm of a conversation. People from other cultures also might expect to stand at a distance closer than we expect. When they stand close, we move back without thinking about it. Again, these differences make coordinating behavior difficult.

Hall (1983) concludes that "1) Conversational distances were maintained with incredible accuracy (to tolerances as small as a fraction of an inch); 2) the process was rhythmic; and 3) human beings were locked together in a dance which functioned almost totally out of awareness" (p. 141). Hall points out that people who use high-context communication are more conscious of their rhythmic movements than are people who use low-context communication. Gudykunst and Ting-Toomey (1988) argue that members of individualistic cultures stress verbal synchronization when they communicate, while members of collectivistic cultures emphasize nonverbal synchronization when they communicate.

Interpersonal syncing is a basis for an *action chain,* a "sequence of events in which usually two or more individuals participate" (Hall, 1976, p. 41). Every action has a beginning, a climax, and an end, and comprises a number of intermediate states. If any of the basic acts are left out or are too greatly distorted, the action must be started all over again. An action chain resembles a dance that is used as a means of reaching a common goal. Greeting, parting, engaging in serious discussion, becoming engaged, and buying something in a store are all examples of action chains of varying complexity. Hall contends that the degree to which one is committed to complete an action chain varies across cultures. People in collectivistic cultures tend to be highly committed to completing action chains because of the high degree of involvement between people; the highly interrelated, cohesive nature of interpersonal relationships; and the overall sensitivity to nonverbal and other contextual cues in their cultures. The strong adherence to interpersonal syncing and completion of action chains by people in collectivistic cultures results in great caution and often reluctance to begin something, particularly in situations or relationships that are not well known. European Americans and other people in individualistic cultures do not ordinarily feel bound to complete action chains regardless of circumstances. Relatively speaking, many European Americans break an action chain readily if they do not like the way things are going or if something or someone better comes along. This behavior can be very frustrating to a stranger from a collectivistic culture emphasizing completion of action chains in interpersonal relationships. European Americans, in contrast, may find the adherence to action chains by people in collectivistic cultures too binding and burdensome.

NONVERBAL CUES IN COMMUNICATING WITH STRANGERS

In the preceding section, we focus on cross-cultural variability in nonverbal behaviors. In this section, we look at the influence of nonverbal behaviors when we communicate with strangers. When we communicate with strangers, they frequently use nonverbal behaviors that are different from ours. These different behaviors often lead to misunderstandings. Burgoon, Buller, and Woodall (1989), for example, point out that the use of different nonverbal behaviors by political leaders can lead to geopolitical embarrassment:

> A prime example is when then vice president Richard Nixon undertook a goodwill tour to Latin America. Photographers at his first airport stop flashed pictures of Nixon holding up both hands in the "A-OK" gesture. Unfortunately, that gesture in many Latin American countries means "screw you." . . . Nearly 15 years later, when Soviet premier Leonid Brezhnev visited the United States to meet with President Nixon, he exited his plane with his hands clenched over his head. This Russian emblem signifies gracious receipt of a tribute, and Brezhnev was acknowledging the welcoming ceremony he was receiving. But this emblem was inappropriate in the host culture, because in North America this emblem denotes superiority and victory. (pp. 27, 189)

Mistakes like these can easily create misunderstandings.

It is not only political leaders who use inappropriate nonverbal behaviors when interacting with members of other cultures. There is an unlimited number of examples of members of one culture or subculture causing miscommunication by using inappropriate nonverbal cues with strangers. In most cases, however, the people are unaware that their nonverbal behavior is inappropriate because nonverbal behavior takes place at low levels of awareness.

Gumperz (1982) illustrates the problems being discussed here with a case study of Indian and Pakistani women working in England:

> In a staff cafeteria at a major British airport, newly hired Indian and Pakistani women were perceived as surly and uncooperative by their supervisor as well as the cargo handlers whom they served. Observation revealed that while relatively few words were exchanged, the intonation and manner in which those words were pronounced were interpreted negatively. For example, when a cargo handler who had chosen meat was asked whether he wanted gravy, a British assistant would say "Gravy" using rising intonation. The Indian assistants, on the other hand, would say the word using falling intonation: "Gravy." (p. 173)

The Indian assistants did not recognize a difference between the way they pronounced "gravy" and the way the British assistants pronounced it. The supervisor, however, recognized the difference and pointed out that saying "gravy" with a falling intonation would be interpreted as "This is gravy," which would be obvious and, therefore, be interpreted as "rude."

Even though nonverbal behavior tends to be unconscious, members of one culture or subculture can learn to use appropriate nonverbal behavior in other cultures or subcultures. People from one culture or subculture who use appropriate nonverbal behavior when interacting with members of another culture or subculture are evaluated more positively than are people who do not adjust their nonverbal behavior (Collett, 1971; Garrett, Baxter, & Rozelle, 1981).

While we can learn the nonverbal behavior used in other cultures or subcultures, we generally do not adapt our nonverbal behavior when communicating with strangers on automatic pilot. If strangers use their own nonverbal behavior and we use ours, we inevitably will violate each other's expectations regarding appropriate nonverbal behavior. In order to understand how violating each other's expections influences our uncertainty and anxiety, we look at Burgoon's (1992) nonverbal expectancy violations theory. We first present her theory and examine its cross-cultural validity; then we apply it to our communication with strangers.

Nonverbal Expectancy Violations Theory

Burgoon and her colleagues (e.g., Burgoon, 1992; Burgoon & Hale, 1988) have been developing a theory of nonverbal expectancy violations (see Burgoon, 1995, for recent evidence and cross-cultural examples). The theory is based on five assumptions and contains five propositions. Bcforc we present the assumptions and propositions, it is important to recognize that Burgoon does not argue that the process she is explaining occurs at high levels of awareness. In other words, we are not necessarily mindful of our interpretations and evaluations of the violations of our nonverbal expectations. Given this caveat, we summarize the theory and discuss the potential for cultural variability regarding the assumptions and propositions.

The first assumption is that "humans have competing approach and avoidance needs" (Burgoon, 1992, p. 56). Burgoon suggests, and we agree, that this assumption should be valid across cultures. This assumption is consistent with our discussion of privacy in Chapter 6 (and our discussion of approach-avoidance tendencies in Chapter 10). While the basic premise should hold across cultures, it is important to keep in mind that there will be cultural variations in how people approach or avoid others. As indicated in Chapter 6, people in individualistic cultures will tend to use physical objects to avoid interaction, while people in collectivistic cultures will use psychological mechanisms to control their privacy.

The second assumption is that "communicators evaluate the reward potential of others" (Burgoon, 1992, p. 57). This assumption is consistent with the perspective we outlined in Chapters 1 and 2. This assumption should hold true across cultures, but there will be variations in the criteria used to define what rewards are. In individualistic cultures, the criteria for evaluating rewards will be based on individual needs. In collectivistic cultures, the focus will be on rewards for the group.

"Communicators develop expectations about the nonverbal behaviors of others" (Burgoon, 1992, p. 57) is the third assumption. There is no reason to question the validity of the assumption across cultures. It is necessary, however, to recognize that the specific expectations which are developed do vary across cultures, as Burgoon points out. Burgoon, for example, notes that cultures that value physical contact will expect to have contact during greetings, while cultures that do not value contact will expect that contact be minimized during greetings.

The fourth assumption is that "nonverbal behaviors have associated evaluations ranging from extremely positive to extremely negative" (Burgoon, 1992, p. 58). Like the earlier assumptions, this assumption should be universal. Burgoon suggests that the evaluations may be instinctive (e.g., feeling fear when threatened), culturally learned, or unique to the individual. She goes on to point out that little firm evidence exists for how nonverbal behaviors are evaluated (e.g., judgments of good/bad) differently across cultures. While there is little research in this area, it is clear that there are cultural variations in how specific nonverbal behaviors are evaluated. Recall, for example, the relationship between contact and immediacy discussed earlier in this chapter. People in high contact cultures value "close" and evaluative it positively and, at the same time, they evaluate "far" negatively.

The final assumption is that "nonverbal behaviors have socially recognized meaning" (Burgoon, 1992, p. 59). There is no reason to question the validity of this assumption across cultures. Burgoon suggests that, in comparison with individualistic cultures, there may be "greater room for multiplicity of meaning and ambiguity in collectivist cultures" (p. 5). While there is multiplicity of meaning, the context provides for relatively agreed-upon meanings for ambiguous messages in collectivistic cultures.

Five propositions are derived from the assumptions outlined above. The first proposition in nonverbal expectancy violation theory is that "expectancy violations are arousing and distracting, diverting attention to communicator and/or relationship characteristics and behaviors" (Burgoon, 1992, p. 60). Burgoon argues that the communicator's characteristics (e.g., group memberships) and the implicit meaning of the nonverbal behavior are more important when our expectations are violated than when they are not. Recall, however, that we may not be highly aware that we have become aroused and our attention has shifted. The process suggested in the proposition should be valid across cultures, but cross-cultural differences in the specific content are to be expected. Burgoon, for example, points out that nonverbal communication is important in determining meaning in collective cultures. Doi (1973) claims that for Japanese, "verbal communication is something that accompanies non-verbal communication and not the other way around" (p. 181). The violation of nonverbal expectations, therefore, should take on greater significance in collectivistic cultures than in individualistic cultures.

"Communicator reward valence [moderates] the interpretation of ambiguous or multi-meaning nonverbal behaviors" (Burgoon, 1992, p. 61) is the second proposition in the theory. Reward valence refers to whether the rewards or the costs associated with the person with whom we are communicating are greater. If the rewards are greater, there is a positive valence; if the costs are greater, there is a negative valence. Burgoon differentiates between nonverbal behaviors that have relatively agreed-upon social meanings within a culture (e.g., averting one's gaze; note that this example is agreed upon only within selected subcultures in the United States) and those that are open to multiple interpretations within a culture (e.g., personal space). When communicators who can provide rewards violate our expectations regarding nonverbal behaviors that are open to multiple meanings, their violations will be interpreted positively, as opposed to the negative violations that would occur with violations committed by people who cannot provide rewards.

The third proposition is that "communicator reward valence [moderates] the evaluation of nonverbal behavior" (Burgoon, 1992, p. 61). Burgoon points out that nonverbal behaviors that have relatively common meanings may be valued differently. The way they are evaluated, however, is influenced by whether the violator can provide rewards. Burgoon argues that the cognitive processes of evaluation should be used by people in all cultures, but that content of the evaluations of specific nonverbal behaviors will vary across cultures (e.g., the different evaluations of "close" and "far" in high and low contact cultures).

The fourth proposition in Burgoon's (1992) expectation violation theory is stated as follows:

> The ultimate evaluation of a violation is a function of the magnitude and direction of the discrepancy between the evaluation of the expected behavior and the evaluation of the actual behavior such that (a) enacted behaviors that are more positively valenced than expected behaviors produce positive violations and (b) enacted behaviors that are more negatively valenced than expected behaviors produce negative violations. (p. 62)

This proposition suggests that we compare the nonverbal behavior that individuals use with our expectations. When actual nonverbal behaviors are viewed more positively than expected behaviors, positive violations occur. When actual behaviors are viewed more negatively than expected behaviors, negative violations occur.

The final proposition in Burgoon's (1992) theory is that "positive violations produce favorable communication outcomes, while negative violations produce negative consequences" (p. 63). Burgoon argues that positive violations of expectations can lead to increases in "credibility, attraction, persuasion, and comprehension" (p. 7).

To summarize, the assumptions and propositions in Burgoon's (1992) theory appear to be valid across cultures. At the same time, however, there are cultural variations regarding the expectations, interpretations, and evaluations of specific nonverbal behaviors. The distance we expect others to stand from us when we are talking, for example, varies between contact and noncontact cultures. People in contact cultures expect others to stand only inches away, while people from noncontact cultures expect others to stand at least an arm's length away. Since we are not highly aware that the expectancy violation processes outlined in the assumption and propositions are occurring, cultural differences in expectations, interpretations, and evaluations create misunderstandings when people from different cultures communicate. In the next section, we focus on what happens when our expectations regarding nonverbal behavior are violated when we communicate with strangers.

Nonverbal Violations in Communicating with Strangers

Nonverbal expectancy violations theory has clear implications for our communication with strangers. We tend to avoid strangers more than we tend to avoid people who are familiar (Assumption 1) because of the uncertainty and anxiety present when we communicate with strangers (we discuss approach-avoidance in Chapter 10). One of the factors that affect our approach-avoidance behavior with strangers, for example, is the cultural/ethnic differences in the ways people indicate that they do not want to be approached. We may be sending signals indicating we do not want to be approached, but strangers do not recognize these signals.

Unless we are attracted to people who are dissimilar to us for some reason, strangers generally have lower reward value than people who are familiar (Assumption 2). The costs of interacting with strangers are generally viewed as greater than any rewards associated with interacting with them (Knapp, cited in Crockett & Friedman, 1980). This view reinforces our desire to avoid strangers rather than seek out interaction with them.

Our expectations for appropriate nonverbal behavior also may be different from those of strangers (Assumption 3). We *may* recognize when strangers violate our expectations, but they probably will not realize that they have violated our expectations unless we tell them. Similarly, strangers *may* recognize when we violate their expectations, but we will not realize we have done so unless we receive some indication from them. It is important to recognize that we will not always consciously recognize that our expectations have been violated. If the violation is not a major one, we will probably negatively interpret the strangers' behavior without consciously thinking about it and we may not consciously realize our expectations were violated. When such a situation occurs, misunderstandings are likely.

We tend consciously to recognize major violations of our expectations. When we consciously recognize these violations, we try to figure them out. If we are mindful of our communication, the possibility of effective communication is increased. Major violations of our nonverbal expectations may not be as problematic as minor violations of our nonverbal expectations when we communicate with strangers.

There is cultural variability in how explicit expectations are. Since rules are less explicit in individualistic cultures than in collectivistic cultures (as indicated in Chapter 3), strangers from collectivistic cultures may have trouble figuring out what the expectations are in individualistic cultures. Further, strangers from collectivistic cultures will emphasize the context more than is appropriate when interpreting the behavior of people in individualistic cultures.

Burgoon (1992) argues that we are aroused and we attune to the characteristics of the person with whom we are communicating when our expectations are violated (Proposition 1). This argument suggests that our uncertainty and anxiety increase when our expectations are violated. We may not, however, be consciously aware that this increase is happening. As indicated in Chapter 2, high uncertainty and anxiety (particularly if they are above our maximum threshold) lead to ineffective communication. Attuning to the characteristics of the person with whom we are communicating also leads to problems when we communicate with strangers. The most prominent characteristic on which we focus is the strangers' group memberships (e.g., their culture or ethnicity). Focusing on strangers' group memberships, in turn, increases the likelihood that we will commit the ultimate attribution error (see Chapter 7).

The other person's reward valence influences how we interpret his or her violations of our expectations. Since strangers generally have negative reward valences, we will tend to interpret their violations of our nonverbal expectations negatively. Consider, for example, the case of someone from the United States (a moderate contact culture) communicating with a stranger from a high contact culture. The stranger from the high contact culture probably will stand closer than the person from the United States expects. Since strangers have negative reward valence, this behavior will be interpreted negatively and the stranger will be viewed as "pushy." If the person from the United States was interacting with his or her boss, the reaction would be different. The boss would have positive reward valence and standing closer than expected would likely be interpreted as the boss's showing that she or he likes the subordinate.

If the nonverbal behavior in which others engage is more positively valenced than the expected behavior, a positive violation of expectations occurs; if the nonverbal behavior in which others engage is more negatively valenced than the expected behavior, a negative violation occurs (Proposition 4). Our expectations regarding strangers' nonverbal behavior are influenced by our stereotypes. If we view the stranger's group as "pushy," for example, and the stranger with whom we interact engages in behavior we interpret as polite, then we will see that behavior as a positive violation of our expectations. Positive violations like this, however, usually lead us to see the particular stranger with whom we are interacting as "an exception to the rule," rather than leading us to change our stereotype of the group. If our stereotype of the stranger's group is that they are "polite" and the stranger is "pushy," in contrast, a negative violation of our expectation occurs. Negative violations like this increase the chance we will make the ultimate attribution error (e.g., they are all like that).

Positive violations of our expectations lead to positive communication outcomes, while negative violations lead to negative outcomes (Proposition 5). Although we do not have data to support our speculation, we believe that negative violations of expectations tend to occur more than positive violations when we communicate with strangers. This speculation suggests that our communication with strangers is likely to have more negative communication outcomes than our communication with people who are familiar. The consequences of negative evaluations include, but are not limited to, an inability to synchronize our behavior with strangers and ineffective communication.

As suggested in the section on the recognition of emotions, the similarity of the stranger's culture and ours, as well as the familiarity we have with his or her culture and the familiarity she or he has with ours may moderate the negative outcomes. The more similar our cultures and the more familiar we are with each other's culture, the greater the chance we will be able to interpret each other's nonverbal cues accurately.

As indicated earlier, we are less aware of our nonverbal behavior than we are of our verbal behavior. We rarely stop and think about what happened when our nonverbal behavior expectations are violated. Rather, we interpret the violation from our own frame of reference. To increase the likelihood of positive outcomes (e.g., effective communication), we must become mindful of our communication. In other words, we must stop and think about what the stranger's behavior that violated our expectation means to the stranger (e.g., we need to reduce our explanatory uncertainty). We cannot do this if we are highly anxious, however. When we become mindful, we must cognitively manage our emotional reaction to the behavior (e.g., our anxiety). Cognitively managing our emotional reaction and understanding what the behavior means to the stranger are necessary for effective communication to occur. We discuss effective communication in more detail in Chapter 10.

SUMMARY

The recognition of at least six primary emotions (anger, disgust, fear, happiness, sadness, and surprise) in facial expressions appears to be universal. In addition to agreement on the emotions expressed, there is agreement on the relative intensity of the emotions across cultures. There also are, however, cross-cultural differences in the display rules guiding the expression of emotions. Recent work suggests that individualism-collectivism and power distance can be used to explain many of the differences.

In addition to the display of emotions, cultures differ in the emphasis they place on the need for contact among members. High contact cultures emphasize close interpersonal distances, extensive touching behavior, and sensory involvement of communicators. Low contact cultures, in contrast, emphasize far interpersonal distances, avoidance of touching, and little sensory involvement between communicators.

One of the major functions that nonverbal behaviors perform is the synchronization of communication. Since people learn different nonverbal behaviors across cultures, it often is difficult for us to synchronize our behavior when we communicate with strangers. Lack of synchronization disrupts communication.

When strangers violate our nonverbal expectations, we tend to interpret those violations negatively. Such negative interpretations decrease the effectiveness of our communication with strangers. To communicate effectively with strangers, we must learn to interpret their nonverbal behavior and their violations of our expectations accurately. Making accurate interpretations requires that we mindfully manage our anxiety and try to reduce our explanatory uncertainty regarding strangers' behavior.

STUDY QUESTIONS

1. What are the similarities and differences between language and nonverbal cues?
2. What are the functions of nonverbal cues?
3. Why are some aspects of the expression and recognition of emotions universal and while other aspects are not?
4. What are the differences between contact and noncontact cultures?
5. What is the role of immediacy in our relationships with others?
6. How does the use of territory differ across cultures?
7. How does the use of interpersonal distance differ across cultures?
8. How does the use of sensory involvement differ across cultures?
9. How does the use of touch differ across cultures?
10. How does the use of interpersonal synchronization differ across cultures?
11. How do nonverbal expectancy violations affect our communication with strangers?

SUGGESTED READING

Hall, E. T. (1959). *The silent language.* New York: Doubleday.

Hall, E. T. (1966). *The hidden dimension.* New York: Doubleday.

Morris, D. (1994). *Body talk: The meaning of human gesture.* New York: Crown.

Poyatos, F. (Ed.). (1988). *Cross-cultural perspectives in nonverbal communication.* Toronto: Hogrede.

Scherer, K., Wallbott, H., & Summerfield, A. (Eds.). (1986). *Experiencing emotion: A cross-cultural study.* Cambridge, UK: Cambridge University Press.

PART FOUR

Interacting with Strangers

In the first two parts of this book, we examined the major influences on our communication with strangers and the ways in which communication patterns vary across cultures. In Part Two, we pointed out that our predictions and interpretations of strangers' behavior and the anxiety we experience are influenced by the culture from which we come and, in addition, by the groups to which we belong, the role expectations we have, and our expectations regarding interpersonal relationships (the sociocultural influences). Further, our anxiety, predictions, and interpretations are influenced by the stereotypes and intergroup attitudes we hold (the psychocultural influences), as well as by the environment in which we are communicating. In Part Three, we examined interpreting and transmitting messages—both verbal messages and nonverbal messages.

The focus of Part Four is on selected aspects of our interaction with strangers. More specifically, in the chapters in this part, we address a series of important questions: What factors increase our effectiveness in communicating with strangers? How do we successfully manage conflict with strangers? What happens when we come into contact with strangers who have personal, social, and cultural differences and begin to communicate with them? How do our relationships (such as friendship and marriage) develop with strangers? What factors contribute to the development of our interpersonal relationships with strangers? How do strangers who find themselves in new and unfamiliar cultural environments cope with and adapt to the many uncertainties of their new lives? What are some of the changes occurring in strangers as a consequence of their adaptive experiences in a new environement? How can we become more "intercultural" as a result of our communication with strangers? How can we develop community with strangers?

In Chapter 10, we focus on factors that contribute to communicating effectively with strangers. Once we understand what is necessary to be effective, we have the basis for successfully managing conflict with strangers, the focus of Chapter 11. Chapters 10 and 11 provide the foundation for examining the development of interpersonal relationships with strangers (Chapter 12). In Chapter 13, we examine how strangers adapt to new cultural environments. Adapting to new cultural environments leads to personal changes, and it provides the foundation for becoming intercultural, the focus of Chapter 14. We conclude by examining how we can build commuity with strangers in Chapter 15.

10

Communicating Effectively with Strangers

To be surprised, to wonder, is to begin to understand.
José Ortega y Gasset

Our desire to communicate with strangers and our relationships with them depend on the degree to which we are effective in communicating with them. We cannot manage conflict with strangers or develop relationships with them if we do not communicate relatively effectively. We, therefore, begin our discussion of interaction with strangers by looking at effective communication.

Our purpose in this chapter is to elaborate on our view of communicating with strangers by examining the factors that contribute to communication effectiveness. We divide our discussion of effectiveness into three sections. In the first section, we define what we mean by effective communication and differentiate it from competence and from being perceived as a competent communicator. Next, we overview ways in which communication effectiveness and intercultural competence have been approached. We present our view of the factors that contribute to being perceived as a competent communicator in the third section.

DEFINING COMMUNICATION EFFECTIVENESS AND COMPETENCE

In the movie *Cool Hand Luke,* Paul Newman plays Luke, a man put in prison for destroying a parking meter. While in prison, Luke constantly gets into trouble with the prison staff. At one point when Luke had not done something that the warden

249

had asked him to do, the warden says to Luke, "What we have here is a failure to communicate." On the surface, the warden's statement makes sense. It is, however, incomplete. The warden and Luke communicated, but they did not communicate effectively.

Communication Effectiveness

To say we communicated does not imply an outcome. Communication is a process involving the exchange of messages and the creation of meaning. No two people ever attach the same meaning to a message. Whether or not a specific instance of communication is effective or not depends on the degree to which the participants attach similar meanings to the messages exchanged. In other words, *effective communication* involves minimizing misunderstandings. "To say that meaning in communication is never totally the same for all communicators is not to say that communication is impossible or even difficult—only that it is imperfect" (Fisher, 1978, p. 257).

When we communicate, we attach meaning to (or interpret) messages we construct and transmit to others. We also attach meaning to (or interpret) messages we receive from others. We are not always aware of this process, but we do it nevertheless. To say that two people communicated effectively requires that the two attach relatively similar meanings to the messages sent and received (i.e., they interpret the messages similarly). Powers and Lowry (1984) refer to interpreting messages similarly as *basic communication fidelity*—"the degree of congruence between the cognitions [or thoughts] of two or more individuals following a communication event" (p. 58). Similarly, Triandis (1977) argues that effectiveness involves making isomorphic attributions (isomorphic implies being similar; attributions involve assigning a quality or characteristic to something).

Ineffective communication can occur for a variety of reasons when we communicate with strangers. We may not transmit our message in a way that can be understood by others, strangers may misinterpret what we say, or both can occur simultaneously. The problems that occur may be due to pronunciation, grammar, familiarity with the topic being discussed, familiarity with the other person, familiarity with the other person's native language, fluency in the other person's language, and/or social factors (Gass & Varonis, 1984). If we are familiar with and/or fluent in the other person's language, for example, we can usually understand that person better when he or she speaks our language than we could if we knew nothing about that person's language.

Generally, the greater our cultural and linguistic knowledge, and the more our beliefs overlap with those of the strangers with whom we communicate, the less the likelihood there will be misunderstandings. Lack of linguistic and cultural knowledge contributes to misunderstandings because we "listen to speech, form a hypothesis about what routine is being enacted, and then rely on social background knowledge and co-occurrence expectations to evaluate what is intended and [the] attitudes [that] are [being] conveyed" (Gumperz, 1982, p. 171).

When we communicate on automatic pilot, we interpret incoming messages on the basis of the symbolic systems we learned as children. A large part of this system is shared with other members of our culture, our ethnic group, our religious group, and our family, to name only a few of our group memberships. A part of our symbolic system, however, is unique because it is based on our specific life experiences. No two people share the same symbolic system. Much of our habitual or scripted behavior involves superficial interactions with other members of our culture or ethnic group, in which we rely mainly on cultural or sociological data. The meanings we attach to specific messages and the meanings others attach to these messages are relatively similar. This similarity is due, in part, to the fact that the scripts we enact provide us with shared interpretations of our behavior. Although there are differences in our meanings, the differences are not large enough to make our communication ineffective. Under these conditions, we do not need to think consciously about our communication to be relatively effective.

In addition to following scripts, placing people in categories can be a source of our going on automatic pilot. We categorize people into groupings that make sense to us. These categories often are based on physical (e.g., gender or race) or cultural (e.g., cultural or ethnic background) characteristics, but we also can categorize others in terms of their attitudes or approaches to life:

> We adopt sets of categories which serve as ways of managing phenomena. The most fully developed products of this tendency are ideologies, the systems of ideas that rationalize, justify, and sanctify our lives. Nationalism, communism, existentialism, Christianity, Buddhism—all provide us with identities, rules of action, and interpretations of how and why things happen as they do. (Trungpa, 1973, p. 6)

Using only *broad* categories to predict and interpret strangers' behavior inevitably leads to ineffective communication.

The categories in which we place others affect our interpretations. Once we place an individual in a category, our stereotype of people in that category influences the predictions we make and how we interpret that individual's behavior. Basing our predictions on broad categories usually leads to mindless behavior. That is, we rely on our expectations of people in that category to guide our behavior and interpretations and we are not conscious of our communication behavior. While categorical information is useful in making predictions, people can be placed into many different categories. To communicate effectively, we have to understand which identity is guiding the other person's communication.

When we are communicating with strangers and basing our interpretations on our symbolic systems, ineffective communication often occurs. Consider a European American teacher interacting with an African American student raised in the lower-class subculture in the United States. The teacher asks the student a question. In answering the question, the student does not look the teacher in the eyes. The teacher, in all likelihood, would interpret the student's behavior as disrespectful and/or assume that the student is hiding something. Establishing eye contact is expected in the European American middle-class subculture in the United States when a person is telling the truth and being respectful. The student's intent, on the other hand, may have been to show respect to the teacher, given that children in the lower-class African American subculture in the United States are taught not to make eye contact with people they respect. Situations like this lead to misunderstanding and ineffective communication.

To summarize, effective communication involves minimizing misunderstandings. To be effective in communicating with strangers, we must be mindful. Communicating effectively and appropriately are important aspects of being perceived as a competent communicator. We can, however, communicate effectively and not be perceived as a competent communicator.

Perceived Competence

There are at least two views of the nature of competence. One view suggests that competence is "within" the communicator, and the second suggests that competence is "between" the communicators. Kim (1991c) takes the first position. She argues that intercultural communication competence

> should be located *within* a person as his or her overall *capacity* or *capability* to facilitate the communication process between people from differing cultural backgrounds and to contribute to successful interaction outcomes. Here [intercultural communication competence] is considered a necessary, but not sufficient, condition for achieving success in intercultural encounters—just as a highly competent driver may not always be able to prevent accidents due to factors external to the driver (such as hazardous road conditions or serious mistakes made by other incompetent drivers). (p. 263)

In this view, competence is internal to the person.

The second view of competence assumes that judgments of competence emerge from the interactions in which we engage. Gudykunst (1991), for example, points out that one communicator's view of her or his communication competence may not be the same as that of the person with whom he or she is communicating. You, for example, might see yourself as a very competent communicator, yet when you interact, your partner may perceive you as not being very competent. An outside observer might have still a different perception of your competence. Understanding communication competence, therefore, minimally requires that we take into consideration our own and the other person's perspective.

If we can have views of our competence different from those of the people with whom we are communicating, then competence is an impression we have of ourselves and others. In other words, "competence is not something intrinsic to a person's nature or behavior" (Spitzberg & Cupach, 1984, p. 115). There are several implications of this view of competence:

> First, competence does not actually reside in the performance; it is an *evaluation* of the performance by someone. . . . Second, the fact that *someone* is making the evaluation means that it is subject to error, bias, and judgment inferences; different judges using the same criteria may evaluate the performance differently. Third, since the

evaluation always must be made with reference to some set of implicit or explicit *criteria,* the evaluation cannot be understood or validated without knowledge of the criteria being employed; thus, the same performance may be judged to be competent by one standard and incompetent by another. (McFall, 1982, pp. 13–14)

This view of competence clearly suggests that the specific skills we have do not ensure that we will be perceived as competent in any particular interaction. Our skills, however, do increase the likelihood that we are able to adapt our behavior so that others see us as competent (Wiemann & Bradac, 1989).

If people from different cultures use the same criteria (e.g., appropriateness) to judge a person's competence, they may still evaluate the same performance differently. Consider the example near the end of Chapter 8 of the Japanese who asked "How old are you?" during an initial interaction with a North American. Another Japanese observing this interaction would likely evaluate the Japanese speaker's question as appropriate. The North American who is asked the question, in contrast, is likely to see the question as inappropriate.

The standards people use to judge competence also vary across cultures. Carroll (1988), for example, argues that the French value animated conversations that are fast-moving, with frequent interruptions. Often, the speakers ask questions and do not wait for answers. North Americans, however, prefer fuller answers to questions, less interruptions, and more continuity in the conversation than the French. The French may interpret North American conversation and readiness to discuss serious topics in social gatherings as inappropriate (and incompetent) because for the French, serious conversations occur in contexts other than social situations and require a strong commitment between individuals. North Americans may view the French style of frequent interruptions and short answers to their questions as inappropriate and, therefore, incompetent.

To further understand differences in perceived competence, consider the role of assertiveness in Japan and the United States (Singhal & Nagao, 1993). People who are perceived as assertive are viewed as competent communicators in the United States, and people who are reticent are not perceived to be highly competent. In Japan, in contrast, people who are reticent are perceived as more competent than people who are assertive. Japanese, therefore, may perceive North American assertiveness as incompetent, and North Americans may perceive Japanese reticence as incompetent.

If we assume that competence is based on impressions then the specific skills we have do not ensure that we are perceived as competent in any particular interaction. Our skills, however, do increase the likelihood that we are able to adapt our behavior so that others see us as competent (Wiemann & Bradac, 1989).

As you can see from the preceding overview of the two positions on the nature of competence, we (the two authors) disagree. Both of us agree, however, that individuals possess motivation, knowledge, and skills that can contribute to the effectiveness of their communication. We both also agree that individuals make judgments of each other's competence. For the purpose of this chapter, we focus, therefore, on effective communication and *perceived competence.*

APPROACHES TO THE STUDY
OF EFFECTIVE COMMUNICATION

There have been several attempts to specify the characteristics of the people who can communicate effectively with strangers (i.e., competence is in the person). Gardner (1962), for example, characterizes people who are effective in communicating with strangers as universal communicators. He describes these people as possessing five characteristics: "(1) an unusual degree of integration or stability, (2) a central organization of the extrovert type, (3) a value system which includes the 'value of all men [and women],' (4) socialized on the basis of cultural universals, and (5) a marked telepathic or intuition sensitivity" (p. 248). Similarly, Kleinjans (1972) takes the position that the effective communicator (1) sees people first and representatives of cultures second, (2) knows people are basically good, (3) knows the value of other cultures as well as that of his or her own, (4) has control over his or her visceral reactions, (5) speaks with hopefulness and candor, and (6) has inner security and is able to feel comfortable being different from other people. Both Gardner and Kleinjans, therefore, characterize competence in communicating with strangers in terms of individual traits within the communicators.

Ruben (1976) suggests that several behavioral dimensions are important to communication competence in intercultural interactions: (1) display of respect involves the ability to show positive regard and express respect for another person, (2) interaction posture is the "ability to respond to others in a descriptive, nonevaluating, and nonjudgmental way" (p. 340), and (3) interaction management "is displayed through taking turns in discussion and initiating and terminating interaction based on a reasonably accurate assessment of the needs and desires of others" (p. 341). Ruben and Kealey (1979) report that successful adaptation to other cultures can be predicted by individuals' empathy, respect, ability to perform role behaviors, nonjudgmentalness, openness, tolerance for ambiguity, and interaction management.

Hawes and Kealey's (1981) research suggests there is a difference between adaptation and effectiveness. People can adapt to other cultures and not be effective. Hawes and Kealey argue that effectiveness is a function of professional expertise, adaptation, and intercultural interaction (i.e., interest in and capacity for interacting with host nationals).

Gudykunst, Wiseman, and Hammer (1977) argue that people who are effective in communicating with strangers do not use the perspective of their own culture when interpreting the behavior of people from other cultures. Rather, effective communicators use a third-culture perspective, which acts as a psychological link between their cultural perspective and that of the stranger.

> We can say that people who have highly developed this perspective can be characterized as follows: (1) they are open-minded toward new ideas and experiences, (2) they are empathic toward people from other cultures, (3) they accurately perceive differences and similarities between the host culture and their own, (4) they tend to describe behavior they don't understand rather than evaluating unfamiliar behavior as bad, nonsensical, or meaningless, (5) they are relatively astute noncritical observers of

their own behavior and that of others, (6) they are better able to establish meaningful relationships with people from the host culture, and (7) they are less ethnocentric (i.e., they try first to understand and then evaluate the behavior of host nationals based upon the standards of the culture they are living in). (p. 424)

Gudykunst, Wiseman, and Hammer recognize that people are not always able to use a third-culture perspective when they communicate. Their view suggests that individuals' knowledge and skills contribute to effective communication, but it does not suggest that such knowledge and skills constitute competence.

Hammer, Gudykunst, and Wiseman (1978) isolate three behavioral dimensions associated with perceived effectiveness: (1) the ability to deal with psychological stress, (2) the ability to communicate effectively, and (3) the ability to establish meaningful interpersonal relationships. The dimension of being able to deal with psychological stress includes the ability to deal with frustration, stress, anxiety, pressures to conform, social alienation, financial difficulties, and interpersonal conflicts. The dimension of being able to communicate effectively includes the ability to enter into meaningful dialogue with other people, to initiate interaction with strangers, to deal with communication misunderstandings, and to deal with different communication styles. The third dimension, the ability to establish meaningful interpersonal relationships, includes the ability to develop satisfying interpersonal relationships with other people, to maintain satisfying relationships with others, to understand the feelings of others, to work effectively with others, and to deal with different social customs. Hammer and his associates suggest that having these skills contributes to effective communication. They do not contend that these skills define competence.

Partial cross-cultural support for these findings comes from Abe and Wiseman's (1983) replication of the study by Hammer, Gudykunst, and Wiseman (1978). Abe and Wiseman's research reveals five dimensions to effectiveness, with all five dimensions being related closely to the three dimensions displayed in the earlier study. The differences that exist in the findings can be explained easily by the length of the individuals' experiences in another culture: The original study examined long-term visitors, while Abe and Wiseman studied tourists. Hammer's (1987) research confirms the three-dimensional explanation. While the dimensions are similar across cultures, the specific behaviors will differ. To illustrate, the behaviors in which people engage to establish relationships across cultures clearly is different (see Chapter 12).

Kealey (1990) proposes a model to explain understanding when we are in other cultures. He contends that our individual skills, desire for contact with members of the host culture, altruistic motives, and positive expectations influence our interactions. The extent to which we are satisfied with our interactions and minimize our stress, in turn, influences our understanding of host nationals.

Individual traits alone can be used as a good predictor of communication effectiveness only if they yield consistent behavior across situations and throughout our lives. That, however, does not appear to be the case. Rather, individual traits often do not lead to consistent behavior across situations or throughout our lives (Mischel, 1973). Explanations of effectiveness, therefore, cannot rely solely on individual traits; they must include other factors, such as the interaction that takes place between the people.

Prior research on effective communication with strangers and/or intercultural competence has not been organized in a systematic way. Given our focus on reducing uncertainty and anxiety when communicating with strangers, we emphasize factors that are related directly to these processes. To isolate these factors, we must look at the components that contribute to being perceived as competent communicators.

COMPONENTS OF PERCEIVED COMPETENCE

Spitzberg and Cupach (1984) isolate three components of perceived competence: motivation, knowledge, and skills. *Motivation* refers to our desire to communicate appropriately and effectively with others. Of particular importance to the present analysis is our motivation to communicate with strangers. *Knowledge* refers to our awareness or understanding of what needs to be done in order to communicate appropriately and effectively. *Skills* are our abilities to engage in the behaviors necessary to communicate appropriately and effectively.

We may be highly motivated and lack the knowledge and/or the skills necessary to communicate appropriately and effectively. We also may be motivated and have the knowledge necessary, but not the skills. Even being motivated and having the knowledge and skills does not ensure that we will communicate appropriately or effectively. Several factors may intervene to affect our behavior. We may, for example, have a strong emotional reaction to something that happens. Our emotional reaction, in turn, may cause us to "act out" a script we learned earlier in life that is dysfunctional in the situation in which we find ourselves. Consider a European American who is served snake meat in another culture. He or she is likely to have a strong negative reaction to eating this meat. If the person is unable to control his or her emotional reaction cognitively, there is little chance that she or he will behave in a way that is perceived as competent by people in the other culture.

The person with whom we are communicating may also be a factor in our ability to be perceived as competent. If the other person communicates with us in a way that suggests we are not competent, we will, in all likelihood, act in an incompetent fashion. It is also possible that we may act appropriately and effectively without actually having the knowledge necessary to engage in the behaviors by imitating the behavior of another person. While this approach can work when we are communicating with people who are different when we do not having sufficient knowledge of the other person's group, it is not the best strategy. Wiemann and Kelly (1981) point out that "knowledge without skill is socially useless, and skill cannot be obtained without the cognitive ability to diagnose situational demands and constraints" (p. 290).

Our motivation, knowledge, and skills interact with outcomes of our communication with others to yield perceptions of competence. We have mentioned two outcomes—appropriateness and effectiveness—already. Other potential outcomes include, but are not limited to, interpersonal attraction, trust, satisfaction with our communication, development of interpersonal relationships (i.e., intimacy), management of conflict, adaptation to other cultures, and the building of community. The remainder of this chapter is devoted to examining motivation, knowledge, and skills—the three components of competence.

Motivation

J. H. Turner (1988) suggests that certain basic needs motivate us to interact with others. *Needs* are "fundamental states of being in humans which, if unsatisfied, generate feelings of deprivation" (p. 23). The needs that serve as motivating factors are (1) our need for a sense of security as a human being, (2) our need for a sense of predictability (i.e., I trust you will behave as I think you will), (3) our need for a sense of group inclusion, (4) our need to avoid diffuse anxiety, (5) our need for a sense of a common shared world, (6) our need for symbolic/material gratification, and (7) our need to sustain our self-conception. We vary in the degree to which we are conscious of our various needs. We are the least conscious of the first three, moderately conscious of the fourth, and the most conscious of the last three.

Our needs, separately and in combination, influence how we want to present ourselves to others, the intentions we form, and the habits or scripts we follow. The needs also can influence each other. Anxiety, for example, can result from not meeting our needs for group inclusion, predictability, security, and/or sustaining our self-concept. J. H. Turner argues that our overall level of motivational energy is a function of our level of anxiety produced by these four needs. Three of these needs are critical in our communication with strangers and warrant further discussion.

Need for Predictability.   One of the major reasons that we are not motivated to communicate with members of other groups is that we often do not see their behavior as predictable. J. H. Turner (1988) contends that we "need to 'trust' others in the sense that, for the purposes of a given interaction, others are 'reliable' and their responses 'predictable'" (p. 56). When others' behavior is predictable, we feel that there is a rhythm to our interactions with them. When others' behavior is not predictable, there is no rhythm to our interaction and we experience diffuse anxiety.

If we do not feel a part of the interaction taking place (i.e., our need for inclusion is not met), we will have a difficult time seeing others' behavior as predictable. One reason we may not feel part of the interaction is that we have learned communication rules that are different from those of people from other groups, and we often follow our own rules, even when communicating in others' languages. If Japanese follow their cultural norms regarding silence in conversations when speaking English, for example, North Americans will feel that the rhythm of the conversation is off and will not feel part of the conversation taking place.

If we do not recognize that predictability will be lower when we are getting to know a person from another group, the low level of predictability will decrease our motivation to communicate. One way that we can deal with this problem is to be mindful when we communicate with members of other groups. When we are mindful, we need to remind ourselves that the lack of predictability may not be due to the other person; rather, group differences may be influencing our communication. After recognizing this possibility, we can try to gather information that will help us understand what is happening and thereby increase the predictability of others' behavior.

Need to Avoid Diffuse Anxiety.   J. H. Turner (1988) views *anxiety* as a "generalized or unspecified sense of disequilibrium" (lack of balance) (p. 61). Anxiety stems from feeling uneasy, tense, worried, or apprehensive about what might happen. It is an emotional (affective) response to situations that is based on a fear of negative consequences (Stephan & Stephan, 1985). Turner argues that feelings of anxiety stem from deprivations in meeting our needs for security, predictability, group inclusion, and self-confirmation. He contends that if we have not met our needs for security, predictability, and group inclusion, the focus of our behavior is in trying to deal with the anxiety associated with not meeting those needs. Because we are not highly aware of our needs for security, predictability, and group inclusion, however, we have a hard time pinpointing the source of the anxiety. The net result is that "considerable interpersonal energy can be devoted to meeting these needs as [people] grope around for a solution to their often vague feelings of discomfort" (p. 63).

Anxiety is an important motivating factor in intergroup encounters. If anxiety is too high, we avoid communicating with members of other groups in order to lower our anxiety. To be motivated to communicate with members of other groups, we have to manage our anxiety if it is too high or if it is too low. This aspect of motivation requires that we be mindful. When we are mindful, there are several things we can do to manage our anxiety. We discuss these techniques in the section on ability to manage anxiety later in this chapter.

Need to Sustain Our Self-Conceptions.   Another consequence of high anxiety is that our need to sustain our self-conceptions becomes important (J. H. Turner, 1988). Sustaining our self-conceptions is much more difficult, however, when we communicate with members of other groups than when we communicate with members of our own groups. Our self-conceptions are made up of the various identities we have and our theories of ourselves:

> Identity, like any theory, is both a *structure,* containing the organized contents of experience, and an active *process* that guides and regulates one's thoughts, feelings, and actions. . . . It influences how information is perceived, processed, and recalled. . . . it acts as a script to guide behavior . . . and it contains the standards against which one's behavior can be compared and evaluated. (Schlenker, 1986, p. 24)

Our self-conceptions, therefore, influence how we communicate with others and the choices (conscious and unconscious) of those with whom we form relationships.

J. H. Turner (1988) contends that we try to maintain our self-conceptions, even going to the point of using defense mechanisms (e.g., denial) to maintain our views of ourselves. Our need for self-concept support directly influences our communication. Cushman, Valentinsen, and Dietrich (1982), for example, suggest that we are attracted to others who have the ability to support our self-concepts. Perceiving that others support our self-concepts is necessary if we are going to form or maintain an interpersonal relationship with them.

One of the problems in intergroup encounters is that one or both of the communicators perceives that the other person does not support his or her self-concept. If we are communicating on automatic pilot, we are likely to respond negatively in this situation. When we are mindful of our communication, however, we can recognize that members of other groups might emphasize aspects of their self-concepts that are different from the aspects that we emphasize. Individualists, for example, stress their personal identities, while collectivists emphasize their social identities. Failure to support each others' self-concepts, therefore, may not be due to lack of concern, but rather, to a failure to understand group differences in what each person considers to be important aspects of the self. To illustrate, Japanese are likely to ask questions about North Americans' social identities when North Americans expect questions about their personal identities. If North Americans perceive this behavior as lack of self-concept support, they will not be motivated to interact with Japanese. If North Americans are mindful of their communication, however, they can recognize that this behavior is just a cultural difference. This interpretation should not have a negative effect on North Americans' motivation to communicate with Japanese.

Approach-Avoidance Tendencies.   Most of us spend the vast majority of our time interacting with people who are relatively similar to us. Our actual contact with people who are different is limited; it is a novel form of interaction (Rose, 1981). If our attempts to communicate with strangers are not successful and we cannot easily get out of the situations in which we find ourselves, then our unconscious need for group inclusion becomes unsatisfied. This situation leads to anxiety about ourselves and our standing in a group context (J. H. Turner, 1988). One way we deal with the anxiety is to retreat into known territory and limit our interactions to people who are similar. At the same time, most of us want to see ourselves as nonprejudiced and caring people. We may, therefore, want to interact with strangers to sustain our self-concept. Holding both attitudes at the same time is not unusual. The combination of our need to avoid diffuse anxiety and our need to sustain our self-conception often leads us to an approach-avoidance orientation toward intergroup encounters.

Knowledge

The knowledge component of communication competence refers to our awareness of what we need to do to communicate in an appropriate and effective way. This aspect of competence includes a specific awareness of the skills discussed later in the chapter and how they can be used when communicating with strangers. When communicating with strangers, we also need to have knowledge about the other person's group. We begin the section on knowledge by looking at how we can gather information about strangers and their groups so that we can interpret their messages accurately. While our focus is on gathering information about strangers, the processes outlined apply equally to gathering information about people who are similar.

Knowledge of How to Gather Information.   Berger (1979) isolates three general types of strategies we can use to gather information about others and to reduce our uncertainty about them and the way they will interact with us: passive, active, and interactive strategies. As an example of this process, let's assume that we want to find out about Yuko, a Japanese to whom we have just been introduced. Although this example is an intercultural one, the strategies discussed can be used to gather information about anyone.

When we use *passive strategies,* we take the role of "unobtrusive observers" (i.e., we do not intervene in the situation we are observing; Berger, 1979). Obviously, the type of situation in which we observe Yuko influences the amount of information we gain about her. If we observe Yuko in a situation where she does not have to interact with others, we will not gain much information about her. Situations in which she is interacting with several people at once, in contrast, allow us to make comparisons of how Yuko interacts with the different people.

If we know any of the people with whom Yuko is interacting, we can compare how Yuko interacts with the people we know and how she might interact with us. It also should be noted that if other Japanese are present in the situation, we can compare Yuko's behavior with theirs to try to determine how she is similar to and different from other Japanese.

There is one other aspect of the situation that will influence the amount of information we obtain about Yuko's behavior. If the situation is a formal one, her behavior is likely to be a function of the role she is filling in the situation and we will not learn much about Yuko as an individual. Informal situations, where behavior is not guided by roles or social protocol, on the other hand, will provide useful information on Yuko's behavior.

The preceding examples all involve our taking the role of an observer. The *active strategies* for reducing uncertainty require us to do something to acquire information about Yuko without actually interacting with her (Berger, 1979). One thing we could do to get information about Yuko is to ask questions of someone who knows her. When we ask others about someone, we need to keep in mind that the information we receive may not be accurate. The other person may intentionally give us wrong information, or the other person may not really know Yuko well.

We can also gather information about other groups by asking questions of people who have had contact with those groups or by doing research in the library. In this example, we could gather information on Japan by questioning someone we know who has lived in Japan, reading a book on Japanese culture, or completing a Japanese cultural assimilator (a programmed learning course that teaches the reader about the Japanese culture). This strategy would give us information about Yuko's cultural background and allow us to make cultural-level predictions about her behavior. Again, we need to keep in mind that our informant may or may not have good information about Japan and that Yuko may not be a typical Japanese.

The possibility of receiving inaccurate information raises the issue of how we can select good informants to learn about other groups. People who have a lot of informal social contact with members of the other group, for example, are better informants than people who have little informal contact or even a lot of contact in formal settings. We also would be well off to select informants who have been successful in their interactions with members of other groups. If, for example, there are two members of our group who have frequent contact with the group in which we are interested, we would select the one who appears to be most successful in interacting with members of the other group (based on our observations of their interactions or their reports of their interactions).

When we use active strategies to gather information, we do not actually interact with the people about whom we are trying to gather information. The *interactive strategies* of verbal interrogation (question asking) and self-disclosure, in contrast, are used when we interact with the other person (Berger, 1979).

One obvious way we can gather information about others is to use *interrogation,* that is, to ask them questions (Berger, 1979). When we are interacting with someone from our own group, there are limitations to this strategy that have to be kept in mind. First, we can ask only so many questions. We may not be sure of what the exact number is, but we always know when we have asked too many.) Second, our questions must be appropriate to the nature of the interaction we are having and the relationship we have with the other person.

When we are communicating with strangers, the same limitations are present, and there are others. The number and type of questions that strangers consider acceptable may not be the same as what we consider acceptable. Strangers also may not be able to answer our questions, especially if our questions deal with why they behave the way they do (the ultimate answer to "why" questions is "because!" or "that is the way we do it here"). When interacting with strangers, we also have the added problem of our not wanting to appear stupid or to be rude. We, therefore, often avoid asking strangers questions.

If we can overcome our fear of appearing stupid, asking questions is an excellent way to gather information about strangers. Generally speaking, strangers will probably respond in a positive way as long as they perceive that our intent is to learn about them personally or about their group and *not* to judge them.

The other way we can gather information about another person when interacting with her or him is through *self-disclosure*—telling the other person information about ourselves (Berger, 1979). Self-disclosure works as an information-gathering strategy because of the reciprocity norm. Essentially, the reciprocity norm states that if I do something for you, you will reciprocate and do something for me. The reciprocity norm appears to be a cultural universal; that is it exists in all cultures.

In conversations between people who are not close (i.e., people we meet for the first time, acquaintances), we tend to reciprocate and tell each other the same information about ourselves that the other person tells us. If one person discloses her or his opinion on a topic when communicating with someone, the other person will probably tell his or her opinion on the same topic. There will, however, be some differences when we communicate with strangers than when we communicate with people from our own group. The topics that are appropriate to be discussed, for example, vary from culture to culture and from ethnic group to ethnic group. If we self-disclose on a topic with a stranger and she or he does not reciprocate, there is a good chance we have found an inappropriate topic of conversation in that person's group. Since the timing and pacing of self-disclosure varies across cultures and ethnic groups, it is also possible that our timing is off or we have tried to self-disclose at an inappropriate pace.

Knowledge of Group Differences.   Many people assume that to communicate effectively with members of other groups, we should focus only on similarities. This, however, is not necessarily the case. If members of another group strongly identify with their group, they will feel that their self-concepts are not being confirmed if we focus only on similarities. Such a response is likely whether the other person comes from a different culture, ethnic group, disability group, age group, or social class. To communicate effectively, we must understand real differences between our group and strangers' groups. We often are aware of differences based on our ethnocentrism, prejudice, sexism, ageism, and stereotypes. These differences, however, may not be real (e.g., our stereotypes may not be accurate, or the person may be an atypical member of his or her group).

Recognizing real differences often facilitates effective communication. Coleman and DePaulo (1991), for example, point out that

> there is evidence to suggest that [nondisabled] people would rather work and socialize with disabled people who acknowledge their disability than with those who do not acknowledge it. . . . Although acknowledgement of the disability on the part of the disabled person does not always lead to acceptance . . . it does reduce uncertainty and tension and enhances the attractiveness of the disabled person. Interactions proceed less problematically when a disabled person "appropriately" self-discloses about the disability. (p. 82)

A similar argument can be made for other group differences.

To communicate effectively, we need to be aware of the actual differences that exist between our group and other groups, and between ourselves and other individuals. One way we can isolate these actual differences is to learn all we can about other groups (e.g., become an expert on another culture or ethnic group). This approach, however, is not practical. How can we be experts on all the groups that the strangers with whom we have contact are members? Obviously, we cannot.

When we are communicating with people from other cultures, we can use the dimensions of cultural variability discussed in Chapter 3 to develop a preliminary understanding of the real differences between our culture and another culture. Gudykunst and Nishida (1994) isolate several cultural differences, for example, that would help North Americans better understand Japanese communication:

> 1. Recognizing that Japan is a collectivistic culture where people conceptualize them-selves as interdependent with one another. This leads to an emphasis on *wa* [harmony] in the ingroup, as well as an emphasis on *enryo* [reticence] and *amae* [dependence] in interactions with others. The importance of *wa* also leads to drawing a distinction be-tween *tatemae* [what is stated in public] and *honne* [what is truly believed].
> 2. High-context messages are used more frequently in Japan than low-context mes-sages. This leads to an emphasis on indirect forms of communication, as opposed to an emphasis on direct forms of communication in the United States. *Sasshi* [the abil-ity to guess] is necessary to understand indirect messages.
> 3. Japan is a high uncertainty avoidance culture. This leads to an emphasis on rituals and the specification of relatively clear rules in most communication situations. Peo-ple who deviate from the rules are viewed as dangerous and, therefore, are avoided whenever possible.
> 4. Japan is a high power distance culture. This leads to an emphasis on status (e.g., position, age) in communication. Power distance also leads to an emphasis on *on* and *giri* [obligations] in relationships between individuals in Japan.
> 5. Japan is a highly masculine culture. This leads to an emphasis on communicating with members of the same sex, and separation of the sexes in many social situations. (p. 112)

These five conclusions are not all-inclusive, but they summarize the way the major dimensions of cultural variability influence Japanese communication.

Broad generalizations like those isolated here can help us understand the dif-ferences between ourselves and members of another culture if the person from the other culture is a relatively typical member of her or his culture. To communicate effectively with a specific stranger, however, we must understand how he or she views his or her culture. We must also go a step further and try to understand per-sonal differences and similarities between us.

Knowledge of Personal Similarities.   While understanding differences is im-portant, we also have to understand similarities if we are going to develop relation-ships with strangers. Understanding similarities at the group level is important, but finding similarities at the individual level is critical if we want to develop a rela-tionship with strangers (this issue is discussed in more detail in Chapter 12). Iso-lating similarities requires that we be mindful of our communication.

One way we can be mindful is by creating new categories (Langer, 1989). One way to create new categories is to develop subcategories of a broader category (e.g., separating Chicanos and Chicanas from Mexican Americans in our stereo-type of people from Mexico). The smaller our categories, the more effectively we can communicate with people in the category. We create new categories when we consciously search for similarities we share with strangers rather than focusing only on differences. Does the person from the other group, for example, have children who go to the same school as ours? Does he or she belong to the same social clubs we do? Does she or he experience similar frustrations in her or his professional and personal life as we do? Does he or she have similar worries about his or her family as we do? The first two questions search for shared group memberships, while the second two focus on shared values, attitudes, or beliefs.

Bellah et al. (1985) point out that we need to seek out commonalities because "with a more explicit understanding of what we have in common and the goals we seek to attain together, the differences between us that remain would be less threatening" (p. 287). Finding commonalities requires that we be mindful of our prejudices. "Racism and sexism and homophobia and religious and cultural intolerance . . . are all ways of denying that other people are the same kind as ourselves" (Brodie, 1989, p. 16).

The position that Bellah and his associates advocate vis-à-vis cultural and/or ethnic differences is consistent with Langer's (1989) contention that

> because most of us grow up and spend our time with people like ourselves, we tend to assume uniformities and commonalities. When confronted with someone who is clearly different in one specific way, we drop that assumption and look for differences. . . . The mindful curiosity generated by an encounter with someone who is different, which can lead to exaggerated perceptions of strangeness, can also bring us closer to that person if channeled differently. (p. 156)

Langer suggests that once individuals satisfy their curiosity about differences, understanding can occur. She argues, therefore, that what is needed is a way to make mindful curiosity about differences not taboo. One way that each of us can contribute to the acceptance of mindful curiosity is by accepting others' questions about us and our groups as "requests for information" until we are certain there is another motivation.

Knowledge of Alternative Interpretations.   Effective communication requires that we minimize misunderstandings or maximize the similarity in the ways messages are interpreted. To accomplish this goal, we must recognize that there are many ways that messages can be interpreted, and often these interpretations involve evaluations of others' behavior. (Note: Awareness of alternative perspectives is one component of being mindful, a skill discussed in the next section.)

The problems of misinterpreting others' behavior are compounded when we communicate with strangers because we tend to interpret strangers' behavior on the basis of our own frame of reference. Lakoff (1990) illustrates the problems that emerge when we interpret strangers' behavior on the basis of our frame of reference:

> We see all behavior from our internal perspective: what would that mean if I did it? And, of course, if I, as a member of my own group, did what that person did in the presence of other members of my group, it would be strange or bad. . . . We don't usu-

ally extrapolate, we don't say, "Yes, but in *his* [or her] frame of reference, what would it mean? We assume the possibility of direct transfer of meaning, that a gesture or act in Culture A can be understood in the same way by members of Culture B. Often this is true: there are universals of behavior, but often that is a dangerous assumption; and by cavalierly ignoring the need for translation, we are making misunderstanding inevitable. (pp. 165–166)

It is important to keep in mind that we tend to make the assumption of direct transfer of meaning when we communicate on automatic pilot. Understanding strangers' perspectives requires that we be mindful of our communication.

When we communicate on automatic pilot, we interpret strangers' behavior using our perspective. Recognizing strangers' perspectives requires understanding the differences between the three cognitive processes involved in our perception of strangers' behavior: description, interpretation, and evaluation. To communicate effectively, we must distinguish between these three processes. By *description,* we mean an actual report of what we have observed with the minimum of distortion and without attributing social significance to the behavior. Description includes what we see and hear and is accomplished by counting and/or recording observations.

In order to clarify these processes, consider the following example:

Description

Kim stood six inches away from me when we talked.

This statement is descriptive in nature. It does not attribute social significance to Kim's behavior; it merely tells what the observer saw. If we attribute social significance to this statement, or make an inference about what we saw, we would be engaged in *interpretation.* In other words, interpretation is what we think about what we see and hear. The important thing to keep in mind is that multiple interpretations can be made for any particular description of behavior. Returning to our example, we have the following:

Description

Kim stood six inches away from me when we talked.

Interpretations

Kim is aggressive.
Kim violated my personal space.
Kim likes me.

Each of these interpretations can have several different evaluations. *Evaluations* are positive or negative judgments concerning the social significance we attribute to behavior, that is, whether or not we like the behavior. To illustrate this process, we can use the first interpretation given above:

Interpretation

Kim is aggressive.

Evaluations

I like that; Kim stands up for her- or himself.
I don't like that; Kim should not violate my rights by standing so close.

Of course, several other evaluations could be made, but these two are sufficient to illustrate potential differences in evaluations that can be made regarding any one interpretation.

If we are unable to distinguish between these three cognitive processes, it is likely that we will skip the descriptive process and jump immediately to either interpretation or evaluation when confronted with different patterns of behavior. Directly interpreting or evaluating leads to misattributions of meaning and, therefore, to ineffective communication. Being able to distinguish among the three processes, on the other hand, increases the likelihood that we are able to see alternative interpretations, thereby increasing our ability to communicate effectively.

If we do not separate descriptive and interpretive processes, misunderstandings are inevitable. When we communicate on automatic pilot, we usually interpret others' behavior without describing it. Our interpretation is based on our cultural, ethnic, and social class upbringing. Our interpretation of someone's behavior, however, may be very different from what he or she intended by the behavior. When we think there might have been a misunderstanding, we need to stop and describe the behavior in question. Once we've described the behavior, we need to look for alternative interpretations. After we have thought of some alternative interpretations, we can ask the other person which interpretation is correct (using the perception checking skill discussed in Chapter 7). If we cannot ask the other person, we can make an educated guess as to what the other person meant on the basis of our knowledge of the other person or the groups of which she or he is a member. Separating descriptions and interpretations, as we are suggesting here, requires that we be mindful.

Skills

The skills necessary to communicate effectively and appropriately with strangers are those that are directly related to reducing our uncertainty and anxiety. Reducing and/or managing our anxiety requires at least three skills: ability to be mindful, ability to tolerate ambiguity, and ability to calm ourselves. Reducing uncertainty minimally requires four skills: ability to be mindful, ability to empathize, ability to adapt our behavior, and ability to make accurate predictions and explanations of others' behavior (the first two skills, however, are necessary to develop the third). Since the ability to be mindful is common to managing both anxiety and uncertainty, we begin with it.

Ability to Be Mindful.   By now, it should be clear that we believe becoming mindful is an important aspect of communicating effectively with strangers. We must be cognitively aware of our communication if we are to overcome our tendency to interpret strangers' behavior on the basis of our own frame of reference. At the outset, it is important to recognize that we are seldom highly mindful of our communication. Even when we communicate with people close to us, we are not mindful of the process. Csikszentmihalyi (1990) contends that

> there are few things as enjoyable as freely sharing one's most secret feelings and thoughts with another person. Even though this sounds commonplace, it in fact requires concentrated attention [mindfulness], openness, and sensitivity. In practice, the degree of investment of psychic energy in a friendship is unfortunately rare. (p. 188)

He goes on to argue that we must control our own lives if we want to improve our relationships with others. Such control requires that we be mindful.

As indicated in Chapter 2, Langer (1989) isolates three qualities of *mindfulness:* "(1) creation of new categories; (2) openness to new information; and (3) awareness of more than one perspective" (p. 62). (Note: Since knowledge of alternative perspectives was discussed in the preceding section, only the first two components are discussed here.)

Langer (1989) points out that "categorizing is a fundamental and natural human activity. It is the way we come to know the world. Any attempt to eliminate bias by attempting to eliminate the perception of differences is doomed to failure" (p. 154). She argues that what we need to do is learn to make more, not fewer, distinctions. To illustrate this point, Langer uses an example of people who are in the category "cripple." If we see all people in this category as the same, we start treating the category in which we place a person as his or her identity. If we draw additional distinctions within this category (i.e., create new categories), on the other hand, it stops us from treating the person as a category. If we see a person with a "lame leg," we do not necessarily treat her or him as a "cripple."

We can become open to new information by modifying our expectations. If, for example, we have an inflexible negative stereotype of another group, we can either modify the content of the stereotype or hold it more flexibly. Harvey, Hunt, and Schroder (1961) argue that people differ in the degree to which they are willing to modify stereotypes they hold, or in other words, the degree of "openness-closedness" of their stereotypes. In applying this concept to interactions across national boundaries, Scott (1965) argues that

> an image is "closed" to the extent that the person regards the attributes included in it as completely defining the object. . . . The more "open" the image, the more is the person willing to entertain the possibility that essential features of the object have not yet been recognized by him [or her], and that these additional attributes would reveal new similarities and differences in relation to other objects. (p. 81)

Holding closed stereotypes is linked directly to inaccurate interpretations and predictions of strangers' behavior. Holding open stereotypes, in contrast, increases the likelihood of making more accurate interpretations and predictions of strangers' behavior. More specifically, if our stereotypes are open, we will be open to perceiving behavior not associated with the stereotype, thereby making it possible for us to interpret and predict the behavior of strangers more accurately. We also need to recognize consciously that our stereotype may be inaccurate and does not apply to *all,* or even most, members of the other group.

Sometimes when we communicate with strangers, we are mindful of our communication. Our focus, however, is usually on the outcome (will I make a fool of myself?), rather than on the process of communication. As you will recall, however, focusing on the outcome does not facilitate effective communication. For effective communication to occur, we must focus on the process. Langer (1989) argues that

> an outcome orientation in social situations can induce mindlessness. If we think we know how to handle a situation, we don't feel a need to pay attention. If we respond to the situation as very familiar (as a result, for example, of overlearning), we notice only minimal cues necessary to carry out the proper scenarios. If, on the other hand, the situation is strange, we might be so preoccupied with the thought of failure ("what if I make a fool of myself?") that we miss nuances of our own and others' behavior. In this sense, we are mindless with respect to the immediate situation, although we may be thinking quite actively about outcome related issues. (p. 34)

Langer believes that focusing on the process (e.g., *how* we do something) forces us to be mindful of our behavior and pay attention to the situations in which we find ourselves. It is only when we are mindful of the process of our communication that we can determine how our interpretations of messages differ from others' interpretations of those messages.

We often are mindful of our behavior when we communicate with strangers because they may act in a deviant or unexpected fashion or we do not have a script to guide our communication with them. The "problem" is that we usually are mindful of the outcome, not the process. Since we tend to interpret others' behavior on the basis of our own frame of reference, to communicate effectively with strangers, we need to become mindful of our process of communication, even when we are engaging in habitual behavior. We are not suggesting that people try to be mindful at all times. That would be impossible. Rather, we are suggesting that when there is a high potential for misunderstanding, we need to be mindful and consciously aware of the process of communication that is taking place.

When we become mindful, there are several things we can do to improve our communication effectiveness. We can, for example, negotiate meanings with the other person. *Negotiating meanings* involves seeking clarification of meanings in the middle of a conversation when we realize a misunderstanding has occurred (Varonis & Gass, 1985). Attempts to negotiate meanings usually are initiated by the person whose native language is being spoken. Another technique we can use is repairs. *Repairs* involve asking the other person to repeat what was said when we do not understand (Gass & Varonis, 1985). Repair sequences usually are initiated by the person speaking in his or her second language.

Negotiating meaning and repairs are forms of metacommunication—communicating about our communication. Another aspect of metacommunication that is relevant when we are mindful of our communication is feedback. When we are mindful, we can give the strangers with whom we are communicating feedback about how we are interpreting their messages and request feedback about how they are interpreting our messages. Closely related is the issue of effective listening. When we communicate on automatic pilot, we do not listen effectively. To listen effectively, we must be mindful of our communication.

Ability to Tolerate Ambiguity.   *Tolerance for ambiguity* implies the ability to deal successfully with situations even when a lot of information needed to interact effectively is unknown. Budner (1962) argues that *lack* of tolerance for ambiguity involves perceiving ambiguous situations as threatening and undesirable. Our tolerance for ambiguity affects the type of information we gather about strangers. If we have a low tolerance for ambiguity, we tend to base our judgments of strangers on first impressions, which are formed prematurely before all information is available (Smock, 1955). We also seek out information that supports our beliefs when we have a low tolerance for ambiguity (McPherson, 1983). If we have a high tolerance for ambiguity, in contrast, we tend to seek objective information about the situation and the people in it. Further, we tend to be open to new information about ourselves and others if we have a high tolerance for ambiguity (Pilisuk, 1963).

The greater our tolerance for ambiguity, the more comfortable we feel in situations where we do not have all the information we would like. Ruben and Kealey (1979) point out that

> the ability to react to new and ambiguous situations with minimal discomfort has long been thought to be an important asset when adjusting to a new culture. . . . Excessive discomfort resulting from being placed in a new or different environment—or from finding the familiar environment altered in some critical ways—can lead to confusion, frustration and interpersonal hostility. Some people seem better able to adapt well in new environments and adjust quickly to the demands of the changing milieu. (p. 19)

Ruben and Kealey's research indicates that the greater our tolerance for ambiguity, the more effective we are in completing task assignments in other cultures.

Our tolerance for ambiguity affects the type of information we try to find out about others. People with a low tolerance for ambiguity try to gather information that supports their own beliefs. People with a high tolerance for ambiguity, in contrast, seek objective information from others (McPherson, 1983). Objective information is necessary to understand strangers and predict their behavior accurately.

Ability to Calm Ourselves.   As indicated earlier, the amount of anxiety we experience when we communicate with strangers influences our motivation to communicate with them. If our anxiety is above our maximum threshold or below our minimum threshold, we will not be able to communicate effectively. If anxiety is too high, we will be too preoccupied with managing our anxiety to communicate effectively. If it is too low, we will not have enough adrenaline flowing to want to communicate.

Kennerley (1990) isolates two general issues in managing anxiety and calming ourselves: (1) controlling bodily symptoms, and (2) controlling worrying thoughts or cognitive distortions. There are several physical symptoms associated with anxiety. When we are highly anxious, we might experience respiratory problems (e.g., difficulty in breathing), palpitations of the heart, dry mouth, muscular tension, or a tension headache.

Prather (1986) suggests the most important thing we can do to manage our anxiety is break away from the situation in which we feel anxious. This approach might mean excusing ourselves to leave the room, or mentally withdrawing for a short period of time. Once we have withdrawn, we need to calm ourselves and remember that our anxiety is not going to harm us. We can allow our anxious feelings to pass and then return to the situation.

If our anxiety does not dissipate quickly, we need to do something that will restore our calm. We can use various techniques to control the physical symptoms associated with our anxiety. These techniques include, but are not limited to, yoga, hypnotism, meditation, and progressive muscular relaxation (i.e., relaxing the various muscle groups in our bodies in a systematic fashion). Respiratory control also can be used to manage the physical symptoms of anxiety. One way to practice controlled breathing is to sit up straight and concentrate on our breathing. Mindfully draw in a long breath and focus on our inhaling. Then let out the breath, focusing on our exhaling.

We can control our worrying thoughts by overcoming our cognitive distortions. When we interpret our own and others' behavior, our perceptions often are distorted because of the ways we think about our feelings and behavior. Burns (1989) isolates ten forms of cognitive distortions that influence the ways we interpret behavior: (1) engaging in all-or-nothing thinking, (2) making overgeneralizations, (3) using mental filters, (4) discounting the positive and focusing only on the negative, (5) jumping to conclusions, (6) magnifying, or making problems bigger than they are, (7) using emotional reasoning, (8) using "should" statements (e.g., I should be a better person), (9) labeling, and (10) blaming ourselves or others. To overcome our worrying thoughts, we need to be mindful of our communication. When we are mindful, we need to replace the worrying thoughts with rational responses. Unless we stop distorting our thought processes, we will *not* be able to manage our anxiety consistently over long periods of time.

Ability to Empathize. The one skill that consistently emerges in discussions of effectively communicating with strangers is empathy. Bell (1987) argues that *empathy* is multifaceted, involving cognitive (thinking), affective (feeling), and communicative components:

> Cognitively, the empathic person takes the perspective of another person, and in so doing strives to see the world from the other's point of view. Affectively, the empathic person experiences the emotions of another; he or she *feels* the other's experiences. Communicatively, the empathic individual signals understanding and concern through verbal and nonverbal cues. (p. 204)

The cognitive, affective, and communicative components are highly interrelated, and all must be present for others to perceive that we are being empathic.

Empathy involves (1) carefully listening to others, (2) understanding others' feelings, (3) being interested in what others say, (4) being sensitive to others' needs, and (5) understanding others' points of view (Hwang, Chase, & Kelly, 1980). While these indicators of empathy include verbal components, we tend to rely on nonverbal behavior more than verbal behavior when we interpret others' behavior as empathic (Bell, 1987).

When we are *empathic,* we imagine how the other person is feeling. Sympathy often is confused with empathy. When we are *sympathetic,* we imagine how we would feel in the other person's situation. Bennett (1979) argues that the Golden Rule—"Do unto others as you would have them do unto you"—which many people are taught as children, involves a sympathetic response to others, not an empathic response. He proposes that we follow the Platinum Rule—"Do unto others as they would have you do unto them"—which involves an empathic response. This is a reasonable approach as long as what others want done unto them does not violate our basic moral principles or universally accepted principles of human rights.

Ability to Adapt Our Behavior. To gather information about and adapt our behavior to strangers requires that we be flexible in our behavior. As suggested in the discussion of knowledge, we must be able to select strategies that are appropriate to gather the information we need about strangers in order to communicate effectively with them. This ability requires that we have different behavioral options for gathering information open to us. Do we sit back and watch the other person or go interact with him or her? Which strategy will provide the information we need to know to communicate effectively?

We also must be able to adapt and accommodate our behavior to people from other groups if we are going to be successful in our interactions with them. Duran's (1983) conceptualization of communication adaptability is consistent with the perspective used here. He argues that *communication adaptability* involves "1) The requirement of both cognitive (ability to perceive) and behavioral (ability to adapt) skills; 2) Adaptation not only of behaviors but also interaction goals; 3) The ability to adapt to the requirements posed by different communication contexts; and 4) The assumption that perceptions of communicative competence reside in the dyad" (p. 320).

Triandis, Brislin, and Hui (1988) provide suggestions for how individualists and collectivists might want to consider adapting their behavior and ways of thinking when communicating with each other. *For individualists to communicate more effectively with collectivists,* Triandis and his associates suggest that individualists

(1) recognize that collectivists pay attention to group memberships and use group memberships to predict collectivists' behavior; (2) recognize that when collectivists' group memberships change, their behavior changes; (3) recognize that collectivists are comfortable in vertical, unequal relationships; (4) recognize that collectivists see competition as threatening; (5) recognize that collectivists emphasize harmony and cooperation in the ingroup; (6) recognize that collectivists emphasize face (public self-image) and help them preserve their face in interactions; (7) recognize that collectivists do not separate criticism from the person being criticized and avoid confrontation whenever possible; (8) cultivate long-term relationships; (9) be more formal than usual in initial interactions; and (10) follow collectivists' guide in disclosing personal information.

For collectivists to interact effectively with individualists, Triandis and his associates suggest that collectivists (1) recognize that individualists' behavior cannot be predicted accurately from group memberships; (2) recognize that individualists will be proud of their accomplishments and say negative things about others; (3) recognize that individualists are emotionally detached from their ingroups; (4) recognize that individualists prefer horizontal, equal relationships; (5) recognize that individualists do not see competition as threatening; (6) recognize that individualists are not persuaded by arguments emphasizing harmony and cooperation; (7) recognize that individualists do not form long-term relationships and that initial friendliness does not indicate an intimate relationship; (8) recognize that individualists maintain relationships when they receive more rewards than costs; (9) recognize that individualists do not respect others on the basis of position, age, or sex as much as collectivists; and (10) recognize that outgroups are not viewed as highly different from the ingroup. Suggestions also could be based on the other dimensions of cultural variability presented in Chapter 3.

Often the adaptations we make when interacting with strangers do not improve the effectiveness of our communication (see, for example, the discussion of communicative distance in Chapter 5). "Adjustments majority speakers make when speaking to minority members often give the impression that the speaker is patronizing and distant and, in turn, affect the recipients' behavior and conversational style" (Kraut & Higgins, 1984, p. 114). If strangers perceive we are patronizing, they will become defensive, and communication cannot be effective when one of the individuals is defensive. To be more effective, we must adapt our messages to the specific person with whom we are communicating. Others understand our messages better when the messages are constructed for them than when we do not adapt our messages.

One important aspect of adapting our behavior is the ability to speak another language (or at least use phrases in another language). If we always expect strangers to speak our language, we cannot be effective in communicating with them. Boyer (1990) points out that we "should become familiar with other languages and cultures so that [we] will be better able to live, with confidence, in an increasingly interdependent world" (p. B4).

Triandis (1983) points out that the importance of speaking another language depends, at least in part, on where we are:

> In some cultures foreigners are expected to know the local language. A Frenchman [or woman] who arrives in the United States without knowing a word of English, or an American who visits France with only a bit of French, is bound to find the locals rather unsympathetic. For example, I have found a discrepancy between my friends' and my own experience in Paris. Their accounts stress discourtesy of the French, while I have found the French to be quite courteous. I suspect the difference is that I speak better French than the majority of visitors and am therefore treated more courteously. In contrast, in other cultures the visitor is not expected to know the local language. In Greece, for example, one is not expected to know the language although a few words of Greek create delight, and increase by order of magnitude (a factor of ten) the normal hospitable tendencies of that population. (p. 84)

Some attempt at using the local language is necessary to indicate an interest in the people and/or culture. It is important to keep in mind, however, that members of other cultures may prefer to speak our language. To illustrate, Ross and Shortreed (1990) report that Japanese who speak English do not view responding in Japanese to non–Japanese-speaking Japanese, even those relatively fluent, to be empathic or efficient.

The need to adapt our behavior is not limited to speaking another language. If a European American is communicating with someone from another culture (e.g., someone from a Latin or Arab culture) who wants to stand closer than the European American wants him or her to stand, the European American has two options if she or he is mindful of his or her communication. First, the European American can choose to try to use his or her own interpersonal distance (e.g., the other person should stand at least at arm's length). If the other person keeps trying to use her or his distance, however, he or she will dance the European American around the room (i.e., the other person moves forward, the European American moves back; to compensate and be at a distance that is comfortable for him or her, the other person moves closer). If the European American is not mindful of his or her communication, this "dance" is likely to occur. Alternatively, the European American can choose to use a different pattern of behavior. The European American can decide to stand closer to the other person than he or she would if she or he was communicating with someone from his or her own culture. This option will, in all likelihood, lead to more effective communication. When people are following different norms, at least one of the parties has to adapt for effective communication to occur.

You may be asking yourself, Why do I have to adapt? Why doesn't the other person adapt, especially if he or she is a foreigner in the United States? The other person could adapt, and people from other cultures visiting or living in the United States usually do to some extent. As members of the human community, nevertheless, we have to make choices about whether to adapt and when to adapt to others. We believe that if we know what can be done to improve the chances for effective communication, have the skills to do what needs to be done, and choose not to adapt our communication, we have to take responsibility for misunderstandings that occur as a result. There are obviously situations where this principle may not hold. If the behavior required, for example, goes against our moral standards or violates another's human rights, some other option must be found.

Ability to Make Accurate Predictions and Explanations.   The final skill is the ability to make accurate predictions and explanations of others' behavior. If we can empathize, have the ability to adapt our communication, and are mindful, we can gather the information necessary to reduce uncertainty. Reducing uncertainty requires that we be able to describe others' behavior, select accurate interpretations of their messages, accurately predict their behavior, and accurately explain their behavior.

Karniol (1990) points out that we assume that others' thoughts, feelings, and behavior are rule-governed. If we do not make such an assumption, we could not ever predict others' thoughts, feelings, or behavior. The problem with the accuracy of our predictions is that we know only a limited number of rules that we can use to understand others' thoughts, feelings, and behavior. Since we may not know the rules that strangers are using, we assume that their rules are the same as ours when we are on automatic pilot. To understand the rules that others are using to guide their thoughts, feelings, and behavior, we must be mindful. When we are mindful, we need to be empathic and use active listening in order to try to understand others' rules. Once we understand the rules strangers are using, we can make accurate predictions and explanations of their behavior.

When we are on automatic pilot, our predictions and explanations for others' behavior are based on our stereotypes, attitudes, and previous experiences with the individuals involved. We may be highly confident of our predictions and explanations when we are on automatic pilot, but our predictions and explanations may *not* be accurate. If our predictions are based only on our stereotypes of another person's group, for example, our predictions will not be accurate if our stereotypes are inaccurate or the person is not typical of his or her group. Accurate predictions or explanations of strangers' behavior require that we use cultural, social, and personal information.

To make accurate predictions and explanations, we must be able to gather accurate information about others. When our anxiety is too high, we are not able to gather accurate information about others (Wilder & Shapiro, 1989). If our anxiety is too low, we also will have problems gathering accurate information about others. To gather accurate information, we must mindfully manage our anxiety so that it is below our maximum threshold and above our minimum threshold. The accuracy of our predictions and explanations for strangers' behavior also depends on our knowledge of group differences, our knowledge of similarities, and our knowledge of alternative interpretations. Our accuracy also is affected by our expectations. If we expect the interactions to be negative, for example, our anxiety will be high, probably above our maximum thresholds, and we will not be able to make accurate predictions or explanations. We also are better able to make accurate predictions and explanations if our needs (see the motivation section of this chapter) have been met.

Another factor that influences the accuracy of our predictions and explanations is our view of our ingroups and outgroups. We tend to view our ingroups as being more differentiated than outgroups. The more familiar we are with outgroups, however, the greater our perceived differentiation of the outgroups (Linville, Fisher, & Salovey, 1989). The more variability we perceive in outgroups, the less will be our tendency to treat all members in a similar negative fashion (Johnston & Hewstone, 1991). The variability we perceive in outgroups provides information about the strangers with whom we are communicating and, therefore, increases the accuracy of our predictions.

Our perceptions of strangers' intentions toward us also affects the accuracy of our predictions and explanations of their behavior. We tend to be more accurate, for example, in perceiving others' intentions when the intentions are negative than when they are positive. "Intentions to convey hostility are perceived more accurately than intentions to convey positive feelings" (Bodenhausen, Gaelick, & Weyer, 1987, p. 159). Our accuracy in interpreting others' intentions also is lower if we have been dissatisfied with our previous interactions with them than if we have been satisfied with our previous interactions.

SUMMARY

Effective communication involves minimizing misunderstandings. To be an effective communicator requires that we be motivated and have the appropriate knowledge and skills. We must be motivated to approach strangers and communicate effectively. Our motivation is a function of meeting our needs for predictability, for avoiding anxiety, and for sustaining our self-conceptions. If we are not able to meet these needs, we will not be motivated to communicate with strangers.

To communicate effectively also requires that we have certain knowledge. We must know how to gather appropriate information about strangers, have knowledge of group differences and personal similarities, and recognize alternative interpretations for others' behavior. If we know how to gather information, we can gain the other types of knowledge from our interaction with strangers.

Several skills are particularly important in reducing our uncertainty and anxiety. To reduce our anxiety, we must be able to be mindful, to tolerate ambiguity, and to calm ourselves. To reduce our uncertainty, we must again be able to be mindful and, in addition, be able to empathize, to adapt our behavior, and to make accurate predictions and explanations of strangers' behavior.

STUDY QUESTIONS

1. How do we know when we have communicated effectively?
2. Why is competence based on our impressions of ourselves and others?
3. What are the components of perceived competence? Why are all three necessary to communicate effectively?
4. How does meeting our needs for predictability, avoiding anxiety, and sustaining our self-conceptions influence our motivation to communicate with strangers?
5. How does our knowledge of how to gather information influence our communication with strangers?
6. How does our knowledge of group differences influence our communication with strangers?

7. How does our knowledge of personal similarities influence our communication with strangers?
8. How does our knowledge of alternative interpretations influence our communication with strangers?
9. How does our ability to be mindful influence our communication with strangers?
10. How does our ability to tolerate ambiguity influence our communication with strangers?
11. How does our ability to manage our anxiety influence our communication with strangers?
12. How does our ability to empathize (not sympathize) influence our communication with strangers?
13. How does our ability to adapt our behavior influence our communication with strangers?

SUGGESTED READING

Gudykunst, W. B., & Nishida, T. (1994). *Bridging Japanese/North American differences.* Thousand Oaks, CA: Sage.

Landis, D., & Bhagat, R. (Eds.). (1996). *Handbook of intercultural training* (2nd edition). Thousand Oaks, CA: Sage.

Spitzberg, B., & Cupach, W. (1984). *Interpersonal communication competence.* Beverly Hills, CA: Sage.

Spitzberg, B., & Cupach, W. (1989). *Handbook of interpersonal competence research.* New York: Springer-Verlag.

Wiseman, R., & Koester, J. (Eds.). (1993). *Intercultural communication competence.* Thousand Oaks, CA: Sage.

11

Managing Conflict
with Strangers

Oftentimes, I have hated in self defense;
but if I were stronger I would not have
used such a weapon.
                              Kahlil Gibran

Elie Wiesel, a recipient of the Nobel Peace Prize, believes that hate directed toward members of different cultural and racial groups, as well as toward members of different political and ideological groups, is the major source of problems between people in the twentieth century. Hate is being expressed toward, and conflict is occurring between, people of different groups everywhere we look. Nationality conflicts, for example, are taking place in the former Soviet Union (e.g., between the Azerbaijanis and the Armenians); ethnic conflict is occurring among the Serbians, Croats, and Muslims in the former Yugoslavia; conflict between neo-Nazis and immigrants in Germany is leading to violence; conflict between Protestants and Catholics in Northern Ireland is still taking place; and conflict between Palestinians and Jews in Israel has not stopped, to name only a few of the intergroup conflicts occurring in the world today. In the United States, racial harassment is taking place on university campuses, hate crimes are being committed against members of certain groups (e.g., members of different ethnic groups, homosexuals), and conflict is continuing between pro-choice and right-to-life groups at abortion clinics. The animosity between the various groups is aggravated by the hate programs appearing on public-access cable television in the United States (e.g., *Race and Reason;* see Zoglin, 1993).

The specific causes of the conflicts occurring throughout the world differ depending upon the situation; nevertheless, all incidents share one thing in common—polarized communication. *Polarized communication* occurs when the communicators have "the inability to believe or seriously consider one's view as wrong and the other's opinion as truth. Communication within [the] human community becomes typified by the rhetoric of 'we' are right and 'they' are misguided or wrong" (Arnett, 1986, pp. 15–16). Polarized communication, therefore, exists when groups or individuals look out for their own interests and have little or no concern for others' interests. Tannen (1993) believes that

> the devastating group hatreds that result in so much suffering in our own country and around the world are related in origin to the small intolerances in our everyday conversations—our readiness to attribute good intentions to ourselves and bad intentions to others; to believe there is one right way and ours is it; and to extrapolate from frustration with an individual in order to generalize to a group. (p. B5)

We express these small intolerances in our everyday conversations without being highly aware of doing so.

The small intolerances in our everyday communication with strangers often lead to conflict. In this chapter, we examine how we can manage conflict with strangers constructively. We begin by looking at the nature of conflict. Next, we look at cultural and ethnic differences in conflict. Then we discuss what is involved in managing conflict constructively. We conclude by providing suggestions for managing our conflicts with strangers.

THE NATURE OF CONFLICT

Conflict "exists whenever incompatible activities occur" (Deutsch, 1973, p. 10). When one person's activities are incompatible with another person's activities, one person or both people are prevented from accomplishing their goals. Such obstruction or interference occurs in a wide range of situations. Conflicts can range from minor disagreements, such as a difference of opinion with someone with whom we have an ongoing relationship, to wars. Knowing how to manage conflict is critical to developing and maintaining our relationships with strangers.

Conflict is inevitable in any ongoing relationship; it is going to happen whether we want it to or not. Roloff (1987) isolates several sources of conflict. First, conflict occurs when people misinterpret each other's behavior. Misinterpreting the partner's intent, for example, is one of the major causes of discontent in marriages (Gottman et al., 1976). Second, conflict can arise from perceptions of incompatibility, such as perceiving that personality or group characteristics are not compatible. Third, conflict arises when people disagree on the causes of their own or other people's behavior. As indicated in Chapter 7, we tend to explain our own positive behavior on the basis of personal characteristics, while we attribute strangers' positive behavior to situational demands. We tend to attribute our own negative behavior to situational demands, and strangers' negative behavior to their personal characteristics.

When a conflict occurs, neither party, only one party, or both parties may recognize that a conflict exists. If neither party recognizes that a conflict exists, the conflict may not create problems for the relationship. If only one party recognizes that a conflict exists, that situation can create problems for the relationship, depending on the conflict and how the person handles it. If, for example, the person decides that the issue is not important, he or she could ignore the conflict and it will not create problems in the relationship. If, however, he or she thinks the conflict *is* important, yet chooses to ignore it, that situation will, in all likelihood, create problems in the relationship. If the conflict does not come out in any other way, it will come out in how the person who chose to ignore it reacts to the other person.

Communication is the medium through which conflict is created and managed. The way we communicate with others often creates conflict. The way we communicate with others reflects whether or not we are having conflicts with them. It also is through communication that we constructively or destructively manage our conflicts.

Conflict in relationships can be overt, or out in the open (manifest conflict), or it can be out of sight (latent conflict). When conflict is out of sight, we easily can avoid addressing the conflict. In fact, avoidance is probably the most widely used strategy for dealing with conflict. Estimates indicate that we avoid 50 percent of our conflicts with others (Sillars et al., 1982). One reason we avoid conflict is that many of us view conflict negatively. Conflict itself, however, is not positive or negative. How we manage the conflicts we have, in contrast, can have positive or negative consequences for our relationships with strangers.

Our conflicts with strangers often seem to get out of control without our realizing it. Donohue (1993) isolates four aspects of conflict development that contribute to this result. First, once conflicts start, they tend to perpetuate themselves, especially if problems already exist between the people involved. Conflict breeds conflict, unless it is managed successfully. Second, conflicts always take place within a context, but we often are not aware of how the context contributes to our conflicts with strangers. To manage conflicts, we have to understand the contexts in which they occur. Third, our conflicts always have implications for our relationships with strangers. When conflicts are over, our relationships change in some way, but we often do not recognize that it is how we manage the conflicts that is critical to how the conflicts will affect our relationships. Fourth, conflicts get out of control because we do not recognize that manifest conflicts actually serve many positive functions in our lives. If two people have conflicts with a common enemy, for example, the shared conflicts bring them closer together. Our conflicts with strangers also help define our roles, help us understand our feelings about strangers, and help make the conflict issues clearer.

CULTURAL AND ETHNIC DIFFERENCES IN MANAGING CONFLICT

One of the reasons that we have difficulty managing conflict with strangers is that strangers often view conflict differently than we do. In this section, we look at the various ways that strangers' views of conflict differ from ours. We begin by looking at cultural differences in managing conflict. Then we examine ethnic differences in managing conflict.

Cultural Differences in Managing Conflict

Many aspects of conflict differ across cultures. We divide our discussion of cultural differences in conflict into two sections. We begin by looking at the assumptions members of different cultures make about the nature of conflict. Then we look at the ways members of different cultures manage conflict.

Assumptions About Conflict. The major reason conflicts occur differs across cultures. Olsen (1978) argues that conflicts arise from either instrumental or expressive sources. *Expressive conflicts* arise from a desire to release tension, usually generated from hostile feelings. *Instrumental conflicts,* in contrast, stem from a difference in goals or practices. Ting-Toomey (1985) believes members of individualistic cultures "are more likely to perceive conflict as instrumental rather than expressive in nature," while members of collectivistic cultures "are more likely to perceive conflict as expressive rather than instrumental in nature" (p. 78).

Members of individualistic cultures often separate the issue on which they are having conflict from the person with whom they have the conflict. Members of collectivistic cultures, in contrast, generally do not make this distinction. To illustrate, Nishiyama (1971) points out that Japanese managers take criticism and objections to ideas they express as personal attacks. North American managers, on the other hand, do not necessarily take criticism of their ideas as personal attacks unless they are highly defensive.

The conditions under which conflicts occur differ across cultures. Ting-Toomey (1985) argues that in individualistic cultures, conflict is likely to occur when an individual's expectation of appropriate behavior is being violated. Conflict in collectivistic cultures, in contrast, is more likely to occur when the group's normative expectations of behavior are being violated. The reason for this difference lies in the role of context in providing information in the two types of cultures. In collectivistic cultures, context plays a crucial role in providing meaning to communication messages, while in individualistic cultures, context plays a less crucial role because more information is provided in the message. The more important the context is, the more often violation of collective normative expectations leads to conflict. The less important the context is, the more often violation of individual expectations leads to conflict.

The attitude of the participants toward dealing with conflict varies across cultures. Ting-Toomey (1985) takes the position that people in individualistic cultures "are more likely to possess a confrontational, direct attitude toward conflicts," while people in collectivistic cultures "are more likely to possess a nonconfrontational, indirect attitude toward conflicts" (p. 79). A direct approach to conflict in individualistic cultures probably stems from the "doing" orientation and the use of linear logic. Members of collectivistic cultures have a strong desire for group harmony and tend to use indirect forms of communication; therefore, they tend to prefer a nonconfrontational approach to conflict.

Ting-Toomey (1994a) argues that the self construal that guides individuals in managing conflicts differs across cultures. Members of individualistic cultures tend to deal with conflict on the basis of an independent self construal, while members of collectivistic cultures tend to deal with conflict on the basis of an interdependent self construal. In using an independent self construal, members of individualistic cultures think only of themselves and the specific person with whom they have a conflict. Members of collectivistic cultures, in contrast, think about themselves and the members of their ingroup when their behavior is guided by an interdependent self construal. Since the self construal is interdependent, members of collectivistic cultures cannot separate themselves from the ingroups of which they are members.

Ting-Toomey (1994a) believes that members of individualistic cultures take a short-term view of managing conflict and members of collectivistic cultures tend to take a long-term view of managing conflict. Members of individualistic cultures are concerned with the immediate conflict situation. Once it is managed, they can move on to other issues in their relationship with the other person. Members of collectivistic cultures, in contrast, focus on the long-term relationship with the other person. The immediate conflict is important, but the critical issue for collectivists is whether they can depend on the other person over the long term.

Ting-Toomey (1994a) also contends that members of collectivistic cultures prefer to use mediators to manage conflicts more than do members of individualistic cultures. The use of mediators allows conflicts to be managed without direct confrontation. If direct confrontation can be avoided, harmony in the relationship can be maintained. When members of individualistic cultures do use mediators to manage conflicts, they prefer formal mediators (e.g., lawyers). Members of collectivistic cultures, in contrast, prefer informal mediators.

Conflict Styles.   *Conflict styles* refer to our typical modes of managing conflict in different situations (Ting-Toomey, 1988). Glenn, Witmeyer, and Stevenson (1977) outline three persuasive styles used to resolve conflicts: factual-inductive, axiomatic-deductive, and affective-intuitive. The *factual-inductive* method begins with the important facts and inductively moves toward a conclusion. This is the predominant style in the United States. The *axiomatic-deductive* style begins with a general principle and deduces the implications for specific situations, and the *affective-intuitive* style is based on the use of emotional or affective messages. These two styles predominate in the former Soviet Union. Ting-Toomey (1985) argues that members of individualistic cultures are likely to use both the factual-inductive and axiomatic-deductive styles in resolving conflict. She believes that members of collectivistic cultures, on the other hand, "are more likely to use affective-intuitive styles in conflict" (p. 82).

Ting-Toomey (1988) predicts cultural differences in conflict on the basis of Rahim's (1983) five styles of conflict. Rahim's styles are based on the degree of concern for self and for others inherent in the way individuals try to manage conflict. An *integrating* style of managing conflict involves a high concern for self and a high concern for others. When we use this style, we try to find solutions that are acceptable to both parties. A *compromising* style involves a moderate concern for self and a moderate concern for others. When we use this style, we try to find an agreement that is acceptable to ourselves and others, but the agreement may not be either party's first choice. Both integrating and compromising styles reflect a solution orientation to conflict (Putnam & Wilson, 1982). A *dominating* style reflects a high concern for self and a low concern for others. When we use this style, we try to control or dominate the conflict situation. An *obliging* style involves a low concern for self and a high concern for others. When we use this style, we give in to what others want in conflict situations. Finally, an *avoiding* style involves a low concern for self and a low concern for others. When we use this style, we avoid the conflict topic or situation. Obliging and avoiding styles involve nonconfrontation of conflict (Putnam & Wilson, 1982).

Ting-Toomey (1988) argues that people in individualistic cultures prefer direct styles of dealing with conflict, such as integrating or compromising. People in collectivistic cultures, on the other hand, prefer indirect styles of dealing with conflict that allow all parties to preserve face. They tend to use obliging and avoiding styles of conflict resolution to avoid the conflict altogether. These predictions are consistent with Barnlund's (1975) description of conflict strategies in Japan and the United States. He concludes that people in the United States

> prefer to defend themselves actively, employing or developing the rationale for positions they have taken. When pushed they may resort to still more aggressive forms that utilize humor, sarcasm, or denunciation. Among Japanese, the reactions are more varied, but defenses tend to be more passive, permit withdrawal, and allow greater concealment. (p. 423)

Ting-Toomey, Trubisky, and Nishida's (1989) study of conflict in Japan and in the United States supports Ting-Toomey's predictions and Barnlund's descriptions of conflict.

Avoiding conflict in order to preserve face and maintain harmony is not limited to the Japanese culture. Leung (1987; Leung & Lind, 1986), for example, report that Chinese prefer bargaining and mediation more than do North Americans, while North Americans prefer adjudicatory procedures more than do Chinese. These findings are explained by the collectivistic emphasis on interpersonal harmony in the ingroup and North American individualistic tendencies. Bond et al.'s (1985) study of Chinese and North Americans, for example, reveals that Chinese would advise an executive to meet with an insulter and the target of the insult separately so that conflict between the two can be avoided. People in the United States, in contrast, would advise an executive to have a joint meeting so that the problem between the insulter and the target of the insult can be resolved. Similar differences emerge when people in the United States and Mexico are compared. Specifically, Mexicans tend to avoid or deny that conflict exists, while people in the United States tend to use direct strategies to deal with it (e.g., McGinn, Harburg, & Ginsburg, 1973).

Not all research is consistent with Ting-Toomey's (1988) predictions. Trubisky, Ting-Toomey, and Lin's (1991) study, for example, suggests that Taiwanese use obliging and avoiding styles more than do people in the United States, but they also use integrating and compromising styles more. Ting-Toomey et al.'s (1991) study also provides inconsistent findings. Gire and Carment (1993) find that Canadians prefer negotiation more than do Nigerians, and Nigerians prefer threats more than do Canadians. One explanation for the inconsistent findings in these studies is that some of the members of the collectivistic cultures might have used independent self construals when dealing with conflict and some of the members of the individualistic cultures may have used interdependent self construals when dealing with conflicts. This explanation is supported by Gire and Carment's research. The Canadians in their study were more collectivistic toward friends (e.g., were more allocentric; see Chapter 3) than the Nigerians, and the conflict studied involved roommates.

A second explanation for the inconsistent findings on conflict styles across cultures is that all people across cultures may want to avoid conflict. Studies of college students in the United States, for example, indicate that students avoid over 50 percent of the conflicts they have with others (Sillars et al., 1982). Similarly, Leung (1987) notes that Chinese and North Americans want to reduce animosity between themselves and the people with whom they have conflict. Chinese, however, see bargaining and mediation as more viable ways to reduce animosity than do North Americans. Gire and Clement (1993), when comparing Nigerians and Canadians, report similar tendencies to want to avoid conflict.

A third explanation for the inconsistent findings on conflict styles predicted on the basis of individualism-collectivism is that other dimensions of cultural variability are involved. Leung et al. (1990), for example, argue that members of feminine cultures prefer harmony-enhancing procedures for managing conflict more than do members of masculine cultures. Members of masculine cultures, in contrast, prefer confrontation procedures such as threats more than do members of feminine cultures. The rationale for this argument is that interpersonal cooperation and a friendly atmosphere are valued in feminine cultures, while achievement and challenging others are valued in masculine cultures.

The research discussed so far has not taken into consideration whether conflict is with a member of the ingroup or a member of an outgroup. Leung (1988) reports that Chinese are less likely to pursue a conflict with an ingroup member and more likely to pursue a conflict with an outgroup member than are people in the United States. Cole (1990) notes that European American students in the United States tend to use integrating and obliging styles more with members of ingroups than with members of outgroups. He also observes that Japanese students studying in the United States tend to use an obliging style more with members of ingroups than with members of outgroups, and they tend to use a dominating style more with members of outgroups than with members of ingroups. Singhal and Nagao (1993) observe that Japanese are more assertive with ingroup members than with outgroup members, while there is no difference between ingroup and outgroup assertiveness in the United States. Han and Park (1995) also report that collectivistic Koreans draw a greater distinction between ingroups and outgroups when managing conflicts than do individualistic Koreans.

To fully understand how conflict operates with respect to ingroups in collectivistic cultures, we must take other dimensions of cultural variability into consideration. Bond et al. (1985) argue that the level of power distance in a culture mediates how collectivists respond to someone who insults members of the ingroup. They note that Chinese are less critical than North Americans of someone who insults ingroup members when the insulter has higher status than the ingroup member than when the status of the insulter is lower than the ingroup members' status. Bond et al. also observe that North Americans make less of a distinction as a function of the insulter's status or group membership.

Ethnic Differences in Managing Conflict

There also are differences in conflict styles across ethnic groups in the United States. African Americans, for example, prefer a controlling conflict resolution style more than do European Americans, while European Americans prefer a solution oriented style more than do African Americans (Ting-Toomey, 1986a). Kagan, Knight, and Martinez-Romero (1982) report that Mexican Americans prefer a passive or avoidance style for dealing with conflict. The style that members of ethnic groups in the United States use to manage conflict, however, is influenced by the strength of their ethnic identity and of their cultural identity (Ting-Toomey et al., 1994). Asian Americans with a weak ethnic identity and a strong cultural identity, for example, use a compromising style more than do Asian Americans with a strong ethnic identity and a weak cultural identity. Asian Americans who strongly identify with their ethnic group and weakly identify with their culture use an avoidance strategy more than do Asian Americans who strongly identify with both their culture and their ethnic group.

Kochman (1981) describes differences in how European Americans and African Americans argue that influence how they manage conflicts. While European Americans "use the relatively detached and unemotional discussion mode to engage an issue, [African Americans] use the more emotionally intense and involving mode of argument. Where [European Americans] tend to underestimate their exceptional talents and abilities, [African Americans] tend to boast about theirs" (Kochman, 1981, p. 106). African Americans favor forceful outputs, such as high volume, while European Americans prefer subdued outputs. African Americans interpret European Americans' subdued responses as lifeless, and European Americans interpret African Americans' responses as being in bad taste (Kochman, 1981).

There are several other areas where European American and African American styles of communication may differ when members of these groups communicate with each other, particularly in a conflict situation. One area of importance for dealing with conflict is how members of the two groups view their responsibilities to the other people's sensibilities and feelings. Differences in reactions to an assignment in an interpersonal communication class where students were told to confront each other and comment on their perceptions of the other person's style of communication illustrate the two approaches (Kochman, 1981). The student responses to the assignment divided basically along ethnic lines:

> Twelve of the fourteen [European American] students argued for the right of students *not* to hear what others might want to say about them—thus giving priority to the protection of individual sensibilities, those of others as well as their own, even if this might result in forfeiting their own chance to say what they felt. . . . The eight [African American] students and the remaining two [European American] students, on the other hand, argued for the rights of those students to express what they had to say about others even if the protection of all individual sensibilities would be forfeited in the process. On this last point, one [African American] woman said: "I don't know about others, but if someone has something to say to me, I want to hear it." (Kochman, 1981, pp. 122–123)

Withdrawing the protection of sensibilities is seen as insensitive or cruel by European Americans, while African Americans see European Americans' failing to say what they think as lack of concern for African American real selves.

One of the major implications of these differences is what happens when African Americans and European Americans are involved in an interethnic conflict situation. African Americans have a tendency to express themselves more forcefully than do European Americans. The tendency "to receive and manipulate the forceful assertions of others gives them greater leverage in interracial encounters" (Kochman, 1981, p. 126). When African Americans offend European Americans' social sensibilities, European Americans demand an apology. African Americans see this demand as weak and inappropriate. Part of the difference is in who is considered responsible when people are upset. When European Americans are upset, they tend to see the cause as the other person. African Americans, in contrast, see themselves as responsible for their feelings. African Americans "will commonly say to those who have become angry, '*Others* did not make you angry'; rather, 'You *let yourself* become angry'" (Kochman, 1981, p. 127).

MANAGING INTERGROUP CONFLICT

Intergroup conflict is occurring at alarming rates throughout the world today (see Boucher, Landis, & Clark, 1987; Horowitz, 1985; for discussions of some of these specific conflicts). Understanding why intergroup conflict occurs and the ways that members of different groups manage conflict is necessary if these conflicts are to be handled constructively. To begin, we look at the characteristics of intergroup conflict.

Characteristics of Intergroup Conflict

Although intergroup conflict is similar in kind to interpersonal conflict in some ways, there are important differences. Condor and Brown (1988) point out that

> intergroup conflict is, by definition, a collective phenomenon, and requires a suitably collective "model of man." The psychological factors associated with intergroup hostility are best sought in *collective* social cognition and motivation. It is an important task . . . to examine the relationship between individual drives and cognition and those associated with the groups to which they belong. (p. 19)

Condor and Brown, therefore, take the position that intergroup conflict is different from interpersonal conflict.

Landis and Boucher (1987) outline several characteristics of interethnic conflict that appear to apply to other forms of intergroup conflict as well. First, intergroup conflict involves perceived (not necessarily real) group differences, which lead to the activation of social identities and stereotypes. Second, intergroup conflict often involves claims to a given territory. Third, intergroup conflict tends to be based on group differences in power and resources. Fourth, intergroup conflict may involve disagreements over language usage or language policies. Fifth, intergroup conflict is exacerbated by group differences in endorsement of the process preferred for resolving conflict (e.g., members of one culture may prefer to resolve conflict through a third party, while members of another culture do not use third parties and prefer direct confrontation). Sixth, intergroup conflict often is exacerbated by religious differences. Conflict is intensified, for example, when religious differences are compounded with other group differences (e.g., in Sri Lanka, the Tamil-Sinhalese conflict is intensified because Tamils are Hindu and Sinhalese are Buddhists).

Lilli and Rehm (1988) point out that social categorization leads individuals to make evaluative judgments about members of the ingroups and outgroups. When conflict occurs, social categorizations are particularly important and their importance heightens the ingroup bias. Social categorizations lead to emphasizing social identities over personal identities. When social identities are enhanced by intergroup comparisons, the devaluation of the outgroup can lead to conflicts. The persistence of "being negatively categorized (labeled) may cause conflicts" (p. 35). Social categorizations also lead to deindividuation. Deindividuation can initiate conflicts or escalate conflicts that already exist. Social categorization also influences the way information about outgroups is processed; it is simplified (e.g., outgroups are seen as homogeneous and only stereotypical information about outgroups is obtained). Simplified information processing can lead to arguments that maintain and justify conflicts.

Contact and Conflict

Intergroup contact often is promoted as a way to manage intergroup conflicts. The contact hypothesis suggests that when contact takes place under favorable conditions (e.g., equal status, intimate contact, rewarding contact; see Stephan, 1987, for a summary), it leads to a decrease in prejudice and discrimination. Tzeng and Jackson's (1994) research further indicates that contact under favorable conditions reduces intergroup hostilities across ethnic groups in the United States.

Related work on norm violations and intergroup hostility (DeRidder & Tripathi, 1992) also suggests that perceptions that their norms have been violated lead members of an ingroup to make negative attributions about outgroups. The negative attributions that ingroup members make lead outgroup members to make negative inferences about ingroup members. Norm violations, therefore, can lead to cycles of escalating conflict. Escalations are most likely when individuals strongly identify with their group, when negative intergroup attitudes exist, when one group has feelings of relative deprivation, and when the group violating the norms has power over the group whose norms are violated.

Harmonious interpersonal contact can take place between members of different groups, even when there is a history of intergroup conflict (e.g., Trew's, 1986, study in Ireland; Taylor, Dube, & Bellerose's, 1986, work in Quebec). Such harmonious contact does not always occur, however, as Foster and Finchilescu's (1986) research in South Africa indicates. Pettigrew (1986) points out that "the use of intergroup contact as a means of alleviating conflict is largely dependent on the social structure that patterns relations between the groups" (p. 191).

To explain cross-cultural variability in this process, we must isolate the dimensions of cultural variability that apply to structural relations. Structural tightness is "the degree of hierarchical structure among sociocultural elements in a society" (Witkin & Berry, 1975, p. 11). Boldt and Roberts (1979) argue that role relatedness (e.g., the degree to which roles are interrelated) defines a culture as loose or tight. Gudykunst (1988a) contends that Ireland and Canada have a high degree of role relatedness with respect to the roles members of different groups fill, while South Africa did not have a high degree of role relatedness between blacks and whites when Foster and Finchilescu's (1986) research was conducted. Gudykunst suggests that contact has a greater influence on reducing intergroup conflict in tight rather than in loose cultures.

CONSTRUCTIVE CONFLICT MANAGEMENT

Conflicts can arise from instrumental sources, such as differences in goals or practices, and from expressive sources, such as tension generated from hostile feelings (Olsen, 1978). Ongoing or recurring conflicts often are indicators of unresolved issues in our relationships (Donohue, 1993). In this case, conflicts may appear instrumental, such as a conflict over the family budget, but may actually be expressive, such as a struggle for control in the marriage. Managing conflict constructively can help us maintain and improve the quality of our relationships with strangers. We begin our discussion of constructive conflict management by looking at how it differs from destructive conflict management.

Constructive Versus Destructive Conflict Management

When we try to manage conflict, our goals are to "reach agreement" and "enhance the relationship" (Hocker & Wilmot, 1991, p. 64). These goals can be accomplished only if we manage conflict constructively. Johnson and Johnson (1982) classify conflicts as constructive or destructive on the basis of the process used in managing them and the outcomes of the conflict. With respect to the *process,* the management of conflicts is *constructive* if the conflict is defined as a mutual problem, and it is defined as a "win-win" situation, where both parties gain. Participants must express their ideas openly and honestly, and all parties must be viewed as equal, with their positions taken seriously, valued, and respected, for conflict to be managed constructively. In constructive conflict management, the participants use effective communication skills, such as responsive listening and perception checking, so that differences in opinions can be clarified and understood. Participants must express their assumptions and perspectives on the problem and not take disagreements as rejection. Finally, similarities in participants' positions on the conflict must be understood and integrated so that the participants can work toward a mutually satisfying solution.

The *processes* involved in the destructive management of conflict are the opposite of those involved in the constructive management of conflict. Johnson and Johnson (1982) argue that the management of conflicts is *destructive* when the conflict is *not* defined as a mutual problem, and instead is defined as a "win-lose" situation, where one person gains and the other loses. When conflict is managed destructively, participants are *not* open or are deceitful, and they do not view each other as equal or respect each other's ideas. In destructive conflict management, participants do *not* use effective communication skills, and differences in opinions are suppressed or ignored. Participants do *not* clarify their assumptions or perspectives on the problem, and they take disagreements as rejection. Finally, when conflict is managed destructively, participants do *not* understand similarities in their positions or try to integrate them and they do *not* work toward a mutually satisfying solution.

With respect to *outcomes,* conflicts are *constructive* when the participants feel understood, think they influenced each other, are committed to the solution, are satisfied with the decision, feel accepted by the other person, and increase their ability to manage future conflicts (Johnson & Johnson, 1982). Conflicts have *destructive outcomes* when participants do *not* feel understood, think they had little influence on each other, are *not* committed to the solution, are *not* satisfied with the solution, do *not* feel accepted, and decrease their ability to manage future conflicts. The outcomes have consequences beyond the immediate conflict situation. Thompson's (1993) research, for example, reports that when members of different groups negotiate mutually satisfactory outcomes in an intergroup conflict situation, such outcomes lead to better relations between the groups.

When we communicate on automatic pilot, many of us tend to manage conflict destructively. We can, however, change the way we manage conflict when we are mindful. One of the guiding principles we need to follow when we are mindful is to be unconditionally constructive.

Being Unconditionally Constructive

Fisher and Brown (1988) believe that one person can change a relationship. If we change the way we react to strangers, they will change the way they react to us. The objective of change is to develop "a relationship that can deal with differences" (p. 3). Achieving change requires that we separate relationship and substantive issues, and pursue goals in each arena separately.

When we are trying to manage conflict, we should always be unconditionally constructive. Fisher and Brown (1988) argue that we should

> [do] only those things that are both good for the relationship and good for us, whether or not [strangers] reciprocate.
> 1. Rationality. Even if [strangers] are acting emotionally, balance emotion with reason.
> 2. Understanding. Even if [strangers] misunderstand us, try to understand them.
> 3. Communication. Even if [strangers] are not listening, consult them before deciding on matters that affect them.
> 4. Reliability. Even if [strangers] are trying to deceive us, neither trust nor deceive them; be reliable.
> 5. Noncoercive modes of influence. Even if [strangers] are trying to coerce us, neither yield to that coercion nor try to coerce them; be open to persuasion and try to persuade them.
> 6. Acceptance. Even if [strangers] reject us and our concerns as unworthy of their consideration, accept them as worthy of our consideration, care about them, and be open to learning from them. (p. 38)

Few, if any, of us follow these six guidelines in our everyday communication with strangers. In order to apply these guidelines, we must be mindful.

Creating Supportive Communication Climates

In managing conflict with strangers, we must develop a supportive climate (Gibb, 1961). Supportive climates facilitate effective communication, while defensive climates inhibit effective communication in our relationships with others. *Defensiveness* is "that behavior which occurs when an individual perceives threat or anticipates threat" (Gibb, 1961, p. 141). The way we communicate creates either a defensive or a supportive communication climate in our relationships. Gibb isolates six characteristics that differentiate the two types of climates: description versus evaluation, problem orientation versus control, being spontaneous versus being strategic, empathy versus neutrality, equality versus superiority, and provisionalism versus certainty.

The first characteristic of a supportive climate is *description* rather than evaluation (Gibb, 1961). We cannot understand strangers if we evaluate them before we understand their positions. Evaluative speech can threaten strangers' self-concepts, and it may cause them to become defensive. Descriptive speech, in contrast, should not make strangers uneasy. If we tell strangers, for example, that "your behavior was insensitive," they will become defensive. If we describe the behavior that led us to think they were insensitive, strangers should not become defensive; in addition, our use of description gives them an opportunity to tell us what they intended.

Taking a *problem orientation* is the second characteristic of a supportive climate (Gibb, 1961). Defining a mutual problem and expressing a willingness to collaborate in finding a solution implies that we have no predetermined outcome we want to see, and leads to a cooperative climate with strangers. If we have a predetermined outcome in mind and try to force this outcome on strangers, we are trying to control them. Attempts to control strangers are inevitably met with resistance. Not controlling strangers is important to maintaining supportive relationships with them.

Being spontaneous, as opposed to being strategic, is the third characteristic of a supportive climate (Gibb, 1961). If we are strategic and appear to have a hidden motive, lie, manipulate, and/or act in what appears to be a strategic way, we will arouse defensiveness in strangers. If we appear spontaneous and not strategic, on the other hand, strangers will not get defensive. Spontaneous messages suggest we are open to strangers' ideas and to being persuaded.

Empathy also is important in establishing a supportive environment (Gibb, 1961). If we convey empathy in our communication with strangers, they will know that we want to understand them and are concerned with their welfare. If we appear neutral toward strangers, they will become defensive. Neutrality is disconfirming (see the discussion of confirmation below) because it emphasizes the content of a discussion over the relationship between the people.

The fifth characteristic of a supportive climate is communicating that we are *equal* (Gibb, 1961). When we communicate equality, we do not talk down to strangers and we do not treat them as though they are superior to us. If we talk in a way that strangers perceive as sounding superior or condescending, they will become defensive. If we truly want to create supportive climates with strangers, we must communicate with them as though we are equal and respect their ideas or opinions.

The final characteristic of a supportive climate is *provisionalism* (Gibb, 1961). If we communicate to strangers that we are open to their viewpoints and willing to experiment with our behavior (try to change it if needed), they will not become defensive. If, on the other hand, we communicate in such a way that indicates that we think we are right and certain of our attitudes and behavior, they will become defensive.

Using Confirming Messages

As indicated in Chapter 10, having our self-concepts confirmed motivates us to communicate with strangers. Having our self-concepts disconfirmed, in contrast, leads us to want to avoid strangers. The same reactions are true for strangers as well. Confirming strangers' self-concepts, therefore, will lead them to want to communicate with us to manage existing conflicts. Laing (1961) defines *confirmation* as "the process through which individuals are recognized, acknowledged, and endorsed" (p. 83). Confirming communication involves recognizing strangers, responding to strangers' messages to us, accepting strangers' experiences as real, and indicating to strangers that we are willing to be involved with them (Cissna & Sieburg, 1981). *Disconfirmation* occurs when strangers are denied, their experiences are denied, or their significance is denied (Cissna & Sieburg, 1981). Disconfirming communication involves not recognizing strangers, not acknowledging that we have a relationship with strangers, not accepting strangers' experiences, and denying the validity of strangers' experiences (Cissna & Sieburg, 1981).

Characteristics of Confirming and Disconfirming Messages.   Cissna and Sieburg (1981) argue that the relationship component of confirming messages implies four meanings: "To me, you exist," "We are relating," "To me, you are significant," and "Your way of experiencing the world is valid" (p. 232). Garvin and Kennedy (1986) contend that we typically use three types of confirming responses in our conversations with others:

> RECOGNITION: A verbal or nonverbal recognition of the other's presence, e.g., eye contact, touch, or a facilitating verbal response, e.g., "uh huh."
> ACKNOWLEDGEMENT: A verbal acknowledgement that one is in a relationship with the other; acknowledgement of the other's perceptions, statements, or questions, e.g., agreement in reply to a question or request for clarification. A different but relevant topic could be introduced only if the previous speaker's content was verbally acknowledged.
> ENDORSEMENT: A verbal endorsement of the other's way of experiencing, especially the other's feelings, e.g., appreciation of the other's feelings or experiences. (pp. 8–9)

The problem is that we use confirming responses less than we think we do when we communicate on automatic pilot.

Cissna and Sieburg (1981) suggest that the relationship component of disconfirming messages sends these relational meanings: "To me, you do not exist," "We are not relating," "To me, you are not significant," and "Your way of experiencing the world is invalid" (p. 232). Garvin and Kennedy (1986) contend we use three types of disconfirming responses in our conversations with others:

> INDIFFERENCE: A response which fails to acknowledge the other's attempt to communicate, e.g., silence, use of impersonal language, monologue, interruption, or change of topic. Indifference conveys the message that the speaker simply does not matter, or does not exist.
> DISQUALIFICATION: A response which indicates the other person, the message, or the self [is] disqualified, e.g., name calling, blaming, laughter at the speaker, tangential response, or an incomplete, qualified or ambiguous response.

IMPERVIOUSNESS: A response which indicates the existence of the other, but fails to respond to the other's experience, e.g., denies the other's feelings, offers false reassurance, or challenges the other's rights to have feelings. (p. 9)

We all use disconfirming messages more than we think we do when we communicate on automatic pilot.

We confirm or disconfirm strangers by the words we choose to use when we talk to them and the way that we say what we do. We often talk in judgmental ways that are disconfirming when we communicate on automatic pilot. All forms of hate speech, such as racist, sexist, ageist, or homophobic language, also disconfirm members of other groups. To overcome our tendency to speak in these ways, we need to be mindful of our communication.

Our relational messages define the relationship between us and strangers. We often are not aware of how strangers interpret our relational messages. We may not intend to transmit a disconfirming message, but strangers may interpret what or how we say something to be disconfirming. This is especially problematic in our communication with strangers because they may interpret the relational component of our messages differently than we intend. We need to make sure that our messages are interpreted as confirming by strangers if we want to communicate effectively. This requires that we be mindful of our communication and watch for signs that strangers may be interpreting our messages as disconfirming. If this occurs, we need to check our perceptions to correct any misperceptions.

Confirming Strangers.   As indicated in the previous section, the words we use and how we say them can disconfirm strangers. If we consistently use male pronouns (he, him) to refer to people in different occupations, for example, it affects the way we think about the occupations to which we refer. To illustrate, if we use the term "mailman," for example, we will think that all people who deliver the mail are men. This obviously is not the case. Women deliver the mail, too. The inclusive term we can use instead of mailman is "mail carrier." Inclusive language makes everyone feel included and confirmed. This may seem like a small thing, but our language usage clearly influences our attitudes toward and thoughts about particular groups (see Chapter 8). It also influences how they respond to us.

Consistently using male pronouns or man-linked words disconfirms women. Additionally, many ethnic idioms we use in our everyday language, such as "Jew them down" or "black magic," disconfirm members of the ethnic groups involved. There also are idioms referring to disabilities, such as "the blind leading the blind," that disconfirm disabled people. To be confirming when we communicate with members of different groups, we need to avoid the use of such terms and idioms. We all use noninclusive language in our everyday interactions when we communicate on automatic pilot. To the extent that we can minimize our use of noninclusive language, we can be more confirming to others. To the extent that we use inclusive language, we can decrease the influence of our stereotypes on our communication. We must be mindful of our communication in order to change our use of noninclusive language. Over time, the use of inclusive language will become automatic.

Managing Anger

We all experience anger at some point in our relationships with strangers. We cannot, however, manage conflict constructively if we are angry with strangers. Experiencing and/or expressing anger can have profound effects on our relationships with strangers. To improve our communication and the quality of our relationships with strangers, we need to understand how we respond when we feel anger.

Lazarus (1991) argues that we get *angry* when we perceive that someone has committed a demeaning offense against us or people close to us. Behavior is interpreted as demeaning when we think that it is arbitrary, inconsiderate, or malevolent. When we get angry, we consciously or unconsciously think that strangers have threatened our identities. The provocation that leads to *anger* is *"a demeaning offense against me or mine"* (Lazarus, 1991, p. 222). The offense involves some slight or injury to our identity, but "even a mere frustration may carry with it the implication that we are less significant or worthy of self-esteem than we would claim or wish" (p. 222).

Lazarus (1991) contends that we see someone (i.e., another person or ourself) as accountable for the threat to our identity. If we see someone else as responsible for the event, we can blame that person and the blame might lead to anger. Blame alone, however, is not sufficient for us to experience anger. We must also see the person we have blamed for the offense as in control. If we blame someone else for the injury to our identity, we must also see that person as able to control what happened for us to be angry. If the person was not able to control what happened, we will view the situation differently and label the feelings as another emotion, such as sadness.

What makes us angry is primarily a function of our upbringing, but our culture also provides guidelines about anger:

> People everywhere get angry, but they get angry in the service of their culture's rules. Sometimes these rules are explicit ("Thou shalt not covet thy neighbor's wife"); more often they are implicit, disguised in the countless daily actions performed because "That's the way we do things around here." These unstated rules are often not apparent until someone breaks them, and anger is the sign that someone has broken them. It announces that someone is not behaving as (you think) she or he *ought.* (Tavris, 1982, p. 47)

When we feel anger, we assume that people are responsible for their behavior and should behave differently. The expression of anger helps us maintain social control over our own and strangers' behavior (Tavris, 1982).

Tavris (1982) isolates two myths regarding anger. First, aggression is the instinctive response when we feel angry. Aggression is a *learned* response to anger; it is not instinctive. Males tend to learn to respond aggressively to anger, while females tend to learn to respond to anger with friendliness. Females, however, can and do learn to respond to anger with aggression. Aggression is not an effective strategy for dealing with anger because it just makes strangers angry or upset. Second, verbally expressing our anger gets rid of it or makes us feel better. Talking about our anger can make us more angry (Tavris, 1982). Expressing our anger to strangers can lead us to like them less than if we do not express our anger to them. We do not mean to suggest that we should *not* express our anger when we experience it. Rather, we need to think about the consequences of expressing our anger. There may be times when we need to express our anger to resolve issues with strangers. The advice "if you can't say something nice about a person, don't say anything at all—at least if you want your anger to dissipate and your associations to remain congenial," however, is worth following (Tavris, 1982, p. 135). Expressing anger puts a damper on our interactions with strangers.

The inappropriate expression of anger hinders our interactions and has a destructive influence on our relationships. As indicated earlier, expressing our anger to strangers is generally not an effective strategy. Rather than expressing our anger, we need to learn to manage it. We need to develop new ways we can deal with our anger when we are mindful of our communication.

Alberty and Emmons (1990) suggest several guidelines that are useful in managing anger. First, it is important to recognize that anger is a natural emotion and we do not need to fear experiencing it. Second, we need to remember that we are responsible for our feeling angry. The other person did not make us feel angry; we unconsciously chose to feel angry. Third, we need to recognize that feeling anger and behaving aggressively are not the same thing. We can respond in an assertive fashion, rather than an aggressive fashion. We need to remember that the other person did not make us angry and work toward a resolution, not a victory. Fourth, we need to know ourselves and what makes us angry. When we know what makes us angry, we can avoid those situations or make sure that we are mindful in those situations.

There are many strategies that we can use to manage our anger. The ability to step back from the situation is an important skill in dealing with our anger. When we step back from the situation, we need to become mindful and not let the anger guide our response. When we are mindful, we need to remember that when we "feel provoked, count to ten; and when [we] are also hot, hungry, exercising, walking along a noisy street, booing the opposition in a crowded stadium, driving a car to (or from) work, or disturbed for the forty-fifth time when [we] have a deadline tomorrow, count to a hundred" (Tavris, 1982, p. 177). If we cannot step back from the situation, we can try to relax when we experience anger (Alberty & Emmons, 1990). Any of the relaxation techniques discussed under managing anxiety in Chapter 10 can be used.

COMMUNICATING TO MANAGE CONFLICT

The way we approach strangers regarding conflicts and how we negotiate solutions to conflicts affect the outcomes. To manage conflicts constructively, we must be mindful of our communication and be concerned with *both* ourselves and the strangers with whom we have conflict. In many ways, managing intergroup conflict is similar to managing conflict with members of our ingroups. To manage intergroup conflicts successfully, however, requires that we adapt our behavior in at least two ways (Gudykunst, 1994). First, we must take strangers' group memberships into consideration. If strangers are collectivist, for example, they may prefer to avoid the conflict. If we are individualists and think it is important to address the conflict, we need to adapt our style of communication to accommodate to collectivists by being more indirect than we usually are. We also must take strangers' group memberships into consideration in interpreting their messages. Second, we must be aware of how our expectations for strangers influence our communication. Our expectations, such as those based on our ethnocentrism, prejudice, or stereotypes, influence how we interpret strangers' messages when we are on automatic pilot. To manage conflict successfully, we must set our group-based expectations aside, understand real group differences, and focus on understanding strangers' perspective on the conflict. To be successful, we must be mindful.

Because there are no set steps to managing conflict successfully, in the remainder of this section, we divide managing conflict into three processes: approaching strangers, defining the conflict, and negotiating solutions. We begin with approaching strangers regarding conflicts.

Approaching Strangers

Johnson (1986) argues that the first process involved in managing conflicts is to *approach* strangers regarding the conflict. We need to approach strangers when we are sure that both of us are available and emotionally capable of discussing the conflict (neither person is emotionally upset, and both people have time to talk). If either person is highly anxious or upset, the conflict cannot be discussed successfully.

Johnson (1986) suggests that the goal of approaching strangers about the conflict is to clarify the issues surrounding the conflict. We want to try to define the problem, establish a cooperative environment, and schedule a negotiation session. Unless the conflict is very minor, we should *not* try to manage the conflict when we approach strangers, but rather, schedule a time later when we can negotiate a solution. The strangers with whom we have conflict need time to think about their goals and the solutions that are acceptable to them before they can negotiate a solution to the conflict with us.

To be effective, our approach needs to be done in a way that does not increase strangers' anxiety or uncertainty, and in a way that allows them to maintain their self-concepts and not become defensive. We must, for example, try to establish a supportive communication climate, listen carefully, be empathic, and so forth. Since most of us do not have scripts for managing conflict, we have to be mindful of our communication, focus on the interaction taking place, and not get distracted by thinking about the outcome of the conflict.

Defining Conflicts

Deutsch (1973) points out that to manage conflicts successfully, we need to be *cooperative,* not competitive. We need to define conflicts as a *mutual problem* that needs to be solved. When we communicate on automatic pilot, we tend to define conflicts as the strangers' problem. We tend to blame strangers for conflicts when we view the conflict issues as important, when conflicts occur frequently, and when we are not satisfied with our relationship with the strangers (Sillars, 1980). We tend to be willing to accept responsibility for conflicts when the topic is not important to us, when conflicts are not frequent, and when we are satisfied with our relationships when we communicate on automatic pilot. It, therefore, is important for us to be mindful when we are engaged in conflict. If we blame strangers, we cannot define the conflict as a mutual problem. When conflicts are defined as a mutual problem to be solved, both parties can win, instead of having one party win and the other party lose. All conflicts are a mutual problem because any problem for one person in a relationship is a problem for both.

Johnson (1986) suggests that in addition to defining conflict as a mutual problem, we need to look for a *common definition of the problem*. If we do not agree on the definition of the problem, we cannot solve it. Many conflicts are due to the involved parties' perceiving that their goals are different or even incompatible. Often people involved in conflicts discover they actually want the same thing. In that case, when they define the problem underlying the conflict, common goals emerge. When the goals actually are different or incompatible, the parties involved must agree on the problem in order to solve it (e.g., the individuals define the problem as "Person A wants X and Person B wants Y").

We need to define conflicts in the most limited way possible (Johnson, 1986). The reason for focusing on limited issues is to increase the likelihood of successful conflict management. If we have a big problem to address, we can break it down into smaller ones, and deal with the smaller problems one at a time.

In order to define a conflict successfully, we must know what our goals are (Hocker & Wilmot, 1991). We cannot find solutions if we do not know what we want. We can alter our goals more easily if they are clear than if they are vague. It is easier to accomplish clear goals than it is to accomplish unclear goals, and only clear goals can be shared.

Negotiating Solutions

Hocker and Wilmot (1991) point out that we have three basic options when it comes to managing conflicts. First, we can try to change strangers. This is a somewhat natural response, but it usually is not very successful. If we try to change strangers and they try to change us, we will both appear rigid and unreasonable to each other. Second, we can try to alter the conditions underlying the conflict. If we "can increase scarce resources, alter the nature of problematic interdependence, change perceptions or incompatible goals, or make some other alteration in the conflict elements," we can change the nature of the conflict and find solutions (Hocker & Wilmot, 1991, p. 180). Third, we can change our own behavior. While we may perceive this option to be the most difficult and least desirable way to manage a conflict, it often is the most successful. If we change our orientation toward strangers with whom we have a conflict, or change our interpretation of the issues, or try to communicate more effectively, we can alter the outcome of the conflict.

By changing our orientation, we can change a win-lose conflict into a win-win outcome.

In managing conflicts, we need to try to communicate as effectively as possible. There are two sides to effective communication: adapting our messages and understanding strangers. We must *adapt our messages* so that strangers can interpret them accurately. We adapt our messages by using language to create a supportive communication environment (as opposed to a destructive environment), establishing a communicative distance of equality (see Chapter 5), and using language with which strangers are familiar. We also need to make sure that we avoid putting strangers down or calling them names if we want to manage the conflict constructively. Another aspect of adapting our messages involves using concrete language, as opposed to abstract language. Abstract language is ambiguous and open to interpretation, and strangers' interpretations of abstract language often are different from our own.

Since conflict produces stress, we generally do not adapt our messages when we are communicating on automatic pilot. To be able to adapt our messages, we have to manage our anxiety. If we feel that our anxiety is above our maximum thresholds, we need to take time to bring our anxiety down below the maximum threshold before we try to manage the conflict. To reduce our anxiety, we can use the skills discussed in Chapter 10.

The second aspect of effective communication during conflicts involves making sure that we *understand strangers.* Such understanding requires that our perceptions be as accurate as possible. Conflict causes anxiety and our anxiety, in turn, causes us to process information more simply than we usually do (Wilder & Shapiro, 1989). When we are managing conflict with strangers on automatic pilot, our perceptions of them tend to be based on our stereotypes and intergroup attitudes, not on the individual strangers with whom we are having conflict. Simple information processing does not allow us to see strangers' points of view. We, therefore, are likely to misinterpret strangers' behavior in conflict situations when we communicate on automatic pilot.

To understand strangers, we need to listen carefully to what they say. Roach and Wyatt (1988) point out that listening is not a natural activity, it is not a passive activity as most of us assume, and most of us are not very skilled listeners. Hearing is a natural, automatic process, while *listening* is the "process of discriminating and identifying which sounds are meaningful or important to us and which aren't" (p. 2). Successful listening, therefore, is a purposive activity (i.e., it requires that we be mindful). More specifically, "real listening involves taking in new information and checking it against what you already know, selecting important ideas from unimportant ideas, searching for categories to store the information in (or creating categories), and predicting what's coming next in order to be ready for it" (p. 4). Bolton (1979) isolates three sets of interrelated skills involved in active listening: attending skills, following skills, and comprehending skills.

Attending skills involve the ways that we attend to the person speaking (Bolton, 1979). One thing we need to do is indicate to the speaker that we are involved in the conversation. Our involvement is indicated by our body posture. If we are leaning backward with our arms crossed, the speaker will probably assume that we are not involved. If, in contrast, we lean forward and face the speaker, he or she will probably assume we are listening. Eye contact also is important. In the European American subculture, "it involves focusing one's eyes softly on the speaker and occasionally shifting the gaze from his [or her] face to other parts of the body" (Bolton, 1979, p. 181). Attending requires that we give the other person our undivided attention. To do this, the environment in which we are communicating needs to be nondistracting.

Following skills indicate to the other person that we are trying to understand her or his perspective (Bolton, 1979). The first thing we need to do is give the other person time to speak. The other person needs time to decide whether she or he wants to talk and to decide what to say. Giving the other person time often requires that we be silent more than we would like. We also need to indicate to the other person that we are interested in what he or she has to say.

Comprehending skills involve ways that we can understand the other person better (Bolton, 1979). Perception checking (discussed in Chapter 7) is one method that we can use to comprehend better what others are saying. Another way we can make sure we are understanding the other person is to *paraphrase* what the other person is saying in our own words. By restating what the other person says in our own words, we ensure that we have not misinterpreted the other person's position (e.g., saying something like "I want to make sure I understand what you're saying"). The other thing we can do to increase our understanding is to use *probing questions*—questions designed to find out who, what, when, where, why, and how. We need to be careful, however, when we ask questions. If we ask too many questions, we end up dealing with our own agenda, rather than understanding the other person.

When we listen to strangers, we must be aware of how our expectations for members of the strangers' group influence our behavior. As indicated in Chapter 5, our predictions of strangers' behavior tend to be inaccurate when we communicate on automatic pilot and base our perceptions and predictions on our stereotypes of strangers' groups. To perceive and predict strangers' behavior accurately, we must recognize the group influences on strangers' behavior, and we must recognize how individual strangers are different from other members of their groups. We cannot make accurate predictions when we communicate on automatic pilot.

When we communicate on automatic pilot, our perceptions are distorted. Ross and Ward (1995) argue that people involved in conflicts are "apt to make overly uncharitable inferences about each other's offers and responses, seeing deviousness and intrasurgence on the part of the other side" (p. 275). When our perceptions are distorted, we may perceive that strangers have negative and hostile feelings toward us, and not perceive the positive feelings they have. We also may see strangers as being more strategic and less sincere than we are (Ross & Ward, 1995). These attitudes lead to a self-fulfilling prophecy when we are communicating on automatic pilot. That is, we assume that strangers are not sincere and are hostile and treat them as such; as a result, they become insincere and hostile, even if they originally were sincere and friendly.

To minimize distortions in our perceptions, we need to adopt a conciliatory orientation toward strangers (Stuart, 1980). This approach involves consciously trying to see strangers' behavior in the most positive way possible, and trying to resolve the conflict equitably. We have to make it clear to strangers that we are interested in finding a solution that is fair to them. If strangers perceive that we care only about ourselves, our chance to manage the conflict constructively decreases.

If we do not understand strangers' positions and they do not understand our position, there is no way we can find a solution acceptable to both parties. To manage conflict successfully, we must be able to predict and explain strangers' behavior as accurately as possible. To accomplish this objective, we need to focus on the present situation, not on the past or on the future (Stuart, 1980). Searching for the cause of the conflict by asking why it occurred is not highly productive. Rather, we need to focus on solutions in the present and ask how can we manage the conflict constructively.

To manage any conflict, we must understand the differences between ourselves and strangers (Johnson, 1986). We must understand both group and individual differences. Group differences in approaches to conflict must be taken into consideration (see the discussion earlier in this chapter). Understanding differences is especially important if our conflict is with strangers who strongly identify with their cultures or ethnic groups. We also have to take into consideration group differences in terms of the content of conflict.

Further, we need to seek out individual differences in opinions and ideas regarding the conflict. If we do not understand the positions on the conflict of the specific strangers with whom we conflict, we cannot find a solution that is acceptable to them. To manage conflict constructively, we also must be able to disagree with strangers and, at the same time, *confirm* them and their views of themselves. If we treat strangers as though they are not valued, they will become defensive, and their anxiety will increase. This response will make it impossible for them to manage conflicts with us constructively.

Once we understand strangers' positions and they understand our position, we may find that there are irreconcilable differences. If we suspect irreconcilable differences are a possibility and we want to continue our relationship with the strangers with whom we have conflict, we need to find an alternative to confronting the issues involved directly. This may be a situation where dealing indirectly with the conflict or avoiding it altogether is the best strategy.

Recognizing similarities and not just focusing on differences also is necessary to manage conflict successfully (Johnson, 1986). If we focus only on differences between our position and strangers' positions, we will never be able to manage the conflict. Finding a solution that will work for us and for strangers requires that we see similarities in our positions and then build on those similarities. To manage conflicts successfully, both parties must understand and see similarities in each other's positions and feelings.

In trying to find a solution for the problem, we need to recognize how our behavior contributed to creating the problem, not focus just on strangers' behavior. Both parties to a conflict contribute to the formation of the conflict. We cannot manage a conflict constructively if we do not understand our contribution to it. In addition to not recognizing our own contribution to conflicts, we have a tendency to devalue solutions that strangers propose (Ross & Ward, 1995). This situation occurs even when the objective evidence would suggest that strangers' proposals are fair. Our perceptions of the fairness of strangers' proposals is influenced by our past interactions with strangers. When our past interactions with strangers have been strained, we tend to view their proposals as unequitable. This perception, in turn, leads to mistrust, which makes managing the conflict even more difficult.

In conclusion, we *cannot* manage conflicts with strangers successfully when we communicate on automatic pilot. To manage conflicts with strangers constructively, we must be mindful of our communication. We also *cannot* manage a conflict constructively by trying to declare a winner. For constructive conflict management, both parties have to win. Constructively managing conflict with strangers is a time-consuming process. There are, however, advantages that result from our time investment. If we are able to manage conflict with strangers constructively, for example, our relationships with them will be strengthened.

Managing Conflicts Between Collectivists and Individualists

Ting-Toomey (1994b) argues that individualists and collectivists can adapt their behavior to increase their effectiveness when they have a conflict. Individualists can make several adaptations that will increase the likelihood of success in managing conflicts with collectivists. First, individualists need to remember that collectivists use an interdependent self construal. Their actions reflect on their ingroup, and they have to take their ingroups into consideration in managing conflicts. Second, individualists should try to deal with conflicts when they are small, rather than allow them to become large issues, and recognize that collectivists may want to use a third party to mediate the conflict. Third, individualists need to help the collectivists maintain face (public image) during the conflict by not humiliating or embarrassing them in public. Fourth, individualists need to pay attention to collectivists' nonverbal behavior and implicit messages. Collectivists generally will not express their opinions directly. Fifth, individualists need to listen when collectivists talk. Sixth, individualists need to use indirect messages more than they typically do. They should use qualifier words such as "maybe" or "possibly," more tentative, and avoid bluntly saying "no." Seventh, individualists need to let go of conflict if collectivists do not want to deal with it (recall that avoiding is the preferred collectivist strategy).

Collectivists also need to make adaptations when dealing with individualists (Ting-Toomey, 1994b). First, collectivists need to recognize that individualists often separate the conflict from the person with whom they are having conflict. Second, collectivists need to focus on the substantive issues involved in the conflict. Third, collectivists need to use an assertive, rather than nonassertive, style when dealing with conflict. Fourth, collectivists need to be more direct than they usually are. This adaptation involves using "I messages" and directly stating their opinions and feelings more than they usually do. Fifth, collectivists need to provide verbal feedback to individualists and focus on the verbal aspects of communication more than they typically do. Sixth, collectivists need to recognize that individualists do not value silence in conversations. Seventh, collectivists need to try to manage conflicts when they arise, rather than avoiding them.

SUMMARY

Conflict, which often arises from the small intolerances expressed in our everyday communication, is inevitable in any ongoing relationship. Our conflicts with strangers often get out of hand before we realize what is happening. Such situations occur, in part, as a result of cultural and ethnic differences in how conflict is viewed and managed.

Members of individualistic cultures tend to separate the conflict issue from the person with whom they have conflict; members of collectivistic cultures tend not to make this distinction. Conflict tends to arise when personal expectations are violated in individualistic cultures and when normative expectations are violated in collectivistic cultures. Members of individualistic cultures tend to approach conflict directly, and members of collectivistic cultures tend to approach conflict indirectly or to avoid it. Members of individualistic cultures tend to take a short-term view of conflict, and members of collectivistic cultures tend to take a long-term view of conflict.

Conflict in and of itself is not positive or negative. When we communicate on automatic pilot, we tend to manage conflict destructively and this has negative consequences on our relationships with strangers. Managing conflict constructively, in contrast, can have positive consequences on our relationships with strangers. To manage conflict with strangers constructively, we need to be mindful of our communication. When we are mindful, we should be unconditionally constructive, create a supportive environment, use confirming messages, and manage our anger.

Managing conflict with strangers is similar to managing conflict with members of our ingroups. When we manage conflict with strangers, however, we must adapt our behavior. We must take strangers' group memberships into consideration, and try to adapt our messages so that strangers can hear what we are saying without becoming anxious or angry. We also have to be aware of how our expectations influence our perceptions of strangers. If we do not communicate mindfully, our stereotypes, ethnocentrism, prejudice, and so forth will guide our perceptions of the strangers with whom we have conflict.

STUDY QUESTIONS

1. Why is conflict inevitable in our relationships with strangers?
2. How do people from individualistic cultures deal with conflict differently than do people from collectivistic cultures?
3. How are constructive and destructive approaches to managing conflict different?
4. Why does the advice "be unconditionally constructive" work in managing conflicts with strangers?

5. How do supportive climates contribute to managing conflict constructively?
6. How does confirming strangers contribute to managing conflict constructively?
7. Why is managing anger critical to managing conflict constructively?
8. Under what conditions should we confront strangers regarding conflicts? What should we try to accomplish when we confront strangers?
9. How do we have to adjust our communication to manage conflict with strangers successfully?
10. Why is it necessary to listen effectively to strangers when we have conflict with them?
11. How can individualists and collectivists adapt their behavior to manage conflict with each other?

SUGGESTED READING

Boucher, J., Landis, D., & Clark, K. (Eds.). (1987). *Ethnic conflict.* Newbury Park, CA: Sage.

Deutsch, M. (1973). *The resolution of conflict.* New Haven, CT: Yale University Press.

Hewstone, M., & Brown, R. (Eds.). (1986). *Contact and conflict in intergroup encounters.* Oxford, UK: Blackwell.

Hocker, J. L., & Wilmot, W. W. (1991). *Interpersonal conflict* (3rd ed.). Dubuque, IA: Wm. C. Brown.

Kochman, T. (1981). *Black and white: Styles in conflict.* Chicago: University of Chicago Press.

Strobe, W., Kruglanski, A., Bar-Tal, D., & Hewstone, M. (Eds.). (1988). *The social psychology of intergroup conflict.* New York: Springer-Verlag.

12

Developing Relationships with Strangers

Under cherry trees
there are
no strangers.
                    Issa

Interpersonal relationships are sources of social contact and intimacy, two integral elements of human survival in any culture. We form many different types of relationships with others. We develop some relationships we call acquaintances and some we call friendships. Friendships, however, should not be confused with friendly relations. Kurth (1970) points out that friendly relations are an outgrowth of role relationships and are possibly a prelude to friendship, while friendships are intimate relationships involving two people as individuals. Friendships, therefore, are more intimate than friendly relations.

Friendly relations involve a present orientation, which focuses on the encounter that is taking place (Kurth, 1970). In a friendship, participants engage in interaction regarding the past and future, as well as the present. The two types of relations also differ with respect to the normative specifications guiding them. There are cultural norms specifying what constitutes friendly relations, but "the development of friendship is based upon private negotiations and is not imposed through cultural values or norms" (Bell, 1981, p. 10). Suttles (1970) takes a similar position; he claims that friendships are the least culturally programmed relationships we form. We do not mean to suggest that culture plays no role in the development of friendships; rather, culture plays a much less important role in friendships than it does in friendly relations.

Wright (1978) argues that friendships are entered into voluntarily and friends informally agree to get together often in the absence of external constraints or pressures. Friendships also involve a focus on the person; friends react to each other as whole persons, not just as members of social groups. The argument we make in this chapter is that our group memberships, including our culture, influence the early stages of our relationships with strangers more than the later stages. If we form close friendships with strangers, they are similar to our close friendships with people from our own groups.

We begin by looking at dimensions of relationships that appear to be universal (i.e., consistent across cultures). Next, we examine cross-cultural variability in communication in interpersonal and romantic relationships. Then we discuss the development of interpersonal relationships with strangers. We conclude this chapter by focusing on romantic relationships with strangers.

UNIVERSAL ASPECTS OF RELATIONSHIPS

Triandis (1977) isolates four dimensions of social relations that appear to be universal. The first dimension is association-dissociation. *Associative behaviors* include being helpful, supportive, or cooperative, while *dissociative behaviors* involve fighting or avoiding another person. The second universal dimension is superordination-subordination. *Superordinate behaviors* include criticizing or giving orders, while *subordinate behaviors* involve asking for help, agreeing, or obeying. The third dimension is intimacy-formality. *Intimate behaviors* include self-disclosure, expressing emotions, or touching, while *formal behaviors* involve sending written invitations to others and similar activities. The final dimension of universal social behavior is overtness-covertness. *Overt behaviors* are visible to others, while *covert behaviors* are not visible to others.

These four behaviors are universal, but the degree to which they are manifested varies across cultures. Triandis (1984) argues that the association-dissociation dimension is related to Kluckhohn and Strodtbeck's (1961) human nature value orientation. Associative behaviors predominate in cultures where people assume that human nature is inherently good, and dissociative behaviors predominate in cultures where people assume that human nature is inherently evil.

The superordination-subordination dimension is similar to Hofstede's (1980) power distance dimension of cultural variability. Triandis (1994) argues that being superordinate and being subordinate are viewed as natural and a function of the characteristics of the people in high power distance cultures. Superordinate and subordinate behaviors are not viewed as natural in low power distance cultures. In low power distance cultures, being superordinate or subordinate is viewed as a function of the roles people play, not as a characteristic with which they are born.

Intimacy-formality can be related to the general issue of contact. Triandis (1984) argues that in contact cultures, "people touch a lot, they stand much closer to each other, they orient their bodies so they face each other, they look each other in the eye, and they employ greater amplitudes of emotional expression" (p. 324). Noncontact cultures involve the opposite pattern: little touching, standing far apart, little eye contact, and low levels of emotional expression. People in contact cultures tend to express their emotions openly, while members of noncontact cultures tend to suppress them.

Triandis (1984) suggests that the overt-covert dimension varies as a function of loose-tight cultural variations. Boldt (1978) defines structural tightness in terms of role diversity (the number of roles and role relationships) and role relatedness (the nature of the bonds among the roles). The more roles there are and the more tightly they are bonded together, the more structurally tight the social structure is. Triandis contends that there is greater overt behavior in loose cultures than in tight cultures.

Adamopoulos and Bontempo (1986) examine the universality of three dimensions of interpersonal relations by using literary material from different historical periods. They note that affiliation and dominance appear to be universal, without much change over the last 3,000 years. Intimacy also appears universal, but the behaviors that are considered intimate have changed over the years.

Foa and Foa (1974) take a different approach to isolating universal dimensions of behavior. They argue that resources individuals exchange during interaction can be classified into six groups arranged in a circle (positions are denoted by using the face of a clock to represent the circle): love (12 o'clock), services (2 o'clock), goods (4 o'clock), money (6 o'clock), information (8 o'clock), and status (10 o'clock). These resources vary along two dimensions: (1) *particularism*—the importance of the individual's (receiver or giver) identity in the exchange (runs vertically on the face of the clock, with least particularism at 6 o'clock and most at 12 o'clock), and (2) *concreteness*—the degree to which the resource has face value versus symbolic value (runs horizontally on the clock's face, with least concreteness at 9 o'clock, and most at 3 o'clock).

In Foa and Foa's (1974) framework, the closer the resources are to each other, the more similar they are perceived to be and the greater the satisfaction that emerges when resources are exchanged. Foa and Foa's research indicates that the resource structure is applicable across cultures.

Fiske (1991) isolates four elementary forms of human relations: communal sharing, equality matching, authority ranking, and market pricing. *Communal sharing* is "a relationship of equivalence in which people are merged (for the purpose at hand) so that the boundaries of individual selves are indistinct" (p. 13). *Equality matching* is an equal relationship between peers who are distinct from each other. *Authority ranking* is an asymmetrical relationship between two people who are not equals. *Market pricing* is a relationship mediated by the values of some "market system." The market system, for example, might be based on people's actions, services, or products. Fiske argues that these four models provide the basic "grammars" for social relationships, and they give order to the way individuals think about their social interactions. Fiske's (1993) research supports this claim. The four elementary forms of social behavior are the basis for all other types of relationships, and are universal across cultures.

Fiske (1991) argues that all forms of behavior can be used in any situation in any culture. Members of cultures, however, learn preferences for particular forms of behavior in particular situations. Triandis (1994) contends that people in collectivistic cultures learn to use communal sharing and authority ranking more than equality matching and market pricing. Members of individualistic cultures, in contrast, learn to use equality matching and market pricing more than the other two forms of behavior. Authority ranking also can be seen to vary as a function of power distance (Triandis, 1994). Smith and Bond (1993) argue that market pricing is related to Hofstede's (1980) masculine orientation and equality matching is related to a feminine orientation.

CROSS-CULTURAL VARIATIONS IN INTERPERSONAL AND ROMANTIC RELATIONSHIPS

While there are dimensions of social relations that appear to be universal, there are many differences in interpersonal relations across cultures. Our focus here is on cultural differences in how we categorize others, differences in the intimacy of interpersonal relationships, self-disclosure and social penetration, anxiety/uncertainty management, face negotiation, and communication in romantic relationships.

Categories of Interpersonal Relationships

The way people categorize types of interpersonal relationships varies across cultures. The type of behavior expected of people in the same category (e.g., friend) may also vary across cultures. Wish, Deutsch, and Kaplan's (1976) research suggests that people in the United States, tend to use four dimensions to distinguish different types of relationships: (1) cooperative-friendly to competitive-hostile, (2) equal to unequal, (3) intense to superficial, and (4) socioemotional-informal to task-oriented-formal. Of primary concern here is the intense-to-superficial dimension. Another way of looking at this dimension is to think of it as addressing the issue of the degree of intimacy present in a relationship.

Nakane (1974) contends that, in contrast to the four dimensions used by people in the United States to categorize interpersonal relationships, the Japanese use three dimensions to distinguish among different categories of people: "(1) those people within one's own group; (2) those whose background is fairly well known; and (3) those who are unknown, the strangers" (p. 124). As one would expect, the style of communication in the first group (the ingroup), which includes not only family members but also coworkers, is generally informal; however, "as a personal relationship becomes more distant, the style becomes more formal, employing more honorific expressions" (p. 125). Nakane (1974) argues that communication with people within one's own group is generally very effective (i.e., there is little "miscommunication"). This result is at least partly due to the stability of people's reference groups in Japan, where individuals may live in the same place and work for the same company all their lives. Since individuals spend the majority of their lives within the same group, they are very concerned with how others react.

With people in the second group (people whose background is known), communication is more formal than with people in the ingroup and "more universal forms of Japanese etiquette" are used (Nakane, 1974, p. 127). This second category includes an indefinite number of people who are not actually known personally, for example, people who went to the same university or grew up in the same rural town. Even though the people may not be known, their backgrounds are. Nakane (who taught at the University of Tokyo at the time) cites an example that illustrates communicating with a person in this group. In the example, she tells of visiting another university (one she had not been to before) to give a series of lectures. When she arrives, she is met by an unknown professor, who greets her by saying, "You must be Professor Nakane. I am also from Tokyo. Please do come into my office." She immediately recognizes that the professor is telling her he went to Tokyo University. Because they share this group membership, the professor moves from being a stranger to being a person whose background is known. Because the professor's background was known, Nakane could make reliable predictions about his behavior.

The third category of people in Japan, strangers, are totally unknown. Japanese "do not feel the necessity of applying any particular code of etiquette" to strangers (Nakane, 1974, p. 128). "Japanese rarely greet or smile at a stranger, even if they share the same table in a crowded restaurant" (p. 128). Contact with strangers is avoided because there is no way to predict how they might behave. Strangers are, to a certain extent, nonpersons. When in a train crowded with strangers, for example, Japanese act as though the other people are not there. If one bumps into strangers, there is no reason to say "excuse me," because strangers are nonpersons.

The interpersonal behavior patterns discussed here are due, at least in part, to the role of context in Japanese communication. Because of the contexting process, people in collectivistic cultures such as Japan draw greater distinctions between insiders and outsiders than do people in individualistic cultures such as the United States. Hall (1976) points out that people in collectivistic cultures expect the person to whom they are talking to know what is on their mind. People in collectivistic cultures will talk indirectly about what is on their mind, giving the other person all the necessary information except the crucial piece. Figuring out the final piece and putting it all together are the responsibility of the other person. Obviously, only insiders can effectively perform these expected functions. Strangers invariably find themselves frustrated in such situations.

Intimacy of Interpersonal Relationships

Gudykunst and Nishida (1986b) compare the intimacy ratings of certain interpersonal and ingroup relationships in the United States with those in Japan on a scale of 1 to 9 (1 equals intimate, 9 equals nonintimate). To illustrate the differences, consider the following findings:

	United States	Japan
Interpersonal Relationships		
Stranger	8.35	7.99
Acquaintance	6.79	4.95
Friend	3.67	3.42
Best friend	2.51	1.73
Boy/girlfriend	1.70	3.32
Lover	1.25	2.81
Ingroup Relationships		
Coworker	5.76	5.27
Colleague	5.33	4.76
Classmate	5.72	3.84

These findings illustrate several of the differences that can be expected based on the dimensions of cultural variability discussed in Chapter 3. In collectivistic cultures, such as that of Japan, ingroup membership is valued highly and there is a greater difference between communication with members of ingroups and communication with members of outgroups than there is in individualistic cultures, such as that of the United States. As expected, the Japanese perceive the three ingroup relationships listed as more intimate than do the respondents in the United States.

Differences due to masculinity-femininity also are illustrated here. The Japanese rate the two opposite-sex interpersonal relationships (boyfriend/girlfriend and lover) as less intimate than do people in the United States. This result is expected because Japan is a high masculine culture and the United States tends to be a feminine culture. In masculine cultures, there is relatively little informal communication in opposite-sex relationships and these relationships, therefore, are not considered highly intimate because of the sex-role rigidity that exists in masculine cultures.

Differences in the intimacy ratings of interpersonal relationships are reflected in the communication that occurs in these relationships. Gudykunst and Nishida (1986b), for example, note that there are greater differences in Japan than in the United States between ingroups and outgroups with regard to the degree to which members of each group talk about personal things, are able to coordinate their communication, and experience difficulties when communicating. This finding is supported by extensive research (Gudykunst, Gao, Schmidt, et al., 1992; Gudykunst, Nishida, & Schmidt, 1989; Gudykunst, Yoon, & Nishida, 1987). Consistent with the masculinity-femininity findings noted above are Gudykunst and Nishida's (1986b) observations of greater differences in Japan than in the United States between communication in same-sex relationships and communication in opposite-sex relationships.

Before we proceed, one additional point needs to be made about Gudykunst and Nishida's (1986b) data. When we look at the scores for the first four interpersonal relationships within each culture, we will note that the same pattern exists in Japan and the United States: Stranger relationships are seen as the least intimate, acquaintance relationships are next, followed by friend and then by best friend relationships. There is consistency in the ratings of the relative intimacy of the four relationships. There is not a consistent pattern, however, when the two romantic relationships are included. People in the United States tend to view boyfriend/girlfriend and lover relationships as more intimate than close friendships, while Japanese tend to view close friendships as more intimate than romantic relationships. These findings are consistent with Gudykunst and Nishida's (1993) research which indicates that North Americans tend to select romantic relationships as their closest relationship and Japanese tend to select friendships as their closest relationship. These differences are consistent with cultural differences in masculinity-femininity.

Anxiety/Uncertainty Management

Anxiety/uncertainty management (AUM) theory (Gudykunst, 1995) suggests that effective interpersonal and intergroup communication is a function of how individuals manage the anxiety and uncertainty they experience when communicating with others. *Uncertainty* involves individuals' ability to predict and/or explain others' feelings, attitudes, and behavior (Berger & Calabrese, 1975). Managing uncertainty is a cognitive process. Berger and Calabrese's (1975) theory of initial interactions uses the notion of uncertainty as its central construct. "Central to the present theory is the assumption that when strangers meet, their primary concern is one of uncertainty reduction or increasing predictability about the behavior of both themselves and others in the interaction" (p. 100). The reduction of uncertainty leads to changes in the nature of the communication that takes place; for example, it brings about increases in the amount of communication and increases in the amount of interpersonal attraction. It also can be argued that if the amount of uncertainty present in initial interactions is not reduced, further communication between the people, in all likelihood, will not take place.

Anxiety is the affective equivalent of uncertainty. It stems from feeling uneasy, tense, worried, or apprehensive about what might happen and is based on a fear of potential negative consequences (Stephan & Stephan, 1985). To date, there is little research on cross-cultural differences in anxiety in interpersonal relationships. It can be argued, however, that members of high uncertainty avoidance cultures experience higher anxiety in communicating with strangers than do members of low uncertainty avoidance cultures (Gudykunst, 1995). Since there are few cross-cultural studies of anxiety, our focus in this section is on cultural and ethnic differences in uncertainty. We begin by looking at cultural differences.

Cultural Differences in Uncertainty. Gudykunst (1983c) suggests that the typical pattern of initial interactions for the individualistic culture of the United States may not be generalizable to collectivistic cultures. Members of collectivistic cultures do reduce uncertainty in initial interactions, but the nature of the information they seek appears to be different from the information sought when two people meet for the first time in the United States. Since much of the information necessary for communication in collectivistic cultures resides in the context or is internalized in the individual (as opposed to being mostly in the message, as in individualistic cultures), people in collectivistic cultures are more cautious concerning what they talk about with strangers than are people in individualistic cultures.

Gudykunst's (1983c) research further indicates that members of collectivistic cultures have a greater tendency to make assumptions about others on the basis of cultural background than do members of individualistic cultures. This finding is similar to Hall's (1976) argument that people in collectivistic cultures are more aware of culture's screening process and, therefore, make greater distinctions between insiders and outsiders than do people in individualistic cultures. Gudykunst's research also suggests that people from collectivistic cultures ask more questions about others' background and engage in less nonverbal activity than do members of individualistic cultures. These findings are consistent with Nakane's (1974) argument that it is the background information that allows people in collectivistic cultures to determine whether or not a person is indeed unknown.

The ways that individuals gather information to reduce uncertainty differ in individualistic and collectivistic cultures. Members of individualistic cultures seek out person-based information to reduce uncertainty about strangers (Gudykunst & Nishida, 1986a). The *person-based* information used to reduce uncertainty involves knowing others' attitudes, beliefs, feelings, values, and past behaviors. Members of collectivistic cultures seek out group-based information to reduce uncertainty (Gudykunst & Nishida, 1986a). The *group-based* information used to reduce uncertainty involves knowing others' age, status, and group memberships. The focus on person-based information leads members of individualistic cultures to search for personal similarities when communicating with outgroup members more than members of collectivistic cultures (Gudykunst, 1995). The focus on group-based information, in contrast, leads members of collectivistic cultures to search for group similarities when communicating with outgroup members more than members of individualistic cultures.

Differences also exist in how members of individualistic and collectivistic cultures explain others' behavior. Members of collectivistic cultures emphasize the importance of context in explaining others' behavior more than do members of individualistic cultures (e.g., Kashima et al., 1992). The emphasis on context in collectivistic cultures affects other aspects of communication as well. Adapting and accommodating to the context in which they are communicating, for example, is an important part of the high-context communication patterns used by people in collectivistic cultures (Hall, 1976).

There also are predictable differences in how uncertainty is managed in ingroup and outgroup relationships in individualistic and collectivistic cultures. Gudykunst and Nishida (1986a), for example, report that Japanese students have more attributional confidence (the inverse of uncertainty) regarding classmates (members of an ingroup in Japan) than do students in the United States, while the reverse pattern exists for strangers (potential members of an outgroup in Japan). Gudykunst, Nishida, and Schmidt (1989) note differences in uncertainty reduction processes between ingroup and outgroup relationships in the Japan sample, but not in the United States sample. Gudykunst, Gao, Schmidt, Nishida, Bond,

Leung, Wang, and Barraclough's (1992) study of uncertainty reduction processes in ingroup and outgroup relationships in Australia, Japan, Hong Kong, and the United States supports the earlier findings. Group membership (ingroup versus outgroup) influenced uncertainty reduction in the Japan and Hong Kong samples, but not in the United States and Australia samples. Uncertainty is lower for communication with members of ingroups than for communication with members of outgroups in Japan and Hong Kong, but there is no difference in Australia and the United States.

Cultural differences also exist in the factors that are related to reducing uncertainty. Gudykunst and Nishida (1986b), for example, report that frequency of communication predicts uncertainty reduction in individualistic cultures, but not in collectivistic cultures. Sanders, Wiseman, and Matz (1991) note that self-disclosure does not predict uncertainty reduction in collectivistic cultures, but it does in individualistic cultures. These findings are compatible with the differences between individualistic and collectivistic cultures discussed in Chapter 3.

Ethnic Differences.   Gudykunst and Hammer (1987) report that there are no differences in the amount of uncertainty European Americans and African Americans experience when communicating with members of their own ethnic group whom they do not know. There are differences, however, in what influences uncertainty reduction. Asking questions leads to uncertainty reduction for European Americans, but not for African Americans. Reducing uncertainty leads to attraction for the other person for European Americans, but not for African Americans.

Sanders and Wiseman (1991) report ethnic differences in predicting uncertainty reduction. Their research suggests that the amount of information others disclose predicts uncertainty reduction across ethnic groups. Positive nonverbal expressiveness predicts uncertainty reduction for European Americans, Latino/Latina Americans, and Asian Americans, but not African Americans. Self-disclosure predicts uncertainty reduction for European Americans and Latino/Latina Americans, but not for the other two groups. Finally, asking questions of the other person reduces uncertainty for European Americans, but not for the other three groups. The finding for question asking is consistent with Gudykunst and Hammer's (1987) research and Gudykunst, Sodetani, and Sonoda's (1987) research, which suggests that the relationship between interrogation and uncertainty reduction may be limited to European Americans.

Self-Disclosure and Social Penetration

Self-disclosure involves individuals' telling information about themselves to others—information that the other people do not know (Altman & Taylor, 1973). Closely related to self-disclosure is Altman and Taylor's notion of social penetration. Altman and Taylor argue that as relationships become more intimate, there is an increase in social penetration; that is, participants engage in self-disclosure on a larger variety of topics and with more intimacy. In this section, we examine cultural and ethnic differences in self-disclosure and social penetration. We begin with cultural differences.

Cultural Differences.   Generally, self-disclosure is associated with the direct communication styles that predominate in individualistic cultures, rather than with the indirect communication styles that predominate in collectivistic cultures (Gudykunst & Ting-Toomey, 1988). Intuitively, it appears that individualists would engage in more self-disclosure than collectivists. Barnlund's (1975) research in Japan and the United States supports this contention. Barnlund begins with the assumption that the Japanese prefer an interpersonal style in which little information about the self is made accessible to others in everyday interactions (i.e., the public self is relatively small), while the majority of information one knows about oneself is kept private (i.e., the private self is relatively large). Barnlund hypothesizes that the preferred interpersonal style in the United States, in contrast, is one in which large portions of information about the self are made available to others (i.e., the public self is relatively large), while little of such information is kept to oneself (i.e., the private self is relatively small).

Barnlund (1975) compares six topics of self-disclosure (interests/tastes, work/studies, opinions on public issues, financial matters, personality, and physical condition) and six targets of self-disclosure (same-sex friend, opposite-sex friend, mother, father, stranger, and untrusted acquaintance) for college students from Japan and the United States. Results of this research suggest there are similarities between the two groups of students in terms of what they consider appropriate topics for self-disclosure. Specifically, tastes and opinions are seen as being most appropriate by both groups, while physical attributes and personality traits are least preferred. Further, the hierarchy of preferences is the same in the United States and Japan: same-sex friend, opposite-sex friend, mother, father, stranger, and untrusted acquaintance. Barnlund, however, finds the level of self-disclosure to be higher for college students from the United States than it is for college students from Japan. This pattern is consistent across all six topics of conversation and all six target persons. Barnlund concludes that "interpersonal distance, as estimated by self-disclosure, was substantially greater among Japanese than Americans" (p. 79).

Consistent with Barnlund's research, Ting-Toomey's (1991) study in France, Japan, and the United States, as well as Chen's (1995) research in China and the United States, indicates that individualists self-disclose more than collectivists. Wheeler, Reis, and Bond (1989), however, report that Chinese in Hong Kong engage in more self-disclosure in everyday communication than do North Americans. On the surface, this finding appears inconsistent with the claim that self-disclosure is associated with direct communication, but this is not necessarily the case. Wheeler, Reis, and Bond point out that most of the Chinese respondents' contacts are with members of their ingroup and communication in ingroups in collectivistic cultures tends to be intimate (e.g., involves high levels of self-disclosure). Most of the North American respondents' contacts, in contrast, are with superficial acquaintances, where high levels of self-disclosure are not expected.

Gudykunst, Gao, Schmidt, et al. (1992) observe more self-disclosure with ingroup members than with outgroup members in two Chinese samples, both high in collectivism. There is, however, no difference in ingroup and outgroup self-disclosure in the Australian and United States samples, both high in individualism. The Japanese data, in contrast, do not fit the expected pattern. Wheeler, Reis, and Bond (1989) argue that this reversal of expectation may be due to other dimensions of self-disclosure mediating the process of self-disclosure. The expected findings, for example, might not be observed in collectivistic cultures, like Japan, that are high in masculinity-femininity and/or uncertainty avoidance (discussed later in the chapter). Alternatively, Wheeler, Reis, and Bond point out that the findings for Japan may be due to the homogeneity of the Japanese culture. Barnlund (1975) contends that "the greater the cultural homogeneity, the greater the meaning conveyed in a single word, the more that can be implied rather than stated" (p. 162).

Gudykunst and Nishida's (1986b) data on social penetration are consistent with Triandis' (1988) description of the focus on ingroup relationships in collectivistic cultures. The Japanese respondents in this study report greater differences in personalization (e.g., knowing personal information), synchronization (e.g., coordination), and difficulty of communication between ingroup (classmate) and outgroup (stranger) relationships than the North American respondents. Gudykunst, Yoon, and Nishida (1987) also examine the influence of individualism on social penetration in ingroup and outgroup relationships in Japan, Korea, and the United States. They note that the greater the degree of collectivism present in a culture, the greater the differences between ingroup (i.e., classmate) and outgroup (i.e., stranger) communication in terms of amount of personalization (e.g., intimacy of communication) and synchronization (e.g., coordination of communication) and difficulty in communication.

Ethnic Differences. The finding that European Americans tend to disclose at higher rates than African Americans is reported by a number of researchers (Diamond & Hellcamp, 1969; Jourard, 1958; Littlefield, 1974; Wolken, Moriwaki, & Williams, 1973). Additionally, Littlefield (1974) finds that African Americans tend to self-disclose at a higher rate than do Mexican Americans. These differences, however, may be attributable to social class rather than to racial factors—an interpretation suggested by Jaffee and Polanski's (1962) finding that no significant differences exist between lower-class African Americans and lower-class European Americans.

Gudykunst and Hammer (1987) report that when social class is controlled for statistically, European Americans engage in more self-disclosure with people they do not know than do African Americans. By the time close friendships are formed, however, the pattern reverses. Gudykunst (1986) observes that African Americans self-disclose more with friends than do European Americans. Hammer and Gudykunst (1987) also note that African Americans engage in more overall social penetration with their best friends than do European Americans. These findings are consistent with Hecht and Ribeau's (1984) research on communication satisfaction. They conclude that "[African Americans] seem to require deeper, more intimate topical involvement than [European American] respondents. This intimacy must be seen as intrinsic to the relationship, therapeutic, and involving trust" (p. 147).

Face Negotiation in Interpersonal Relationships

Face involves the projected image of oneself in a relational situation. More specifically, face is conceptualized as the interaction between the degree of threats or considerations a member offers to another party, and the degree of claim for a sense of self-respect (or the demand of respect) by the other party in a given situation (Ting-Toomey, 1988). Ting-Toomey (1988) presents theoretical propositions to account for the relationship between individualism-collectivism and face management. Ting-Toomey contends that members of individualistic cultures emphasize self-face maintenance more than do members of collectivistic cultures. Members of collectivistic cultures, in comparison, emphasize mutual-face and other-face maintenance more than do members of individualistic cultures.

Ting-Toomey, Gao, Trubisky, Yang, Kim, Lin, and Nishida's (1991) study is not consistent with the theoretical predictions. They observe, for example, that students in the United States are concerned more with other-face than are students in Japan, while students in Japan are concerned more with self-face than are students in the United States. These findings may be due to the measurement of facework used in the study (i.e., it was a measure developed in the United States and not modified for use in collectivistic cultures), or the respondents from the collectivistic cultures may have been more individualistic than the respondents from the United States.

Other research supports Ting-Toomey's (1988) theoretical propositions (see Ting-Toomey, 1994c, for alternative conceptualizations of face across cultures). Holtgraves and Yang (1992), for example, note that in determining when to be polite, Koreans are influenced by others' power and the relational distance more than are North Americans. Cocroft and Ting-Toomey (1994) report that North Americans use antisocial, self-presentation, and self-attribution face-maintenance strategies more than do Japanese, while Japanese use indirect face-maintenance strategies more than do North Americans. Cupach and Imahori (1993) note that North Americans are more likely than Japanese to use humor and aggression to manage social predicaments, while Japanese are more likely than North Americans to apologize. Imahori and Cupach (1994) observe that North Americans use humor as a way to maintain face in embarrassing situations more than do Japanese. Japanese, in contrast, use remediation (e.g., the correction of behavior) as a way to manage face more than do North Americans.

Holtgraves (1992) argues that the relative power two people have and the relationship between them influence the amount of politeness behavior across cultures. Even though the factors that contribute to politeness behavior are consistent across cultures, cultural differences in the way people look at these factors can lead to intercultural misunderstandings. He argues, for example, that people in the United States emphasize the distance between themselves and others less than do Koreans. North Americans, therefore, may assume a closer distance than do Koreans when they interact and use less politeness behavior than Koreans expect. Koreans may interpret the lack of politeness as a claim to greater power in the relationship. Scollon and Scollon (1981) also report that European Americans are less polite than Athabaskan Indians when members of the two groups interact. European Americans' politeness behavior is guided by how close they think they are to the other person. They often use less politeness than Athbaskan Indians expect. The Athabaskan Indians interpret the lack of politeness as being due to the European Americans' thinking that they are culturally superior.

Communication in Romantic Relationships

Dion and Dion (1988) suggest that individualism-collectivism is the major dimension of cultural variability that influences similarities and differences in romantic relationships across cultures. They point out that in individualistic cultures like the United States, the idea of being dependent upon someone else is either viewed negatively or receives a neutral response. That, however, is not the case in collectivistic cultures. Doi (1973), for example, relates the Japanese concept of *amae* to love. *Amae* refers to the tendency to depend upon another person and/or presume upon that person's benevolence. Doi claims that "*amae*, generally speaking, is an inseparable concomitant of love" (p. 118). Hsu (1953/1981) makes a similar observation about love in Chinese culture.

Dion and Dion (1988) isolate several problems that arise in individualistic cultures regarding love relationships:

> First, one can "lose" one's self and the feeling of personal autonomy in a love relationship, feeling used and exploited as a result. Second, satisfying the autonomous needs of two "separate" individuals in a love relationship obviously becomes a balancing act. Third, the spirit of [North] American individualism makes it difficult for either partner in a relationship to justify sacrificing or giving to the other more than one is receiving. Finally, and inevitably, [North] Americans confront a fundamental conflict trying to reconcile personal freedom and individuality, on the one hand, with obligations and role requirements of marital partner and parent, on the other. (p. 286)

These problems would not necessarily arise in collectivistic cultures where dependence on others is valued.

Dion and Dion (1993) suggest that romantic love is less likely to be considered an important reason for marriage in collectivistic cultures than it is in individualistic cultures. In individualistic cultures, romantic love is considered the main reason for marriage. In collectivistic cultures, however, having a family tends to be the main reason for marriage. If having a family is the most important consideration, then the acceptability of the potential mate to the family is critical. This consideration explains the emphasis on arranged marriages in collectivistic cultures (Note: There is a tendency in many collectivistic cultures for young people to want to marry on the basis of love). Dion and Dion also contend that psychological intimacy is more important to marital satisfaction in individualistic cultures than in collectivistic cultures.

Dion and Dion's research (cited in Dion & Dion, 1993) suggests that the greater our psychological individualism, the less positive our attitudes toward marriage are. Dion and Dion's research (1991) indicates that the greater our self-contained individualism (e.g., the tendency to dislike any form of dependency and to want total control over our lives), the less love, care, need, trust, and physical attraction we experience with partners in romantic relationships.

Dion, Pak, and Dion (1990) suggest that individualism-collectivism influences the stereotyping of members of the opposite sex on the basis of physical attractiveness. They contend that collectivism leads individuals to stereotype members of the opposite sex on group-related attributes (e.g., the other person's position in a social network and family memberships) rather than on individual attributes such as physical attractiveness.

Sprecher et al. (1994) report that North Americans emphasize romantic, passionate love and love based on friendship more than do Japanese and Russians. North Americans and Russians score higher on romantic beliefs than Japanese. Further, North Americans rate physical appearance, similarity, family and friend approval, personality, affection, and mystery as important more than do Russians and Japanese. With the exception of friend and family approval, these findings support Dion and Dion's (1993) speculations.

Gao (1993) notes that individualism-collectivism influences love and intimacy in romantic relationships. Specifically, partners in romantic relationships in the United States report more passion than do partners in romantic relationships in China. Partners in Chinese romantic relationships, in contrast, report more intellectual intimacy than do partners in North American relationships.

Gao and Gudykunst (1995) observe greater high-context attributional confidence (i.e., indirect reduction of uncertainty) in Chinese romantic relationships than in European American romantic relationships. They also note that perceived attitude similarity is higher among European Americans than among Chinese. Finally, they observe that others react socially to European American romantic partners as a couple more than they do to Chinese romantic partners.

In addition to the research cited here, there is research on the use of power strategies (i.e., ways of persuading others to do something) in romantic relationships that is consistent with individualism-collectivism. Belk et al. (1988) suggest that individuals in the United States use direct power strategies, such as persistence, persuasion, and telling more than do Mexicans. Mexicans, in contrast, use bilateral-indirect strategies more than do people in the United States. Belk et al. also report that Mexican men use more indirect-unilateral power strategies than do men in the United States. This last difference may be a function of masculinity-femininity.

Most of the research to date supports Dion and Dion's (1988, 1991, 1993) speculations regarding differences in love in individualistic and collectivistic cultures (see Levine et al., 1995, for an 11-culture study). There is, however, one study that does not support their speculations. Doherty et al.'s (1994) research indicates that individual-level individualism is correlated negatively with passionate love among members of different ethnic groups in Hawaii.

THE DEVELOPMENT OF INTERPERSONAL RELATIONSHIPS WITH STRANGERS

Most of our close interpersonal relationships are with people who are relatively similar to us. We tend to develop close relationships with members of our own culture and members of our ethnic group (Pogrebin, 1987). Safilios-Rothchild (1982) also points out that "there is considerable evidence that very often people do not want to enter unpredictable, and therefore, stressful interactions with visibly disabled people, and they avoid doing so by extending only 'fictional acceptance' which does not go beyond a polite, inhibited, and overcontrolled interaction" (p. 44). Fussell (1983) claims that class differences similarly hinder members of different social classes from developing close relationships. Tamir (1984) argues that age segregation in society "has hampered the opportunity for young and old to come to know one another. Hence, when they do come into contact, well-worn and often detrimental stereotypes may persist, and participants must make an active effort to dispel these preconceptions for a healthy dialogue to take place" (p. 39).

One reason we do not have close relationships with members of other groups is that we do not have a lot of contact with strangers. Another reason is that our initial interactions and superficial contacts with strangers often result in ineffective communication. Since our communication with strangers is not as effective and satisfying as we would like, we do not *try* to develop intimate relationships with strangers. If we understand the process of relationship development, however, we can make an informed conscious decision as to whether or not we want to have intimate relationships with strangers. In making such a decision, we must keep in mind that the more we know about strangers, the more accurately we can predict their behavior (Honeycutt, Knapp, & Powers, 1983).

In examining how communication influences the development of interpersonal relationships with strangers, we must keep in mind that there are both similarities and differences in communication across cultures. In this section, we examine how our expectations influence the relationships we form, how we reduce uncertainty and anxiety in communicating with strangers, as well as the roles of similarity and self-disclosure in relationship development. We also discuss linguistic/cultural knowledge, communication satisfaction, and quality of communication. We conclude by presenting a summary of the patterns of the relationship development process. To begin, we look at how our expectations influence our interactions with strangers.

Expectations

Since proximity is one of the major factors involved in interpersonal attraction (Berscheid & Walster, 1969), strangers may be attracted to us simply because we are nearer to them than are members of their own group. In interacting with us, strangers may expect that they have nothing to lose. "The costs of pursuing a dissimilar relation are negligible relative to the rewards [for strangers]" (Knapp cited in Crockett & Friedman, 1980, p. 91). We may, however, expect that we have something to lose when interacting with strangers since the rewards may be negligible and the costs high. Specifically, we may expect that if we interact with strangers, we may be looked down on by members of our group. Regardless of any actual or potential sanctions, however, some of us expect positive interactions with strangers.

Hoyle, Pinkley, and Insko (1989) report that people expect interpersonal encounters (i.e., interactions with ingroup members) to be more agreeable and less abrasive than intergroup encounters. These expectations generalize to Japan (Gudykunst, Nishida, & Morisaki, 1992) and Greece (Broome, 1990). In Greece, for example, ingroup members are expected to be cooperative, polite, reliable, and warm, while outgroup members are expected to be competitive, deceitful, hostile, and untrustworthy. Gudykunst and Shapiro (in press), however, report that expectations become more positive as relationships with strangers become more intimate. Hubbert, Guerrero, and Gudykunst (1995) also observe that expectations become more positive over time in intergroup encounters simply as a function of the communication that takes place.

Our expectations for interactions with strangers can create self-fulfilling prophecies. Negative expectations can lead us to want to avoid interacting with strangers or keep our interactions as short as possible. Positive expectations, in contrast, can lead us to look for the positive aspects of our interactions with strangers. If we find the positive aspects of the interaction, we want to interact more. Whether we want to continue our interaction also depends on our ability to manage our anxiety and uncertainty.

Uncertainty and Anxiety Management

Once a decision is made to interact with strangers, our major concern during the initial stages of interaction is the management of uncertainty and anxiety. Reducing uncertainty is necessary if we are to arrive at a basis for predicting strangers' responses to our communication behavior and accurately interpreting strangers' behavior. Reducing anxiety is necessary to decrease our tendency to avoid interacting with strangers and to motivate us to want to communicate.

Uncertainty.   There are differences in uncertainty reduction processes used when we communicate with strangers as opposed to when we communicate with people who are familiar. Initial interactions with people who are familiar are different from initial interactions with strangers. Gudykunst (1983a) reports that students in the United States tend to make more assumptions about others on the basis of cultural background in initial interactions with strangers than they do in initial interactions with people who are familiar. This result is to be expected, given that the major difference between the two forms of interaction is the communicators' cultural background. Gudykunst also notes that students in the United States prefer to do more of the talking in initial encounters with people who are familiar, while they prefer to ask more questions in initial encounters with strangers.

Lee and Boster's (1991) research indicates that people in the United States perceive strangers from other cultures as less attractive than people from their own culture and have less confidence in predicting the behavior of strangers in initial interactions than people who are familiar. Lee and Boster also note that individuals ask for more intimate information from partners who are familiar than from strangers.

Consistent with earlier research, Gudykunst and Shapiro (in press) report that there is greater uncertainty in intergroup encounters (interethnic and intercultural) than in intragroup encounters. They also observe that uncertainty is associated negatively with positive expectations, communication satisfaction, and quality of communication. Uncertainty is associated positively with the degree to which social identities are activated in the interaction, and with the amount of anxiety experienced. Hubbert, Guerrero, and Gudykunst (1995) note that uncertainty decreases over time in intergroup encounters. Gudykunst, Nishida, and Chua (1986) report that uncertainty decreases as the intimacy of intercultural relationships increases. Similarly, Gudykunst (1985c) notes that there is less uncertainty in intercultural friendships than in intercultural acquaintance relationships.

Research (Gudykunst & Hammer, 1988b; Gudykunst, Sodetani, & Sonoda, 1987) suggests that our social identities affect the reduction of uncertainty when we communicate with strangers. Gudykunst and Hammer, for example, report that the more positive individuals' relevant social identities (e.g., ethnic identity when interacting with someone from a different ethnic group) are, the more those individuals are able to reduce uncertainty when communicating with strangers. This finding, however, holds only when the stranger is seen as typical of his or her group and when group differences are recognized. If the other person is viewed as atypical of her or his group and/or group differences are not recognized, personal identity, not social identity, influences the interaction.

Anxiety.   Actual or anticipated interaction with members of other ethnic groups can lead to anxiety. Stephan and Stephan (1985) argue that individuals fear four types of negative consequences: negative psychological consequences (e.g., frustration), negative behavioral consequences (e.g., exploitation), negative evaluations by members of outgroups (e.g., negative stereotyping), and negative evaluations by members of their ingroups (e.g., disapproval).

Stephan and Stephan (1985, 1989, 1992) argue that the amount of anxiety we experience when interacting with strangers is, in part, a function of our intergroup attitudes. The greater our prejudice and ethnocentrism, for example, the greater our anxiety about interacting with strangers. Contact with strangers, however, also leads to decreases in anxiety (Islam & Hewstone, 1993; Stephan & Stephan, 1992).

Gudykunst and Shapiro (in press) note that greater anxiety is experienced in intergroup encounters (interethnic and intercultural) than in intragroup encounters. They report that anxiety, like uncertainty, is associated negatively with positive expectations, communication satisfaction, and quality of communication. Anxiety is associated positively with the degree to which social identities are activated in the interaction, and with the amount of uncertainty experienced. Hubbert, Guerrero, and Gudykunst (1995) report that anxiety decreases over time in intergroup encounters with strangers as a function of the communication that takes place.

As indicated earlier, we experience more anxiety in our initial interactions with members of other groups than with members of our own group. Managing anxiety is associated closely with developing trust. *Trust* is "confidence that one will find what is desired from another, rather than what is feared" (Deutsch, 1973, p. 149). When we trust others, we expect positive outcomes from our interactions with them; when we have anxiety about interacting with others, we fear negative outcomes from our interactions with them. When we first meet someone, "trust is often little more than a naive expression of hope" (Holmes & Rempel, 1989, p. 192). For us to have hope about the relationship, our anxiety must be below our maximum threshold. For relationships to become close,

> most people need to act *as if* a sense of [trust] were justified, and set their doubts aside. To do so requires a "leap of faith" in the face of evidence that can never be conclusive. Thus trust becomes . . . an emotionally charged sense of closure. It permits an illusion of control . . . where one can plan ahead without anxiety. (Holmes & Rempel, 1989, p. 204)

Without some minimal degree of trust, relationships cannot become close.

Language and Cultural Knowledge

If strangers approach us and do not speak our language, it will be almost impossible to reduce uncertainty about their behavior and it will inhibit the development of any possible relationship between us (Kertamus, Gudykunst, & Nishida, 1991; Gudykunst et al., 1991; Sudweeks et al., 1990). In Gudykunst et al.'s (1991) study, the North Americans' acceptance of the Japanese partners' inability to speak English well and/or the North Americans' offering help to the Japanese partners in improving their English was one of the major factors in allowing relationships to move past the acquaintance stage.

The development of personal relationships with strangers requires more than knowledge of linguistic codes. Knowledge of culturally appropriate rules for conducting the process of acquaintance formation also is necessary. Strangers, in all likelihood, have learned rules for the process of acquaintance formation that are different from those we have learned. Lack of knowledge of strangers' cultures inhibits the development of interpersonal relationships. Miller and Sunnafrank (1982), for example, argue that "knowledge about another person's culture—its language, dominant values, beliefs, and prevailing ideology—often permits predictions of the person's probable response to certain messages. . . . Upon first encountering . . . [people from another culture], cultural information provides the only grounds for communicative predictions" (pp. 226–227).

Similarity

The ease with which initial interactions take place depends, at least in part, on the degree of similarity (including cultural, racial, sexual, and attitudinal) between the two participants. It is not the actual similarity between participants that is important, but the degree of *perceived similarity,* the degree to which people think they are similar to others. As would be expected, the degree of perceived similarity is higher in intragroup relationships than in intergroup relationships (Gudykunst, 1986; Gudykunst, Chua, & Gray 1987).

Rokeach (1960) argues that the primary factor in the social distance between two people is the degree of similarity perceived. Similarly, Byrne (1971) views attraction as a function of the proportion of similar opinions two people hold. Brewer (1968) reports that similarity of beliefs accounts for social distance among East African tribes. Byrne et al. (1971) note that although culture influences the level of attraction, similarity also has a significant influence on attraction to strangers. Tan and Singh's (1995) study also suggests that the similarity-attraction hypothesis generalizes to collectivistic cultures. H. K. Kim's (1991) research also suggests that perceived attitude similarity is a stronger predictor of attraction to strangers than even perceived competence in the ingroup language.

Knapp points out that dissimilarity "is enjoyable when the interaction is brief, when the differences are few and on peripheral beliefs, and when the chance of rejection is small, that is, when the costs of pursuing dissimilar relations are negligible relative to the rewards" (cited in Crockett & Friedman, 1980, p. 91). Knapp (1978) also suggests several qualifications that must be made with respect to the general principle of similarity and attraction:

> In the early stages of a relationship, similarity may be based upon a wide range of background factors and relatively superficial opinions and interests. As the relationship intensifies, certain topics, beliefs, and values may emerge as the most critical areas of similarity; those areas must be similar if the relationship is to continue. . . . Other qualifications include those people who are attracted to others dissimilar from themselves. . . . There are instances in which we seek out people who are known to be different. (pp. 102–103)

In Knapp's view, then, dissimilarities may not hinder our initial interactions with strangers.

Rogers and Bhowmik (1971) argue that "in a free choice situation, when a source can interact with any one of a number of different receivers, there is a strong tendency for him [or her] to select a receiver who is like himself [or herself]" (p. 528). They go on to suggest that communication between people who are similar is generally more effective than communication between dissimilar people. Although this finding is accepted widely, moderate dissimilarities between communicators who are generally similar may lead to the most effective communication (Simons, Berkowitz, & Moyer, 1970).

Simard's (1981) study of French/English intraethnic and interethnic initial interactions in Canada indicates that when focusing on a potential friend from the other group [French and English subjects] perceive it as more difficult to know how to initiate a conversation, to know what to talk about during interaction, to be interested in the other person, and to guess in which language they should talk, than when they considered a person from their own group. (p. 183)

Further, Simard's research suggests that both groups (Anglophones and Francophones in Canada) find attitude and language similarity more important than occupational and social class similarity in the development of interethnic acquaintances. Results of her research "may imply that the dissimilarity in terms of ethnic affiliation may have been compensated for by increased similarity along a number of other dimensions or that so much dissimilarity was expected that after the actual encounters the overall similarity surprised the [respondents]" (p. 187).

Sunnafrank and Miller's (1981) report that "individuals paired with an attitudinally similar partner were more attracted to the partner than individuals paired with an attitudinally dissimilar partner, but only when they had not engaged in initial interaction" (p. 22). People are attracted to dissimilar strangers if they have a chance to interact with them, but they are not attracted to them if interaction does not take place. Hubbert, Guerrero, and Gudykunst's (1995) research supports this argument. They report that perceived similarity increases over time as a function of the communication that takes place.

We filter potential relational partners on the extent to which we perceive that they are similar to us (Duck, 1977). In the initial stages of getting to know others, we probably focus on general attitudes and opinions that we hold. If we perceive that our attitudes are similar to others', we will be attracted to them because the similarity in attitudes validates our view of the world (Byrne, 1971). As we get to know others, we search for similarities in central aspects of our world views (e.g., our core values).

Probably one of the most important similarities we search for in potential relational partners is similarity in our orientations toward interpersonal interactions (Sunnafrank, 1991). If we perceive similarities in our orientations toward communication, we are likely to form close relationships with others. Burleson, Samter, and Lucchetti's (1992) research suggests that close friends have similar orientations toward five specific communication activities: conflict management, ways to comfort each other, ways to persuade each other, ways to support each other's self-concepts, and ways to tell stories and jokes.

In summary, while cultural dissimilarity may complicate initial interactions, it clearly does not preclude the development of more intimate relationships. Following Rokeach, Smith, and Evans (1960), it appears reasonable to argue that cultural similarity is not a necessary prerequisite for friendship formation. In the absence of cultural similarity, however, similarity in other areas (e.g., attitudes, interests) may be necessary for friendships to develop. The degree of similarity between communicators plays another important role in initial interactions in that it influences the reduction of uncertainty (Berger & Calabrese, 1975) and the reduction of anxiety present when we communicate with strangers (Stephan & Stephan, 1985).

It appears reasonable to argue that our initial interactions with strangers will move toward the development of more intimate relationships if we perceive some minimum level of similarity between ourselves and the strangers and are able to reduce some of the uncertainty present in our initial interactions. If we do not perceive sufficient similarity, on the other hand, the relationship probably will not change in level of intimacy over time; for example, we may remain acquaintances for the entire length of time we know each other.

Self-Disclosure and Social Penetration

One of the major factors contributing to the development of personal relationships with strangers is self-disclosure. One type of interaction where self-disclosure is an important issue is when nondisabled and disabled people communicate. Thompson (1982), for example, argues that nondisabled people react more positively to disabled people who self-disclose than those who do not self-disclose, especially when the self-disclosure is about the disability. Thompson and Seibold (1978), however, point out that self-disclosure does not necessarily reduce tension, but it does increase the nondisabled people's acceptance of disabled people. Braithwaite (1991) contends that disabled people tend to disclose about their disability in response to nondisabled people's questions about their disabilities if they perceive that the disclosure is appropriate to the relationship and the context in which they are communicating. Disabled people, however, prefer to have nondisabled people get to know them as individuals before answering questions about their disabilities. To accomplish this, disabled people may try to direct the conversation and suggest topics for conversation other than their disabilities. If disabled people perceive that a nondisabled person with whom they are communicating is experiencing great discomfort, they may choose to disclose about their disabilities to make the other person more comfortable (Braithwaite, 1991).

The age of the communicators also affects self-disclosure. Dickson-Markman (1986), for example, believes that older people tend to disclose more than younger people, especially with respect to negative feelings. Self-disclosure in intergenerational encounters does not necessarily follow the same patterns as it does in encounters with members of the same generation (Giles et al., 1992). When older people interact with younger people, they tend to self-disclose more than younger people, especially about painful information such as accidents, deaths in the family, and medical problems. When older people self-disclose to younger people they do not know, the younger people do not necessarily reciprocate self-disclosures at the same rate they do when communicating with other younger people. When young people self-disclose, in contrast, older people tend to reciprocate.

Gudykunst and Nishida (1984) report that there is a greater intention to disclose information in initial intercultural encounters than in initial encounters with people from the same culture. This pattern, however, does not hold when self-disclosure in intracultural and intercultural acquaintances and friendships are compared. Gudykunst (1985c), for example, observes no difference between the amount of self-disclosure in intercultural and intracultural acquaintances and/or friendships. There is, nevertheless, more self-disclosure in both intracultural and intercultural friendships than in intracultural or intercultural acquaintances. Gudykunst's (1985b) research also reveals moderate to high associations between social penetration in close friendships with culturally similar partners and social penetration in close friendships with culturally dissimilar partners.

The research summarized here can be explained by using Altman and Taylor's (1973) conceptualization of the social penetration process. Communication in close friendships is characterized by freewheeling and loose exchange and "facile switching from one mode of communication to another" (p. 139). They also point out that in close friendships "the dyad has moved to the point where interaction is relatively free in both peripheral and in more central areas of the personality. Cultural stereotypy is broken down in these more intimate areas and there is a willingness to move freely in and out of such exchanges" (pp. 139–140). If cultural stereotypy is indeed broken down, the culture from which a person comes should not be a major factor influencing the interaction. Close relationships between culturally similar communicators, therefore, should not be expected to differ dramatically from those between culturally dissimilar ones.

Another explanation for the research on self-disclosure comes from Miller and Steinberg's (1975) developmental theory of interpersonal communication. Specifically, it can be inferred that when communicators making predictions move from the cultural and sociocultural levels of data to the use of psychocultural data, the culture from which people come is not a major variable affecting the predictions made about their communication behavior. Given this theory, it would be expected that when predictions are made mainly on the basis of psychocultural data (e.g., in close friendships), the degree of social penetration should not necessarily differ in culturally similar and dissimilar relationships. The differences that do exist in close friendships are best attributed to the specific characteristics of the dyad and the people involved, not to their cultural background.

Gudykunst, Nishida, and Chua's (1986) study of social penetration processes in intercultural dyads supports the argument made here. It reveals that as intercultural relationships become more intimate (i.e., move from acquaintance to friend to close friend), social penetration increases. Social penetration in intercultural relationships influences the degree of communication satisfaction individuals have when they communicate with strangers.

Quality of Communication

Quality of communication refers to the extent our communication is relaxed, smooth, involves understanding, and a minimum of communication breakdowns (Duck et al., 1991). Gudykunst and Shapiro (in press) report that perceptions of the quality of communication are higher in intragroup relationships than in intergroup relationships. Hubbert, Guerrero, and Gudykunst (1995) observe that perceived quality of communication increases over time as a function of the interaction. Gudykunst and Shapiro also note that perceived quality increases as intergroup relationships become more intimate.

Gudykunst (1995) argues that the effectiveness of communication with strangers is a function of our ability to manage our anxiety and uncertainty. Hubbert, Guerrero, and Gudykunst's (1995) research indicates that the perceived quality and perceived effectiveness of communication is affected by the amount of uncertainty and anxiety present in the interaction. The less the uncertainty and anxiety, the greater the perceived quality and effectiveness of communication. This pattern holds across time, and it holds for both European Americans and non-European Americans.

Communication Satisfaction

Whether we are able to manage uncertainty and anxiety, find similarities, and engage in social penetration influences whether participants are satisfied with our communication. *Satisfaction* is an affective (i.e., emotional) reaction to communication that meets or fails to meet our expectations (Hecht, 1978). The way strangers respond to us influences our satisfaction in communicating with them. Hodges and Byrne (1972), for example, point out that responses to strangers are most positive when they express attitudes in open-minded, rather than dogmatic (closed-minded) terms. Broome (1981) argues that "responses to differences stated in an open manner will be less defensive than responses stated in a non-open manner" (p. 231).

Hecht and Ribeau and their associates study satisfaction with interethnic conversations in the United States. Hecht, Ribeau, and Alberts (1989), for example, isolate factors that contribute to African Americans' satisfaction with their conversations with European Americans. To be satisfied, African Americans need to feel that they are respected, confirmed, and accepted by the European Americans with whom they communicate. Satisfying conversations with European Americans also include emotional expression and the European Americans' being authentic (i.e., European Americans in satisfying conversations are perceived as genuine and European Americans in dissatisfying conversations are perceived as evasive). African Americans also perceive that there is understanding (i.e., shared meanings) and goal attainment in satisfying conversations. They perceive negative stereotyping and feel powerless (e.g., manipulated or controlled) in dissatisfying conversations.

Hecht, Ribeau, and Sedano (1990) report a similar study with Latino/Latina Americans. Similar to African Americans, Latino/Latina Americans see acceptance as an important aspect of satisfying conversations. Satisfying conversations with European Americans also include the expression of feelings and rational behavior. The presence of self-expression and relational solidarity also contribute to satisfaction in conversations. Negative stereotyping and failure to discover a shared world view (i.e., absence of perceived similarities) emerge as important factors in dissatisfying conversations.

Gudykunst, Nishida, and Chua's (1986, 1987) research indicates that the more communication in a relationship is personalized and synchronized, and the less difficulty people experience in communicating with their partner, the more satisfied they are with the communication in their relationship. It also suggests that the more partners self-disclose to each other, the more they are attracted to each other, the more similarities they perceive, and the more uncertainty they reduce about each other, the more satisfied they are. Finally, the more competent the partners judge each other's communication to be, the more satisfied they are.

Gudykunst and Shapiro (in press) report that satisfaction is higher in intragroup encounters than in intergroup encounters. They also note that satisfaction increases as relationships become more intimate. Hubbert, Guerrero, and Gudykunst (1995) also observe that satisfaction increases over time in intergroup encounters for non-Europeans, but it remains relatively constant for European Americans.

Patterns of Relationship Development

What is it about our initial interactions and our communication with acquaintances who are from other groups that allows the relationship to develop into a friendship? Research suggests that we must communicate in a way that signals we accept the other person, we must express our feelings, and we must avoid negative stereotyping. All these factors combined suggest that our communication with the other person helps him or her have positive personal and social identities. In other words, we support the other person's self-concept.

As pointed out earlier, research (Kertamus, Gudykunst, & Nishida 1991; Gudykunst et al., 1991; Sudweeks et al., 1990) suggests that there must be linguistic competence, some degree of cultural knowledge, and the perception of some degree of similarity between ourselves and the other person if an intimate relationship is to develop. The display of empathy and mutual accommodation regarding differences in communication styles (i.e., adapting each other's style to that of the other person) also appear to be critical.

Other factors that appear to be important are similar to those in developing relationships with people from our own groups. We must, for example, make time available to interact with the other person (Kertamus, Gudykunst, & Nishida, 1991; Gudykunst et al., 1991; Sudweeks et al., 1990). In addition to making time to interact, consciously or unconsciously attempting to increase the intimacy of our communication (i.e., talking about things that are important to us) is necessary if we are going to develop interpersonal relationships with strangers.

The stages that relationships go through provide additional insight into the development of interpersonal relationships with strangers. Altman and Taylor (1973), for example, propose a four-stage model of interpersonal relationship development: (1) orientation, (2) exploratory affective exchange, (3) full affective exchange, and (4) stable exchange. The orientation stage is characterized by responses that often are stereotypical and reflect superficial aspects of the personalities of the actors involved. The content of the interaction at this stage is limited to the "outer public areas" of the individuals' personalities. The second stage, exploratory affective exchange, is typified by those relationships labeled casual acquaintances and nonintimate friends. Relationships at this stage, according to Altman and Taylor, are generally friendly and relaxed, but commitments are only temporary. The third stage, full affective exchange, is characteristic of close friendships and courtship relationships. These relationships involve loose and freewheeling verbal interaction and an increase of self-disclosure concerning the central areas of the individuals' personalities. As was pointed out previously, in this stage is where cultural stereotypy is broken down. The final stage, stable exchange, is achieved in very few relationships. If it is achieved, however, Altman and Taylor argue that there are very few instances of miscommunication between the partners because they have fully described themselves to each other.

Given Altman and Taylor's (1973) model, it can be argued that the initial stages of our relationships (i.e., the first two stages) with strangers are different from those of our relationships with people who are familiar. These differences arise because the early stages are dominated by cultural stereotypes, and, therefore, when we communicate with strangers, differences are bound to emerge. That is not to say that our relationships with strangers do not go through these stages, because they do. Rather, the argument is that they may go through them in different ways.

If cultural stereotypy is indeed broken down in the stage of full affective exchange, it can be argued that the culture from which a person comes will not be a major factor influencing such relationships. Once a relationship reaches the stage of friendship, the majority of interaction has a personalistic focus, a focus on the other person as a unique communicator (Wright, 1978). In other words, the communicators in a friendship have moved from using cultural and sociocultural levels of data for making predictions to using psychocultural data (Miller & Steinberg, 1975). When the data used in making predictions is at the psychocultural level, the culture from which strangers come is not a major factor influencing our predictions.

Our relationships with strangers and those with people who are familiar are not the same. No two friendships are exactly the same; friendships are based on private negotiations, follow idiosyncratic rules, and are all slightly different. The argument put forth is that since friendship is a relationship in which cultural stereotypy is broken down and in which there is a personalistic focus, the differences in our behavior in the two types of friendships can be attributed to personal characteristics of the person with whom we are interacting or to other factors, not to the person's cultural background.

Before concluding, we should note that relationships do not always develop along a smooth course from superficial to intimate. Altman, Vinsel, and Brown (1981) point out that "although people may exhibit relatively stable openness (or closedness) for a time, it is likely that openness eventually gives way to closedness and that closedness is eventually followed by openness. Such cyclical variations in accessibility of people to one another are affected by factors internal and external to an individual" (p. 139). They go on to argue that different patterns of openness-closedness may be adaptive over the life span of a relationship. Lerner (1979) makes the additional point that relationships go through cycles with respect to other dimensions, including affection, trust, and sharing. How a particular relationship ultimately develops, therefore, is influenced by the degree to which the people involved have synchrony in timing and content with respect to the openness-closedness in their interaction (Altman, Vinsel, & Brown, 1981), as well as by whether or not there is synchrony with respect to their display of affection and trust (Lerner, 1979). Following Hall (1983), we believe establishing synchrony is easier with people who are familiar than it is with strangers. It can be established with strangers, however.

When we communicate on automatic pilot, we often filter out members of other groups as potential friends simply because they are different and our communication with them is not as effective as our communication with people from our own group. Whether or not we want to act differently depends on our motivation. Pogrebin (1987) points out that pluralistic friendships celebrate

> *genuine* differences arising out of life experiences and culture but reject *socially constructed* differences resulting from stereotypes or discrimination. . . .
>
> Ethnicity is friendship-enhancing when it does not make another group into an "Other" group.
>
> Ethnicity is friendship-enhancing when we make it an "and" not a "but." The difference is palpable: "She's my friend *and* she's Jewish" allows me the pride of difference that a "but" would destroy.
>
> Group pride spawns both pride *and* prejudice. What makes a group special also makes it different. For some people, "different" must mean "better" or it is experienced as "worse." But people who do not need ethnic supremacy to feel ethnic pride find comfort and attitudinal regeneration among their "own kind" and also are able to make friends across racial and ethnic boundaries. (pp. 187–188)

Pogrebin's comments on ethnicity apply to other group differences (e.g., disability, age, social class) that affect relationship development as well.

Do we want to approach people who are different, or continue to avoid them? We believe that relationships with strangers provide a chance for us to grow as individuals (see Chapter 14). The choice about developing these relationships, however, is an individual one. We encourage you to make a conscious choice about whether or not you want to communicate effectively and develop relationships with strangers rather than relying on your unconscious, mindless decisions. If you choose to approach strangers and are mindful of your communication, you will recognize real differences and eventually discover similarities between yourselves and the strangers with whom you communicate. The similarities you discover provide the foundation for developing intimate relationships.

ROMANTIC RELATIONSHIPS WITH STRANGERS

Much of the material discussed in the preceding section on the development of interpersonal relationships also applies to the development of romantic relationships with strangers. In this section we focus, therefore, on selected aspects of communication with strangers that are unique to romantic relationships. We begin by examining dating relationships with strangers. We conclude with an examination of intercultural marriages.

Intercultural Dating Relationships

Research by Lampe (1982) on interethnic dating (European American–African American, European American–Latino/Latina American, African American–Latino/Latina American) in the United States indicates that the major motivation for interethnic dating is the same as for intraethnic dating, namely, personal liking for the other person. In fact, in Lampe's study, no other reason for interethnic dating comes close to personal liking in terms of the percentage of respondents giving it (personal liking is reported by 60 percent of the respondents; no other reason is given by more than 16 percent of the respondents). Lampe's study, in contrast, reveals no consistent reason against interethnic dating. "The most commonly cited reason given by both males and females was a lack of desire" (p. 118); however, this response was given by less than 35 percent of the respondents. The most common reasons against interethnic dating given by European Americans in Lampe's study are "no desire," "don't know any well enough," and "no chance." The most common reasons given by African Americans are "no desire," "hadn't thought of it," and "no chance." Mexican Americans give "don't know any well enough," "no desire," and "no chance" as the most common reasons against interethnic dating.

Kitano et al. (1984) point out that Asian Americans marry out of their group more than any other non-European American ethnic group in the United States. Their research also indicates that Asian Americans who are born in the United States are more likely to date out of their group than are Asian Americans who immigrate to the United States. They also note that Asian American females are more likely to date and marry out of their group than are Asian American males. The latter finding is supported by extensive research (e.g., Kitano & Chai, 1982; Lee & Yamanaka, 1990; Weiss, 1970). Johnson and Ogasawara (1984) also report that individuals from higher socioeconomic groups are more likely to date and marry out of their groups than are individuals from lower socioeconomic groups.

One possible reason that Asian American females date out of their own ethnic group more than males has to do with the stereotypes individuals hold. Weiss (1970), for example, points out that European American males have positive stereotypes of Chinese American females (e.g., "sexy," "quiet," "subservient") and Chinese American females have negative stereotypes of Chinese American males (e.g., "weak," "traditional," "old-fashioned"). This combination of stereotypes facilitates interethnic dating for Chinese American females. Chung (1990) also argues that individuals who hold negative stereotypes of members of the opposite sex in the in-group are more likely to date out of their group than those who hold favorable stereotypes.

Tucker and Mitchell-Kernan (1995) report that over half of the African Americans, Latino/Latina Americans, and European Americans in the survey in southern California date members of other ethnic groups. Their survey indicates that interethnic dating is associated with young males who are highly educated, and with people who perceive the possibility of marrying with members of other ethnic groups. Their data also suggest that African Americans and Latino/Latina Americans are more likely to engage in interethnic dating than are European Americans.

Alba (1976) argues that the strength of individuals' ethnic identities is related to their outgroup dating and marriage. Specifically, he contends that those with weaker identities have a greater tendency to date/marry out of their group than do those with strong identities. Parsonson's (1987) research supports this contention, but also suggests there may be ethnic differences. Her data suggest that this relationship may not hold for non-Anglos in Canada.

Chung (1990) applies Cross' (1970) model of ethnic identity transformation to explain interethnic dating. Cross argues that individuals go through four stages of ethnic identity transformation: (1) preencounter—individuals view the world as being against their ethnic group and behave in ways which devalue their ethnic identity; (2) encounter—individuals become aware of what it means to be a member of their ethnic group and begin to validate themselves in terms of their ethnic identity; (3) immersion-emersion—individuals reject nonethnic values and immerse themselves in their ethnic culture; and (4) internalization—individuals develop a self-confident and secure ethnic identity and, at the same time, are comfortable expressing nonethnic interests. Chung argues that individuals in the preencounter and internalization stages are more likely to date out of their ethnic group than are individuals in the encounter or immersion-emersion stages.

Another factor that influences the decision to date strangers is the degree to which strangers are perceived to be typical members of their culture. Gudykunst and his associates (1991) report that individuals in intercultural romantic relationships see their partners as atypical of their culture. The Japanese respondents, for example, view their North American partners as different from other North Americans and as possessing some Japanese characteristics.

Intergroup Marriages

The decision to date or become friends with a stranger is not the same as the decision to marry such a person. A marriage with a stranger requires a lifelong commitment to live with a person who is culturally different. While any marriage calls for adjustments, marriages to strangers generally demand more adjustments on the part of both partners than do marriages to people who are familiar. One of the adjustments necessary is adjusting to the ingroup's reaction to intergroup couples. Research (National Opinion Research Center, 1991), however, suggests that European Americans in the United States are becoming more tolerant of interethnic marriages. In 1970, European American disapproval of laws prohibiting interethnic marriages was only 48 percent. In 1990, 77 percent of European Americans disapproved of such laws. Even though there is more disapproval of these laws, many people still consider interethnic relationships taboo (Johnson & Warren, 1994). Also, interethnic marriages are still relatively rare; for example, the U.S. Bureau of the Census (1992) reports that only 1.9 percent of all marriages are interethnic. This figure, nevertheless, is about three times larger than the percent of interethnic marriages in 1970.

People get married for a wide variety of reasons. When one chooses to marry a stranger, the choice, like the decision to date, is often based on the same reasons for which one would choose to marry a person who is familiar (e.g., for love or upward mobility). People in interracial marriages, for example, report being attracted to their partners because they hold similar values and have similar interests (Kouri & Lasswell, 1993), or because they get along well (Rosenblatt, Karis, & Powell, 1995). There are, however, other motivations coming into play in marriages to strangers that may not be factors in marriages to people who are familiar (Char, 1977). To illustrate, while chance and availability play a major role in any marriage, these reasons often take on increased importance in marriages to strangers. When strangers are living in or visiting another culture, they are in close proximity to potential marriage partners from the host culture and far away from any from their home culture (Char, 1977). Often marriages to strangers take place simply because people from another culture are the only available partners; for example, United States military personnel living overseas may marry host-country nationals because they are the only available candidates.

Related to chance and availability are practical reasons for marrying strangers. Char (1977) cites the following as an example of a practical reason: "A poor . . . German girl may consent to marry [an African American] soldier stationed in post-war Germany for the material benefits he can give her, and the opportunity to escape from her unhappy home and come to America" (p. 35). In citing this example, Char does not imply these are the only reasons a white German woman might marry an African American serviceman from the United States, only that they are possible reasons.

Another reason for marrying strangers is the beliefs we hold about their culture. These beliefs, of course, may be based on actual characteristics of the strangers' culture or they may be beliefs not grounded in reality. To illustrate, a European American "male might marry a Japanese woman because he feels a Japanese female can better satisfy his desire to have a wife who is willing to wait on him" (Char, 1977, p. 37). Such a belief may be based on messages given by his parents or the mass media. Parents, for example, may consciously or unconsciously suggest that members of another culture are desirable or undesirable marriage partners.

No matter what the motivation for entering into a marriage, once married, the partners must learn to adjust to living with each other. Disapproval of family, friends, and members of the community are not problems unique to intercultural marriages, but the resulting rejection and discrimination are (Stuart & Abt, 1973). Fontaine and Dorch's (1980) research reveals that interethnic marriages have more severe problems than intraethnic marriages. Similarly, Markoff (1977) observes that partners in intercultural marriages have difficulty in communicating and in coping with external disapproval. Graham, Moeai, and Shizuru (1985) also report that there are more external problems in intercultural marriages than in intracultural marriages even though both groups were equally satisfied with their marriages.

In addition to partners' ability to adjust to external demands, the success of a marriage depends on the ability of each party to adjust to living with the other person. In interracial marriages, the problem of racism cannot be ignored. Partners' racists beliefs may come out accidentally when they are angry. Rosenblatt, Karis, and Powell (1995) point out that overcoming racism, even in interracial marriages, is a lifelong project.

Another problem in marriages between strangers is that very often the individuals are not prepared to recognize cultural differences (Tseng, 1977). When confronted with a particular situation, both partners react on the basis of their cultural backgrounds, neither recognizing that the other is reacting from a different set of cultural standards. Tseng argues that

> any problems or differences which may exist within an intercultural marriage will not be solved easily just because cognitively the persons are aware of the reason for the differences and strategically there is a prescribed solution for it. Culture is something which is learned through experiences in early life. An individual has developed strong emotional attachments to his [or her] culture—associated with his [or her] belief system, values, and habits—his [or her] style of life. In the process of intercultural marriage adjustment, he [or she] has to learn how to overcome, correct, and adjust his [or her] emotional reaction to the necessary change and expansion of his [or her] cultural behavior. (pp. 96–97)

What Tseng says about marriage between culturally dissimilar partners can also be applied to the development of friendships between strangers.

Tseng (1977) describes five general patterns of adjustment in marriages between culturally dissimilar partners: (1) one-way adjustment, (2) alternative adjustment, (3) mid-point compromise, (4) mixing, and (5) creative adjustment. The *one-way adjustment* pattern takes place when one spouse totally adopts the cultural patterns of the other. Such an adjustment may be with regard to one particular aspect of a culture (e.g., religion, food, or language) or the whole constellation of cultural behaviors. This pattern of adjustment is common when one culture is extremely dominant; also, it often is selected because of the practicality of everyday life.

Alternative adjustment occurs when both spouses insist that their cultural patterns be followed and when it is impossible for either to mix or give up cultural behavior, according to Tseng (1977). Again, this pattern may involve only one aspect of a culture or both cultures as wholes. Tseng cites an example of a couple (one Catholic, one Buddhist) who decide to have two wedding ceremonies to meet the requirements of both their cultures.

Mid-point compromise occurs when the partners compromise or meet in the middle. Tseng (1977) cites a couple of which the husband is from China and the wife is from the United States. The husband feels an obligation to send his family in China $100 a month (the extended family is most important), but the wife objects because she thinks they cannot spare the money (the nuclear family is most important). In order to address both of their needs, they settle on a mid-point compromise—the husband sends his family $50 a month rather than $100 as he originally planned.

Couples also can mix the two cultures in their marriage. This *mixing* might be random and awkward, or balanced and harmonious. While such a mixing is most obvious in concrete matters (e.g., home furnishings, eating patterns, religious behavior), it may also involve concepts and ideas, according to Tseng. That is, the partners may develop their own values, norms, and rules of behavior, which are a mix of their original cultures.

Creative adjustment takes place when a couple gives up both of the original cultures and decides to "invent" new behaviors for their marriage (Tseng, 1977). This pattern of adjustment may be necessary because of conflict between the couple's cultures (e.g., traditional dinner-eating patterns in the United States and in some Eastern cultures are not highly compatible), or it may come about because neither partner is satisfied with his or her own culture.

Marriages between culturally dissimilar partners do have unique problems of adjustment, but they should not be viewed simply as problematic. There is also a positive side to such marriages. They can be a source of personal growth for the partners, as well as a source of social change for the culture in which they take place.

SUMMARY

In this chapter, we examine selected aspects of the interpersonal relationships we develop with strangers. Cultural similarity is not a requirement for the development of an interpersonal relationship. In the absence of cultural similarity, linguistic similarity and similarity along other dimensions (e.g., occupation, attitudes) may be necessary. If sufficient similarity is perceived during initial interactions, culturally dissimilar communicators may meet again, thereby making it possible for the development of a more intimate relationship.

The initial stages of our relationships with strangers may be different from those of our relationships with people who are familiar. Depending on the culture from which strangers come, for example, they may reduce uncertainty differently than we do. Strangers from collectivistic cultures will seek demographic information, while those from individualistic cultures will seek information regarding attitudes and values.

If our relationships with strangers reach the stage of friendship, then the culture from which the strangers come becomes less important. In other words, since friendships have a personalistic focus in which cultural stereotypes are broken down, the culture from which the stranger comes is not a major factor in predicting behavior in a close relationship. Friendships with strangers and with people who are familiar, therefore, exhibit more similarities than differences. What differences do exist are best attributed to the idiosyncratic rules and structure of particular relationships.

There are similarities and differences in romantic relationships across cultures. It appears that openness, involvement, shared nonverbal meanings, and relational assessment are themes in romantic relationships across cultures. At least some of the differences which do exist are related to individualism-collectivism. Physical attractiveness of partners, for example, is more important in individualistic cultures than in collectivistic cultures.

While people in the United States appear to be more tolerant of intercultural marriages than in the past, intercultural couples still face discrimination. If intercultural marriages are to succeed, the partners must learn to accommodate to each others' cultural patterns of behavior.

STUDY QUESTIONS

1. How are friendships different from friendly relations?
2. What are the elementary forms of social relationships that exist across cultures?
3. How do the categories of relationships used in the United States and Japan differ?
4. How do the intimacy ratings of relationships differ in Japan and the United States?
5. How is uncertainty reduced in individualistic and collectivistic cultures?
6. How does self-disclosure differ in individualistic and collectivistic cultures?
7. How does face negotiation differ in individualistic and collectivistic cultures?
8. How do romantic relationships differ in individualistic and collectivistic cultures?
9. Why do we have relatively few relationships with strangers?
10. How does uncertainty reduction differ when we communicate with strangers from when we communicate with people who are familiar?
11. What factors influence our anxiety when we communicate with strangers?
12. How do linguistic and cultural knowledge contribute to developing relationships with strangers?
13. How does perceived similarity contribute to developing relationships with strangers?
14. What factors contribute to African Americans' and Latino/Latina Americans' satisfaction when communicating with European Americans?
15. What are the major patterns of adjustment used in marriages in which the partners come from dissimilar cultures?

SUGGESTED READING

Gudykunst, W. B., & Ting-Toomey, S., with Chua, E. (1988). *Culture and interpersonal communication.* Beverly Hills, CA: Sage.

Gudykunst, W. B., Ting-Toomey, S., & Nishida, T. (Eds.). (1996). *Communication in personal relationships across cultures.* Thousand Oaks, CA: Sage.

Hatfield, E., & Rapson, R. (1995). *Love and sex: A cross-cultural perspective.* Boston: Allyn & Bacon.

Pogrebin, L. (1987). *Among friends.* New York: McGraw-Hill.

Rosenblatt, P., Karis, T., & Powell, R. (1995). *Multiracial couples.* Thousand Oaks, CA: Sage.

Ting-Toomey, S. (Ed.). (1994). *The challenge of facework.* Albany: State University of New York Press.

Ting-Toomey, S., & Korzenny, F. (Eds.). (1991). *Cross-cultural interpersonal communication.* Newbury Park, CA: Sage.

13

Adapting to New Cultures

Be bent, and you will remain straight.
Be vacant, and you will remain full.
Be worn, and you will remain new.
Lao Tsu

In the preceding chapter, we discuss various aspects of developing interpersonal relationships with strangers. We now focus our attention on strangers and examine how they adapt to a new and unfamiliar cultural environment and how their communication activities influence their adaptation. Conversely, we become strangers ourselves and must undergo the same adaptation process as we move to an unfamiliar culture. Usually this adaptation is associated with major cultural gaps that occur as a result of strangers' relocation from one society or subsection of a society to another, as well as with changes in their social environments.

A list of examples of situations that involve cross-cultural adaptation is presented by Taft (1977) under five headings: sojourning, settling, subcultural mobility, segregation, and change in society. While the first two involve geographic mobility, the other three do not. Examples of *in situ* changes requiring adaptation include such situations as starting at a university, making a transition from school to work, changing professions, getting married, getting divorced, retiring, and aging (Moos, 1976). Also included are the processes of accepting major social and technological innovations such as computerized information-processing systems. There are also situations in which strangers are incorporated into a new social system, including the military services, religious orders, residential universities, mental hospitals, rehabilitation centers, prisons, and concentration camps.

Situations that result from moving to new locations include those encountered by international students, Peace Corps volunteers, foreign business personnel, missionaries, military personnel stationed in foreign countries, diplomats, and technical advisors or administrators, as well as increasing numbers of individuals who seek employment for prolonged periods of time overseas. There are also immigrants and refugees who have voluntarily or involuntarily moved to another country intending to start a new life on a more or less permanent basis. Also, individuals moving from a small rural town to a large metropolitan area, or vice versa, are in a situation that requires a degree of cross-cultural adaptation.

International migration, whether for a long or short term, represents a classic situation where the newly arrived strangers are required to face substantial challenges of uncertainty. Because of the relatively greater severity of cultural change, the experiences of international immigrants, refugees, and sojourners provide us with comprehensive insights into the process of cross-cultural adaptation that can be extended to understanding the situations of other less drastic adaptation situations. The following examination, therefore, focuses on the adaptation process that takes place in the context of international migration and is based primarily on Y. Kim's theory that describes and explains the cross-cultural adaptation process from an interdisciplinary, communication perspective (Y. Kim, 1979c, 1988, 1991a, 1995a, 1995b, in press).

CROSS-CULTURAL ADAPTATION

Situations involving international migration and motives for such migration vary widely (Berry, 1990; Furnham, 1988; Volkan, 1993). Abrupt and involuntary cultural transitions, for instance, are experienced by refugees around the world who have left their homeland involuntarily as a result of war or natural disasters. Owing to the sudden nature of their departure, most refugees have little chance to prepare themselves for life in the host country. At least during the initial resettlement phase, many suffer from a deep psychological dislocation and sense of loss (Chan & Lam, 1987; Y. Kim, 1980, 1989a, 1989d).

Even when the transition is made voluntarily, international migrants differ in their motivation to relocate and to make the host society their "second home." The motivation to adapt depends largely on the degree of permanence of the new residence. In the case of immigrants, they must reestablish their life conditions and attain a permanent membership in the host society. They need to be concerned with their relationship to the new environment in the same way as the members of the native population are. A peripheral contact with the new culture, on the other hand, is typical of the situation of many sojourners. Reasons for a sojourn are often specifically to pursue a vocation, to obtain a degree, or merely to enhance one's prestige in the eyes of the folks back home. Such reasons may require less motivation to adapt to the host cultural system. International students, for example, can reduce their adaptation to the bare minimum as they pursue a degree by confining their social contact to fellow students from their home country. Similarly, military personnel and their families in foreign countries may perceive less need to adapt to the host culture since their stay is only temporary and their contacts confined largely to the military base.

Regardless of the circumstantial and motivational variations, every stranger in a new environment must respond to the challenges of finding ways to function in that environment. Every stranger must undergo a process of adaptation that makes such functioning possible.

The Process of Adaptation

Throughout the socialization process, we learn and acquire "all the factors and processes which make one human being fit to live in the company of others" (Kelvin, 1970, p. 270). Socialization involves conditioning and programming in the basic processes of communication, including decoding (perceptual and cognitive) patterns and encoding (verbal and nonverbal) training. The form of this training depends on the particular culture and is embedded in the process of *enculturation*. Berger and Luckmann (1967) point out that the forms for expressing and comprehending basic social behavior are internalized from the teachings of early "significant others" and become "the world, the only existent and conceivable world" (p. 134), with a strong emotional overtone and identification. The process of socialization provides children with an understanding of their world and with the culturally patterned modes of responding to it. The familiar culture, then, is the "home world," which is associated closely with the family or significant others. An unfamiliar culture, in contrast, is one that is out of harmony with one's basic understanding of self and reality.

When strangers move into a new and unfamiliar culture and interact in it, the process of resocialization, or *acculturation*, occurs. Gradually, strangers begin to detect similarities and differences within the new surroundings. They become acquainted with and adopt some of the norms and values of salient reference groups of the host society. As acculturation takes place, however, some unlearning of old cultural patterns occurs as well, at least in the sense that new responses are adopted in situations that previously would have evoked different ones. This unlearning of the original cultural habits is called *deculturation*.

As the dynamic interplay of acculturation and deculturation continues, newcomers gradually undergo a cross-cultural adaptation process. Of course, a change in their basic values is extremely difficult, slow, and rare. Brim (in Brim & Wheeler, 1966) suggests that more common adaptive changes in strangers take place in more superficial areas, such as overt role behavior. A person can be pressed to conform to requirements in social interactions but cannot be forced to accept and appreciate the underlying values. Goffman (1961) also doubts whether true resocialization occurs in practice, even in a "total institution" such as prison.

Even with the limit in acculturative changes, a new culture does have a substantial influence on the psychological and social behaviors of strangers. Through group support, institutional legitimization of the new identity, and the presence of new significant others to replace those of childhood, strangers may adopt the cultural patterns of the host society to a significant degree. Even then, the acculturative change is accomplished only slowly and in stages. It normally brings conflict, a struggle between the desire to retain old customs and to keep the original cultural identity on the one hand, and the desire to adopt new ways to seek harmony with the changed milieu on the other (Boekestijn, 1988). This conflict is, in essence, between the need for acculturation and the resistance to deculturation, the push of the new culture and the pull of the old, and between the existing conditions inside the strangers and the demands of the external environment. It is, then, a conflict that is not unlike the experiences of members of the older generations who often find themselves in the situation of "involuntary immigrants from the past to the present" (Mead, 1963).

Adaptation and Change

The core of cross-cultural adaptation is change (Dyal & Dyal, 1981). Unlike the native-born members of the host society, who often attempt to change and succeed in changing portions of the environment to better suit their needs, strangers are almost exclusive bearers of the burden of making adjustments themselves. The power of individual strangers to change the host environment is miniscule, at least in the short run, when compared with the pervasive influence the host culture has on them. Clearly, a reason for the essentially one-sided change is the diffference between the size of the population sharing a given stranger's original culture and that of the population sharing the host culture. To the extent the dominant power of the host culture controls the daily survival and functioning of strangers, it presents a coercive pressure on them to adapt.

The direction of acculturative change in strangers is toward *assimilation,* that is, a state of a high degree of acculturation into the host milieu and a high degree of deculturation of the original culture. It is a state that reflects a maximum convergence of strangers' internal conditions with those of the natives and of a minimum maintenance of the original cultural habits. Indeed, studies of historical change in immigrant communities have demonstrated the long-term assimilative trend of the cross-cultural adaptation process, particularly across generations (e.g., Barnett & Kincaid, 1983; Y. Kim, 1977a, 1977b, 1978a, 1978b, 1980, 1989a, 1989d; McGuire & McDermott, 1988; Subervi-Velez, 1986; Szalay & Inn, 1988). A study by the American Jewish Committee, for example, shows a significant increase in the members' merging into non-Jewish organizations and a substantial decrease in their Jewish identification (Zweigenhaft, 1979–1980). Masuda (1970) further demonstrates that ethnic identification of Japanese Americans in the United States shows a gradual decrease from the first generation to the third.

As summarized in Figure 13.1, the cross-cultural adaptation process involves a continuous interplay of deculturation and acculturation that brings about change in strangers in the direction of assimilation, the highest degree of adaptation theoretically conceivable. It is that process by which strangers are resocialized into a new culture, so as to attain an increasing compatibility and functional fitness. For most people, even for natives, complete adaptation is a lifetime goal and individuals vary in the degree of adaptation achieved. The adaptation of

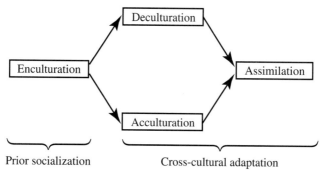

Prior socialization   Cross-cultural adaptation

Figure 13.1   Key terms associated with cross-cultural adaptation.

strangers, therefore, should be properly thought of as falling at some point on a continuum ranging from minimally adapted to maximally adapted (Taft, 1966, 1977, 1988).

THE ROLE OF COMMUNICATION

Underlying the adaptation process is the communication process: Adaptation occurs in and through communication. Just as natives have acquired their cultural patterns through interaction with others, strangers over time acquire the new cultural patterns through participating in the host communication activities. Conversely, strangers' communication patterns reveal their adaptation. Through prolonged and varied experiences in communication, strangers gradually learn and internalize the symbols and practices of the host communication system. The acquired communicative capabilities, in turn, serve as a set of adaptive tools assisting strangers to satisfy their personal and social needs. Through effective communication, strangers are able to increase control over their own behavior and over the host environment.

Because communication involves interaction of the person and the environment, we can examine the role of strangers' communication in the adaptation process in terms of two interrelated processes: personal communication and social communication (Ruben, 1975).

Personal Communication

Personal (or intrapersonal) communication refers to the three interrelated psychological processes—cognitive, affective, and operational—by which we organize ourselves in a sociocultural milieu. Through personal communication, we develop ways of understanding and responding to our environment. Ruben (1975) notes that "personal communication is thought of as sensing, making sense [of], or acting toward the objects and people in one's milieu. It is the process by which the individual informationally fits himself [or herself] into (adapts and adapts to) his [or her] environment" (pp. 168–169).

In the context of cross-cultural adaptation, personal communication can be viewed as the process of organizing adaptive experiences into identifiable cognitive, affective, and operational patterns that are consistent or compatible with the cultural patterns of the host environment. Strangers' personal communication patterns, thus, can be viewed in terms of their *host communication competence,* that is, the capability to communicate in ways that are compatible and consistent with the communication codes and rules operating in the host culture. As strangers develop host communication competence, they are increasingly empowered to participate in the cultural processes of the host environment with fidelity and effectiveness. The level of strangers' host communication competence at a given time, in turn, should reflect their overall adaptation level, while the lack of such competence manifests itself in various forms of "miscommunication" on the part of strangers (Banks, Gao, & Baker, 1991; Gass & Varonis, 1991).

The Cognitive Process.   One of the most fundamental adaptive changes in personal communication (or host communication competence) occurs in the cognitive structure through which strangers process information from the environment. Communication between strangers and hosts is successful to the extent that the strangers are able to comprehend the categorizing system of the hosts and match their own cognitive activities to those of the hosts.

Because of their unfamiliarity with the cognitive process of the host culture, strangers frequently find the mindset of the natives difficult to understand. Their difficulty stems from the fact that, particularly during the initial phases of adaptation, their perception of the host environment is simplistic. Gross stereotypes are salient in the strangers' perception of the host cultural patterns. The "thinking-as-usual," as we may call it, often becomes unworkable in dealing with the host environment since strangers do not share the common underlying assumptions of the native population. Schuetz (1944) argues that

> the cultural pattern of the approached group is to the stranger not a shelter but a field of adventure, not a matter of course but a questionable topic of investigation, not an instrument for disentangling problematic situations but a problematic situation itself and one hard to master. (p. 108)

The uncertainty and the accompanying anxiety, thus, are two of the most basic challenges that confront strangers. As such, Gudykunst and associates (Gao & Gudykunst, 1990; Gudykunst, 1988b, 1995; Gudykunst & Hammer, 1988b; Gudykunst & Sudweeks, 1992) have identified these two factors as central to explaining intercultural communication effectiveness in general and cross-cultural adaptation in particular.

Yet, to the extent that culture is a learned phenomenon, we recognize that strangers over time increase their understanding of the host cognitive system. Cultural learning enables them to recognize their cognitive structures as distinct from those of the host culture and to increase their ability in "perspective taking" (Fogel, 1979) and develop a "coorientation relation" with members of the host society (H. S. Kim, 1986; Pearce & Stamm, 1973). Empirical data from Y. Kim's study (1977a) of Korean immigrants suggest that, as the strangers' cultural knowledge becomes increasingly extensive, accurate, and refined, their cognitive structure in perceiving the host culture also becomes more discriminating and integrative. The increased cognitive complexity, in turn, has been found to lead to a greater capacity to understand the host culture and seek information from appropriate sources (Yum, 1982).

The Affective Process.   Over time, strangers learn to acquire not only cognitive complexity but also the affective patterns of the host culture. The affective cultural patterns are embodied in the common emotional orientations, aesthetic sensibilities, motivational drives, attitudes, and values held by the native members of the host society. Taft (1977) identifies this affective process as the "dynamic" aspect of culture:

> There are certain universal human needs and modes of functioning that must be satisfied in all cultures. In broad terms, these needs refer to the maintenance of life processes, the need to maintain a structural society to enhance as well as regulate social relationships, and to provide for the self-expressive needs of individuals. While these needs are universal, each culture prescribes different models for satisfying them. (p. 134)

Because all personal and social activities in the host society involve some measure of affective experiences, strangers must understand and participate in these activities not only intellectually, but also affectively.

Mansell (1981) argues that the fulfillment of aesthetic needs is important in an alien culture:

> The concept of aesthetic awareness is linked with ineffable, intuitive feelings of appreciation and celebration. This form of awareness creates a consciousness which transforms individuals' perceptions of the world and imparts a sense of unity between self and surrounding. . . . It is in this transformative mode of experiencing that many people create access to the momentary peaks of fulfillment which make life meaningful. (p. 99)

Because needs of this sort are often difficult to gratify within an unfamiliar culture, many newly arrived strangers experience decline in emotional well-being (Ying & Liese, 1991). One way they can compensate for this psychological difficulty is by withdrawing from the host nationals and by affiliating with other conationals or by communicating with their family and friends back home. In fact, ethnic communities commonly serve as the refuge for emotionally and aesthetically needy immigrants by offering a range of familiar cultural elements—from food, language, music, and entertainment to activities of socializing through churches and social clubs.

It is when the affective process is integrated successfully with the cognitive process that strangers achieve an adequate psychological and social orientation that enables them to appreciate and participate in the natives' experiences of joy, hope, and excitement, as well as their anger, pain, and disappointment.

The Operational Process.   What is ultimately required of strangers in the host society is the operational (or behavioral) capacity that enables them to carry out behaviors externally in accordance with the host cultural patterns (Ruben, 1976; Ruben & Kealey, 1979). Doing so requires a capacity to act and react appropriately in various social situations in addition to the relevant cognitive and affective abilities. Taft (1977) describes such behavioral capacity in terms of two types of skills: technical and social. *Technical skills* are basic practical skills, such as language skills, job skills, academic skills, and others that are essential to performing one's particular social role. A study of Japanese sojourners in the United States (Diggs & Murphy, 1991), for example, shows that the inability to drive a car is one of the significant factors that correlated with the strangers' level of satisfaction. *Social skills* are more general and crucial to all social interactions in that they encompass a wide range of capabilities, from initiating a simple conversation and adjusting to the behavioral patterns of different interaction partners to developing and solidifying a relationship and managing conflicts.

Strangers who are competent in technical skills may find it difficult to detect the patterns of communication behavior that are practiced. Even the natives of a culture who perform various social roles naturally are often unable to explain the specific patterns involved in certain situations. Strangers, therefore, need to formulate "action plans" before dealing with situations they face. North American businesspeople visiting a Japanese company also must rely on their own understanding of the way Japanese business is conducted in figuring out how to behave in performing their role as business negotiators.

Through trial and error, and through cumulative acquisition of cognitive and affective orientations of the host culture, strangers can and do increase their operational capabilities to enact appropriate and effective technical and social behaviors. Their action plans gradually become refined and integrated into sequences that can be used in a relatively automatic form. Well-adapted strangers can perform the required social roles without having to formulate a mental plan of action in accordance with the cultural rules and norms of the host society. This ability means they have internalized many culturally patterned behaviors that allow them to achieve synchronic harmony in their social transactions with the native-born individuals (Y. Kim, 1992, 1993). Insofar as these automatic actions are executed successfully, strangers experience satisfaction and success in performing their daily transactions.

The operational skills, together with the cognitive and affective orientations, constitute the overall host communication competence. As previously noted, this competence is the very capacity of a stranger to cope with various challenges of the new life and to achieve a cohesive functional relationship with the host society and enjoy participating in the emotional/aesthetic experiences of host nationals. Mastery of this competence, then, is equivalent to a full membership in the host communication system: This mastery, after all, is one of the key features that distinguish strangers from the host nationals.

Social Communication

Personal communication, or host communication competence, is linked to social communication in a reciprocal relationship. Strangers interacting with their new environment, knowingly or not, have opportunities to learn and regulate the cognitive, affective, and behavioral patterns of themselves and of host nationals. Strangers' improved communication competence, in turn, increases the likelihood of greater success in subsequent encounters.

Participation in the host social communication processes can take many forms—from simple observations of people on the street or reading about people and events in newspapers and magazines, to actively engaging in face-to-face encounters with people. There are two general forms of social communication: *interpersonal communication* and *mass communication*. Interpersonal communication occurs in the context of direct, one-on-one interpersonal relationships. Mass communication, on the other hand, is a more generalized form of social communication by which individuals interact with their environment without direct relational involvement with any particular person. Individuals participate in mass communication processes through various media, such as radio, television, newspapers, magazines, movies, theater, museums, and lectures, as well as audio- and videotapes, among others.

Interpersonal Communication.   Communication in interpersonal relationships is central to life. Fogel (1993) argues that individuals develop through their relationships with others. Communication in this context is particularly vital to strangers' cognitive, affective, and behavioral learning. Through formal and informal contacts and relationships, strangers can also find social support in attempting to handle difficulties as well as opportunities for finding additional contacts (Adelman, 1988; Y. Kim, 1986a, 1987; Pescosolidio, 1992; Wellman, 1992). At the same time, interpersonal networks exert social control by determining the language strangers must use and by conveying implicit or explicit messages of social approval and disapproval (Heckathorn, 1990; Ho & Sung, 1990; Milroy, 1980).

One can infer strangers' level of adaptation from their interpersonal communication activities involved in the relationships they have in their social network at a given time. An immigrant with a mainly ethnic relational network, for example, tends to be less adapted and probably less competent in the host communication system than someone whose associates are primarily members of the host society. Also, the degree of intimacy in the relationships developed with members of the host society is an important indicator of strangers' acculturative communication competence.

Considerable evidence exists to link strangers' adaptation level and their interpersonal relationship patterns. Studies of international students and visitors indicate a positive association between the number of natives in strangers' relational network and their positive feelings toward the host society at large. Also, the degree of interpersonal involvement has been found to be an important indicator of sojourners' cognitive learning. Selltiz and her associates (1963), for example, report that international students in the United States who associate extensively with and form close friendships with host nationals score higher on measures of adjustment than do those who have less association with host nationals or who do not have host friends. In Morris' (1960) study, students who are high on measures of social relations with host nationals score high on an index of satisfaction with various aspects of their experience in the host country (see also Coelho, 1958; Pool, 1965).

A similar linkage between interpersonal communication and elements of host communication competence has been observed in studies of long-term settlers in the United States and elsewhere (e.g., Y. Kim, 1976, 1977a, 1979a, 1980, 1989a; Y. Kim & Gudykunst, 1988a; Oehlkers, 1991; Searle & Ward, 1990; Shah, 1991). A consistent conclusion from these studies is a positive relationship between participation in host interpersonal communication activities and other aspects of adaptation, such as variables of host communication competence and psychological health. The immigrants who are most active in their host social communication activities, for example, tend also to show more favorable attitudes toward the new environment and enjoy greater satisfaction in their new life. Wen (1976) observed that the degree of mental illness Chinese immigrants experience tends to vary with the degree of social isolation from the host culture. Yum's (1982) study of Korean immigrants in Hawaii further suggests that the immigrants' ability to acquire information necessary for their functioning in the United States is influenced positively by the level of integration of Hawaiians in the immigrants' information sources. In addition, a study of Native Americans in Oklahoma (Kim, Lujan, & Shaver, 1994) indicates that the psychological adaptation in the predominantly European American environment is linked closely to the level of inclusion of non-Native American acquaintances and friends in the Native Americans' relational network.

With respect to intraethnic communication activities, researchers generally agree that extensive and prolonged intraethnic involvements tend to retard the adaptation process in the long run. This observation is made despite the fact that the ethnic community often plays a vital role in assisting during the initial stages of adaptation of many newly arrived strangers. In many ethnic communities in the United States, new arrivals often find necessary emotional and social support and information from their family members, relatives, and other fellow compatriots (Mortland & Ledgerwood, 1988). Y. Kim's studies of Korean immigrants (1977a, 1977b, 1978a) and of Indochinese refugees (1979a, 1980, 1989a, 1989d) also have shown the heavy reliance on ethnic ties during the first several years in the United States, even though the numbers of both ethnic and host acquaintances tend to increase simultaneously during this period.

Supporting the adaptation-retarding effect of ethnic communication systems are the findings in various studies of immigrants conducted in the United States, including Bates' (1994) study of Asian immigrants' support networks; Hsu, Grant, and Huang's (1993) study of foreign students; Shah's (1991) study of Asian Indians; and Okazaki-Luff's study (1991) of Japanese sojourners. This insulating effect has been found to be even stronger when the strangers' ethnic ties consist primarily of coethnics who are themselves poorly adapted (Hsu, Grant, & Huang, 1993).

On the basis of these and related research findings, Y. Kim (1986b, 1987, 1988, 1995a, in press) postulates that strangers' interpersonal network changes over time from a primarily intraethnic composition to an increasing integration of ties with members of the host society. In this regard, the role of involvement with persons from the same culture is considered to promote ethnicity and, in the long run, slow their adaptation in the host society. This conclusion concurs with the observation of Shibutani and Kwan (1965) that "to the extent that . . . a minority group participated in different sets of communication channels, they develop different perspectives and have difficulty in understanding each other" (p. 582). Broom and Kitsuse (1955) similarly argue that "a large part of the acculturation experience of the members of an ethnic group may be circumscribed by the ethnic community" (p. 45).

Mass Communication.   Many studies of immigrants in the United States have shown that, along with the development of nonethnic interpersonal ties, the use of the mass media of the host society increases over time and that such an increased media use facilitates the adaptation process (e.g., Hong, 1980; Kapoor & Williams, 1979; J. Kim, 1980; J. Kim, Lee, & Jeong, 1982; Y. Kim, 1977a, 1977b, 1978a, 1979b, 1980; Pedone, 1980; Ryu, 1976; Subervi-Velez, 1986; Walker, 1993; Yang, 1988). Participation in the host mass communication processes enables strangers to learn about a broader spectrum of the elements of the host culture not easily discernible from their immediate environment. In transmitting messages that reflect aspirations, historical forces, myths, work and play, and specific issues and events, the mass media explicitly and implicitly convey societal values, norms, and traditional perspectives for interpreting the larger environment.

Exposure to information oriented media messages such as news items, analyses of social issues, and documentaries is particularly indicative of adaptation, as compared with exposure to primarily entertainment oriented messages (Y. Kim, 1976, 1979a). The overall adaptation function of mass communication is relatively more limited than that of interpersonal channels (Y. Kim, 1976, 1979a). This limitation is due to the often stereotypical, undifferentiated images of the host culture that mass media depict (G. Miller, 1988). In addition, interpersonal communication activities (particularly those that take place in direct face-to-face encounters) provide strangers with unsolicited feedback messages that subtly, yet powerfully, let the strangers recognize inadequacies in their behaviors.

The intensity inherent in many face-to-face communication situations may be too stressful to strangers poorly equipped in host communication competence. They may shy away from participating in such direct encounters with the natives. Accordingly, mass media provide alternative, less stressful channels of communication through which strangers with inadequate communication competence can absorb some elements of the host culture. Along with the mass media of the host society, ethnic media, including newspapers, magazines, audiotapes, and video-taped television programs and movies imported from the home country, are avail-able to most strangers. Many large ethnic communities in the United States also offer locally produced radio and television programs (S. Miller, 1987; Subvervi-Velez, 1986). Research has shown consistently that, in direct contrast to the in-creasing use of the host mass media over time, the level of interest and the per-ceived utility of ethnic media decreases as strangers become familiar with the host language and culture.

The processes of personal and social communication discussed above are summa-rized in Figure 13.2. Communication processes are essential to the cross-cultural adaptation process. Just as native-born people undergo their enculturation process through communication, strangers undergo the deculturation-acculturation inter-play. In this process, strangers acquire and internalize some of the cognitive, affective, and behavioral communication patterns operating in the host society. The acquired communication competence, in turn, facilitates their participation in the host social communication processes, both interpersonally and via mass media.

FACTORS INFLUENCING ADAPTIVE COMMUNICATION

Strangers respond differently to a new cultural environment in terms of their prior experiences, accepting what promises to be rewarding and rejecting what seems un-workable or disadvantageous. At the same time, strangers' experiences are condi-tioned further by the host environment. The nature of the dynamic interaction be-tween personal factors and environmental factors shapes the patterns of subsequent adaptive changes in strangers.

Predisposition

An important factor that needs to be considered in understanding strangers' adap-tation is the degree of difference (or similarity) between their *ethnicity* and the dominant ethnicity in the host society. Strangers from the United States, for exam-ple, have a greater adaptive potential when they move to Canada than to Thailand. To the extent that the original ethnic patterns coincide with those of the host na-tionals, less adjustment is necessary. The greater the disparity between the two, the more difficulty there is in strangers' adaptation and the larger the numerous gaps that must be bridged. Differences in language, verbal and nonverbal behaviors, rules and norms of social engagement, economic and political ideology, as well as religious beliefs, ceremonies, and rituals are some of the major ethnicity gaps to be overcome in the adaptation process.

    Students from Europe have an easier time developing social relationships with North Americans than do other international students studying in the United States. Lysgaard (1955) and Sewell and Davidsen (1961) describe Scandinavian

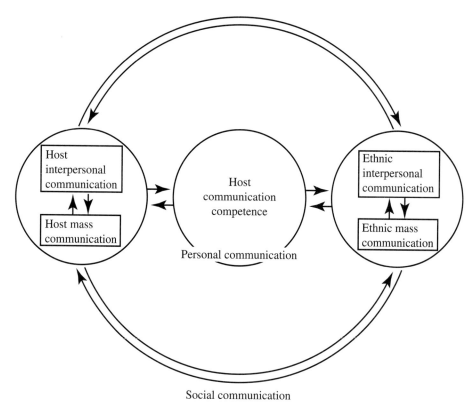

Figure 13.2   Interrelated processes of personal and social communication
(*Source:* Y. Kim, 1988, p. 65).

students as having little difficulty in adapting to life in the United States, while Lambert and Bressler (1956) and Bennett, Passin, and McKnight (1958) report considerable difficulty on the part of students from India and Japan, respectively. Similar results are reported by Furnham and Bochner (1982) for international students in England.

Another important factor of ethnicity is the degree of *salience* of *physical distinctiveness* (Y. Kim, 1986a, 1989c). Outstanding attributes such as skin color, facial features, and physique often add to the overall "foreignness" of strangers, playing a favorable or unfavorable role in the strangers' subsequent communication with host nationals. An Irish immigrant in the United States, for example, is likely to present less of a psychological distance to native-born North Americans than someone from India.

Along with ethnicity, the *personality* of individual strangers plays an important role in their adaptation. Everyone possesses a set of certain basic dispositions that are more or less enduring and adaptive. Personality patterns make all individuals unique, and such uniquenesses reveal themselves dramatically when strangers are struggling to adapt to a new environment. When strong prejudice or actual enmity exists toward strangers, for instance, some strangers are able to win a position of respect and the good will of host nationals while others respond with hostility and withdrawal.

Various personality attributes have been observed in empirical research to be associated with adaptation. Among such attributes are tolerance for ambiguity and risk taking (Fiske & Maddi, 1961), gregariousness (Bradburn, 1969), internal locus of control (Johnson & Sarason, 1978; Yum, 1988a), and a hardy or resilient personality (Quisumbing, 1982). Yum (1988a), for example, reports a finding that immigrants' internal locus of control (the tendency to place the responsibility for events within themselves) is associated positively with the extent to which they develop host national acquaintances. In addition, behavioral characteristics that reflect extroversion, positive orientation, respect for people in general, and self-control have been identified as contributing to effective adaptation in the new culture.

These and related personal attributes share considerable semantic redundancy, and are consolidated by Y. Kim (1988, 1995a, in press) into two higher-level constructs, *openness* and *strength*. Openness as a personality construct serves as the inclusive generic baseline for specific attributes, such as flexibility, open-mindedness, tolerance for ambiguity, gregariousness, optimism, and extroversion. Correspondingly, strength as a personality construct represents concepts of narrower meanings, such as internal locus of control, persistence, hardiness, resourcefulness, and self-confidence.

In addition to the factors of personality and ethnicity, the adaptive potential of strangers is further a matter of *preparedness* for change prior to entering the new environment (Y. Kim, 1976, 1977a, 1988, 1995a, in press). Strangers move to a new environment with differing levels of realism in their expectations and knowledge about the environment (Brabant, Palmer, & Gramling, 1990). Many cross-cultural training and orientation programs, thus, emphasize familiarizing trainees with their host culture (Brislin & Yoshida, 1994; Landis & Brislin, 1983). Peace Corps volunteers are among the best prepared for cross-cultural adaptation in that they go through an intensive screening process and extensive language and cultural training before being given an overseas assignment. Sewell and Davidsen (1961) also have found that the guidance international students receive prior to coming to the United States positively influences their academic adjustment and satisfaction with the sojourn.

Certain demographic characteristics also tend to increase strangers' adaptive potential. In studies of immigrants, *age* is considered a critical element in subsequent adaptation in the host society. The older strangers are, the greater the difficulty they experience in adapting to a new culture and the slower they are in acquiring new cultural elements (Y. Kim, 1976, 1977a; Rogler et al., 1980; Szapocznik & Kurtines, 1980; Szapocznik, Kurtines, & Fernandez, 1980; Searle & Ward, 1990). This inverse relationship between age and adaptation can be attributed to the greater rigidity (or lesser openness) of the personality structure that tends to grow as we grow older.

Another important demographic factor is the *educational level* of strangers prior to migration. Education, regardless of its cultural context, appears to expand our mental capacity for new learning and for the challenges of life in general. In many cases, strangers' education in their home country includes training in the language of the host country, which provides an added leverage for building communication competencies after moving into the new system (Y. Kim, 1976, 1977a, 1980; Yum, 1982).

Environment

The adaptation process is influenced not only by strangers' adaptive predisposition but also by the conditions existing or developing in the host society (Y. Kim, 1979c, 1988, 1991a, 1994a, 1995a, 1995b, in press). The adaptation process involves an interactive "push and pull" between the strangers and the environment. The adaptation experiences of two very similar persons may differ in two different environments.

The environment influences strangers' adaptation by way of defining the *interaction potential*, the degree of opportunity provided by the immediate physical and social environment for strangers to communicate with hosts (Y. Kim, 1976, 1977a, 1978b; Y. Kim, Lujan, & Shaver, 1994). Ordinarily, if a situation is to have any interaction potential at all, it must provide for physical proximity. Beyond this basic requirement, social contexts differ greatly in interaction potential. People in the United States, for example, do not usually talk to strangers sitting next to them in the subway or on a bus. If, on the other hand, strangers are assigned to work with people on a collaborative task, they soon cease to be unknown. Such social contexts are high in interaction potential, almost demanding communication of some sort and making it easy to go beyond superficial exchange if strangers so wish.

Thus, international students who live without host roommates in buildings not predominantly occupied by host students are likely to have relatively little interaction with host nationals outside of classrooms. Ting-Toomey (1981), in her study of Chinese American college students, reports that the students' friendship formation is influenced significantly by the availability of European Americans within their school environment. Similarly, U.S. military personnel who live in a predominantly military town have limited access to local people in their daily activities. Peace Corps volunteers, in contrast, have a greater interaction potential and develop more meaningful interpersonal relationships with the host nationals.

The interaction potential for cultural strangers depends on the *receptivity* of the host society toward them (Y. Kim, 1988, 1995a, 1995b, in press). Receptivity refers to the attitude present in the host environment that shows openness and acceptance toward strangers. Strong hostility against a group minimizes the receptivity of the host society toward individual members of that group and, consequently, makes communication more difficult for them. The attitudes of the native population toward a specific group may be due to a long-standing historical animosity. New developments in international relationships may abruptly change a traditionally held attitude between groups, as has been the case recently in the increased openness among Americans toward Russians and the increased suspicion toward some of the Middle Easterners.

Sometimes, the attitude or sentiment of the host society toward an outside group may be influenced by its own domestic economic or political situation, such as a high unemployment rate or a prevailing conservative ideology. Mass media play a particularly important role in determining the emotional mood of the host society toward other cultural groups. Media news coverage of various international and domestic events tends to influence public sentiment and opinion concerning various target groups. Once a societal climate is developed, some unusual situations may arise in the host society regarding specific groups of strangers, such as direct social segregation in housing, discrimination in employment, and social isolation by exclusion from intimate and sympathetic social contacts. These and other discriminatory practices in the host environment can make the already difficult cultural adaptation of strangers even more trying.

The adaptive experiences of strangers are further influenced by the degree of *conformity pressure* the host society places on the strangers (Y. Kim, 1988, 1995a, in press). The extent that the host society expects strangers to conform to its existing cultural norms and values varies from society to society. Strangers entering a totalitarian society or one that follows some ideological orthodoxy may be forced to conform rapidly to assigned roles that cover many aspects of their daily activities. Relatively freer and more pluralistic societies such as the United States, on the other hand, allow a greater latitude or tolerance for cultural differences.

A similar observation can be made about the differences in the cultural rigidity of the small rural town and the openness of the large metropolitan area toward diverse lifestyles. The heterogeneous and cosmopolitan cultural milieu of the metropolitan area exhibits greater freedom for new and different elements. One cannot point to this or that particular type of relationship and behavior as forming the basis of the social and cultural system of a city since many types contribute to this end, no one of which may be excluded. Yet, the presence of strangers can be a matter of keen interest in villages, and they may be subjected to close scrutiny. If strangers are to be accepted by the villagers, they are likely to find it hard not to learn and conform to the accepted practices of the local people.

The degree to which a given host environment extends receptivity to and exerts conformity pressure on a stranger is closely influenced by *the strength of the stranger's ethnic group* relative to the host environment at large (Y. Kim, 1994a, 1995a, in press). An insight into ethnic group strength has been provided by a number of investigators, such as sociologists Clarke and Obler (1976), who describe ethnic communities developing from the stages of initial economic adjustment and community building to the subsequent stage of aggressive self-assertion and promotion of identity. An additional insight has been offered in theories of institutional completeness (Breton, 1964, 1991; Goldenberg & Haines, 1992) and of ethnolinguistic vitality and intergroup behavior (Giles & Johnson, 1987). These theories point to the ecological conditions of a strong ethnic group and its influence on the psychology and communication behavior of its individual members.

In the long run, the strength of an ethnic group tends to discourage the strangers' development of host communication competence and their participation in the host social communication processes. Inglis and Gudykunst (1982) have examined the interpersonal communication patterns of Korean immigrants in the Hartford, Connecticut, area and compared them with the findings from Y. Kim's (1976, 1977a, 1978a, 1978b) studies of the same group in the Chicago area. The comparison yields a significant difference in the Korean immigrants' interaction with other Koreans. Members of the smaller and less organized Hartford-area Korean community have far fewer Korean acquaintances than do members of the Chicago-area community, where a more established system of ethnic organizations and communication activities exists. A more recent study of Korean communities in southern California (Shim, 1994) has reported a similar ethnicity-reinforcing influence of the immigrants' usage of Korean newspapers.

ADAPTATION AND PSYCHOLOGICAL HEALTH

Individuals in a new environment change naturally and inevitably as long as they remain in contact with the host environment. Adaptive changes are not necessarily planned or preferred by strangers. As Taft (1977) explains, even those who interact with the natives with the intention of confining themselves to only superficial relationships are likely to become at least minimally adapted to the host culture in time "in spite of themselves" (p. 150). Nor do adaptive changes necessarily serve to pursue or achieve clear goals concerning tasks to be accomplished. Adaptive changes, instead, are a cumulative result of all conceivable communication activities—conscious, unconscious, instrumental, noninstrumental, personal, and interpersonal. Large or sudden modifications are more likely during the initial phase of adaptation, producing intense stress in strangers' internal conditions (Moos, 1976).

An important outcome of strangers' adaptive transformation is psychological or mental health (Y. Kim, 1988, in press). When we are fully in control of ourselves in a new environment, we possess a high level of host communication competence—cognitive, affective, and operational. These psychological processes not only are present simultaneously but also are well coordinated and balanced. For a long time, however, strangers are likely to be lacking in any one or more of the three processes, resulting in frequent experiences of internal imbalance and lack of harmony. Some strangers may be quite knowledgeable about the host culture and yet may be lacking in ability to relate to members of the host society on the affective level. Others may be adequately skilled in performing specific jobs in the host society but may find some of the values operative in their job performance disagreeable.

When such internal imbalance is severe, maladjustment may occur (Wong-Rieger, 1984). The cognitive, affective, and behavioral processes of an individual's personal communication system are linked closely with many of the psychological problems associated with the stranger status. The negative self-image, low self-esteem, feeling of alienation, dissatisfaction with life and with the host environment, as well as other related psychological problems of strangers are associated primarily with their inability to relate to the people in the host society in any one or more of the three processes of personal communication. Thayer (1968) explains that

> successful communication with self and others implies correction by others as well as self-correction. In such a continuous process, up-to-date information about the self, the world, and the relationship of the self to the world leads to the acquisition of appropriate techniques, and eventually increases the individual's chances of mastery of life. Successful communication therefore becomes synonymous with adaptation and life. (p. 18)

Effective communication with members of the host culture, therefore, is critical to adaptation.

Inquiries on mental health of immigrants have emphasized the extent to which the adaptation experiences challenge the individual with stressful psychosocial demands. Aside from psychological distress, immigrants, at least initially, are considered to be prone to behavior impairment in social productivity. Many investigations have been made to assess different mental health issues related to maladaptation or to present specific clinical cases of mental illness and counseling (Berry & U. Kim, 1987; Dyal & Dyal, 1981; Hurh & K. Kim, 1988). Empirical studies have assessed psychological health (or illness) of immigrants. Hurh and K. Kim (1988), for example, measured mental health in terms of the immigrants' overall life satisfaction and directly linked it to their psychological, social, and economic adaptation.

Psychological health is clearly an important consequence of cumulative adaptive experiences. Increased psychological health, however, does not always take place in everyone. There is that small group of people who are unsuccessful in coping with various challenges of the host environment. Yet most people who struggle and find their way into more benign circumstances are likely to "weather" the challenges, and achieve an increasingly healthy psychological integration.

SUMMARY

The process of adapting to a new and unfamiliar culture is essentially a journey of personal change in which strangers who are socialized in one culture (enculturation) cultivate inroads into another culture. Once strangers enter the new environment, the adaptation process is set in motion, and will continue as long as they stay in direct contact with that environment. Gradually and imperceptively, strangers acquire and internalize new learning (acculturation) as well as suspend and unlearn some of the old practices (deculturation), so as to move in the direction of an increased functional fitness and ultimately into a state of assimilation in the host society. At the heart of the adaptation process lie the communication activities linking newcomers to the new environment. In turn, the stranger's cognitive, affective, and operational capacity to communicate (host communication competence) enables the stranger to partake in the various social communication processes (interpersonal and mass communication) of the host society.

Even as we acknowledge the central role of personal and social communication processes in cross-cultural adaptation of all strangers, we also must recognize that each stranger's adaptation experiences are somewhat unique. The nature of the stranger's communicative relationship with the host environment is influenced by the interplay of factors attributable to both the strangers themselves and the environment. We can predict that those strangers who possess a cultural background similar to that of the host culture, those who are familiar with the host culture prior to immigration, and those whose personality is characteristically open and strong are more likely to be successful in their acculturation process. Also, those who are better educated and younger will find it easier to adapt to a new cultural environment. If all other factors are equal, the strangers are likely to be better adapted in an environment that provides greater receptivity toward them but, at the same time, exerts a greater conformity pressure on them. Strangers, however, are less likely to feel the pressure of the host environment when their own ethnic community enjoys a strong presence and exerts its own conformity pressure on its members.

The cross-cultural adaptation process is seldom a smooth and easy process. Yet it is a process that strangers must undertake if they are to carry on their life activities in sync with the forces of the host milieu and to attain a state of mind that is healthy and at ease.

STUDY QUESTIONS

1. Describe the various cross-cultural situations that require at least some level of cross-cultural adaptation.
2. Compare the situations identified above in terms of the relative degree of strangers' adaptation that is generally expected to take place.
3. Define and compare the meanings of these key terms: *acculturation, adaptation, enculturation, deculturation,* and *assimilation.* How are these terms interrelated?
4. What role does personal communication, or host communication competence, play in the cross-cultural adaptation process? Explain the three processes of personal communication—cognitive, affective, and operational.
5. What role do the two social communication processes, interpersonal and mass communication, play in cross-cultural adaptation? What deliberate efforts can strangers make in each area to facilitate their cross-cultural adaptation?
6. How do strangers' active and prolonged communication activities within their ethnic communities affect their adaptation to the larger society?
7. What factors in the stranger's predisposition facilitate or retard his or her communication and adaptation in the host environment? Explain how these factors affect the stranger's communication behavior.
8. What are the factors in the host environment that facilitate or retard the stranger's communication and adaptation? How do these environmental factors affect the stranger's communication behavior?
9. How is the stranger's increased adaptation to the host environment related to his or her psychological health? Why?

SUGGESTED READING

Kim, Y. Y. (1988). *Communication and cross-cultural adaptation: An integrative theory.* Clevedon, U.K.: Multilingual Matters.

Kim, Y. Y., & Gudykunst, W. B. (Eds.). (1988). *Cross-cultural adaptation.* Newbury Park, CA: Sage.

Moos, R. (Ed.). (1976). *Human adaptation: Coping with life crisis.* Lexington, MA: Heath.

Torbiorn, I. (1982). *Living abroad.* New York: Wiley.

14

Becoming Intercultural

There is a tide in the affairs of men [or women]
Which, taken at the flood, leads on to fortune. . . .
On such a sea we are now afloat,
And we must take the current when it serves,
or lose our ventures .
Julius Caesar, William Shakespeare

We live in a "world of simultaneous events and overall awareness" (McLuhan, 1962, p. 40). Through remarkable advancements in communications technology, we constantly are exposed to international affairs. What happens in a small nation anywhere in the world can be, directly and indirectly, a significant factor in the political and economic reality of many other nations around the world. Diplomats and international business personnel work closely with strangers from other cultures and need to be aware of the changing conditions of the world. In urban centers, many of us find ourselves working side by side with strangers from various national, racial, ethnic, and religious backgrounds.

In addition to adjusting to the technological connectedness of our international and domestic environments, each of us has to make changes in many aspects of our lives—in social structure, values, politics, and, most of all, in our human relations. Even in less technologically advanced societies, change has encroached on nearly every pattern of traditional values, the structure and functions of the family, and the relations between generations, genders, and other social groups. Every index suggests that the rate of change will continue to increase up to the as yet untested limits of human adaptability. Our relationship to our personal and collective past is increasingly becoming one of dislocation, of that peculiar mixture of freedom and loss that inevitably leads to massive change. The culture of our youth can no longer be depended on to produce reliable predictions about what other people are going to do next. Indeed, "modernity has made all of us immigrants in our own homes" (Pearce & Kang, 1988, p. 40).

When faced with new circumstances, however, most of us prefer to continue in our familiar cultural ways without a clear and objective vision and without a readiness to embrace the different and the unfamiliar. Each of us acquires a personality and a culture in childhood, long before we are capable of comprehending either of them (Barnlund, 1991). Efforts to cope with the changes and complexities of the contemporary world often lack an understanding of its fundamental dynamics and direction for change. Even though the problems we face demand a new orientation and new ways of dealing with one another, we often try to force our own cultural ways on others. Such is the case with many international and domestic clashes of divergent cultural forces as well as our attempts to resolve them.

In order to be more effective in this changing world, we need to make a conscious decision concerning our basic views of ourselves and our relationships to others and to the world at large. Accepting this challenge means we need to search for a new definition of ourselves that will help us develop specific strategies for daily activities and problems. Reorienting ourselves is, of course, a serious challenge. Most of us who have been enculturated into one culture during our formative years find it extremely difficult to change the inertia of our habits even if we are willing to do so. Yet it is crucial that we do our utmost in reassessing our customary, ethnocentric ways and in reformulating our habitual practices if we are to increase our functional fitness and psychological health in this changing world. To be profitable business managers in a multinational company, for example, we cannot insist on our own ways of doing business. To be effective teachers in a multiethnic urban school, we must be able to deal with children and parents whose cultural attributes are different from our own. To be successful ambassadors overseas, we must be effective communicators with a great deal of cultural sensitivity and understanding, and with the necessary social skills of the local culture.

In this chapter, we extend our discussion from Chapter 13 on cross-cultural adaptation and examine how it is possible for individuals to undergo a fundamental psychic transformation through prolonged intercultural communication and adaptation experiences. Information and insights we gain from the experiences of immigrants and sojourners will serve as a main source of our understanding of the psychodynamics of change. We will also examine the concept of the "intercultural person" (Y. Kim, 1988, 1991c, 1994b, 1995a, 1995b, in press; Y. Kim & Ruben, 1988) as a model of human development in this increasingly interconnected world.

ENCOUNTERING DIFFERENT CULTURES

All of us came into this world knowing literally nothing of what we need to know to function acceptably in human society. Through the process of enculturation, cultural patterns are etched into our nervous system and become part of our personality and behavior. This internalized learning enables us to interact easily with other members of our culture, who share a similar image of reality. That is, the culture of our youth provides a common pattern for our cognitive, affective, and behavioral structure and processes so that people belonging to the same culture tend to have a similar understanding of and responses to reality. It is culture that programs us to define what is real, what is true, what is right, what is beautiful, and what is good.

Cultural Unconscious

We remain largely unconscious of the cultural imprinting that governs our personality and behavior. Our cultural unconscious can be understood only by detailed analysis. We automatically treat what is most characteristically our own as though it were innate. We are programmed to think, feel, and behave as though anyone whose behavior is not predictable or is peculiar in any way is strange, improper, irresponsible, or inferior. In this sense, all of us have a natural tendency to be ethnocentric as a result of our very profound and inseparable relationship to our culture.

The only time we become aware of our hidden control system is when things do not follow the hidden program. Boulding (1956) argues that the human nervous system is structured in such a way that the patterns that govern behavior and perception come into consciousness only when there is a deviation from the familiar. To be functional and mature in a given culture, we must experience a multitude of challenges, and the full impact of the process is not experienced until we have "cut the apron strings" and established ourselves as separate from our parents (Hall, 1976, p. 225). Similarly, the only time we become fully aware of the hidden control system of our own culture is when we distance ourselves mentally or physically from our own culture and face experiences that challenge our taken-for-granted images and assumptions.

Encounters with strangers bring surprises (uncertainty) and stresses (anxiety). Some of the surprises may shake our self-concept and cultural identity and bring the anxiety of temporary rootlessness. Similarly, when we are strangers in other cultures, we are confronted with situations in which our mental and behavioral habits are called into question. Such situations produce a conflict in which we are forced temporarily to suspend or abandon our identification with the cultural patterns that have symbolized who we are and what we are. Ill-equipped to deal with such inconsistencies, most of us are, temporarily at least, in a state of mental and physical disturbance. The many examples of confusion experienced by international students, Peace Corps volunteers, and international business personnel suggest a wide spectrum of responses and reactions to new cultural surroundings. Similarly, someone who returns to work after many years of being out of the work force may experience some of these transitional problems.

Culture Shock

Reactions to new situations has been called culture shock. Fictional as well as first-person accounts have been written depicting the bewildering experiences of being foreign in foreign lands (e.g., Dublin, 1993; Lewis & Jungman, 1986). It is Oberg

(1958), however, who first coined the term *culture shock,* in connection with the experience of anthropologists who must learn to manage the violation of their social reality implicit in alien social norms, values, and mores. This violation represents a challenge to their primary socialization. Lundstedt (1963) describes culture shock as "a form of personality maladjustment, a reaction to a temporary unsuccessful attempt to adjust to new surroundings and people" (p. 8).

In an overview of various studies of culture shock, Taft (1977) has identified a number of common reactions, including (1) "cultural fatigue," manifested by irritability, insomnia, and other psychosomatic disorders; (2) a sense of loss arising from being uprooted from one's familiar surroundings; (3) rejection by the individual members of the new environment; and (4) a feeling of impotence from being unable to deal competently with the environmental unfamiliarity. Others describe the reactions of people to stressful situations under more severe conditions, such as those of concentration camp inmates, hostages captured by political terrorists, and returned prisoners of war. In each of these cases, the features associated with the change are the "shock" effects involving heightened emotions and intense suffering.

Bennett (1977) expanded the meaning of culture shock and regarded it as a part of the general *transition shock,* a natural consequence of the state of a person's inability to interact with the new and changed environment in an effective manner. Bennett contends that transition shock occurs in various situations, such as divorce, relocation, death of a loved one, and change of values associated with rapid social innovation, as well as the loss of a familiar frame of reference in intercultural encounters. Further, the concepts culture shock and transition shock have been extended to include *reentry shock,* or the emotional and physiological difficulties an individual may experience on returning home from overseas. Gullahorn and Gullahorn (1963) suggest that reentry difficulties are likely to be more severe a short time after return than immediately on return to the home culture.

At the heart of these "shock" phenomena is the lack of fitness between strangers' subjective experiences and the commonly accepted modes of experience in the unfamiliar surroundings. Everyone requires the ongoing validation of his or her experiences, and being unable to meet this basic human need can lead to symptoms of mental, emotional, and physical disturbance (Berger & Kellner, 1970; Williams & Westermeyer, 1986). The shifting of the self-world relationship brings about heightened levels of inner conflict through an increased awareness of the split between internal, subjective experiences and external, objective circumstances. In this sense, our experiences of culture shock and related phenomena are basically a form of so-called "self-shock" (Zaharna, 1989), a form of existential dilemma in response to the painful discrepancy between what is and what should be.

THE PROCESS OF INTERCULTURAL TRANSFORMATION

Many investigators of sojourner adaptation have attempted to understand what short-term adaptive changes follow the initial shock phase. Oberg (1958), for example, has identified four stages: (1) a "honeymoon" stage characterized by fascination, elation, and optimism; (2) a stage of hostility and emotionally stereotyped attitudes toward the host society and increased association with fellow sojourners; (3) a recovery stage characterized by increased language knowledge and ability to get around in the new cultural environment; (4) a final stage in which adjustment is about as complete as possible, anxiety is largely gone, and new customs are accepted and enjoyed.

These and other similar characterizations of adaptation stages also have been described in "curves" that indicate the patterns of adaptive change over time. Researchers have measured adaptive change mainly in terms of the level of satisfaction or positive attitudes toward the host environment, and their findings generally support a "U-curve" hypothesis to predict the psychological change of sojourners. The U-curve depicts the initial optimism and elation in the host culture, the subsequent dip in the level of adaptation, and the following gradual recovery (Deutsch & Won, 1963). As shown in Figure 14.1, this popularized U-curve pattern of adaptive change in the new environment has been extended to the "W-curve" (Gullahorn & Gullahorn, 1963; Trifonovitch, 1977) with the addition of a reentry (or return-home) phase of the sojourn experience.

The U-curve and W-curve patterns of adaptive change have not always been observed consistently in empirical studies. Church (1982) notes that support for the U-curve hypothesis is somewhat inconclusive and overgeneralized. Not all studies, for instance, report that sojourners begin their intercultural experiences with a period of elation and optimism (Klineberg & Hull, 1979). Even those supporting the hypothesis show marked differences in the time parameters of the curve, making the U-curve description too variable to be useful.

Figure 14.1   The U-curve and W-curve adaptive change of sojourners.

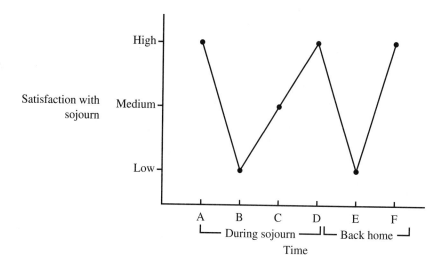

The Stress-Adaptation-Growth Dynamic

Despite the difficulty in identifying the adaptive process with precision, the process as a whole often is one of the most profound and even painful life experiences. Adler (1982/1987) argues that culture shock is not necessarily a "disease for which adaptation is the cure, but is at the very heart of the cross-cultural learning experience, self-understanding, and change" (p. 29). Intercultural learning and growth are, in this view, the core or essence of the sojourn experience. Strangers are capable not only of adapting to new cultures but also, and more importantly, of undertaking modifications within themselves. Through culture shock experiences, individuals confront the physiological, psychological, social, and philosophical discrepancies between their own internalized dispositions and those of the host culture. The sojourn experience, accordingly, is an experience of personal transformation, or a psychological "movement from a state of low self- and cultural awareness to a state of high self- and cultural awareness" (Adler, 1982/1987, p. 15).

How can a person brought up through the primary enculturation process to be a certain type of cultural being ever overcome the existing barriers in order to cope with an unfamiliar culture? An answer lies in the profound plasticity and adaptability of the human organism. From the moment of birth, we are active agents in our own development, constructing the very reality in which we live. As we change, there is a progression of stages, where each stage in the developmental sequence is a necessary result of the preceding stage and integrates previous behaviors, concepts, and actions into a present condition. We simultaneously go through qualitative changes and maintain integrity throughout our life span, although it is still not clearly understood how such qualitative changes occur between stages.

In this framework of human development, successive levels and forms of equilibrium are conceived as levels of adaptation, with change being caused by a mismatch or discrepancy between our internal world and the external reality (Fogel, 1979; Ford & Lerner, 1992). This adaptive principle governing the human organism is evidenced most dramatically in individuals who have gone through such extreme life circumstances as prisons and death camps. Many inmates manage to cope in such settings with resilience. Numerous immigrants, refugees, and missionaries also demonstrate that they gradually learn to create for themselves appropriate situations and relationships.

Because cross-cultural adaptation necessitates both acculturation (learning) and deculturation (unlearning), the psychological movement of strangers often produces forms of *stress*. Stress, after all, is a natural human response whenever one has to let go of familiar and routine habits and whenever one's internal capabilities are challenged by the demands of the environment (Y. Kim, 1988). Because strangers' cultural identity and habits are placed against the systematic forces of the host culture, the strangers are, at least temporarily, in an unsettling state of "disequilibrium" manifested in many emotional "lows" of uncertainty and confusion. Indeed, the challenges of handling daily activities are most severe during the initial phases, as has been shown in culture shock studies.

In the state of stress, a so-called defense mechanism is activated in strangers to hold the internal structure in balance. They try to avoid or minimize the anticipated or actual "pain" of disequilibrium by some kind of psychological maneuvering, such as selective attention, self-deception, denial, avoidance, and withdrawal, as well as hostility, cynicism, and compulsive altruism (Lazarus, 1966; Lazarus, Averill, & Opton, 1974; Lazarus et al., 1980). Yet, defensive stress reactions such as these are generally temporary; if prolonged, they are counterproductive to the strangers' functioning in the host environment. Such reactions must, and generally do, accompany adaptive responses as well.

Temporary psychic disintegration is identified by Y. Kim (1988, 1995a, 1995b, in press) as the very basis for subsequent *adaptation*. She argues that experiences of stress prompt adaptation because, when the environment continues to threaten internal conditions, individuals by necessity strive to meet the challenge by adding to the existing system of ideas and reconfiguring it into a new set of coping abilities. As a result of the reflexive and self-reflexive capacity of the human mind, which reviews, anticipates, generalizes, analyzes, and plans, we are capable of creatively transforming our internal conditions. What follows such adaptive responses is a subtle internal *growth,* according to Y. Kim. The periods of stress will pass in time as the strangers work out new ways of handling problems. A crisis, once managed, presents the strangers an opportunity for a strengthening of their internal capacity.

The interdependence of stress, adaptation, and subsequent internal transformation is referred to by Y. Kim as the *stress-adaptation-growth dynamic.* As depicted in Figure 14.2, this psychological process is one that is fueled by a

Figure 14.2   The stress-adaptation-growth dynamic (*Source:* Y. Kim, 1988, p. 56).

continual and cyclic tension between stress and adaptation, resulting in a form of psychic growth. Each stressful experience is responded to with a "draw back," which then activates the adaptive energy to help reorganize oneself and "leap forward." The process presents a continual resolution of the dialectic relationship between push and pull, or engagement and disengagement, in which the "opposite" psychological forces bring about a qualitative transformation—a greater personality integration and maturity (Heath, 1977; Kao, 1975; Wrightsman, 1994).

The process, if successful, means that the individual grows into a new kind of person at a higher level of integration. Even extreme mental illness, on the other hand, can be viewed as a process of a potentially positive disintegration followed by reintegration with new material at a higher level (Dabrowski, 1968). Jourard (1974) refers to this phenomenon as the "integration-disintetgration-reintegration" process:

> Growth is the disintegration of one way of experiencing the world, followed by a reorganization of this experience, a reorganization that includes the new disclosure of the world. The disorganization, or even shattering, of one way to experience the world, is brought on by new disclosures from the changing being of the world, disclosures that were always being transmitted, but were usually ignored. (p. 456)

The stress-adaptation-growth dynamic, central to Y. Kim's theory of intercultural transformation, echoes Mezirow's (1984, 1991) idea of "transformation learning" of adults. Mezirow emphasizes the capacity of adults to develop a higher level of self-understanding through reflection, and in so doing, "emancipate" themselves from the constraints of various limited, conventional perspectives. Kim's theory further converges with what Hall (1976) calls the "identity-separation-growth dynamics," and what Phinney (1993) refers to as the "differentiation-conflict-integration" process.

Research Evidence

Few systematic studies actually have examined the phenomenon of the process of intercultural identity development described above. Yet, some scientific evidence is available offering indirect support for the phenomenon of the process of intercultural transformation. Among such studies is the report by Eaton and Lasry (1978) that the stress level of more upwardly mobile immigrants tends to be greater than those who are less upwardly mobile. Similarly, among Japanese Americans (Marmot & Syme, 1976) and Mexican American women (Miranda & Castro, 1977), the better-adapted immigrants initially experience a somewhat greater frequency of stress-related symptoms (such as anxiety and need for psychotherapy) than the less-adapted group. Some of the findings from the study of Ruben and Kealey (1979) further suggest that, even in the case of temporary sojourners (Canadian technical advisors in Nigeria), those who are ultimately the most effective in the new environment tend to be those who have undergone the most intense culture shock during the transition period.

These and other similar research findings lack the important detail concerning the subtle and intricate psychological dynamic of stress, adaptation, and growth, and the gradual and often unquantifiable identity transformation depicted in Figure 14.2. Yet they do offer valuable "snapshots" of the evolutionary process, particularly when we examine them in the context of the many studies (some of which have been discussed in this chapter and in the preceeding chapter) that consistently point to the upward-forward progression accompanying an increased level of functional fitness (greater adaptation) and of psychological health (less adaptive stress). As noted earlier, these studies point to the fact that, once the initial phase has been managed successfully, strangers almost always develop increasingly refined and positive views toward the host society and toward themselves. They also have been found to develop, over time, more behavioral capacities to manage themselves and function effectively in the host environment and experience less feelings of alienation and hostility vis-à-vis the environment.

An additional source of validation of the stress-adaptation-growth dynamic is provided by the extensive body of research studies that have investigated the phenomenon of personal constructs and cognitive complexity originally theorized by Kelly (1955). Kelly argues that personal constructs are the conceptual tools we use in understanding and differentiating between similar or adjacent objects in the psychological environment. The cognitive schemes we employ define our intentions and imply alternative lines of action in a given situation. The greater the number of constructs present in our cognitive system, the more discriminating and mindful we are in experiencing each communicative reality accurately and fully. Bieri (1955) applies the term cognitive complexity to describe this psychological construct. He defines *cognitive complexity* as the "degree of differentiation of the construct system" (Bieri, 1955, p. 263). From subsequent research, three structural features of the complexity-simplicity continuum have been identified: (1) differentiation of the number of dimensions in one's personal constructs; (2) the relative articulation (or abstraction) of dimensions or the number of categories in a behavioral dimension that a person can discriminate (Rigney, Bieri, & Tripodi, 1964); and (3) integration of various dimensions of cognition into a meaningful whole, which is called "integrative complexity" (Schroder, Driver, & Streufert, 1967).

An important aspect of human cognition relevant to the present discussion is the intrinsically social and developmental nature of its structure. Schroder and his associates (1967) argue that the level of cognitive complexity in a given area is not necessarily static over time but develops further with new learning experiences. In other words, our cognitive structure is developed through various social experiences, creating a relatively differentiated, articulated (or abstracted), and integrated schematic structure. This developmental principle has been demonstrated in the research on immigrant adaptation. Just as comparative analyses of children, adolescents, and adults reveal an increasing cognitive complexity, research indicates that, in general, immigrants' perception of the new culture becomes more complex and refined in time with increased interactions with the host environment. Through the cumulative experiences of adaptation, strangers gradually attain a significant degree of cognitive capacity to differentiate between the original culture and the host culture along increasingly more dimensions and categories, and to synthesize the cultures and their dimensions into an integrated whole.

What is significant about successfully adjusted immigrants and sojourners is that, as strangers in the host culture, they separate themselves mentally and physically from their original culture. As they become less like strangers and more familiar with the host society, they simultaneously go through a process of transforming their original cultural identity and of becoming intercultural. This transformation means their psychic patterns are reorganized on a higher level of cognitive complexity, allowing for a greater capacity to overcome cultural parochialism. Empirical validation that is of particular significance to this development has been offered in Y. Kim's (1976, 1977a) study of Korean immigrants. When asked to compare the meaning of "friendship" among Koreans with that among Americans, the subjects who were relatively new to the United States were able to offer fewer and more stereotypical comments, focusing only on the differences between the two cultures. On the other hand, the subjects who had lived in the United States longer addressed both the similarities and the differences in a more elaborate, differentiated, and accurate manner. This research finding clearly suggests a pattern of perceptual development in strangers over time toward greater clarity, depth, scope, balance, and integration (see also Grotevant, 1993).

INTERCULTURAL PERSONHOOD

Emerging from the process of intercultural transformation is the image of *intercultural personhood,* a special kind of personal orientation that promises greater fitness in our increasingly intercultural world (Y. Kim, 1994b, 1995b, in press; Y. Kim & Ruben, 1988). The "intercultural person" projects the fundamental outlook of someone who has achieved a high level of identity transformation through a prolonged process of stress, adaptation, and growth experiences through intercultural encounters.

Some Psychological Characteristics

The intercultural person possesses internal attributes that are not rigidly defined by any single culture. Instead, he or she is someone who has internalized different cultural elements and is open to further intercultural growth. The term intercultural person is employed here as a generic term that embraces other similar concepts, such as "international" person (Lutzker, 1960), "universal" person (Walsh, 1973), "multicultural" person (Adler, 1982/1987), and "species identity" (Boulding, 1990), as well as "meta-identity" and "transcultural identity." Walsh's (1973) concept of "universal" person, for instance, emphasizes three aspects of a "cosmopolitan" viewpoint: (1) respect for all cultures, (2) understanding of what individuals in other cultures think, feel, and believe, and (3) appreciation for differences among cultures. Adler (1982/1987) explains the unique characteristics of the multicultural person:

> The identity of multicultural [person] is based, not on "belongingness" which implies either owning or being owned by culture, but on a style of self-consciousness that is capable of negotiating ever new formations of reality. In this sense multicultural [person] is a radical departure from the kinds of identities found in both traditional and mass societies. He [or she] is neither totally a part of nor totally apart from his [or her] culture; he [or she] lives, instead, on the boundary. (p. 391)

All these terms indicate a *nondualistic, noncategorical, and metacontextual definition of self and others* rather than rigid boundedness within any particular category. As such, the intercultural person manifests a mindset that is less stereotypical, less ethnocentric, and more individualized. Having experienced the conflict between identity maintenance and adaptive change, they possess a mental outlook that exhibits greater cognitive differentiation (Amerikaner, 1978; Boekestijn, 1988; Y. Kim, 1988, 1995a, 1995b, in press). Such an outlook allows the openness that embraces different cultural and group-based characteristics without being dictated by them. The intercultural person can thus step into and "imaginatively participate in the other's world view" (Bennett, 1977, p. 49).

As we become increasingly intercultural in our internal system, we gain new perspectives and outlooks that reflect *an integrative and creative "third-culture" perspective* (Gudykunst, Wiseman, & Hammer, 1977). In this realm of psychic growth, differences and distinctions between human groups are taken less as polarities and opposites without relationships. The intercultural person is better able to seek and find creative ways to reconcile seemingly contradictory elements of groups of people and of cultures and transform them into complementary parts of an integrated whole. The nature of this psychic evolution presents a potential for achieving what Harris (1979, 1980) defines as "optimal communication competence." As one achieves a significant level of interculturalness, one may be better able to make deliberate choices of actions in specific situations rather than simply being bound by the culturally normative courses of behavior. Harris argues that optimally competent communicators have a sophisticated metasystem for critiquing their own managing system and interpersonal system.

The achievement of an increasingly *inclusive and transcendental perception and awareness* is seen as one of the highest aims of humans in the spiritual traditions of the eastern cultures. Suzuki (1968) writes:

> The fundamental idea of Buddhism is to pass beyond the world of opposites, a world built up by intellectual distinctions and emotional defilements, and to realize the spiritual world of non-distinction, which involves achieving an absolute point of view. (p. 18)

As such, a virtuous person in the eastern philosophical tradition is not one who undertakes the impossible task of striving for the good and eliminating the bad, but rather, one who is able to maintain a dynamic balance between good and bad. This notion of dynamic balance is emphasized extensively by the Chinese sages in their symbolism of the archetypal poles of yin and yang. They call the unity lying beyond yin and yang the tao, and see it as a process that brings about the interplay of the two poles (Yoshikawa, 1988).

In becoming intercultural, we rise above the hidden forces of culture and discover that there are many ways to be "good," "true," and "beautiful." In this developmental process, we acquire a greater capacity to overcome cultural parochialism and develop *a wider circle of identification,* approaching the limit of many cultures and ultimately of humanity itself. The process of becoming intercultural, then, is like climbing a high mountain. As we reach the mountaintop, we see that all paths below ultimately lead to the same summit and that each path presents unique scenery. Becoming intercultural is a gradual process of liberating ourselves from our limited and exclusive interests and viewpoints and of striving to attain a perspective in which we see ourselves as part of a larger, more inclusive whole.

Case Illustrations

Bearing concrete witness to the concept of the intercultural person are many individuals' experiences of crossing cultures that have been told in case studies, memoirs, biographical stories, and essays of self-reflection and self-analysis (e.g., Ainslie, 1994; Copelman, 1993; Keene, 1994; Miller, 1988; O'Halloran, 1994; Schwimmer & Warren, 1993). Such accounts often present vivid testimonials and special insights into the emotional ebb and flow and the progressive and eventual realization of intercultural transformation.

One story of intercultural transformation is told by a Cambodian refugee described by Sheehy (1986). At the age of 12, Mohm was one of the first Cambodian refugees to be settled in New York City in September 1982. Having lived through the genocidal regime of Pol Pot, during which her entire family, with the possible exception of a brother, was wiped out, Mohm became the author's adopted daughter. Mohm's diary during the first two years in the United States is interspersed with the author's own reflections, and tells a compelling account of Mohm's stress, adaptation, and growth experiences. Her inner conflict continues throughout the period, although in an increasingly hopeful and confident tone.

After one month:

> I don't like to live here, all Americans, all big apartments, no children, and I can't speak. Everything I know seems so far away, cannot ever get it back. My family is gone, part of me is torn away. I'm already broken. But I healed some of that wound, brought some of those parts back together and made the beginning of a new life. (p. 214)

After three months:

> My mind is still in my little world, of the [refugee] camp, where you could walk to everything. Anything you need, you could just call out for it and people will hear you and you can hear them. When I walk down the street in New York, there's another street like it and another and another as far as I look—it's endless. But I'm beginning to know which direction is right and wrong. I want to find my way. (p. 234)

After six months:

> Things begin to fall into place little by little. And I'm not scared anymore of doing things, that I'll make a bad mistake. Even I'm able to communicate with people, a little bit. It isn't going to be as bad as I think. I have the feeling if I want to be myself badly enough, I can be someday—but not soon. Life is not as ugly as I think. It could be as beautiful as I want, if I make it. (p. 243)

Clearly, over time, Mohm was able to affirm herself and her new world, as she began to reinvent herself. Toward the end of her first two years in the United States, an intercultural identity begins to emerge in Mohm. The author reflects:

> Mohm did not emerge as a little cutout of an American teenager, made to order to fit some empty place in a middle-aged woman's life, with a miserable Cambodian child inside screaming to get out. She was, and is today, able to embrace her brand new American-ness while retaining her essential Cambodian-ness, knowing that is what makes her special. (p. xvii)

This story clearly illustrates how individuals can reinvent themselves.

Another story is told by Yoshikawa (1978), who was born in Japan and has been teaching at a university in the United States for many years. Yoshikawa's following observation on his development captures the essential elements of intercultural personhood discussed earlier.

> I am now able to look at both cultures with objectivity as well as subjectivity; I am able to move in both cultures, back and forth without any apparent conflict. . . . I think that something beyond the sum of each [cultural] identification took place, and that it became something akin to the concept of "synergy"—when one adds 1 and 1, one gets three, or a little more. This something extra is not culture-specific but something unique of its own, probably the emergence of a new attribute or a new self-awareness, born out of an awareness of the relative nature of values and of the universal aspect of human nature. . . . I really am not concerned whether others take me as a Japanese or [a North] American; I can accept myself as I am. I feel I am much freer than ever before, not only in the cognitive domain (perception, thoughts, etc.), but also in the affective (feeling, attitudes, etc.) and behavioral domains. (p. 220)

This case illustrates how integration of indentities can have a freeing effect for the individual.

PROMOTING INTERCULTURAL GROWTH

The process of intercultural development exemplified in the two personal stories above can be credited in large part to the individual. The power and responsibility for the transformation ultimately rests within the individual, as each one is the captain of her or his own intercultural journey. The stories clearly demonstrate that becoming intercultural is not a mere theoretical possibility or a romantic ideal, but a concrete reality—one that all of us can attain if we are prepared to undergo the stressful challenges inherent in the process.

Intercultural persons play a special role in our increasingly pluralistic world as the "cross-links" (Molina, 1978), "mediating persons" (Bochner, 1981), and the sustaining core of agents of positive social change (Lum, 1982). They provide the hub and glue of the moral infrastructure that is necessary to hold together divergent groups, to facilitate individual freedom, to discourage excessive claims for social categories, and to help build communities where individuals of disparate identities are given their respective places without losing sight of common aspirations. They possess the creative mindset that can reconcile and unite cultural differences and integrate the roles required by each cultural context. Such a mindset embodies the requisite attributes of an effective facilitator and catalyst. Even short-term sojourners such as exchange students who have returned home from abroad have been observed to have developed the capacity to serve as mediating persons (Wilson, 1985).

Just as democracy is an ideal state of government, the intercultural person is an ideal toward which we can strive. The process of psychic growth from being monocultural to being intercultural is a process of change in which we continually integrate new elements of life. The process necessitates openness to the dynamics of change and possession of attitudes that welcome new cultural learning, with a commitment to the "uncommitted potentiality for change" (Bateson, 1972, p. 497) and to doubt our own culturally colored perception by suspending our own value priorities.

Each of us is different, of course, in the degree to which our perceptions and interests are flexible. Some react with curiosity to unpredictable events. Others are disturbed or uncomfortable in the presence of confusing and complex information. Some show strong resilience and tolerance for ambiguity, while others become extremely insecure. A crucial factor influencing the rigidity or flexibility of our psyche is age. As discussed in Chapter 13, age at the time of sojourn or immigration significantly affects the subsequent adaptation in the host society. A study of children of Hispanic cultural background (Seelye & Wasilewski, 1981) suggests that well-adjusted immigrant children already manifest a type of character structure on which a different but integrated intercultural personality can be built. Some of the children in the study demonstrate a noticeable amount of "situational flexibility" and a wide enough behavioral repertoire to negotiate differences of opinion in the multitude of cultural contexts of their daily activities, including home, school, and street environments.

Efforts to promote intercultural development can be directed most effectively to younger generations. The educational system has a monumental task of projecting and cultivating a new direction for human character formation. If sucessful, the educational system can help members of future generations embrace the intercultural world and its diversity and give up outdated national, racial, ethnic, and territorial perspectives. The educational system of the United States has begun to respond to this challenge by emphasizing the international/intercultural dimension throughout the curricula and by developing special programs, such as foreign language programs, bilingual-bicultural education programs, ethnic studies, area studies, and studies of world regions and cultures.

If intercultural personhood is deemed a valid educational goal, and we believe that it is, an extensive search for ways to articulate and implement intercultural human development must be undertaken. The propagation of the goal must go beyond the educational process directly to the political processes and the mass media. Media, in particular, can play a pivotal role in the spread of interculturalness as a human social value and thus produce a gradual change in the mindset of the general public. Y. Kim and Ruben (1988) state that

> there is a special privilege to think, feel, and behave beyond the parameters of any single culture. This accomplishment . . . has an intrinsic merit in dealing with our increasingly complex intercultural world. In this frame of mind, the tension, stress, and effort necessarily present in overcoming intercultural difficulties can be more willingly accepted and endured. (p. 318)

Ultimately, each of us must bear the responsibility for developing the frame of mind that leads to intercultural personhood.

SUMMARY

In this chapter, we examine the process of the development of intercultural personhood through the experience of intercultural communication. In this process, we witness the human spirit at work, at once struggling and being triumphant as individuals undergo the dynamic interplay of stress, adaptation, and growth. Intercultural personhood presents a model of human development toward less cultural rigidity and more openness, less ethnocentrism and more understanding of the fundamental oneness of all human beings. We argue that this kind of fundamental personal change is necessary for us to be functional in our increasingly intercultural world, that is, to be better able to accept and appreciate cultural variations, to resolve and integrate conflicting views from the basis of a perspective broader than any one particular cultural perspective.

Reaching this goal would take a lifetime commitment, and visible short-term results may be limited. Yet, numerous immigrants and sojourners around the world already have accomplished the long and difficult journey of becoming intercultural, leaving us with little doubt that becoming an intercultural person is a viable goal toward which all of us may strive. Through the personal testimonials of Mohm, Yoshikawa, and many others with similar transformative experiences, we learn about the reality of the continual juxtapositions of stress and adaptation. Despite the often unsettling nature of the transformation process, we see in their experiences the triumphant human spirit that embraces new elements of life. While the process of becoming intercultural is largely the work of each individual, it needs to be promoted as an important public value that can be propagated through the educational and mass communciation institutions of each society.

STUDY QUESTIONS

1. Explain how the changing circumstances of today's world necessitate a new self-definition and a new orientation toward others.
2. What are the various symptoms of culture shock?
3. What are the general stages that strangers tend to undergo in the face of culture shock? How have they been characterized graphically in the research literature?
4. Describe Kim's theory of psychic growth. How do intercultural experiences facilitate the growth process?
5. What kinds of research evidence are available concerning Kim's theory?
6. Identify at least one prominent person whom you consider to be highly intercultural. What characteristics of this person qualify him or her to be an intercultural person?
7. How can intercultural persons benefit the community on local, national, and international levels?
8. How can the people in leadership positions promote intercultural personhood as a public value? How can ordinary citizens in a democratic society participate in this effort?

SUGGESTED READING

Bochner, S. (Ed.). (1981). *The mediating person.* Cambridge, MA: Schenkman.

Furnham, A., & Bochner, S. (1986). *Culture shock: Psychological reactions to unfamiliar environments.* London: Methuen.

Keene, D. (1994). *On familiar terms: A journey across cultures.* New York: Kodansha International.

Kim, Y. Y. (in press). *Becoming intercultural: An integrative theory of cross-cultural adaptation.* Newbury Park, CA: Sage.

Walsh, J. (1979). *Humanistic culture learning.* Honolulu: University of Hawaii Press.

15

Building Community

In and through community lies the salvation of the world.
M. Scott Peck

Conflict between people of different ethnic and cultural groups is occurring throughout the world today. While the specific causes of intergroup conflict differ depending upon the situation, all incidents share one thing in common: They involve polarized communication. As indicated in Chapter 11, polarized communication occurs when we are not willing to question our assumption that we are right and others are wrong (Arnett, 1986). Polarized communication, therefore, exists when groups or individuals look out for their own interests and have little concern for others' interests.

Lack of concern for others' interests leads to moral exclusion. Lack of concern for others and moral exclusion are a function, at least in part, of the spiritual deprivation (i.e., the feeling of emptiness associated with separation from our fellow humans) that Mother Teresa sees as the major problem facing the world today (Jampolsky, 1989).

There is a tendency for many of us to think that cultural and ethnic diversity inevitably lead to polarized communication and hinder the development of community. That, however, is not the case. Diversity is necessary for community to exist. For community to develop, group differences must be dealt with in a constructive fashion.

The term *community* is derived from the Latin *communitas*, which has two related, but distinct, interpretations: (1) the quality of "common interest and hence the quality of fellowship," and (2) "a body of people having in common an external bond" (Rosenthal, 1984, p. 219). Yankelovich (1981) argues that community evokes the "feeling that 'Here is where I belong, these are my people, I care for them, they care for me, I am part of them' . . . its absence is experienced as an achy loss, a void . . . feelings of isolation, falseness, instability, and impoverishment of spirit" (p. 227). Selznick (1992) argues that "communities provide settings within which people grow and flourish and within which subgroups are nourished and protected" (p. 360). Wuthnow (1991), however, points out that even though people in the United States talk a lot about community, they live their lives in ways that say individual freedom is more important.

Our purpose in this chapter is to show why diversity is necessary for feelings of community to develop, and to provide suggestions for developing community with strangers. We begin by examining Buber's suggestions for developing community.

WALKING A NARROW RIDGE

Buber (1958, 1965) sees community as a choice around a common center, the voluntary coming together of people in a direct relationship that involves a concern for the self, the other, and the group. He believes that community must begin in small groups and that it cannot be forced on organizations or nations. At the same time, Buber contends that some form of community is necessary to make life worth living.

In Buber's view, a community is *not* a group of like-minded people; rather, it is a group of individuals with complementary natures who have differing minds. Extending Buber's analysis, Friedman (1983) draws a distinction between a community of otherness and a community of affinity. A *community of affinity* is a group of like-minded people who have come together for security. Friedman argues that they feel safe because they use a similar language and the same slogans, but they do not have close relations with one another. A *community of otherness,* on the other hand, begins from the assumption that each member has a different point of view that contributes to the group. Members are not alike, but they share common concerns.

Buber sees openness, *not* intimacy, as one of the keys to developing community. "A real community need not consist of people who are perpetually together; but it must consist of people who, precisely because they are comrades, have mutual access to one another and are ready for one another" (quoted by Friedman, 1986, p. xiii). The importance of openness becomes clear when we look at the distinctions Buber draws among three forms of communication: monologue, technical dialogue, and dialogue.

Monologues are self-centered conversations in which the other person is treated as an object. When we engage in monologues, we do not see others as unique human beings and we do not take their needs into consideration. *Technical dialogues* are information-centered conversations. In technical dialogues, our goal is to exchange information with others, not to establish a contact with them. Monologues and technical dialogues are necessary and appropriate at times, but problems emerge when they are used too frequently (e.g., there is a lack of connection between the participants) and community, therefore, cannot develop.

For community to develop, dialogue is necessary (Buber, 1958). *Dialogue* involves communication between individuals. The goal of a dialogue is not to change others, but to understand them. In a dialogue, there is a search for mutuality. The focus is on what is happening between the two people. In a dialogue, each participant's feeling of control and ownership is minimized; each participant confirms the other, even when conflict occurs. Buber argues that it is the mutual confirmation that occurs in dialogues that allows us to feel human.

When we communicate on automatic pilot, most of our conversations are monologues or technical dialogues. Engaging in these types of conversations exclusively does not allow us to make contact with others. For most of us, engaging in dialogue requires that we be mindful of our communication. When we are mindful, we need to focus on the process of communication, not worry about an outcome. If we focus on what is happening between ourselves and others and we do not think about our goals, we can engage in dialogue with others.

Developing community requires engaging in dialogue with others; it also requires a commitment to values higher than our own (Arnett, 1986). Tinder (1980) suggests that the values of civility and of tolerance of plurality and diversity are necessary for community. Holding these values requires that we accept that our own needs are not always met (Arnett, 1986).

The key to building community in Buber's view is for individuals to walk a narrow ridge. The concept of *narrow ridge* involves taking both our own and others' viewpoints into consideration in our dealings with others. Arnett (1986) uses the metaphor of a tightrope walker to illustrate the narrow ridge concept. If tightrope walkers lean too much in one direction, they will begin to lose their balance. To regain their balance, tightrope walkers must compensate by leaning in the other direction. The same is true of walking the narrow ridge in our dealings with others. If we give our own opinions too much weight in a conversation, we must compensate by considering others' opinions with equal weight if we are going to walk a narrow ridge.

In walking the narrow ridge, we must try to understand others' points of view. Buber does *not* advocate that we take a nonjudgmental or relativistic attitude toward others. Rather, he argues that we openly listen to others, but if we are not persuaded by their arguments, we should maintain our original position; if we are persuaded, we should modify our opinions. There is a subtle difference between listening openly and not changing our minds, and being close-minded. The difference depends on our intentions. If our intentions are to consider others' opinions seriously, we are walking the narrow ridge; if our intentions are not to consider others' opinions, then we are close-minded. It is the dual concern for self and others in walking the narrow ridge that stops polarized communication and allows community to develop (Arnett, 1986).

Buber argues that we should avoid giving in and accepting others' opinions just for the sake of peace. Rather, he suggests that we should accept others' opinions or compromise if that is the way to the best solution. Our commitment must be to principles, not false peace. It also is important to note that Buber does not suggest that we accept everything others say unquestioningly. Suspicion is sometimes warranted, but problems occur when suspicion becomes a norm of communication. When suspicion is always present, existential mistrust exists.

One factor that contributes to mistrust in individualistic cultures like the United States, which value direct communication, is looking for hidden meanings. Suspicion and looking for hidden meanings are only two of the factors that lead to mistrust. No mater how mistrust comes about, it always polarizes communication. Understanding people from other cultural or ethnic groups requires "a willing suspension of disbelief" (Trilling, 1968, p. 106).

CHARACTERISTICS OF COMMUNITY

Peck (1987) takes a slightly different, but compatible, approach to community. He sees community as critical to peace and intergroup harmony.

> In and through community lies the salvation of the world. Nothing is more important. Yet it is virtually impossible to describe community meaningfully to someone who has never experienced it—and most of us have never had an experience of true community. The problem is analogous to an attempt to describe the taste of artichokes to someone who has never eaten one. (p. 17)

Peck restricts the use of the term *community* to "a group of individuals who have learned how to communicate honestly with each other, whose relationships go deeper than their masks of composure, and who have developed some significant commitment to 'rejoice together, mourn together' and to 'delight in each other, make others' conditions our own'" (p. 59). Peck isolates several characteristics of a true community. Six are important here:

1. *Inclusivity.* Consistent with Buber's argument that communities are not made up of the like-minded is Peck's contention that different types of people, ideas, and emotions must be present in a community. Exclusivity is the enemy of a community. When individuals are excluded, cliques are formed, and cliques are defensive bastions against community.

2. *Commitment.* Peck argues that commitment involves "a willingness to co-exist together and hang in there when the going gets rough" (p. 62). It is commitment to the community that allows the differences among the individuals in the group to be absorbed.

3. *Consensus.* Communities seek agreement among all the members. Developing a consensus requires that differences be confronted and discussed. A consensus cannot emerge if differences are ignored or if conflict is suppressed. In a community, differences are transcended, *not* obliterated or demolished. "Perhaps the most necessary key to transcendence is the appreciation of differences. In community, instead of being ignored, denied, hidden, or changed, human differences are celebrated as gifts" (p. 62).

4. *Contemplation.* Members of a community examine it. "The essential goal of contemplation is increased awareness of the world outside oneself, the world in-

side oneself, and the relationship between the two" (p. 66). The need for contemplation is consistent with Socrates' claim that "the life which is unexamined is not worth living." Nozick (1989) believes that this position is unnecessarily harsh, but he does argue that it is necessary to examine *our* lives, if we are to live our own lives, not someone else's.

5. *Vulnerability.* As indicated earlier, for community to develop, members must drop their masks of composure. Peck contends that the development of community requires that we expose our inner selves to others and that we are affected by others when they expose their inner selves to us.

6. *Graceful fighting.* A community cannot exist without conflict. The management of the conflict which occurs, however, must be based on a real desire to listen to and understand each other's opinions, not on an insistence on being right. Peck makes the point that people tend to believe the fantasy that "if we can resolve our conflicts, then someday we will be able to live together in a community" (p. 72). He suggests, however, that this fantasy has the relationship between conflict and community backwards. The goal should be: "If we can live together in community, then someday we shall be able to resolve our conflicts" (p. 72).

Peck contends that while community can occur by accident, it also can occur by design. He sees the process through which a group becomes a community as a lawful one and one that can be taught and learned. Peck isolates four stages in the development of community: pseudocommunity, chaos, emptiness, and community. In the first stage, members of the group are pleasant to each other and avoid conflict. What emerges is not true community, but pseudocommunity, because conflict is avoided. The focus of the second stage, chaos, involves misguided attempts to help others or convert them to our way of thinking. In this stage, individual differences are out in the open and there is a perceived vacuum in leadership.

Peck specifies two ways out of the chaos stage. One way is through organization (e.g., assigning a leader). While organization will help a group out of chaos, it does not lead to community. Community emerges from "emptiness." By emptiness, Peck is referring to "the need to empty [ourselves] of barriers to [effective] communication" (p. 95). These barriers to effective communication include expectations and preconceptions; prejudices; ideology, theology, and solutions; the need to heal, convert, fix, or solve; and the need to control. When the individuals in the group overcome the barriers to effective communication, community can emerge.

The barriers to effective communication that Peck isolates are consistent with those discussed by many other authors. Prather (1986), for example, makes the point that all expectations are judgments and that for people to unite, they must let go of their expectations. While we agree with Prather's sentiment, we also think it is important to recognize that we cannot let go of all our expectations, prejudices, and the like. Being aware of our expectations and prejudices and how they influence the way we communicate (e.g., being mindful), however, is necessary for effective communication and community building.

COMMUNITY AND PUBLIC LIFE

Bellah et al. (1985) argue that without community, "there may be very little future to think about at all" (p. 286). They see a community as an inclusive group of people who share their public and private lives, or more specifically, as "a group of people who are socially interdependent, who participate together in discussion and decision-making and who share certain practices that both define the community and nurture it" (p. 333). A genuine community (e.g., a marriage, a university, a whole society) is defined by its practices.

Practices refer to "shared activities that are not undertaken as a means to an end but are ethically good in themselves" (Bellah et al., 1985, p. 335; this definition is similar to Aristotle's use of the term *praxis*). Bellah and his associates argue that genuine practices virtually always involve commitment because they involve activities that are ethically good.

Consistent with Buber and Peck, Bellah and his associates (1985) view communities as consisting of different types of people, even though there is a tendency to want to be with people who are similar. They point out that "the [North] American search for spontaneous community with the like-minded is made urgent for fear that there may be no way at all to relate to those who are different. . . . the public realm still survives, even though with difficulty, as an enduring association of the different" (p. 251). At times, the associations in the public realm may approach community. Bellah and his associates cite the civil rights movement and the response to Martin Luther King, Jr., as an example:

> The powerful response King elicited, transcending simple utilitarian calculations, came from the reawakened recognition by many [North] Americans that their own sense of self was rooted in companionship with others who, though not necessarily like themselves, nevertheless shared with them a common history and whose appeals to justice and solidarity made powerful claims on their loyalty. (p. 252)

Developing community, therefore, requires that we value justice and loyalty, and recognize the commonalities we share.

Selznick (1992) argues that there are two sources of moral integration that serve as the foundation for community: civility and piety. *Civility* involves being "guided by the distinctive virtues of public life. These include, especially, moderation in pursuit of one's own interests, and concern for the common good. More particularly, civility signals the community's commitment to dialogue as the preferred means of social decision" (p. 391). Selznick contends that civility "presumes diversity, autonomy, and potential conflict" and that "norms of civility are predicated on a regard for the integrity and independence of individuals and groups" (p. 391). Peck (1993) argues that civility emerges out of being conscious of our behavior (i.e., mindful) and is based on ethical behavior toward others. *Piety* involves a "reflection of the need for coherence and attachment. The distinctive virtues of piety are humility and loyalty" (Selznick, 1992, p. 387). Dewey (1934) views piety as a respect for human interdependence.

Bellah and his associates (1985) believe that commitment to public life and community will not emerge unless large numbers of individuals go through personal transformations (i.e., are willing to change). These transformations must not only be transformations of consciousness, but also transformations of actions.

One of the transformations of actions necessary for the development of community is giving of ourselves to others. Gandhi states that "consciously or unconsciously, every one of us does render some service or other. If we cultivate the habit of doing this service deliberately, our desire for service will steadily grow stronger, and will make not only for our own happiness, but for that of the world at large" (quoted by Lynberg, 1989, p. 19). Lynberg points out that

> the importance of giving, the path to a greater sense of success and fulfillment, is also a central lesson of the world's great religions. "They who give have all things," says a Hindu proverb, "they who withhold have nothing." In the Buddhist scriptures it is written, "The man [or woman] of wisdom who did good, the man [or woman] of morals who gave gifts, in this world and the next one too, they will advance to happiness." In the Koran, Mohammed conveys that "a man's [or woman's] true wealth is the good he [or she] does in this world." In the Torah, it is said that the Lord gives to every man [or woman] according to his [or her] ways, according to the fruit of his [or her] doings." And in Christianity we learn that "it is more blessed to give than to receive" and that "he [or she] who is greatest among you shall be your servant." (p. 18)

Lynberg concludes that it is not possible to live a "great life" without serving others.

Wuthnow (1991) points out that serving others is not inconsistent with individualism. He reports that both people who value "being able to do what you want" and people who do not value "being able to do what you want" in the United States say that helping people in need also is important. Wuthnow argues that individualism "embodies inner strength, a strong and clear sense of personal identity. It is this self-confidence that allows one to give. . . . It is, therefore, possible to live in community without giving up one's individuality" (p. 114).

While individuals must give of their own accord, the support of a community engaging in the same behavior makes it easier. Bellah and his associates (1985) point out that "individuals need the nurture of groups that carry a moral tradition reinforcing their own aspirations" (p. 286). They also contend that we need to develop a conception of the common good because "with a more explicit understanding of what we have in common and the goals we seek to attain together, the differences between us that remain would be less threatening" (p. 287). Finding commonalities requires that we be mindful of our prejudices. "Racism and sexism and homophobia and religious and cultural intolerance . . . are all ways of denying that other people are the same kind as ourselves" (Brodie, 1989, p. 16).

The position that Bellah and his associates advocate vis-à-vis cultural and/or ethnic differences is consistent with Langer's (1989) contention that

> because most of us grow up and spend our time with people like ourselves, we tend to assume uniformities and commonalities. When confronted with someone who is

> clearly different in one specific way, we drop that assumption and look for differences. . . . The mindful curiosity generated by an encounter with someone who is different, which can lead to exaggerated perceptions of strangeness, can also bring us closer to that person if channeled differently. (p. 156)

Langer's research suggests that once individuals satisfy their curiosity about differences, understanding can occur. Harman (1987) points out that "with modernity has come the need on behalf of the modern stranger to recognize community with potential others and negotiate membership on the basis of minimal indicators of commonality" (p. 127).

Bellah and his associates do not identify the practices or moral traditions necessary for commitment to the group and developing community. We, therefore, turn to a discussion of the ethical issues to identify practices necessary for building community with strangers.

ETHICAL ISSUES IN BUILDING COMMUNITY WITH STRANGERS

The practices in which we engage are critical to the development of community. One area where there may be a conflict in practices when we communicate with strangers is in the area of ethical behavior. Barnlund (1980) suggests that

> the moral issues that attend intercultural encounters are not simply more complicated, they are of an entirely new dimension. Despite the pervasiveness of cross-cultural contact, these complications remain overlooked and unexplored in any systematic way. The ethical vacuum that confronts us reflects not merely a failure of specialists within this evolving field, nor the negligence of outside agencies to give support to such ethical study, but is due in large part to difficulties that are inherent in the cross-cultural context. (pp. 9–10)

He goes on to argue that there is not a metaethic that can be used by people from different cultures when ethical dilemmas arise. Since ethical principles tend to be culture-specific, Barnlund suggests that when we communicate with strangers, we tend to approach ethical questions in one of two ways: (1) we make ethical judgments using our own cultural standards, or (2) we use the frame of reference of the strangers' culture. Both of these methods are unsatisfactory because

> either fosters a truncated morality that is incomplete and ethnocentric, for it subordinates the ethical premises of one culture or the other. And it thereby fails to fully illuminate or to fairly adjudicate conflicts in which people of different moral orientations must accommodate their differences and create ways of collaborating on common tasks. (p. 10)

Barnlund contends that what is needed is a metaethic, one prescribing standards applicable to both cultures.

One reason Barnlund (and others) argues that ethical judgments cannot be made regarding people in one culture by people in another culture is that he (and others) have extended the descriptive theory of cultural relativity to the domain of ethics. The theory of cultural relativism asserts that the behavior of people in different cultures can be understood only in the context of those cultures (see Chapters 1 and 5). In other words, if we want to understand the behavior of people in other cultures, we have to do it from their frame of reference (i.e., we have to avoid being ethnocentric). Many of the early writers discussing cultural relativism, however, incorporated the idea of tolerance of different practices in their discussions of cultural relativism. Herskovits (1973), for example, maintains that cultural relativism "is a philosophy which, in recognizing the values set up by every society to guide its own life, lays stress on the dignity in every body of custom, and on the need for tolerance of conventions though they may differ from one's own" (p. 76).

Renteln (1988) points out that incorporating tolerance in the theory of cultural relativity was due to the time in which the theory was developed. She points out that "cultural relativism was introduced in part to combat . . . racist, Eurocentric notions of progress" (p. 37), for example, viewing people from "less developed" cultures as "savages" or as "primitive." Barnsley (1972) points out, however, that it is necessary to draw a distinction between the evaluative and descriptive aspects of ethical relativity:

> Descriptive relativism . . . merely asserts the factual diversity of customs, of moral beliefs and practices. . . . The thesis itself, however, is purely a factual one. It may be termed, therefore, cultural relativism. . . . Ethical relativism proper, on the other hand, is an evaluative thesis, affirming that the value of actions and the validity of moral judgments are dependent upon their sociocultural context. The two theses are logically distinct, though not unrelated. (pp. 326–327)

In other words, Barnsley takes the position that saying that ethics develop out of culture and vary across cultures (cultural relativism) is different from saying that valid moral judgments can be made only within a particular cultural context (ethical relativism).

Berger argues that cultural relativity "does not, of course, free the individual from finding his [or her] own way morally. That would be another instance of 'bad faith,' with the objective fact of relativity being taken as an alibi for the subjective necessity of finding those single decisive points at which one engages one's whole being" (cited by Barnsley, 1972, p. 355). Like Berger, Renteln (1988) contends that cultural relativism

> does not force its adherents to foreswear moral criticism. Relativists, like everyone else, are ethnocentric . . . and remain true to their own convictions. There is no reason why the relativist should be paralyzed [from making moral judgments]. . . . But the relativist will acknowledge that the criticism is based on his [or her] own ethnocentric standards and realizes also that the condemnation may be a form of cultural imperialism. Under extreme circumstances, meaning that an action in another culture

violates one of the relativists' most deeply held beliefs, the relativist may decide that criticism and even intervention are lesser evils than either ethnocentrism or cultural imperialism" (pp. 63–64).

Even if we accept cultural diversity, in other words, we must still make ethical judgments in our interactions with strangers.

There is not a metaethic upon which there is agreement to guide our moral judgments, but there are cultural universals that can be used to guide our behavior when we communicate with strangers. Bidney (1968), for example, suggests that there may be universals regarding prohibitions against activities such as treason, murder, rape, and incest because "in all cultures the perpetuation of society takes precedence over the life of the individual" (p. 545). Selznick (1992) argues that a long list of moral universals can be constructed. Such a list would include "the ideal of preserving human life; looking to the well-being of close relatives; prohibiting murder and theft; valuing affection and companionship; reciprocity in helping and being helped; and hospitality" (p. 96). Selznick goes on to point out that "there can be no effective social life without widespread commitment to responsible conduct, which requires virtues of truthfulness, courage, fidelity, and respect" (p. 101). Although there is general agreement on these values across cultures, the ways that the values are practiced may differ.

In discussing the moral constraints necessary for peace, Bok (1989) suggests additional areas where there may be cultural universals in ethical behavior:

> Of the four, two are the widely acknowledged curbs on violence and deceit. . . . To cement agreement about how and to whom those curbs apply, and to keep them from being ignored or violated at will, a third constraint—on breaches of valid promises, contracts, laws, and treaties—is needed.
>
> Whether expressed in religious or secular form, these three values are shared by every civilization, past and present. Any community, no matter how small or disorganized, no matter how hostile toward outsiders, no matter how cramped its perception of what constitutes, say, torture, has to impose at least *some* internal curbs on violence, deceit, and betrayal in order to survive. But because persons acting clandestinely easily bypass or ignore these constraints, a fourth is necessary on excessive secrecy. (pp. 81–82)

The practice of Bok's moral constraints in a group provides an environment in which peace and community can be nurtured (for extended discussions of the importance of nonviolence, see Gandhi, 1948; King, 1958).

PRINCIPLES OF COMMUNITY BUILDING

To review, a community consists of diverse individuals who are honest and open with each other, trust each other, engage in ethical behavior, and are committed to living together. Members of a community are civil to each other, and they value diversity while, at the same time, they search for the commonalities humans share.

Community makes life worth living, and the existence of community makes peace and intergroup harmony possible. While community occurs in groups, individuals must take the responsibility for building community in their marriages, workplaces, schools, cities, and nations, as well as in the world. Finally, members of a community behave ethically.

To conclude our discussion of community, we synthesize the information presented in this chapter into a set of principles for community building (this section is based on Gudykunst, 1994). The principles we will present are based on several *assumptions:*

1. Community is necessary to make life worth living and to increase the potential for peace in the world. Peace is not possible without community. "Our experience of connection and community shape who we are, how we experience other people, and how we bear the stresses of both ordinary and extraordinary events" (Staub, 1989, p. 269).

2. Developing community is the responsibility of the individual. All of us must take the responsibility for building community in our own lives. "People who fully develop and harmoniously integrate their capabilities, values, and goals will be connected to others. The full evolution of the self . . . requires relationships and the development of deep connections and community—as well as the capacity for separateness" (Staub, 1989, p. 269).

3. Cultural and ethnic diversity (and all other forms of diversity, as well) are necessary resources for building community. Lippmann (1937) argues that we need to work toward developing communities that respect and encourage diversity. A true community cannot exist without diversity. Gardner (1991), however, points out that "to prevent the wholeness from smothering diversity, there must be a philosophy of pluralism, an open climate for dissent, and an opportunity for subcommunities to retain their identity and share in setting of larger goals" (p. 11).

4. Communities can be any size (e.g., a marriage, social organization, university, town, country, or even the world), but we must start building community in the smaller groups of which we are members (e.g., families) and work toward developing community in the larger groups (e.g., universities, societies).

5. We are what we think. Jampolsky (1989), among others, points out that "everything in life depends on the thoughts we choose to hold in our minds and our willingness to change our belief systems" (p. 31). Similarly, in *The Dhammapada,* Buddha said that "our life is shaped by our minds; we become what we think."

6. Community cannot exist without conflict. Hampshire (1989) argues that we should expect "ineliminable and acceptable conflicts, and . . . rationally controlled hostilities, as the normal condition" (p. 189). We need to be able to manage and reconcile the conflicts that occur, especially the conflicts that emerge from the diversity of our community (Lippmann, 1937). Peck (1987) points out that we tend to assume that "if we can resolve our conflicts, then someday we will be able to live together in community" (p. 72). He argues that this assumption is mistaken. Actually, "if we can live together in community, then someday we shall be able to resolve our conflicts" (p. 72). To develop community, therefore, we must engage in graceful fighting; we must try to persuade each other, but not coerce each other.

7. As Fisher and Brown (1988) suggest, one person can change a relationship and/or start the development of community. If one person follows the principles suggested below, people with whom this person comes in contact eventually will change the way they interact.

Given these assumptions and the material summarized throughout the book, we present seven *community building principles:*

1. *Be committed.* We must be committed to the principle of building community in our lives, as well as to the individuals with whom we are trying to develop a community (Peck, 1987). Commitment to others is a prerequisite for community to exist. If we are not committed, others will sense our lack of commitment and it will affect the quality of our relationships with them. We also need to be committed to dialogue as a way of solving problems (Selznick, 1992). Without commitment to our relationships with others and to dialogue, we cannot manage our conflicts constructively with others. It is the commitment present in a community that allows the differences inherent in its diversity to be absorbed (Peck, 1987). We need to be committed to our collective (social) identities associated with our communities and to a participatory mode of politics within the community (Taylor, 1991). We must be committed to adhering to cooperating with others on our shared goals. We also need to be committed to principles, not to insisting on being right (Buber, 1958).

2. *Be mindful.* We must pay attention to what we do and say. Bellah et al. (1991) point out that "when we are giving our full attention to something, when we are really attending, we are calling on all of our resources of intelligence, feeling, and moral sensitivity. . . . We are not thinking about ourselves, because we are completely absorbed in what we are doing" (p. 254). If we communicate on automatic pilot, we will interpret others' behavior by using our own frame of reference and evaluate others, rather than try to understand them. If we are not mindful of our communication, we will interpret others' behavior from our own frame of reference and be more concerned for ourselves than others. Interpreting others' behavior using our frame of reference makes it impossible to develop community. When we are mindful, we need to focus on the process of our communication, not the outcome (Langer, 1989). Our emphasis should be on adapting our messages so that others can understand them and on interpreting others' messages by using their frame of reference.

3. *Be unconditionally accepting.* For community to develop, we must accept others as they are, and not try to change or control them (Fisher & Brown, 1988). If we try to change others, they will become defensive and building community will not be possible. We must accept others' diversity and not judge them only on the basis their group memberships. We need to recognize and support the personal and social identities others claim for themselves. If we do not support others' self-concepts, we cannot develop satisfying relationships with them. We need to minimize our expectations, prejudices, suspicion, and mistrust (Peck, 1987). Bellah et al. (1991) point out that trusting others is necessary for community to develop.

4. *Be concerned for both ourselves and others.* Communities are inclusive; they are *not* groups of like-minded people. We must walk a narrow ridge in our in-

teractions with others whenever practical (Buber, 1958). Doing so means that we must avoid polarizing our communication (Arnett, 1986), actively listen to others when they speak, and engage in dialogue whenever possible (Buber, 1958, 1965). Our survival depends on the survival of the communities of which we are members (Loewry, 1993). Being authentic (e.g., self-fulfilled, empowered) and identifying with others and our communities are *not* incompatible (Taylor, 1991). We need to be concerned with our own and others' personal and social identities. We must consult others on issues that affect them, and be open to their ideas (Fisher & Brown, 1988). We must take others into consideration when there is conflict, and fight gracefully (Peck, 1987). We also need to be contemplative in examining our own behavior and that of the other members of the communities of which we are a part (Peck, 1987).

5. *Be understanding.* We need to strive to understand others as completely as possible. As Martin Luther King, Jr., (1963) said, "shallow understanding from people of good will is more frustrating than absolute misunderstanding from people of ill will" (p. 88). To be understanding, we must determine how others' interpretations of events and/or behaviors are different from and similar to our own. We also must recognize how culture, ethnicity, and other forms of diversity affect the way we think and behave. We must understand real differences between our group and others' groups, not base our interpretations of differences on our stereotypes and prejudices. Building community requires "the appreciation of differences. In community, instead of being ignored, denied, hidden, or changed, human differences are celebrated as gifts" (Peck, 1987, p. 62). We also need to search for commonalities on which community can be built (Bellah et al., 1985). In our communication, we must balance emotion, anxiety, and fear with reason (Fisher & Brown, 1988).

6. *Be ethical.* We must engage in behavior that is not a means to an end, but behavior which is morally right in and of itself (Bellah et al., 1985). We have to be reliable in what we say and do (Fisher & Brown, 1988). We must be morally inclusive (Opotow, 1990) and engage in service to others (Lynberg, 1989). Staub (1989) points out that "starting with common everyday acts and moving on to acts requiring greater sacrifice . . . can lead to genuine concern and a feeling of responsibility for people" (p. 276). That is not to say that we should not make moral judgments. We cannot avoid making ethical judgments, but we need to understand strangers' behavior in their frame of reference before we make such judgments. A community is based on its moral principles (Etzioni, 1993).

7. *Be peaceful.* We must *not* be violent or deceitful, breach valid promises, or be secretive (Bok, 1989). Even if others engage in these behaviors toward us, we are not justified in engaging in these behaviors toward them (Fisher & Brown, 1988). As Socrates pointed out, retaliation is never justified (Vlastos, 1991). We must strive for internal harmony (Prather, 1986) and harmony in our relations with others. "Practicing mindfulness in each moment of our daily lives, we can cultivate our own peace. With clarity, determination, and patience . . . we can sustain a life of action and be real instruments of peace" (Hanh, 1991, p. 99). If we are peaceful, everyone with whom we come into contact will benefit from our peace.

These seven principles are ideals toward which we can strive. The more we are able to put them into practice individually, the greater the chance for community and peace in the world. We must not punish ourselves, however, when we fail to achieve the ideal. Achieving these ideals is a lifetime's work and requires extensive practice. If we are to tolerate others, we must begin by accepting our own mistakes. Prather (1986) points out that when we find that we are not engaging in behaviors we want to practice (e.g., building community), we must forgive ourselves and start anew at practicing the behaviors. For most of us, this process will occur numerous times a day initially, especially when the behaviors suggested in the ideals are different from those we have learned from birth. To engage in these behaviors consistently, we may have to unlearn many of our normal behaviors (e.g., behaviors that occur at low levels of awareness, such as reacting defensively and looking out only for ourselves). The critical thing is *not* the outcome, but the process. If we behave in a way consistent with these ideals (the process), community (the desirable outcome) will occur.

SUMMARY

Polarized communication predominates in the world today. There is a lack of concern for others present in the world today which often leads to strangers' being morally excluded. Communities, however, are inclusive, and cultural and ethnic diversity are resources for building community. The development of community requires that we walk a narrow ridge when communicating with others. To develop community in our lives, we must be committed, mindful, unconditionally accepting, concerned for both ourselves and others, understanding, ethical, and peaceful.

In conclusion, we have tried to present the material that we think will help you understand your communication with strangers. Understanding is a necessary prerequisite for effective communication. If we do not understand how strangers are different from and similar to ourselves, we cannot communicate effectively with them. To understand strangers (and people who are familiar), we must be able to manage the anxiety we experience when we communicate with them. Understanding strangers (and people who are familiar), therefore, requires that we be mindful of our communication.

We generally are not mindful when we communicate with strangers or with people who are familiar. When we are mindful, however, we can manage our anxiety cognitively and figure out how our interpretations of messages differ from those of the strangers with whom we are communicating. Deciding whether we want to make the effort is up to each of us. We can continue our normal patterns of communication—communicating on automatic pilot and interpreting strangers' messages by using our own frame of reference. Making this choice ensures that a large portion of our communication with strangers will be ineffective. If, on the other hand, we choose to try to understand strangers, the likelihood that our communication with them will be effective increases. Understanding strangers does not mean that we have to accept behavior we find objectionable. Rather, we need to understand what the behavior means to the strangers before we judge them and to realize that our judgment may be ethnocentric.

Attempting to understand strangers increases the chance that we will be able to build community in our lives and foster peace on the planet. While these are idealistic goals, they are achievable, if we all do our part. Let us begin!

STUDY QUESTIONS

1. Why are communities *not* composed of people who are like-minded?
2. What are the differences between monologues, technical dialogues, and dialogues? Which contributes to building community? Why?
3. What is involved in walking a narrow ridge?
4. What are the characteristics of community?
5. What is the role of civility in building community?
6. Why are individualism and community not inconsistent?
7. Why are diversity and commonality important in developing community?
8. Why is ethical relativity not necessary for building community?
9. What are potential universals of ethical principles?
10. Why is conflict a necessary part of building community?
11. What are the principles of building community?

SUGGESTED READING

Arnett, R. (1986). *Communication and community.* Carbondale: Southern Illinois University Press.

Bellah, R., Madsen, R., Sullivan, W., Swidler, A., & Tipton, S. (1985). *Habits of the heart.* Berkeley: University of California Press.

Bellah, R., Madsen, R., Sullivan, W., Swidler, A., & Tipton, S. (1991). *The good society.* New York: Knopf.

Etzioni, A. (1993). *The spirit of community.* New York: Crown.

Peck, M. S. (1987). *The different drum: Community making and peace.* New York: Simon and Schuster.

Selznick, P. (1992). *The moral commonwealth.* Berkeley: University of California Press.

Staub, E. (1989). *The roots of evil.* New York: Cambridge University Press.

Taylor, C. (1992). *The ethics of authenticity.* Cambridge, MA: Harvard University Press.

References

Abe, H., & Wiseman, R. (1983). Cross-cultural confirmation of the dimensions of intercultural effectiveness. *International Journal of Intercultural Relations, 7,* 53–68.

Abelson, R. (1976). Script processing in attitude formation and decision making. In J. Carroll & J. Payne (Eds.), *Cognition and social behavior.* Hillsdale, NJ: Erlbaum.

Abrahams, R. (1976). *Talking black.* Rowley, MA: Newbury House.

Adamopoulos, J., & Bontempo, R. (1986). Diachronic universals in interpersonal structures. *Journal of Cross-Cultural Psychology, 17,* 169–189.

Adelman, M. B. (1988). Cross-cultural adjustment. *International Journal of Intercultural Relations, 12,* 183–204.

Adelman, M. B., & Lustig, W. (1981). Intercultural communication problems as perceived by Saudi Arabian and American managers. *International Journal of Intercultural Relations, 5,* 365–381.

Adler, P. S. (1975). The transitional experience: An alternative view of culture shock. *Journal of Humanistic Psychology, 15,* 13–23.

Adler, P. S. (1982/1987). Beyond cultural identity: Reflections on cultural and multicultural man. In L. Samovar & R. Porter (Eds.), *Intercultural communication: A reader* (4th ed.). Belmont, CA: Wadsworth.

Agar, M. (1994). *Language shock.* New York: Morrow.

Ainslie, R. (1994). Notes on the psychodynamics of acculturation. *Mind & Human Interaction, 5*(2), 6–67.

Aitken, T. (1973). *The multinational man: The role of the manager abroad.* New York: Wiley.

Alba, R. (1976). Social assimilation among American Catholic national origin groups. *American Sociological Review, 41,* 1030–1046.

Alba, R. (1990). *Ethnic identity.* New Haven, CT: Yale University Press.

Albert, E. (1972). Culture patterning in Burundi. In J. Gumperz & D. Hymes (Eds.), *Directions in sociolinguistics.* New York: Holt, Rinehart and Winston.

Alberty, R., & Emmons, M. (1990). *Your perfect right* (6th ed.). San Louis Obispo, CA: Impact.

Allen, B. P. (1976). Race and physical attractiveness as criteria for white subjects' dating choices. *Social Behavior and Personality, 4,* 289–296.

Allen, I. (1983). *The language of ethnic conflict.* New York: Columbia University Press.

Allport, G. W. (1954). *The nature of prejudice.* New York: Macmillan.

Almaney, A., & Alwan, A. (1982). *Communicating with the Arabs.* Prospect Heights, IL: Waveland.

Altman, I. (1975). *The environment and social behavior.* Monterey, CA: Brooks/Cole.

Altman, I. (1977). Privacy regulation. *Journal of Social Issues, 33,* 66–84.

Altman, I., & Chemers, M. (1980a). *Culture and environment.* Monterey, CA: Brooks/Cole.

Altman, I., & Chemers, M. (1980b). Cultural aspects of environment-behavior relationships. In H. Triandis & R. Brislin (Eds.), *Handbook of cross-cultural psychology* (Vol. 5). Boston: Allyn and Bacon.

Altman, I., & Gauvain, M. (1981). A cross-cultural dialectical analysis of homes. In L. Luben, A. Patterson, & N. Newcombe (Eds.), *Spatial representation and behavior across the life span.* New York: Academic Press.

Altman, I., & Taylor, D. (1973). *Social penetration.* New York: Holt, Rinehart, and Winston.

Altman, I., Vinsel, A., & Brown, B. (1981). Dialectical conceptions in social psychology: An application to social penetration and privacy regulation. In L. Berkowitz (Ed.), *Advances in experimental social psychology* (Vol. 14). New York: Academic Press.

Amerikaner, M. (1978). *Personality integration and the theory of open systems.* Unpublished doctoral dissertation, University of Florida, Gainesville.

Andersen, P., Lustig, M., & Andersen, J. (1990). Changes in latitude, changes in attitude. *Communication Quarterly, 38,* 291–311.

Applegate, J., & Sypher, H. (1983). The constructivist approach. In W. Gudykunst (Ed.), *Intercultural communication theory.* Beverly Hills, CA: Sage.

Argyle, M. (1982). Intercultural communication. In S. Bochner (Ed.), *Cultures in contact.* Elmsford, NY: Pergamon.

Argyle, M. (1991). *Cooperation.* London: Routledge.

Argyle, M., Furnham, A., & Graham, J. (1981). *Social situations.* Cambridge, UK: Cambridge University Press.

Argyle, M., & Henderson, M. (1984). The rules of relationships. In S. Duck & D. Perlman (Eds.), *Understanding personal relationships.* Beverly Hills, CA: Sage.

Argyle, M., Henderson, M., Bond, M., Iizuka, Y., & Contarelo, A. (1986). Cross-cultural variations in relationship rules. *International Journal of Psychology, 21,* 287–315.

Arnett, R. (1986). *Communication and community.* Carbondale: Southern Illinois University Press.

Arnoff, C. (1974). Old age in prime time. *Journal of Communication, 24,* 86–87.

Aronson, E. (1972). *The social animal.* San Francisco: W. H. Freeman.

Ashcraft, N., & Scheflen, E. (1976). *People space: The making and breaking of human boundaries.* Garden City, NY: Anchor Press.

Atkenson, P. (1970). Building communication in intercultural marriage. *Psychiatry, 33,* 396–408.

Atwater, E. (1983). *Psychology and adjustment.* Englewood Cliffs, NJ: Prentice Hall.

Austin, C. (1983). *Cross-cultural reentry: An annotated bibliography.* Abilene, TX: Abilene Christian University.

Baddassare, M., & Feller, S. (1975). Cultural variation in personal space. *Ethos, 3,* 481–503.

Baker, J., & Gudykunst, W. (1990). *Privacy regulation in Japan and the United States.* Paper presented at the International Communication Association convention, Dublin.

Ball-Rokeach, S. (1973). From pervasive ambiguity to definition of the situation. *Sociometry, 36,* 378–389.

Ball-Rokeach, S., Rokeach, M., & Grube, J. (1984). *The great American values test.* New York: Free Press.

Banks, S. (1987). Achieving "unmarkedness" in organizational discourse. *Journal of Language and Social Psychology, 6,* 171–190.

Banks, S., Gao, G., & Baker, J. (1991). Intercultural encounters and miscommunication. In N. Coupland, H. Giles, & J. Wiemann (Eds.), *"Miscommunication" and problematic talk.* Thousand Oaks, CA: Sage.

Barbato, C., & Feezel, J. (1987). The language of aging in different age-groups. *Gerontological Society of America, 27,* 527–531.

Barnes, J. (1954). Class and communities in a Norwegian island parish. *Human Relations, 7,* 39–58.

Barnett, G., & Kincaid, D. L. (1983). A mathematical theory of cultural convergence. In W. Gudykunst (Ed.), *Intercultural communication theory.* Beverly Hills, CA: Sage.

Barnlund, D. (1962). Toward a meaning-centered philosophy of communication. *Journal of Communication, 2,* 197–211.

Barnlund, D. (1968). *Interpersonal communication.* Boston: Houghton Mifflin.

Barnlund, D. (1975). *Public and private self in Japan and the United States.* Tokyo: Simul Press.

Barnlund, D. (1980). The cross-cultural arena: An ethical void. In N. Asuncion-Lande (Ed.), *Ethical perspectives and critical issues in intercultural communication.* Falls Church, VA: Speech Communication Association.

Barnlund, D. (1991). Communication in a global village. In L. Samovar & R. Porter (Eds.), *Intercultural communication: A reader* (6th ed.). Belmont, CA: Wadsworth.

Barnsley, J. (1972). *The social reality of ethics.* London: Routledge and Kegan Paul.

Barringer, F. (1993, May 16). Pride in a soundless world. *New York Times,* pp. 1, 14.

Barth, F. (1969). *Ethnic groups and boundaries.* London: Allen and Unwin.

Basso, K. (1970). To give up on words. *Southern Journal of Anthropology, 26,* 213–230.

Bates, T. (1994). Social resources generated by group support networks may not be beneficial to Asian immigrant-owned small businesses. *Social Forces, 72,* 671–689.

Bateson, G. (1972). *Steps to an ecology of mind.* New York: Ballantine Books.

Bateson, G. (1978). The pattern which connects. *Co-Evolution Quarterly, 18,* 4–15.

Bateson, G. (1979). *Mind and nature.* New York: Dutton.

Beardsley, R. K. (1965). Cultural anthropology. In J. Hall & R. Beardsley (Eds.), *Twelve doors to Japan.* New York: McGraw-Hill.

Beck, A. (1976). *Cognitive therapy and the emotional disorders.* New York: International Universities Press.

Beck, A. (1988). *Love is never enough.* New York: Harper and Row.

Beebe, L., & Takahashi, T. (1989). Sociolinguistic variations in face threatening acts. In M. Eisenstein (Ed.), *The dynamic interlanguage.* New York: Plenum.

Beier, E., & Zautra, A. (1972). Identification of vocal communication of emotion across cultures. *Journal of Consulting and Clinical Psychology, 34,* 166.

Belk, S., Snell, W., Garcia-Falconi, R., Hargrove, L., & Holzman, W. (1988). Power strategies used in the intimate relationships of women and men from Mexico and the United States. *Personality and Social Psychology Bulletin, 14,* 439–447.

Bell, R. (1981). *Worlds of friendship.* Beverly Hills, CA: Sage.

Bell, R. (1987). Social involvement. In J. McCrosky & J. Daly (Eds.), *Personality and interpersonal communication.* Beverly Hills, CA: Sage.

Bellah, R., Madsen, R., Sullivan, W., Swidler, A., & Tipton, S. (1985). *Habits of the heart.* Berkeley: University of California Press.

Bellah, R., Madsen, R., Sullivan, W., Swidler, A., & Tipton, S. (1991). *The good society.* New York: Knopf.

Bem, S. (1970). Case study of nonconscious ideology. In D. Bem (Ed.), *Beliefs, attitudes, and human affairs.* Belmont, CA: Brooks/Cole.

Bem, S. (1974). The measurement of psychological androgyny. *Journal of Consulting and Clinical Psychology, 42,* 155–162.

Bem, S. (1993). *The lens of gender.* New Haven, CT: Yale University Press.

Benedict, R. (1934). *Patterns of culture.* Boston: Houghton Mifflin.

Benedict, R. (1946). *The chrysanthemum and the sword.* Boston: Houghton Mifflin.

Bennett, J. (1977). Transition shock. In N. Jain (Ed.), *International and intercultural communication annual* (Vol. IV). Falls Church, VA: Speech Communication Association.

Bennett, J., Passin, J., & McKnight, R. (1958). *In search of identity: Japanese overseas scholars in the United States.* Minneapolis: University of Minnesota Press.

Bennett, M. (1979). Overcoming the golden rule: Sympathy and empathy. In D. Nimmo (Ed.), *Communication yearbook 3.* New Brunswick, NJ: Transaction.

Benson, P., & Vincent, S. (1980). Development and validation of the sexist attitude toward women scale. *Psychology of Women Quarterly, 5,* 276–291.

Berger, C. (1979). Beyond initial interaction. In H. Giles & R. St. Clair (Eds.), *Language and social psychology.* Oxford, UK: Blackwell.

Berger, C., & Bradac, J. (1982). *Language and social knowledge.* London: Edward Arnold.

Berger, C., & Calabrese, R. (1975). Some explorations in initial interaction and beyond. *Human Communication Research, 1,* 99–112.

Berger, C., & Douglas, W. (1982). Thought and talk: "Excuse me, but have I been talking to myself?" In F. Dance (Ed.), *Human communication theory.* New York: Harper and Row.

Berger, C., Gardner, R., Parks, M., Schulman, L., & Miller, G. (1976). Interpersonal epistemology and interpersonal communication. In G. Miller (Ed.), *Explorations in interpersonal communication.* Beverly Hills, CA: Sage.

Berger, P., & Kellner, H. (1970). Marriage and construction of reality. In H. Dreitzel (Ed.), *Recent sociology, no. 2: Patterns of communication behavior.* New York: Macmillan.

Berger, P., & Luckman, T. (1967). *The social construction of reality.* New York: Doubleday.

Berger, J., Wagner, D., & Zelditch, M. (1985). Introduction: Expectation states theory. In J. Berger & M. Zelditch (Eds.), *Status, rewards, and influence.* San Francisco: Jossey-Bass.

Berlin, B., & Kay, P. (1969). *Basic color terms: Their universality and evolution.* Berkeley: University of California Press.

Berlo, D. K. (1960). *The process of communication.* New York: Holt, Rinehart and Winston.

Berlyne, D. (1980). Psychological aesthetics. In H. Triandis & W. Lambert (Eds.), *Handbook of cross-cultural psychology* (Vol. 3). Boston: Allyn and Bacon.

Bernstein, B. (1966). Elaborated and restricted codes. In A. Smith (Ed.), *Communication and culture.* New York: Holt, Rinehart and Winston.

Bernstein, B. (1971). *Class, codes and control.* Boston: Routledge and Kegan Paul.

Berreman, G. (1972). Race, caste and other invidious distinctions in social stratification. *Race, 13,* 385-414.

Berry, J. (1980). Acculturation as varieties of adaptation. In A. Padilla (Ed.), *Acculturation: Theory, models and some new findings.* Boulder, CO: Westview Press.

Berry, J. (1990). Psychology of acculturation. In R. Brislin (Ed.), *Applied cross-cultural psychology.* Newbury Park, CA: Sage.

Berry, J., & Kim, U. (1987). Acculturation and mental health. In P. Dasen, J. Berry, & N. Sartorious (Eds.), *Health and cross-cultural psychology.* Thousand Oaks, CA: Sage.

Berry, J., Kim, U., & Boski, P. (1988). Psychological acculturation of immigrants. In Y. Kim & W. Gudykunst (Eds.), *Cross-cultural adaptation.* Newbury Park, CA: Sage.

Berscheid, E. (1985). Interpersonal attraction. In G. Lindzey & E. Aronson (Eds.), *Handbook of social psychology* (3rd ed., Vol. 2). New York: Random House.

Berscheid, E., Granziano, W., Monson, T., & Dermer, M. (1976). Outcome dependency. *Journal of Personality and Social Psychology, 34,* 978–989.

Berscheid, E., & Walster, E. (1969). *Interpersonal attraction.* Reading, MA: Addison-Wesley.

Best, D., & Williams, J. (1984). A cross-cultural examination of self and ideal self descriptions in Canada, England, and the United States. In R. Diaz-Guerrero (Ed.), *Cross-cultural and national studies in social psychology.* New York: Elsevier.

Bezooijen, R., Otto, S., & Heenan, T. (1983). Recognition of vocal expressions of emotions. *Journal of Cross-Cultural Psychology, 14,* 387–406.

Bidney, D. (1968). Cultural relativism. In D. Sills (Ed.), *International encyclopedia of the social sciences.* (Vol. 3). New York: Free Press.

Bieri, J. (1955). Cognitive complexity-simplicity and predictive behavior. *Journal of Abnormal and Social Psychology, 51,* 263–268.

Billig, M. (1987). *Arguing and thinking.* Cambridge, UK: Cambridge University Press.

Billig, M. (1995). *Banal nationalism.* London: Sage.

Billig, M., Condor, S., Edwards, D., Gane, M., Middleton, D., & Radley, A. (1988). *Ideological dilemmas.* Newbury Park, CA: Sage.

Birdwhistell, R. (1963). The kinesis level in the investigation of the emotions. In P. H. Knapp (Ed.), *Expressions of the emotions in man.* New York: International University Press.

Birdwhistell, R. (1970). *Kinesics in context.* Philadelphia: University of Pennsylvania Press.

Birenbaum, A., & Sagarin, E. (1976). *Norms and human behavior.* New York: Praeger.

Biswas, A. (1984). *Climate and development.* Dublin: Tycoly.

Blanchard, F., Lilly, T., & Vaughn, L. (1991). Reducing the expression of racial prejudice. *Psychological Science, 2,* 101–105.

Blau, P., & Schwartz, B. (1984). *Cross-cutting social circles.* New York: Academic Press.

Boas, F. (1911). Introduction. In *Handbook of American Indian languages* (Vol. 40). Washington, DC: Smithsonian Institute.

Bochner, S. (Ed.). (1981). *The mediating person.* Cambridge, MA: Schenkman.

Bochner, S. (1994). Cross-cultural differences in self-concept. *Journal of Cross-Cultural Psychology, 25,* 273–283.

Bodenhausen, G., Gaelick, L., & Wyer, R. (1987). Affective and cognitive factors in intragroup and intergroup communication. In C. Hendrick (Ed.), *Group processes and intergroup relations.* Newbury Park, CA: Sage.

Boekestijn, C. (1988). Intercultural migration and the development of personal identity. *International Journal of Intercultural Relations, 12*(2), 83–105.

Bogardus, E. (1959). *Social distance.* Yellow Springs, OH: Antioch Press.

Bok, S. (1989). *A strategy for peace.* New York: Pantheon.

Boldt, E. (1978). Structural tightness and cross-cultural research. *Journal of Cross-Cultural Psychology, 9,* 151–165.

Boldt, E., & Roberts, L. (1979). Structural tightness and social conformity. *Journal of Cross-Cultural Psychology, 10,* 221–230.

Bolton, R. (1979). *People skills.* New York: Simon and Schuster.

Bond, M. (1988). Finding universal dimensions of individual variations in multinational studies of values. *Journal of Personality and Social Psychology, 55,* 1009–1015.

Bond, M. (1993). Emotions and their experience in Chinese culture. *Journal of Nonverbal Behavior, 17,* 245–262.

Bond, M., & Cheung, T. (1983). College students' spontaneous self-concept. *Journal of Cross-Cultural Psychology, 14,* 153–171.

Bond, M., & Venus, C. (1991). Resistance to group or personal insults in an ingroup and out-group context. *International Journal of Psychology, 26,* 83–94.

Bond, M., Wan, K., Leung, K., & Giacalone, R. (1985). How are the responses to verbal insults related to cultural collectivism? *Journal of Cross-Cultural Psychology, 16,* 111–127.

Bosmajian, H. (1974). *The language of oppression.* Washington, DC: Public Affairs Press.

Bostain, J. (1973). *"How to read a foreigner."* Videotaped presentation. Intercultural Relations Course, Naval Amphibious School, Coronado, CA.

Boucher, J., Landis, D., & Clark, K. (Eds). (1987). *Ethnic conflict.* Newbury Park, CA: Sage.

Boulding, E. (1990). *Building a global civic culture.* Syracuse, NY: Syracuse University Press.

Boulding, K. (1956). *The image.* Ann Arbor: University of Michigan Press.

Bourhis, R. (1985). The sequential nature of language choices in cross-cultural communication. In R. Street & J. Cappella (Eds.), *Sequence and pattern in communicative behavior.* London: Edward Arnold.

Bourhis, R., Giles, H., Leyens, J., & Tajfel, H. (1979). Psycholinguistic distinctiveness. In H. Giles & R. St. Clair (Eds.), *Language and social psychology.* Oxford, UK: Blackwell.

Bourhis, R., Giles, H., & Rosenthal, D. (1981). Notes on the construction of a "subjective vitality questionnaire" for ethnolinguistic groups. *Journal of Multilingual and Multicultural Development, 2,* 145–155.

Bourhis, R., & Sachdev, I. (1984). Vitality perceptions and language attitudes. *Journal of Language and Social Psychology, 3,* 97–126.

Boyer, E. (1990, June 20). Letter to the editor. *Chronicle of Higher Education,* p. B4.

Brabant, S., Palmer, C., & Grambling, R. (1990). Returning home. *International Journal of Intercultural Relations, 14,* 387–404.

Bradac, J. (1990). Language attitudes and impression formation. In H. Giles & P. Robinson (Eds.), *Handbook of language and social psychology.* London: Wiley.

Bradburn, N. (1969). *The structure of psychological well-being.* Chicago: Aldine.

Braithwaite, D. (1991). "Just how much did that wheelchair cost?" *Western Journal of Speech Communication, 55,* 254–274.

Bram, J. (1955). *Language and society.* Garden City, NY: Doubleday.

Branham, R. (1980). Ineffability, creativity and communication competence. *Communication Quarterly, 3,* 11–21.

Branscombe, N., & Wann, D. (1994). Collective self-esteem consequences of outgroup derogation when a values social identity is on trial. *European Journal of Social Psychology, 24,* 641–657.

Brein, M., & David, K. (1971). Intercultural communication and the adjustment of the sojourner. *Psychological Bulletin, 76,* 215–230.

Breton, R. (1964). Institutional completeness of ethnic communities and the personal relations of immigrants. *American Journal of Sociology, 40,* 193–205.

Breton, R. (1991). *The governance of ethnic communities.* Westport, CT: Greenwood.

Brewer, M. (1968). Determinants of social distance among East African tribal groups. *Journal of Personality and Social Psychology, 10,* 279–289.

Brewer, M. (1979). Ingroup bias in the minimal intergroup situation. *Psychological Bulletin, 86,* 307–324.

Brewer, M. (1991). The social self. *Personality and Social Psychology Bulletin, 17,* 475–482.

Brewer, M., & Campbell, D. (1976). *Ethnocentrism and intergroup attitudes.* New York: Wiley.

Brewer, M., & Miller, N. (1988). Contact and cooperation. In P. Katz & D. Taylor (Eds.), *Eliminating racism.* New York: Plenum.

Brim, O., & Wheeler, S. (1966). *Socialization through the life cycle.* New York: Wiley.

Brislin, R. (1979). Increasing the range of concepts in intercultural research: The example of prejudice. In W. Davey (Ed.), *Intercultural theory and practice.* Washington, DC: Society for Intercultural Education, Training and Research.

Brislin, R. (1981). *Cross-cultural encounters.* Elmsford, NY: Pergamon.

Brislin, R., Cushner, K., Cherrie, C., & Yong, M. (1986). *Intercultural interactions.* Beverly Hills, CA: Sage.

Brislin, R., & Yoshida, T. (1994). *Intercultural communication training.* Thousand Oaks, CA: Sage.

Brodie, H. (1989, September 9). No we're not taught to hate, but we can overcome the instinct to fear "the other." *Los Angeles Times,* Part II, p. 16.

Broom, L., & Kitsuse, J. (1955). The validation of acculturation. *American Anthropologist, 57,* 44–48.

Broome, B. (1981). Facilitating attitudes and messages characteristic in the expression of differences in intercultural encounters. *International Journal of Intercultural Relations, 5,* 215–238.

Broome, B. (1990). "Palevome": Foundations of struggle and conflict in Greek interpersonal communication. *Southern Journal of Communication, 55,* 260–275.

Brown, P., & Fraser, C. (1979). Speech as a marker of situation. In K. Scherer & H. Giles (Eds.), *Social markers in speech.* Cambridge, UK: Cambridge University Press.

Brown, R. (1966). *Words and things.* Glencoe, IL: Free Press.

Bruner, J. (1957). On perceptual readiness. *Psychological Review, 64,* 123–152.

Bruner, J. (1958). Social psychology and perception. In E. Maccoby, T. Newcomb, & E. Hartley (Eds.), *Readings in social psychology* (3rd ed.). New York: Holt, Rinehart and Winston.

Bruner, J., Goodnow, J., & Austin, G. (1956). *A study of thinking.* New York: Wiley.

Bruner, J., & Perlmutter, H. (1957). Compatriot and foreigner. *Journal of Abnormal and Social Psychology, 55,* 253–260.

Bruner, J., Oliver, R., & Greenfield, P. (1966). *Studies in cognitive growth.* New York: Wiley.

Buber, M. (1958). *I and thou.* New York: Scribner.

Buber, M. (1965). *Between man and man.* New York: Macmillian.

Budner, S. (1962). Intolerance of ambiguity as a personality variable. *Journal of Personality, 30,* 29–50.

Burgoon, J. (1992). Comparatively speaking: Applying a comparative approach to nonverbal expectancy violations theory. In J. Blumler, J. McCleod, & K. Rosengren (Eds.), *Communication and culture across time and space.* Newbury Park, CA: Sage.

Burgoon, J. (1995). Cross-cultural and intercultural applications of expectancy violations theory. In R. Wiseman (Ed.), *Intercultural communication theory.* Thousand Oaks, CA: Sage.

Burgoon, J., Buller, D., & Woodall, W. (1989). *Nonverbal communication.* New York: Harper and Row.

Burgoon, J., & Hale, J. (1988). Nonverbal expectancy violations. *Communication Monographs, 55,* 58–79.

Burgoon, M., Dillard, J., Doran, N., & Miller, J. (1982). Cultural and situational influences on the process of persuasive strategy selection. *International Journal of Intercultural relations, 6,* 85–99.

Burk, J. (1976). The effects of ethnocentrism on intercultural communicators. In F. Casmir (Ed.), *International and intercultural communication annual* (Vol. III). Falls Church, VA: Speech Communication Association.

Burleson, B., Samter, W., & Lucchetti, A. (1992). Similarity in communication values as predictors of friendship choices. *The Southern Communication Journal, 57,* 260–276.

Burns, D. (1989). *The feeling good handbook.* New York: William Morrow.

Burridge, K. (1956). Friendship in Tangu. *Oceana,* 177–189.

Butler, R. (1969). Age-ism: Another form of bigotry. *Gerontologist, 9,* 243–246.

Byers, P., & Byers, H. (1972). Nonverbal communication and the education of children. In C. Cozden et al. (Eds.), *Functions of language in the classroom.* New York: Teachers College Press.

Byrne, D. (1971). *The attraction paradigm.* New York: Academic Press.

Byrne, D., Gouaux, C., Griffitt, W., Lamberth, J. Murakawa, N. Prasad, M., Prasad, A., & Ramirez, M. (1971). The ubiquitous relationship: Attitude similarity and attraction. *Human Relations, 24,* 201–207.

Byrne, D., & Wong, T. (1962). Racial prejudice, interpersonal attraction and assumed dissimilarity of attitudes. *Journal of Abnormal and Social Psychology, 65,* 246–253.

Campbell, D. T., & Levine, R. A. (1968). Ethnocentrism and intergroup relations. In R. Abelson, E. Aronson, W. McGuire, T. Newcomb, M. Rosenberg, & P. Tannenbaum (Eds.), *Theories of cognitive consistency: A sourcebook.* Chicago: Rand McNally.

Cantor, N., Mischel, W., & Schwartz, J. (1982). Social knowledge. In A. Isen & A. Hastorf (Eds.), *Cognitive social psychology.* New York: Elsevier.

Capra, F. (1975). *The tao of physics.* Boulder, CO: Shambhala.

Carbaugh, D. (1993). Competence as cultural pragmatics. In R. Wiseman & J. Koester (Eds.), *Intercultural communication competence.* Thousand Oaks, CA: Sage.

Carroll, R. (1988). *Cultural misunderstandings.* Chicago: University of Chicago Press.

Catton, W. R. (1961). The functions and dysfunctions of ethnocentrism. *Social Problems, 8,* 201–211.

Cegala, D., & Waldron, V. (1992). A study of the relationship between communicative performance and conversational participants' thoughts. *Communication Studies, 43,* 105–123.

Chaika, E. (1982). *Language: The social mirror.* Rowley, MA: Newbury House.

Chan, K., & Lam, L. (1987). Psychological problems of Chinese Vietnamese refugees resettling in Quebec. In K. Chan & D. Indra (Eds.), *Uprooting, loss, and adaptation.* Ottawa: Canadian Public Health Association.

Char, W. (1977). Motivations for intercultural marriages. In W. Tseng, J. McDermott, & T. Maretzki (Eds.), *Adjustment in intercultural marriage.* Honolulu: University of Hawaii Press.

Chen, G. (1995). Differences in self-disclosure patterns among Americans versus Chinese. *Journal of Cross-Cultural Psychology, 26,* 84–91.

Cheng, A. (1974). Clashes in courtship across cultures. *East-West Center Magazine,* Summer, 11–12.

Chinese Culture Connection. (1987). Chinese values and the search for culture-free dimensions of culture. *Journal of Cross-Cultural Psychology, 18,* 143–164.

Chung, L. (1990). *An analysis of cultural identity and stereotypes as factors influencing interethnic dating.* Unpublished paper, Department of Speech Communication, California State University, Fullerton.

Church, A. (1982). Sojourner adjustment. *Psychological Bulletin, 91,* 540–572.

Cissna, K., & Sieburg, E. (1981). Patterns of interactional confirmation and disconfirmation. In C. Wilder-Mott & J. Weakland (Eds.), *Rigor and imagination.* New York: Praeger.

Clark, H. (1985). Language use and language users. In G. Lindzey & E. Aronson (Eds.), *Handbook of social psychology* (3rd ed., Vol. II). New York: Random House.

Clark, H., & Marshall, C. (1981). Definite reference and mutual knowledge. In A. Joshi, B. Webber, & I. Sag (Eds.), *Elements of discourse understanding.* New York: Cambridge University Press.

Clark, R., & Delia, J. (1977). Cognitive complexity, social perspective-taking and functional persuasive skills in second-to-ninth grade children. *Human Communication Research, 3,* 128–134.

Clarke, S., & Obler, J. (1976). Ethnic conflict, community building, and the emergence of ethnic political traditions in the United States. In S. Clarke & J. Obler (Eds.), *Urban ethnic conflict.* Chapel Hill: University of North Carolina Press.

Clatterbuck, G. (1979). Attributional confidence and uncertainty in initial interactions. *Human Communication Research, 5,* 147–157.

Cocroft, B., & Ting-Toomey, S. (1994). Facework in Japan and the United States. *International Journal of Intercultural Relations, 18,* 469–506.

Cody, M., & McLaughlin, M. (1985). The situation as a construct in interpersonal communication. In M. Knapp & G. Miller (Eds.), *Handbook of interpersonal communication.* Beverly Hills, CA: Sage.

Coelho, G. (1958). *Changing images of America.* Glencoe, IL: Free Press.

Cohen, E. (1972). Toward a sociology of international tourism. *Social Research, 39,* 164–182.

Cohen, R. (1987). Problems in intercultural communication in Egyptian-American diplomatic relations. *International Journal of Intercultural Relations, 11,* 29–47.

Cole, M. (1990). *Relational distances and personality influences on conflict communication styles.* Paper presented at the Speech Communication Association convention, Chicago.

Coleman, L., & DePaulo, B. (1991). Uncovering the human spirit: Moving beyond disability and "missed" communication. In N. Coupland, H. Giles, & J. Wiemann (Eds.), *"Miscommunication" and problematic talk.* Newbury Park, CA: Sage.

Collett, P. (1971). On training Englishmen in the nonverbal behavior of Arabs. *International Journal of Psychology, 6,* 209–215.

Collier, M., Ribeau, S., & Hecht, M. (1986). Intracultural communication rules and outcomes within three domestic cultures. *International Journal of Intercultural Relations, 10,* 439–458.

Condon, J., & Kurata, K. (1973). *In search of what's Japanese about Japan.* Tokyo: Shufunotomo.

Condon, J., & Yousef, F. (1975). *An introduction to intercultural communication.* Indianapolis, IN: Bobbs-Merrill.

Condor, S., & Brown, R. (1988). Psychological processes in intergroup conflict. In W. Strobe, A. Kruglanski, B. Bar-Tal, & M. Hewstone (Eds.), *The social psychology of intergroup conflict.* New York: Springer-Verlag.

Copelman, D. (1993). The immigrant experience. *Mind & Human Interaction, 4* (2), 76–82.

Coupland, J., Nussbaum, J., & Coupland, N. (1991). The reproduction of aging and ageism in intergenerational talk. In N. Coupland, H. Giles, & J. Wiemann (Eds.), *"Miscommunication" and problematic talk.* Newbury Park, CA: Sage.

Coupland, N. (1980). Style-shifting in a Cardiff work setting. *Language in Society, 9,* 1–12.

Coupland, N., Coupland, J., Giles, H., & Henwood, K. (1988). Accommodating the elderly. *Language in Society, 17,* 1–42.

Cousins, S. (1989). Culture and self perception in Japan and the United States. *Journal of Personality and Social Psychology, 56,* 124–131.

Covey, H. (1988). Historical terminology used to represent old people. *Gerontologist, 28,* 291–297.

Crocker, J., & Luhtanen, R. (1990). Collective self-esteem and ingroup bias. *Journal of Personality and Social Psychology, 58,* 60–67.

Crockett, W., & Friedman, P. (1980). Theoretical explorations of the process of initial interactions. *Western Journal of Speech Communication, 44,* 86–92.

Crosby, F., Bromley, S., & Saxe, L. (1980). Recent unobtrusive studies of black and white discrimination and prejudice. *Psychological Bulletin, 87,* 546–563.

Cross, W. (1970). The Negro to black conversion experience. *Black World, 20,* 13–27.

Csikszentmihalyi, M. (1990). *Flow: The psychology of optimal experiences.* New York: Harper and Row.

Cupach, W., & Imahori, T. (1993). Managing social predicaments created by others. *Western Journal of Communication, 57,* 431–444.

Cushman, D., Valentinsen, B., & Dietrich, D. (1982). A rules theory of interpersonal relationships. In F. Dance (Ed.), *Human communication theory.* New York: Harper and Row.

Cushman, D., & Whiting, G. (1972). An approach to communication theory: Toward a consensus on rules. *Journal of Communication, 22,* 217–233.

Dabrowski, K. (1968). *Theory of positive disintegration.* Audio recording. Big Sur Recordings No. 1120.

Dance, F. (1982). A speech theory of human communication. In F. Dance (Ed.), *Human communication theory.* New York: Harper and Row.

Dance, F., & Larson, C. (1972). *Speech communication.* New York: Holt, Rinehart and Winston.

Darwin, C. (1872). *Journal of researches into natural history and geology of the countries visited during the voyage of H.M.S. "Beagle" round the world, under the command of Capt. Fitzroy, R.N.* London: Ward, Lock and Bowden.

Davidson, A. (1975). Cognitive differentiation and culture training. In R. Brislin, S. Bochner, & W. Lonner (Eds.), *Cross-cultural perspectives on learning.* Beverly Hills, CA: Sage.

Davidson, A., & Thompson, E. (1980). Cross-cultural studies of attitudes and beliefs. In H. Triandis & R. Brislin (Eds.), *Handbook of cross-cultural psychology* (Vol. 5). Boston: Allyn and Bacon.

Davis, F. (1977). Deviance disavowal. In J. Stubbins (Ed.), *Social and psychological aspects of disability.* Baltimore: University Park Press.

Deaux, K. (1991). Social identities. In R. Curtis (Ed.), *The relational self.* New York: Guilford.

Deaux, K. (1993). Reconstructing social identity. *Personality and Social Psychology Bulletin, 19,* 4–12.

Deaux, K., & Ethier, K. [Dimensions of social identity]. Unpublished raw data reported in Deaux (1991).

Deaux, K., Reid, A., Mizirahi, K., & Ethier, K. (1995). Parameters of social identity. *Journal of Personality and Social Psychology, 68,* 280–291.

deBono, E. (1991). *I am right you are wrong.* New York: Viking.

Deregowski, J. (1980). Perception. In H. Triandis & W. Lonner (Eds.), *Handbook of cross-cultural psychology* (Vol. 3). Boston: Allyn and Bacon.

DeRidder, R., & Tripath, R. (1992). *Rules to live by: Escalation and de-escalation of inter-group hostility.* Oxford, UK: Clarendon.

Detweiler, R. (1975). On inferring the intentions of a person from another culture. *Journal of Personality, 43,* 591–611.

Detweiler, R. (1978). Culture, category width and attributions. *Journal of Cross-Cultural Psychology, 9,* 259–284.

Detweiler, R. (1980). Intercultural interaction and the categorization process. *International Journal of Intercultural Relations, 4,* 275–293.

Deutsch, M. (1954). Field theory in social psychology. In G. Lindzey (Ed.), *Handbook of social psychology* (Vol. 1). Reading, MA: Addison-Wesley.

Deutsch, M. (1961). The interpretation of praise and criticism as a function of their social context. *Journal of Abnormal and Social Psychology, 62,* 391–400.

Deutsch, M. (1973). *The resolution of conflict.* New Haven, CT: Yale University Press.

Deutsch, S., & Won, G. (1963). Some factors in the adjustment of foreign nationals. *Journal of Social Issues, 19*(3), 115–122.

Devine, P. (1989). Stereotypes and prejudice. *Journal of Personality and Social Psychology, 56,* 5–18.

DeVos, G. (1975). Ethnic pluralism. In G. DeVos & L. Romanucci-Ross (Eds.), *Ethnic identity.* Palo Alto, CA: Mayfield.

DeVos, G. (1978). Selective permeability and reference group sanctioning. In J. Yinger & S. Cutler (Eds.), *Major social issues.* New York: Free Press.

Dewey, J. (1934). *A common faith.* New Haven, CT: Yale University Press.

Diamond, R., & Hellcamp, D. (1969). Race, sex, ordinal position of both and self-disclosure in high school students. *Psychological Report, 25,* 235–238.

Dickson-Markman, F. (1986). Self-disclosure with friends across the life cycle. *Journal of Social and Personal Relationships, 3,* 259–264.

Diggs, N., & Murphy, B. (1991). Japanese adjustment to American communities. *International Journal of Intercultural Relations, 15,* 103–116.

Dion, K. K., & Dion, K. L. (1991). Psychological individualism and romantic love. *Journal of Social Behavior and Personality, 6,* 17–33.

Dion, K. K., & Dion, K. L. (1993). Individualistic and collectivistic perspectives on gender and the cultural context of love and intimacy. *Journal of Social Issues, 49*(3), 53–69.

Dion, K. K., Pak, A., & Dion, K. L. (1990). Stereotyping and physical attractiveness. *Journal of Cross-Cultural Psychology, 21,* 378–398.

Dion, K. L. (1990). The joy of ethnicity. *International Society for the Study of Personal Relationships Bulletin, 7*(1), 3–7.

Dion, K. L., & Dion, K. K. (1988). Romantic love: Individual and cultural perspectives. In R. Sternberg & M. Barnes (Eds.), *The psychology of love.* New Haven, CT: Yale University Press.

Doherty, K., Hatfield, E., Thompson, K., & Choo, P. (1994). Cultural and ethnic influences on love and attachment. *Personal Relationships, 1,* 391–398.

Doi, T. (1973). *The anatomy of dependence.* Tokyo: Kodansha.

Doi, T. (1976). The Japanese patterns of communication and the concept of amae. In L. Samovar & R. Porter (Eds.), *Intercultural communication: A reader* (2nd ed.). Belmont, CA: Wadsworth.

Doi, T. (1986). *The anatomy of the self.* Tokyo: Kodansha.

Donohue, W., with Kolt, R. (1993). *Managing interpersonal conflict.* Newbury Park, CA: Sage.

Douglis, C. (1987, November). The beat goes on. *Psychology Today,* pp. 37–42.

Dovido, J., Mann, J., & Gaertner, S. (1989). Resistance to affirmative action. In F. Blanchard & F. Crosby (Eds.), *Affirmative action perspective.* New York: Springer-Verlag.

Downs, J. (1971). *Cultures in crisis.* Chicago: Glencoe Press.

Downs, R., & Stea, D. (Eds.). (1973). *Image and environment.* Chicago: Aldine.

Downs, R., & Stea, D. (1977). *Maps in minds.* New York: Harper and Row.

Driberg, H. (1935). The "best friend" among the Dianja. *Man, 35,* 101–102.

Driver, E. (1973). Self-conceptions in India and the United States. *Sociological Quarterly, 14,* 576–588.

Dublin, T. (1993). *Immigrant voices.* Urbana: University of Illinois Press.

Dubos, R. (1981). *Celebrations of life.* New York: McGraw-Hill.

Ducci, L., Arcuri, L., W/Georgis, T., & Sineshaw, D. (1982). Emotion recognition in Ethiopia. *Journal of Cross-Cultural Psychology, 13,* 340–351.

Duck, S. (1977). *The study of acquaintance.* Farnborough, UK: Saxon House.

Duck, S., Rutt, D., Hurst, M., & Strejc, H. (1991). Some evident truths about conversations in everyday relationships. *Human Communication Research, 18,* 228–267.

Duncan, B. (1976). Differential social perception and attribution of intergroup violence. *Journal of Personality and Social Psychology, 34,* 590–598.

Duran, R. (1983). Communicative adaptability. *Communication Quarterly, 31,* 230–326.

Dyal, J., & Dyal, R. (1981). Acculturation, stress and coping. *International Journal of Intercultural Relations, 5,* 301–328.

Eaton, W., & Lasry, J. (1978). Mental health and occupational mobility in a group of immigrants. *Science and Medicine, 12,* 53–58.

Edgerton, R. (1985). *Rules, expectations, and social order.* Berkeley: University of California Press.

Edwards, J. (1985). *Language, society, and identity.* Oxford, UK: Blackwell.

Efron, D. (1941/1972). *Gestures and environment.* New York: King's Crown Press.

Ehrenhaus, P. (1983). Culture and the attribution process. In W. Gudykunst (Ed.), *Intercultural communication theory.* Beverly Hills, CA: Sage.

Ehrlich, H. (1973). *The social psychology of prejudice.* New York: Wiley.

Eibl-Eibesfeldt, L. (1979). Similarities and differences between cultures in expressive movements. In S. Weitz (Ed.), *Nonverbal communication* (2nd ed.). New York: Oxford University Press.

Eisenstadt, E. (1954). *The absorption of immigrants.* London: Routledge and Kegan Paul.

Ekman, P. (1972). Universals and cultural differences in facial expressions of emotion. In J. Cole (Ed.), *Nebraska symposium on motivation* (Vol. 19). Lincoln: University of Nebraska Press.

Ekman, P. (1978). Facial expressions. In A. Siegman & S. Feldstein (Eds.), *Nonverbal behavior and communication.* Hillsdale, NJ: Erlbaum.

Ekman, P., & Friesen, W. (1969). The repertoire of nonverbal behavior: Categories, origins, usage, and coding. *Semiotica, 1,* 49–98.

Ekman, P., & Friesen, W. (1971). Constants across cultures in the face and emotion. *Journal of Personality and Social Psychology, 17,* 124–129.

Ekman, P., Friesen, W., O'Sullivan, M., Chan, A., Diacoyanni-Tarlatzis, I., Heider, K., Krause, R., LeCompte, W., Pitcairn, T., Ricci-Bitti, P., Scherer, K., Tomita, M., & Tzavaras, A. (1987). Universals and cultural differences in the judgment of facial expressions of emotions. *Journal of Personality and Social Psychology, 53,* 712–717.

Ellingsworth, H. (1977). Conceptualizing intercultural communication. In B. Ruben (Ed.), *Communication yearbook 1.* New Brunswick, NJ: Transaction.

Embree, J. (1950). Thailand—A loosely structured social system. *American Anthropologist, 52,* 181–193.

Emerson, R. (1960). *From empire to nation.* Cambridge, MA: Harvard University Press.

Engebretson, D., & Fullmer, D. (1970). Cross-cultural differences in territoriality. *Journal of Cross-Cultural Psychology, 1,* 261–269.

Enloe, W., & Lewin, P. (1987). Issues of integration abroad and readjustment to Japan of Japanese returnees. *International Journal of Intercultural Relations, 11,* 223–248.

Epstein, S. (1984) Controversial issues in emotion theory. In P. Shaver (Ed.), *Review of personality and social psychology* (Vol. 5). Beverly Hills, CA: Sage.

Erickson, F. (1981). *Anecdote, rhapsody, and rhetoric.* Paper presented at the Georgetown University Roundtable on Linguistics, Washington, DC.

Ervin-Tripp, S. (1964). Interaction of language, topic, and listener. *American Anthropologist, 66,* 86–102.

Ethier, K., & Deaux, K. (1994). Negotiating social identity when contexts change. *Journal of Personality and Social Psychology, 67,* 243–251.

Etzioni, A. (1993). *The spirit of community.* New York: Crown.

Farb, P. (1979). Man at the mercy of language. In D. Mortensen (Ed.), *Basic readings in communication theory* (2nd ed.). New York: Harper and Row.

Faulkender, P. (1985). Relationship between Bem sex-role inventory and attitudes of sexism. *Psychological Reports, 57,* 227–235.

Feather, N. (1990). Bridging the gap between values and action. In E. Higgins & R. Sorrentino (Eds.), *Handbook of motivation and cognition* (Vol. 2). New York: Guilford.

Feather, N. (1995). Values, valences, and choice. *Journal of Personality and Social Psychology, 68,* 1135–1151.

Feig, J., & Blair, J. (1975). *There is a difference.* Washington, DC: Meriden International House.

Feldman, R. (1968). Response to compatriot and foreigner who seek assistance. *Journal of Personality and Social Psychology, 10,* 202–214.

Fernandez-Collado, C., Rubin, R., & Hernandez-Sampieri, R. (1991). *A cross-cultural examination of interpersonal communication motives in Mexico and the United States.* Paper presented at the International Communication Association convention.

Festinger, L. (1957). *A theory of cognitive dissonance.* Evanston, IL: Row, Peterson.

Fisher, B. A. (1978). *Perspectives on human communication.* New York: Macmillan.

Fisher, R., & Brown, S. (1988). *Getting together.* New York: Houghton Mifflin.

Fiske, A. (1991). *Structures of social life.* New York: Free Press.

Fiske, A. (1993). Social errors in four cultures. *Journal of Cross-Cultural Psychology, 24,* 463–494.

Fiske, D., & Maddi, S. (Eds.). (1961). *Functions of varied experiences.* Homewood, IL: Dorsey.

Foa, U., & Foa, E. (1974). *Societal structures of the mind.* Springfield, IL: Charles Thomas.

Fogel, A. (1993). *Developing through relationships.* Chicago: University of Chicago Press.

Fogel, D. (1979). *Human development and communication competencies.* Paper presented at the Speech Communication Association convention, San Antonio, TX.

Fontaine, G., & Dorch, E. (1980). Problems and benefits of close interpersonal relationships. *International Journal of Intercultural Relations, 4,* 329–338.

Ford, D., & Lerner, R. (1992). *Developmental systems theory.* Newbury Park, CA: Sage.

Forgas, J., & Bond, M. (1985). Cultural influences on perceptions of interaction episodes. *Personality and Social Psychology Bulletin, 11,* 75–88.

Foster, D., & Finchilescu, G. (1986). Contact in a "noncontact" society. In M. Hewstone & R. Brown (Eds.), *Contact and conflict in intergroup encounters.* Oxford, UK: Blackwell.

Frey, D., & Gaertner, S. (1986). Helping and the avoidance of inappropriate interracial behavior. *Journal of Personality and Social Psychology, 50,* 1083–1090.

Friedman, M. (1974). *The hidden human image.* New York: Dell.

Friedman, M. (1983). *The confirmation of otherness.* New York: Pilgrim Press.

Friedman, M. (1986). Foreward. In R. Arnett, *Communication and community.* Carbondale: Southern Illinois University Press.

Friesen, W. (1972). *Cultural differences in facial expression in a social situation.* Unpublished doctoral dissertation, University of California, San Francisco.

Frymier, A., Klopf, D., & Ishii, S. (1990). Japanese and Americans compared on the affect orientation construct. *Psychological Reports, 66,* 985–986.

Fuentes, C. (1992). *The buried mirror.* Boston: Houghton Mifflin.

Furnham, A. (1986). Situational determinants of intergroup communication. In W. Gudykunst (Ed.), *Intergroup communication.* London: Edward Arnold.

Furnham, A. (1988). The adjustment of sojourners. In Y. Kim & W. Gudykunst (Eds.), *Cross-cultural adaptation.* Newbury Park, CA: Sage.

Furnham, A., & Bochner, S. (1982). Social difficulty in a foreign culture. In S. Bochner (Ed.), *Cultures in contact.* Elmsford, NY: Pergamon.

Furnham, A., & Bochner, S. (1986). *Culture shock.* New York: Routledge.

Fussell, P. (1983). *Class.* New York: Summit Books.

Gabrenya, W., & Wang, Y. (1983). *Cultural differences in self schemata.* Paper presented at the Southeast Psychological Association convention.

Gaertner, S. & Bickman, L. (1971). Effects of race on the elicitation of helping behavior. *Journal of Personality and Social Psychology, 20,* 218–222.

Gaertner, S., & Dovidio, J. (1986). The aversive form of racism. In J. Dovidio & S. Gaertner (Eds.), *Prejudice, discrimination, and racism.* Orlando, FL: Academic Press.

Gaetz, L., Klopf, D., & Ishii, S. (1990). *Predispositions toward verbal behavior of Japanese and Americans.* Paper presented at the Communication Association of Japan conference.

Gallois, C., Franklyn-Stokes, A., Giles, H., & Coupland, N. (1988). Communication accommodation theory and intercultural encounters. In Y. Kim & W. Gudykunst (EDs.), *Theories in intercultural communication.* Newbury Park, CA: Sage.

Gallois, C., Giles, H., Jones, F., Cargile, A., & Ota, H. (1995). Accommodating intercultural encounters. In R. Wiseman (Ed.), *Intercultural communication theory.* Thousand Oaks, CA: Sage.

Galston, (1991). Rights do not equal rightness. *Responsive Community, 1,* 78.

Gandhi, M. (1948). *Nonviolence in peace and war.* Ahmedabad, India: Garland.

Gans, H. (1979). Symbolic ethnicity. *Ethnic and Racial Studies, 2,* 1–20.

Gao, G. (1990). *A dyadic analysis of romantic relationships in China and the United States.* Unpublished doctoral dissertation, Arizona State University, Tempe.

Gao, G. (1991). Stability of romantic relationships in China and the United States. In S. Ting-Toomey & F. Korzenny (Eds.), *Cross-cultural interpersonal communication.* Newbury Park, CA: Sage.

Gao, G. (1993). *A test of the triangular theory of love in Chinese and EuroAmerican romantic relationships.* Paper presented at the International Communication Association convention.

Gao, G., & Gudykunst, W. B. (1990). Uncertainty, anxiety, and adaptation. *International Journal of Intercultural Relations, 14,* 301–317.

Gao, G., & Gudykunst, W. B. (1995). Attributional confidence, perceived similarity, and network involvement in Chinese and European American romantic relationships. *Communication Quarterly, 43,* 431–445.

Gao, G., Schmidt, K., & Gudykunst, W. (1994). The influence of strength of ethnic identity on perceived ethnolinguistic vitality. *Hispanic Journal of Behavioral Sciences, 16,* 332–341.

Gardner, G. (1962). Cross-cultural communication. *Journal of Social Psychology, 58,* 241–256.

Gardner, J. (1991). *Building community.* Washington, DC: Independent Sector.

Gardner, R. (1985). *Social psychology and second language learning.* London: Edward Arnold.

Garratt, G., Baxter, J., & Rozelle, R. (1981). Training university police in black-American nonverbal behavior. *Journal of Social Psychology, 113,* 217–229.

Garrett, P., Giles, H., & Coupland, N. (1989). The contexts of language learning. In S. Ting-Toomey & F. Korzenny (Eds.), *Language, communication, and culture.* Newbury Park, CA: Sage.

Garvin, B., & Kennedy, C. (1986). Confirmation and disconfirmation in nurse-physician communication. *Journal of Applied Communication Research, 14,* 1–19.

Gass, S., & Varonis, E. (1984). The effect of familiarity on the comprehensibility of nonnative speech. *Language Learning, 34,* 65–89.

Gass, S., & Varonis, E. (1985). Variations in native speaker speech modification on nonnative speakers. *Studies in Second Language Acquisition, 7,* 37–58.

Gass, S., & Varonis, E. (1991). Miscommunication in nonnative speaker discourse. In N. Coupland, H. Giles, & J. Wiemann (Eds.), *"Miscommunication" and problematic talk.* Thousand Oaks, CA: Sage.

Geertz, C. (1966). *Person, time, and conduct in Bali.* New Haven, CT: Yale Southeast Asia Studies Program.

Geertz, C. (1973). *The interpretation of culture.* New York: Basic Books.

Geertz, C. (1975). On the nature of anthropological understanding. *American Scientist, 63,* 47–53.

Genesse, F., & Bourhis, R. (1982). The social psychological significance of code switching in cross-cultural communication. *Journal of Language and Social Psychology, 1,* 1–28.

Gerbner, G. (1978). The dynamics of cultural resistance. In G. Tuchman et al. (Eds.), *Health and home.* New York: Oxford University Press.

Gerbner, G., Gross, L., Morgan, M., & Signorielli, N. (1980). The "mainstreaming" of America. *Journal of Communication, 30,* 10–29.

Gibb, J. (1961). Defensive communication. *Journal of Communication, 11,* 141–148.

Gibbs, J. (1965). Norms: The problem of definition and classification. *American Journal of Sociology, 70,* 586–594.

Giles, H. (1973). Accent mobility. *Anthropological Linguistics, 15,* 87–105.

Giles, H., Bourhis, R., & Taylor, D. (1977). Toward a theory of language in ethnic group relations. In H. Giles (Ed.), *Language, ethnicity and intergroup relations.* London: Academic Press.

Giles, H., & Byrne, J. (1982). The intergroup theory of second language acquisition. *Journal of Multilingual and Multicultural Development, 3,* 17–40.

Giles, H., Coupland, N., Coupland, J., Williams, A., & Nussbaum, J. (1992). Intergenerational talk and communication with older people. *International Journal of Aging and Human Development, 34,* 271–297.

Giles, H., Coupland, N., & Wiemann, J. (1992). "Talk is cheap . . . " but "my word is my bond." In R. Bolton & H. Kwok (Eds.), *Sociolinguistics today.* London: Routledge.

Giles, H., & Hewstone, M. (1982). Cognitive structures, speech, and social situations. *Language Sciences, 4,* 187–219.

Giles, H., & Johnson, P. (1981). The role of language in ethnic relations. In J. Turner & H. Giles (Eds.), *Intergroup behavior.* Chicago: University of Chicago Press.

Giles, H., & Johnson, P. (1987). Ethnolinguistic identity theory. *International Journal of the Sociology of Language, 68,* 69–90.

Giles, H., Mulac, A., Bradac, J., & Johnson, P. (1986). Speech accommodation theory. In M. McLaughlin (Ed.), *Communication yearbook 10.* Newbury Park, CA: Sage.

Giles, H., Rosenthall, D., & Young, L. (1985) Perceived ethnolinguistic vitality: The Anglo- and Greek-Australian setting. *Journal of Multilingual and Multicultural Development, 6,* 253–269.

Giles, H., & Smith, P. (1979). Accommodation theory. In H. Giles & R. St. Clair (Eds.), *Language and social psychology.* Oxford, UK: Blackwell.

Gimenez, M., Lopez, F., & Munoz, C. (Eds.). (1992). The politics of ethnic construction. *Latin American Perspectives, 19*(4).

Gire, J., & Carment, D. (1993). Dealing with disputes. *Journal of Social Psychology, 133,* 81–95.

Glazer, N., & Moynihan, D. (1975). *Ethnicity.* Cambridge, MA: Harvard University Press.

Glenn, E. (1981). *Man and mankind.* Norwood, NJ: Ablex.

Glenn, E., Witmeyer, D., & Stevenson, K. (1977). Cultural styles and persuasion. *International Journal of Intercultural Relations, 1,* 52–66.

Glidden, H. (1972). The Arab world. *American Journal of Psychiatry, 128,* 984–988.

Goffman, E. (1959). *The presentation of self in everyday life.* Hammondsworth, UK: Penguin.

Goffman, E. (1961). *Asylums.* New York: Doubleday.

Goffman, E. (1963). *Stigma.* Englewood Cliffs, NJ: Prentice Hall.

Goldenberg, S., & Haines, V. (1992). Social networks and institutional completeness. *Canadian Journal of Sociology, 17,* 301–312.

Gonzalez, D. (1992, November 15). What's the problem with Hispanics? Just ask a Latino. *Los Angeles Times,* p. E6.

Gorden, M. (1964). *Assimilation in American life.* Oxford, UK: Oxford University Press.

Gorden, R. (1974). *Living in Latin America.* Skokie, IL: National Textbooks.

Gotanda, P. K. (1991). Interview with Philip Kan Gotanda. *Los Angeles Performing Arts, 25* (1), pp. 10–11.

Gottman, J., Notarius, C., Markman, H., Bank, S., Yoppi, B., & Rubin, M. (1976). Behavioral exchange theory and marital decision making. *Journal of Personality and Social Psychology, 34,* 14–23.

Gouldner, A. (1960). The norm of reciprocity. *American Sociological Review, 25,* 161–179.

Graham, M., Moeai, J., & Shizuru, L. (1985). Intercultural marriages. *International Journal of Intercultural Relations, 9,* 427–434.

Grant, P., & Holmes, J. (1981). The integration of implicit theory schemes and stereotype images. *Social Psychology Quarterly, 44,* 107–115.

Grice, H. (1975). Logic and conversation. In P. Cole & J. Morgan (Eds.), *Syntax and semantics* (Vol. 3). New York: Academic Press.

Grotevant, H. (1993). The integrative nature of identity. In J. Kroger (Ed.), *Discussions on ego identity.* Hillsdale, NJ: Erlbaum.

Grove, T., & Werkman, D. (1991). Communication with able-bodied and visually disabled strangers. *Human Communication Research, 17,* 507–534.

Gudykunst, W. B. (1983a). Similarities and differences in perceptions of initial intracultural and intercultural encounters. *Southern Speech Communication Journal, XLIX,* 49–65.

Gudykunst, W. B. (1983b). Toward a typology of stranger-host relationships. *International Journal of Intercultural Relations, 7,* 401–415.

Gudykunst, W. B. (1983c). Uncertainty reduction and predictability of behavior in low- and high-context cultures. *Communication Quarterly, 31,* 49–55.

Gudykunst, W. B. (1985a). A model of uncertainty reduction in intercultural encounters. *Journal of Language and Social Psychology, 4,* 79–98.

Gudykunst, W. B. (1985b). An exploratory comparison of close intracultural and intercultural friendships. *Communication Quarterly, 33,* 236–251.

Gudykunst, W. B. (1985c). The influence of cultural similarity, type of relationship, and self-monitoring on uncertainty reduction processes. *Communication Monographs, 52,* 203–217.

Gudykunst, W. B. (1986). Toward a theory of intergroup communication. In W. B. Gudykunst (Ed.), *Intergroup communication.* London: Edward Arnold.

Gudykunst, W. B. (1987). Cross-cultural comparisons. In C. R. Berger & S. Chaffee (Eds.), *Handbook of communication science.* Newbury Park, CA: Sage.

Gudykunst, W. B. (1988a). Intergroup communication across cultures. In M. Bond (Ed.), *The cross-cultural challenge to social psychology.* Beverly Hills, CA: Sage.

Gudykunst, W. B. (1988b). Uncertainty and anxiety. In Y. Y. Kim & W. B. Gudykunst (Eds.), *Theories in intercultural communication.* Newbury Park, CA: Sage.

Gudykunst, W. B. (1989). Culture and communication in interpersonal relationships. In J. Anderson (Ed.), *Communication yearbook 12.* Newbury Park, CA: Sage.

Gudykunst, W. B. (1991). *Bridging differences.* Newbury Park, CA: Sage.

Gudykunst, W. B. (1993). Toward a theory of interpersonal and intergroup communication. In R. Wiseman & J. Koester (Eds.), *Intercultural communication competence.* Thousand Oaks, CA: Sage.

Gudykunst, W. B. (1994). *Bridging differences* (2nd ed.). Thousand Oaks, CA: Sage.

Gudykunst, W. B. (1995). Anxiety/uncertainty management (AUM) theory. In R. Wiseman (Ed.), *Intercultural communication theory.* Thousand Oaks, CA: Sage.

Gudykunst, W. B., Chua, E., & Gray, A. (1987). Cultural dissimilarities and uncertainty reduction processes. In M. McLaughlin (Ed.), *Communication yearbook 10.* Newbury Park, CA: Sage.

Gudykunst, W. B., Gao, G., & Franklyn-Stokes, A. (in press). Self-monitoring in China and England. In J. Pandy, D. Sinha, & D. Bhawuk (Eds.), *Asian contributions to cross-cultural psychology.* New Delhi: Sage.

Gudykunst, W. B., Gao, G., Nishida, T., Bond, M. H., Leung, K., Wang, G., & Barraclough, R. A. (1989). A cross-cultural study of self-monitoring. *Communication Research Reports, 6*(1), 7–12.

Gudykunst, W. B., Gao, G., Nishida, T., Nadamitsu, Y., & Sakai, J. (1992). Self-monitoring in Japan and the United States. In S. Iwaki, Y. Kashima, & K. Leung (Eds.), *Innovations in cross-cultural psychology.* The Hague: Swets and Zeitlinger.

Gudykunst, W. B., Gao, G., Schmidt, K. L., Nishida, T., Bond, M. H., Leung, K., Wang, G., & Barraclough, R. (1992). The influence of individualism-collectivism on communication in ingroup and outgroup relationships. *Journal of Cross-Cultural Psychology, 23,* 196–213.

Gudykunst, W. B., Gao, G., Sudweeks, S., Ting-Toomey, S., & Nishida, T. (1991). Developmental themes in opposite-sex Japanese-North American relationships. In S. Ting-Toomey & F. Korzenny (Eds.), *Cross-cultural interpersonal communication.* Newbury Park, CA: Sage.

Gudykunst, W. B., & Hammer, M. (1987). The effect of ethnicity, gender, and dyadic composition on uncertainty reduction in initial interactions. *Journal of Black Studies, 18,* 191–214.

Gudykunst, W. B., & Hammer, M. (1988a). Strangers and hosts. In Y. Kim & W. Gudykunst (Eds.), *Cross-cultural adaptation.* Newbury Park, CA: Sage.

Gudykunst, W. B., & Hammer, M. (1988b). The influence of social identity and intimacy of interethnic relationships on uncertainty reduction processes. *Human Communication Research, 14,* 569–601.

Gudykunst, W. B., & Lim, T. S. (1985). Ethnicity, sex, and self-perceptions of communicator style. *Communication Research Reports, 2,* 68–75.

Gudykunst, W. B., & Lim, T. S. (1986). A perspective for the study of intergroup communication. In W. Gudykunst (Ed.), *Intergroup communication.* London: Edward Arnold.

Gudykunst, W. B., Matsumoto, Y., Ting-Toomey, S., Nishida, T., Kim, K., & Heyman, S. (1996). The influence of cultural individualism-collectivism, self construals, and individual values on communication styles across cultures. *Human Communication Research.*

Gudykunst, W. B., & Nishida, T. (1983). Social penetration in close friendships in Japan and the United States. In R. Bostrom (Ed.), *Communication yearbook 7.* Beverly Hills, CA: Sage.

Gudykunst, W. B., & Nishida, T. (1984). Individual and cultural influences on uncertainty reduction. *Communication Monographs, 51,* 23–36.

Gudykunst, W. B., & Nishida, T. (1986a). Attributional confidence in low-and high-context cultures. *Human Communication Research, 12,* 525–549.

Gudykunst, W. B., & Nishida, T. (1986b). The influence of cultural variability on perceptions of communication behavior associated with relationship terms. *Human Communication Research, 13,* 147–166.

Gudykunst, W. B., & Nishida, T. (1993). Closeness in interpersonal relationships in Japan and the United States. *Research in Social Psychology, 8*(2), 85–97.

Gudykunst, W. B., & Nishida, T. (1994). *Bridging Japanese/North American differences.* Thousand Oaks, CA: Sage.

Gudykunst, W. B., Nishida, T., & Chua, E. (1986). Uncertainty reduction in Japanese-North American dyads. *Communication Research Reports, 3,* 39–46.

Gudykunst, W. B., Nishida, T., & Chua, E. (1987). Perceptions of social penetration in Japanese-North American dyads. *International Journal of Intercultural Relations, 11,* 171–190.

Gudykunst, W. B., Nishida, T., Chung, L., & Sudweeks, S. (1992). *The influence of strength of cultural identity and perceived typicality on individualistic and collectivistic values in Japan and the United States.* Paper presented at the Asian Regional Congress of the International Association for Cross-Cultural Psychology,

Gudykunst, W. B., Nishida, T., Koike, H., & Shiino, N. (1986). The influence of language on uncertainty reduction: An exploratory study of Japanese-Japanese and Japanese-North American interactions. In M. McLaughlin (Ed.), *Communication yearbook 9.* Beverly Hills, CA: Sage.

Gudykunst, W. B., Nishida, T., & Morisaki, S. (1992). *The influence of personal and social identity on expectations for interpersonal and intergroup encounters in Japan and the United States.* Paper presented at the International Communication Association convention.

Gudykunst, W. B., Nishida, T., & Schmidt, K. (1989). Cultural, relational, and personality influences on uncertainty reduction processes. *Western Journal of Speech Communication, 53,* 13–29.

Gudykunst, W. B., & Shapiro, R. (in press). Communication in everyday interpersonal and intergroup encounters. *International Journal of Intercultural Relations.*

Gudykunst, W. B., Sodetani, L. L., & Sonoda, K. T. (1987). Uncertainty reduction in Japanese-American/Caucasian relationships in Hawaii. *Western Journal of Speech Communication, 51,* 256–278.

Gudykunst, W. B., & Sudweeks, S. (1992). Applying a theory of intercultural adaptation. In W. Gudykunst & Y. Kim (Eds.), *Readings on communicating with strangers.* New York: McGraw-Hill.

Gudykunst, W. B., & Ting-Toomey, S. (1988). *Culture and interpersonal communication.* Newbury Park, CA: Sage.

Gudykunst, W. B., & Ting-Toomey, S. (1990). Ethnicity, language, and communication breakdowns. In H. Giles & P. Robinson (Eds.), *Handbook of language and social psychology.* London: Wiley.

Gudykunst, W. B., Ting-Toomey, S., Hall, B. J., & Schmidt, K. L. (1989). Language and intergroup communication. In M. K. Asante & W. B. Gudykunst (Eds.), *Handbook of international and intercultural communication.* Newbury Park, CA: Sage.

Gudykunst, W. B., Ting-Toomey, S., Sudweeks, S., & Stewart, L. (1995). *Building bridges: Interpersonal skills for a changing world.* Boston: Houghton Mifflin.

Gudykunst, W., Wiseman, R., & Hammer, M. (1977). Determinants of a sojourner's attitudinal satisfaction. In B. Ruben (Ed.), *Communication yearbook 1.* New Brunswick, NJ: Transaction.

Gudykunst, W. B., Yang, S. M., & Nishida, T. (1985). A cross-cultural test of uncertainty reduction theory. *Human Communication Research, 11,* 407–454.

Gudykunst, W. B., Yang, S. M., & Nishida, T. (1987). Cultural differences in self-consciousness and self-monitoring. *Communication Research, 14,* 7–36.

Gudykunst, W. B., Yoon, Y. C., & Nishida, T. (1987). The influence of individualism-collectivism on perceptions of communication in ingroup-outgroup relationships. *Communication Monographs, 54,* 295–306.

Gulick, S. (1962). *The East and the West: A study of their psychic and cultural characteristics.* Rutland, VT: Charles E. Tuttle.

Gullahorn, J. T., & Gullahorn, J. E. (1963). An extension of the U-curve hypothesis. *Journal of Social Issues, 19*(3), 33–47.

Gumperz, J. (1982). *Discourse strategies.* New York: Cambridge University Press.

Gumperz, J., & Hernandez-Chavez, E. (1972). Bilingualism, bidialectism and classroom interaction. In C. Cazden et al. (Eds.), *Functions of language in the classroom.* New York: Teacher's College Press.

Gumperz, G., & Hymes, D. (1972). *Directions in sociolinguistics.* New York: Holt, Rinehart and Winston.

Gumperz, J., & Tannen, D. (1979). Individual and social differences in language use. In C. Fillmore, D. Kempler, & W. Wang (Eds.), *Individual differences in language ability and language behavior.* New York: Academic Press.

Gutmann, A. (1992). Introduction. In A. Gutmann (Ed.), *Multiculturalism and the politics of recognition.* Princeton, NJ: Princeton University Press.

Hale, C. L. (1980). Cognitive complexity-simplicity as a determinant of communication effectiveness. *Communication Monographs, 47,* 304–311.

Hall, B. J., & Gudykunst, W.B. (1986). The intergroup theory of second language ability. *Journal of Language and Social Psychology, 5,* 291–302.

Hall, E. T. (1959). *The silent language.* New York: Doubleday.

Hall, E. T. (1966). *The hidden dimension.* New York: Doubleday.

Hall, E. T. (1976). *Beyond culture.* New York: Doubleday.

Hall, E. T. (1983). *The dance of life.* New York: Doubleday.

Hall, E. T., & Whyte, W. F. (1979). Intercultural communication. In C. D. Mortenson (Ed.), *Basic readings in communication theory* (2nd ed.). New York: Harper and Row.

Hallinan, M., & Smith, S. (1985). The effects of classroom racial composition on students' interracial friendliness. *Social Psychology Quarterly, 48,* 3–16.

Hamilton, D., Sherman, S., & Ruvolo, C. (1992). Sterotyped based expectancies. In W. Gudykunst & Y. Kim (Eds.), *Readings on communicating with strangers.* New York: McGraw-Hill. (Originally published in *Journal of Social Issues, 46*(2), 35–60).

Hammer, M. (1987). Behavioral dimensions of intercultural effectiveness. *International Journal of Intercultural Relations, 11,* 65–88.

Hammer, M., & Gudykunst, W. (1987). The influence of ethnicity, sex, and dyadic composition on communication in friendships. *Journal of Black Studies, 17,* 418–437.

Hammer, M., Gudykunst, W., & Wiseman, R. (1978). Dimensions of intercultural effectiveness. *International Journal of Intercultural Relations, 2,* 382–393.

Hampshire, S. (1989). *Innocence and experience.* Cambridge, MA: Harvard University Press.

Han, G., & Park, B. (1995). Children's choice in conflict. *Journal of Cross-Cultural Psychology, 26,* 298–313.

Han, S., & Shavitt, S. (1994). Persuasion and culture. *Journal of Experimental Social Psychology, 30,* 326–350.

Hanh, T. N. (1991). *Peace in every step.* New York: Bantam.

Harman, L. (1987). *The modern stranger.* New York: Mouton de Gruyter.

Harris, L. (1979). *Communication competence: An argument for a systematic view.* Paper presented at the International Communication Association convention,

Harris, L. (1980). *Communication competence: An empirical test of a systematic model.* Paper presented at the International Communication Association convention,

Harris, P., & Moran, R. (1979). *Managing cultural differences.* Houston, TX: Gulf.

Harvey, O., Hunt, D., & Schroder, H. (1961). *Conceptual systems and personality organization.* New York: Wiley.

Haselden, K. (1968). *Morality and the mass media.* Nashville, TN: Broadman Press.

Haslett, B. (1990). Social class, social status, and communicative behavior. In H. Giles & W. Robinson (Eds.), *Handbook of language and social psychology.* Chichester, UK: Wiley.

Hass, R., Katz, I., Rizzo, N., Bailey, J., & Moore, L. (1992). When racial ambivalence evokes negative affect. *Personality and Social Psychology Bulletin, 18,* 786–797.

Hawes, F., & Kealey, D. (1981). An empirical study of Canadian technical assistance. *International Journal of Intercultural Relations, 5,* 239–258.

Hayashi, R. (1990). Rhythmicity, sequence, and synchrony of English and Japanese face-to-face conversations. *Language Sciences, 12,* 155–195.

Hearn, L. (1956). *Japan: An attempt at interpretation.* Tokyo: Charles Tuttle.

Heath, D. (1977). *Maturity and competence.* New York: Gardner.

Hecht, M. (1978). The conceptualization and measurement of communication satisfaction. *Human Communication Research, 4,* 253–264.

Hecht, M., Andersen, P., & Ribeau, S. (1989). Cultural dimensions of nonverbal communication. In M. Asante & W. Gudykunst (Eds.), *Handbook of international and intercultural communication.* Newbury Park, CA: Sage.

Hecht, M., & Ribeau, S. (1984). Sociocultural roots of ethnic identity. *Journal of Black Studies, 21,* 501–513.

Hecht, M., Ribeau, S., & Alberts, J. (1989). An Afro-American perspective on interethnic communication. *Communication Monographs, 56,* 385–410.

Hecht, M., Ribeau, S., & Sedano, M. (1990). A Mexican-American perspective on interethnic communication. *International Journal of Intercultural Relations, 14,* 31–55.

Heckathorn, D. (1990). Connective sanctions and compliance norms. *American Sociological Review, 55,* 366–384.

Heider, F. (1958). *The psychology of interpersonal relations.* New York: Wiley.

Heimann, B. (1964). *Facets of Indian thought.* New York: Schocken.

Henley, N., Hamilton, M., & Thorne, B. (1985). Womanspeak and manspeak. In A. Sargent (Ed.), *Beyond sex roles.* New York: West.

Henley, N., & Kramarae, C. (1991). Gender, power, and miscommunication. In N. Coupland, H. Giles, & J. Wiemann (Eds.), *"Miscommunication" and problematic talk.* Thousand Oaks, CA: Sage.

Henry, W. (1990, April 9). Beyond the melting pot. *Time,* pp. 28–31.

Herman, S., & Schield, E. (1960). The stranger group in a cross-cultural situation. *Sociometry, 24,* 165–176.

Herskovits, M. (1955). *Cultural anthropology.* New York: Knopf.

Herskovits, M. (1966). *Cultural dynamics.* New York: Knopf.

Herskovits, M. (1973). *Cultural relativism.* New York: Random House.

Hewstone, M., & Brown, R. (1986). Contact is not enough. In M. Hewstone & R. Brown (Eds.), *Contact and conflict in intergroup encounters.* Oxford, UK: Blackwell.

Hewstone, M., & Giles, H. (1986). Stereotypes and intergroup communication. In W. Gudykunst (Ed.), *Intergroup communication.* London: Edward Arnold.

Hewstone, M., & Jaspars, J. (1984). Social dimensions of attributions. In H. Tajfel (Ed.), *The social dimension* (Vol. 2). Cambridge, UK: Cambridge University Press.

Hirokawa, R., & Miyahara, A. (1986). A comparison of influence strategies utilized by managers in American and Japanese organizations. *Communication Quarterly, 34,* 250–265.

Ho, T., & Sung, K. (1990). Role of infrastructure networks in supporting social values to sustain economic success in newly-industrialized nations. *International Journal of Psychology, 25,* 887–900.

Hocker, J., & Wilmot, W. (1991). *Interpersonal conflict* (3rd ed.). Dubuque, IA: Wm. C. Brown.

Hockett, C. (1958). *A course in modern linguistics.* New York: Macmillan.

Hockett, C. F. (1968). Chinese vs. English. In P. Gleeson & N. Wakefield (Eds.), *Language and culture.* Columbus, OH: Merrill.

Hodges, H. H. (1964). *Social stratification.* Cambridge, UK: Schenkman.

Hodges, L., & Byrne, D. (1972). Verbal dogmatism as a potentiator of intolerance. *Journal of Personality and Social Psychology, 21,* 312–317.

Hoebel, E. (1960). *The Cheyennes.* New York: Holt, Rinehart and Winston.

Hoffman, E. (1985). The effect of race-relation composition on the frequency of organizational communication. *Social Psychology Quarterly, 48,* 17–26.

Hofman, T. (1985). Arabs and Jews, blacks and whites. *Journal of Multilingual and Multicultural Development, 6,* 217–237.

Hofstede, G. (1979). Value systems in forty countries. In L. Eckensberger, W. Lonner, & Y. Poortinga (Eds.), *Cross-cultural contributions to psychology.* Lisse, The Netherlands: Swets and Zeitlinger.

Hofstede, G. (1980). *Culture's consequences.* Beverly Hills, CA: Sage.

Hofstede, G. (1983). Dimensions of national cultures in fifty countries and three regions. In J. Deregowski, S. Dzuirawiec, & R. Annis (Eds.), *Explications in cross-cultural psychology.* Lisse, The Netherlands: Swets and Zeitlinger.

Hofstede, G. (1991). *Cultures and organizations.* London: McGraw-Hill.

Hofstede, G., & Bond, M. (1984). Hofstede's culture dimensions. *Journal of Cross-Cultural Psychology, 15,* 417–433.

Hogg, M., Joyce, N., & Abrams, D. (1984). Diglossia in Switzerland. *Journal of Language and Social Psychology, 3,* 185–196.

Hoijer, H. (1954). *Language in culture.* Chicago: University of Chicago Press.

Hoijer, H. (1976). The Sapir-Whorf hypothesis. In L. Samovar & R. Porter (Eds.), *Intercultural communication: A reader* (2nd ed.). Belmont, CA: Wadsworth.

Holmes, J., & Rempel, J. (1989). Trust in close relationships. In C. Hendrick (Ed.), *Close relationships.* Newbury Park, CA: Sage.

Holmes, L. (1965). *Anthropology.* New York: Ronald Press.

Holtgraves, T. (1992). The linguistic realization of face management. *Social Psychology Quarterly, 55,* 141–159.

Holtgraves, T., & Yang, J. (1992). The interpersonal underpinnings of request strategies. *Journal of Personality and Social Psychology, 62,* 246–256.

Honess, T. (1976). Cognitive complexity and social prediction. *British Journal of Social and Clinical Psychology, 15,* 22–31.

Honeycutt, J., Knapp, M., & Powers, W. (1983). On knowing others and predicting what they say. *Western Journal of Speech Communication, 47,* 157–174.

Hong, K. S. (1980). The interest level and exposure to informational contents of mass media. *Shin-Moon-Hak-Bo (Journal of Mass Communication),* 83–93.

Horowitz, D. (1985). *Ethnic groups in conflict.* Berkeley: University of California Press.

Howell, W. (1982). *The empathic communicator.* Belmont, CA: Wadsworth.

Hoyle, R., Pinkley, R., & Insko, C. (1989). Perceptions of social behavior. *Personality and Social Psychology Bulletin, 15,* 365–376.

Hraba, J., & Hoiberg, E. (1983). Origins of modern theories of ethnicity. *Sociological Quarterly, 24,* 381–391.

Hsu, F. (1953/1981). *Americans and Chinese* (3rd ed.). Honolulu: University of Hawaii Press.

Hsu, F. (1971). *The challenge of the American dream: The Chinese in the United States.* Belmont, CA: Wadsworth.

Hsu, T., Grant, A., & Huang, W. (1993). The influence of social networks on the acculturation behavior of foreign students. *Connections, 16*(1–2), 23–30.

Hubbert, K., Guerrero, S., & Gudykunst, W. (1995). *Intergroup communication over time.* Paper presented at the International Communication Association convention.

Hudson Institute (1987). *Workforce 2000.* Washington, DC: United States Department of Labor.

Huntington, E. (1945). *Mainsprings of civilizations.* New York: Wiley.

Hurh, W., & Kim, K. (1988). *Uprooting and adjustment.* Washington, DC: National Institute of Mental Health.

Huston, T. (1973). Ambiguity of acceptance, social desirability, and dating choice. *Journal of Experimental Social Psychology, 9,* 32–42.

Hwang, J., Chase, L., & Kelly, C. (1980). An intercultural examination of communication competence. *Communication, 9,* 70–79.

Hymes, D. (1971). Sociolinguistics and the ethnography of speaking. In E. Ardener (Ed.), *Social anthropology and language.* New York: Tavistock.

Hymes, D. (1974). Ways of speaking. In R. Bauman & J. Sherzer (Eds.), *Explorations in the ethnography of speaking.* Cambridge, UK: Cambridge University Press.

Hymes, D. (1979). On communication competence. In J. Pride & J. Holmes (Eds.), *Sociolinguistics.* New York: Penguin.

Imahori, T., & Cupach, W. (1994). A cross-cultural comparison of the interpretation and management of face. *International Journal of Intercultural Relations, 18,* 193–220.

Inglis, M., & Gudykunst, W. (1982). Institutional completeness and communication acculturation. *International Journal of Intercultural Relations, 6,* 251–272.

Inkeles, A. (1974). *Becoming modern.* Cambridge, MA: Harvard University Press.

Islam, M., & Hewstone, M. (1993). Dimensions of contact as predictors of intergroup anxiety, perceived outgroup variability, and outgroup attitude. *Personality and Social Psychology Bulletin, 19,* 700–710.

Ittelson, W. (1973). Environment perception and contemporary perceptual theory. In W. Ittelson (Ed.), *Environment and cognition.* New York: Seminar Press.

Ittelson, W., & Cantril, H. (1954). *Perceptions, a transactional approach.* Garden City, NY: Doubleday.

Ittelson, W., Prochansky, H., Rivlin, L., & Winkel, G. (1974). *Introduction to environmental psychology.* New York: Holt, Rinehart and Winston.

Izard, C. (1968). *The emotions as a culture-common framework of motivational experiences and communicative cues.* Washington, DC: Office of Naval Research.

Izard, C. (1971). *The face of emotion.* New York: Apppleton-Century-Crofts.

Izard, C. (1980). Cross-cultural perspectives on emotion and emotion communication. In H. Triandis & W. Lonner (Eds.), *Handbook of cross-cultural psychology* (Vol. 3). Boston: Allyn and Bacon.

Jackman, M., & Jackman, R. (1983). *Class awareness in the United States.* Berkeley: University of California Press.

Jackson, J. (1964). The normative regulation of authoritative behavior. In W. Grove & J. Dyson (Eds.), *The making of decisions.* New York: Free Press.

Jacobson, E., Kumata, H., & Gullahorn, J. (1960). Cross-cultural contributions to attitude research. *Public Opinion Quarterly, 24,* 205–233.

Jaffee, L., & Polanski, N. (1962). Verbal inaccessibility in young adolescents showing delinquent trends. *Journal of Health and Social Behavior, 3,* 105–111.

Jahoda, G. (1980). Theoretical and systematic approaches. In H. Triandis & W. Lambert (Eds.), *Handbook of cross-cultural psychology* (Vol. 1). Boston: Allyn and Bacon.

Jampolsky, G. (1989). *Out of darkness and into the light.* New York: Bantam.

Janis, I. (1971). *Stress and frustration.* New York: Harcourt Brace Jovanovich.

Janis, I., & Mann, L. (1977). *Decision making.* New York: Free Press.

Janis, I., & Smith, M. (1965). Effects of education and persuasion on national and international images. In H. Kelman (Ed.), *International behavior.* New York: Holt, Rinehart and Winston.

Jantsch, E. (1980). *The self-organizing universe: Scientific and human implications of the emerging paradigm of evolution.* New York: Pergamon.

Jaspars, J., & Hewstone, M. (1982). Cross-cultural interaction, social attribution, and intergroup relations. In S. Bochner (Ed.), *Cultures in contact.* Elmsford, NY: Pergamon.

Jaspars, J., & Warnaen, S. (1982). Intergroup relations, social identity, and self-evaluation in India. In H. Tajfel (Ed.), *Social identity and intergroup relations.* Cambridge, UK: Cambridge University Press.

Jeffries, L., & Hur, K. K. (1981). Communication channels within ethnic groups. *International Journal of Intercultural Relations, 5,* 115–132.

Johnson, C., & Johnson, F. (1975). Interaction rules and ethnicity. *Social Forces, 54,* 452–466.

Johnson, D. (1986). *Reaching out* (3rd ed.). Englewood Cliffs, NJ: Prentice Hall.

Johnson, D., & Johnson, F. (1982). *Joining together* (2nd ed.). Englewood Cliffs, NJ: Prentice Hall.

Johnson, H. G., Ekman, P., & Friesen, W. V. (1975). Communicative body movements: American emblems. *Semiotica, 15,* 335–353.

Johnson, J., & Sarason, I. (1978). Life stress, depression and anxiety. *Journal of Psychosomatic Research, 22,* 205–208.

Johnson, K. (1976). Black kinesics. In L. Samovar & R. Porter (Eds.), *Intercultural communication: A reader* (2nd ed.). Belmont, CA: Wadsworth.

Johnson, R., & Ogasawara, G. (1984). Group size and group income as influences on marriage patterns in Hawaii. *Social Biology, 31,* 101–107.

Johnson, W., & Warren, D. (1994). Introduction. In W. Johnson & D. Warren (Eds.), *Inside the mixed marriage.* Lanham, MD: University Press of America.

Johnston, L., & Coolen, P. (1995). A dual processing approach to stereotype change. *Personality and Social Psychology Bulletin, 21,* 660–673.

Johnston, L., & Hewstone, M. (1991). Intergroup contact. In D. Abrahms & M. Hogg (Eds.), *Social identity theory.* New York: Springer-Verlag.

Johnston, L., & Macrae, C. (1994). Changing social stereotypes. *European Journal of Social Psychology, 24,* 581–592.

Jones, E., & Davis, K. (1965). From acts to dispositions. *Personality and Social Psychology Bulletin, 4,* 200–206.

Jones, E., Gallois, C., Barker, M. & Callan, V. (1994). Evaluations of interaction between students and academic staff: Influence of Communication accommodation, ethic group, and status. *Journal of Language and Social Psychology, 13,* 158–191.

Jones, E., & Nisbett, R. (1972). *The actor and the observer.* Morristown, NJ: General Learning Press.

Jones, T., & Remland, M. (1982). *Cross-cultural differences in self-reported touch avoidance.* Paper presented at the Eastern Communication Association convention.

Jourard, S. (1958). A study of self-disclosure. *Scientific American, 198,* 77–82.

Jourard, S. (1961). Self-disclosure patterns in British and American college females. *Journal of Social Psychology, 54,* 315–320.

Jourard, S. (1971). *Self-disclosure.* New York: Wiley.

Jourard, S. (1974). Growing awareness and the awareness of growth. In B. Patton & K. Giffin (Eds.), *Interpersonal communication.* New York: Harper and Row.

Kagan, S., Knight, G., & Martinez-Romero, S. (1982). Culture and the development of conflict negotiation style. *Journal of Cross-Cultural Psychology, 13,* 43–59.

Kanouse, D., & Hanson, L. (1972). Negativity in evaluations. In E. Jones, D. Kanouse, H. Kelley, R. Nisbett, S. Valms, & B. Weiner (Eds.), *Attribution.* Morristown, NJ: General Learning Press.

Kanter, R. (1977). *Men and women of the corporation.* New York: Basic Books.

Kao, C. (1975). *Search for maturity.* Philadelphia: Westminister.

Kapoor, S., & Williams, W. (1979). *Acculturation of foreign students by television.* Paper presented at the International Communication Association convention, Philadelphia.

Karniol, R. (1990). Reading people's minds. In M. Zanna (Ed.), *Advances in experimental social psychology* (Vol. 23). New York: Academic Press.

Kashima, Y. (1989). Conceptions of persons. In C. Kagitcibasi (Ed.), *Growth and progress in cross-cultural psychology.* The Hague: Swets and Zeitlinger.

Kashima, Y., Siegel, M., Tanaka, K., & Kashima, E. (1992). Do people believe behaviors are consistent with attitudes? *British Journal of Social Psychology, 31,* 111–124.

Kashima, Y., & Triandis, H. C. (1986). The self-serving bias in attributions as a coping strategy. *Journal of Cross-Cultural Psychology, 17,* 83–97.

Katz, D. (1960). The functional approach to the study of attitudes. *Public Opinion Quarterly, 24,* 164–204.

Kealey, D. (1990). *Cross-cultural effectiveness.* Quebec: International Development Agency.

Keene, D. (1994). *On familiar terms.* Tokyo: Kodansha.

Keesing, R. (1974). Theories of culture. *Annual Review of Anthropology, 3,* 73–97.

Kellermann, K. (1993). Extrapolating beyond. In S. Deetz (Ed.), *Communication yearbook 16.* Newbury Park, CA: Sage.

Kelley, H. (1967). Attribution theory in social psychology. *Nebraska Symposium on Motivation, 15,* 192–238.

Kelley, H. (1972). Causal schemata and the attribution process. In E. Jones, D. Kanouse, H. Kelley, R. Nisbett, S. Valins, & L Petrullo (Eds.), *Attribution.* Morristown, NJ: General Learning Press.

Kelly, C., Sachdev, I., Kottsieper, P., & Ingram, M. (1993). The role of social identity in second language proficiency and use. *Journal of Language and Social Psychology, 12,* 288–301.

Kelly, G. A. (1955). *The psychology of personal constructs.* New York: Norton.

Kelvin, P. (1970). *The bases of social power.* New York: Holt, Rinehart and Winston.

Kennerley, H. (1990). *Managing anxiety.* New York: Oxford University Press.

Kertamus, L., Gudykunst, W., & Nishida, T. (1991). *Themes in male-male Japanese-North American relationships.* Paper presented at the Conference on Communication in Japan and the United States, California State University, Fullerton.

Kim, H. K. (1991). Influence of language and similarity on initial intercultural attraction. In S. Ting-Toomey & F. Korzenny (Eds.), *Cross-cultural interpersonal communication.* Newbury Park, CA: Sage.

Kim, H. S. (1986). Coorientation and communication. In B. Dervin & M. Voight (Eds.), *Progress in communication science* (Vol. VII). Norwood, NJ: Ablex.

Kim, J., Lee, B., & Jeong, W. (1982). *Uses of mass media in acculturation.* Paper presented at the Association for Education in Journalism convention.

Kim, J. K. (1980). Explaining acculturation in a communication framework. *Communication Monographs, 47,* 155–179.

Kim, J. K., Lee, B. H., & Jeong, W. J. (1982, July). *Use of mass media in acculturation.* Paper presented at the Association for Education in Journalism conference, Athens, OH.

Kim, M. S. (1994). Cross-cultural comparisons of the perceived importance of conversational constraints. *Human Communication Research, 21,* 128–151.

Kim, M. S., Sharkey, W., & Singelis, T. (1994). The relationship between individuals' self construals and perceived importance of interactive constraints. *International Journal of Intercultural Relations, 18,* 117–140.

Kim, M. S., & Wilson, S. (1994). A cross-cultural comparison of implicit theories of requesting. *Communication Monographs, 61,* 210–235.

Kim, Y. Y. (1976). *Communication patterns of foreign immigrants in the process of acculturation.* Unpublished doctoral dissertation, Northwestern University, Evanston, IL.

Kim, Y. Y. (1977a). Communication patterns of foreign immigrants in the process of acculturation. *Human Communication Research, 4,* 66–77.

Kim, Y. Y. (1977b). Interethnic and intraethnic communication. In N. Jain (Ed.), *International and intercultural communication annual* (Vol. 4). Falls Church, VA: Speech Communication Association.

Kim, Y. Y. (1978a). *Acculturation and patterns of interpersonal communication relationships.* Paper presented at the Speech Communication Association convention, Minneapolis, MN.

Kim, Y. Y. (1978b). Toward a communication approach to the acculturation process. *International Journal of Intercultural Relations, 2,* 197–224.

Kim, Y. Y. (1979a). *Mass media and acculturation.* Paper presented at the Eastern Communication Association convention, Philadelphia.

Kim, Y. Y. (1979b). Toward an interactive theory of communication-acculturation. In D. Nimmo (Ed.), *Communication yearbook 3.* New Brunswick, NJ: Transaction.

Kim, Y. Y. (1979c). *Dynamics of intrapersonal and interpersonal communication: A study of Indochinese refugees in the initial phase of acculturation.* Paper presented at the Speech Communication Association convention, San Antonio, TX.

Kim, Y. Y. (1980). *Psychological, social, and cultural adjustment of Indochinese refugees.* Vol. IV of Indochinese refugees in the State of Illinois (5 vols.). Chicago: Travelers Aid Society of Metropolitan Chicago.

Kim, Y. Y. (1985). Communication, information, and adaptation. In B. Ruben (Ed.), *Information and behavior* (Vol. 1). New Brunswick, NJ: Transaction.

Kim, Y. Y. (Ed.). (1986a). *Interethnic communication.* Newbury Park, CA: Sage.

Kim, Y. Y. (1986b). Understanding the social context of intergroup communication: A personal network approach. In W. Gudykunst (Ed.), *Intergroup communication.* London: Edward Arnold.

Kim, Y. Y. (1987). Facilitating immigrant adaptation: The role of communication. In T. Albrecht & M. Adelman (Eds.), *Communicating social support.* Newbury Park, CA: Sage.

Kim, Y. Y. (1988). *Communication and cross-cultural adaptation: An integrative theory.* Clevedon, UK: Multilingual Matters.

Kim, Y. Y. (1989a). Intercultural adaptation. In M. Asante & W. Gudykunst (Eds.), *Handbook of international and intercultural communication.* Newbury Park, CA: Sage.

Kim, Y. Y. (1989b). Communication and adaptation of Asian Pacific refugees in the United States. *Journal of Pacific Rim Communication, 1,* 191–207.

Kim, Y. Y. (1989c). Psychological, social, and economic adaptation: The case of 1975–1979 arrivals in Illinois. In D. Haines (Ed.), *Refugees as immigrants: Survey research on Cambodians, Laotians, and Vietnamese in America.* Totowa, NJ: Rowman and Littlefield.

Kim, Y. Y. (1989d). Interethnic conflict: An interdisciplinary overview. In J. Gittler (Ed.), *Annual review of conflict knowledge and conflict resolution* (Vol. 1). New York: Garland.

Kim, Y. Y. (1991a). Communication and adaptation. In L. Samovar & R. Porter (Eds.), *Intercultural communication: A reader* (6th ed.). Belmont, CA: Wadsworth.

Kim, Y. Y. (1991b). Intercultural personhood. In L. Samovar & R. Porter (Eds.), *Intercultural communication: A reader* (6th ed.). Belmont, CA: Wadsworth.

Kim, Y. Y. (1991c). Intercultural communication competence. In S. Ting-Toomey & F. Korzenny (Eds.), *Intercultural interpersonal communication.* Newbury Park, CA: Sage.

Kim, Y. Y., (1992). Synchrony and intercultural communication. In D. Crookall & K. Arai (Eds.), *Global interdependence.* New York: Springer-Verlag.

Kim, Y. Y. (1993). *Synchrony and intercultural communication competence.* Paper presented at the International Communication Association convention.

Kim, Y. Y. (1994a). Interethnic communication. In S. Deetz (Ed.), *Communication yearbook 17.* Thousand Oaks, CA: Sage.

Kim, Y. Y. (1994b). Intercultural personhood. In L. Samovar & R. Porter (Eds.), *Intercultural communication: A reader* (7th ed.). Belmont, CA: Wadsworth.

Kim, Y. Y. (1995a). Cross-cultural adaptation. In R. Wiseman (Ed.), *Intercultural communication theory.* Thousand Oaks, CA: Sage.

Kim, Y. Y. (1995b). Identity development. In H. Mokros (Ed.), *Information and behavior* (Vol. 5). New Brunswick, NJ: Transaction.

Kim, Y. Y. (in press). *Becoming intercultural.* Thousand Oaks, CA: Sage.

Kim, Y. Y., & Gudykunst, W. B. (Eds.). (1988a). *Cross-cultural adaptation: Current approaches.* Newbury Park, CA: Sage.

Kim, Y. Y., & Gudykunst, W. B. (Eds.). (1988b). *Theories in intercultural communication.* Newbury Park, CA: Sage.

Kim, Y. Y., Lujan, P., & Shaver, L. (1994). *"I can walk both ways": Identity integration of American Indians in Oklahoma.* Paper presented at the Conference on Language and Social Psychology.

Kim, Y. Y., & Ruben, B. (1988). Intercultural transformation: A systems theory. In Y. Kim & W. Gudykunst (Eds.), *Theories in intercultural communication.* Newbury Park, CA: Sage.

King, M. L., Jr. (1958). *Stride toward freedom.* New York: Harper and Row.

King, M. L., Jr. (1963). Letter from Birmingham jail. In *Why we can't wait.* New York: Harper and Row.

Kitano, H., & Chai, L. (1982). Chinese interracial marriage. *Marriage and Family Review, 5,* 75–89.

Kitano, H., Young, W., Chai, L., & Hatanaka, H. (1984). Asian American interracial marriage. *Journal of Marriage and the Family, 46,* 179–190.

Kitayama, S., & Burnstein, E. (1988). Automaticity in conversations. *Journal of Personality and Social Psychology, 54,* 219–224.

Klass, M., & Hellman, H. (1971). *The kinds of mankind.* New York: Lippincott.

Kleg, M. (1993). *Hate, prejudice, and racism.* Albany: State University of New York Press.

Kleinjans, E. (1972). Opening remarks at a conference on world communication held at the East-West Center, Honolulu, HI.

Klineberg, O., & Hull, W. F. (1979). *At a foreign university.* New York: Praeger.

Kluckhohn, F., & Strodtbeck, F. (1961). *Variations in value orientations.* New York: Row, Peterson.

Knapp, M. (1978). *Social intercourse.* Boston: Allyn and Bacon.

Knapp, M. (1983). Dyadic relationship development. In J. Wiemann & R. Harrison (Eds.), *Nonverbal interaction.* Beverly Hills, CA: Sage.

Knapp, M., Ellis, D., & Williams, B. (1980). Perceptions of communication behavior associated with relationship terms. *Communication Monographs, 47,* 262–278.

Knapp, M., & Hall, J. (1992). *Nonverbal communication in human interaction* (3rd ed.). New York: Harcourt Brace.

Kochman, T. (1981). *Black and white: Styles in conflict.* Chicago: University of Chicago Press.

Kochman, T. (1990). Force fields in black and white communication. In D. Carbaugh (Ed.), *Cultural communication and intercultural contact.* Hillsdale, NJ: Erlbaum.

Kohn, M. (1969). *Class and conformity: A study in values.* Homewood, IL: Dorsey Press.

Korten, D. (1972). *Planned change in a traditional society.* New York: Praeger.

Korzybski, A. (1948). *Science and sanity* (3rd ed.). Lakeville, CT: International Non-Aristotelian Library.

Kouri, K., & Lasswell, M. (1993). Black-white marriage. *Marriage and Family Review, 19,* 241–255.

Kraft, C. (1978). Worldview in intercultural communication. In F. Casmir (Ed.), *International and intercultural communication.* Washington, DC: University Press of America.

Krauss, R., & Fussell, S. (1991). Constructing shared communicative environments. In L. Resnick, J. Levine, & S. Behend (Eds.), *Perspectives on socially shared cognition.* Washington, DC: American Psychological Association.

Kraut, R., & Higgins, E. (1984). Communication and social cognition. In R. Wyer & T. Srull (Eds.), *Handbook of social cognition* (Vol. 3). Hillsdale, NJ: Erlbaum.

Kristeva, J. (1991). *Strangers to ourselves.* New York: Colombia University Press.

Kruglanski, A. (1989). *Lay epistemics and human knowledge.* New York: Plenum.

Kurth, S. (1970). Friendships and friendly relations. In G. McNall (Ed.), *Social relationships.* Chicago: Aldine.

LaBarre, W. (1947). The cultural basis of emotions and gestures. *Journal of Personality, 16,* 49–68.

LaBarre, W. (1976). Paralinguistics, kinesics, and cultural anthropology. In L. Samovar & R. Porter (Eds.), *Intercultural communication: A reader* (2nd ed.). Belmont, CA: Wadsworth.

Labrie, N., & Clement, R. (1986). Ethnolinguistic vitality, self-confidence, and second language proficiency. *Journal of Multilingual and Multicultural Development, 7,* 269–282.

Lackoff, R. (1975). *Language and woman's place.* New York: Harper and Row.

Lackoff, R. (1990). *Talking power.* New York: Basic Books.

LaFrance, M., & Mayo, C. (1978). Cultural aspects of nonverbal behavior. *International Journal of Intercultural Relations, 2,* 71–89.

Laing, D. (1961). *The self and others.* New York: Panthem.

Lambert, R., & Bressler, M. (1956). *Indian students on an American campus.* Minneapolis: University of Minnesota Press.

Lambert, W. (1963). Psychological approaches to the study of language. *Modern Language Journal, 14,* 51–62.

Lambert, W. (1972). *Language, psychology, and culture.* Stanford, CA: Stanford University Press.

Lampe, P. (1982). Interethnic dating: Reasons for and against. *International Journal of Intercultural Relations, 6,* 115–126.

Landis, D., & Boucher, J. (1987). Themes and models of conflict. In J. Boucher, D. Landis, & K. Clark (Eds.), *Ethnic conflict.* Newbury Park, CA: Sage.

Landis, D., & Brislin, R. (Eds.). (1983). *Handbook of intercultural training* (Vol. I-III). New York: Pergamon.

Lane, H. (1993). The medicalization of cultural deafness in historical perspective. In R. Fisher & H. Lane (Eds.), *Looking back.* Hamburg: Signum Press.

Langer, E. (1978). Rethinking the role of thought in social interaction. In J. Harvey, W. Ickes, & R. Kidd (Eds.), *New directions in attribution research* (Vol. 2). Hillsdale, NJ: Erlbaum.

Langer, E. (1989). *Mindfulness.* Reading, MA: Addison-Wesley.

Larkey, L., Hecht, M., & Martin, J. (1993). What's in a name? *Journal of Language and Social Psychology, 12,* 302–317.

Lazarsfeld, P., & Merton, R. (1954). Friendship as a social process. In M. Berger et al. (Eds.), *Freedom and control in modern society.* New York: Octagon Books.

Lazarus, R. (1966). *Psychological stress and the coping process.* New York: McGraw-Hill.

Lazarus, R. (1991). *Emotions and adaptation.* New York: Oxford University Press.

Lazarus, R., Averill, J., & Opton, E. (1974). The psychology of coping. In G. Coelho, D. Hamburg, & J. Adams (Eds.), *Coping and adaptation.* New York: Basic Books.

Lazarus, R., Cohen, R., Folkman, S., Kanner, A., & Schaefer, C. (1980). Psychological stress and adaptation. In H. Selye (Ed.), *Seyle's guide to stress research* (Vol 1). New York: Van Nostrand Reinhold.

Leary, M., Kowalski, R., & Bergen, D. (1988). Interpersonal information acquisition and confidence in first encounters. *Personality and Social Psychology Bulletin, 14,* 68–77.

Lebra, T. (1987). The cultural significance of silence in Japanese communication. *Multilingua, 6,* 343–357.

Lee, D. (1950). Lineal and nonlineal codifications of reality. *Psychosomatic Medicine, 12,* 89–97.

Lee, D. (1959). *Freedom and culture.* Englewood Cliffs, NJ: Prentice Hall.

Lee, H., & Boster, F. (1991). Social information for uncertainty reduction during initial interactions. In S. Ting-Toomey & F. Korzenny (Eds.), *Cross-cultural interpersonal communication.* Newbury Park, CA: Sage.

Lee, S., & Yamanaka, K. (1990). Patterns of Asian American intermarriage and marital assimilation. *Journal of Comparative Studies,* 287–305.

Lerner, R. (1979). A dynamic interactional concept of individual and social relationship development. In R. Burgess & T. Huston (Eds.), *Social exchange in developing relationships.* New York: Academic Press.

Leung, K. (1987). Some determinants of reaction to procedural models for conflict resolution. *Journal of Personality and Social Psychology, 53,* 898–908.

Leung, K. (1988). Some determinants of conflict avoidance. *Journal of Cross-Cultural Psychology, 19,* 125–136.

Leung, K., & Bond, M. (1982). How Chinese and Americans reward task-related contributions. *Psychologia, 25,* 32–39.

Leung, K., & Bond, M. (1984). The impact of cultural collectivism on reward allocation. *Journal of Personality and Social Psychology, 49,* 793–804.

Leung, K., Bond, M., Carment, D., Krishman, L., & Liebrand, W. (1990). Effects of cultural femininity on preference for methods of conflict processing. *Journal of Experimental Social Psychology, 26,* 373–388.

Leung, K., & Lind, E. (1986). Procedure and culture. *Journal of Personality and Social Psychology, 50,* 1134–1140.

Levin, J., & Levin, W. (1980). *Ageism.* Belmont, CA: Wadsworth.

Levine, D. (1965). *Wax and gold.* Chicago: University of Chicago Press.

Levine, D. (1979). Simmel at a distance. In W. Shack & E. Skinner (Eds.), *Strangers in African societies.* Berkeley: University of California Press.

Levine, D. (1985). *The flight from ambiguity.* Chicago: University of Chicago Press.

Levine, R., & Campbell, D. (1972). *Ethnocentrism.* New York: Wiley.

Levine, R., Sato, S., Hashimoto, T., & Verma, J. (1995). Love and marriage in eleven cultures. *Journal of Cross-Cultural Psychology, 26,* 554–571.

Lewin, K. (1936). *Principles of topological psychology.* New York: McGraw-Hill.

Lewin, K. (1948). Some social-psychological differences between the United States and Germany. In G. Lewin (Ed.), *Resolving social conflicts.* New York: Harper.

Lewin, K. (1951). *Field theory in social science.* New York: Harper and Row.

Lewis, T., & Jungman, R. (Eds.). (1986). *On being foreign.* Yarmouth, ME: Intercultural Press.

Liem, N. D. (1980). *Vietnamese-American intercultural communication.* Paper presented at the International Communication Association convention, Acapulco, Mexico.

Lilli, W., & Rehm, J. (1988). Judgmental processes as bases of intergroup conflict. In W. Strobe, A. Kruglanski, D. Bar-Tal, & M. Hewstone (Eds.), *The social psychology of intergroup conflict.* New York: Springer-Verlag.

Lindgren, H., & Marrash, J. (1970). A comparative study of intercultural insight and empathy. *Journal of Social Psychology, 80,* 135–141.

Linville, P., Fisher, G., & Salovey, P. (1989). Perceived distriburtions of the charactcristics of in-group and out-group members. *Journal of Personality and Social Psychology, 57,* 165–188.

Lippman, W. (1922). *Public opinion.* New York: Macmillan.

Lippman, W. (1937). *The good society.* Boston: Little, Brown.

Lipset, S. (1963). The value patterns of democracy. *American Sociological Review, 28,* 515–531.

Little, K. (1968). Cultural variations in social schemata. *Journal of Personality and Social Psychology, 10,* 1–7.

Littlefield, R. (1974). Self-disclosure among Negro, white and Mexican-American adolescents. *Journal of Counseling Psychology, 21,* 133–136.

LoCastro, V. (1987). *Aizuchi:* A Japanese conversational routine. In L. Smith (Ed.), *Discourse across cultures.* Englewood Cliffs, NJ: Prentice Hall.

Loewry, E. (1993). *Freedom and community.* Albany: State University of New York Press.

Longmore, P. (1987). Screening stereotypes. In A. Gartner & T. Jol (Eds.), *Images of the disabled.* New York: Praeger.

Lonner, W. (1980). The search for psychological universals. In H. Triandis & W. Lambert (Eds.), *Handbook of cross-cultural psychology* (Vol. 1). Boston: Allyn and Bacon.

Loomis, C. (1938). Political and occupational cleavages in a Hanoverian village. *Sociometry, 1,* 375–419.

Loveday, L. (1982). Communicative interference. *International Review of Applied Linguistics in Language Teaching, 20,* 1-16.

Luhtanen, R., & Crocker, J. (1992). A collective self-esteem scale. *Personality and Social Psychology Bulletin, 18,* 302–318.

Lukens, J. (1978). Ethnocentric speech. *Ethnic Groups, 2,* 35–53.

Lum, J. (1982). Marginality and multiculturalism. In L. Samovar & R. Porter (Eds.), *Intercultural communication: A reader* (3rd ed.). Belmont, CA: Wadsworth.

Lundstedt, S. (1963). An introduction to some evolving problems in cross–cultural research. *Journal of Social Issues, 14,* 1–9.

Lutzker, D. (1960). Internationalism as a predictor of cooperative behavior. *Journal of Conflict Resolution, 4,* 426–430.

Lynberg, M. (1989). *The path with heart.* New York: Fawcett.

Lysgaard, S. (1955). Adjustment in a foreign society. *International Social Science Bulletin, 7,* 45–51.

Mahler, I., Greenberg, L., & Hayashi, H. (1981). A comparative study of rules of justice. *Psychologia, 24,* 1–8.

Maltz, D., & Borker, R. (1982). A cultural approach to male-female miscommunication. In J. Gumperz (Ed.), *Language and social identity.* Cambridge, UK: Cambridge University Press.

Mansell, M. (1981). Transcultural experience and expressive response. *Communication Education, 30,* 93–108.

Mare, L. (1990). *Ma* and Japan. *Southern Communication Journal, 55,* 319–328.

Markoff, R. (1977). Intercultural marriage. In W. Tseng, J. McDermott, & T. Martzki (Eds.), *Adjustment in intercultural marriages.* Honolulu: University of Hawaii Press.

Markus, H., & Kitayama, S. (1991). Culture and the self. *Psychological Review, 98,* 224–253.

Markus, H., & Kitayama, S. (1994a). The cultural construction of self and emotion. In S. Kitayama & H. Markus (Eds.), *Culture, self, and emotion.* Washington, DC: American Psychological Association.

Markus, H., & Kitayama, S. (1994b). A collective fear of the collective. *Personality and Social Psychology Bulletin 20,* 568–579.

Marmott, M., & Syme, S. (1976). Acculturation and coronary heart disease in Japanese-Americans. *American Journal of Epidemiology, 104,* 225–247.

Martin, J. (1984). The intercultural reentry. *International Journal of Intercultural Relations, 8,* 115–134.

Martin, J. (1986). Communication in the intercultural reentry. *International Journal of Intercultural Relations, 10,* 1–22.

Maslow, A. H. (1954/1970). *Motivation and personality* (2nd ed.). New York: Harper and Row.

Maslow, A. H. (1971). *The farther reaches of human nature.* New York: Viking.

Masuda, M. (1970). Ethnic identity in three generations of Japanese Americans. *Journal of Social Psychology, 81,* 199–207.

Matsumoto, D. (1989). Cultural influences on the perception of emotion. *Journal of Cross-Cultural Psychology, 20,* 92–104.

Matsumoto, D. (1991). Cultural influences on the facial expression of emotions. *Southern Communication Journal, 56,* 128–137.

Matsumoto, D., & Kudoh, T. (1993). American-Japanese cultural differences in attributions based on smiles. *Journal of Nonverbal Behavior, 17,* 231–243.

Matsumoto, D., Wallbott, H., & Scherer, K. (1989). Emotions in intercultural communication. In M. Asante & W. Gudykunst (Eds.), *Handbook of international and intercultural communication.* Newbury Park, CA: Sage.

Mazur, A. (1977). Interpersonal spacing on public benches in contact vs. noncontact cultures. *Journal of Social Psychology, 101,* 53–58.

McArthur, L. (1982). Judging a book by its cover. In A. Hastorf & A. Isen (Eds.), *Cognitive social psychology.* New York: Elsevier.

McClelland, D. (1961). *The achieving society.* Princeton, NJ: Van Nostrand.

McConahay, J. (1986). Modern racism, ambivalence, and the modern racism scale. In J. Dovidio & S. Gaertner (Eds.), *Prejudice, discrimination, and racism.* New York: Academic Press.

McConnell-Ginet, S. (1978). Address forms in sexual politics. In D. Butturff & E. Epstein (Eds.), *Women's language and styles.* Akron, OH: L&S Books.

McFall, R. (1982). A review and reformulation of the concept of social skills. *Behavior Assessment, 4,* 1–33.

McGill, M. (1986). *The McGill report on male intimacy.* New York: Harper and Row.

McGinn, N., Harburg, E., & Ginsburg, G. (1973). Responses to interpersonal conflict by middle class males in Guadalajara and Michigan. In F. Jandt (Ed.), *Conflict resolution through communication.* New York: Harper and Row.

McGuire, M., & McDermott, S. (1988). Communication in assimilation, deviance, and alienation states. In Y. Kim & W. Gudykunst (Eds.), *Cross-cultural adaptation.* Newbury Park, CA: Sage.

McGuire, W. (1969). The nature of attitudes and attitude change. In G. Lindzey & E. Aronson (Eds.), *Handbook of social psychology* (2nd ed., Vol. 3). Reading, MA: Addison-Wesley.

McLemore, S. (1970). Simmel's 'stranger': A critique of the concept. *Pacific Sociological Review, 13,* 86–94.

McLuhan, M. (1962). *The Gutenberg galaxy.* New York: New American Library.

McPherson, J. (1991). *Opportunities for contact and network diversity.* Paper presented at the Sunbelt Social Network conference.

McPherson, K. (1983). Opinion-related information seeking. *Personality and Social Psychology Bulletin, 9,* 116–124.

Mead, M. (1963). Culture change and character structure. In M. Stein et al. (Eds.), *Identity and anxiety.* Glencoe, IL: Free Press.

Meggers, B. J. (1954). Environmental limitations on the development of culture. *American Anthropologist, 56,* 801–824.

Mehrabian, A. (1971). *Silent messages.* Belmont, CA: Wadsworth.

Melikan, L. (1962). Self-disclosure among university students in the Middle East. *Journal of Social Psychology, 57,* 257–263.

Merton, R. K. (1957). *Social theory and social structure.* New York: Free Press.

Mezirow, J. (1984). A critical theory of adult learning and education. In S. Merriam (Ed.), *Selected writings on philosophy and adult education.* Malabar, FL: Robert E. Krieger.

Mezirow, J. (1991). *Transformative dimensions of adult learning.* San Francisco: Jossey-Bass.

Milgram, S. (1970). The experience of living in cities. *Science, 167,* 1461–1468.

Miller, G. (1988). Media messages and information processing in interpersonal communication. In B. Ruben (Ed.), *Information and behavior* (Vol. 2). New Brunswick, NJ: Transaction.

Miller, G., & Steinberg, M. (1975). *Between people.* Chicago: Science Research Associates.

Miller, G., & Sunnafrank, M. (1982). All is for one but one is not for all: A conceptual perspective of interpersonal communication. In F. Dance (Ed.), *Human communication theory.* New York: Harper and Row.

Miller, J. (1984). Culture and the development of everyday social explanations. *Journal of Personality and Social Psychology, 46,* 961–978.

Miller, S. (1987). *The ethnic press in the United States.* New York: Greenwood.

Milroy, L. (1980). *Language and social networks.* Baltimore, MD: University Park Press.

Milroy, L. (1984). Comprehension and context. In P. Trudgill (Ed.), *Applied sociolinguistics*. London: Academic Press.

Mintz, N. (1956). Effects of aesthetic surroundings II. *Journal of Personality, 41,* 459–466.

Miranda, M., & Castro, F. (1977). Culture distance and success in psychotherapy with Spanish-speaking clients. In J. Martinez (Ed.), *Chicano Psychology*. New York: Academic Books.

Mischel, W. (1973). Toward a cognitive social learning reconceptualization of personality. *Psychological Review, 80,* 252–283.

Miyahara, A. (1995). Metatheoretical issues in conceptualization of Japanese communication competence. *Keio Communication Review, 17,* 63–82.

Mizutani, O. (1981). *Japanese: The spoken language*. Tokyo: Japan Times.

Molina, J. (1978). Cultural barriers and interethnic communication in a multiethnic neighborhood. In E. Ross (Ed.), *Interethnic communication*. Athens: University of Georgia Press.

Montagu, A. (1952). *Man's most dangerous myth*. New York: Harper and Row.

Montagu, A. (1972). *Statement on race*. New York: Oxford University Press.

Moos, R. (1976). *Human adaptation*. Lexington, MA: Heath.

Morris, M. L. (1981). *Saying and meaning in Puerto Rico*. Elmsford, NY: Pergamon.

Morris, R. T. (1960). *The two-way mirror*. Minneapolis: University of Minnesota Press.

Morrison, T. (1992). *Playing in the dark*. Cambridge, MA: Harvard University Press.

Morsbach, H. (1976). Aspects of nonverbal communication in Japan. In L. Samovar & R. Porter (Eds.), *Intercultural communication: A reader* (2nd ed.). Belmont, CA: Wadsworth.

Mortland, C., & Ledgerwood, J. (1988). Refugee resource acquisition. In Y. Kim & W. Gudykunst (Eds.), *Cross-cultural adaptation*. Newbury Park, CA: Sage.

Mosel, J. (1973, May 17). *Status and role analysis*. Lecture to Japan and East Asia Area Studies Course, Foreign Service Institute, Washington, DC.

Myrdal, G. (1944). *An American dilemma* (2 vols.). New York: Harper and Row.

Nakane, C. (1970). *Japanese society*. Berkeley: University of California Press.

Nakane, C. (1974). The social system reflected in interpersonal communication. In J. Condon & M. Saito (Eds.), *Intercultural encounters with Japan*. Tokyo: Simul Press.

National Opinion Research Center. (1991). Race relations responses to General Social Survey. Reported in *Los Angeles Times,* January 9, 1991, p. A15.

Nayo, L. (1995, July 7). Making monsters of ordinary men. *Los Angeles Times,* p. B7.

Neisser, U. (1976). *Cognition and reality*. San Francisco: W. H. Freeman.

Neuberg, S. (1989). The goal of forming accurate impressions. *Journal of Personality and Social Psychology, 56,* 374–386.

Nilsen, A. (1977). Sexism as shown through English vocabulary. In A. Nilsen, H. Bosmajian, H. Gershuny, & J. Stanley (Eds.), *Sexism and language*. Urbana, IL: National Council of Teachers of English.

Nilsen, A., Bosmajian, H., Gershuny, H., & Stanley, J. (Eds.). (1977). *Sexism and language*. Urbana, IL: National Council of Teachers of English.

Nisbett, R., Caputo, C., Legant, P., & Marecek, J. (1973). Behavior as seen by the actor and as seen by the observer. *Journal of Personality and Social Psychology, 27,* 154–165.

Nishida, H. (1985). Japanese intercultural communication competence and cross-cultural adjustment. *International Journal of Intercultural Relations, 9,* 247–270.

Nishiyama, K. (1971). Interpersonal persuasion in a vertical society. *Speech Monographs, 38,* 148–154.

Noesjirwan, J. (1978). A rule-based analysis of cultural differences in social behavior. *International Journal of Psychology, 13,* 305–316.

Noller, P. (1980). Misunderstanding in marital communication. *Journal of Personality and Social Psychology, 39,* 1135–1148.

Noller, P. (1993). Gender and emotional communication in marriage. *Journal of Language and Social Psychology, 12,* 132–152.

Norton, R. (1978). Foundations of a communicator style construct. *Human Communication Research, 4,* 99–112.

Nozick, R. (1989). *The examined life.* New York: Simon and Schuster.

Nuessel, F. (1984). Ageist language. *Maledicta, 8,* 17–28.

Oberg, K. (1958). *Culture shock and the problem of adjustment to new cultural environments.* Washington, DC: Department of State, Foreign Service Institute.

Oberg, K. (1960). Culture shock and the problems of adjustment to new cultural environments. *Practical Anthropology, 7,* 170–179.

Oehlkers, P. (1991). *Networks of social support and the adjustment of Japanese sojourners in the United States.* Paper presented at the Speech Communication Association convention.

O'Halloran, M. (1994). *Pure heart, enlightened mind.* Tokyo: Tuttle.

Okabe, K. (1987). Indirect speech acts of Japanese. In D. Kincaid (Ed.), *Communication theory from eastern and western perspectives.* New York: Academic Press.

Okabe, R. (1983). Cultural assumptions of east and west: Japan and the United States. In W. Gudykunst (Ed.), *Intercultural communication theory: Current perspectives.* Beverly Hills, CA: Sage.

Okazaki-Luff, M. (1991). On the adjustment of Japanese sojourners. *International Journal of Intercultural Relations, 15,* 85–102.

O'Keefe, D., & Sypher, H. (1981). Cognitive complexity measures and the relationship of cognitive complexity to communication. *Human Communication Research, 8,* 72–92.

Oliver, R. (1962). *Culture and communication.* Springfield, IL: Charles C. Thomas.

Oliver, R. (1971). *Communication and culture in ancient India and China.* Syracuse, NY: Syracuse University Press.

Olsen, M. (1978). *The process of social organization* (2nd ed.). New York: Holt, Rinehart and Winston.

Opotow, S. (1990). Moral exclusion and injustice. *Journal of Social Issues, 46* (1), 1–20.

Ornstein, R. (1972). *The psychology of consciousness.* New York: Pelican Books.

Ortega y Gasset, J. (1957). *Man and people* (W. Trask, Trans.). New York: Norton.

Osgood, C., May, H., & Miron, S. (1972). *Cross-cultural universals of affective meaning.* Urbana: University of Illinois Press.

Palisi, B. (1966). Ethnic patterns of friendship. *Phylon,* 217–225.

Palmore, E. (1962). Ethnophaulisms and ethnocentrism. *American Journal of Sociology, 67,* 442–445.

Palmore, E. (1982). Attitudes toward the aged. *Research on Aging, 4,* 333–348.

Pandy, J. (1990). The environment, culture, and behavior. In R. Brislin (Ed.), *Applied cross-cultural psychology.* Newbury Park, CA: Sage.

Park, R. (1939). Reflections on communication and culture. *American Journal of Sociology, 44,* 191–205.

Park, R. (1950). Our racial frontier in the Pacific. In R. Park (Ed.), *Race and culture.* New York: Free Press.

Parrillo, V. N. (1980). *Strangers to these shores.* Boston: Houghton Mifflin.

Parsons, T. (1951). *The social system.* Glencoe, IL: Free Press.

Parsons, T. (1953). Some comments on the state of the general theory of action. *American Sociological Review, 18,* 618–631.

Parsons, T., & Shils, E. (1951). *Toward a general theory of action.* Cambridge, MA: Harvard University Press.

Parsonson, K. (1987). Intermarriage. *Journal of Cross-Cultural Psychology, 18,* 363–371.

Pascale, R., & Athos, A. (1981). *The art of Japanese management.* New York: Simon and Schuster.

Patai, R. (1976). *The Arab mind.* New York: Scribner.

Patterson, O. (1977). *Ethnic chauvinism.* New York: Stein and Day.

Pearce, W. B., & Kang, K. (1988). Conceptual migrations. In Y. Kim & W. Gudykunst (Eds.), *Cross-cultural adaptation.* Newbury Park, CA: Sage.

Pearce, W. B., & Stamm, K. (1973). Communication behavior and coorientation relations. In P. Clark (Ed.), *New models for communication research.* Beverly Hills, CA: Sage.

Peck, M. S. (1987). *The different drum: Community making and peace.* New York: Simon and Schuster.

Peck, M. S. (1993). *A world waiting to be born: Civility rediscovered.* New York: Bantam.

Pedone, R. (1980). *The retention of minority language in the United States.* Washington, DC: National Center for Educational Statistics.

Pelto, P. (1968, April). The difference between "tight" and "loose" societies. *Transaction,* pp. 37–40.

Peng, F. (1974). Communicative distance. *Language Sciences, 31,* 32–38.

Pescosolidio, B. (1992). Beyond rational choice. *American Journal of Sociology, 97,* 1096–1138.

Pettigrew, T. (1958). Personality and sociocultural factors in intergroup attitudes. *Journal of Conflict Resolution, 2,* 29–42.

Pettigrew, T. (1978). Three issues in ethnicity. In J. Yinger & S. Cutler (Eds.), *Major social issues.* New York: Free Press.

Pettigrew, T. (1979). The ultimate attribution error. *Personality and Social Psychology Bulletin, 5,* 461–476.

Pettigrew, T. (1982). Cognitive styles and social behavior. In L. Wheeler (Ed.), *Review of personality and social psychology* (Vol. 3). Beverly Hills, CA: Sage.

Pettigrew, T. (1986). The intergroup contact hypothesis reconsidered. In M. Hewstone & R. Brown (Eds.), *Contact and conflict in intergroup encounters.* Oxford, UK: Blackwell.

Phillips, H. (1965). *Thai peasant personality.* Berkeley: University of California Press.

Phinney, J. (1993). Multiple group identities. In J. Kroger (Ed.), *Discussions on ego identity.* Hillsdale, NJ: Erlbaum.

Pike, K. L. (1966). Etic and emic standpoints for the description of behavior. In A. Smith (Ed.), *Communication and culture.* New York: Holt, Rinehart and Winston.

Piker, S. (1968). Friendship to the death in rural Thai society. *Human Organization,* 200–204.

Pilusuk, M. (1963). Anxiety, self acceptance, and open-mindedness. *Journal of Clinical Psychology, 19,* 386–391.

Pinker, S. (1994). *The language instinct.* New York: Harper.

Planalp, S., Rutherford, D., & Honeycutt, J. (1988). Events that increase uncertainty in relationships. *Human Communication Research, 14,* 516–547.

Pleck, J. (1977). The psychology of sex roles. *Journal of Communication, 26,* 193–200.

Plog, S. (1965). The disclosure of self in the United States and Germany. *Journal of Social Psychology, 65,* 193–203.

Pogrebin, L. (1987). *Among friends.* New York: McGraw-Hill.

Pool, I. de Sola (1965). Effects of cross-national contact on national and international images. In H. Kelman (Ed.), *International behavior.* New York: Holt, Rinehart and Winston.

Powers, W., & Lowry, D. (1984). Basic communication fidelity. In R. Bostrom (Ed.), *Competence in communication.* Beverly Hills, CA: Sage.

Prather, H. (1986). *Notes on how to live in the world and still be happy.* New York: Doubleday.

Presidential Commission on Foreign Language and International Studies. (1979). *Strength through wisdom.* Washington, DC: U.S. Government Printing Office.

Pritchard, M. (1991). *On becoming responsible.* Lawrence: University of Kansas Press.

Putnam, L., & Wilson, C. (1982). Communication strategies in organizational conflicts. In M. Burgoon (Ed.), *Communication yearbook 6.* Beverly Hills, CA: Sage.

Pyszczynski, T., & Greenberg, J. (1981). Role of disconfirmed expectancies in the instigation of attributional processing. *Journal of Personality and Social Psychology, 40,* 31–38.

Quisumbing, M. (1982). *Life events, social support and personality: Their impact upon Filipino psychological adjustment.* Unpublished doctoral dissertation, University of Chicago, Chicago.

Rahim, A. (1983). A measure of styles of handling interpersonal conflict. *Academy of Management Journal, 26,* 368–376.

Rahula, W. (1959). *What the Buddha taught.* New York: Grove Press.

Ralston, D. (1985). Employee ingratiation. *Academy of Management Review, 10,* 447–487.

Rapoport, A. (1969). *House form and culture.* Englewood Cliffs, NJ: Prentice Hall.

Read, K, (1995). Morality and the concept of the person among the Gahuku-kama. *Oceana, 25,* 233–282.

Reagan, T. (1995). A sociocultural understanding of deafness. *International Journal of Intercultural Relations, 19,* 239–281.

Reina, R. (1959). Two patterns of friendship in a Guatemalan community. *American Anthropologist, 44–61.*

Renteln, A. (1988). Relativism and the search for human rights. *American Anthropologist, 90,* 56–72.

Rigney, J., Bieri, J., & Tripodi, T. (1964). Social concept attainment and cognitive complexity. *Psychological Reports, 15,* 503–509.

Riley, P. (1989). Well don't blame me! On the interpretation of pragmatic errors. In W. Oleksy (Ed.), *Contrastive pragmatics.* Philadelphia: John Benjamins.

Roach, C., & Wyatt, N. (1988). *Successful listening.* New York: Harper and Row.

Rodriguez, R. (1982). *The hunger of memory.* New York: Bantam.

Rogers, E. M., & Bhowmik, D. K. (1971). Homophily-heterophily. *Public Opinion Research, 34,* 523–531.

Rogers, E. M., & Shoemaker, F. (1971). *Communication of innovations* (2nd ed.). New York: Free Press.

Rogler, L. H., (1980). Intergenerational change in ethnic identity in Puerto Rican family. *International Migration Review, 14,* 193–214.

Rokeach, M. (1951). A method for studying individual differences in "narrow-mindedness." *Journal of Personality, 20,* 219–233.

Rokeach, M. (Ed.) (1960). *The open and closed mind.* New York: Basic Books.

Rokeach, M. (1972). *Beliefs, attitudes and values.* San Francisco: Jossey-Bass.

Rokeach, M. (1973). *The nature of human values.* New York: Free Press.

Rokeach, M., Smith, P., & Evans, R. (1960). Two kinds of prejudice or one? In M. Rokeach, (Ed.), *The open and closed mind.* New York: Basic Books.

Roloff, M. (1987). Communication and conflict. In C. Berger & S. Chaffe (Eds.), *Handbook of communication science.* Newbury Park, CA: Sage.

Roosens, E. (1989). *Creating ethnicity.* Newbury Park, CA: Sage.

Root, M. (Ed.). (1995). *The multiracial experience.* Thousand Oaks, CA: Sage.

Rose, A. (1965). The subculture of aging. In A. Rose & W. Peterson (Eds.), *Older people and their social world.* Philadelphia: F. A. Davis.

Rose, T. (1981). Cognitive and dyadic processes in intergroup contact. In D. Hamilton (Ed.), *Cognitive processes in stereotyping and intergroup behavior.* Hillsdale, NJ: Erlbaum.

Roseman, I., Dhawan, N., Rettek, S., Naidu, R., & Thapa, K. (1995). Cultural differences and cross-cultural similarities in appraisals and emotional responses. *Journal of Cross-Cultural Psychology, 26,* 23–48.

Rosenblatt, P. C. (1964). Origins and effects of group ethnocentrism and nationalism. *Journal of Conflict Resolution, 8,* 131–146.

Rosenblatt, P., Karis, T., & Powell, R. (1995). *Multiracial couples.* Thousand Oaks, CA: Sage.

Rosenfeld, H. (1978). Conversational control functions of nonverbal behavior. In A. Siegman & S. Feldstein (Eds.), *Nonverbal behavior in communication.* Hillsdale, NJ: Erlbaum.

Rosenthal, P. (1984). *Words and values.* Cambridge, UK: Cambridge University Press.

Rosenthal, R., Hall, J., Dimatteo, M., Rogers, P., & Archer, D. (1979). *Sensitivity to nonverbal communication.* Baltimore, MD: Johns Hopkins University Press.

Ross, L., & Ward, A. (1995). Psychological barriers to dispute resolution. In M. Zanna (Ed.), *Advances in experimental social psychology* (Vol. 27). New York: Academic Press.

Ross, L. D. (1977). The intuitive psychologist and his shortcomings: Distortions in the attribution process. In L. Berkowitz (Ed.), *Advances in experimental psychology* (Vol. 10). New York: Academic Press.

Ross, S., & Shortreed, I. (1990). Japanese foreigner talk. *Journal of Asian Pacific Communication, 1,* 134–145.

Ruben, B. D. (1975). Intrapersonal, interpersonal and mass communication process in individual and multi-person systems. In B. Ruben & J. Kim (Eds.), *General systems theory and human communication.* Rochelle Park, NJ: Hayden.

Ruben, B. D. (1976). Assessing communication competency for intercultural adaptation. *Group and Organizational Studies, 1,* 334–354.

Ruben, B. D., & Kealey, D. J. (1979). Behavioral assessment of communication competency and the prediction of cross-cultural adaptation. *International Journal of Intercultural Relations, 3,* 15–48.

Ryan, E., Giles, H., & Sebastian, R. (1982). An integrative perspective for the study of attitudes toward language. In E. Ryan & H. Giles (Eds.), *Attitudes toward language variation.* London: Edward Arnold.

Ryan, E., Hewstone, M., & Giles, H. (1984). Language and intergroup attitudes. In J. Eiser (Ed.), *Attitudinal judgment.* New York: Springer-Verlag.

Ryu, J. S. (1976). *New-socialization function of mass media working among foreign students.* Paper presented at the Western States Speech Communication Association convention, San Francisco.

Saarinen, E. (1948). *The search for form.* New York: Reinhold.

Sachdev, I., & Bourhis, R. (1990). Bilinguality and multilinguality. In H. Giles & P. Robinson (Eds.), *Handbook of language and social psychology.* London: Wiley.

Sacks, H., Schegloff, E., & Jefferson, G. (1974). A simplist systematics for the organization of turn-taking in conversations. *Language, 50,* 696–735.

Safilios-Rothchild, C. (1982). Social and psychological parameters of friendship and intimacy for disabled people. In M. Eisenberg, C. Giggins, & R. Duval (Eds.), *Disabled people as second class citizens.* New York: Springer.

Salamon, S. (1977). Family bonds and friendship bonds. *Journal of Marriage and the Family, 39,* 807–820.

Saleh, S., & Gufwoli, P. (1982). The transfer of management techniques and practices. In R. Rath, H. Aschana, D. Sinha, & J. Sinha (Eds.), *Diversity and unity in cross-cultural psychology.* Lisse, The Netherlands: Swets and Zeitlinger.

San Antonio, P. (1987). Social mobility and language usage in an American company in Japan. *Journal of Language and Social Psychology, 6,* 191–200.

Sanders, J., & Wiseman, R. (1991). *Uncertainty reduction among ethnicities in the United States.* Paper presented at the International Communication Association convention, Chicago.

Sanders, J., Wiseman, R., & Matz, I. (1991). Uncertainty reduction in acquaintance relationships in Ghana and the United States. In S. Ting-Toomey & F. Korzenny (Eds.), *Cross-cultural interpersonal communication.* Newbury Park, CA: Sage.

Sapir, E. (1925/1970). *Culture, language and personality.* Berkeley: University of California Press.

Sarbaugh, L. (1979). *Intercultural communication.* Rochelle Park, NJ: Hayden.

Sarbin, T., & Allen, V. (1968). Role theory. In G. Lindzey & E. Aronson (Eds.), *Handbook of social psychology* (2nd ed.). Reading, MA: Addison-Wesley.

Schaefer, R. (1979). *Racial and ethnic groups.* Boston: Little, Brown.

Scheflen, A. E. (1976). *Human territories.* Englewood Cliffs, NJ: Prentice Hall.

Scherer, K., & Wallbott, H. (1994). Evidence for universality and cultural variation of differential emotion response patterning. *Journal of Personality and Social Psychology, 66,* 310–328.

Schild, E. (1962). The foreign student as stranger, learning the norm of the host culture. *Journal of Social Issues, 18,* 41–54.

Schlenker, B. (1986). Self-identification. In R. Baumeister (Ed.), *Public self and private self.* New York: Springer-Verlag.

Schmidt, K. (1991). *Exit, voice, loyalty, and neglect: Responses to sexist communication in dating relationships.* Unpublished doctoral dissertation, Arizona State University, Tempe.

Schneider, J., & Hacker, S. (1973). Sex role imagery and the use of generic "man" in introductory texts. *American Sociologist, 8,* 12–18.

Schneider, M., & Jorden, W. (1981). Perception of the communicative performance of Americans and Chinese in intercultural dyads. *International Journal of Intercultural Relations, 5,* 175–192.

Schroder, H., Driver, M., & Streufert, S. (1967). *Human information processing: Individuals and groups functioning in complex social situations.* New York: Holt, Rinehart and Winston.

Schuetz, A. (1944). The stranger. *American Journal of Sociology, 49,* 499–507.

Schuetz, A. (1945). The homecomer. *American Journal of Sociology, 50,* 369–376.

Schwartz, J. (1980). The negotiation for meaning. In D. Larsen-Freeman (Ed.), *Discourse analysis in second language research.* Rowley, MA: Newbury House.

Schwartz, S. (1990). Individualism-collectivism. *Journal of Cross-Cultural Psychology, 21,* 139–157.

Schwartz, S. (1992). Universals in the content and structure of values. In M. Zanna (Ed.), *Advances in experimental social psychology* (Vol. 25). New York: Academic Press.

Schwartz, S. (1994a). Are there universal aspects of the structure and content of values? *Journal of Social Issues, 50* (4), 19–45.

Schwartz, S. (1994b). Beyond individualism-collectivism. In U. Kim, H. Triandis, C. Kagitcibasi, S. Choi, & G. Yoon (Eds.), *Individualism and collectivism.* Thousand Oaks, CA: Sage.

Schwartz, S., & Bilsky, W. (1987). Toward a psychological structure of human values. *Journal of Personality and Social Psychology, 53,* 550–562.

Schwartz, S., & Bilsky, W. (1990). Toward a theory of the universal content and structure of values. *Journal of Personality and Social Psychology, 58,* 878–891.

Schwartz, S., & Sagiv, L. (1995). Identifying culture-specifics in the content and structure of values. *Journal of Cross-Cultural Psychology, 26,* 92–116.

Schwartz, T. (Ed.). (1976). *Socialization as cultural communication.* Berkeley: University of California Press.

Schwimmer, B., & Warren, D. (Eds.). (1993). *Anthropology and the Peace Corp.* Ames: Iowa State University Press.

Scollon, R., & Scollon, S. (1981). *Narrative, literacy, and face in interethnic communication.* Norwood, NJ: Ablex.

Scollon, R., & Wong-Scollon, S. (1990). Athabaskan-English interethnic communication. In D. Carbaugh (Ed.), *Cultural communication and intercultural contact.* Hillsdale, NJ: Erlbaum.

Scott, J. (1993, September 24). On-line, and maybe out of line. *Los Angeles Times,* pp. A1, 32–33.

Scott, W. (1965). Psychological and social correlates of international images. In H. Kelman (Ed.), *International behavior.* New York: Holt, Rinehart and Winston.

Scotton, C. (1983). The negotiation of identities in conversation. *International Journal of the Sociology of Language, 44,* 115–136.

Scotton, C. (1990). The sociolinguistics of language switching. In R. Jacobson (Ed.), *Codeswitching as a worldwide phenomenon.* New York: Peter Lang.

Searle, W., & Ward, C. (1990). The prediction of psychological and sociocultural adjustment during cross-cultural transitions. *International Journal of Intercultural Relations, 14,* 485–506.

Sears, D. (1988). Symbolic racism. In P. Katz & D. Taylor (Eds.), *Eliminating racism.* New York: Plenum.

Sechrest, L. (1969). Nonreactive assessment of attitudes. In E. Williams & H. Raush (Eds.), *Naturalistic viewpoints in psychological research.* New York: Holt, Reinhart and Winston.

Seelye, H., & Wasilewski, J. (1981). *Social competency development in multicultural children, aged 6–13.* Washington, DC: National Institute for Education.

Selltiz, C., Christ, J., Havel, J., & Cook, S. (1963). *Attitudes and social relations of foreign students in the United States.* Minneapolis: University of Minnesota Press.

Selznick, P. (1992). *The moral commonwealth.* Berkeley: University of California Press.

Sewell, W., & Davidsen, O. (1961). *Scandinavian students on an American campus.* Minneapolis: University of Minnesota Press.

Shack, W. (1979). Open systems and closed boundaries. In W. Shack & E. Skinner (Eds.), *Strangers in African society.* Berkeley: University of California Press.

Shah, H. (1991). Communication and cross-cultural adaptation patterns among Asian Indians. *International Journal of Intercultural Relations, 15,* 311–321.

Sharkey, W., & Singelis, T. (1993). *Embarrassability and relational orientation.* Paper presented at the International Network on Personal Relationships.

Sheehy, G. (1986). *The spirit of survival.* New York: Bantam Books.

Sherif, M., & Sherif, C. (1953). *Groups in harmony and tension.* New York: Harper.

Shibutani, T., & Kwan, M. (1965). *Ethnic stratification.* New York: Macmillan.

Shim, J. (1994). *Community orientations and newspaper use.* Paper presented at the International Communication Association convention.

Shouby, E. (1970). The influence of the Arabic language on the psychology of the Arabs. In A. Lutifiyya & C. Churchill (Eds.), *Readings in the Arab middle eastern societies and cultures.* The Hague: Mouton.

Shuter, R. (1976). Proxemics and tactility in Latin America. *Journal of Communication, 26,* 46–52.

Shuter, R. (1982). Initial interaction of American blacks and whites in interracial and intraracial dyads. *Journal of Social Psychology, 117,* 45–52.

Sigman, S. (1980). On communication rules from a social perspective. *Human Communication Research, 7,* 37–51.

Sillars, A. (1980). Attribution and communication in roommate conflicts. *Communication Monographs, 47,* 180–200.

Sillars, A., Coletti, S., Parry, D., & Rogers, M. (1982). Coding verbal conflict tactics. *Human Communication Research, 9,* 83–95.

Simard, L. M. (1981). Cross-cultural interaction: Potential invisible barriers. *Journal of Social Psychology, 113,* 171–192.

Simard, L. M., & Taylor, D. M. (1973). The potential for bicultural communication in a dyadic situation. *Canadian Journal of Behavioral Science, 5,* 211–225.

Simard, L. M., Taylor, D. M., & Giles, H. (1976). Attributional processes and interpersonal accommodation. *Language and Speech, 19,* 374–387.

Simmel, G. (1908/1950). The stranger. In K. Wolff (Trans. and Ed.), *The sociology of Georg Simmel.* New York: Free Press.

Simons, H., Berkowitz, N., & Moyer, R. (1970). Similarity, credibility, and attitude change: A review and a theory. *Psychological Bulletin, 73,* 1–16.

Singelis, T., & Brown, W. (1995). Culture, self, and collectivist communication. *Human Communication Research, 21,* 354–389.

Singelis, T., & Sharkey, W. (in press). Culture, self construal, and embarrassability. *Journal of Cross-Cultural Psychology.*

Singhal, A., & Nagao, M. (1993). Assertiveness as communication competence. *Asian Journal of Communication, 3,* 1–18.

Skevington, S. (1989). A place for emotion in social identity theory. In S. Skevington & D. Baker (Eds.), *The social identity of women.* London: Sage.

Smalley, W. (1963). Culture shock, language shock and the shock of self-discovery. *Practical Anthropology, 10,* 49–56.

Smith, E. (1994). Social identity and social emotions. In D. Mackie & D. Hamilton (Eds.), *Affect, cognition, and stereotyping.* New York: Academic Press.

Smith, H. (1976). *The Russians.* New York: Ballantine Books.

Smith, P., & Bond, M. (1993). *Social psychology across cultures.* New York: Harvester.

Smith, S., & Whitehead, G. (1984). Attributions for promotions and demotions in the United States and India. *The Journal of Social Psychology, 30,* 526–537.

Smock, C. (1955). The influence of psychological stress on the intolerance of ambiguity. *Journal of Abnormal and Social Psychology, 50,* 177–182.

Smutkupt, S., & Barna, L. (1976). Impact of nonverbal communication in an intercultural setting: Thailand. In F. Casmir (Ed.), *International and intercultural communication annual* (Vol. III). Falls Church, VA: Speech Communication Association.

Smuts, J. C. (1926/1967). *Holism and evolution.* New York: Viking.

Snyder, M. (1974). Self-monitoring of expressive behavior. *Journal of Personality and Social Psychology, 30,* 526–537.

Snyder, M., & Haugen, J. (1995). Why does behavioral confirmation occur? *Personality and Social Psychology Bulletin, 21,* 963–974.

Sodetani, L. L., & Gudykunst, W. B. (1987). The effects of surprising events on intercultural relationships. *Communication Research Reports, 4*(2), 1–6.

Sommer, R. (1968). Intimacy ratings in five countries. *International Journal of Psychology, 3,* 109–114.

Sorrentino, R., & Short, J. (1986). Uncertainty orientation, motivation, and cognition. In R. Sorrentino & E. T. Higgins (Eds.), *Handbook of motivation and cognition.* New York: Guilford.

Southworth, F. (1980). Indian bilingualism. *Studies in Child Language and Multilingualism, 345,* 121–135.

Spitzberg, B., & Cupach, W. (1984). *Interpersonal communication competence.* Beverly Hills, CA: Sage.

Spradley, J. P. (Ed.). (1972). *Culture and cognition.* San Francisco: Chandler.

Sprecher, S., Aron, A., Hatfield, E., Cortesa, A., Potapova, E., & Levitskaya, A. (1994). Love: American style, Russian style, and Japanese style. *Personal Relationships, 1,* 349–369.

Srivastava, S. (1960). Patterns of ritual friendship in tribal India. *International Journal of Comparative Sociology,* 239–247.

Stanfield, J. (Ed.). (1995). Theories of ethnicity. *American Behavioral Scientist, 38* (3)(whole issue).

Stangor, C., & Lange, J. (1994). Mental representations of social groups. In M. Zanna (Ed.), *Advances in experimental social psychology* (Vol. 26). New York: Academic Press.

Stanley, J. (1977). Paradigmatic women. In D. Shores & C. Hines (Eds.), *Papers in language variation.* Tuscaloosa: University of Alabama Press.

Staub, E. (1989). *The roots of evil.* New York: Cambridge University Press.

Stephan, C., & Stephan, W. (1992). Reducing intercultural anxiety through intercultural contact. *International Journal of Intercultural Relations, 16,* 89–106.

Stephan, W. (1985). Intergroup relations. In G. Lindzey & E. Aronson (Eds.), *Handbook of Social Psychology* (3rd ed., Vol. 2). New York: Random House.

Stephan, W. (1987). The contact hypothesis in intergroup relations. In L. Hendrick (Ed.), *Group processes and intergroup relations.* Thousand Oaks, CA: Sage.

Stephan, W., & Rosenfield, D. (1982). Racial and ethnic stereotyping. In A. Millar (Ed.), *In the eye of the beholder.* New York: Praeger.

Stephan, W., & Stephan, C. (1985). Intergroup anxiety. *Journal of Social Issues, 41,* 157–166.

Stephan, W., & Stephan, C. (1989). Antecedents of intergroup anxiety in Asian-Americans and Hispanic-Americans. *International Journal of Intercultural Relations, 13,* 203–219.

Stephenson, G. (1981). Intergroup bargaining and negotiation. In J. Turner & H. Giles (Eds.), *Intergroup behavior.* Chicago: University of Chicago Press.

Stewart, E. C. (1972). *American cultural patterns: A cross-cultural perspective.* Chicago: Intercultural Network.

Strassberg, D., & Anchor, K. (1975). Rating intimacy of self-disclosure. *Psychological Reports, 37,* 562.

Stryker, S., & Stratham, A. (1985). Symbolic interactions and role theory. In G. Lindzey & E. Aronson (Eds.), *Handbook of social psychology* (3rd ed., Vol. I). New York: Random House.

Stuart, I., & Abt, E. (1973). *Interracial marriage.* New York: Grossman.

Stuart, R. (1980). *Helping couples change.* New York: Guilford.

Subervi-Velez, F. (1986). The mass media and ethnic assimilation and pluralism. *Communication Research, 13,* 71–86.

Sudweeks, S., Gudykunst, W. B., Ting-Toomey, S., & Nishida, T. (1990). Developmental themes in Japanese-North American relationships. *International Journal of Intercultural Relations, 14,* 207–233.

Suleiman, M. W. (1973). The Arabs and the west: Communication gap. In M. Prosser (Ed.), *Intercommunication among nations and peoples.* New York: Harper and Row.

Sumner, W. G. (1940). *Folkways.* Boston: Ginn.

Sunnafrank, M. J. (1991). Interpersonal attraction and attitude similarity. In J. Andersen (Ed.), *Communication yearbook 14.* Newbury Park, CA: Sage.

Sunnafrank, M. J., & Miller, G. R. (1981). The role of initial conversation in determining attraction to similar and dissimilar strangers. *Human Communication Research, 8,* 16–25.

Sussman, N., & Rosenfeld, H. (1982). Influence of culture, language, and sex on conversational distance. *Journal of Personality and Social Psychology, 42,* 66–74.

Suttles, G. (1970). Friendship as a social institution. In G. McNall (Ed.), *Social relationships.* Chicago: Aldine.

Suzuki, D. T. (1968). *The essence of Buddhism.* Kyoto, Japan: Hozokan.

Swann, W. (1983). Self-verification. In J. Suls & A. Greenwald (Eds.), *Psychological perspectives on the self* (Vol. 2). Hillsdale, NJ: Erlbaum.

Szalay, L. B., & Deese, J. (1978). *Subjective meaning and culture.* Hillsdale, NJ: Erlbaum.

Szalay, L., & Inn, A. (1988). Cross-cultural adaptation and diversity. In Y. Kim & W. Gudykunst (Eds.), *Cross-cultural adaptation.* Newbury Park, CA: Sage.

Szapocznik, J., et al. (1975). *Acculturation: Theory, measurement and clinical implications.* Rockville, MD: National Institute on Drug Abuse.

Szapocznik, J., & Kurtines, W. (1980). Acculturation, biculturalism and adjustment of Cuban Americans. In A. Padilla (Ed.), *Acculturation.* Boulder, CO: Westview.

Szapocznik, J., Kurtines, W., & Fernandez, T. (1980). Bicultural involvement and adjustment of Hispanic-Americans. *International Journal of Intercultural Relations, 4,* 353–365.

Tafoya, D. (1983). Perceptions of the roots of conflict: A theory and typology. In W. Gudykunst (Ed.), *Intercultural communication theory.* Beverly Hills, CA: Sage.

Taft, R. (1966). *From stranger to citizen.* London: Tavistock.

Taft, R. (1977). Coping with unfamiliar cultures. In N. Warren (Ed.), *Studies in cross-cultural psychology* (Vol. 1). New York: Academic Press.

Taft, R. (1988). The psychological adaptation of Soviet immigrants in Australia. In Y. Kim & W. Gudykunst (Eds.), *Cross-cultural adaptation.* Newbury Park, CA: Sage.

Tagore, R. (1961). *Toward universal man.* New York: Asia Publishing House.

Tajfel, H. (1958). Second thoughts about cross-cultural research and international relations. *International Journal of Psychology, 3,* 213–219.

Tajfel, H. (1969a). Social and cultural factors in perception. In G. Lindzey & A. Aronson (Eds.), *The handbook of social psychology* (2nd ed.). Reading, MA: Addison-Wesley.

Tajfel, H. (1969b). Cognitive aspects of prejudice. *Journal of Social Issues, 25,* 79–97.

Tajfel, H. (1972). Experiments in a vacuum. In J. Israel & H. Tajfel (Eds.), *The context of social psychology.* London: Academic Press.

Tajfel, H. (1974). Social identity and intergroup behavior. *Social Science Information, 13,* 65–93.

Tajfel, H. (1978). Social categorization, social identity, and social comparisons. In H. Tajfel (Ed.), *Differentiation between social groups.* London: Academic Press.

Tajfel, H. (1981). Social stereotypes and social groups. In J. Turner & H. Giles (Eds.), *Intergroup behavior.* Chicago: University of Chicago Press.

Tajfel, H. (1982). *Human groups and social categories.* Cambridge, UK: Cambridge University Press.

Tajfel, H., & Turner, J. (1979). An integrative theory of intergroup conflict. In W. Austin & S. Worchel (Eds.), *The social psychology of intergroup relations.* Monterey, CA: Brooks/Cole.

Tamir, L. (1984). The older person's communicative needs. In R. Dunkle, M. Heig, & M. Rosenberg (Eds.), *Communications technology and the elderly.* New York: Springer.

Tan, D., & Singh, R. (1995). Attitudes and attraction. *Personality and Social Psychology Bulletin, 21,* 975–986.

Tannen, D. (1975). Communication mix and mixup or how linguistics can ruin a marriage. *San Jose State Occasional Papers on Linguistics,* 205–211.

Tannen, D. (1979). Ethnicity and conversational style. In *Working papers on sociolinguistics* (No. 55). Austin, TX: Southwest Educational Development Laboratory.

Tannen, D. (1990). *You just don't understand.* New York: Ballentine.

Tannen, D. (1993). Commencement address at State University of New York at Binghamton. Printed in *Chronicle of Higher Education,* June 9, 1993, p. B5.

Tavris, C. (1982). *Anger: The misunderstood emotion.* New York: Simon and Schuster.

Taylor, C. (1991). *The ethics of authenticity.* Cambridge, MA: Harvard University Press.

Taylor, D., Wright, S., & Porter, L. (1994). Dimensions of perceived discrimination. In M. Zanna & J. Olsen (Eds.), *The psychology of prejudice.* Hillsdale, NJ: Erlbaum.

Taylor, D. M., Dube, L., & Bellerose, J. (1986). Intergroup contact in Quebec. In M. Hewstone & R. Brown (Eds.), *Contact and conflict in intergroup encounters.* Oxford, UK: Blackwell.

Taylor, D. M., & Gardner, R. C. (1970). Bicultural communication: A study of communicational efficiency and person perception. *Canadian Journal of Behavioral Science, 2,* 67–81.

Taylor, D. M., & Simard, L. M. (1975). Social interaction in a bilingual setting. *Canadian Psychological Review, 16,* 240–254.

Taylor, S. E., & Fiske, S. T. (1975). Point of view and perceptions of causality. *Journal of Personality and Social Psychology, 32,* 439–445.

Taylor, S. E., & Fiske, S. T. (1978). Salience, attention, and attribution. In L. Berkowitz (Ed.), *Advances in experimental social psychology* (Vol. 11). New York: Academic Press.

Taylor, S. E., & Koivumaki, J. H. (1976). The perception of self and others. *Journal of Personality and Social Psychology, 33,* 403–408.

Tessler, M. A., O'Ban, W. M., & Spain, D. H. (1973). *Tradition and identity in changing Africa.* New York: Harper and Row.

Thayer, L. (1968). *Communication and communication systems.* Homewood, IL: Irwin.

Thomas, J. (1983). Cross-cultural pragmatic failure. *Applied Linguistics, 4,* 91–112.

Thomas, K. (1983). Conflict and its management. In M. Dunnette (Ed.), *Handbook of industrial and organizational psychology.* New York: Wiley.

Thompson, L. (1993). The impact of negotiation on intergroup relations. *Journal of Experimental Social Psychology, 29,* 304–325.

Thompson, T. (1982). Disclosure as a disability management strategy. *Communication Quarterly, 30,* 196–202.

Thompson, T., & Siebold, D. (1978). Stigma management in normal-stigmatized interaction. *Human Communication Research, 4,* 231–242.

Tinder, G. (1980). *Community.* Baton Rouge: Louisiana State University Press.

Ting-Toomey, S. (1980). Talk as a cultural resource in the Chinese-American speech community. *Communication, 9,* 193–203.

Ting-Toomey, S. (1981). Ethnic identity and close friendship in Chinese–American college students. *International Journal of Intercultural Relations, 5,* 383–406.

Ting-Toomey, S. (1985). Toward a theory of conflict and culture. In W. Gudykunst, L. Stewart, & S. Ting-Toomey (Eds.), *Communication, culture, and organizational processes.* Beverly Hills, CA: Sage.

Ting-Toomey, S. (1986a). Conflict styles in black and white subjective cultures. In Y. Kim (Ed.), *Current research in interethnic communication.* Beverly Hills, CA: Sage.

Ting-Toomey, S. (1986b). Japanese communication patterns. *World Communication, 15,* 113–126.

Ting-Toomey, S. (1988). A face negotiation theory. In Y. Kim & W. Gudykunst (Eds.), *Theories in intercultural communication.* Newbury Park, CA: Sage.

Ting-Toomey, S. (1989). Identity and interpersonal bonding. In M. Asante & W. Gudykunst (Eds.), *Handbook of international and intercultural communication.* Newbury Park, CA: Sage.

Ting-Toomey, S. (1991). Intimacy expression in three cultures. *International Journal of Intercultural Relations, 15,* 29–46.

Ting-Toomey, S. (1994a). Managing conflict in intimate intercultural relationships. In D. Cahn (Ed.), *Intimate conflict in personal relationships.* Hillsdale, NJ: Erlbaum.

Ting-Toomey, S. (1994b). Managing intercultural conflicts effectively. In L. Samovar & R. Porter (Eds.), *Intercultural communication: A reader* (7th ed.). Belmont, CA: Sage.

Ting-Toomey, S. (Ed.). (1994c). *The challenge of facework.* Albany: State University of New York Press.

Ting-Toomey, S. (in press). Intercultural conflict competence. In W. Cupach & D. Canary (Eds.), *Competence in interpersonal conflict.* New York: McGraw-Hill.

Ting-Toomey, S., Gao, G., Trubisky, P., Yang, Z., Kim, H., Lin, S., & Nishida, T. (1991). Culture, face maintenance, and styles of handling conflict. *International Journal of Conflict Management, 2,* 275–296.

Ting-Toomey, S., & Korzenny, F. (Eds.). (1989). *Language, communication, and culture.* Newbury Park, CA: Sage.

Ting-Toomey, S., Trubisky, P., & Nishida, T. (1989). *An analysis of conflict styles in Japan and the United states.* Paper presented at the Speech Communication Association convention.

Ting-Toomey, S., Yee-Jung, K., Shapiro, R., Garcia, W., & Wright, T. (1994). *Ethnic identity salience and conflict styles in four ethnic groups.* Paper presented at the Speech Communication Association convention.

Tiryakian, E. A. (1973). Perspectives on the stranger. In S. TeSelle (Ed.), *The rediscovery of ethnicity.* New York: Harper and Row.

de Tocqueville, A. (1945). *Democracy in America.* New York: Knopf.

Toffler, A. (1980). *The third wave.* New York: Bantam Books.

Torbiorn, I. (1982). *Living abroad.* New York: Wiley.

Trager, G. L., & Hall, E. T. (1954). Culture and communication. *Explorations, 3,* 137–149.

Trew, K. (1986). Catholic-Protestant conflict in Northern Ireland. In M. Hewstone & R. Brown (Eds.), *Contact and conflict in intergroup encounters.* Oxford, UK: Blackwell.

Triandis, H. C. (1964). Cultural influences upon cognitive processes. In L. Berkowitz (Ed.), *Advances in experimental social psychology* (Vol. 1). New York: Academic Press.

Triandis, H. C. (1967). Interpersonal relations in international organizations. *Journal of Organizational Behavior and Human Performance, 7,* 316–328.

Triandis, H. C. (1972). *The analysis of subjective culture.* New York: Wiley.

Triandis, H. C. (1975). Culture training, cognitive complexity and interpersonal attitudes. In R. Brislin, S. Bochner, & W. Lonner (Eds.), *Cross-cultural perspectives on learning.* New York: Wiley.

Triandis, H. C. (1977). *Interpersonal behavior.* Monterey, CA: Brooks/Cole.

Triandis, H. C. (1980). Values, attitudes, and interpersonal behavior. In M. Page (Ed.), *Nebraska symposium on motivation* (Vol. 27). Lincoln: University of Nebraska Press.

Triandis, H. C. (1983). Essentials of studying culture. In D. Landis & R. Brislin (Eds.), *Handbook of intercultural training* (Vol. 1). Elmsford, NY: Pergamon.

Triandis, H. C. (1984). A theoretical framework for the more efficient construction of cultural assimilators. *International Journal of Intercultural Relations, 8,* 301–330.

Triandis, H. C. (1988). Collectivism vs. individualism. In G. Verma & C. Bagley (Eds.), *Cross-cultural studies of personality, attitudes, and cognition.* London: Macmillian.

Triandis, H. C. (1989). The self and social behavior in differing cultural contexts. *Psychological Review, 96,* 506–517.

Triandis, H. C. (1990). Cross-cultural studies of individualism-collectivism. In J. Berman (Ed.), *Nebraska symposium on motivation* (Vol. 37). Lincoln: University of Nebraska Press.

Triandis, H. C. (1994). *Culture and social behavior.* New York: McGraw-Hill.

Triandis, H. C. (1995). *Individualism-collectivism.* Boulder, CO: Westview.

Triandis, H. C., Bontempo, R., Villareal, M., Asai, M., & Lucca, N. (1988). Individualism-collectivism: Cross-cultural studies of self-ingroup relationships. *Journal of Personality and Social Psychology, 54,* 323–338.

Triandis, H. C., Brislin, R., & Hui, C. H. (1988). Cross-cultural training across the individualism-collectivism divide. *International Journal of Intercultural Relations, 12,* 269–289.

Triandis, H. C., Leung, K., Villareal, M., & Clack, F. (1985). Allocentric versus idiocentric tendencies. *Journal of Research in Personality, 19,* 395–415.

Triandis, H. C., & Vassiliou, V. (1972). Interpersonal influence and employee selection in two cultures. *Journal of Applied Psychology, 56,* 140–145.

Triandis, H. C., Vassiliou, V., & Nassiakou, M. (1968). Three cross-cultural studies of subjective culture. *Journal of Personality and Social Psychology, 8* (Monograph Supplement No. 4), 1–42.

Trifonovitch, G. (1977). Culture learning/culture teaching. *Educational Perspectives, 16,* 18–22.

Trilling, L. (1968). *Beyond culture.* New York: Viking.

Trubisky, P., Ting-Toomey, S., & Lin, S. (1991). The influence of individualism-collectivism and self-monitoring on conflict styles. *International Journal of Intercultural Relations, 15,* 65–84.

Trungpa, C. (1973). *Cutting through spiritual materialism.* Boulder, CO: Shambhala.

Tseng, W. (1977). Adjustment in intercultural marriage. In W. Tseng, J. McDermott, & T. Maretzki (Eds.), *Adjustment in intercultural marriage.* Honolulu: University of Hawaii Press.

Tucker, M., & Mitchell-Kernan, C. (1995). Social structure and psychological correlates of interethnic dating. *Journal of Social and Personal Relationships, 12,* 341–361.

Turnbull, C. (1961). *The forest people.* New York: Simon and Schuster.

Turner, J. C. (1982). Towards a cognitive redefinition of the social group. In H. Tajfel (Ed.), *Social identity and intergroup relations.* Cambridge, UK: Cambridge University Press.

Turner, J. C. (1987). *Rediscovering the social group.* Oxford, UK: Blackwell.

Turner, J. H. (1987). Toward a sociological theory of motivation. *American Sociological Review, 52,* 15–27.

Turner, J. H. (1988). *A theory of social interaction.* Stanford, CA: Stanford University Press.

Turner, R. H. (1987). Articulating self and social structure. In K. Yardley & T. Honess (Eds.), *Self and society.* Chichester, UK: Wiley.

Tyrwhitt, J. (1960). The moving eye. In E. Carpenter & M. McLuhan (Eds.), *Explorations in communication.* Boston: Beacon.

Tzeng, O., & Jackson, J. (1994). Effects of contact, conflict, and social identity on intergroup hostilities. *International Journal of Intercultural Relations, 18,* 259–276.

Uehara, A. (1986). The nature of American student reentry adjustment and perceptions of sojourn experience. *International Journal of Intercultural Relations, 10,* 415–438.

U.S. Bureau of the Census. (1992). Marital status and living arrangements: March 1991. *Current Population Reports,* Series P–20, No. 461.

Van den Berghe, P. L. (1971). The benign quota. *The American Sociologist, 6,* 40–43.

Vander Zanden, J. W. (1965). *Sociology: A systematic approach.* New York: Ronald Press.

van Dijk, T. (1984). *Prejudice in discourse.* Amsterdam: Benjamins.

Varonis, E., & Gass, S. (1985). Nonnative/native conversations. *Applied Linguistics, 6,* 71–90.

Vassiliou, V., Triandis, H., Vassiliou, G., & McGuire, H. (1972). Interpersonal contact and stereotyping. In H. Triandis (Ed.), *The analysis of subjective culture.* New York: Wiley.

Verbrugge, L. M. (1977). The structure of adult friendship choices. *Social Forces, 56,* 576–597.

Verkuyten, M., deJung, W., & Masson, K. (1994). Racial discourse, attitude, and rhetorical manoeuvres. *Journal of Language and Social Psychology, 13,* 278–298.

Vlastos, G. (1991). *Socrates, ironist and moral philosopher.* Ithaca, NY: Cornell University Press.

Volkan, V. (1993). Immigrants and refugees. *Mind & Human Interaction, 4,* 63–69.

von Hippel, W., Sekaquaptewa, D., & Vargas, P. (1995). On the role of the encoding process in stereotype maintenance. In M. Zanna (Ed.), *Advances in experimental social psychology* (Vol. 27). New York: Academic Press.

Waley, A. (Trans.). (1938). *The analects of Confucius.* New York: Vintage Books.

Walker, D. (1993). *The role of the mass media in the adaptation of Haitian immigrants in Miami.* Unpublished doctoral dissertation, Indiana University.

Wallace, A. (1952). Individual differences and cultural uniformities. *American Sociological Review, 17,* 747–750.

Wallach, M. A. (1959). The influence of classification requirements on gradients of response. *Psychological Monographs, 73,* 478.

Walsh, J. E. (1973). *Intercultural education in the community of man.* Honolulu: University of Hawaii Press.

Walsh, J. E. (1979). *Humanistic culture learning.* Honolulu: University of Hawaii Press.

Waterman, A. (1984). *The psychology of individualism.* New York: Praeger.

Waters, M. (1990). *Ethnic options.* Berkeley: University of California Press.

Watson, J., & Lippitt, R. (1955). *Learning across cultures.* Ann Arbor: University of Michigan.

Watson, O. M. (1970). *Proxemic behavior: A cross-cultural study.* The Hague: Mouton.

Watson, O., & Graves, T. (1966). Quantitative research in proxemic behavior. *American Anthropologist, 68,* 971–985.

Watters, E. (1995, September 17). Claude Steele has scores to settle. *New York Times Magazine,* pp. 45–47.

Watts, A. (1966). *The book: On the taboo against knowing who you are.* New York: Pantheon.

Watzlawick, P., Beavin, J., & Jackson, D. (1967). *The pragmatics of human communication.* New York: Norton.

Wegner, D., & Vallacher, R. (1977). *Implicit psychology.* New York: Oxford University Press.

Wei, A. (1980). *Cultural variations in perception.* Paper presented at the 6th Annual Third World Conference, Chicago.

Weiner-Davis, M. (1992). *Divorce busting.* New York: Summit Books.

Weinstock, A. (1964). Some factors that retard or accelerate the rate of acculturation. *Human Relations, 17,* 321–340.

Weiss, W. (1970). Selective acculturation and the dating process. *Journal of Marriage and the Family, 32,* 273–278.

Wellman, B. (1992). Which types of ties and networks provide what kinds of social support? *Advances in Group Processes, 17(2),* 28–45.

Wen, K. (1976). Theories of migration and mental health. *Social Science and Medicine, 10,* 297–306.

Wendt, J. (undated). Description, interpretation and evaluation. Unpublished paper, Department of Speech Communication, University of Minnesota.

Werner, H. (1957). The concept of development from a comparative and organismic point of view. In D. Harris (Ed.), *The concept of development.* Minneapolis: University of Minnesota Press.

Westin, A. (1970). *Privacy and freedom.* New York: Atheneum.

Wetherall, M. (1982). Cross-cultural studies of minimal groups. In H. Tajfel (Ed.), *Social identity and intergroup relations.* Cambridge, UK: Cambridge University Press.

Wheeler, L., Reis, H., & Bond, M. (1989). Collectivism-individualism in everyday social life. *Journal of Personality and Social Psychology, 57,* 79–86.

White, S. (1989). Back channels across cultures. *Language in Society, 18,* 59–76.

Whorf, B. (1952). *Collected papers on metalinguistics.* Washington, DC: Department of State, Foreign Service Institute.

Whorf, B. L. (1956). *Language, thought, and reality.* New York: Wiley.

Whorf, B. L. (1968). An American Indian model of the universe. In P. Gleeson & N. Wakefield (Eds.), *Language and culture.* Columbus, OH: Merrill.

Wiemann, J. (1985). Interpersonal control and regulation in conversation. In R. Street & J. Cappella (Eds.), *Sequence and pattern in communicative behavior.* London: Edward Arnold.

Wiemann, J., & Backlund, P. (1980). Current theory and research in communication competence. *Review of Educational Research, 50,* 185–199.

Wiemann, J., & Bradac, J. (1989). Metatheoretical issues in the study of communicative competence. In B. Dervin (Ed.), *Progress in communication science* (Vol. 9). Norwood, NJ: Ablex.

Wiemann, J., Chen, V., & Giles, H. (1986). *Beliefs about talk and silence in cultural context.* Paper presented at the Speech Communication Association convention, Chicago.

Wiemann, J., & Kelly, C. (1981). Pragmatics of interpersonal competence. In C. Wilder-Mott & J. Weaklund (Eds.), *Rigor and imagination.* New York: Praeger.

Wilder, D. (1994). The role of anxiety in facilitating stereotypic judgment of outgroup behavior. In D. Mackie & D. Hamilton (Eds.), *Affect, cognition, and stereotyping.* New York: Academic Press.

Wilder, D., & Shapiro, P. (1989). Effects of anxiety on impression formation in a group context. *Journal of Experimental Social Psychology, 25,* 481–499.

Wilder, D., & Shapiro, P. (1991). Facilitation of outgroup stereotypes by enhanced ingroup identity. *Journal of Experimental Social Psychology, 27,* 431–452.

Williams, C., & Westmeyer, J. (1986). Psychiatric problems among adolescent Asian refugees. *Pacific/Asian Mental Health Research Center Newsletter, 4*(3/4), 22–24.

Williams., J. (1984). Gender and intergroup behavior. *British Journal of Social Psychology, 23,* 311–316.

Williams, R. M. (1947). *The reduction of intergroup tensions.* New York: Social Science Research Council.

Williams, R. M. (1974). *Strangers next door: Ethnic relations in American communities.* Englewood Cliffs, NJ: Prentice Hall.

Wilmont, W. (1980). *Dyadic communication* (2nd ed.). Reading, MA: Addison-Wesley.

Wilson, A. (1985). Returned exchange students. *International Journal of Intercultural Relations, 9,* 285–304.

Wirth, L. (1945). The problem of minority groups. In R. Linton (Ed.), *The science of man in the world crisis.* New York: Columbia University Press.

Wiseman, R., & Abe, H. (1986). Cognitive complexity and intercultural effectiveness. In M. McLaughlin (Ed.), *Communication yearbook 9.* Beverly Hills, CA: Sage.

Wish, M., Deutsch, M., & Kaplan, S. (1976). Perceived dimensions of interpersonal relations. *Journal of Personality and Social Psychology, 33,* 409–421.

Witkin, H. A., & Berry, J. (1975). Psychological differentiation in cross-cultural perspective. *Journal of Cross-Cultural Psychology, 6,* 4–87.

Witkin, H. A., Dyk, R. B., Faterson, H. F., Goodenough, D. R., & Karp, S. A. (1962). *Psychological differentiation.* New York: Wiley.

Witkin, H. A., Lewis, H. B., Hertzman, M., Machover, K., Missner, P., & Wapner, S. (1954). *Personality through perception.* New York: Harper and Row.

Wolfgang, A., & Weiss, D. (1980). Locus of control and social distance: Comparison of Canadian and West Indian-born students. *International Journal of Intercultural Relations, 4,* 295–305.

Wolken, G., Moriwaki, S., & Williams, K. (1973). Race and social class as factors in the orientation toward psychotherapy. *Journal of Counseling Psychology, 20,* 312–316.

Wong-Rieger, D. (1984). *Testing a model of emotional and coping responses to problems in adaptation.* Paper presented at Society for Intercultural Education, Training, and Research conference, Long Beach, CA.

Wood, M. M. (1934). *The stranger: A study in social relationships.* New York: Columbia University Press.

Worchel, S., & Norwell, N. (1980). Effect of perceived environmental conditions during cooperation on intergroup attraction. *Journal of Personality and Social Psychology, 38,* 764–772.

Wright, P. H. (1978). Toward a theory of friendship based upon a conception of self. *Human Communication Research, 4,* 196–207.

Wrightsman, L. (1994). *Adult personality development* (Vol. 1). Thousand Oaks, CA: Sage.

Wuthnow, R. (1991). *Acts of compassion.* Princetion: Princeton University Press.

Yamada, H. (1990). Topic management and turn distributions in business meetings. *Text, 10,* 271–295.

Yamaguchi, S. (1994). Collectivism among the Japanese. In U. Kim, H. Triandis, C. Kagitcibasi, S. Choi, & G. Yoon (Eds.), *Individualism and collectivism.* Thousand Oaks, CA: Sage.

Yamaguchi, S., Kuhlman, D., & Sugimori, S. (1992). *Universality of personality correlates of person's collectivistic tendencies.* Paper presented at the International Congress of Psychology.

Yang, S. (1988). *The role of mass media in immigrants' political socialization.* Unpublished doctoral dissertation, Stanford University, Stanford, CA.

Yankelovich, D. (1981). *New rules.* New York: Random House.

Ying, Y., & Liese, L. (1991). Emotional well-being of Taiwan students in the U.S. *International Journal of Intercultural Relations, 15,* 345–366.

Yinger, M. J. (1960). Contraculture and subculture. *American Sociological Review, 25,* 625–635.

Yinger, M. J. (1994). *Ethnicity.* Albany: State University of New York Press.

Yoshikawa, M. (1978). Some Japanese and American cultural characteristics. In M. Prosser, *The cultural dialogue.* Boston: Houghton Mifflin.

Yoshikawa, M. (1988). Cross-cultural adaptation and perceptual development. In Y. Kim & W. Gudykunst (Eds.), *Cross-cultural adaptation.* Newbury Park, CA: Sage.

Young, L., Giles, H., & Pierson, H. (1986). Sociopolitical change and perceived vitality. *International Journal of Intercultural Relations, 10,* 459–469.

Yum, J. O. (1982). Communication diversity and information acquisition among Korean immigrants in Hawaii. *Human Communication Research, 8,* 154–169.

Yum, J. O. (1988a). Locus of control and communication patterns of immigrants. In Y. Kim & W. Gudykunst (Eds.), *Cross-cultural adaptation.* Newbury Park, CA: Sage.

Yum, J. O. (1988b). The impact of Confucianism in interpersonal relationships and communication in East Asia. *Communication Monographs, 55,* 374–388.

Zaharna, R. (1989). Self-shock. International Journal of *Intercultural Relations, 13,* 501–525.

Zajonc, R. (1952). Aggressive attitudes of the "stranger" as a function of conformity pressures. *Human Relations, 5,* 205–216.

Zajonc, R. (1980). Feeling and thinking. *American Psychologist, 35,* 151–175.

Zavalloni, M. (1980). Values. In H. Triandis & R. Brislin (Eds.), *Handbook of cross-cultural psychology* (Vol. 5). Boston: Allyn and Bacon.

Zax, M., & Takahashi, S. (1967). Cultural influences on response style. *Journal of Social Psychology, 71,* 3–10.

Zerubavel, E. (1991). *The fine line.* New York: Free Press.

Zoglin, R. (1993, June 21). All you need is hate. *Time,* p. 63.

Zurcher, L. (1968). Particularism and organizational position: A cross-cultural analysis. *Journal of Applied Psychology, 52,* 139–144.

Zweigenhaft, R. L. (1979–1980). American Jews: In or out of the upper class? *Insurgent Sociologist, 9,* 24–37.

Index